The Bird in Art

Caroline Bugler

The Bird in Art

MERRELL
LONDON • NEW YORK

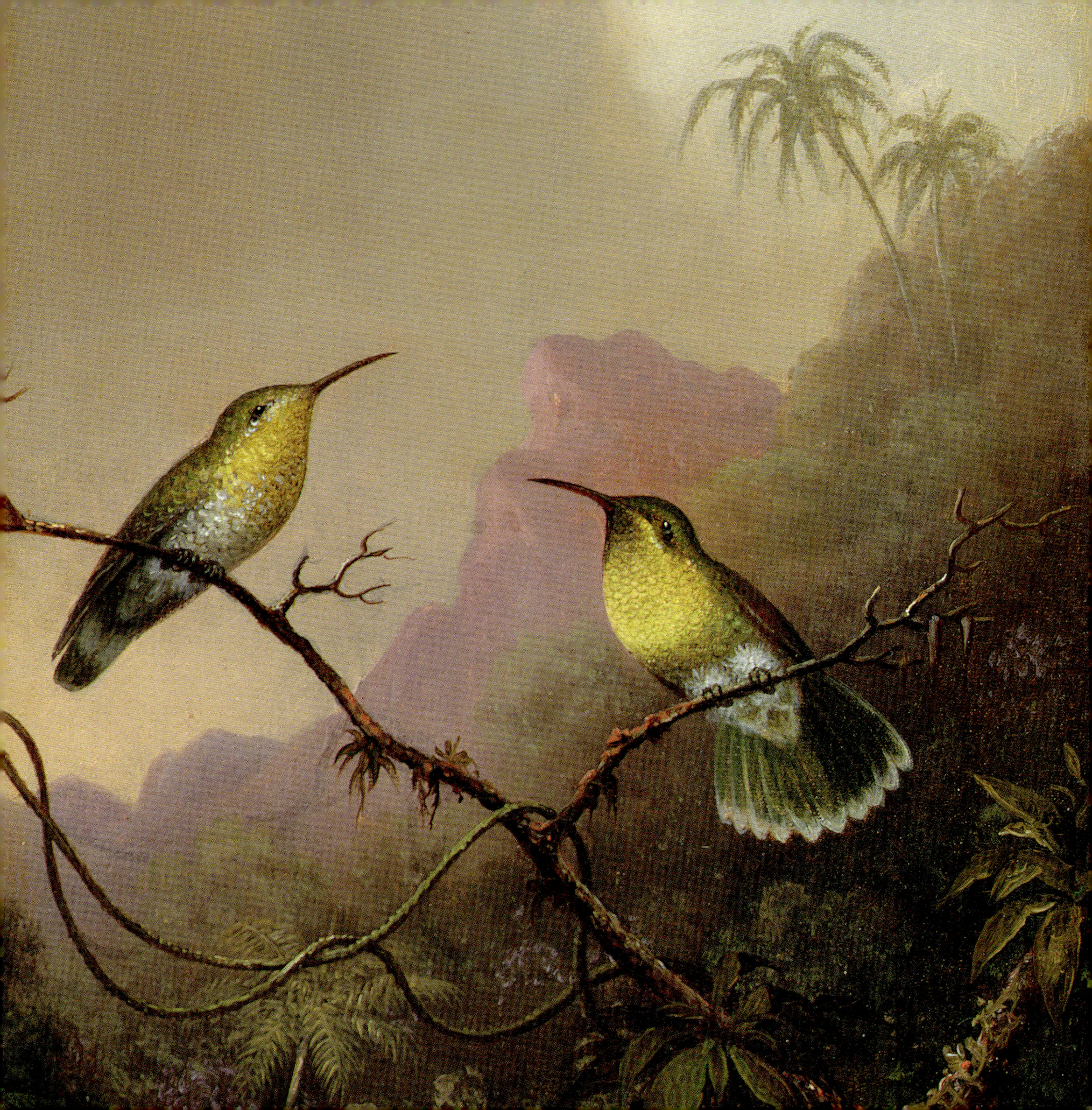

CONTENTS

'Hope' is the thing with feathers –
That perches in the soul –
And sings the tune without the words –
And never stops – at all –

Emily Dickinson

INTRODUCTION

For the American poet Emily Dickinson, hope is a bird that sings through the gale and storm, keeping others warm but asking not a crumb in return. Birds embody our aspirations, fears and spiritual yearnings. They may be a familiar part of our daily life, as providers of food, feathers and entertainment, but their ability to sing and fly is mysterious, setting them apart from all other creatures. Their enviable freedom to escape the everyday by soaring into the beyond may explain why they are at the heart of many of the world's creation myths, and why images of them have been used to represent the human soul ascending to Paradise, the divine spirit descending to Earth, or communication between men and gods.

Many pagan divinities and Christian saints have particular birds as their attributes. Some rely on avian transport to wheel about the heavens, or transform themselves into birds to carry out special missions. Other gods are hybrid creatures: half-human, half-bird. And, since the skies are connected with divine providence, birds have frequently been used as oracles to foretell the future, their flight patterns seen as auguries of good or ill. Angels, messengers of God, are also blessed with the gift of flight, and it is no accident that they are often depicted in art with remarkably realistic birds' wings. Humans have always wanted to fly as birds do: the myth of Daedalus and Icarus, who attempted to escape captivity by strapping on pairs of wings, is one poetic interpretation of this desire (p. 98). Leonardo da Vinci's efforts to develop a flying machine based on his observation of birds' wings were an attempt to realize the same ambition.

This book sets out to explore how artists have reflected the changing imaginative relationship between people and birds. Over the centuries, different birds have attracted a wealth of symbolic associations, often loosely based on characteristic behaviour. The eagle, for example, a dominant bird of prey, has been adopted in various forms as an emblem of power and victory by empires and nations from ancient Rome to the United States. But the significance of birds is complex and often contradictory. So the owl, which from Classical times has been associated with wisdom through its link with the Greek goddess Athena, can signify foolishness in seventeenth-century Dutch paintings. The peacock can stand for such opposing attributes as vanity and immortality, and for Christ's Resurrection. The dove can represent love, lust, peace and the Holy Spirit. And while the ancient Egyptians may have placed vultures as protective symbols on the doorways of their temples, in modern viewers the birds prompt a feeling of doom. Scientists, as well as artists and writers, have shaped the wider cultural significance of birds. The humble mockingbird of the Galapagos Islands played a central part in the most shocking theory to emerge in Victorian Britain: Charles Darwin's theory of evolution.

EARLY BIRDS

The earliest known depictions of birds appear on the walls of caves from the Palaeolithic era, although they are hard to date with any accuracy. There was great

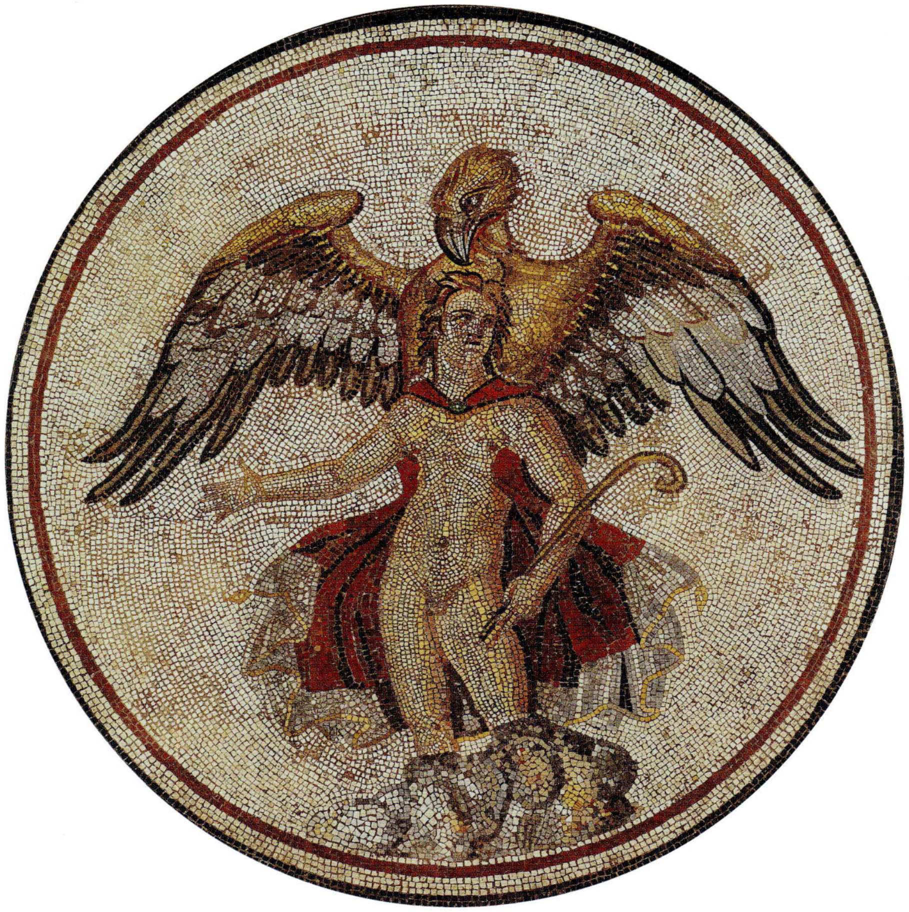

Roman
The Abduction of Ganymede
2nd–3rd century AD
Mosaic
Musée Saint-Pierre, Vienne, France

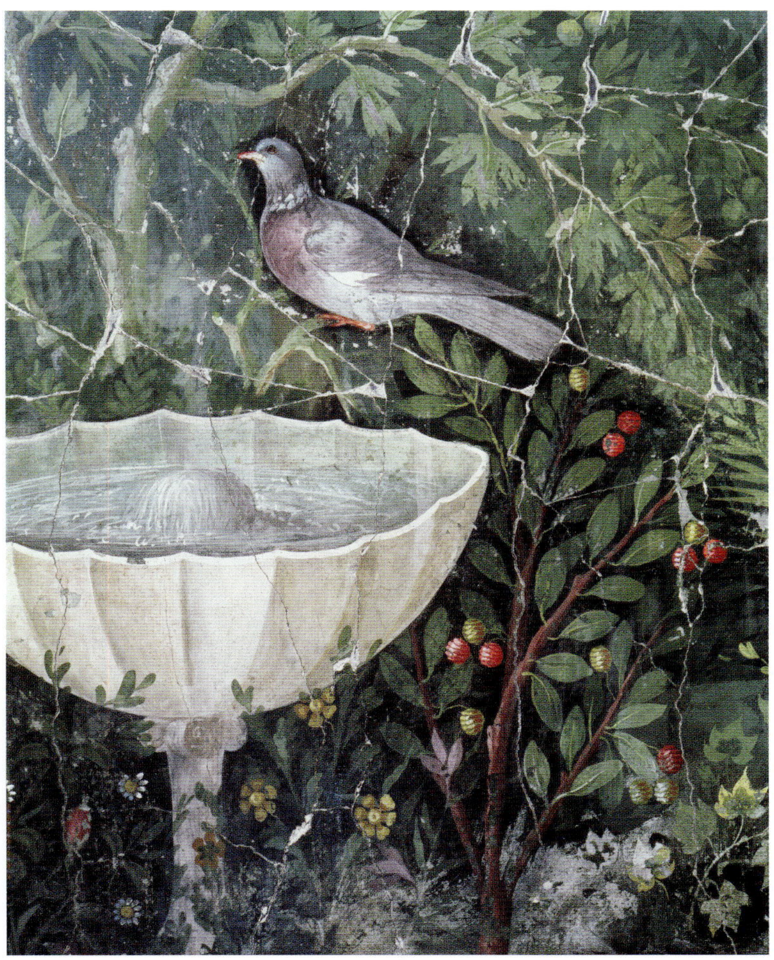

Roman villas of Pompeii and Herculaneum were painted for the enjoyment of the living. Birds fly around or perch among the flowers, trees and fountains in elaborate garden scenes (left, bottom, and p. 56), and dead ones appear in larder scenes or still lifes showing the ingredients for banquets. The Romans appreciated birds both for their gastronomic possibilities and for their beauty. They kept aviaries containing peacocks, doves and green parrots, and ostriches from Africa, and valued birds as pets.

The wealthy householders and their guests who admired such paintings would have been well versed in the Classical myths featuring birds. Zeus or Jupiter is associated with the eagle, and uses this guise to abduct Ganymede, cup-bearer to the gods (left, top, and p. 103). He also disguises himself as a swan in order to seduce the wife of the king of Sparta, Leda (p. 94), who later gives birth to two eggs that produce two sets of twins: Castor and Clytemnestra, and Pollux and Helen. Juno, Jupiter's jealous wife, is credited with giving the peacock its glorious eye-studded tail (p. 104); the Greek goddess Aphrodite (Roman: Venus) is usually seen with two doves (p. 101); and Athena (Minerva) is inextricably linked with the owl.

BIRDS ON THE PAGE

Mythical birds flitted through the stories of antiquity, while the philosophers and natural historians of the Classical world made the first attempts to develop a scientific system for classifying real ones. The Greek

English
A brown bird, hoopoe and red cock, from a medieval bestiary (MS 379 f. 24r)
1300–25
Vellum
The Fitzwilliam Museum, Cambridge

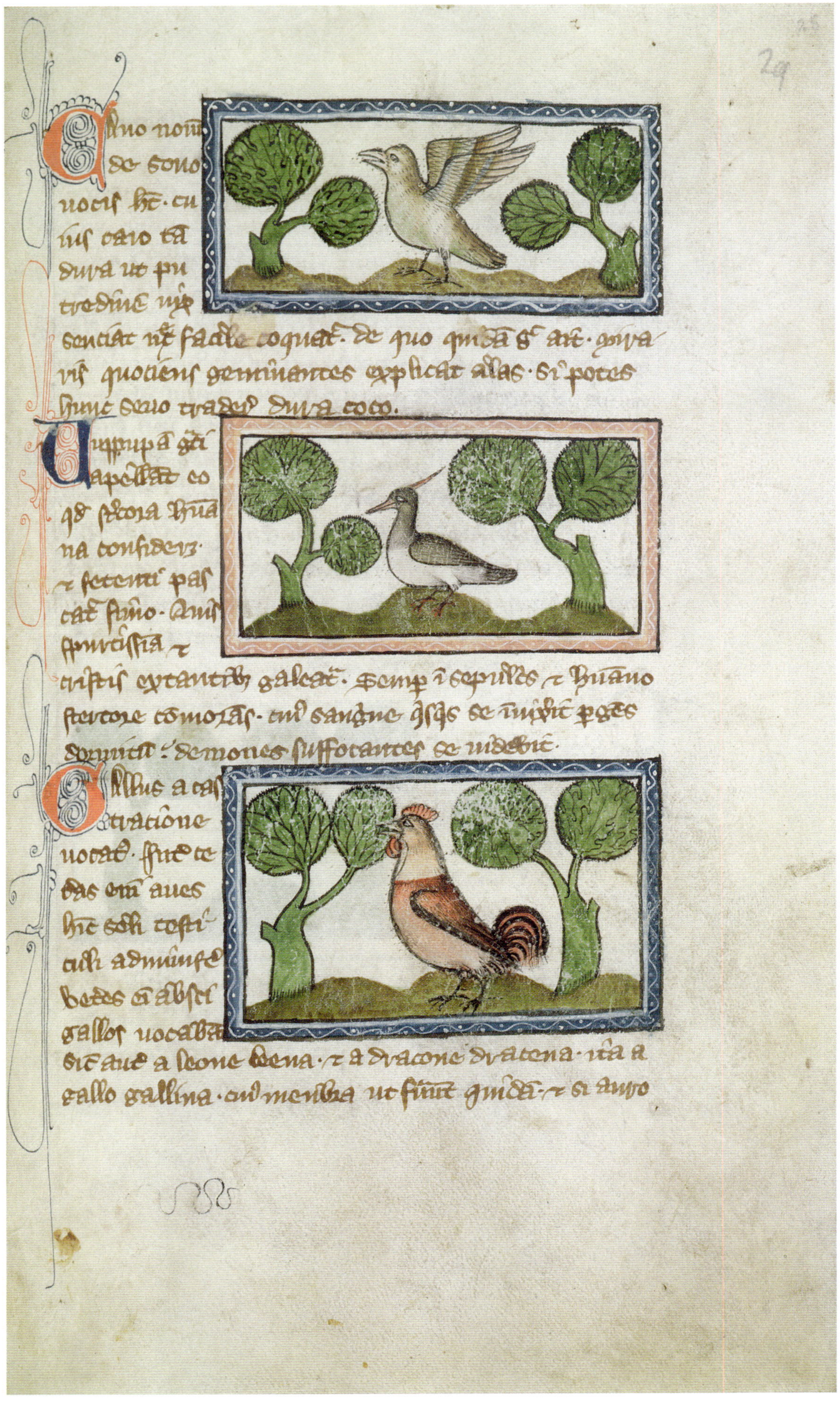

philosopher Aristotle (384–322 BC) devoted four books of his multi-volume *Historia Animalium* to birds, describing some 140 species that he recognized. His work was elaborated on by the Roman writer Pliny the Elder (AD 23–79), who devoted one volume of his *Historia Naturalis* to them. Much of the material that appears in medieval bestiaries can be traced back to him, via a didactic text called *Physiologus*, which was assembled by an anonymous Greek in Alexandria some time in the fourth or fifth century.

Bestiaries – early natural-history books – enjoyed great popularity in Britain in the thirteenth and fourteenth centuries. These compendia of beasts and birds combined illustrations of and text about each creature depicted: its character, its place in history, and titbits of myth and folklore. The one illustrated on the right shows a hoopoe and a cockerel beneath a large eagle with spread wings. But some of the birds depicted in bestiaries were purely imaginary, such as the phoenix and the caladrius bird (p. 91). The birds are rarely portrayed with much accuracy, and appear exaggerated or crude to modern eyes, but the bestiary's prime aim was to illustrate a moral tale rather than record scientific observation.

Illuminated manuscripts abound with birds, both imaginary and real: one scholar has identified more than eighty-three species of bird in manuscripts made between 698 and 1482. In early Celtic gospel books, such as the Lindisfarne Gospels and the Book of Kells (created in the late seventh and the eighth or ninth centuries respectively), schematic birds are often woven

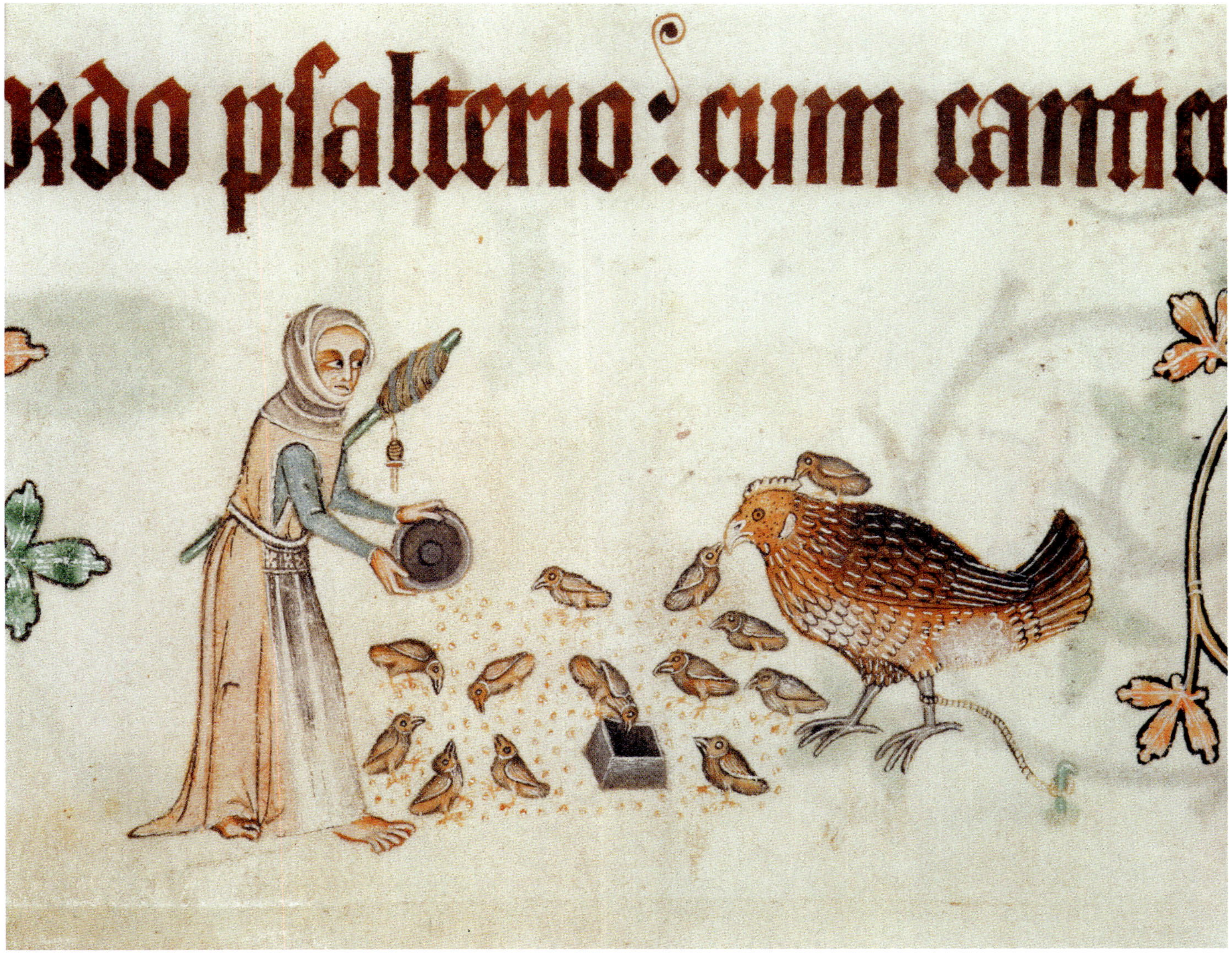

English
Woman throwing corn to hens and chickens, from the Luttrell Psalter (Add 42130 f. 166v)
c. 1340
Vellum
Whole page 36 × 24.5 cm (14⅛ × 9⅝ in.)
British Library, London

into the dense interlacing patterns that cover the pages. More naturalistic birds appear in manuscripts from the twelfth century onwards. They enliven the pages of the large, sumptuously illustrated bibles that were read out to church congregations, and smaller psalters (books of psalms) intended for personal use by clergy and laity from around the thirteenth century. The scenes of everyday life that appear at the foot of the pages of the Luttrell Psalter show birds in a domestic context: hawks set off on a hunt, rooks follow a ploughman, and a housewife scatters corn for her poultry (above).

A number of particularly fine birds can be seen cavorting among the flowers and other wildlife in the margins of books of hours for private devotions produced in England and Flanders from the fourteenth to the sixteenth centuries (overleaf). While some of these birds may have been based on those kept in aviaries by the monarchs and nobles who commissioned the books, by no means all the bird depictions in manuscripts were observed at first hand. Artists and illuminators frequently copied one another, so the same birds tend to crop up regularly in the same poses. Furthermore, the artists were not ornithologists, but made liberal use of their imagination to come up with their own embellishments and invent hybrid creatures.

Birds also appear in hunting treatises. Before the advent of firearms they were caught by hand, knocked down by sticks, trapped in nets or pursued with spears and arrows, or by other birds. The excitement of a medieval hunt is conveyed in a leaf from an Italian manuscript written in the fourteenth century for the instruction of children. It shows men and boys setting

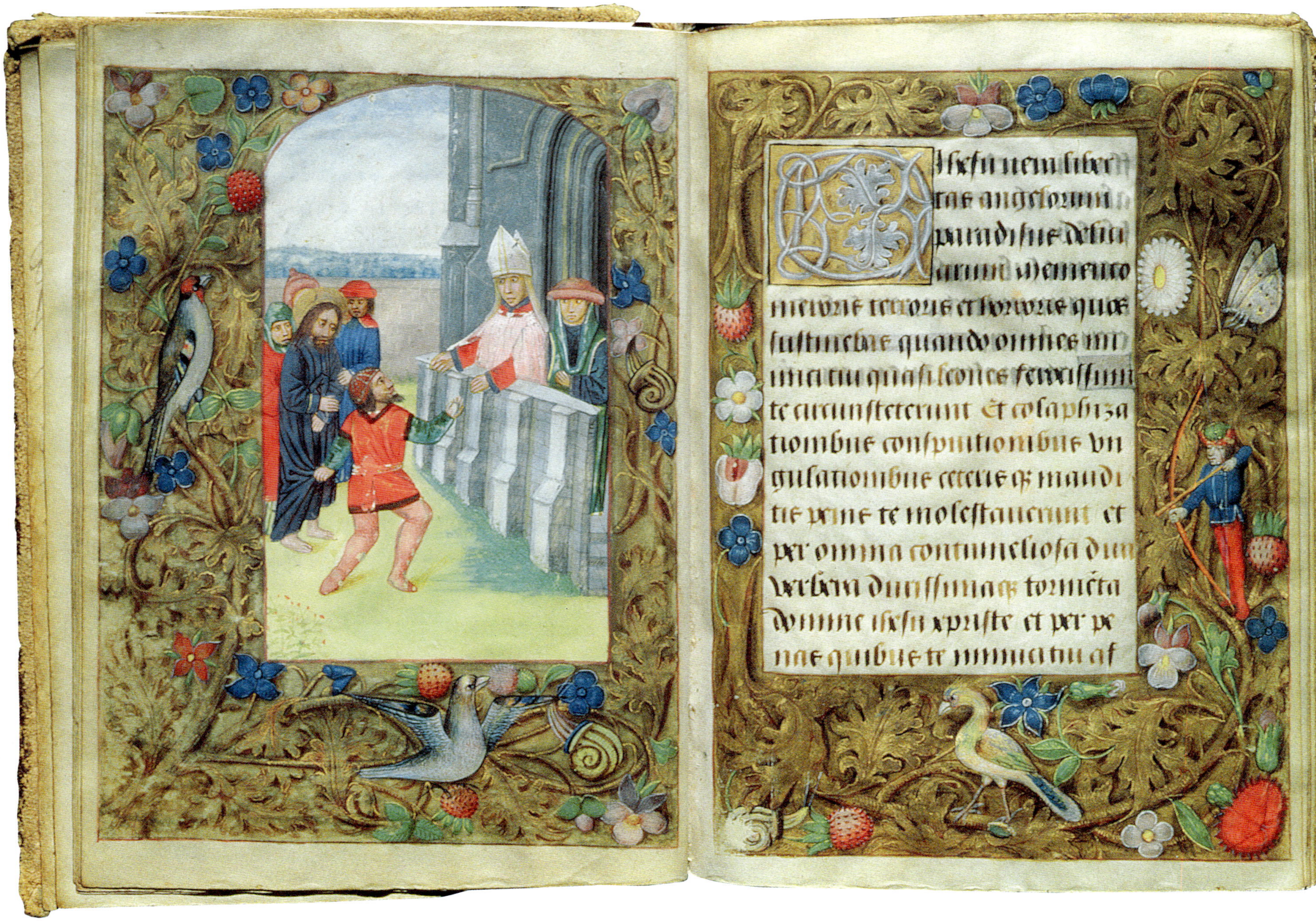

Flemish
Christ Accused, from the
Staffordshire Prayer Book
16th century
Vellum
Dimensions unknown
Arundel Castle, West Sussex

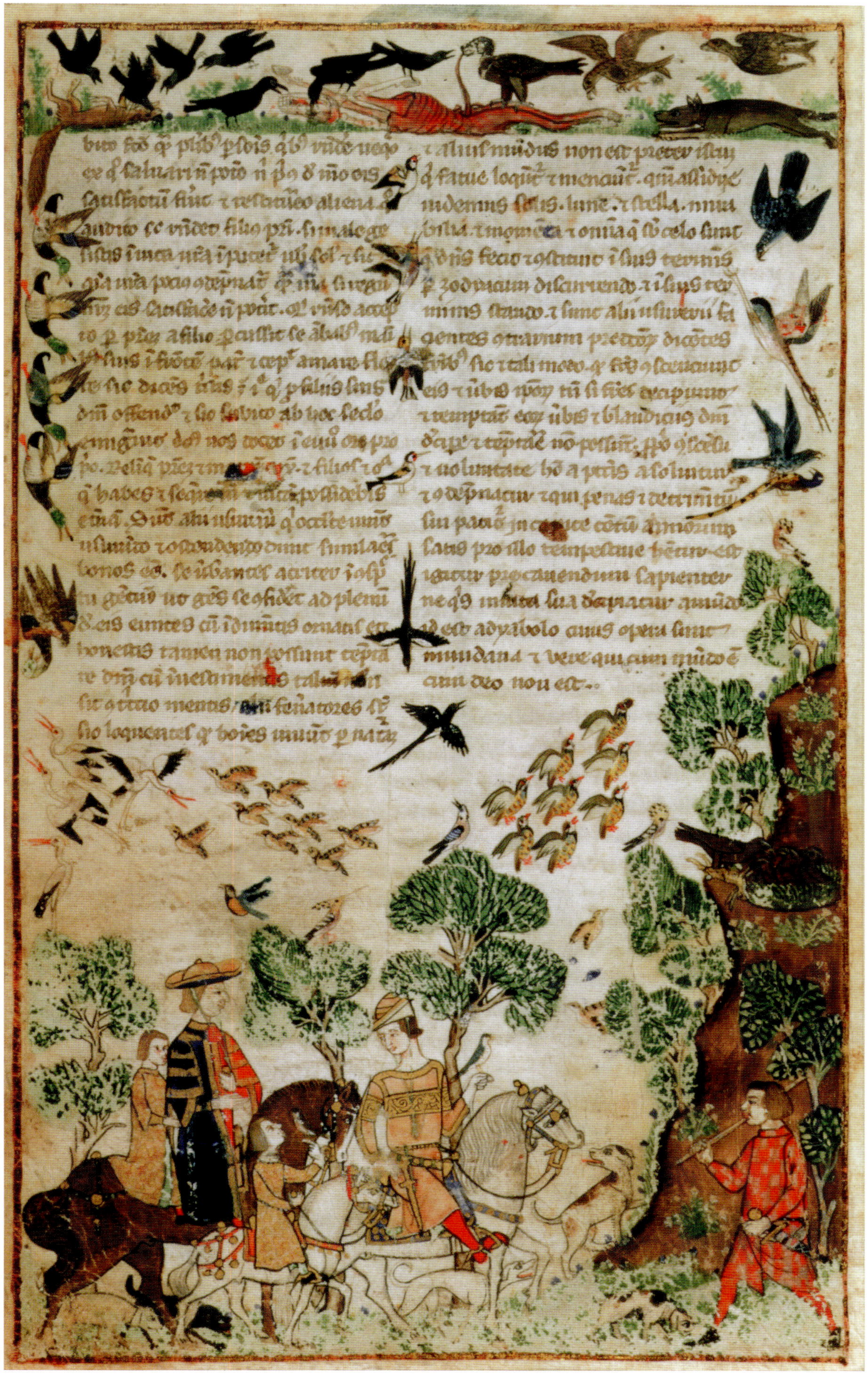

Italian
Men and Boys Hawking,
from the Cocharelli treatise
(Eg 3127 f. 1v)
c. 1330–40
Vellum
17 × 10.5 cm (6⅝ × 4⅛ in.)
British Library, London

out on a hunt, while the hawks dart and dive in pursuit of a host of smaller birds (left). The birds on this page are lively, if schematic, and could have been copied from another source, but some of those in the drawings made by Renaissance artists as preparatory studies for paintings, tapestries and frescoes were clearly based on observation (overleaf, left).

FROM SACRED TO SECULAR

The Bible contains numerous references to birds, scattered through the various books from Genesis to Revelation. Birds are there at the very beginning of everything; indeed, the spirit of God is said to 'hover over the surface of the waters', conjuring up a bird-like image at the very moment of creation. Birds themselves come into being on the fifth day, when God creates birds to 'fly above the earth in the open expanse of sky' and fish to fill the sea (p. 15). Adam is given dominion over the birds and names all the living creatures, becoming the first naturalist.

The raven is the first bird to be mentioned by name in the Bible, but the bird referred to most often is the dove. It is the embodiment of the Holy Spirit (p. 16, bottom), and it is the bird that returns to the Ark bearing the olive branch that tells Noah the flood waters are subsiding – whereas the raven sent by Noah returns with nothing. The dove is often present in paintings of the Creation, the Annunciation and the Baptism of Christ. The eagle also makes frequent appearances as one of the four beasts of Revelation, and is associated

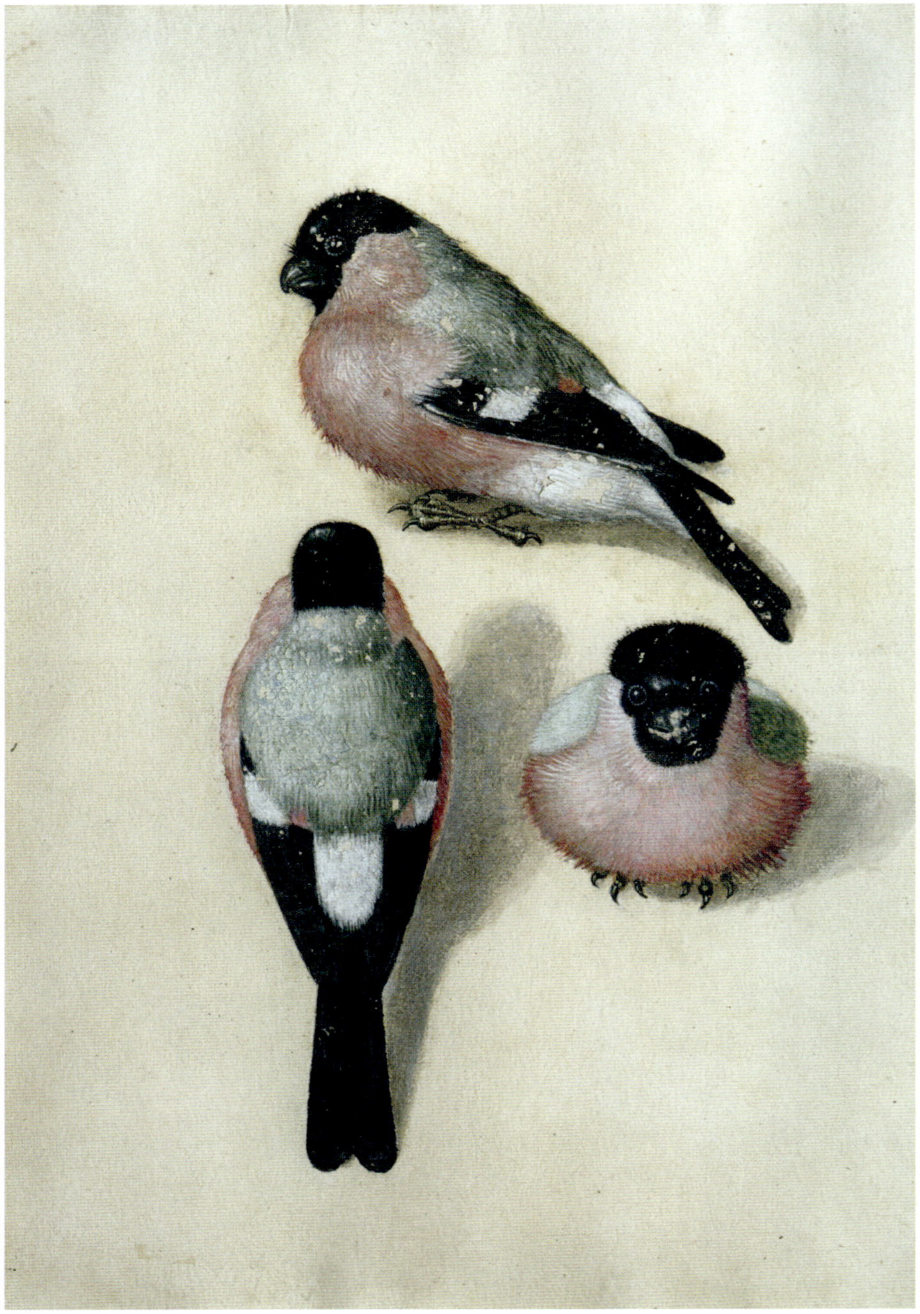

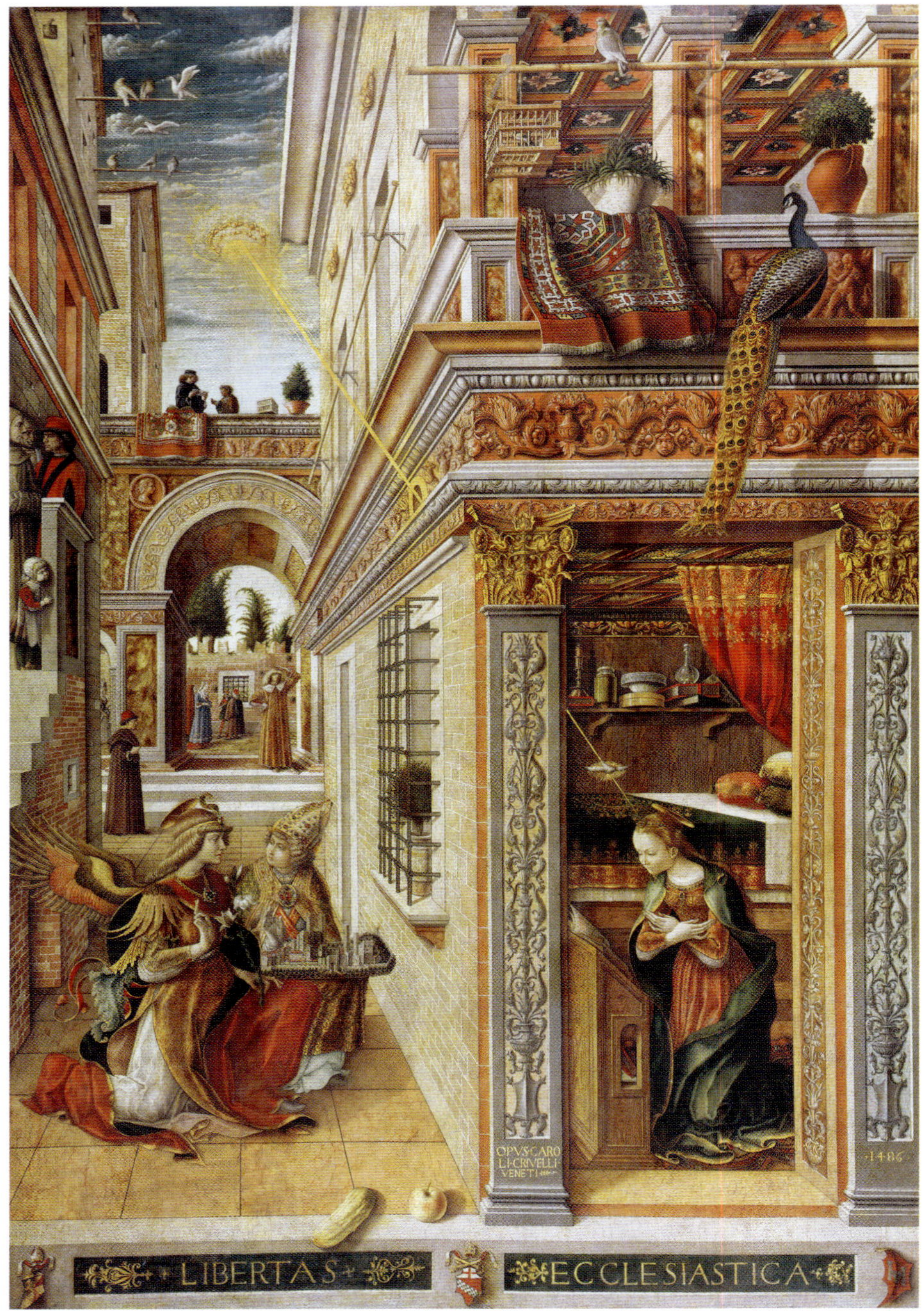

Albrecht Dürer
(1471–1528)
Three studies of a bullfinch

Early 16th century
Watercolour and gouache on paper
Dimensions unknown
Real Monasterio de El Escorial, San Lorenzo de El Escorial, Spain

Carlo Crivelli
(*c.* 1430/35–1494)
The Annunciation, with St Emidius

1486
Egg and oil on canvas
207 × 146.7 cm (81½ × 57¾ in.)
The National Gallery, London

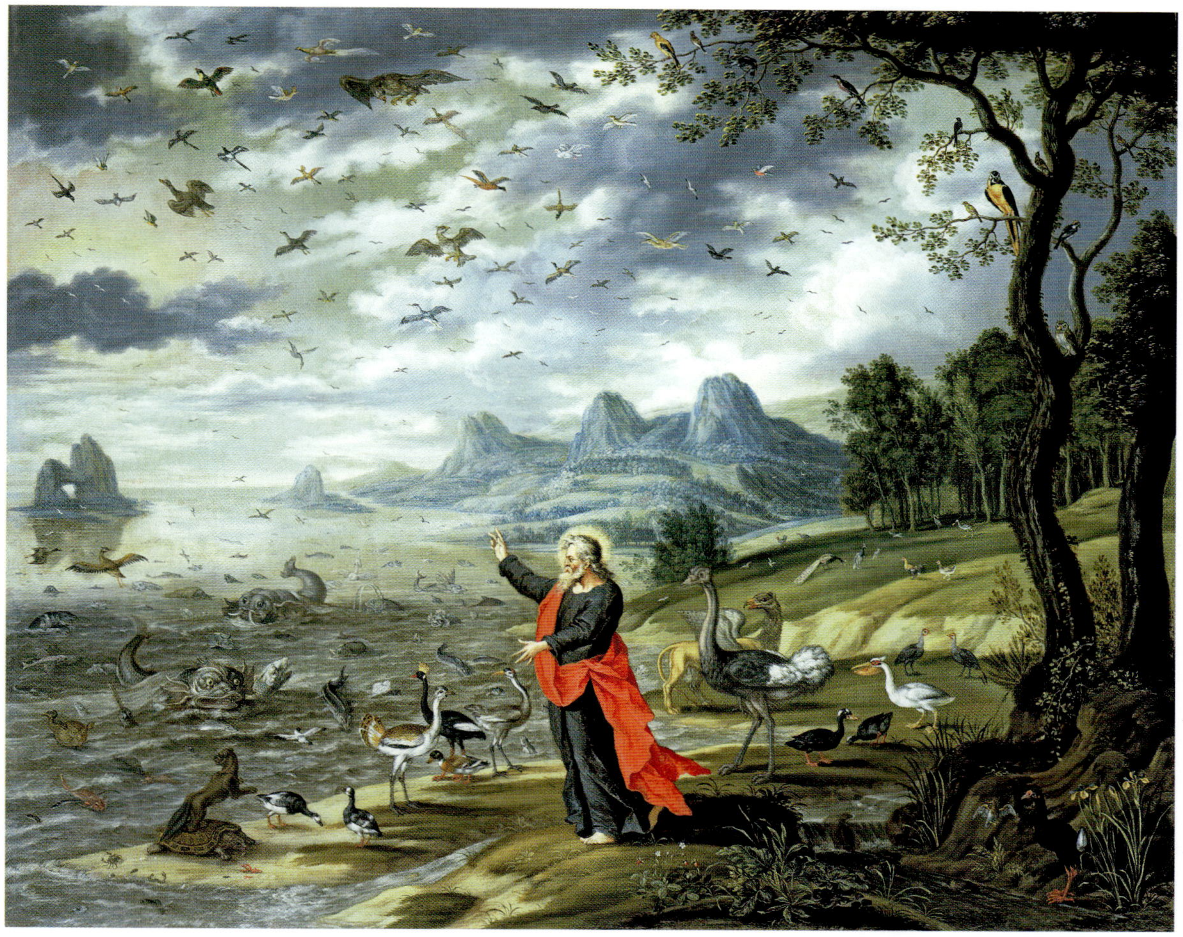

with St John. The brilliantly coloured goldfinch crops up in the margins of manuscripts and in paintings of the Madonna and Child, where it serves as a reminder of the fate that awaits the baby in Mary's lap. It is said to have acquired the vivid red on its head when it flew down to pluck a thorn from Christ's crown as he was on the road to Calvary, and was splashed with a drop of the Saviour's blood (p. 75). The fact that goldfinches were once popular pets among European children must have added to the poignancy of the association.

While birds themselves are not generally the central subjects of Renaissance paintings, their presence often adds a layer of symbolic meaning, or enigma, to the narrative. In Carlo Crivelli's *Annunciation, with St Emidius* (opposite, right) we see the dove of the Holy Spirit descending through the clouds to Mary in her chamber, while other birds flutter about a dovecote on the house opposite, and a peacock, the Christian symbol of immortality and the Resurrection, perches on the balcony above her chamber. Near the peacock is a caged goldfinch, which prefigures Christ's Passion, and another dove, representing purity. Two further religious paintings in the National Gallery, London – Giovanni Bellini's *Madonna of the Meadow* (*c.* 1500) and Andrea Mantegna's *Agony in the Garden* (1458) – contain vultures as symbols of death. In Raphael's *Miraculous Draught of Fishes* (1515–16), a working drawing for a set of tapestries commissioned by Pope Leo X for the Sistine Chapel, the foreground is dominated by three lifelike cranes, which stand for vigilance (p. 76), while the ravens in the background could represent the banishment of sin and deceit.

One of the most captivating Renaissance bird scenes is that commissioned for the ceiling of a garden pavilion at the Villa Medici in Rome used by Cardinal Ferdinando de' Medici, which was decorated in the 1570s by Jacopo Zucchi (overleaf). It shows a *trompe l'œil* vine-clad pergola with a variety of birds playing as though in an aviary. This scene harks back to similar wall paintings produced in ancient Rome

Isaak van Oosten
(1613–1661)
The Creation of the Birds and Fishes
17th century
Oil on copper
Dimensions unknown
Private collection

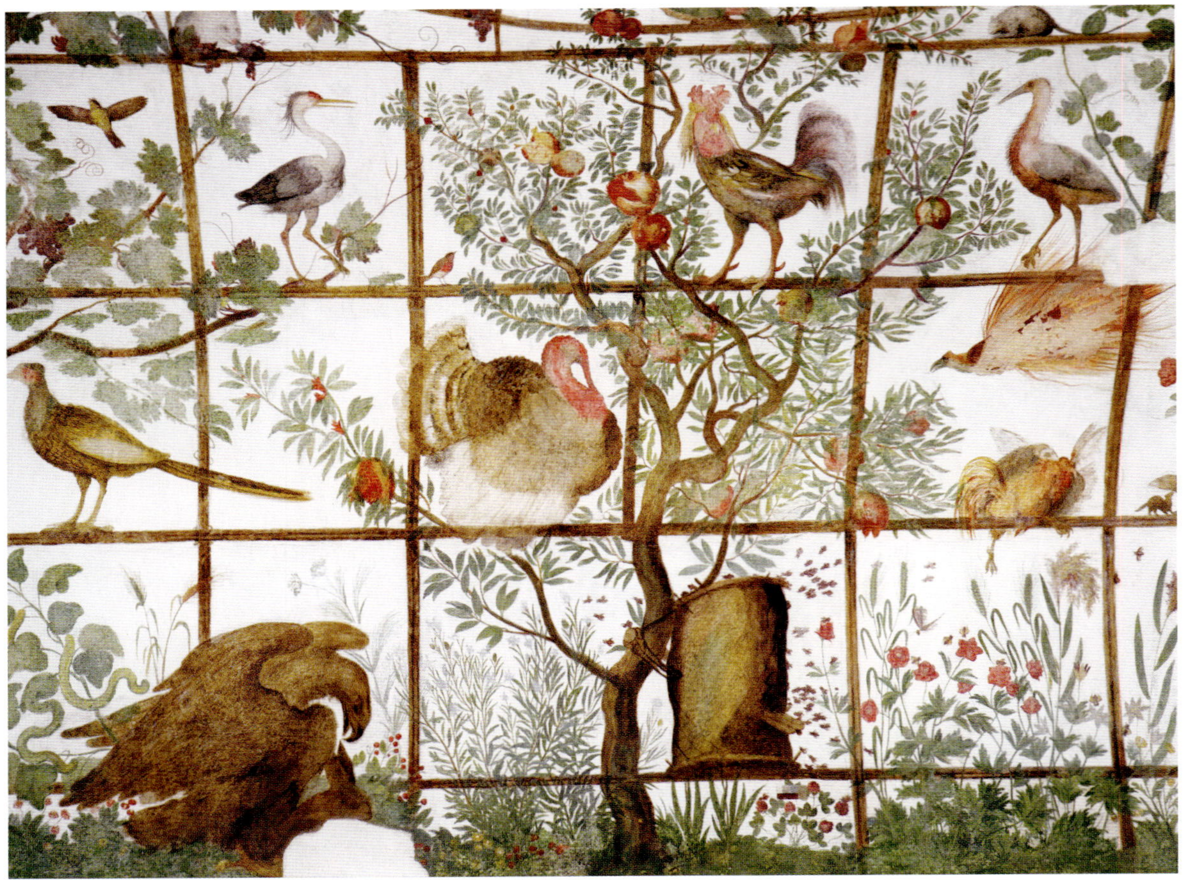

Jacopo Zucchi
(*c.* 1540–1596)
Ceiling in the antechamber of Ferdinando de' Medici's studiolo
1570s
Fresco
Villa Medici, Rome

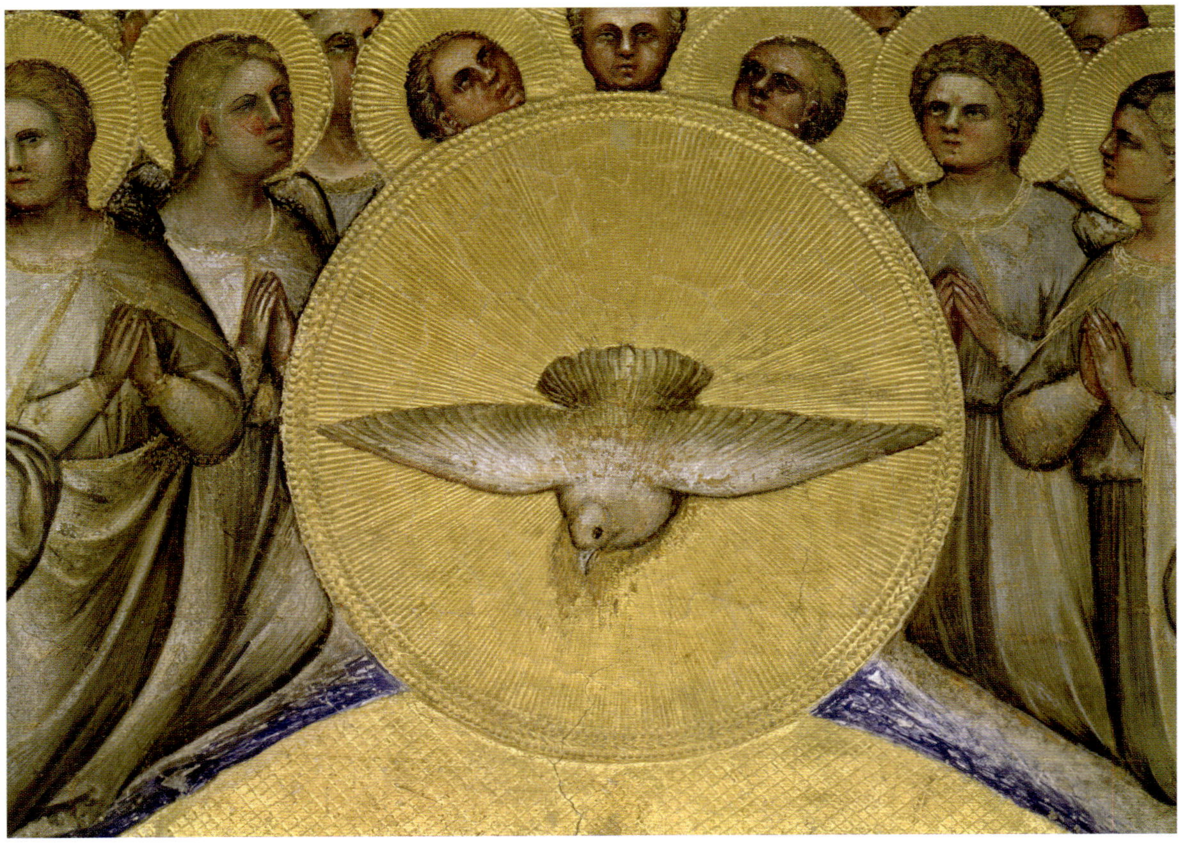

and Pompeii, conceived as illusionistic extensions of gardens. Although commissioned by a man of the church, the scene is determinedly secular. During the sixteenth century, while religious subjects continued to provide an opportunity to portray birds en masse – in scenes of the Creation, Noah's Ark and the Garden of Eden, for example – the links between artists and the Catholic Church were being loosened in Protestant areas of Europe. Painters gradually began to relegate the religious content to the background of their bird and animal pictures; eventually, they could abandon it altogether.

Birds proliferated in portraits of individuals from the Renaissance onwards, often making a subtle statement about the identity of a sitter. Vittore Carpaccio's *Young Knight in a Landscape* (1510; opposite, left) contains many highly decorative birds, with carefully observed flowers, plants and animals. In the sky, a hawk battles with a heron. Various interpretations have been proposed for this enigmatic vignette. The motif of these battling birds often represents the conflict of virtue and vice in medieval and Renaissance art. But here it could simply be that the heron caught by the hawk or eagle represents the death of the young man in battle, and that this is a funerary portrait. The unidentified young man (who may be Francesco Maria della Rovere, 3rd Duke of Urbino) is geared up to fight: a scroll to the left is inscribed 'Better die than lose one's honour', and the peacock perching on the helmet of the mounted man on horseback (perhaps the sitter in action) is a reference

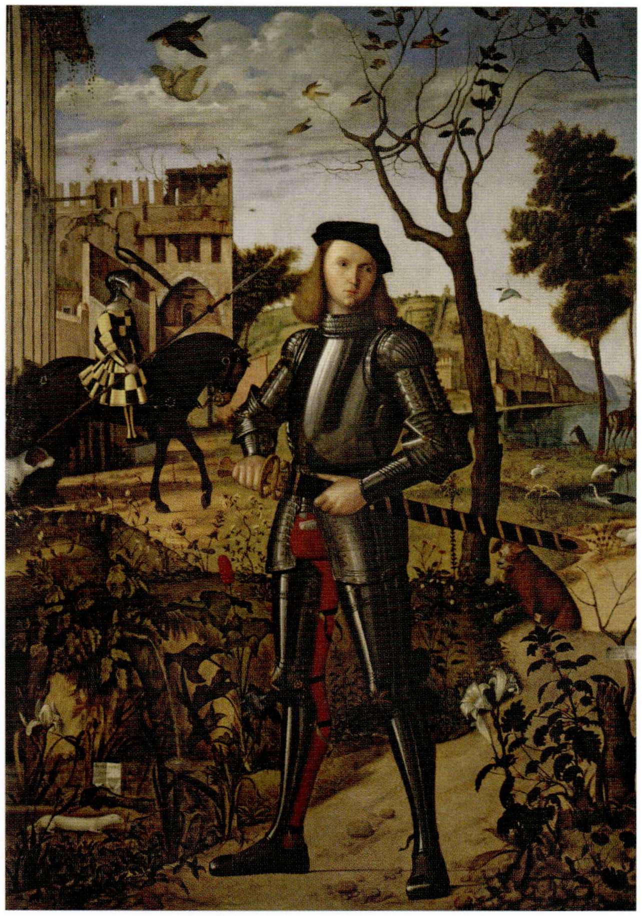

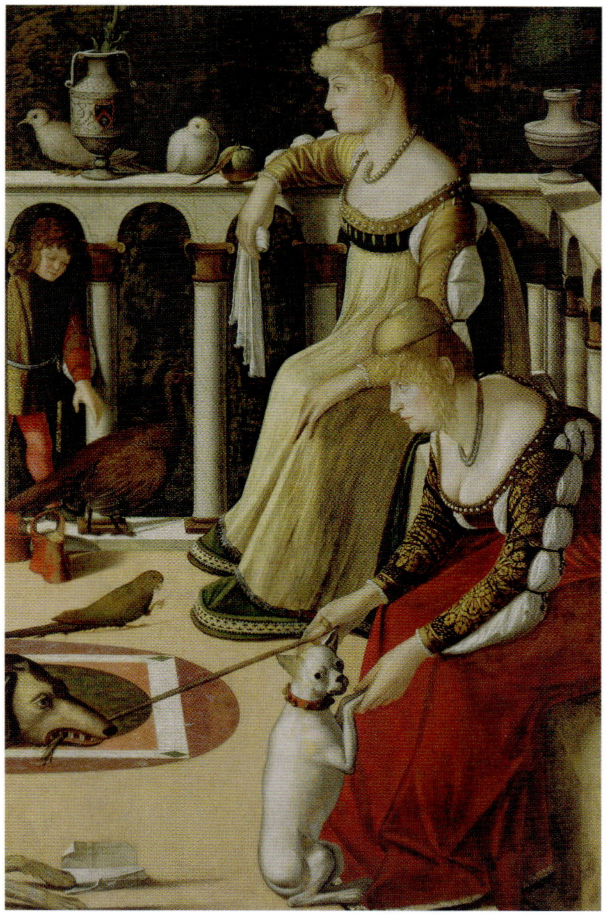

to immortality. But the painting's ultimate meaning continues to tantalize. The birds in the same artist's portrait of two Venetian ladies may also contain clues to the painting's meaning (above, right). The peahen is emblematic of a happy marriage, and the doves on the balustrade are the birds of Venus. Another fragment of the same painting, in the J. Paul Getty Museum in Los Angeles, shows young men in the lagoon fishing with the aid of cormorants, adding a further layer of complexity to the bird theme. But since these panels are only part of a whole work, they are hard to interpret.

Also puzzling is the meaning of the dead bittern Rembrandt holds up in his self-portrait of 1639 (overleaf, left). The artist's face is obscured by shadow while the light shines on the bird's plumage. It is an enigma: Rembrandt presents himself as a hunter, when there is no evidence that he took part in the sport. Hunting such birds as bitterns was an aristocratic privilege, and perhaps by showing himself in this way Rembrandt was indicating his rising social status. Alternatively, he may simply have been showing the viewer the superbly painted dead bird as evidence of his artistic skill.

The significance of a bird in a portrait is often more straightforward. In Hans Holbein's portrait of a woman thought to be Anne Ashby, Lady Lovell (p. 19), the starling (then a common pet) could be a wordplay on East Harling in Norfolk, where the family lived. (The squirrel refers to the family's coat of arms, which included three squirrels.) Elizabethan portraits were redolent with symbolism: when Nicholas Hilliard painted a portrait of the Virgin Queen, he showed her wearing a brooch in the form of a pelican. The bird had long been associated with Christ's sacrifice, since it was believed that the female fed her young with her own blood, so the implication was that Elizabeth was mother to her own people.

Birds were sometimes included in formal portraits simply as fashionable accessories. When Willem Wissing portrayed James II's queen, Mary of Modena, in about 1685, around the time of her coronation, he

OPPOSITE, BOTTOM

Giusto de' Menabuoi
(*c.* 1320–1391)
The Dove of the Holy Spirit
c. 1376–78
Fresco
Baptistery of the Cathedral, Padua

ABOVE, LEFT

Vittore Carpaccio
(?1460/66–1525/26)
Young Knight in a Landscape
1510
Oil on canvas
218.5 × 151.5 cm (86 × 59⅝ in.)
Museo Thyssen-Bornemisza, Madrid

ABOVE, RIGHT

Vittore Carpaccio
(?1460/66–1525/26)
Two Venetian Ladies
c. 1495
Oil on panel
94 × 64 cm (37 × 25⅛ in.)
Museo Correr, Venice

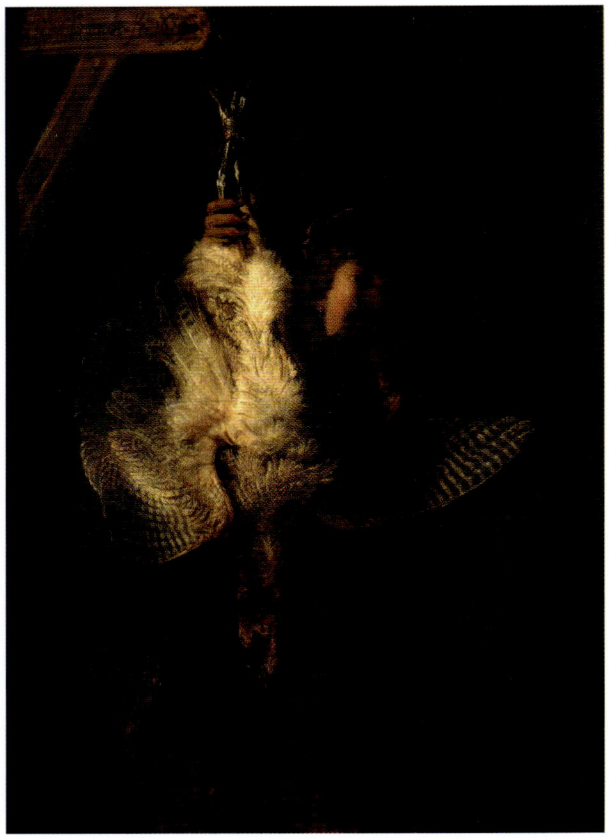

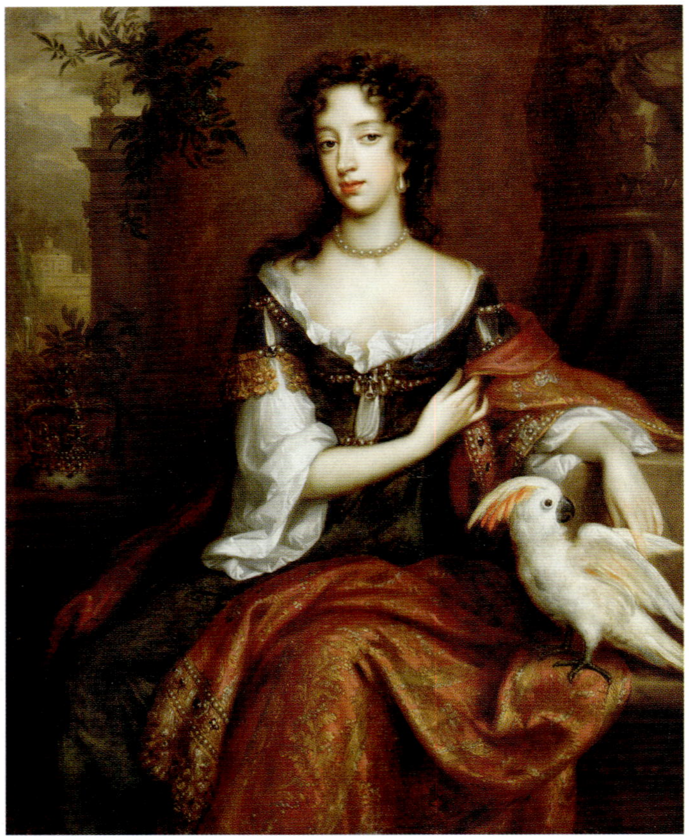

perched a cockatoo on her gown (above, right). Other versions of the composition feature a dog, and the fact that Mary is stroking her bird indicates that she had a similar fondness for it. By this time, the English royal family had its own menagerie and aviary in St James's Park, so the bird could have been a favourite housed there. Mary fled England with her husband in 1689, and the English throne was taken over by William of Orange, who employed the talents of his own bird artist, Melchior de Hondecoeter. Two remarkable bird paintings by Hondecoeter in Holkham Hall in Norfolk might be thought of as allegorical portraits of William III – or at least his naval victories – as the countries he vanquished in his lowland wars are personified as birds. In one of the canvases (p. 20, top), the brown eagle stands for Russia, the heron for The Netherlands, the raven for Denmark, the goose for England and the cock for France.

Birds are given starring roles in many Baroque landscape paintings and still lifes (p. 20, bottom). Live birds, such as hawks, are depicted as active participants in hunting, and dead ones are shown heaped up in the countryside (p. 21, top) or on tables as trophies. They can form the appetizing components of a feast in kitchen scenes (p. 21, bottom) or hang from hooks as the basis of a humbler meal. They are also portrayed as pets, caged or otherwise. The goldfinch that features in the upper right-hand corner of Abraham Mignon's exuberant still life has even been taught to perform a trick: lifting a minute bucket on a chain from a glass of water so that it can drink (p. 22). The contemporary viewer would have recognized the goldfinch's link with the Passion of Christ, and perhaps associated its drinking trick with the Eucharistic wine; the squirrel, long associated with the devil, might have brought to mind the foolish sinner.

Many of the finest seventeenth-century bird paintings were produced by Dutch and Flemish artists, and a number feature recently discovered exotic species imported to Europe by explorers of and traders

ABOVE, LEFT

Rembrandt Harmensz. van Rijn (1606–1669)
Self-portrait with Bittern
1639
Oil on panel
121 × 89 cm (47⅝ × 35 in.)
Gemäldegalerie Alte Meister, Dresden

ABOVE, RIGHT

Willem Wissing (1656–1687)
Mary of Modena
c. 1685
Oil on canvas
125.6 × 102.6 cm (49⅜ × 40⅜ in.)
Yale Center for British Art, New Haven, Connecticut

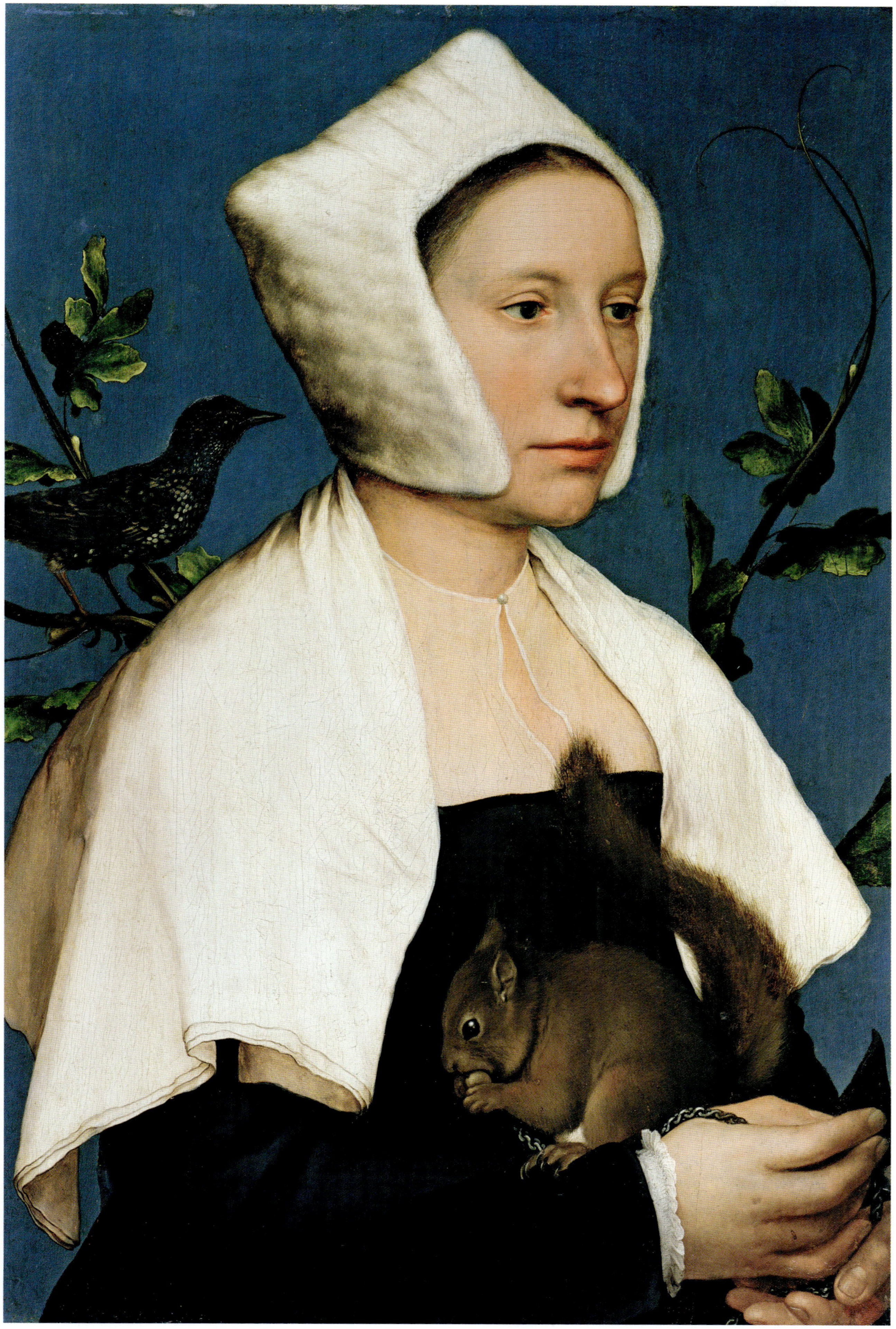

Hans Holbein the Younger
(1497/98–1543)
Lady with a Squirrel and a Starling
c. 1526–28
Oil on panel
56 × 38.8 cm (22 × 15¼ in.)
The National Gallery, London

Melchior de Hondecoeter
(1636–1695)
William III's Lowland Wars
Last quarter of the 17th century
Oil on canvas
Dimensions unknown
Holkham Hall, Norfolk

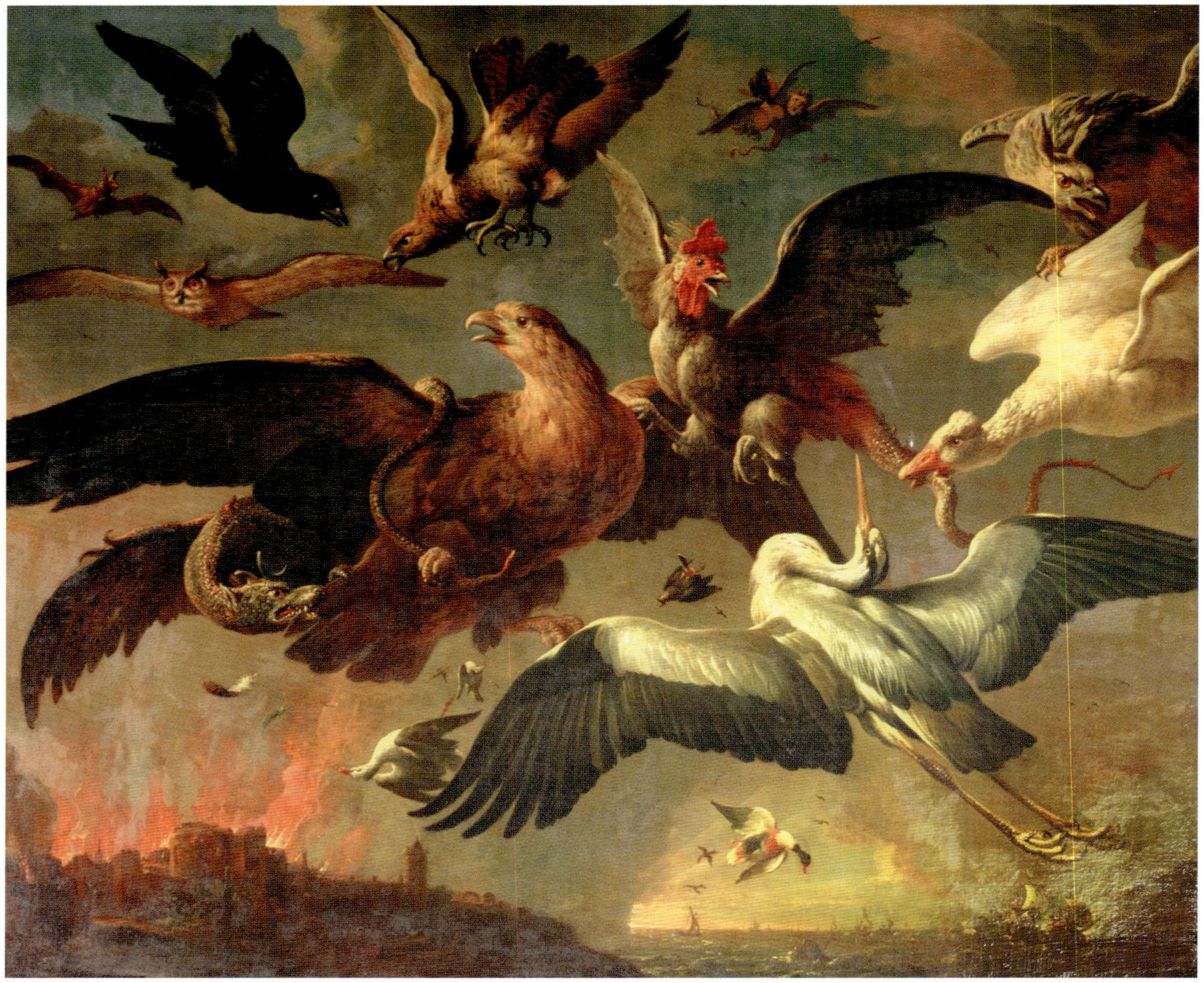

Balthasar van der Ast
(?1593/94–1657)
Still Life with Fruit and Macaws
1622
Oil on copper
20.6 × 26.7 cm (8 1/8 × 10 1/2 in.)
The Fitzwilliam Museum, Cambridge

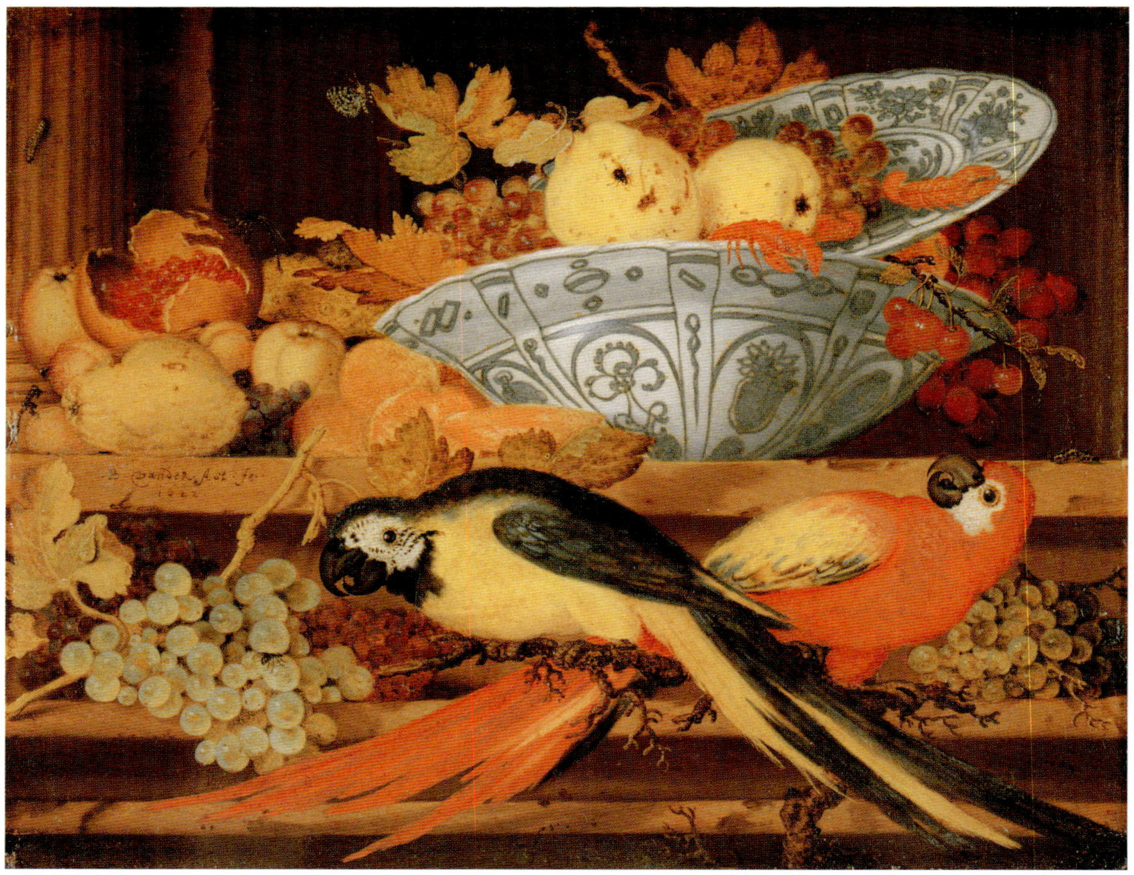

Jan Fyt (1611–1661)
Still Life of Swan and Game in a Landscape
First half of the 17th century
Oil on canvas
Dimensions unknown
Private collection

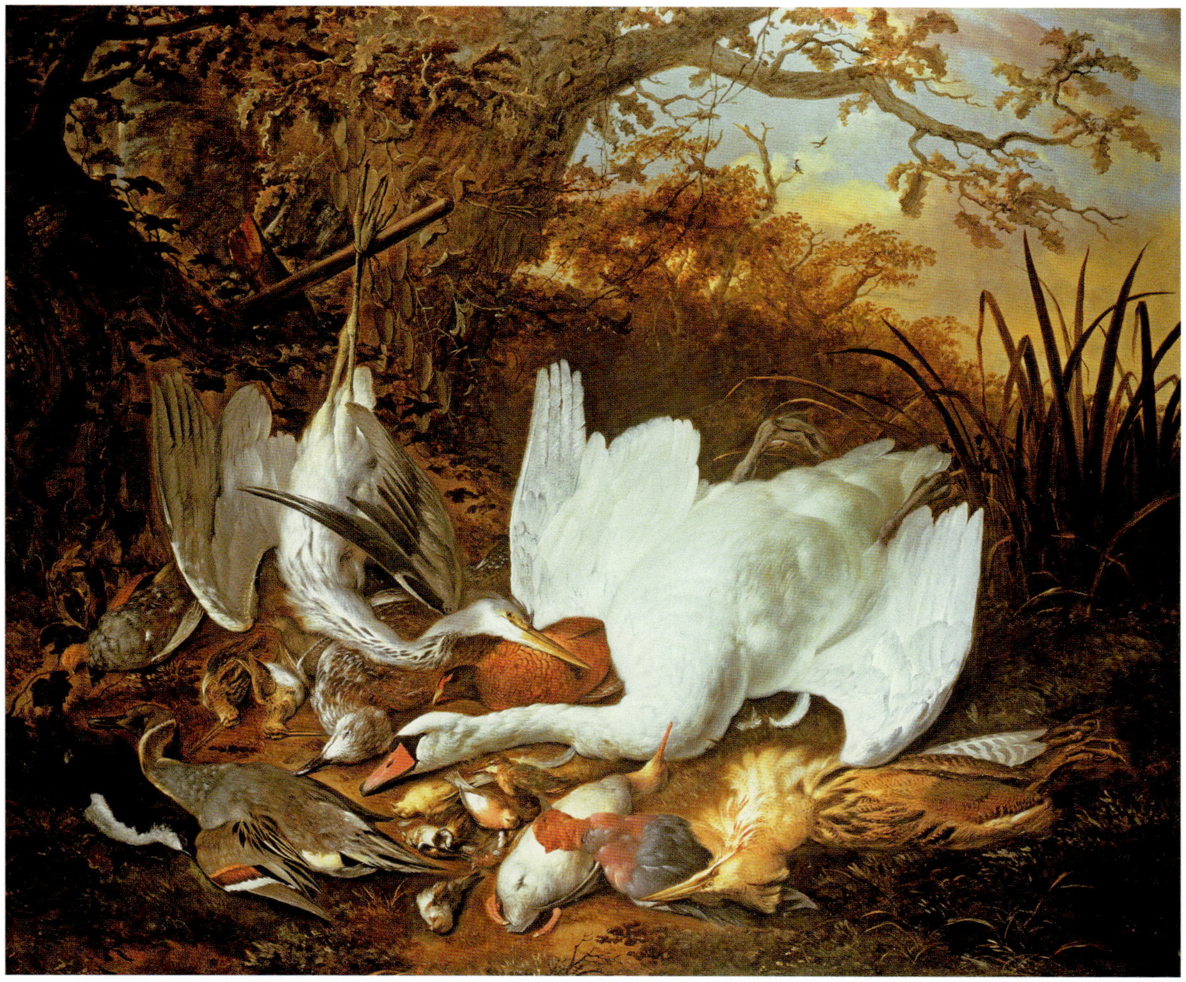

Sir Nathaniel Bacon (1585–1627)
The Cookmaid
c. 1620–25
Oil on canvas
Dimensions unknown
Private collection

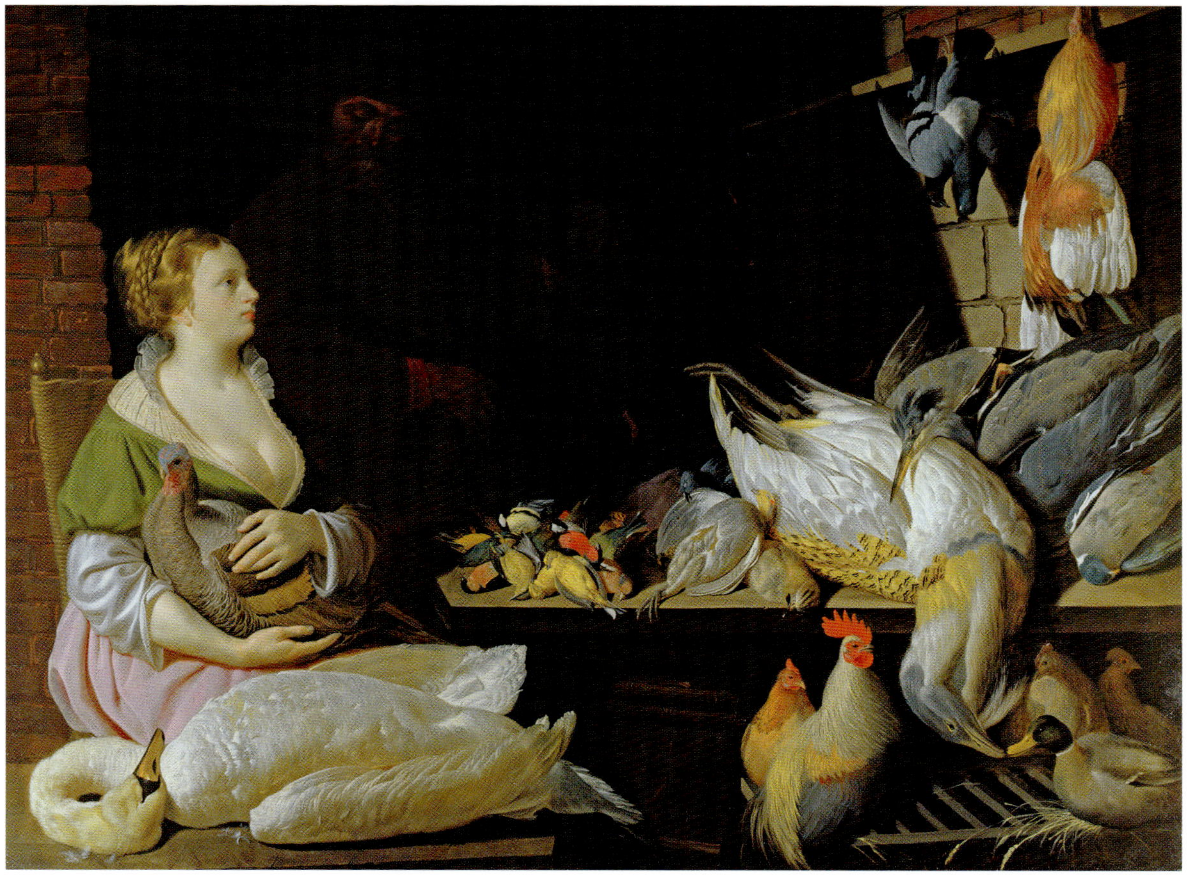

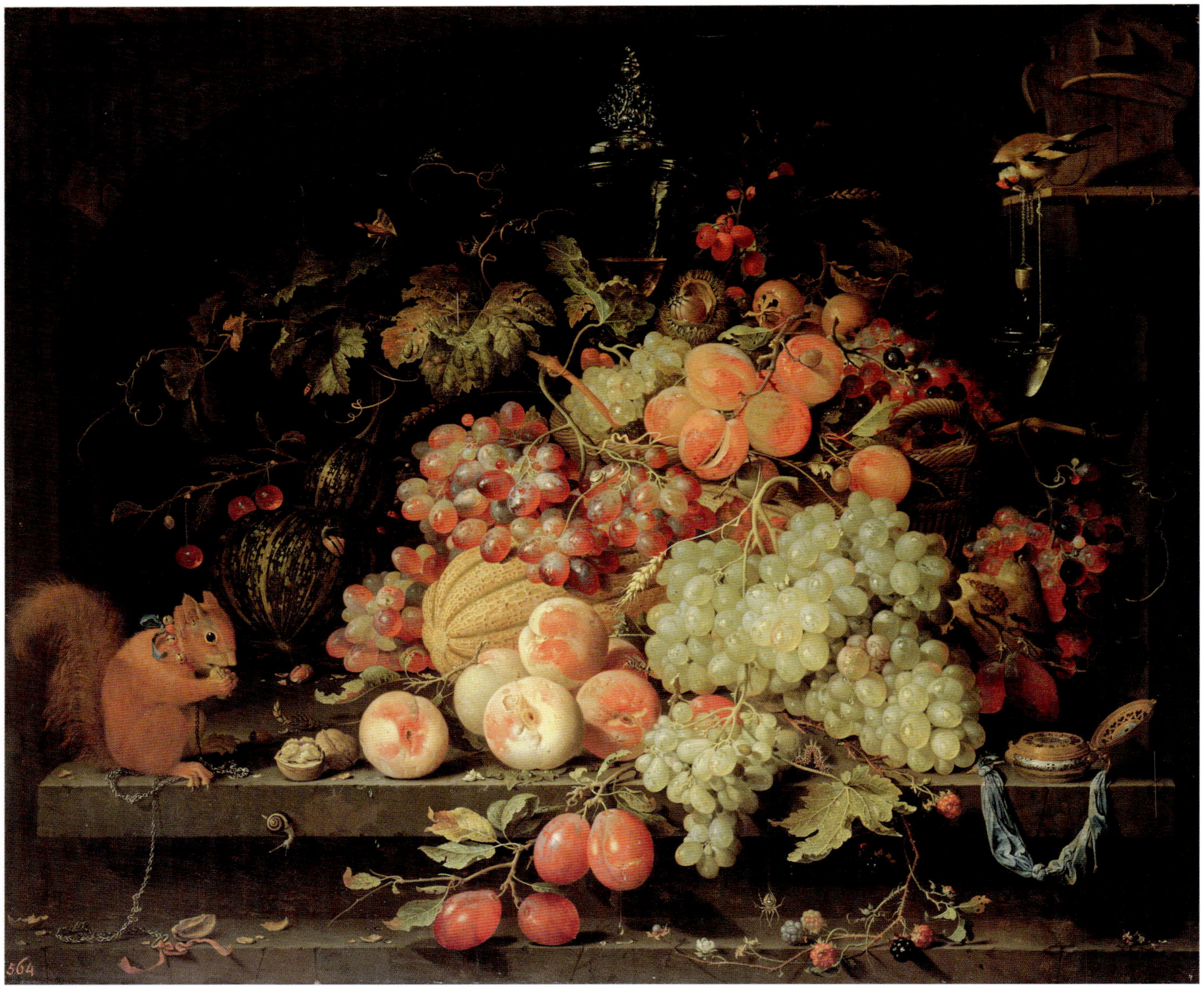

Abraham Mignon
(1640–1679)
Still Life with Fruit, Squirrel and Goldfinch
n.d.
Oil on canvas
80.5 × 99.5 cm (31⅝ × 39⅛ in.)
Gemäldegalerie Alte Meister, Kassel

with the New World. Artists were commissioned to record the colourful and unfamiliar plumage of parrots, cassowaries and other exotic species housed in the menageries of royalty or aristocrats. Where they were not able to observe the live birds, they could base their studies on bird skins preserved in alcohol or salt and later plumped out with wadding. (The practice sometimes produced comical results: the skins of birds of paradise arrived without legs attached, leading to the curious belief that they were constantly airborne, like angels.)

In northern Europe, there was considerable demand for decorative paintings of exotic species from South America, Africa and Asia, as they made extravagantly ornamental pieces for the large houses of newly rich merchants. The birds were not generally shown in their native habitats, but rather more usually placed in such fanciful settings as palace gardens (p. 24). Just as the Dutch flower painters paid no attention to the seasons when they included flowers in bloom at different times of year in the same composition, so birds from South America, the Caribbean and Indonesia were shown keeping company with native species, and scant regard was paid to relative scale. Truthfulness was less important than visual impact. A humorous sub-genre also developed in which birds were shown gathered in concert, under the baton of a wise old owl, or

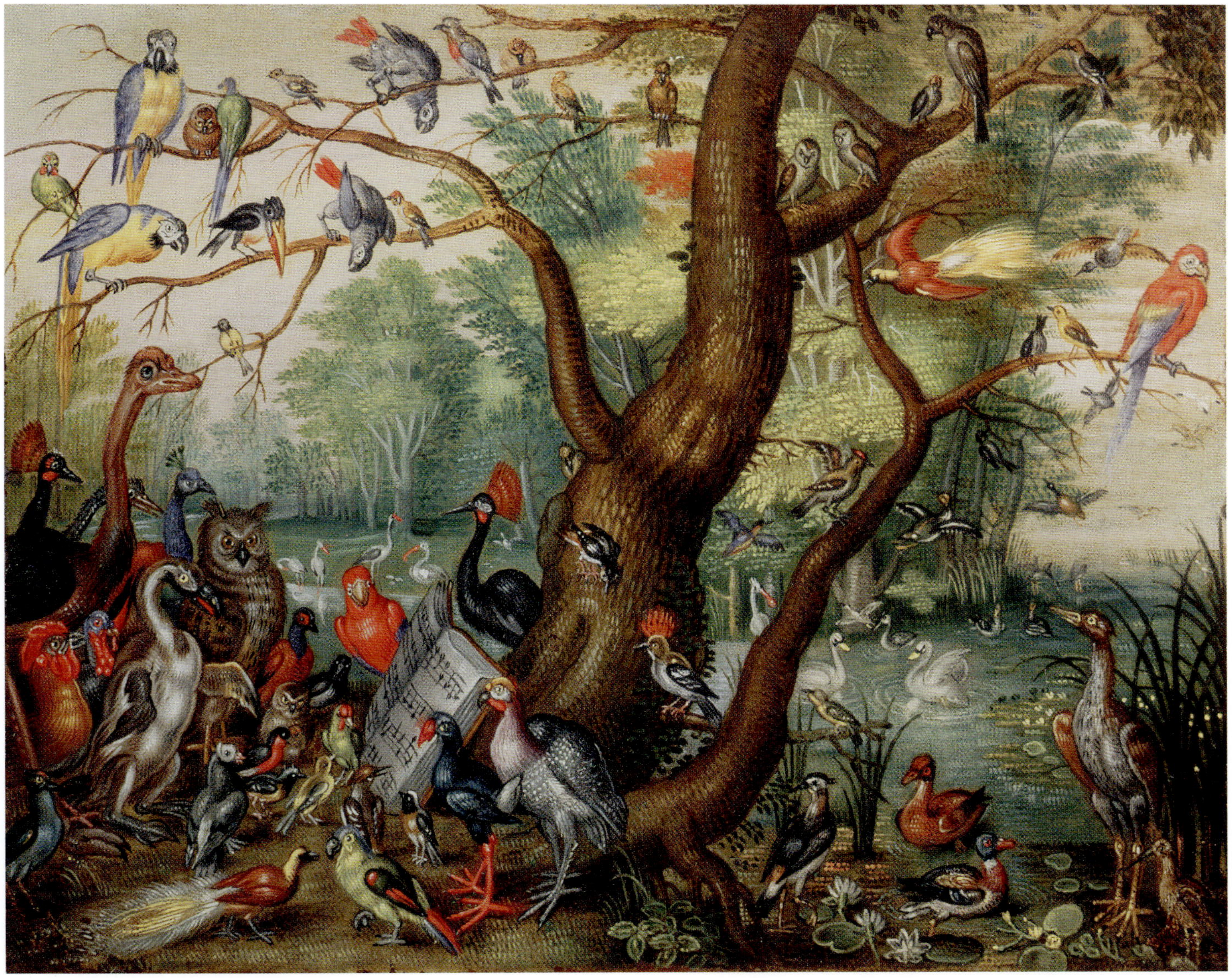

Jan van Kessel the Elder
(1626–1679)
Concert of Birds
c. 1660–70
Oil on copper
13.5 × 17 cm (5¼ × 6⅝ in.)
Galerie De Jonckheere, Paris

assembling as though in a parliamentary debate. Those people who could not afford to commission the most expensive artists to paint scenes of exotic birds could buy less showy paintings of native species. But by the mid-seventeenth century, even the previously exotic parrot was not an uncommon sight in bourgeois homes in the Low Countries (p. 215).

In the eighteenth century, large canvases crammed with birds of all types gradually fell out of fashion, and artists were more frequently asked for simpler, intimate pictures better suited to private apartments than to grand reception rooms. Paintings showing domestic poultry or game – alive or dead – became increasingly popular, and artists were quick to portray the new breeds of domestic bird that were starting to appear. Some of the finest still lifes of this quieter variety were produced by French painters. Jean-Baptiste Oudry's beautifully observed *White Duck* (p. 27, right) is one of the best examples, its carefully modulated white hues forming part of a tonal exercise that presents an interesting contrast with Jean-Siméon Chardin's more traditional composition showing a dead mallard (p. 27, left).

Birds were an increasing presence in paintings of domestic life, too, especially those of women and children with pets (p. 29). Sometimes the bird (very often a parrot) sits quietly on its perch while the mistress of the house is absorbed in her task, at ease

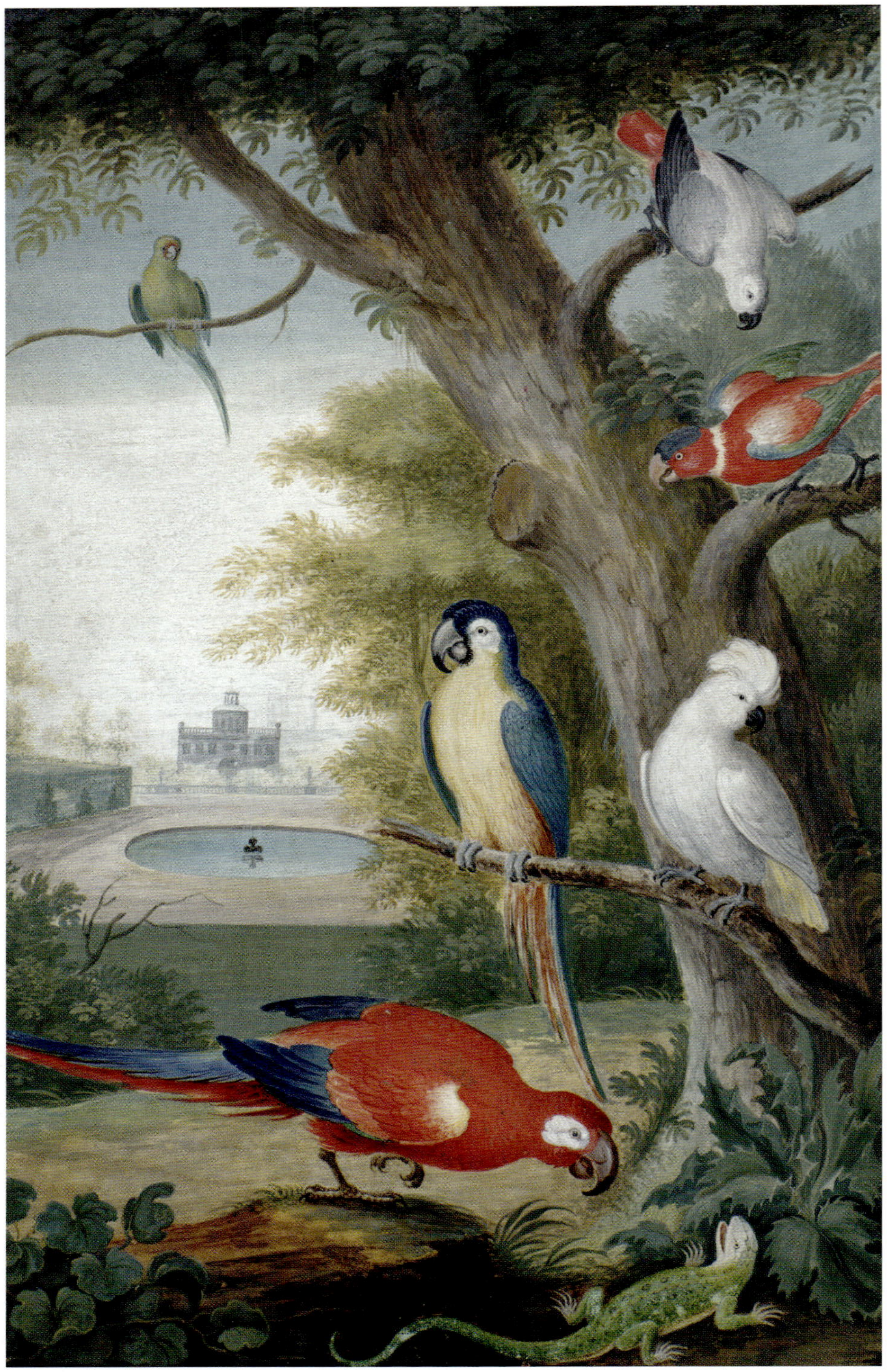

Jakob Bogdány
(1660–1724)
Parrots and Lizard in a Picturesque Park
Early 18th century
Gouache on paper
Dimensions unknown
Private collection

BELOW
Melchior de Hondecoeter
(1636–1695)
Palace of Amsterdam with Exotic Birds
c. 1670
Oil on canvas
Dimensions unknown
Private collection

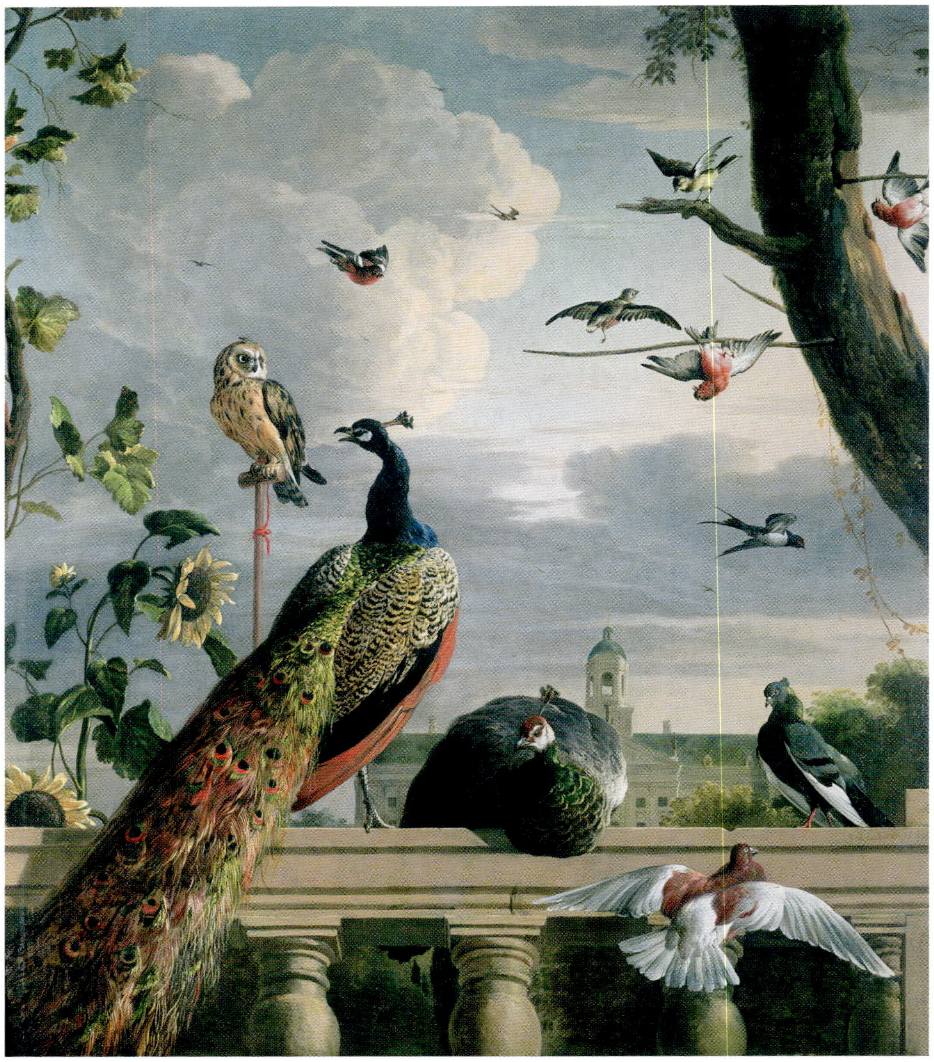

Philip van Dijk
(1680–1753)
A Musical Company
n.d.
Oil on panel
50.9 × 35.6 cm (20 × 14 in.)
Private collection

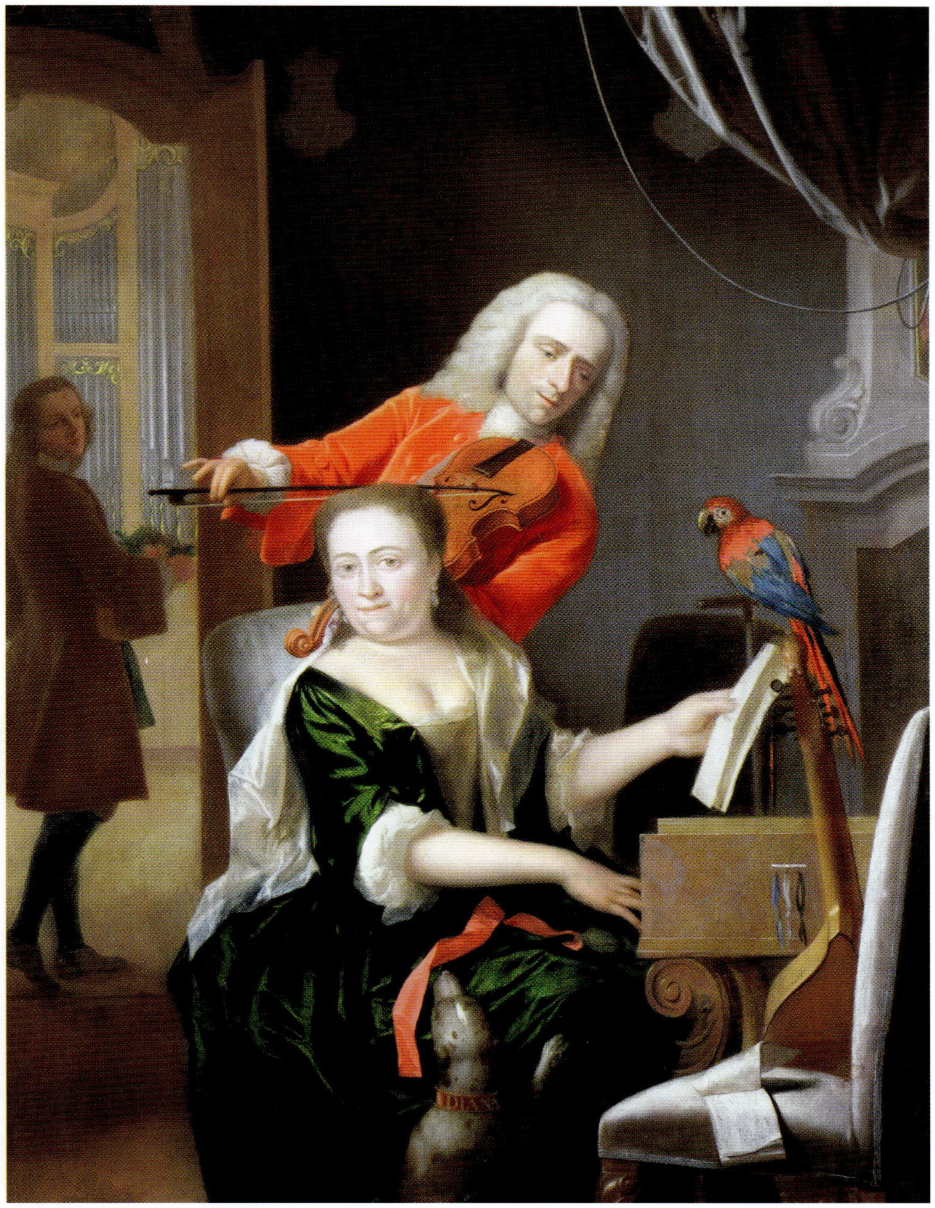

with the world. Sometimes the bird's owner plays with it, teaches it to sing or gets it to join in a human concert (right and p. 222). Sometimes a bird escapes from its cage, while its owner looks on wistfully as it enjoys its newly acquired freedom (p. 26). And sometimes, far from signifying liberty, an open birdcage suggests wantonness.

ORNITHOLOGICAL ENQUIRY

During this period a growing spirit of scientific enquiry was filtering through to fine art and illustration, whetting the public's appetite for ornithological books and prints of birds. In 1676 Francis Willughby and John Ray had laid the foundations of modern ornithology with their three-volume illustrated *Ornithologia*, but the first bird book illustrated with hand-coloured etchings was Eleazar Albin's three-volume *Natural History of Birds*, published in 1731–38, followed shortly by George Edwards's four-volume *Natural History of Uncommon Birds* (1743–51). Edwards based his bird illustrations on the bird skins and mounted specimens belonging to Sir Hans Sloane, whose collection was to provide the founding core of the British Museum and the Natural History Museum.

When Captain James Cook went on his voyages of exploration in the 1770s, he took with him trained artists to record the flora and fauna of the newly discovered lands. Scientists did not want to see fanciful compositions of birds in imaginary Italian landscapes; they sought a more accurate record of birds in their

Willem van Mieris (1662–1747)
Portrait of a Woman
1687
Oil on panel
20.5 × 16.9 cm (8 × 6⅝ in.)
Hamburger Kunsthalle, Hamburg

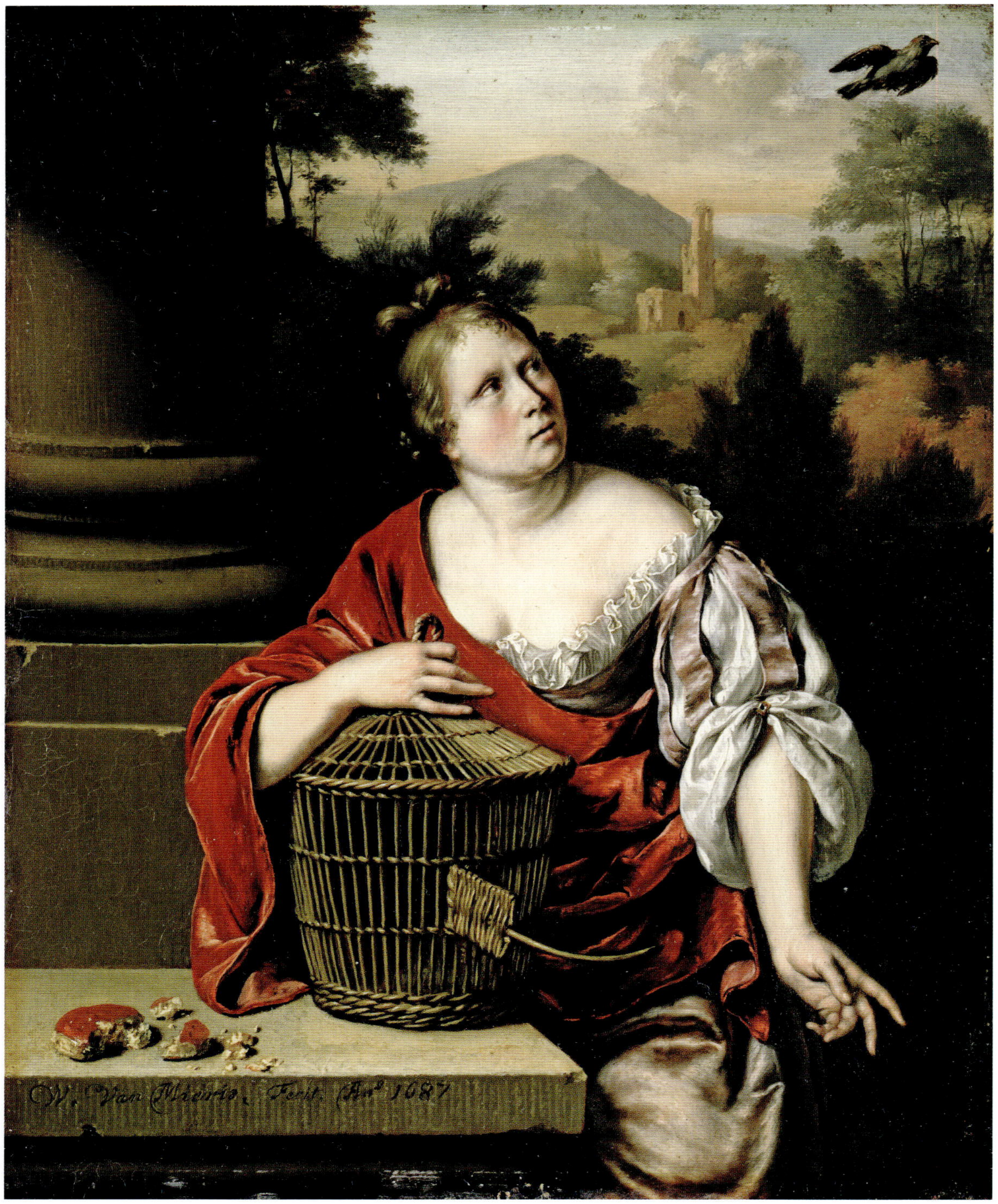

native habitats. This desire for veracity eventually extended into oil paintings, encouraging artists to depict birds in natural settings appropriate to their origins. The English artist George Stubbs even dissected birds and animals, determined to arrive at a better understanding of anatomy and to give his painted creatures a more lifelike appearance.

The number of recognized bird species was rapidly increasing: in 1758, when the naturalist Carl Linnaeus produced the tenth edition of his *Systema Naturae*, he included 564 birds. By 1801 three thousand birds were known (the number is now closer to 10,000). New species discovered in the colonies were increasing the corpus of birds, and inspiring ever more lavish publishing projects. A pioneering Scot, Alexander Wilson, travelled through America gathering material for his book *American Ornithology* (1808–14), the first comprehensive guide to birds in the country. But when he tried to sell a copy in a shop in Louisville, Kentucky, the shopkeeper decided that he could go one better, and set out on his own quest to paint the avian life of the continent north of Mexico.

That reluctant shopkeeper, whose real passion lay in depicting birds, was John James Audubon. He is now regarded by many as the greatest bird illustrator ever to have existed, and plates from his multi-volume *Birds of America* (1827–38), engraved by Robert Havell from Audubon's watercolours, sell for record-breaking prices. Audubon's depictions convey a feeling of theatricality and movement that had not been seen before in printed images of birds, injecting a new sense

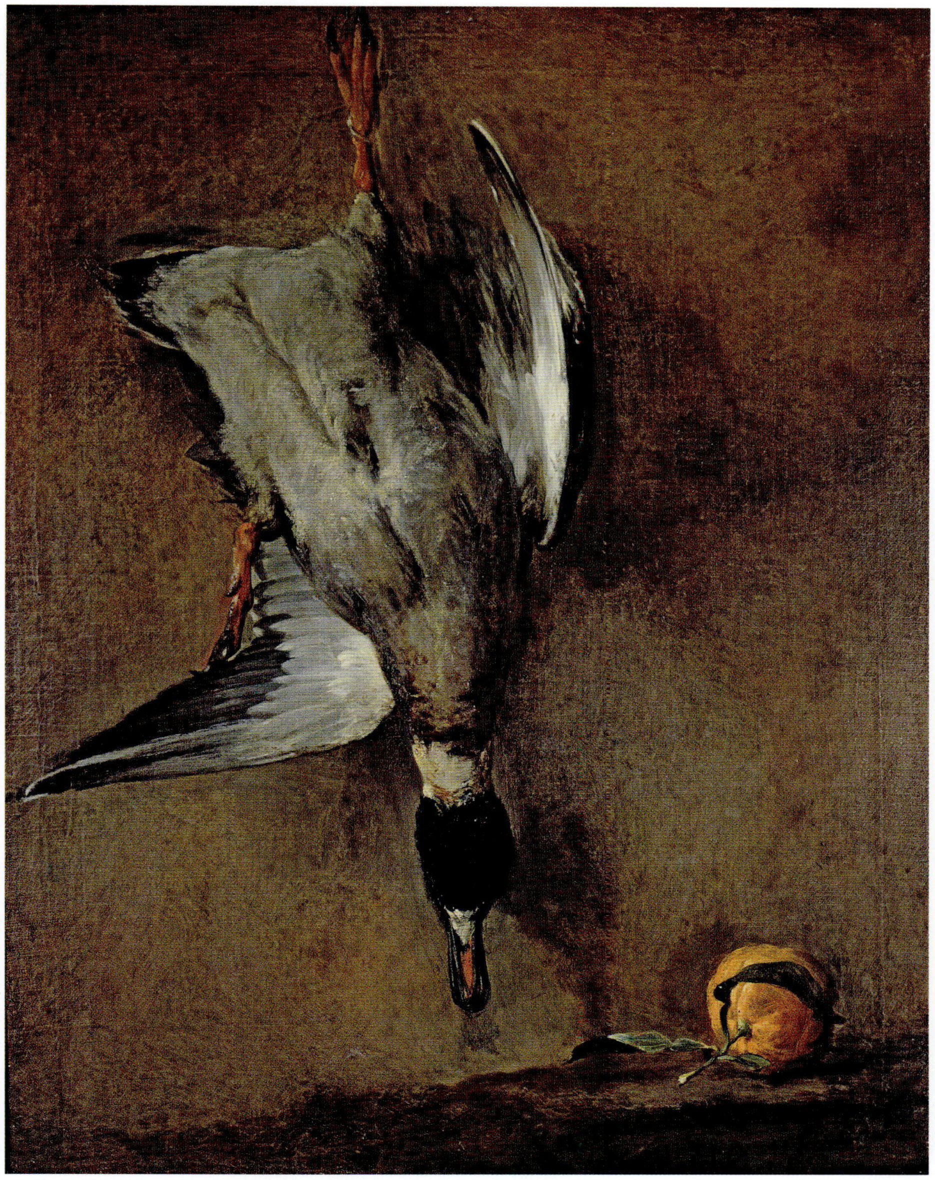

BELOW

Jean-Baptiste Oudry
(1686–1755)
The White Duck
1753
Oil on canvas
97.7 × 63.7 cm (38⅜ × 25 in.)
Private collection

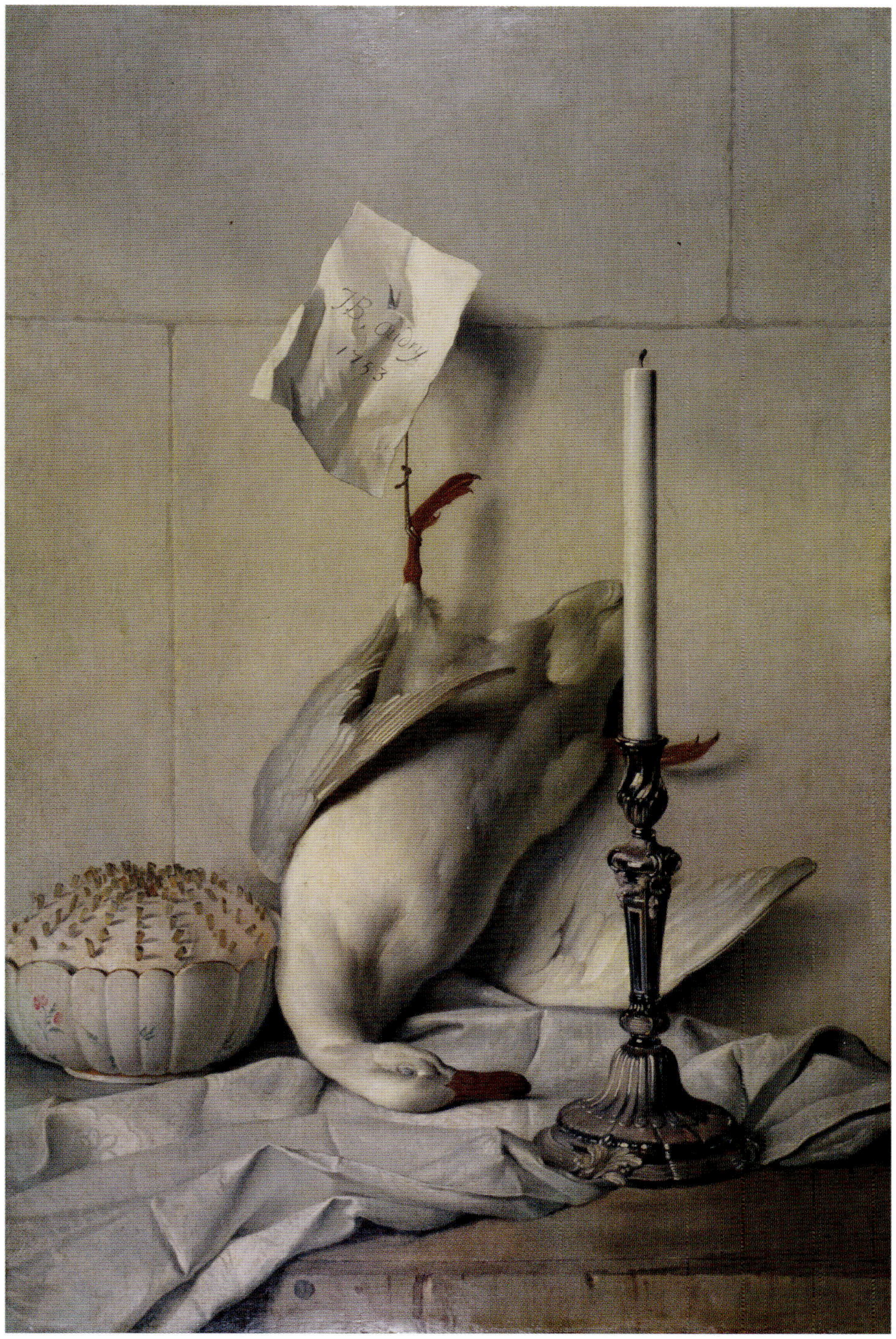

ABOVE

Jean-Siméon Chardin
(1699–1779)
A Mallard Duck Hanging on a Wall with a Seville Orange
1720–30
Oil on canvas
80.5 × 64.5 cm (31⅝ × 25⅜ in.)
Musée de la Chasse et de la Nature, Paris

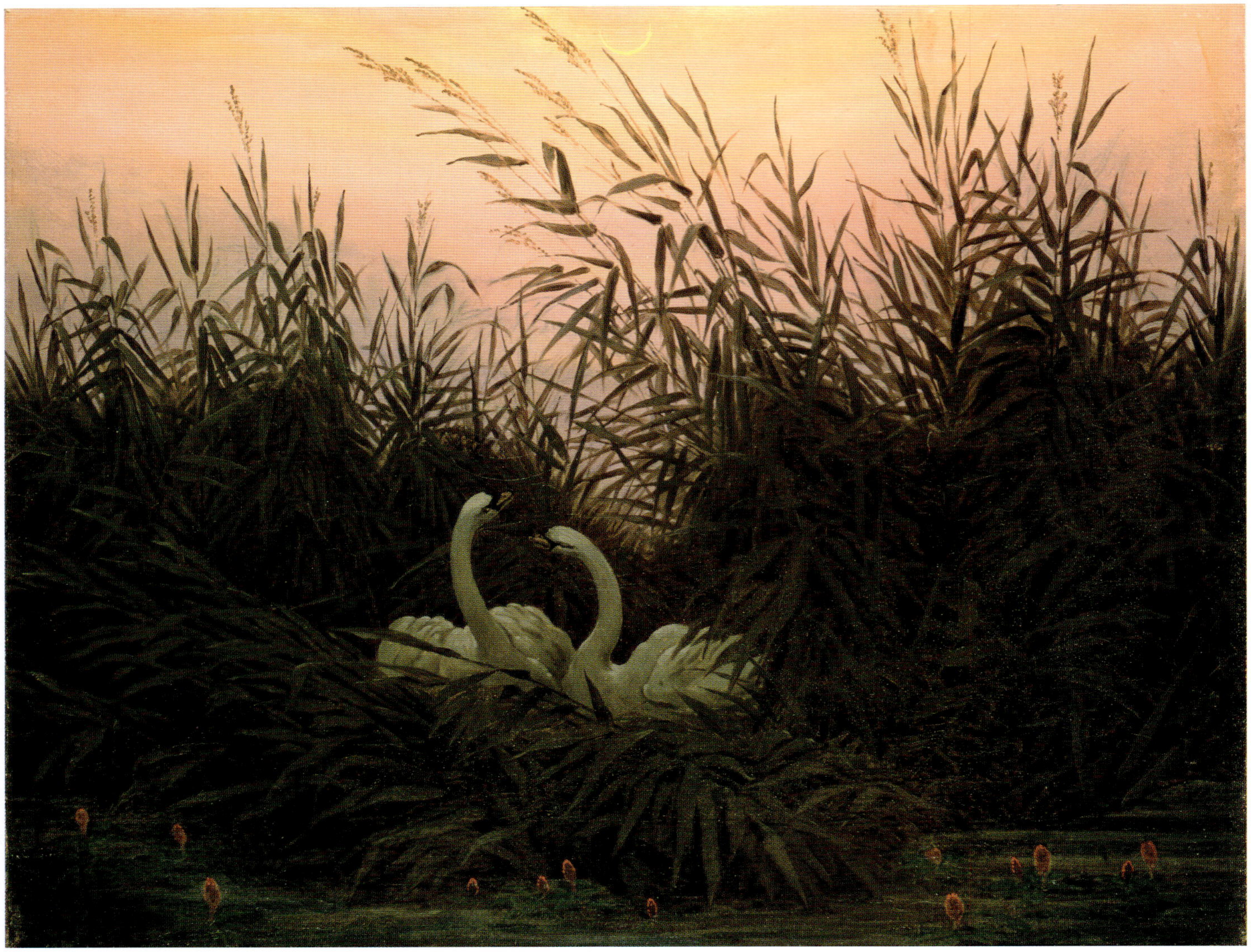

Caspar David Friedrich
(1774–1840)
Swans in the Reeds
c. 1820
Oil on canvas
34 × 44 cm (13⅜ × 17¼ in.)
The State Hermitage Museum, St Petersburg

of excitement into the genre (opposite, right, and p. 155). During the same decade that Audubon's book was produced, the young Edward Lear spent hours sketching exotic birds closer to home, in the newly established Zoological Gardens in London, in preparation for his first major book, *Illustrations of the Family of Psittacidae, or Parrots* (1830–32). Lear, always bespectacled and increasingly rotund, caricatured himself as an owl in later life, and created a series of fantasy 'nonsense' birds in the same vein as his nonsense verses.

THE ROMANCE OF BIRDS

The familiarity of birds, and the fact that they were kept as household pets and in zoos, did nothing to rob them of their poetry and potential for mystery. Indeed, in the hands of some creative souls, they were being annexed for a wide range of new symbolic ends that were far removed from mundane reality and scientific analysis. Caspar David Friedrich's two swans in the rushes seen by the light of the moon are reminders of divinity, death and immortality – a meaning reinforced by the presence of the evening star (above). The artist was reflecting the particular resonance of swans in Germany at the time. In the poetry of Friedrich Hölderlin and Heinrich Heine and the opera of the Romantic period, swans were associated with death, perhaps because of the song they sing as they expire. Later, the composer Richard Wagner incorporated a Swan Knight into his opera *Lohengrin* (1850), and the

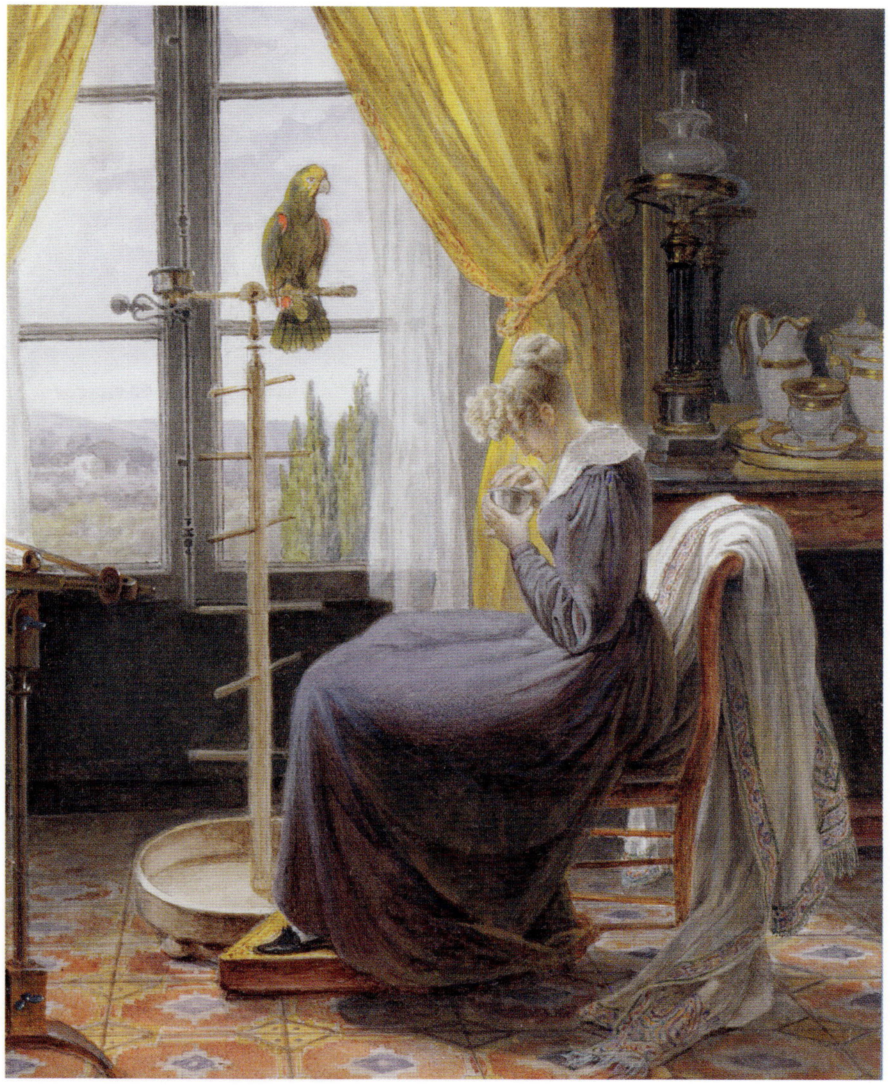

French
A Woman Feeding a Parrot in an Interior
c. 1820
Watercolour with gouache on paper
19.2 × 16.6 cm (7½ × 6½ in.)
Private collection

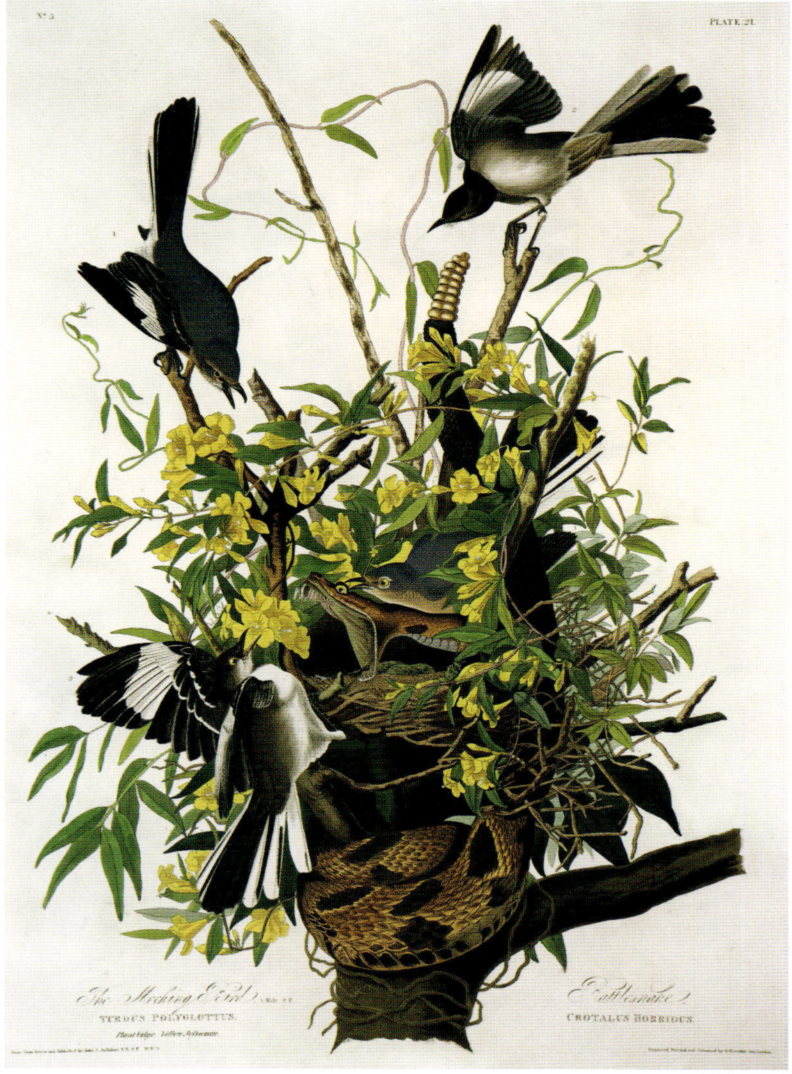

John James Audubon
(1785–1851)
Mockingbirds and Rattlesnake, from *Birds of America*
1827–38
Coloured engraving
33.3 × 23.5 cm (13⅛ × 9¼ in.)
Private collection

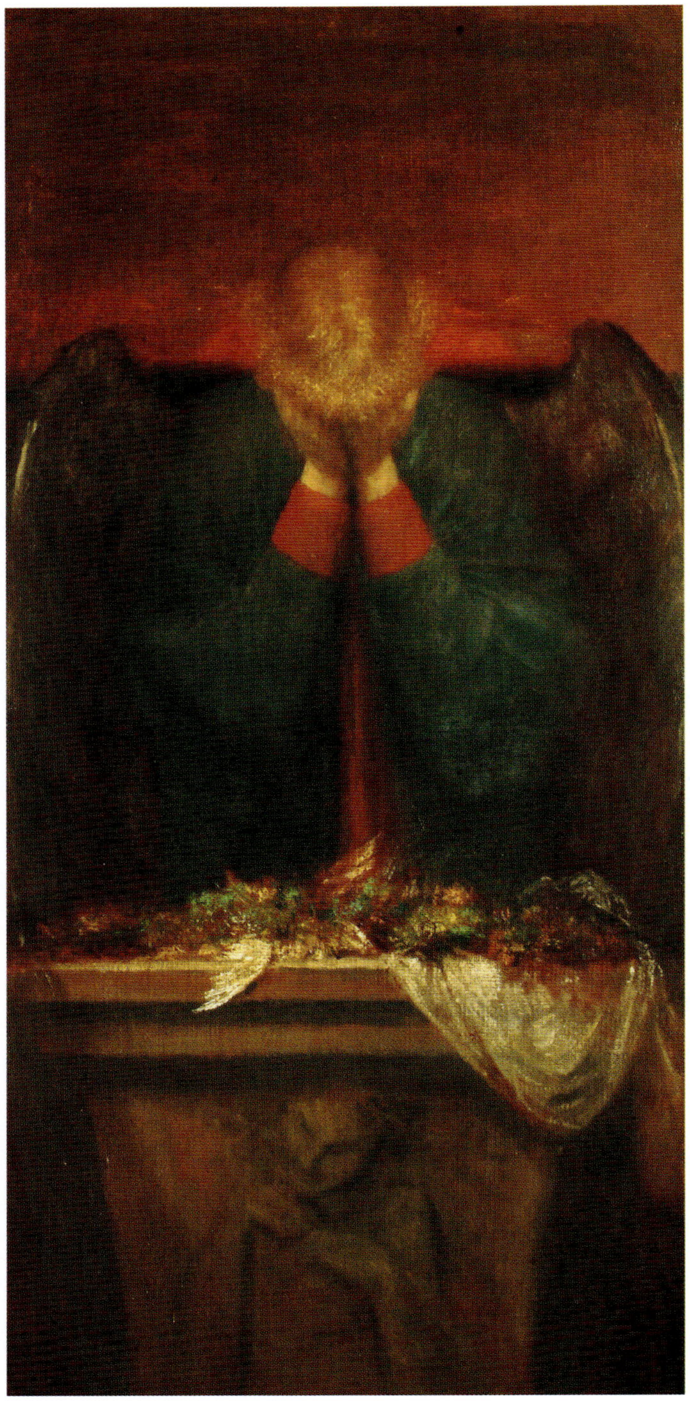

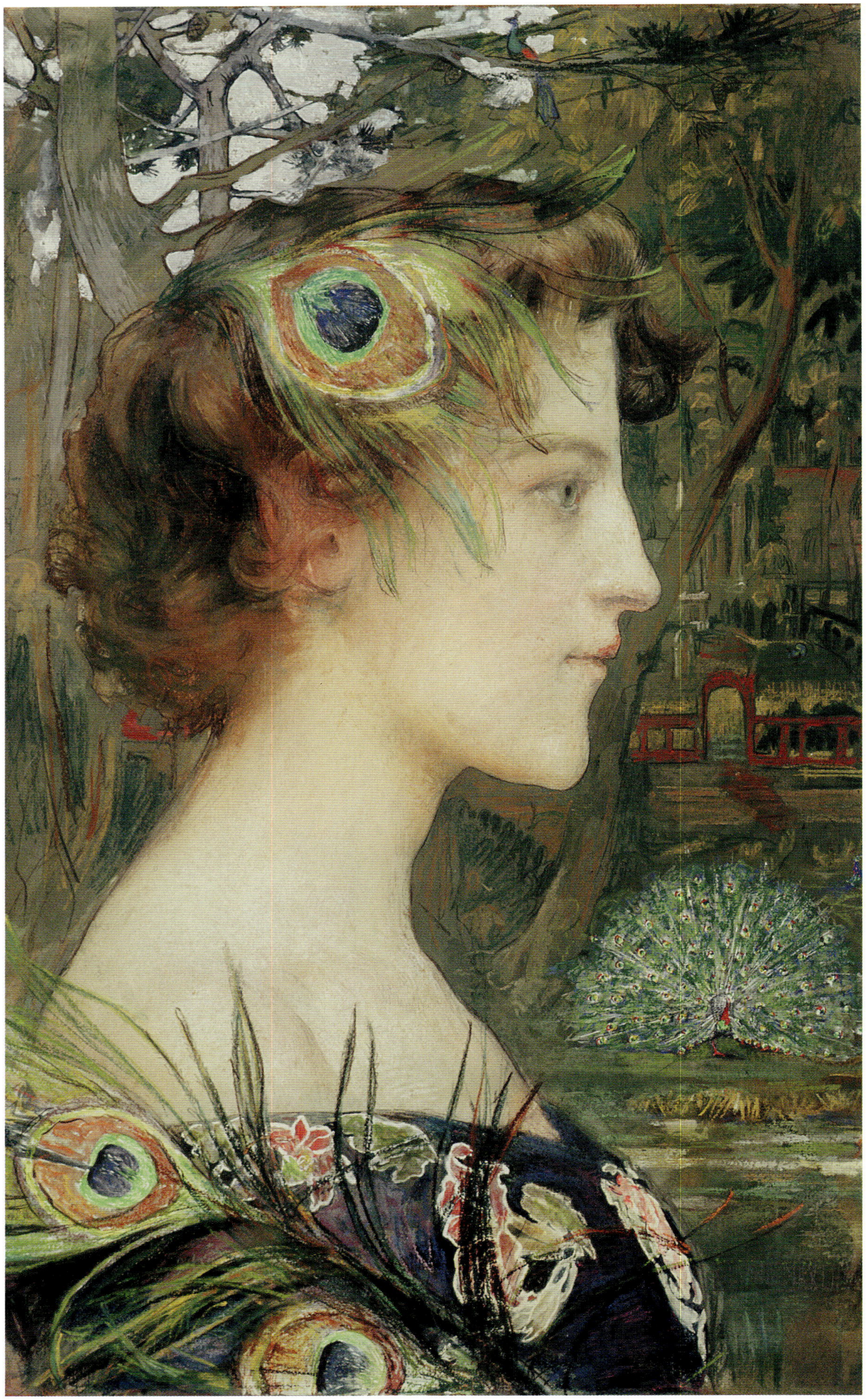

George Frederic Watts
(1817–1904)
A Dedication

1898–99
Oil on canvas
137.2 × 71 cm (54 × 28 in.)
Watts Gallery, Compton, Surrey

swan motif inspired his patron 'Mad' King Ludwig of Bavaria to call himself the 'Swan King'.

Ludwig was also fond of peacocks; he even had a throne in the form of a peacock installed in the garden kiosk of his Linderhof Castle. But the peacock's apotheosis really came at the end of the nineteenth century, when it was adopted as the motif par excellence of designers and artistic adherents to the Aesthetic movement and Art Nouveau. The English painter Dante Gabriel Rossetti kept a menagerie that included peacocks in the garden of his house in London, and the American-born J.A.M. Whistler even produced an entire peacock-themed decorative scheme for the London house of his patron Frederick Leyland. The showy, apparently impractical bird with its extravagant plumage was the perfect embodiment of 'art for art's sake'.

Edgard Maxence's profile portrait of a young French woman (opposite, right) shows her sporting a fascinator made of peacock feathers, but in Britain there was growing concern about the use of feathers for personal adornment. In 1889 one Emily Williamson founded a group to protest against the use of feathers from rare birds in clothing. Originally called the 'Plumage League', it became the Royal Society for the Protection of Birds (RSPB), the members of which dedicated themselves to discouraging the wanton destruction of birds, and pledged to refrain from wearing feathers of any bird not killed for food (apart from the unfortunate ostrich). A decade later, G.F. Watts recorded his own revulsion against the use of feathers in fashion in his painting *A Dedication*, which is subtitled: 'To those who love the beautiful and mourn over the senseless and cruel destruction of bird life and beauty'. Bird feathers lie on an altar decorated with a grimacing satyr, while a winged angel mourns (opposite, left).

This artistic sensitivity towards birds continued into the twentieth century, manifesting itself in various ways. One of these was the increase in the number of wildlife artists, who committed their observations of different species to paper and canvas as faithfully as possible. Such artists as Bruno Liljefors and Archibald Thorburn painted birds in their natural habitats to convey a true sense of how they behave and move in the wild, and how they blend into the landscape (pp. 137 and 164). This naturalistic approach was carried forward by Charles Frederick Tunnicliffe, one of the outstanding modern painters and illustrators who have dedicated themselves to the portrayal of birds. Brought up on a farm and acutely aware of the wildlife around him, he kept a visual diary of the birds he saw every day. His watercolour of bartailed godwit and dunlin on the shore of an estuary (p. 33) is satisfying both as a lively painting of the birds themselves and as a superbly designed composition that transcends dry scientific record. Hundreds of wildlife artists working today continue this tradition of faithful observation, aided by improved scientific knowledge, field guides, photography and film.

Nor have artists at the forefront of the avant-garde neglected birds as a subject. In fact, avian motifs are

Edgard Maxence (1871–1954)
Peacock Profile
1896
Pastel and gouache on paper
46 × 30 cm (18⅛ × 11¾ in.)
Private collection

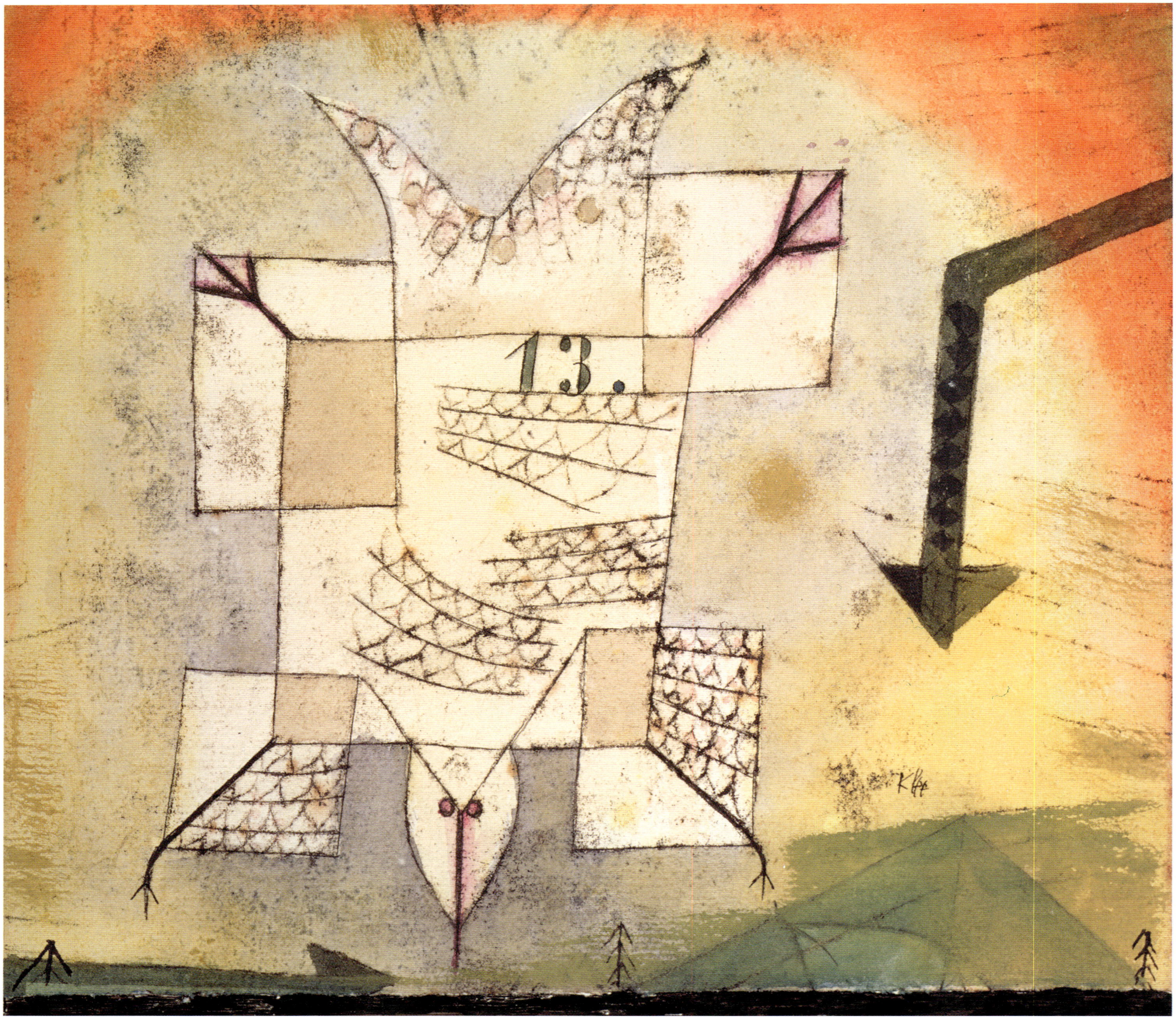

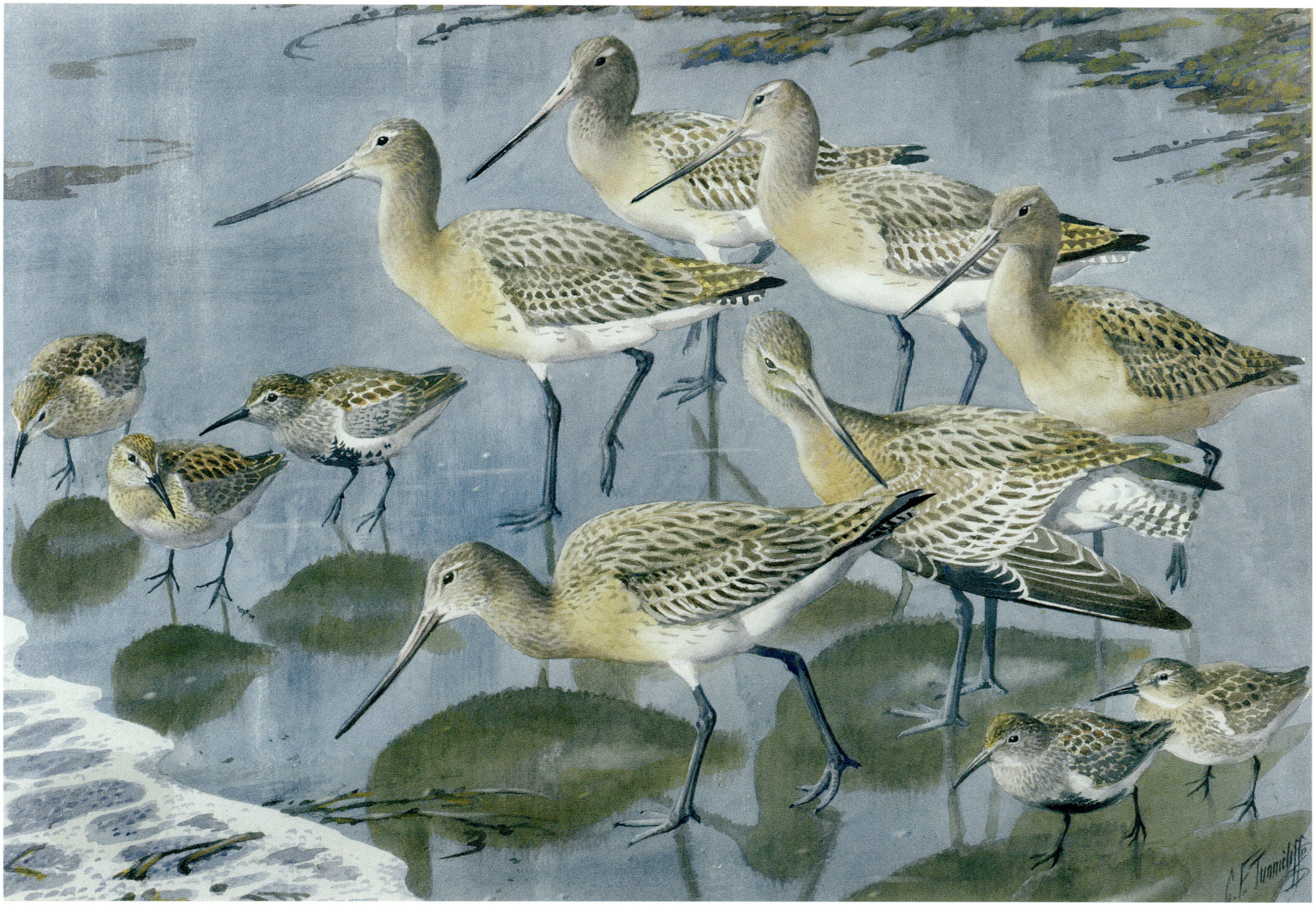

Paul Klee
(1879–1940)
Falling Bird
1919
Watercolour, transferred printing ink and ink on paper, bordered with ink
16.2 × 18.7 cm (6⅜ × 7⅜ in.)
The Metropolitan Museum of Art, New York

Charles Frederick Tunnicliffe
(1901–1979)
Bartailed Godwit and Dunlin at the Water's Edge
c. 1952
Watercolour
Dimensions unknown
Private collection

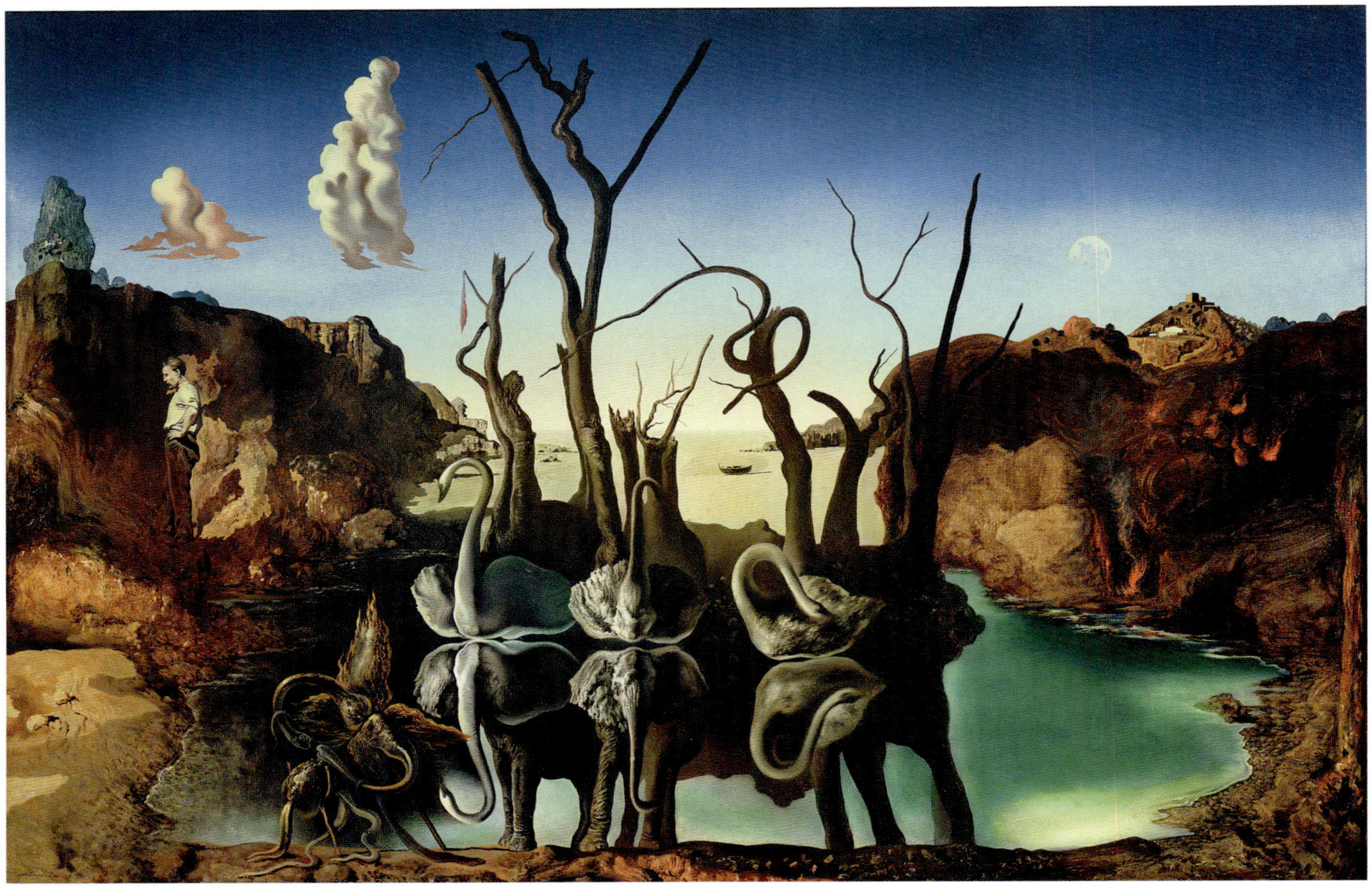

Salvador Dalí
(1904–1989)
Swans Reflecting Elephants
1937
Oil on canvas
51 × 77 cm (20 × 30¼ in.)
Private collection

prominent in works by artists associated with the major art movements of the first half of the twentieth century: Cubism, Futurism and especially Surrealism. But, unlike the wildlife painters, these artists were not concerned with accurately noting every detail of plumage or behaviour. Birds are stripped down to their very essence in the minimalist sculptures of Constantin Brancusi (p. 251); they appear as flattened cutouts in Georges Braque's still lifes (p. 258); their flight patterns are analysed in graphic form by the Futurist artist Giacomo Balla (p. 243). They are cartoon-like inhabitants of Paul Klee's exotic night gardens (p. 246) and elements in twittering machines, or they crash like aeroplanes in an ironic take on the gift of flight for which birds had so long been envied (p. 32).

The most startling explosion of twentieth-century bird imagery occurred in the work of artists who used imaginary birds as symbols of their own inner worlds. Max Ernst's early childhood memory of his pet cockatoo dying at the moment his sister was born led to a mysterious conflation of humans and birds (p. 253) that manifested itself in his development of an avian alter ego, Loplop. Roosters, cockerels and doves signify love and happiness in Marc Chagall's personal universe (p. 248). Salvador Dalí portrayed swans metamorphosing into elephants in a nightmarish vision only he could have conjured up (above). But the most famous bird images of the last century are probably the various versions of the dove of peace created by Pablo Picasso (opposite). Adopted as the emblem of the World Peace Congress in Paris in 1949, the dove appeared overnight on posters all over the French capital. In a post-war world, this gentle bird's most ancient and noble symbolism – freedom from conflict – seemed more relevant than ever.

Pablo Picasso
(1881–1973)
The Dove of Peace
1962
Pastel on paper
Dimensions unknown
Private collection

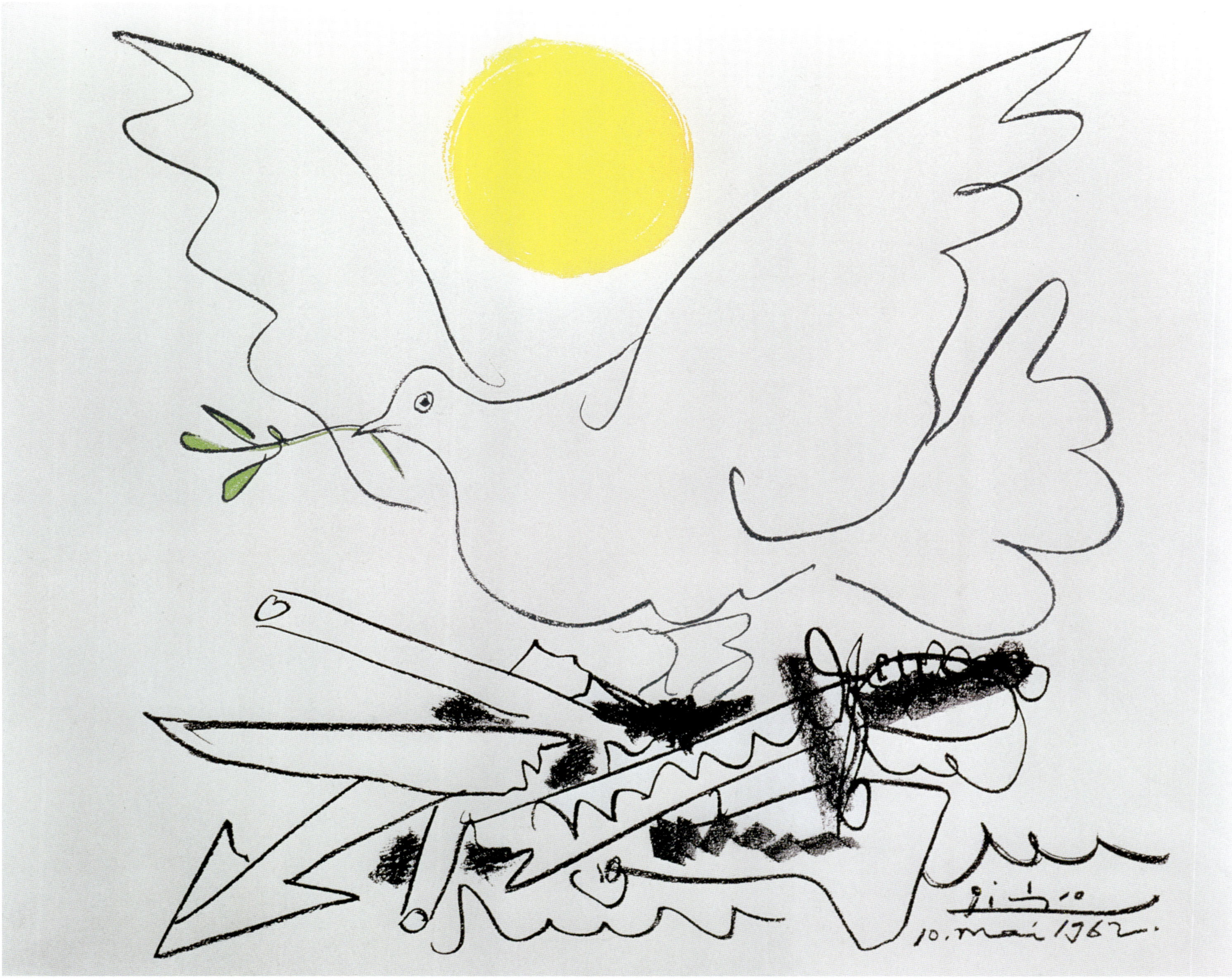

Birds of Antiquity

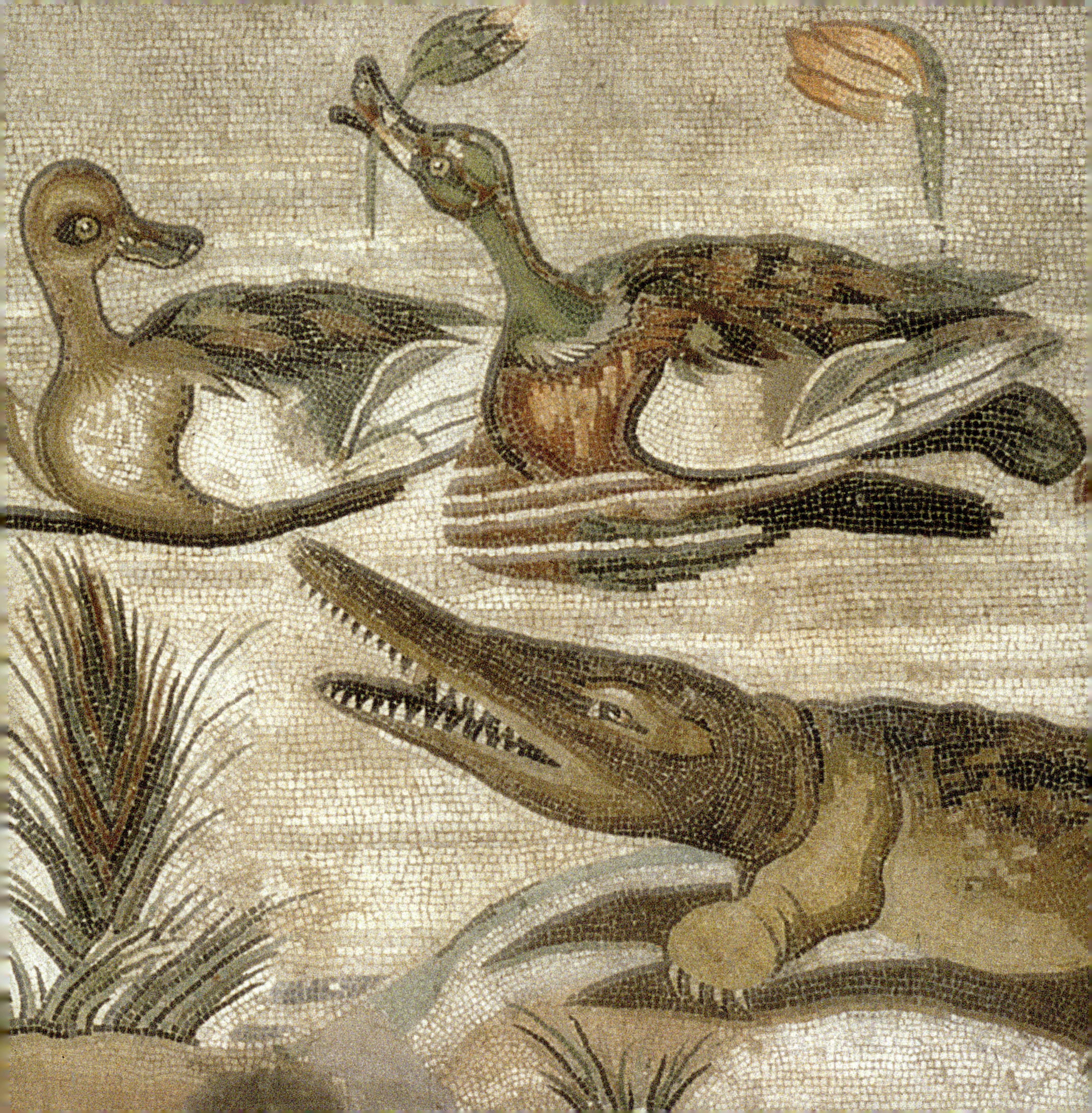

Apart from a scattering of birds etched into or daubed on the walls of Palaeolithic caves, the earliest bird images familiar to us are those produced millennia ago in Egypt. It is a testimony to the abundant avian life that flourished along the banks of the Nile – including falcons, kites, plovers, pigeons, ibises, vultures and owls – that well over seventy species of bird have been identified in Egyptian art. Some birds were evidently fair game for hunters, while others, such as geese, pigeons, ducks and quails, were also domesticated for the table, just as songbirds were caged for the pleasure of their melodies. Egyptian artists were capable of quite detailed ornithological observation: whoever painted the walls of the tomb of Nefermaat and Atet at Meidum took care to ensure that the three different types of goose had their own distinguishing features (detail opposite).

In ancient Egypt, birds were intimately linked with gods and the afterlife. Flocks of sacred birds, particularly ibises, were bred and kept near temples. The ibis was sacred to the god Thoth (p. 43), and the hieroglyph that represents it stands for 'transfiguration' or 'to be radiant': a good metaphor for the transfigured dead. The mummies of ibises and falcons have been found at the great necropolis in Saqqara; they were probably offered for sale to the pilgrims who visited the cult centre.

Falcons were a barometer of the well-being of Egyptian society as a whole. Egyptian civilization depended on a mild annual flooding of the Nile to irrigate the riverbanks and surrounding fields, ensuring a successful harvest. The flood waters also brought plenty of the small migratory birds and other creatures on which falcons feed, but when there was drought or excessive flooding the natural balance was upset, and the falcon population diminished. Small wonder, then, that Horus, the most powerful god in the Egyptian pantheon, has the head of a falcon, and that pharaohs are often shown in his company (p. 40). In the Late Period the identity of the sun god Ra merged with that of Horus, and he too appears as a falcon (p. 45). The benu bird, which was linked with both Ra and Osiris (the god of the underworld), was another divine creature, said to appear each morning in the form of the rising sun, and to renew itself constantly, anticipating the phoenix of Greek mythology, which rose from the ashes (p. 41).

Birds feature as accessories of the gods in the Greek and Roman pantheon, too: Zeus (Roman form: Jupiter) has his powerful eagle; Athena (Minerva) her wise owl; Aphrodite (Venus) her doves; and Hera (Juno) her many-eyed peacock. But Classical artists did not neglect the importance of birds in everyday life. We know from the evidence of the wall paintings of Pompeii that birds were an intrinsic part of daily routine. They are shown in gardens, flying above vegetation or walking on the ground, and it is clear that artists often tried to depict them in their natural habitat (pp. 52–53). Most of the birds shown on the walls of Pompeii are so carefully represented, with great attention to detail, that it is possible to identify individual species (p. 56).

Roman mosaics and paintings showing birds hanging in larders also confirm the fact that they were hunted or domesticated for the table (p. 51). In the cookery book known as *Apicius* (sixth century AD), there is an entire chapter of recipes for poultry and wild birds, showing that the ancient Romans enjoyed dishes made from chickens, geese, ducks, partridges, guineafowl, pheasants, ostriches, thrushes and pigeons, and even cranes, peacocks and flamingoes. Other birds, including parrots, were kept in aviaries and enjoyed for their exotic plumage.

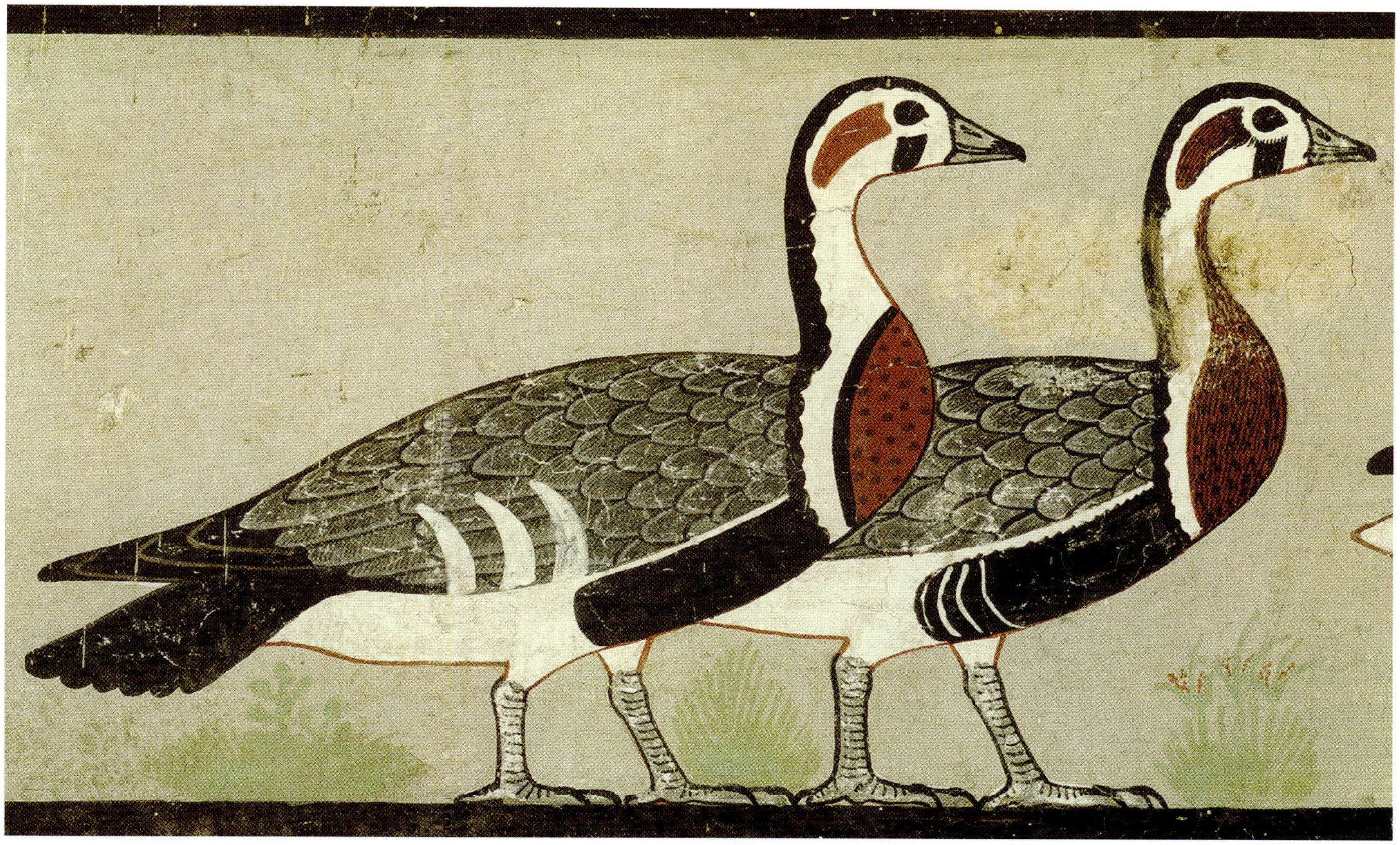

Egyptian
Meidum Geese, from the tomb of Nefermaat and Atet (detail)
c. 2620 BC
Painted stucco
Museum of Egyptian Antiquities, Cairo

This famous panel is one of the masterpieces of Egyptian wall painting. It shows six geese, three facing left and three facing right, and those at either end pecking at the ground. It has been suggested that this represents the unification of Upper and Lower Egypt. It might equally have a more general religious significance, since geese were used as sacred offerings and the goose was dedicated to Geb, father of Isis. Some variety is introduced into the symmetrical composition by the variation in the birds' feathers. Three separate species can be identified: the white-fronted goose, the bean goose and the red-breasted goose. The painting comes from the tomb of an Egyptian prince, Nefermaat, and his wife, Atet, and it was removed by the French scholar and archaeologist Auguste Mariette, who recognized its superlative quality when he excavated the site in 1871. A fragment from another scene shown in the tomb, depicting a man trapping a duck in a clap net, is in the British Museum in London.

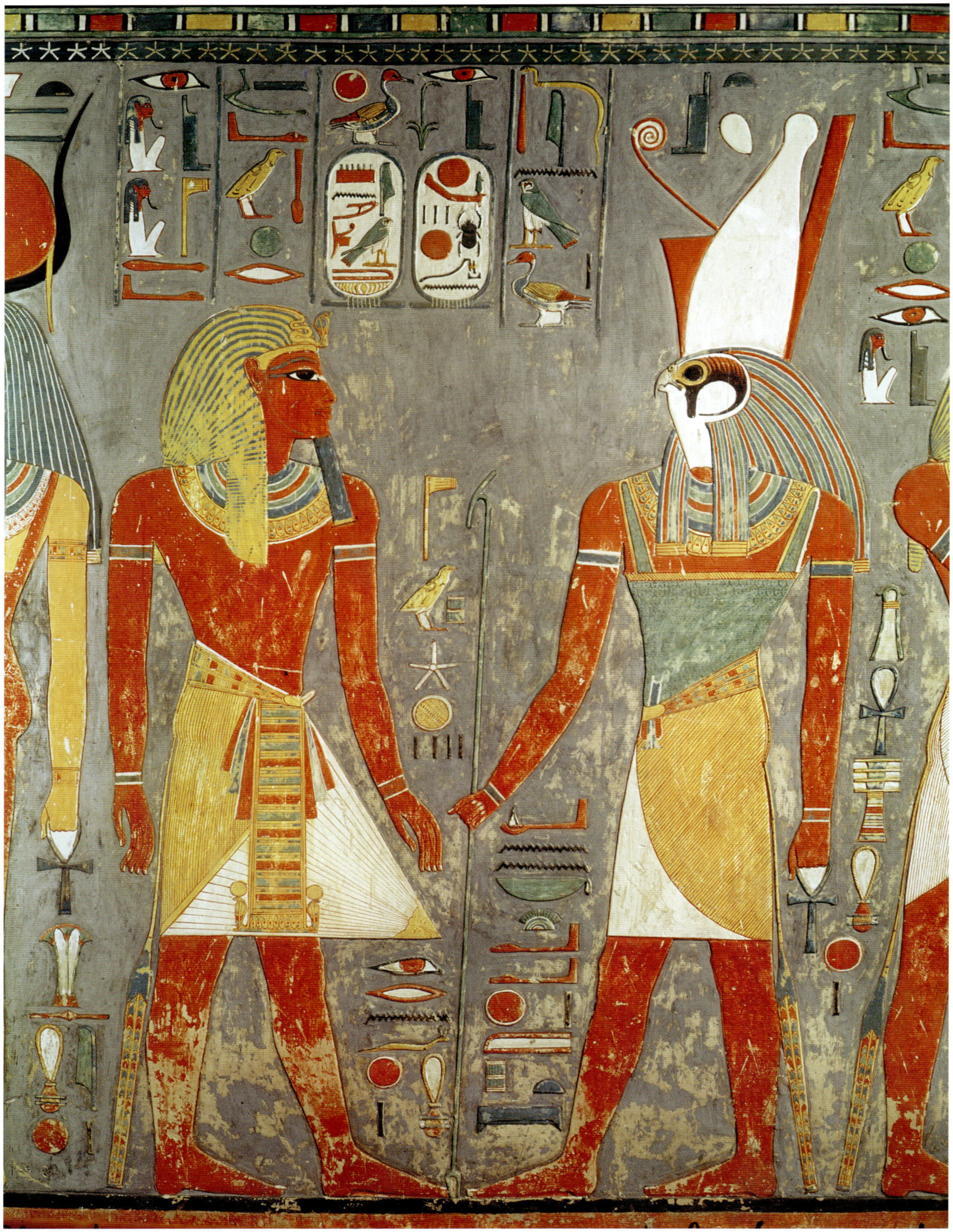

Egyptian
Horemheb before Horus

c. 1567–1320 BC
Painted limestone
Tomb of Horemheb, Valley of the Kings, Thebes

Horemheb, who was commander-in-chief of the Egyptian army, became ruler of Egypt some years after Tutankhamun's early death. He was probably of common birth, and his coronation text thanks the god Horus for placing him on the Egyptian throne. In this painted relief from Horemheb's tomb, he is shown with the falcon-headed god, who sports the red-and-white double crown of Upper and Lower Egypt, signifying national unity. Horus is one of the most ancient and important Egyptian gods. During the long course of Egyptian history, ideas about his role changed, and he was shown in many forms: sometimes as a falcon, particularly in hieroglyphics, and sometimes as a man with a falcon head, as here. He became closely associated with pharaohs, and at one time Egyptian rulers were even said to be Horus in human form.

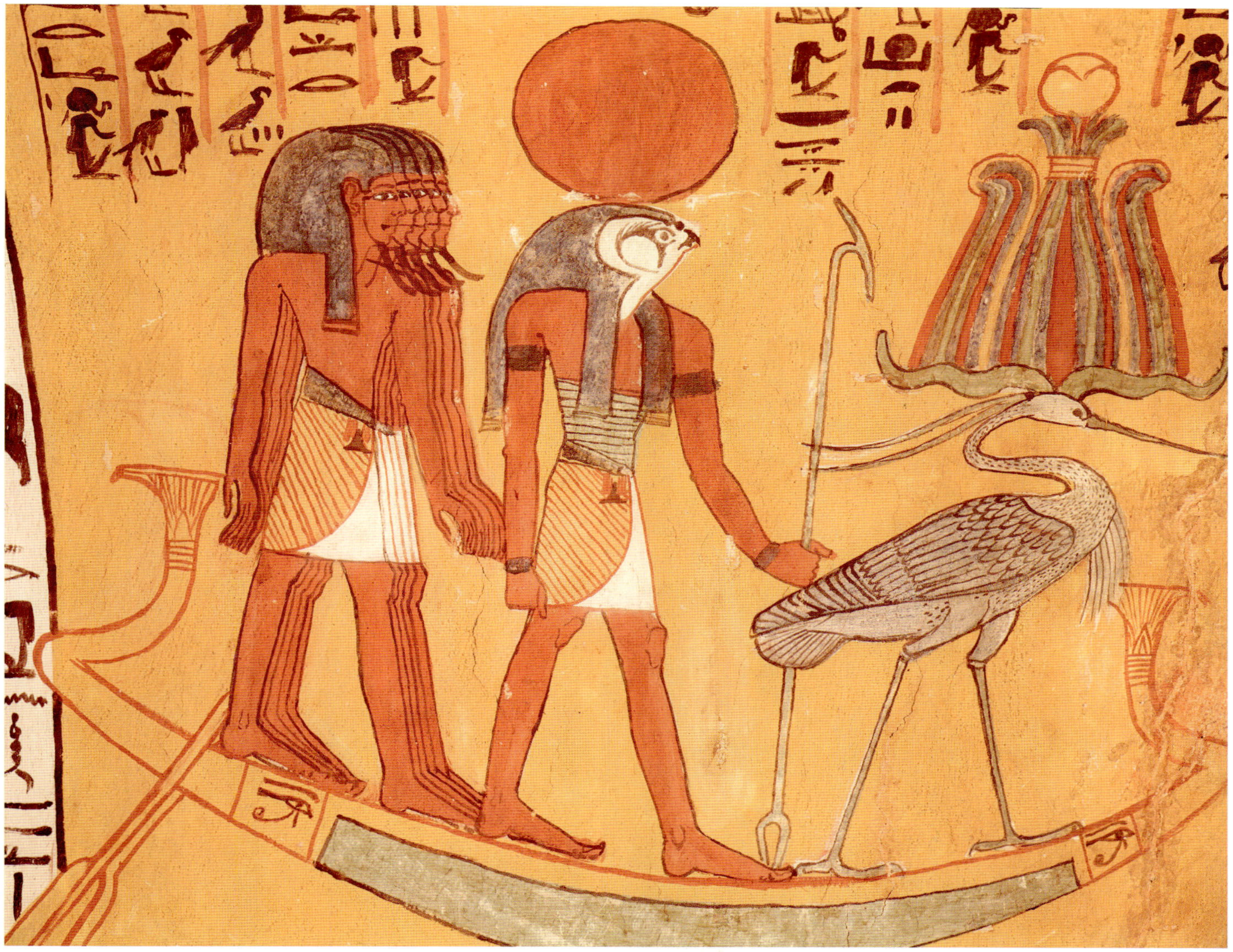

Egyptian
Solar barque with Re-Horakhty, the benu bird and five other deities

c. 1297–1185 BC
Painted limestone
Tomb of Sennedjem, Deir el-Medina, Egypt

The benu bird is the Egyptian version of the phoenix, and is associated with the Creation. Standing alone on high ground during the first floods, the heron-like bird was believed to be the first life to have appeared on the primeval mound that rose from the watery chaos; its cry at the creation of the world marked the beginning of time. The benu was also associated with the *ba* or soul of Ra. Like that of the sun god, its own birth was attributed to self-generation, and it was believed to rise renewed each morning, just like the sun. This most probably led to the concept of its long life and later identification with the Greek phoenix, which also renewed itself from a fiery death. The connection with resurrection eventually led to the benu bird's association with Osiris, the Egyptian god of the underworld. The bird, which was first depicted as resembling a yellow wagtail or an eagle, was later portrayed as a grey heron, and sometimes shown wearing on its head the feathered crown of Osiris (as it is here) or the sun disc. This wall painting from a tomb in the workers' village of Deir el-Medina shows the benu bird on the solar barque of Ra (Re-Horakhty), who is shown as a falcon-headed man crowned by a solar disc.

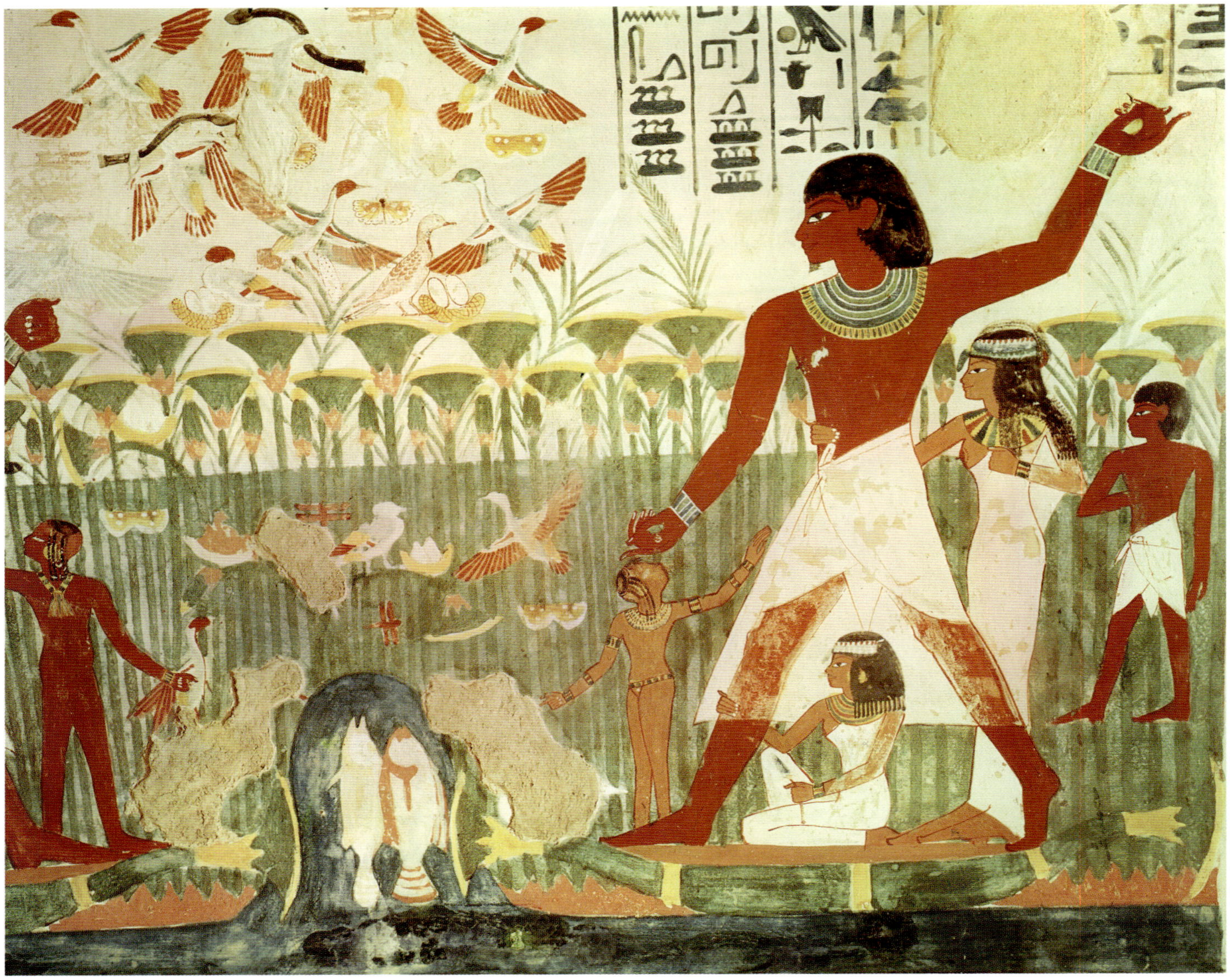

Egyptian
Hunting and Fishing
c. 1567–1320 BC
Painted plaster
Tomb of Nakht, Valley of the Nobles, Thebes

Among the scenes of daily life shown in ancient Egyptian tombs are a number that depict hunting and fowling in the marshes of the Nile. This vignette is from the tomb of Nakht, a scribe. It shows the deceased and his family in a papyrus thicket by the river pursuing birds, which are taking flight in a desperate attempt to escape. Among the papyrus plants are two nests containing eggs. The entire family – Nakht, his wife, Tawy, and their children – are enjoying the sport, although this is probably a symbolic representation of family unity, since in reality it is highly unlikely that they would all have hunted together. Nakht stands in a papyrus skiff, his posture suggesting that he is about to throw a spear at the birds, although the artist has neglected to paint such a weapon. Further scenes show Nakht and his wife being offered birds and fish, the mass capture of birds using a large net, and birds being plucked and cleaned in preparation for the table.

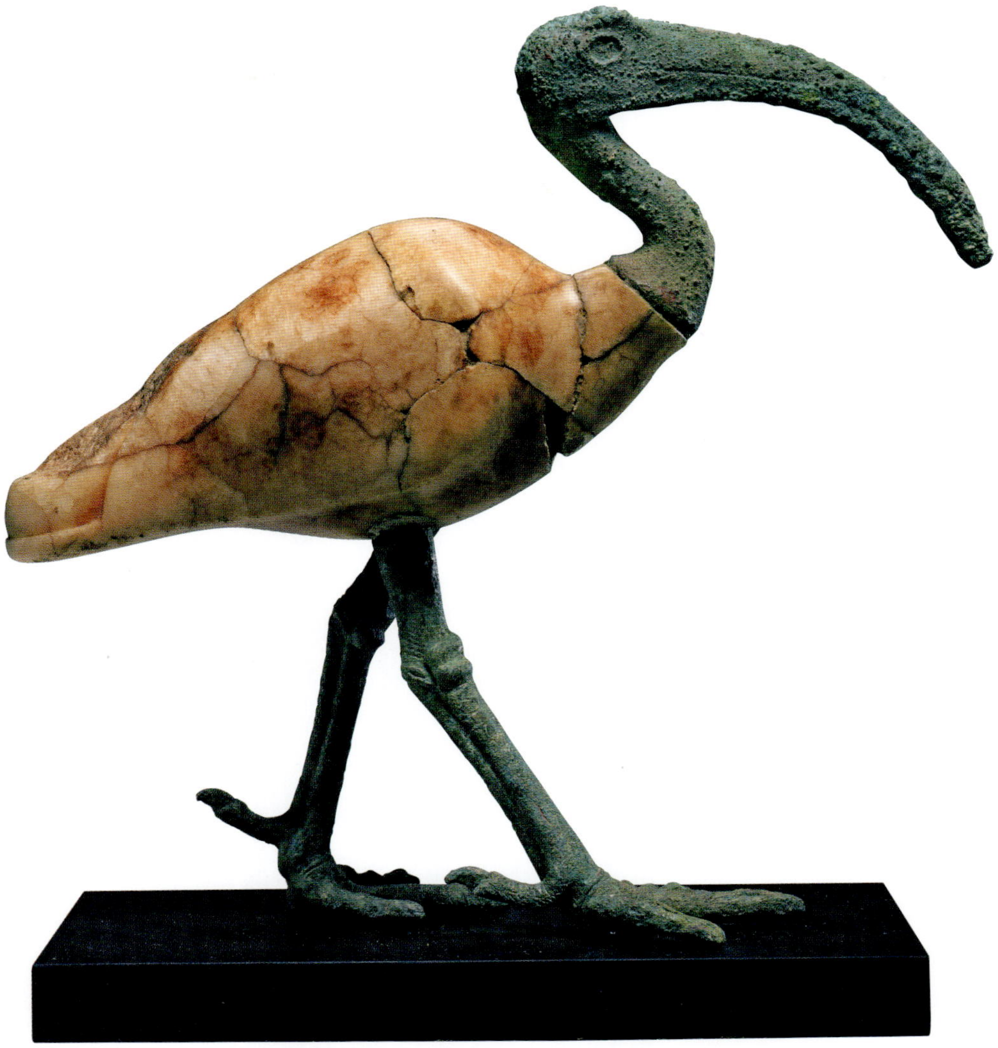

Egyptian
Ibis

715–332 BC
Bronze and alabaster
21.4 cm (8⅜ in.) high
Private collection

The ibis, a wading bird with a slender, curved beak, was the sacred bird of ancient Egypt because it was seen as an incarnation of the god Thoth. In the Late Period, when the cult of Thoth reached its peak, millions of these birds were mummified as offerings to the god, and huge numbers of votive statues and amulets were produced. It may be that the popularity of the ibis can be traced back to its ability to rid homes, shops and grain stores of snakes and vermin (as was the case with the cat, whose skills as a mouser ultimately made it an object of veneration). According to the Greek historian Herodotus, the penalty for killing an ibis was death. Since the ibis-headed Thoth was the patron of scribes (see overleaf), many of the administrators who ran the country had a statue of him at their place of work. The ibis was fairly common in Egypt until the nineteenth century, but is now restricted to a few areas of the country.

Egyptian
Thoth

c. 1187–1186 BC
Painted limestone
Tomb of Prince Khaemwaset II,
Valley of the Queens, Thebes

The Egyptian god Thoth is depicted in various forms, but the version most frequently seen shows him as a man with the head of an ibis. Thoth was thought to be the master of physical and divine law, the inventor of writing, scribe to the underworld and the author of works on science, religion, magic and philosophy. When he is shown with a lunar disc sitting in a crescent moon on top of his head, as here, the artist is referring to his role as the reckoner of times and seasons. This relief of Thoth comes from the tomb of the eldest son of Rameses III, one of the most beautifully preserved in the Valley of the Queens. The wall decorations show the king himself and the young prince making offerings to Thoth and other gods. When he is depicted in tombs, Thoth is usually shown recording the final judgement on the deceased.

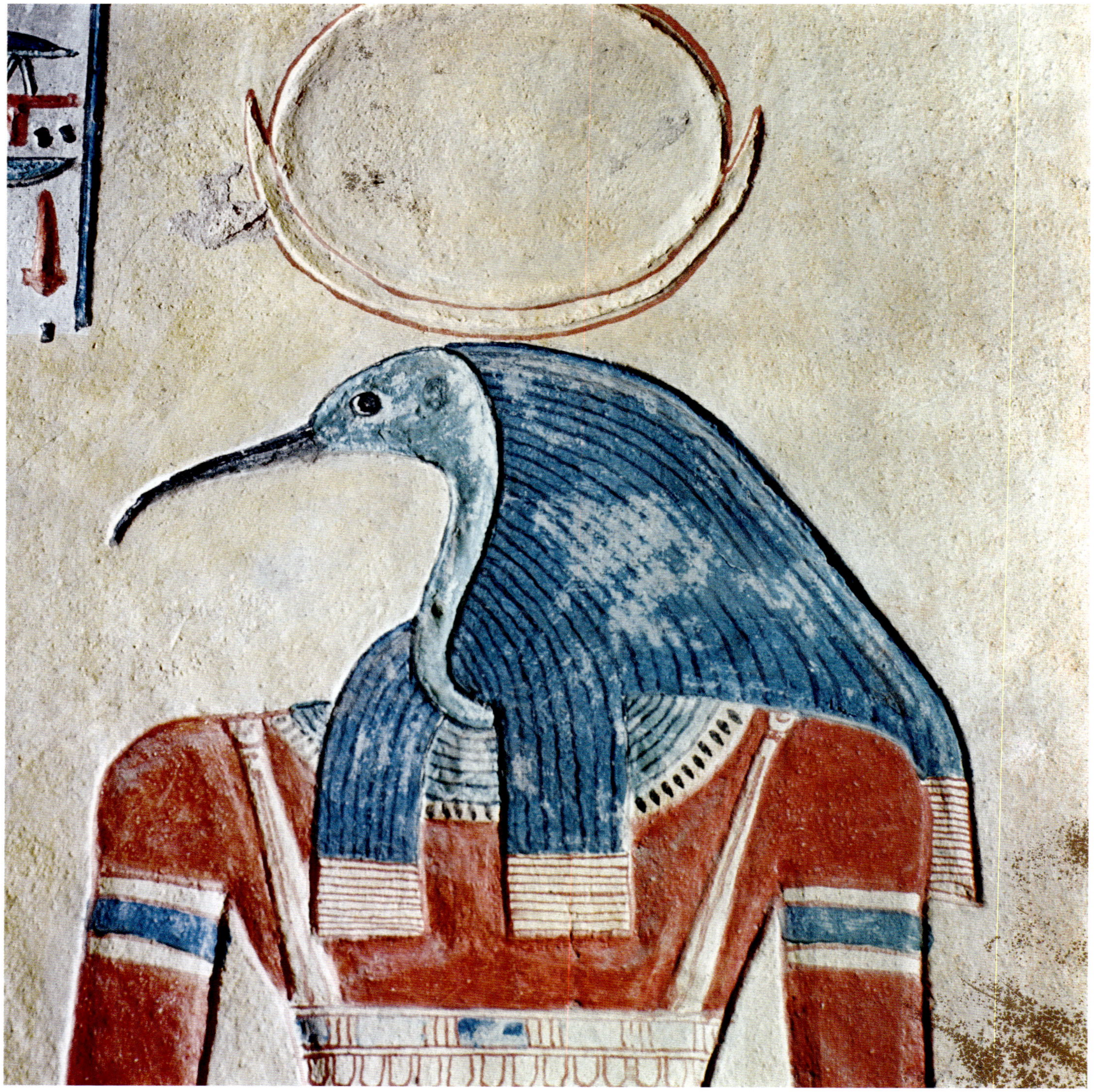

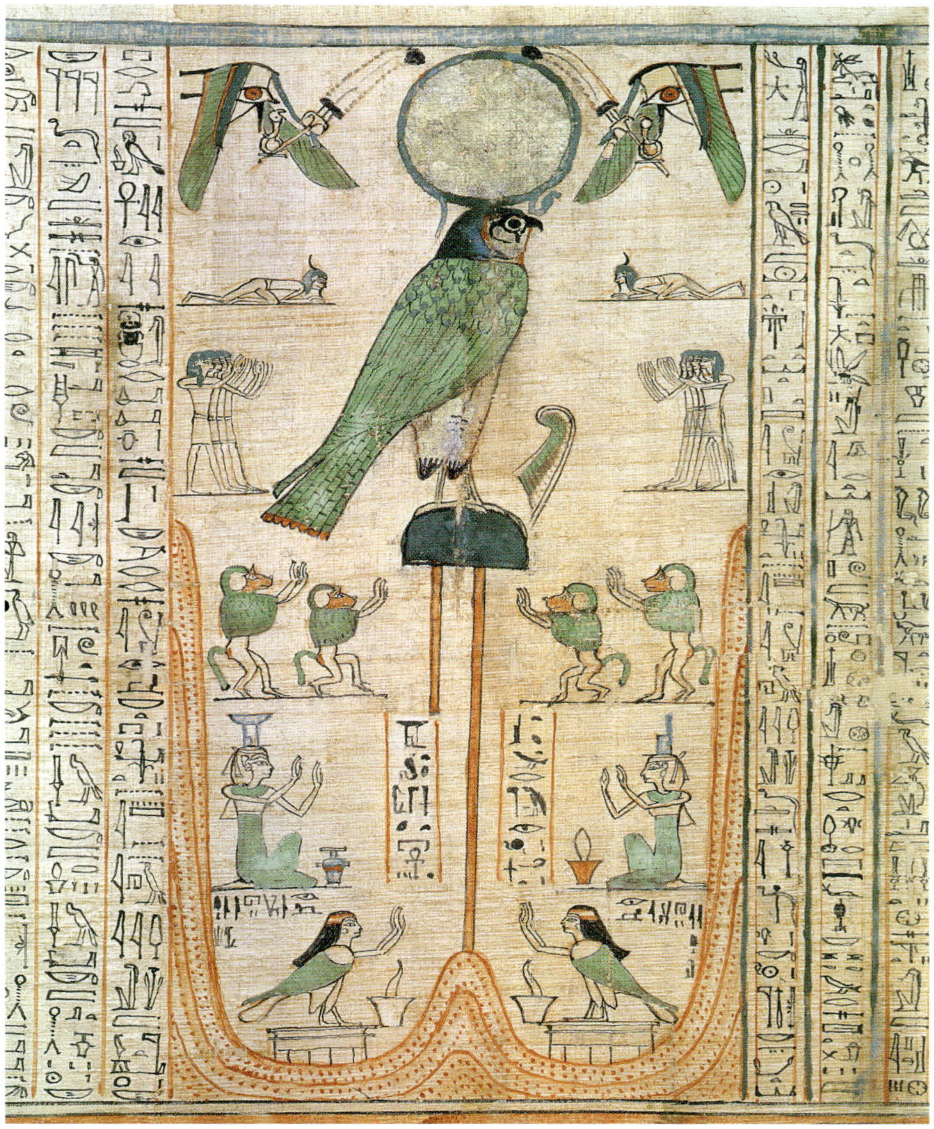

Egyptian
Adoration of the Rising Sun in the form of Re-Horakhty
c. 1050 BC
Papyrus
The British Museum, London

Horus, one of the earliest and most significant Egyptian gods, was traditionally represented as a falcon, or a falcon-headed man. The pharaoh was identified with him, and was considered to be a manifestation of Horus in life. Under the later Egyptian dynasties, Horus's identity became merged with that of Ra (or Re), the sun god, and he re-emerged as Re-Horakhty. In this vignette from the funerary papyrus of the high priestess Anhai, the god represents the rising sun, and is depicted in the form of a falcon with a solar disc on his head, standing on a sign representing the west. He is protected by two winged Eyes of Horus carrying ostrich-feather fans at the top of the composition. Further down is a row of dancing baboons, thought to represent the dawn, and beneath them Isis and her sister Nephthys kneel in adoration. At the bottom, the spirit of the deceased Anhai, shown twice as a composite bird–woman, raises its arms.

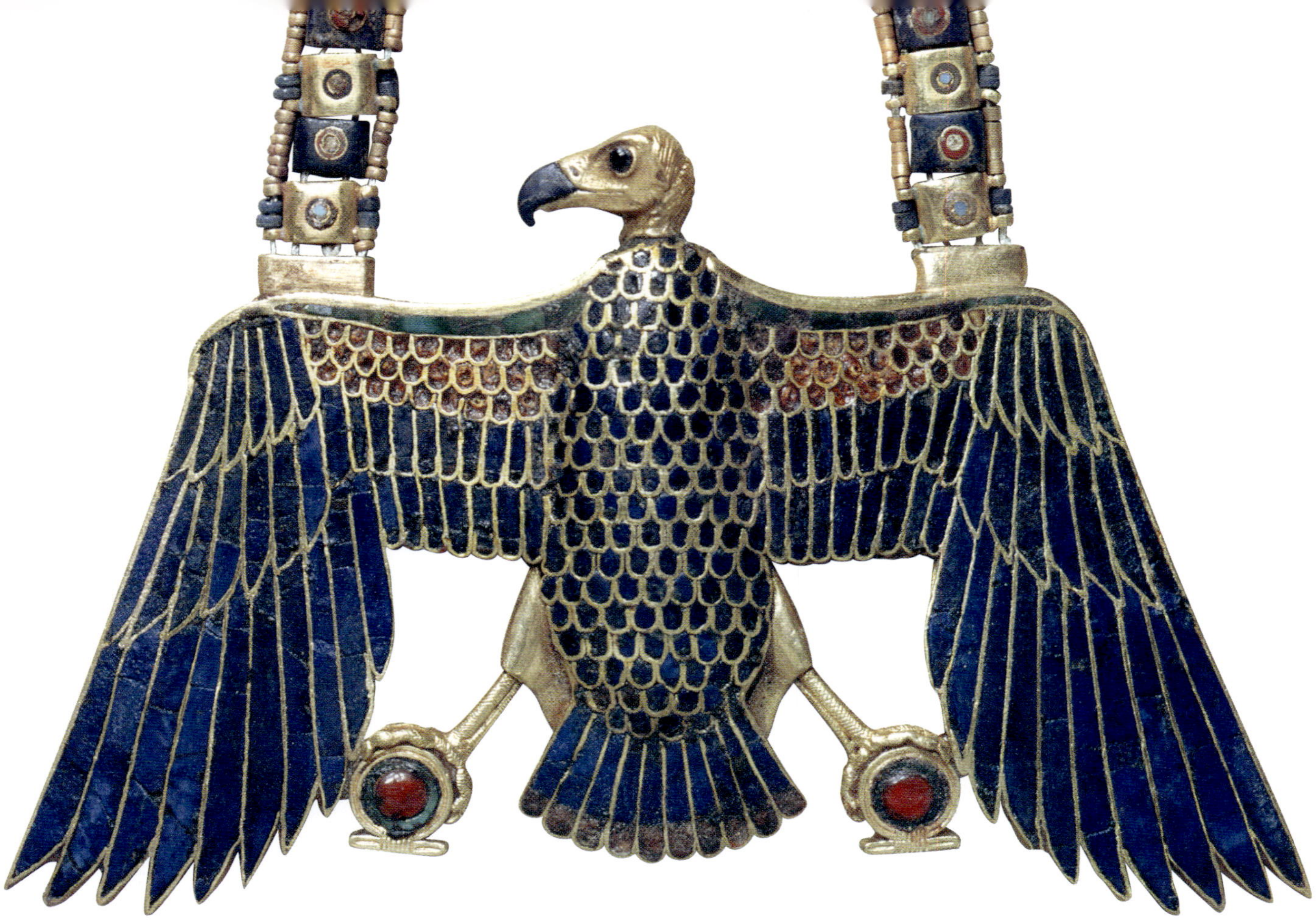

Egyptian
Vulture pendant from the tomb of Tutankhamun

c. 1567–1320 BC
Gold encrusted with lapis lazuli and cornelian
6.5 × 11 cm (2½ × 4⅜ in.)
Museum of Egyptian Antiquities, Cairo

Among the 100 or so items of jewellery that the English Egyptologist Howard Carter found when he unwrapped Tutankhamun's mummy in 1925 was this pendant in the form of a vulture. It represents Nekhbet, the vulture goddess of Upper Egypt and protector of the pharaoh. The goddess was variously represented as a woman with the head of a griffon vulture, or as a vulture wearing the crown of Upper Egypt, and was often shown with her counterpart, Uatchet, the snake goddess of Lower Egypt. (The vulture and snake appear as joint symbols on the headdress of Tutankhamun's famous gold mask.) The head of the bird is rendered with surprising naturalism, while the wings are spread like a protective cloak. In the talons are *shenu* signs – loops of rope that surrounded the cartouches of the pharaohs, protecting their names. Since the amulet was placed in the innermost layers, close to the body, it was probably worn by the pharaoh during his lifetime.

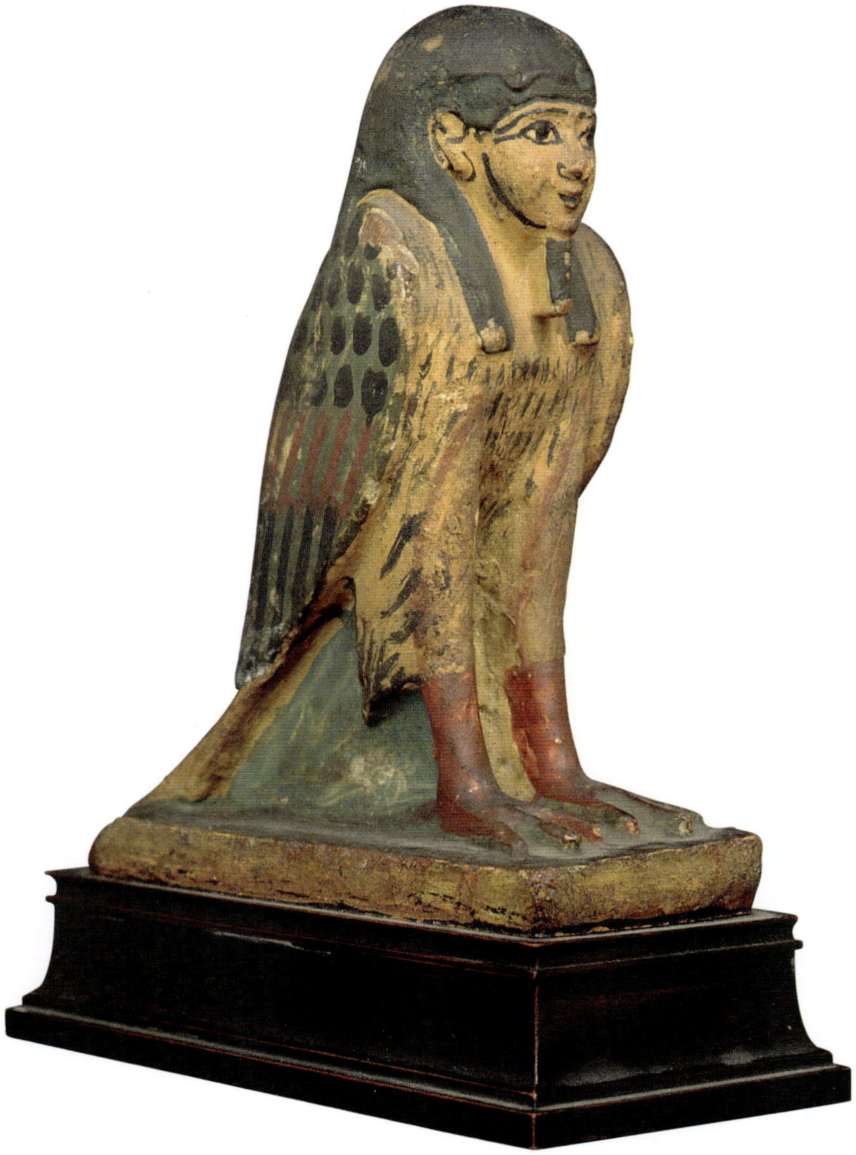

Egyptian
Human-headed *ba* bird

332–330 BC
Gessoed and painted wood
14 cm (5½ in.) high
Freud Museum, London

For the ancient Egyptians, the *ba* was the individual spirit or personality that survived in eternity after a person died. Tomb paintings, papyri and statues depict it as a bird – usually a falcon or hawk – with a human head. Since it had wings, it could travel anywhere it wished before returning to the dead body in the tomb every night, and it was often shown hovering above the mummy or re-entering the tomb to take up residence in the body, having flown around in the world outside. Such wooden figures as this would have been attached to a coffin or shrine – the kind of place where a bird might naturally have perched. One spell in the ancient Egyptian Books of the Dead – a series of funerary texts – recommended that a golden *ba* bird be placed on the chest of the mummy to ensure that the *ba* was reunited with the body.

Greek
Corinthian *aryballos* in the form of an owl

c. 640 BC
Ceramic
5 cm (2 in.) high
Musée du Louvre, Paris

This charming little ceramic owl with huge staring eyes is an *aryballos* – a flask used to store perfume or oil. The liquid would have been poured through an opening underneath its tail, and the flask would have been suspended on a cord threaded through holes in its base. It was made in Corinth, which in the seventh century BC specialized in the production of small perfume vessels, often in the shape of animals. The shape of the vessel and the design of its black-and-red decoration work perfectly in harmony. The owl had a special place in Greek mythology as the bird of Athena, goddess of wisdom and warfare. Owls were said to protect Greek armies in war, and when one flew over soldiers before battle it was taken to foretell victory. Owls were also associated with commerce, and a number of Athenian coins (called 'owls') bear their image.

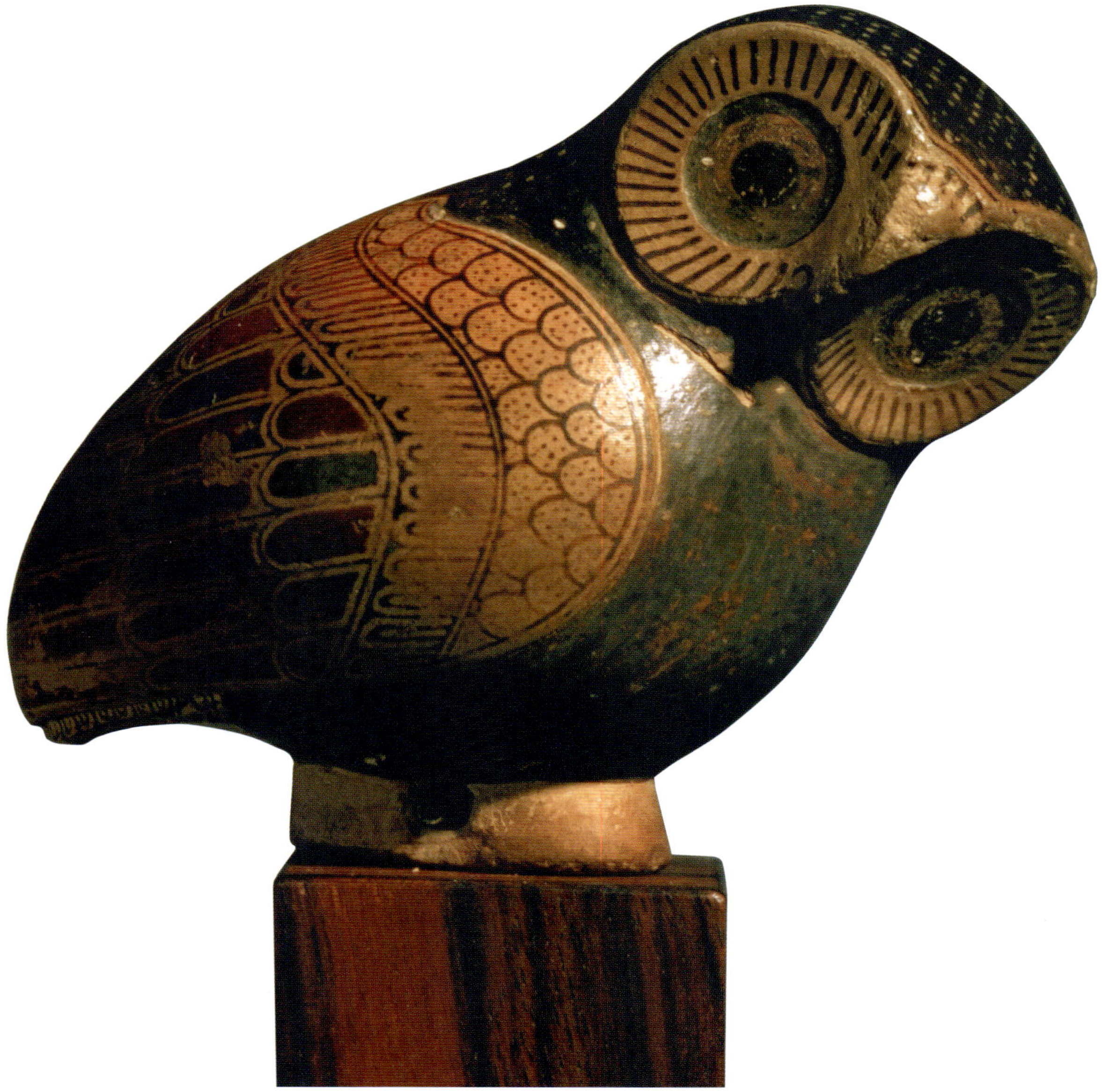

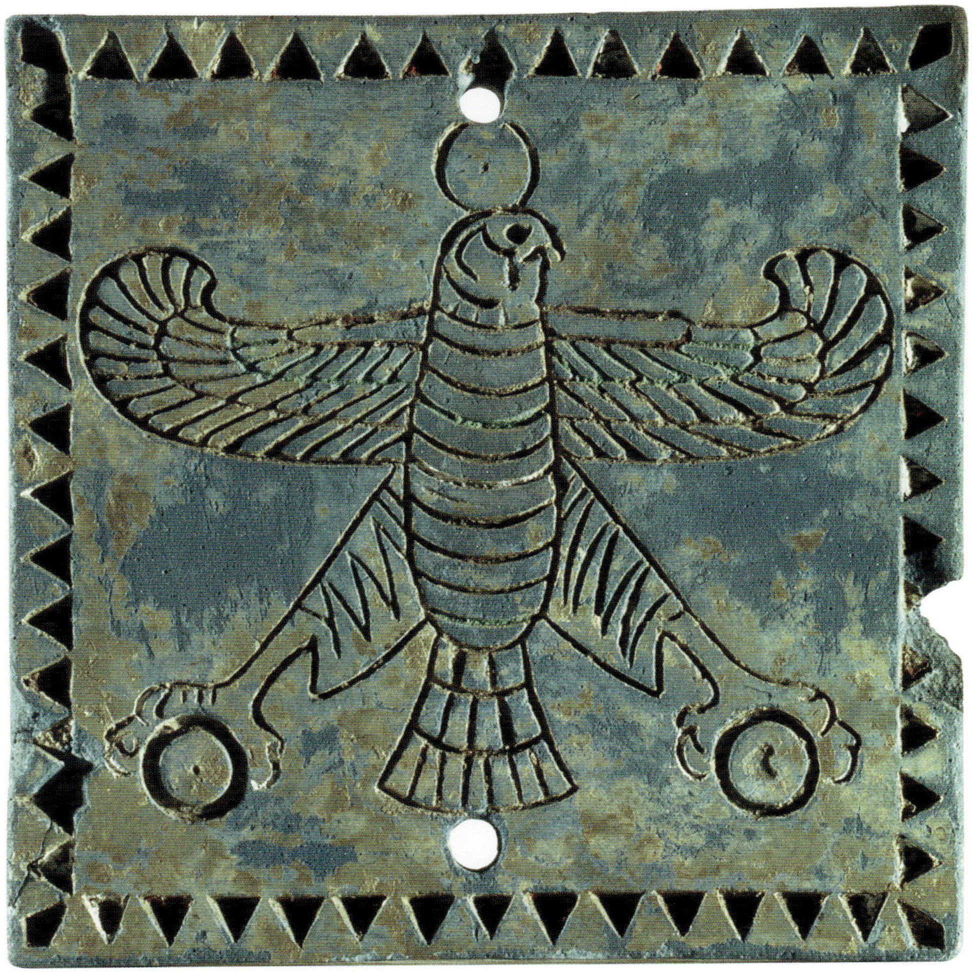

Achaemenid
Tile depicting an eagle

c. 500–480 BC
Ceramic
12.5 × 12.6 cm (4⅞ × 5 in.)
National Museum of Iran, Teheran

This blue faience tile showing an eagle with outstretched wings comes from the ancient Persian capital of Persepolis, founded about 515 BC by Darius the Great. The eagle seems to have been an important symbol for the Achaemenid Persian rulers: the Greek historian Xenophon (*c.* 430–354 BC) reported that the standard carried by the Persian king Artaxerxes II bore the image of a golden eagle with spread wings. Such standards were brightly coloured and carried into battle on long poles or spears to identify the positions of the individuals who carried them. The Persians may have been the first people to use the eagle as a national symbol, but the bird's power and majesty have led to its being adopted by countless empires and nations since, from Imperial Rome to Nazi Germany.

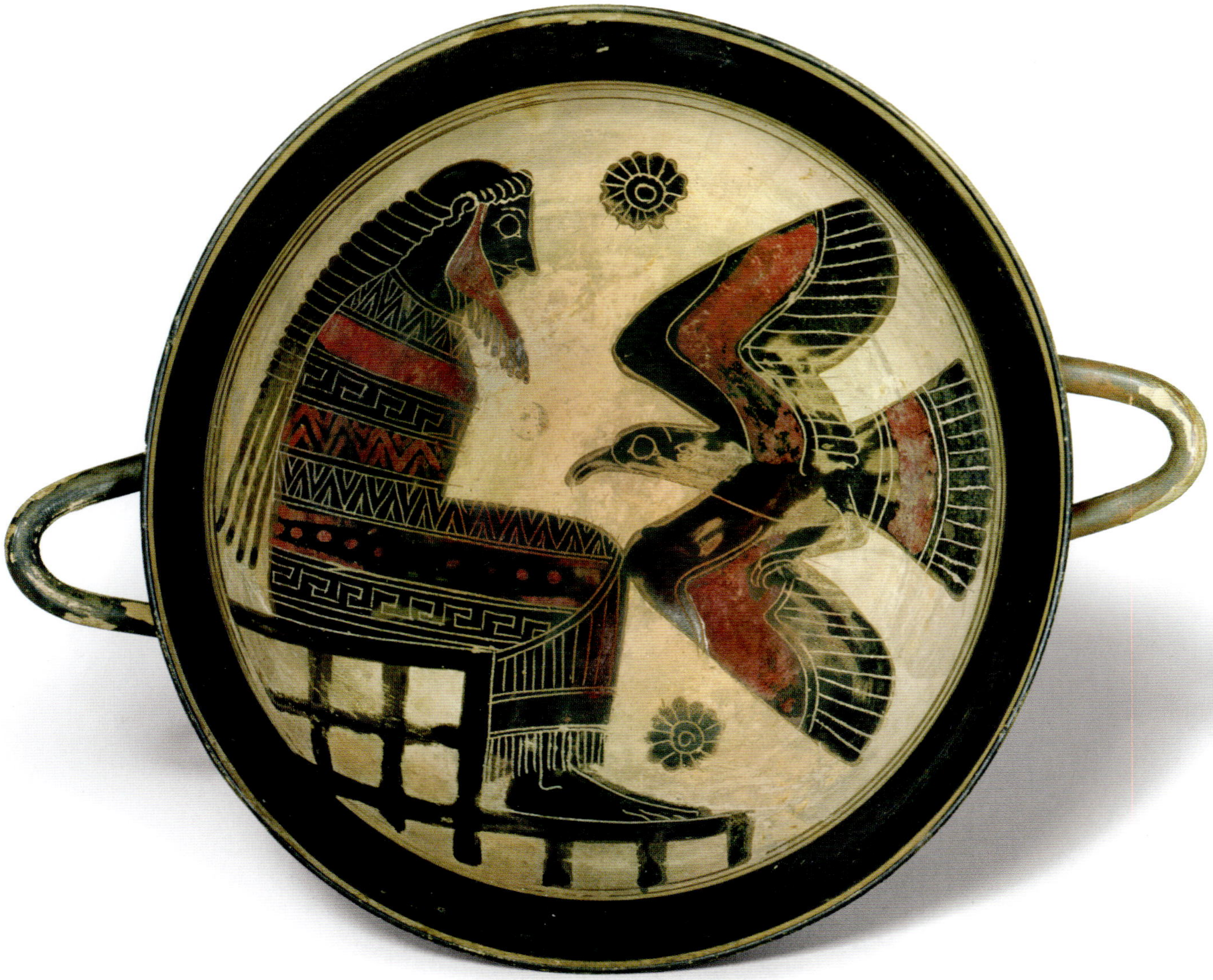

Naukratis painter
(active 575–550 BC) (attrib.)
Laconian cup depicting Zeus
and the eagle
6th century BC
Ceramic
12.7 × 25 cm (5 × 9¾ in.)
Musée du Louvre, Paris

This drinking cup was probably produced in the southern Greek province of Laconia. The central tondo shows Zeus – the supreme ruler of the Greek pantheon and god of the sky – with his characteristic eagle. The bird served him as messenger and companion, helping him to carry out his mission to abduct the youth Ganymede and inflict punishment on Prometheus (see pp. 9, top, 103 and 110, bottom). Sometimes Zeus, who was capable of changing into a variety of beasts, even transformed himself into an eagle. Some Greek legends say that Zeus adopted the bird as his symbol when it flew towards him as he was about to make war on the Titans, as an augury of his victory. Another myth relates that the eagle was originally a human king named Periphas, who incurred the jealousy of Zeus and was turned into a bird.

Roman
Five thrushes in a ring from El-Jem (Thysdrus)

2nd century AD
Mosaic
96 × 100 cm (37¾ × 39⅜ in.)
Musée National du Bardo, Le Bardo, Tunisia

A verse in one of the sonnets written by the Roman poet Virgil recalls a visit to a Roman villa in the city of Carthage in modern-day Tunisia, where this mosaic was found:

The immense cryptoportico, the square peristyle,
The uncountable flowers, octagonal garden,
I remember, O soul, the smiling young patrician,
Playing with the song thrushes near the bluish pond.

However, these dead thrushes strung up on a cord were appreciated for rather more than just their song. They were intended for the table, since the mosaic was in the villa's dining area, where it was usual to depict the delicacies a master would serve to his guests. The Roman writer Martial speaks of setting nets to catch thrushes, and they were also kept in cages and fattened up for eating. The Roman recipe book *Apicius* gives one recipe for thrushes that involves stuffing them and tying their necks with a string – rather as the birds are shown here – as well as a more extravagant one, for a sow stuffed with live thrushes.

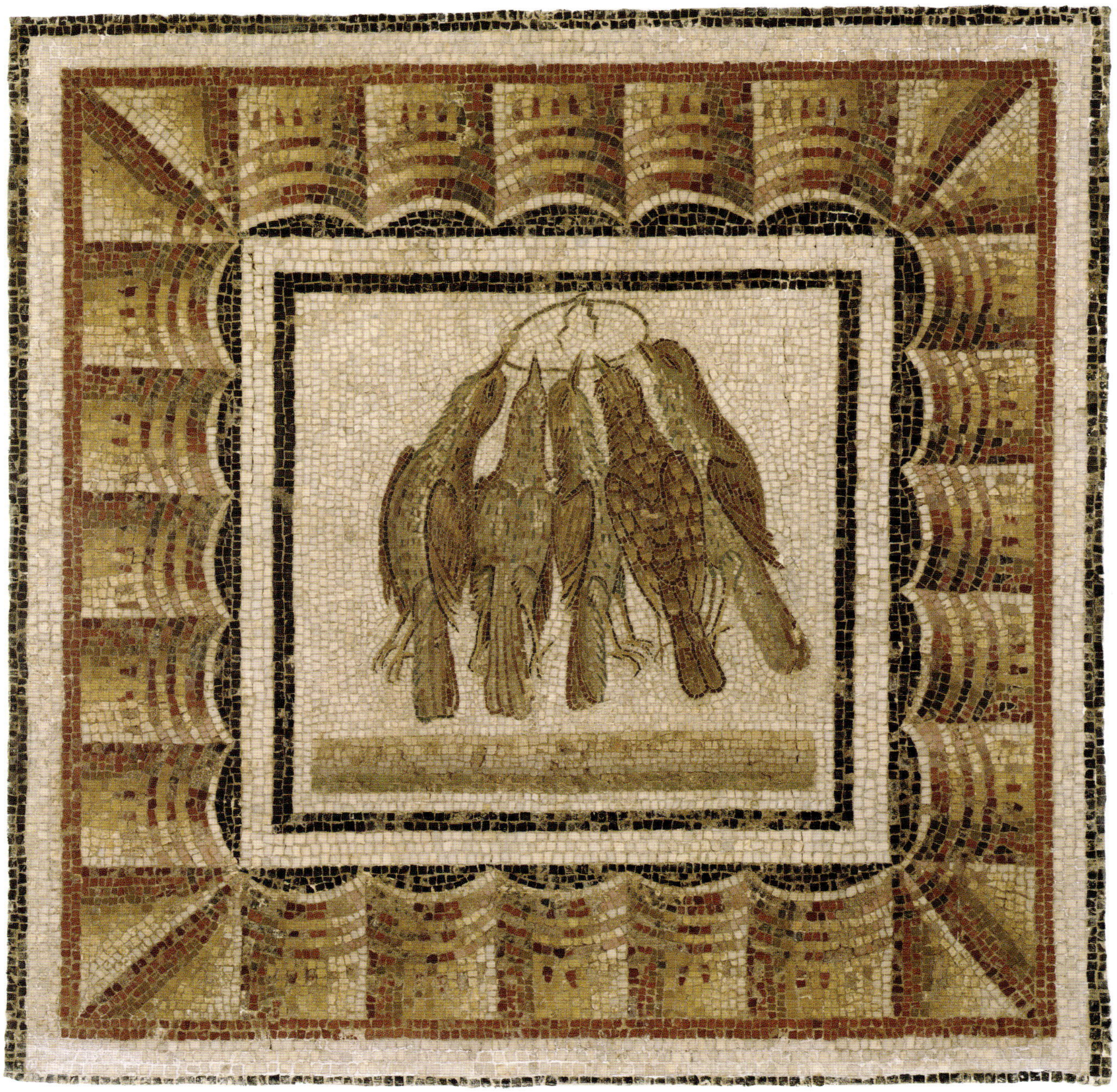

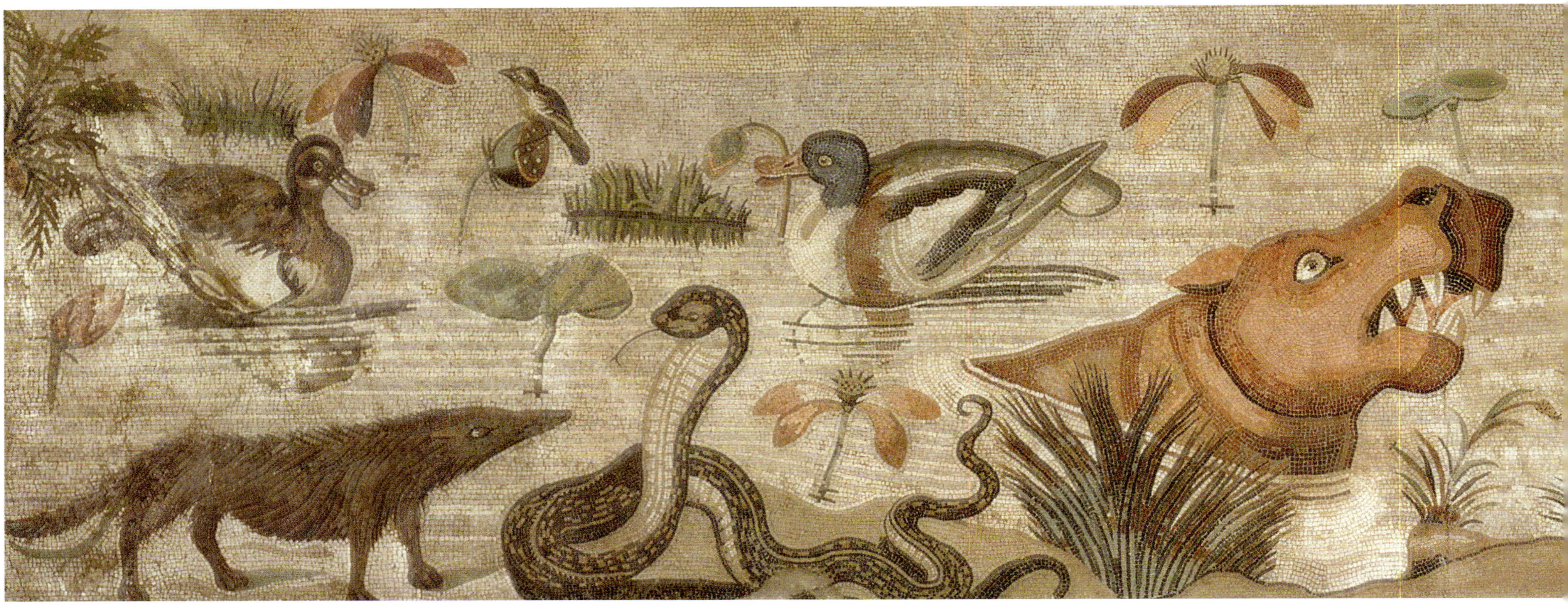

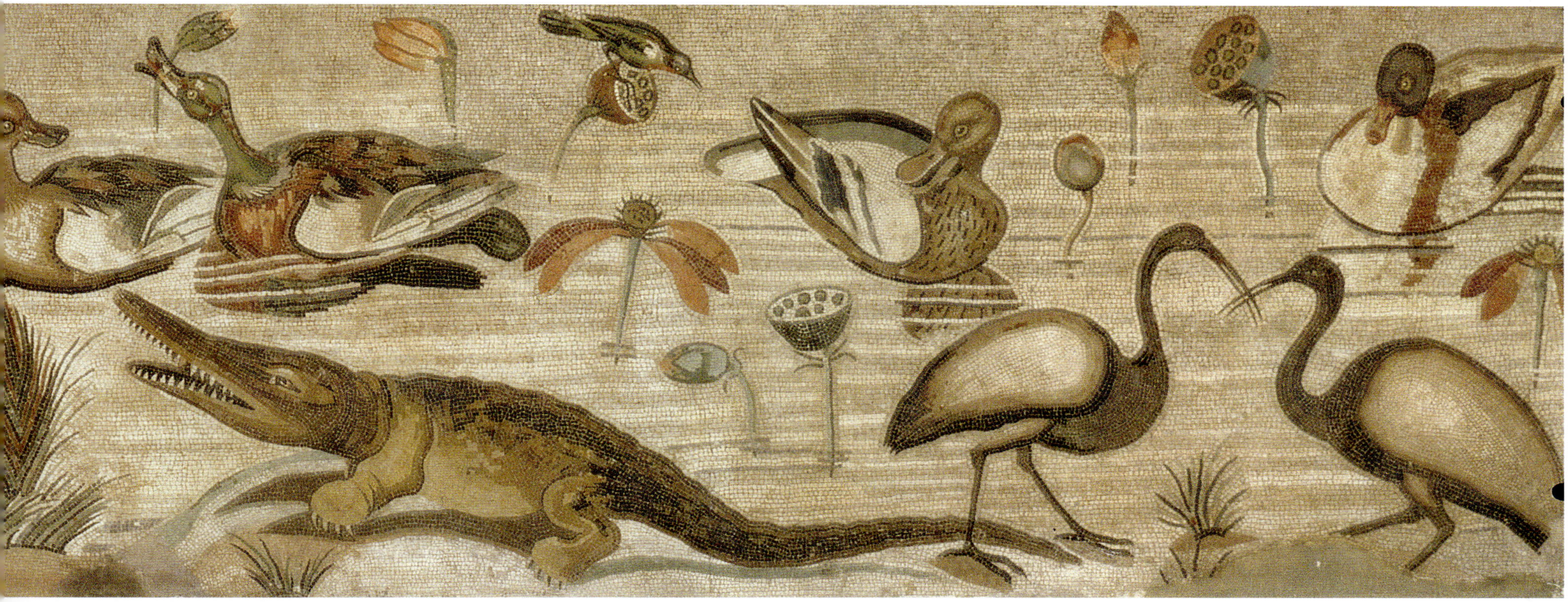

Roman
Nile Scene
1st century BC
Mosaic
Museo Archeologico Nazionale di Napoli, Naples

The walls and mosaics of Pompeiian villas were lavishly decorated with scenes, many of which include birds and mammals. This mosaic from the Casa del Fauno (House of the Faun) illustrates the flora and fauna of Egypt. A hippopotamus, a crocodile, snakes and birds all disport themselves in the waters of the Nile; the ducks and ibis seem quite unperturbed by their fiercer neighbours. The aristocratic House of the Faun was one of the most impressive in Pompeii, and several of its fine mosaics, including a famous one of Alexander in battle, have been removed to the National Archaeological Museum in Naples. Other birds illustrated in mosaics from the house are a kingfisher, poised to dive from the shore on to fish writhing in the sea, drake teals, mallards, chaffinches and an unfortunate partridge in the claws of a cat.

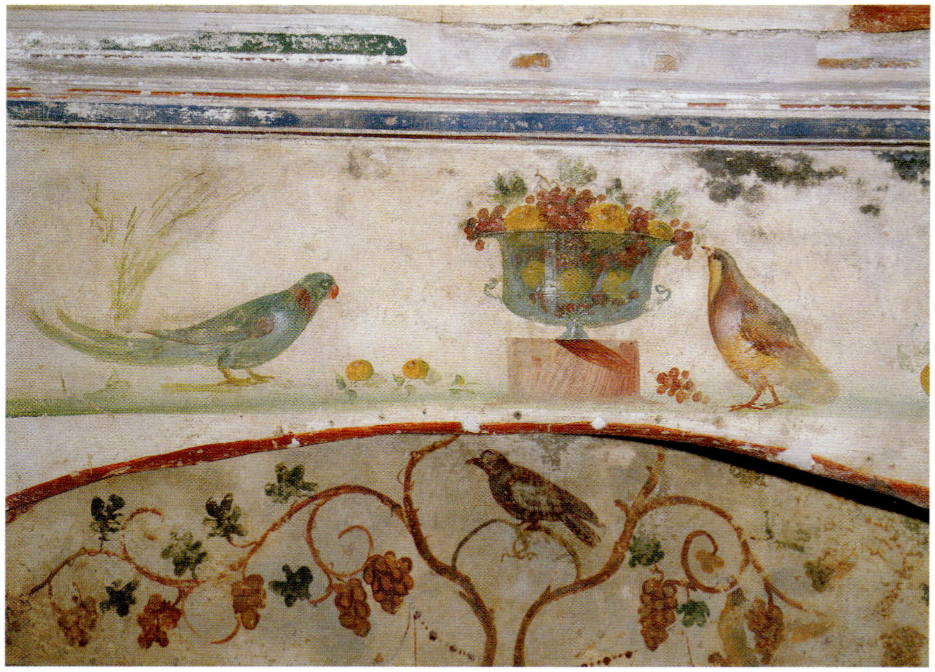

Roman
Birds and fruit

2nd or 3rd century AD
Fresco
Catacombs of San Sebastiano, Rome

There are a number of fine frescoes in the catacombs beneath the basilica of San Sebastiano Fuori le Mura in Rome, a series of tunnels constructed as a burial ground and place of worship for early Christians. This one shows three beautifully painted birds playing in a vine, which in early Christian art is an emblem of the Eucharist. On the left is a green parrot. These birds first appeared in Europe after Alexander the Great's invasion of the Punjab in 327 BC, from which he brought back a green parrot with a pink collar (the Alexandrine Parrot). They became popular pets in the Classical world: the Roman poet Ovid (born 43 BC) even wrote an elegy on the death of his mistress Corinna's pet parrot, which rather touchingly managed to squawk a final farewell to her. The bird in the branches here looks like a pigeon, and that on the right could be a quail, which sometimes stood for the human soul – although it is rather large. Since it is pecking at one of the grapes overflowing from the glass bowl, it could represent the human soul nourishing itself with Communion wine.

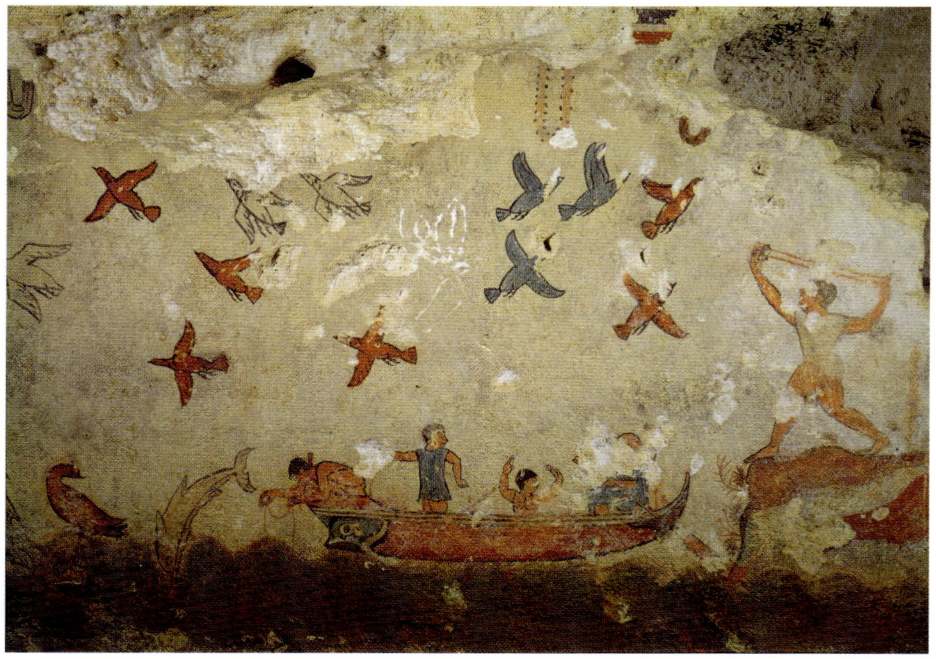

Etruscan
Fishermen in boats and birds flying

c. 520–510 BC
Fresco
Tomb of Hunting and Fishing, Tarquinia, Italy

This lively fresco comes from an Etruscan tomb in the Italian province of Lazio, just north of Rome. The scene takes place on a river, where four boys in a boat set about the business of fishing by casting nets into the water, while dolphins leap above the waves. Another youth, standing on the shore, hurls stones at the birds – possibly ducks – which scatter in the sky. The fresco gives the impression of an enjoyable day out, and was perhaps intended to re-create the youthful pursuits of the tomb's inhabitant. The sense of fun and light-heartedness is reminiscent of Egyptian tomb paintings of hunting in the marshes of the Nile (see p. 42). As with the much older Egyptian scenes, the composition is essentially flat, and little attempt is made to create depth or perspective. The birds are also enormous in comparison to the figures, but their movement in flight conveys a great sense of energy.

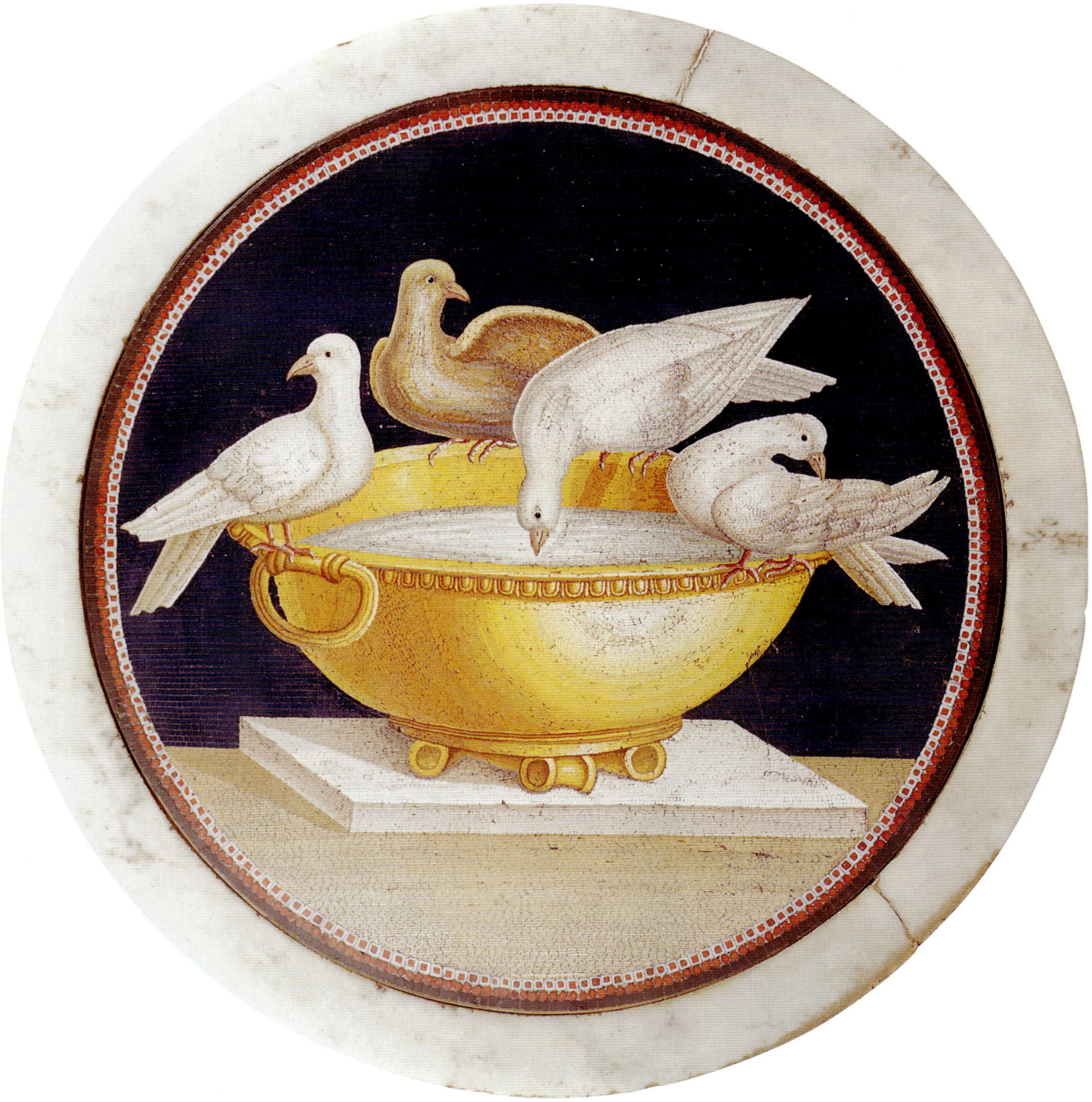

The Doves of Pliny
Early 19th-century copy of an antique original
Micro-mosaic
Diameter: 34.5 cm (13½ in.)
Musée Condé, Chantilly, France

Four doves perch on the rim of a copper bowl. One stoops to drink, while two sun themselves and a fourth preens its feathers. This mosaic, composed of tiny oblong pieces, was made in a Roman workshop, probably that of the celebrated mosaic artist Giacomo Raffaelli, in the early nineteenth century. It is a version of the so-called 'Doves of Pliny' composition, invented by the Hellenic mosaic artist Sosos of Pergamon (who was active in the second century BC) and described by Pliny the Elder in his *Historia Naturalis* (*c.* AD 77–79) as a supreme example of illusionism in mosaic art. The composition was much admired both in antiquity and in later eras, and became a very popular motif. A Roman copy of this Greek original was discovered in 1737 in Hadrian's Villa near Rome, sparking great interest and a number of copies.

Roman
A bird in a garden

1st century AD

Fresco

Casa del Bracciale d'Oro, Pompeii

The Casa del Bracciale d'Oro (House of the Golden Bracelet) in Pompeii had one of the most breathtaking Roman frescoes, covering the entire wall of an outdoor dining room, and framing a central niche, which may have contained a fountain. It depicts a garden with abundant foliage filled with different species of bird, such as the warbler-like creature shown here among the roses. Other birds fly through the air, hide in the foliage, walk along the ground or drink from a fountain. Pompeii's frescoes suggest that the Romans were consciously trying to attract birds, as they are shown feeding on fruit and berries placed on shelves, or perched on the rims of fountain bowls, and provided with places for bathing and drinking in the gardens.

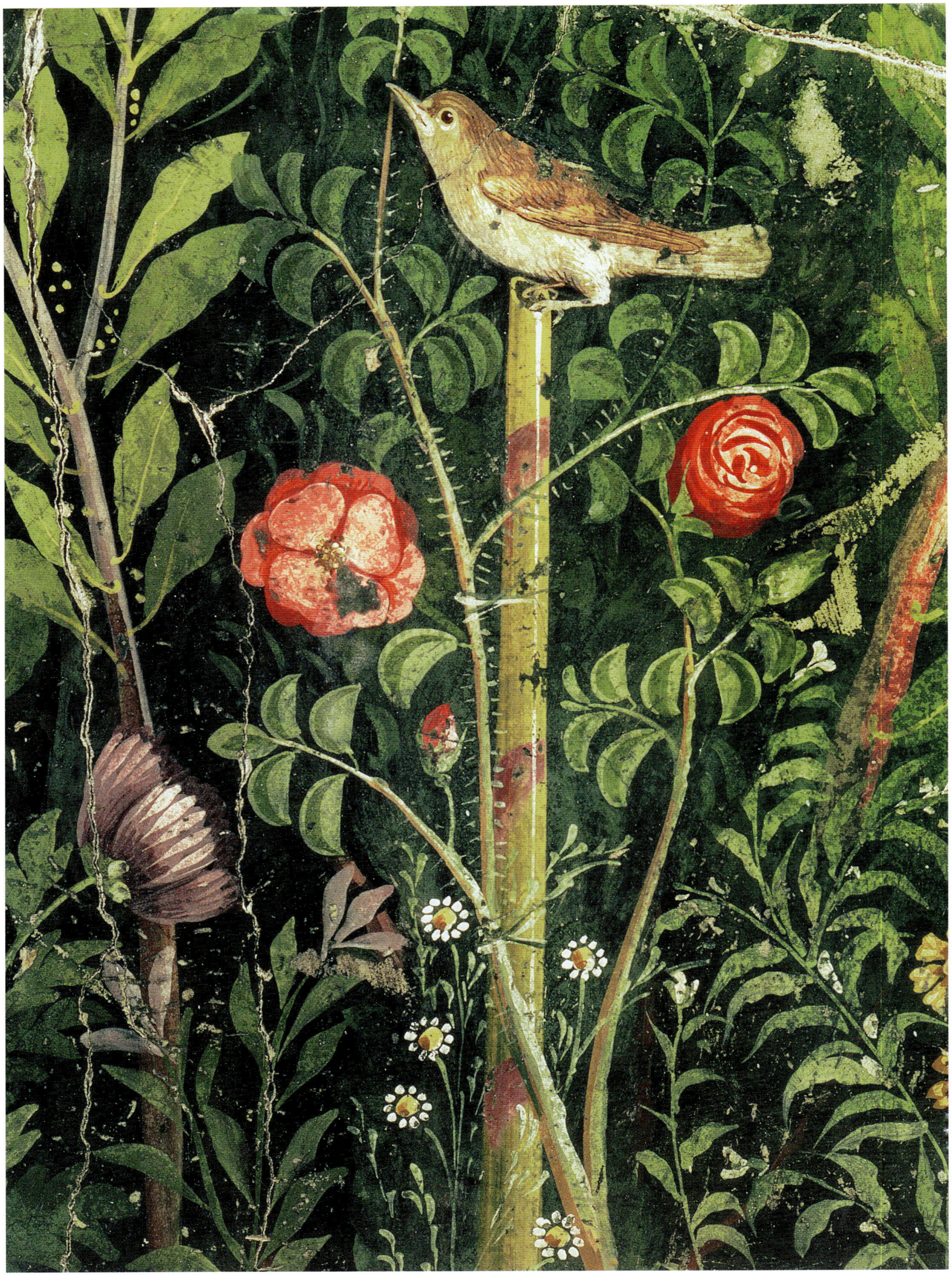

Sir Edward John Poynter (1836–1919)

Feeding the Sacred Ibis in the Halls of Karnac

1871
Oil on canvas
93.5 × 70 cm (36¾ × 27½ in.)
Private collection

The Victorian painter Edward Poynter had a distinguished career, which included stints as director of the National Gallery and president of the Royal Academy in London. But he is chiefly remembered today for the canvases in which he attempted to reconstruct events and situations in the ancient world with painstaking archaeological accuracy. This composition shows a young, bare-breasted priestess dishing out small fish to a flock of sacred ibis (which are distinguished from other species of ibis by their black heads, necks and wing tips) in the temple of Karnac in Thebes (modern-day Luxor). The columns and walls of Hypostyle Hall in this vast religious complex are shown coloured, as they would have been originally, and birds appear in the hieroglyphic decoration. The birds were sacred to Thoth, the god of knowledge, who is generally depicted as an ibis-headed man. In his *Histories*, the Greek historian Herodotus said that the Egyptians venerated the birds because they attacked the flying serpents that appeared at the beginning of spring.

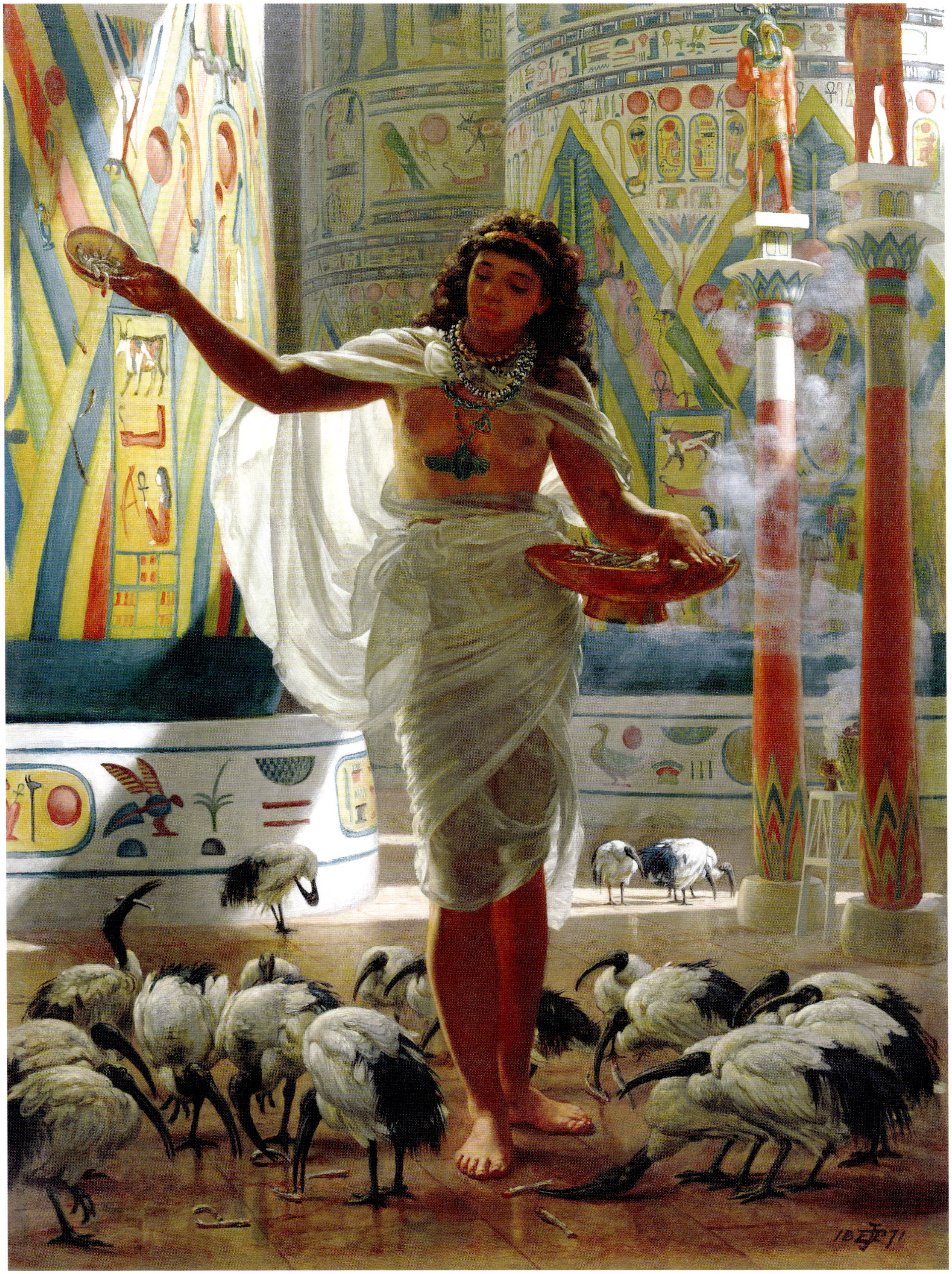

The Christian Bird

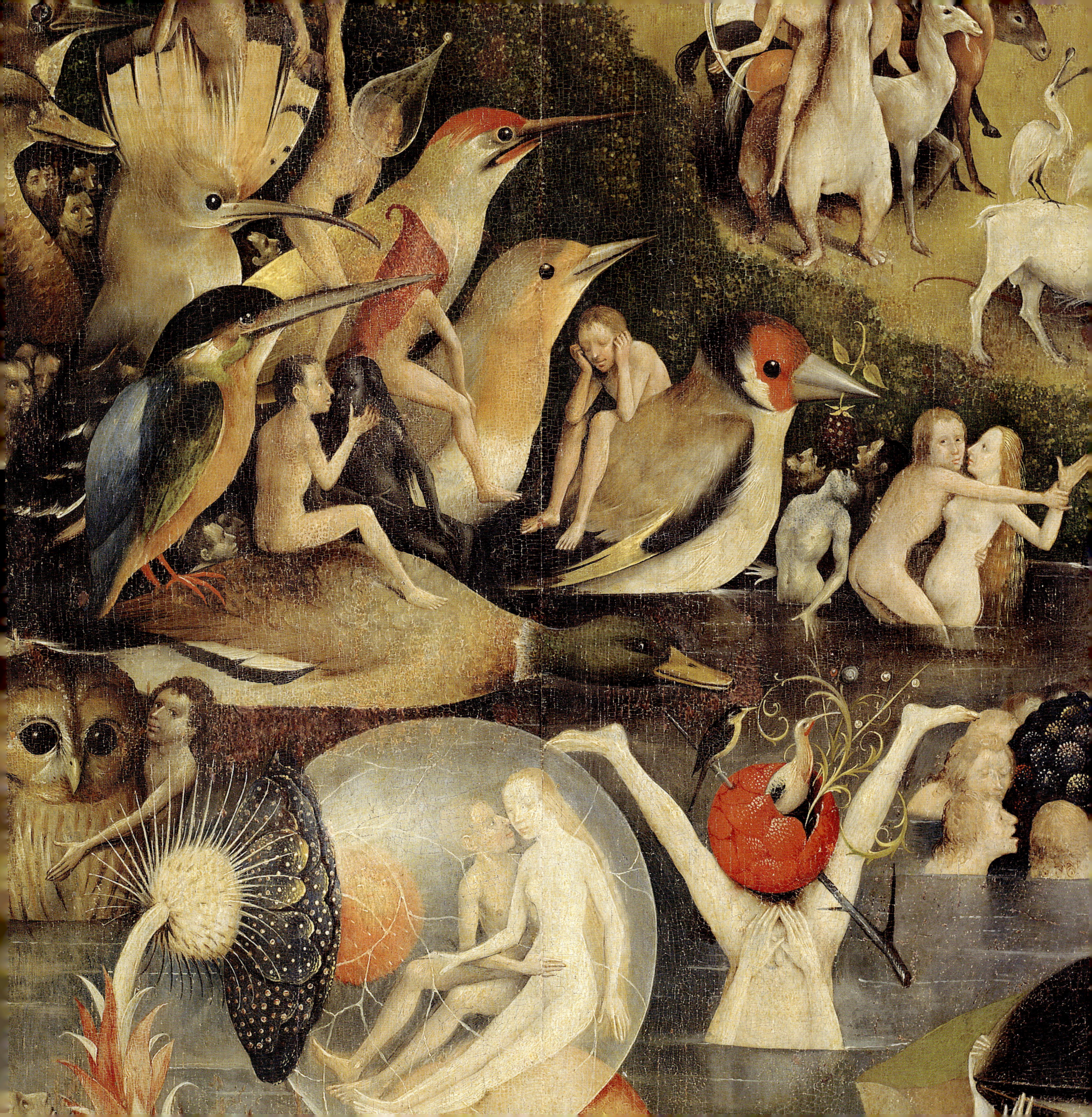

Scores of symbolic birds flit through Christian narratives. The borders of many gospel books, missals and books of hours are a riot of foliage and bird life (opposite), and thousands of the world's most famous religious paintings contain birds, some of them included because they are mentioned in the Bible, and others based on apocryphal stories. Angels, those divine messengers blessed with flight, often sport elaborate wings based on those of real birds.

Birds are at the centre of the most important events in the Bible. In the book of Genesis, they come into existence on the fifth day of Creation, so that they can fly above the Earth in the open firmament of Heaven (p. 79). Adam and Eve's Garden of Eden would be unimaginable if it were not filled with colourful plumage and birdsong: a Paradise scene that has understandably long appealed to artistic imaginations (p. 81). The story of Noah's Ark, with its pairs of animals and birds lining up to be loaded on to the ship, is another subject that has provided an excellent pretext for portraying an avian extravanganza (pp. 62, bottom, 80 and 84). As the waters of the deluge begin to subside, it is the dove bearing an olive branch that tells Noah that he is near dry land, an event that provides a further poignant moment full of visual possibility (p. 86).

Certain birds are favoured in religious art. God manifests Himself in the form of a pure-white dove in scenes of the Creation, the Annunciation, Baptism and Pentecost (pp. 65, 70 and 77), and Mary sacrifices two doves in the temple following the birth of her son. The dove even dictates the word of God to St Gregory the Great as he writes (p. 82). The exotic parrot occurs in Renaissance paintings as a symbol of the Virgin Birth, perhaps because of its ability to speak and the ancient notion of conception occurring through the ear, or possibly because of the strange notion that the words a parrot uttered to Julius Caesar after the Battle of Actium in 31 BC – 'Ave Caesar' – prefigured the Ave Maria with which God hailed Mary at the Annunciation (p. 78). Christ himself is associated with the pelican, which was once mistakenly thought to nourish its young on blood drawn from its breast, just as Christ sacrificed Himself in order to redeem mankind (p. 64). The swallow, too, is linked with the Resurrection because of its habit of reappearing in Europe every spring (p. 71), while the goldfinch, clutched by the baby Jesus in hundreds of Renaissance images of the Madonna and Child, is another reference to Christ's eventual Crucifixion (p. 75). Similarly, the cock that crows to herald St Peter's denial of Christ has led to the bird being associated with the Passion (p. 87).

Birds sometimes intervene in the lives of holy men and saints. The desert saints Elijah, Paul the Hermit, Anthony and Onuphrius were fed on bread brought to them every day by ravens when they retreated to the wilderness (p. 83), while a raven intervened to carry away a loaf of poisoned bread when an envious priest tried to kill St Benedict. The eagle, one of the four beasts of the Apocalypse, which utters cries of woe at the sound of the last trumpet, is often shown sitting beside St John the Evangelist as he writes his Gospel (p. 68). Just as the eagle is the bird that flies closest to Heaven, so the saint is said to have been the closest to God.

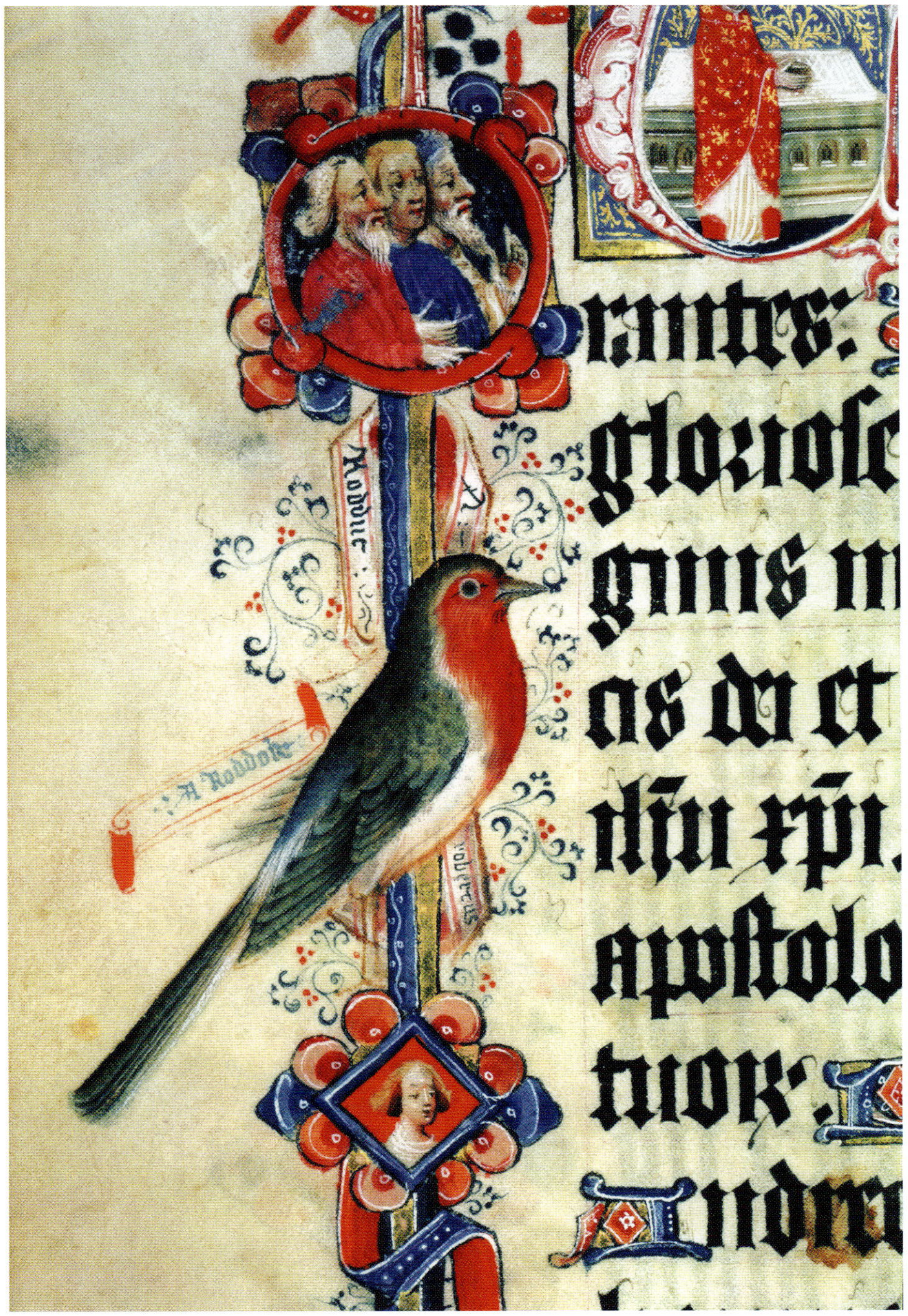

English
The Sherborne Missal (detail)

c. 1400–1407
Vellum
British Library, London

A missal is a book containing the text and music needed to celebrate the Mass, and the example known as the Sherborne Missal is one of the masterpieces of medieval English art. It was made for the Benedictine Abbey of St Mary in Sherborne, Dorset, and contains 694 pages. One of its distinguishing features is a series of forty-eight illustrations of wild birds, which are depicted realistically and identified by name in Middle English rather than Latin. About forty species can be identified, including gannets, moorhens, storks, cormorants, wagtails and woodpeckers, giving an insight into the natural history of Dorset in about 1400. This charming robin (called a 'roddok') decorates the margin of one of the pages from the Canon, which contains the prayers said in the central part of the Mass. The artists who decorated most medieval manuscripts are anonymous, but we do know the name of the chief illuminator of the Sherborne Missal: John Siferwas, a Dominican friar. He was assisted by at least four other artists.

English
The Angel Summons Birds to Eat the Flesh of Men
The Lambeth Apocalypse
f. 33v

c. 1260
Vellum
Lambeth Palace Library, London

The Lambeth Apocalypse is one of a number of Apocalypse manuscripts produced in England in the thirteenth and fourteenth centuries. It is a richly illustrated text of the book of Revelation, describing the visions of St John, foretelling the destruction of the wicked, the overthrow of Satan and the establishment of Christ's kingdom on Earth. This illumination relates to the Battle of Armageddon, when St John sees an angel standing in the sun, who invites all the birds of the sky to a banquet to eat the flesh of kings, generals, mighty men, horses and all people. The illuminator (whose identity is unknown) depicts this terrifying scene with great vividness, showing different species of bird swooping down to devour the naked corpses strewn across the ground. St John, seated at the left, transcribes the scene.

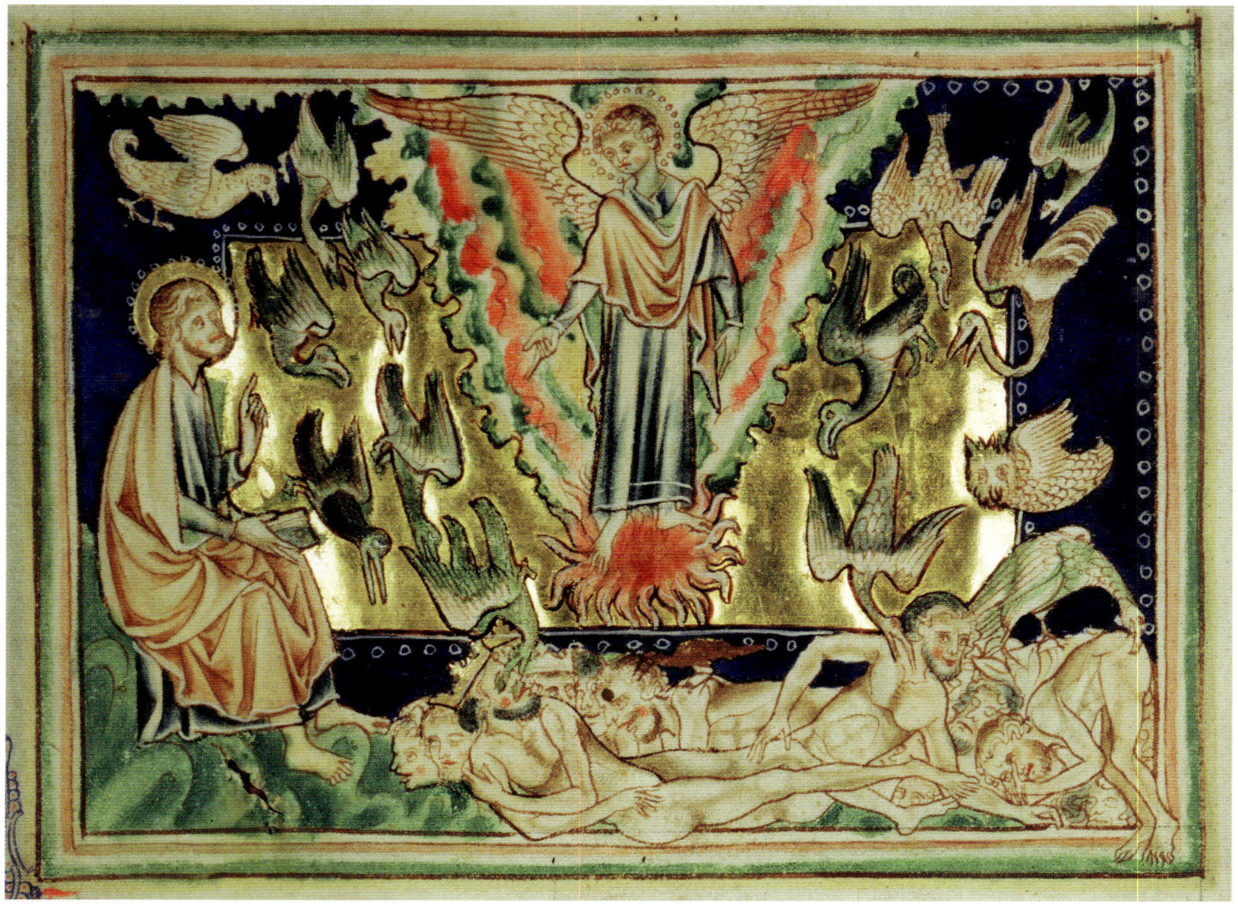

Byzantine
Noah Putting Birds on the Ark

13th century
Mosaic
Basilica di San Marco, Venice

The basilica of St Mark, which dominates Venice's famous piazza, is richly decorated with mosaics depicting biblical scenes. In the vestibule, or narthex, is the story of Noah and the Flood, which is told in Genesis 6–9. When God decided to cleanse the Earth of mankind's wickedness by sending a great flood to obliterate all living things, he instructed the righteous man Noah to build a great Ark and fill it with pairs of every animal and bird, to ensure the survival of their species, as well as his wife, his sons and his sons' wives. Here Noah loads pairs of birds on to the Ark: two peacocks are being bundled on while other birds, including ducks, cockerels and pigeons, line up ready to board. In further scenes, Noah is shown releasing the dove from the Ark, and the humans and animals are seen disembarking on to dry land while birds fly out from their confinement.

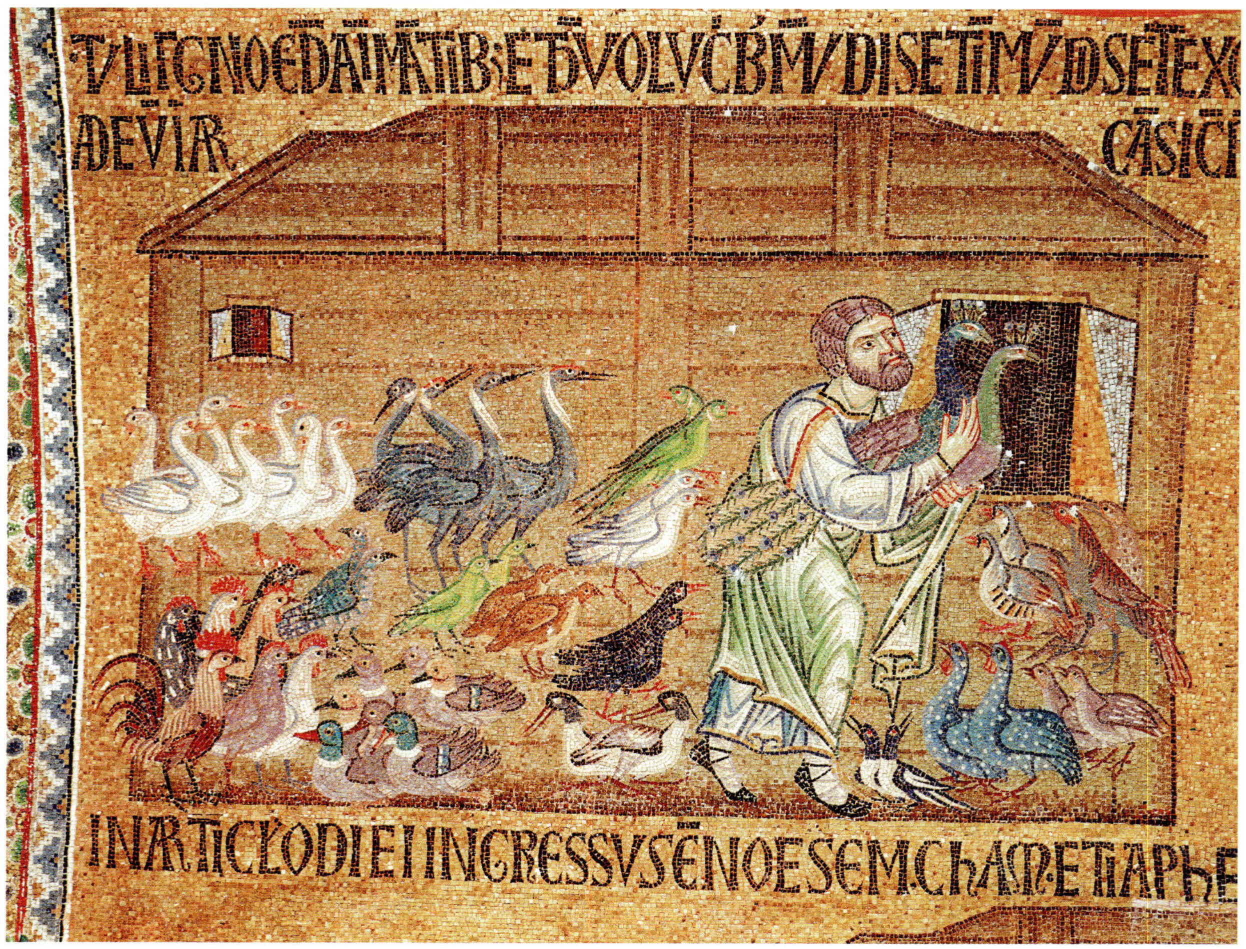

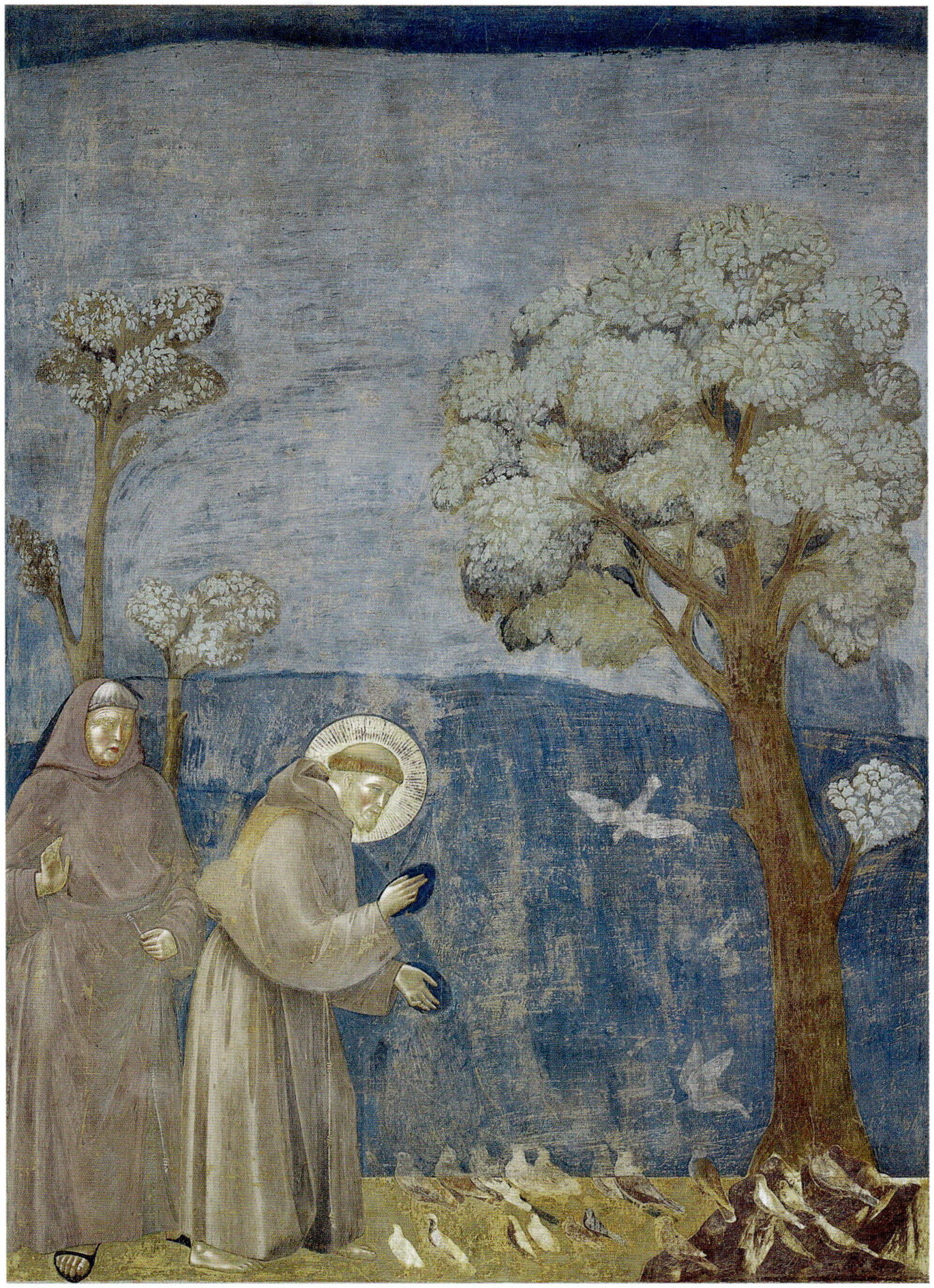

Giotto di Bondone
(*c.* 1267–1337) (attrib.)
St Francis Preaching to the Birds

1297–99
Fresco
San Francesco, Assisi, Upper Church

The walls of the Upper Church of San Francesco in Assisi are decorated with a fresco cycle attributed to Giotto. It depicts various episodes in the life of St Francis (1181/82–1226), the famous Tuscan saint who abandoned a life of privilege to embrace that of a poor friar and preacher. According to a medieval story, soon after Francis's conversion to Christianity, he stopped on the road to Bevagna, near Assisi, to preach a sermon to some birds he had spotted in the trees. Addressing the birds as 'my little sisters', he exhorted them to sing the praises of their Creator, who had given them the liberty to fly about, and who had made sure that they were provided with sustenance, clothing and places to nest. The birds, which had gathered around him and listened silently while he spoke, opened their beaks, spread their wings and bowed their heads, to show their joy. They then rose into the air, singing sweetly, following a sign of the cross the saint had made.

Lorenzo Monaco (Piero di Giovanni) (*c.* 1370–*c.* 1425)

Crucifixion

c. 1410–15
Tempera on panel
50 × 27 cm (19⅝ × 10⅝ in.)
Galleria dell'Accademia, Florence

Writing in the fourth century AD, St Jerome gave voice to a common myth that when a pelican's young were killed by serpents the mother bird could revive them by piercing her breast to feed them on her blood. (This curious notion may have been based on the observation that adult pelicans feed their young on macerated food – mistakenly thought to be blood – stored under their bills.) In the Middle Ages the pelican became a symbol of the sacrifice of Christ on the cross, since Christ shed his blood to redeem mankind. The connection is made explicit in this Crucifixion scene, which shows a pelican on top of the cross, while angels hold up cups to gather the blood from Christ's wounds. Lorenzo Monaco (the name means 'Lorenzo the Monk') was one of the leading painters in Florence at the beginning of the fifteenth century.

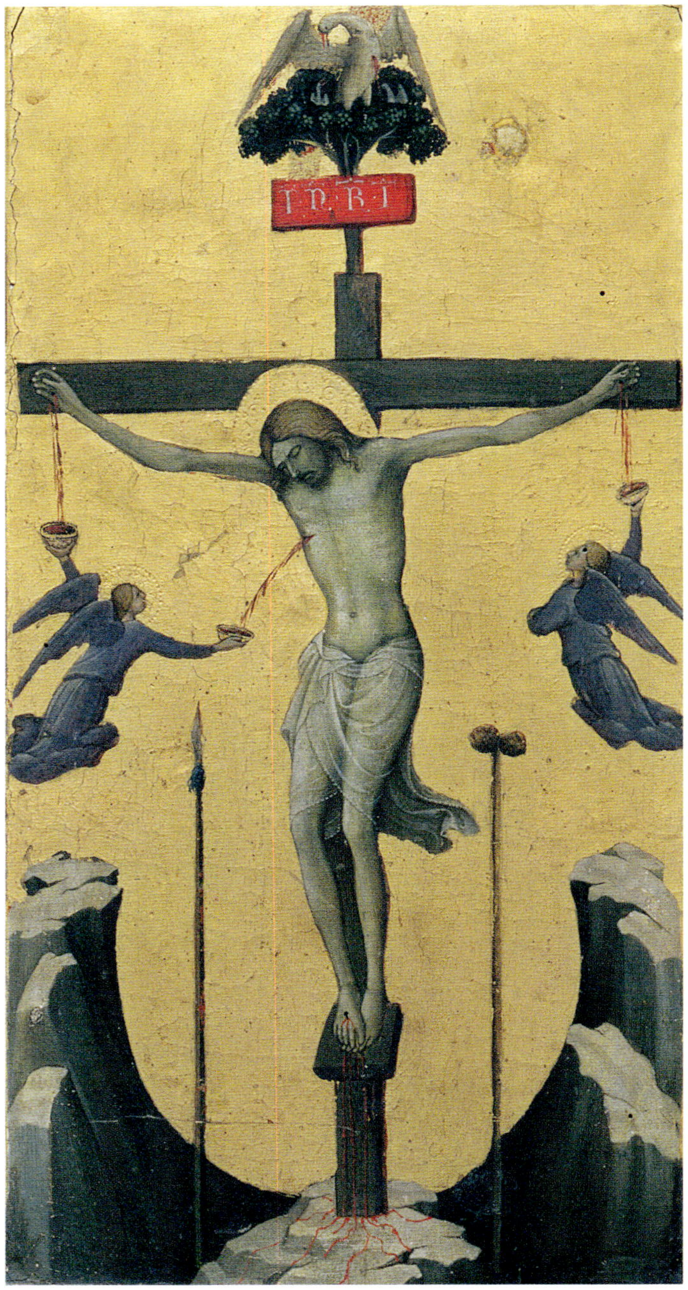

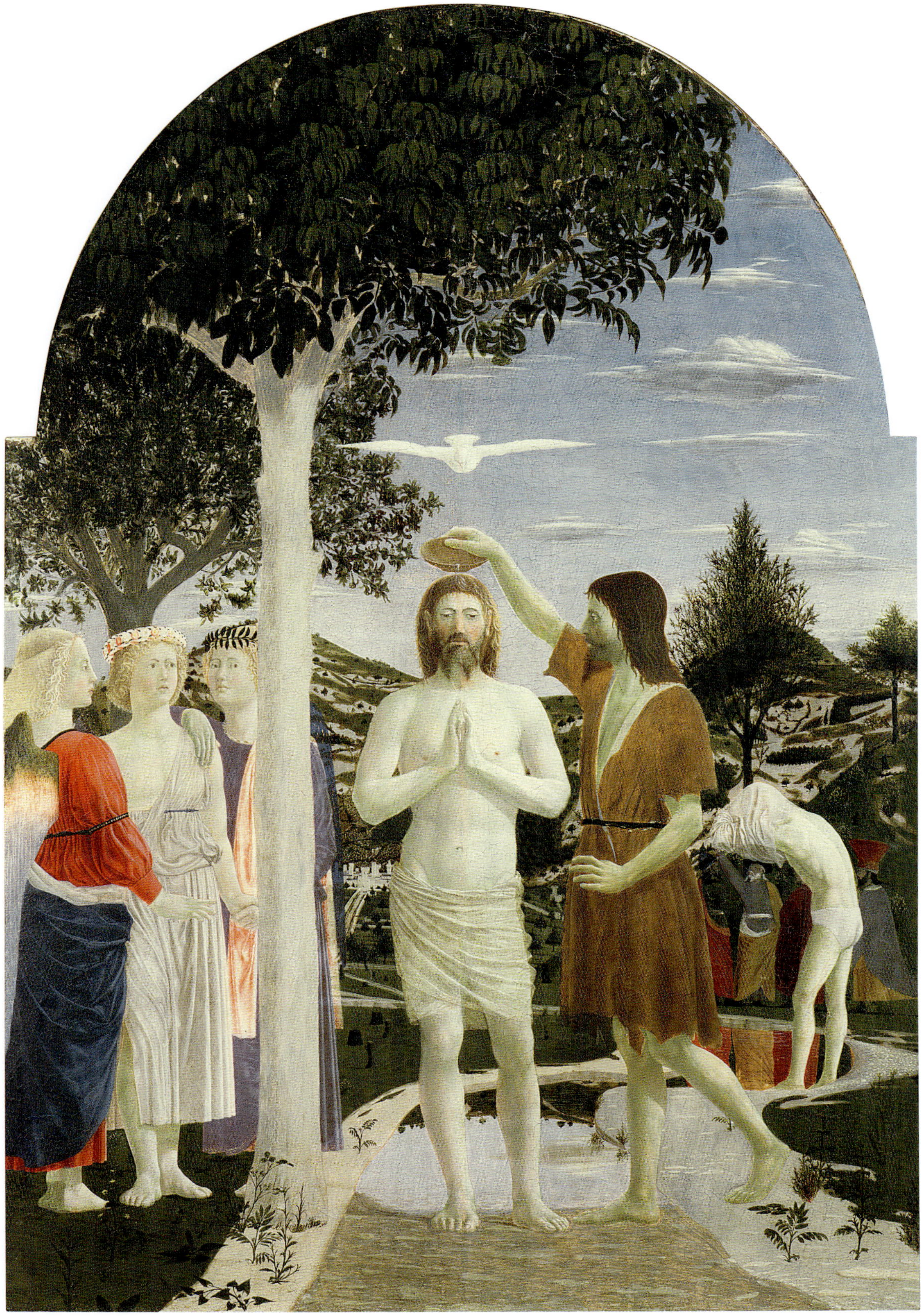

Piero della Francesca
(*c.* 1415–1492)
The Baptism of Christ
1450s
Egg on poplar
167 × 116 cm (65¾ × 45⅝ in.)
The National Gallery, London

Since they symbolize the Holy Spirit, doves often feature in paintings of the Baptism of Christ, reflecting accounts in the Bible. The connection is made explicit in the Gospel of St John the Evangelist, which quotes St John the Baptist: 'I saw the Spirit coming down on him from Heaven like a dove and resting on him. I did not know him myself, but he who sent me to baptize with water had said to me, "The man on whom you see the Spirit come down and rest is the one who is going to baptize with the Holy Spirit."' (1:32–34). Piero della Francesca shows St John the Baptist baptizing Jesus, as the spiritual dove descends from the heavens to hover above Christ's head. Seen from the front, its shape echoes the clouds in the distance. The panel was the central part of an altarpiece, painted for the chapel of St John the Baptist in the abbey of the Tuscan town of Borgo Sansepolcro, where Piero was born.

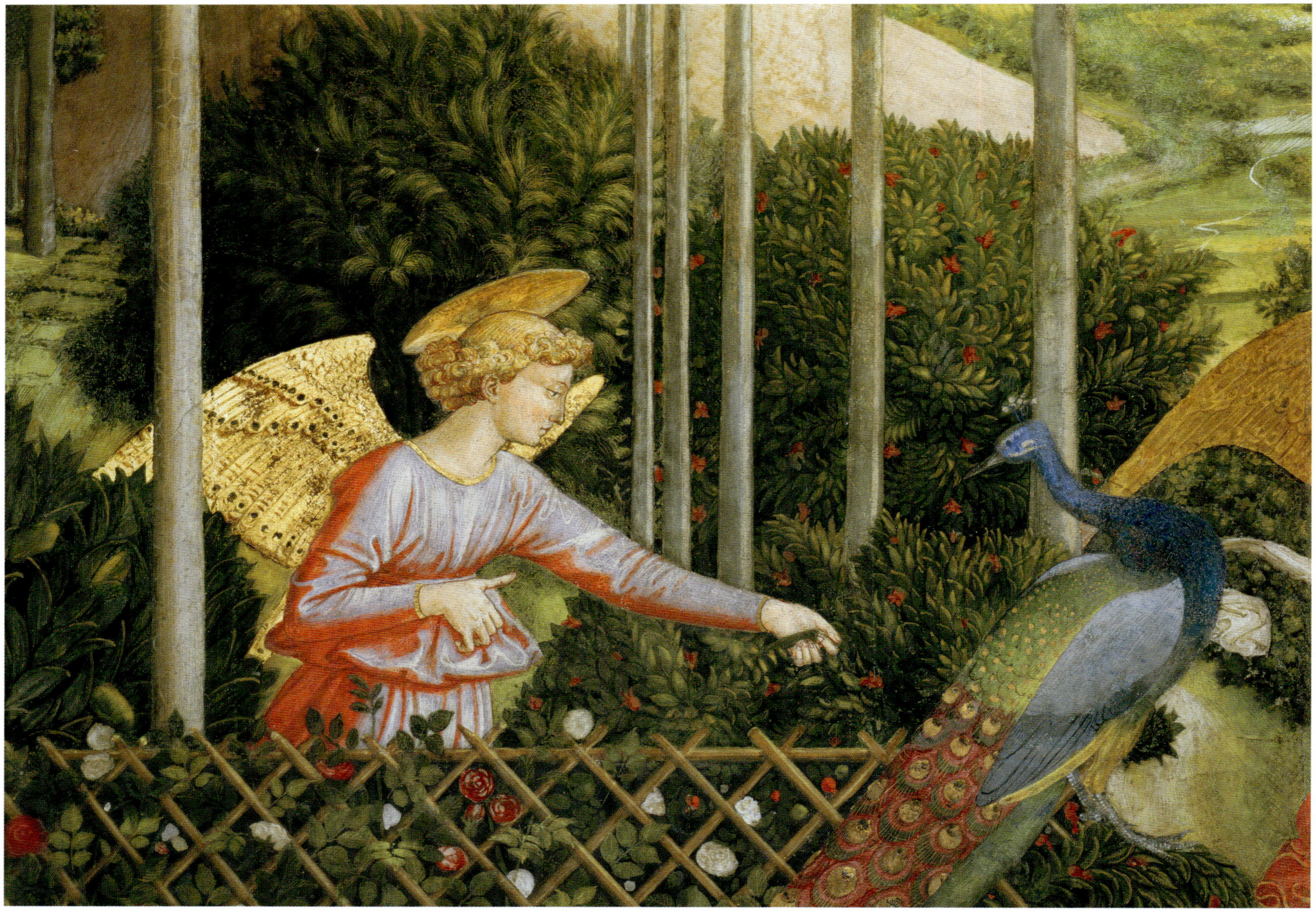

Benozzo Gozzoli
(*c.* 1420–1497)
The Journey of the Magi (detail)
1459–61
Fresco
Palazzo Medici-Riccardi, Florence

Benozzo Gozzoli's frescoes in the private devotional chapel of the Palazzo Medici-Riccardi are among the outstanding masterpieces of Florentine Renaissance art. The wealthy Medici banking family effectively ruled Florence at the time, and they clearly meant to impress visitors with their beautiful chapel, which was also used to receive dignitaries. The main part of the chapel shows the Journey of the Magi, featuring members of the family as part of an exotic cavalcade that winds its way along mountain paths towards Bethlehem. In the sanctuary are two scenes of Paradise, which is portrayed as a place of extravagant vegetation and pretty Italian hill towns populated by angels with brilliantly coloured and ornamented wings. There are a number of birds in these idyllic scenes, but the most eye-catching is a peacock, which is being fed by an angel. Because of the ancient myth that its flesh never decays, the bird is an appropriate choice to represent eternity.

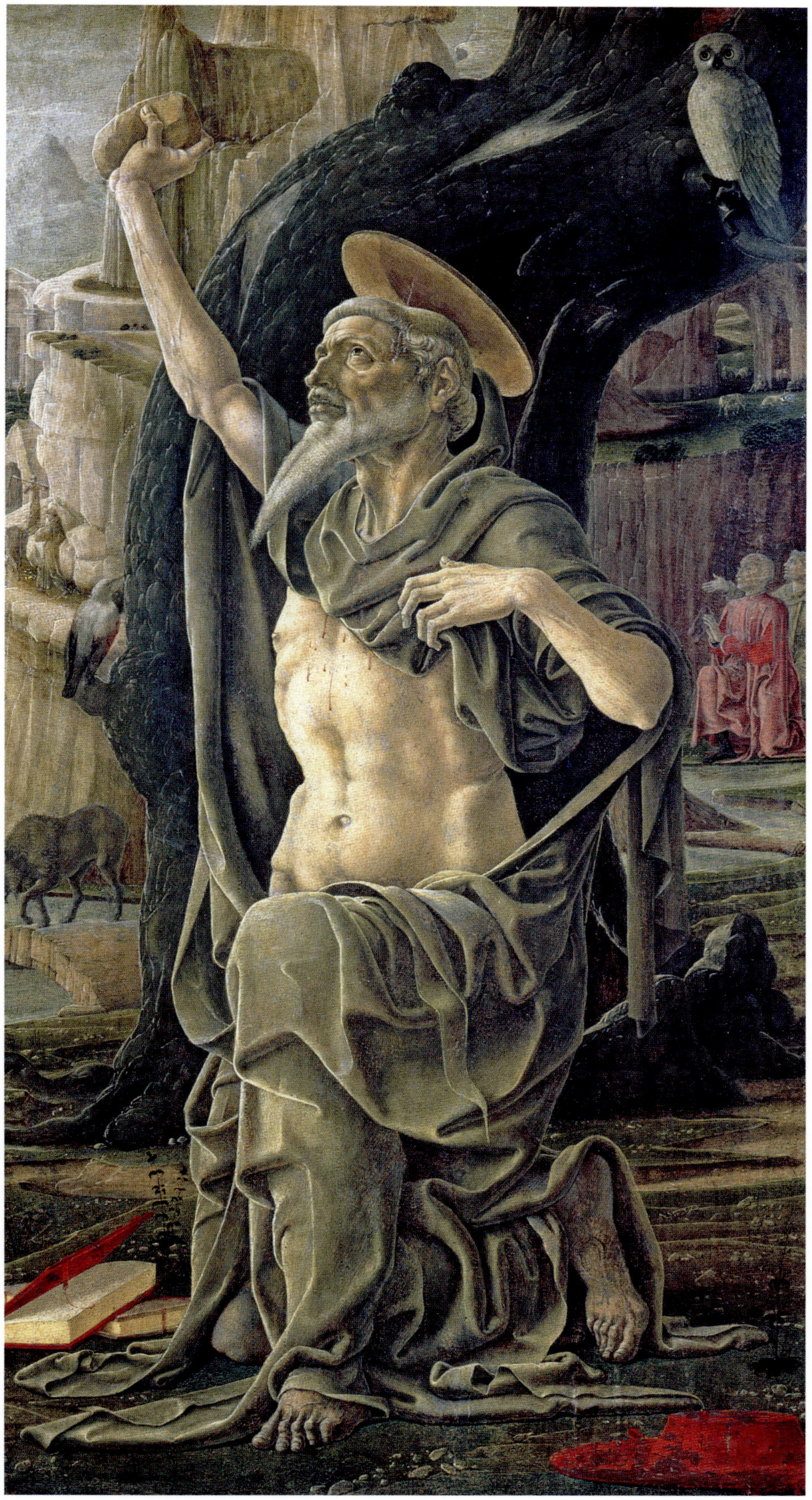

Cosimo Tura
(?1430–1495)
St Jerome

c. 1470
Oil and egg on poplar
101 × 57.2 cm (39¾ × 22½ in.)
The National Gallery, London

St Jerome (*c.* 342–420) spent four years living as a hermit in the Syrian desert, repenting of his sins. While he was there he experienced wild sexual hallucinations, and would beat his breast until the torment abated. The Ferrarese artist Cosimo Tura shows him holding a stone for the purpose, and casting his anguished gaze towards the heavens. The lion that Jerome befriended (a medieval story tells how he removed a thorn from its paw) is skulking on the left, and a white barn owl holding a frog in its talons sits on a branch above the saint. The artistic symbolism of the owl is complex and contradictory, and it is hard to be certain what it means in this context. The owl can evoke evil, since the bird's nocturnal habits were sometimes associated with sin. On the other hand, it is also associated with scholarship, which would make it an entirely suitable companion for one of the Latin Fathers of the Church. A wallcreeper, perching on a branch near the saint's breast, may also suggest evil, or simply represent the desert habitat.

Pedro Berruguete
(*c.* 1450–*c.* 1500)
St John the Evangelist

c. 1493–99
Oil on panel
Dimensions unknown
Convent of San Tomás, Ávila, Spain

The eagle is the principal attribute of St John the Evangelist, the presumed author of the Gospel of St John, who is also associated with the three Epistles and the book of Revelation. (John's fellow Evangelists have their particular symbols, too: St Luke's is the ox; St Matthew's a man or angel; and St Mark's a lion.) Of all the birds, the eagle is the one that flies closest to Heaven, and it is said to represent John because he was alleged to be closest to God. In art, John's eagle is sometimes shown holding a pen or inkhorn in its beak, as an allusion to his writings. The Spanish artist Pedro Berruguete portrays the Evangelist at work on his Gospel, accompanied by the bird – a white-bellied eagle rather than the more usual golden one – which holds an inkwell. The panel is part of an altarpiece devoted to St Thomas, painted for the convent church of San Tomás in Ávila.

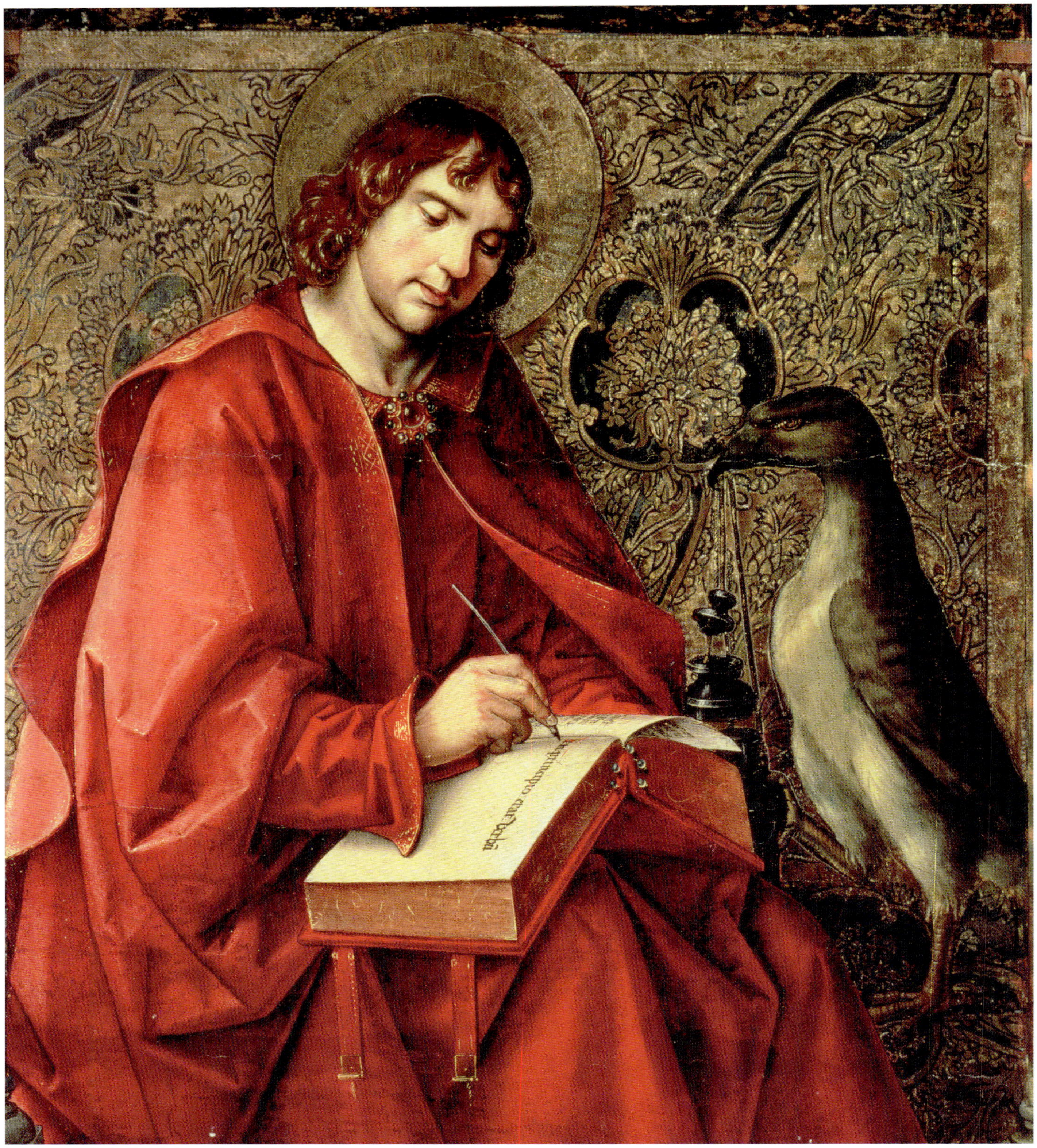

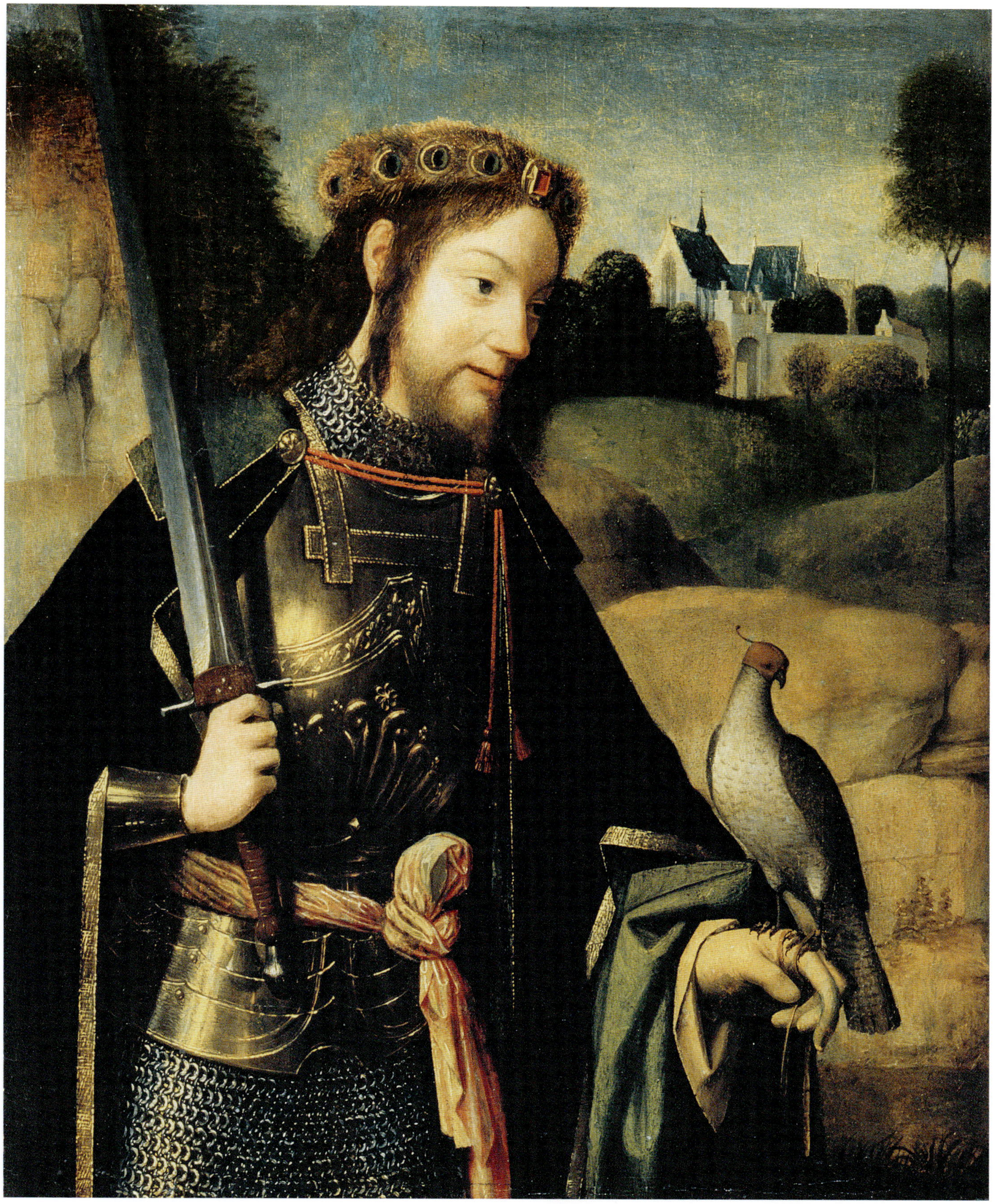

Geertgen tot Sint Jans
(1455/65–*c.* 1495)
St Bavo of Ghent

c. 1490
Oil on canvas
36.5 × 30 cm (14⅜ × 11¾ in.)
The State Hermitage Museum, St Petersburg

Bavo, who lived in the seventh century, was a Flemish aristocrat and soldier, whose youthful years were wild and selfish. He repented after hearing a sermon by St Amand of Maastricht, and determined to mend his ways, building an abbey on his estate and becoming a monk, handing over his belongings to the poor and living as a hermit until his death. Paintings and sculptures often show Bavo as a knight with a sword and a falcon on his wrist – hunting being a sport of nobles – and, by association, he has become the patron saint of falconry. He is also the patron saint of the Belgian city of Ghent and the Dutch city of Haarlem, and there are cathedrals named for him in both cities. The artist's name, Geertgen tot Sint Jans, means 'little Gerard of St John', and refers to the Brethren of St John at Haarlem, a lay order to which the artist probably belonged. Little is known about his life, but about a dozen works are attributed to him.

Vittore Carpaccio (?1460/66–1525/26)

The Annunciation

1504
Oil on panel
127 × 139 cm (50 × 54⅝ in.)
Galleria Franchetti, Ca' d'Oro, Venice

The dove of the Holy Spirit plays a central role in scenes of the Annunciation, the moment described in the Gospel of St Luke when Mary is told by the angel Gabriel that she will conceive and bear a son, and that he will be named Jesus. The Venetian artist Carpaccio shows God in the upper left-hand corner sending a dove zooming down to the Virgin in a ray of light, while three more doves perch on a rail above her head. Artists commonly show Mary reading in her chamber, and her demure demeanour here is typical of such scenes, as is Gabriel's lily, symbolic of spring and purity. Carpaccio must have loved birds: he frequently includes them in his paintings (see p. 17), and he has not been able to resist adding more here, where they strut about the garden outside Mary's room. He has also clearly taken great pleasure in depicting Gabriel's exotic, multicoloured wings.

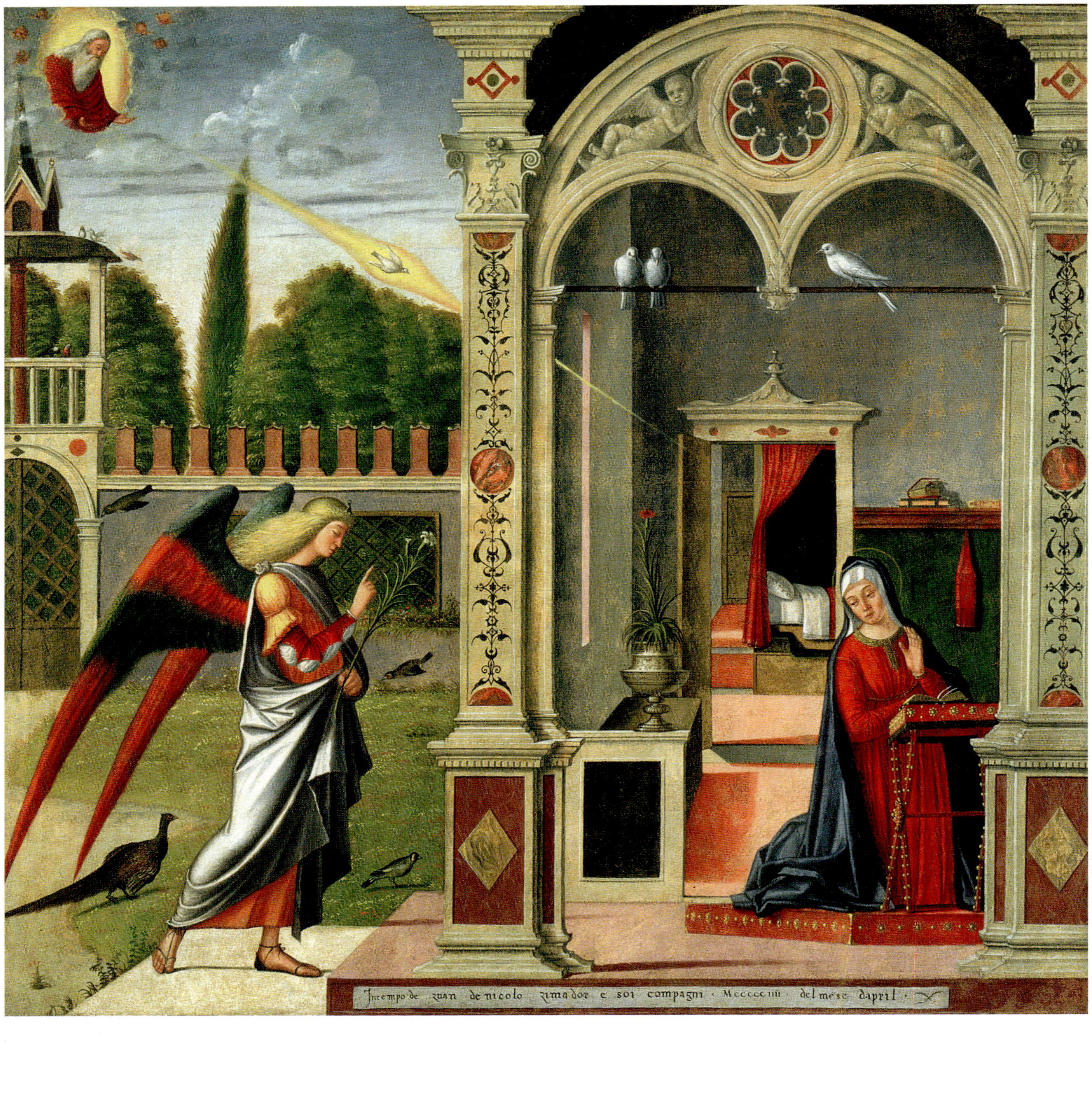

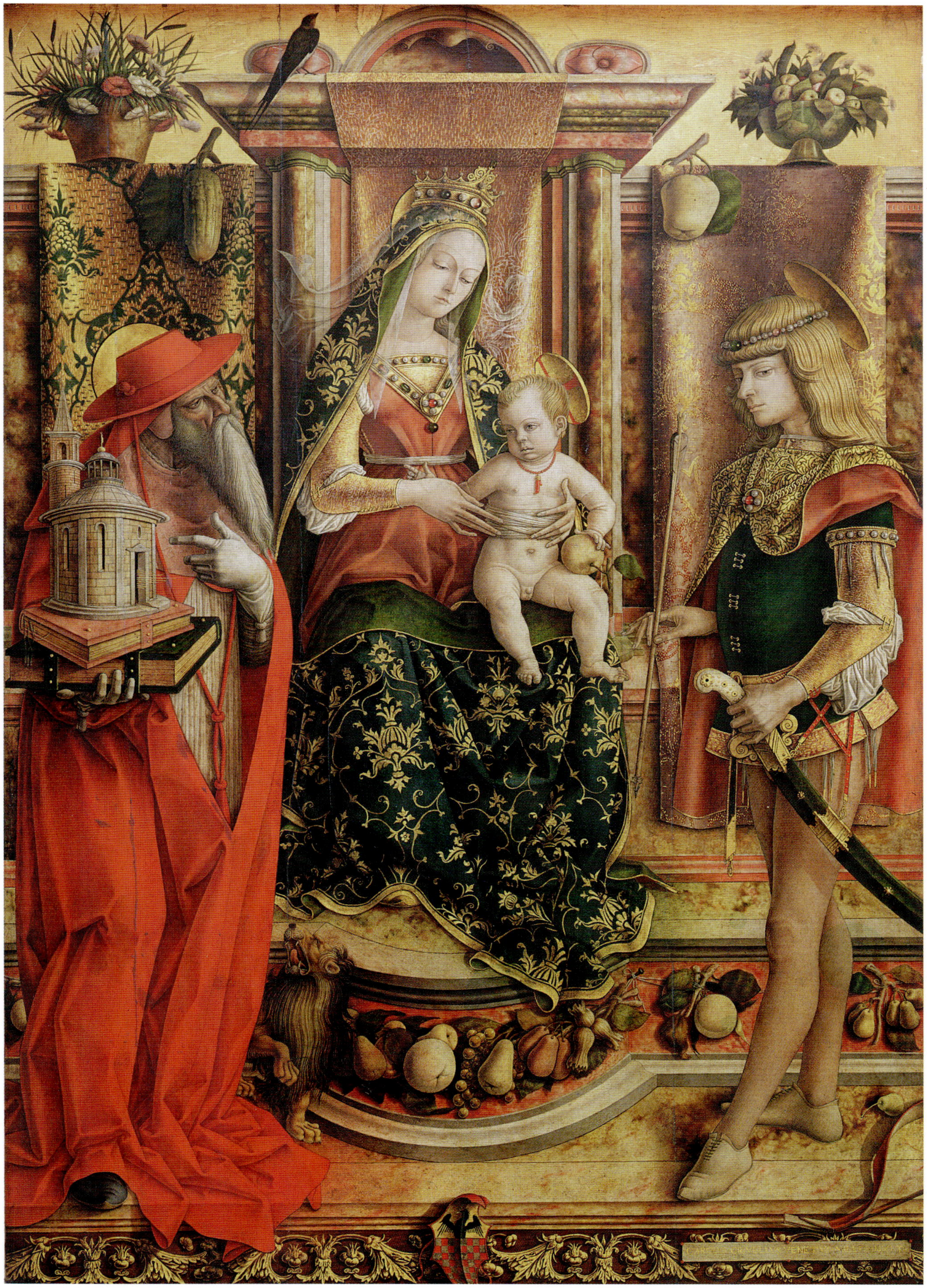

Carlo Crivelli
(*c.* 1430/35–1494)
The Madonna of the Swallow
(La Madonna della Rondine)

After 1490
Oil and egg on paper
150.5 × 107.3 cm (59¼ × 42¼ in.)
The National Gallery, London

This altarpiece is named for the swallow (*rondine*) that perches above the Virgin, who sits enthroned, holding the Christ Child in her lap. The bird symbolizes the Resurrection, perhaps because of its reappearance every spring. Jesus's hand rests on an apple, also foretelling his future, since it alludes to the Tree of Knowledge, and by extension to his future role as the Redeemer of mankind from original sin. St Jerome, kitted out in his traditional cardinal's robes, stands to the left, while St Sebastian is on the right. The panel was painted for the church of San Francesco in Matelica in the Marche (eastern central) area of Italy, where the Venetian artist Carlo Crivelli carried out much of his work. His paintings are characterized by a strong linear style, brilliant colour and a minute observation of detail; they often feature swags of fruit and flowers and carefully portrayed birds.

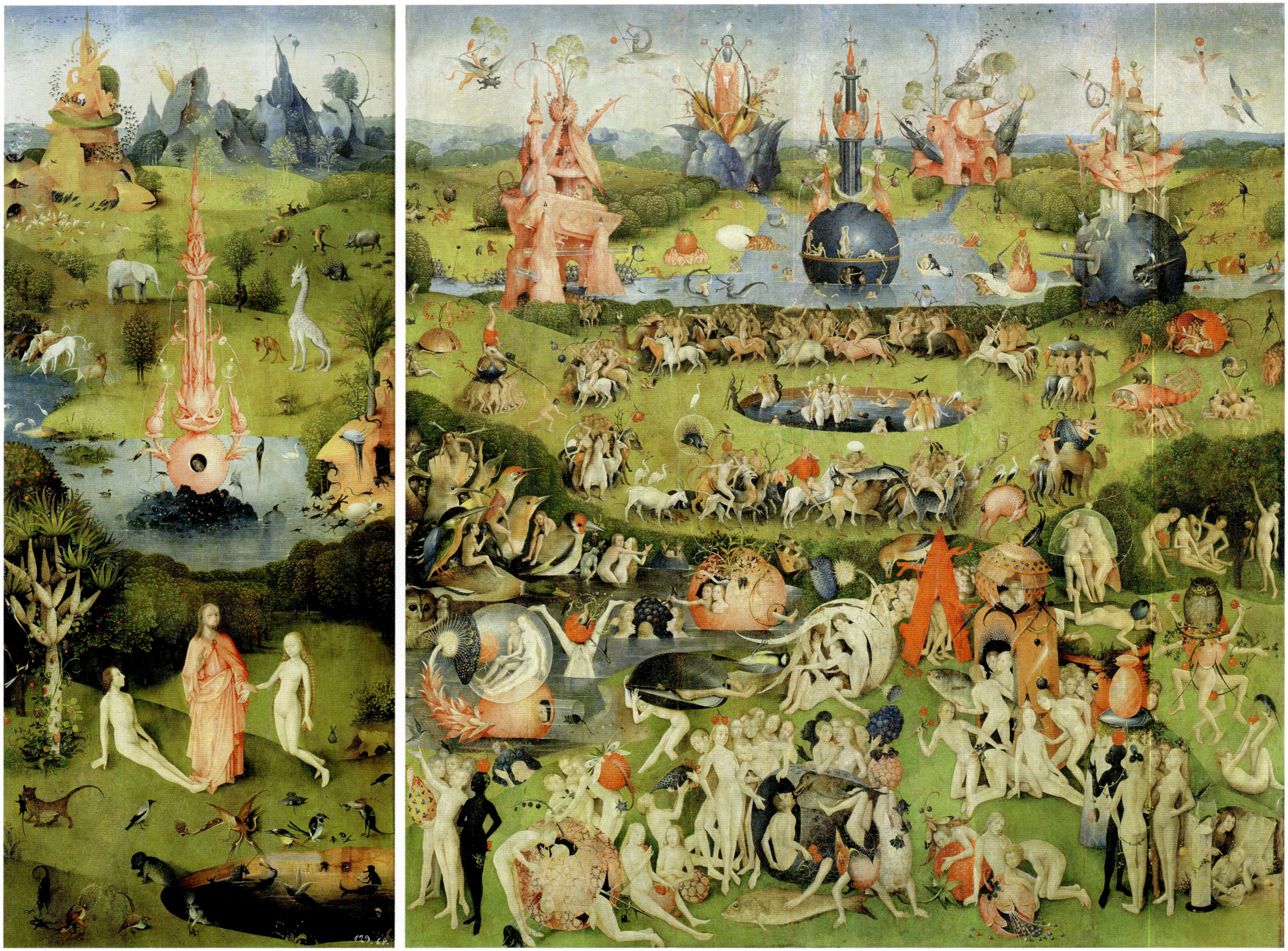

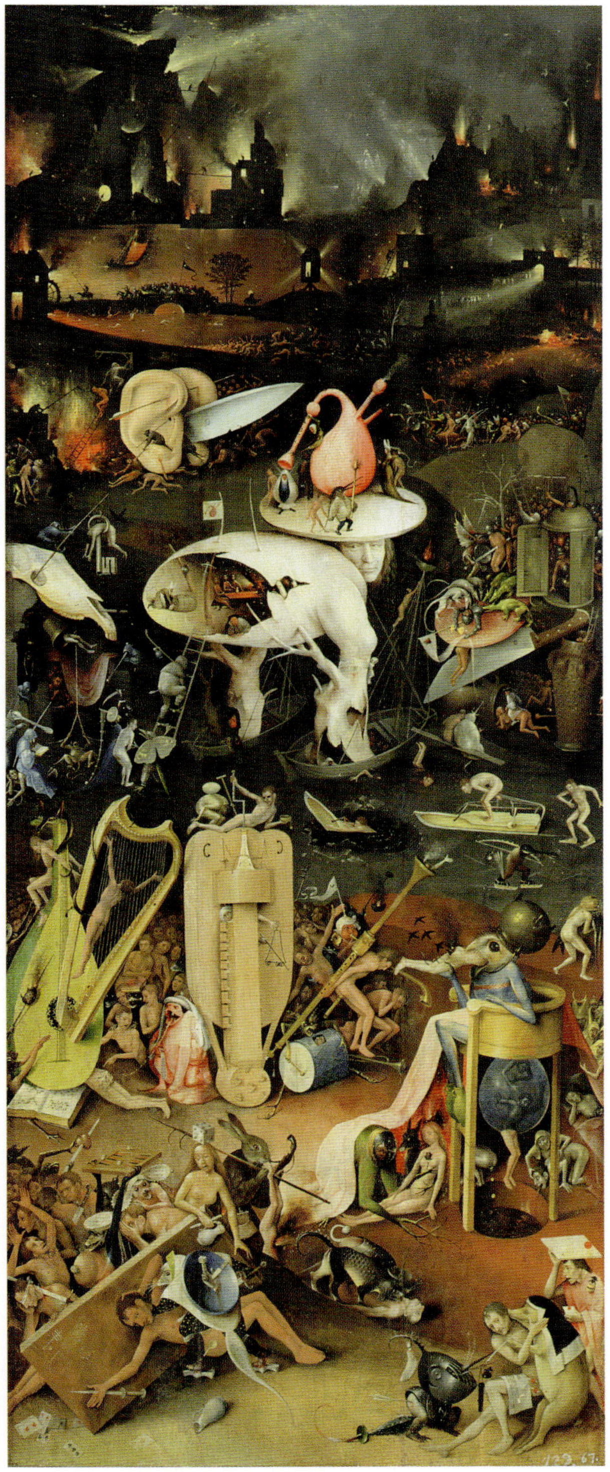

Hieronymus Bosch (*c.* 1450–1516) *The Garden of Earthly Delights*

c. 1500
Oil on panel
220 × 389 cm (86⅝ × 153⅛ in.)
Museo Nacional del Prado, Madrid

Bosch's famous triptych *The Garden of Earthly Delights* is full of ornithological delights, despite its doom-laden message. Its three parts trace the downfall of mankind, from the creation of Adam and Eve in the left panel, through the hedonistic, ephemeral pleasure of the world in the centre, to the hellish torture that awaits sinful humanity in the right-hand panel. The work contains several recognizable creatures, including birds, as well as many that are hybrids or pure fantasy. In the central panel we can see a short-eared owl, a goldfinch, a robin, a green woodpecker, a kingfisher, a hoopoe, mallards, a spoonbill and an ibis. Because of their improbable scale they have become the stuff of nightmares, as they are tenderly (and improbably) embraced by diminutive naked humans, who abandon themselves to the sensual pleasures of the world with little thought of virtue and the hereafter. Birds do not feature in the final panel, showing Hell, although it does contain a terrifying vision of a monstrous bird-man swallowing and excreting human beings (right).

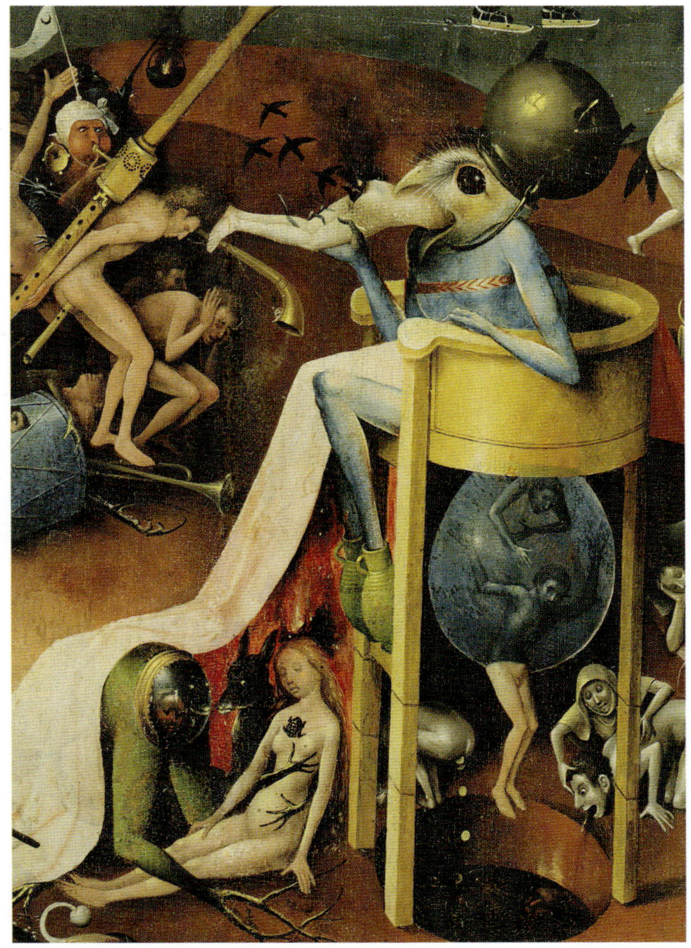

Piero di Cosimo
(1461/62–1521)
Madonna and Child with a Dove

c. 1490–1500
Oil on panel
87 × 58 cm (34¼ × 22¾ in.)
Musée du Louvre, Paris

Piero di Cosimo's Mary is a simple girl in a blue linen headdress, attempting to read a prayer book while restraining her squirming child, who is trying to escape from her clutches. The Christ Child reaches towards the white dove perching on the ledge beside the book, but this is no ordinary bird. We can see from the nimbus around its head that it is the Holy Spirit – which appears, as a symbolic bird, in countless scenes of the Annunciation and the Baptism of Christ. The Tuscan painter Piero di Cosimo is an obscure figure, and much of what is known about him depends on the account given in Giorgio Vasari's sixteenth-century *Lives of the Painters*, which portrays him as an eccentric character who subsisted on a diet of hard-boiled eggs.

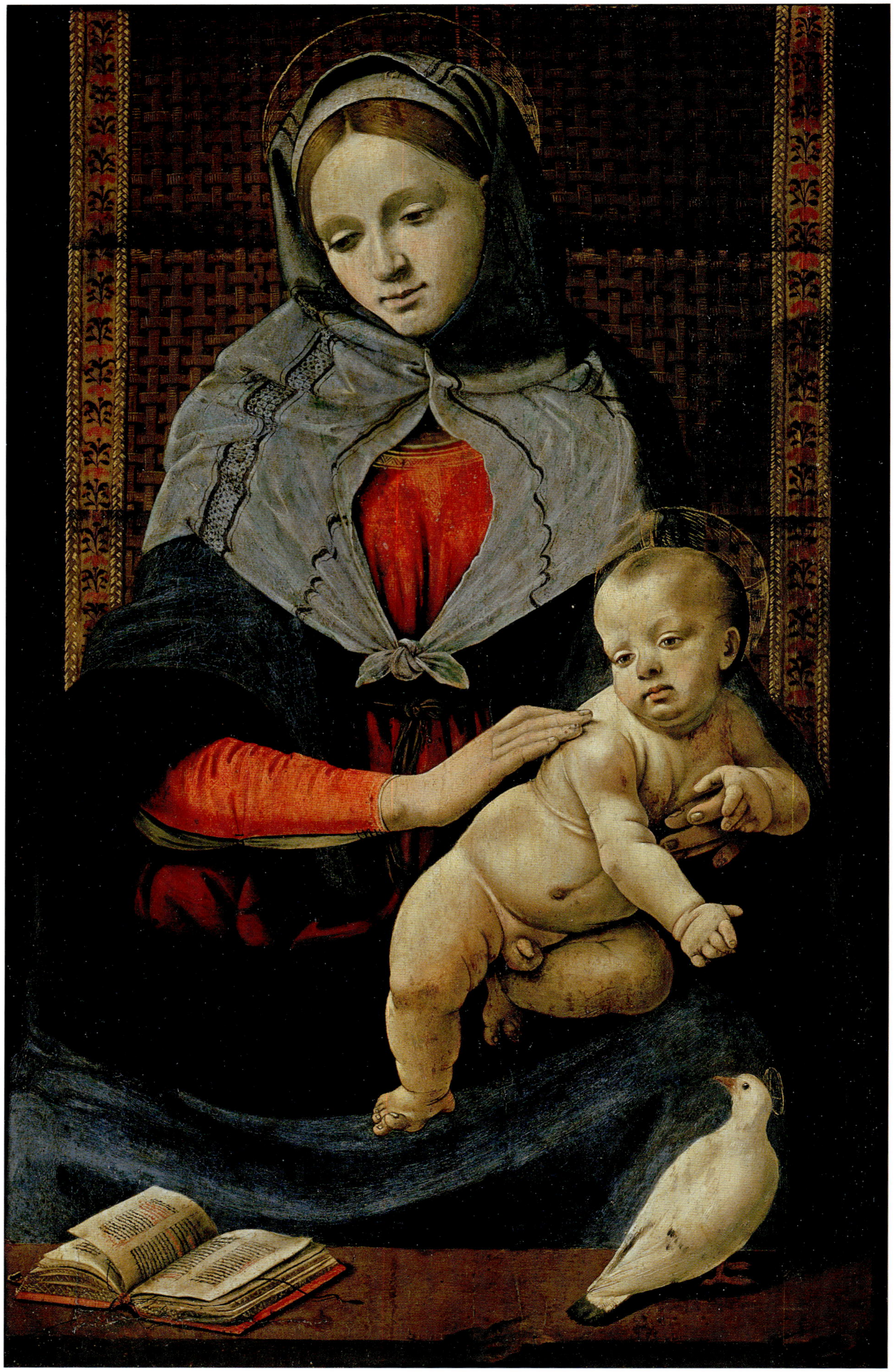

Raphael (Raffaello Sanzio) (1483–1520)

The Madonna of the Goldfinch

c. 1506
Oil on panel
107 × 77 cm (42⅛ × 30¼ in.)
Galleria degli Uffizi, Florence

The goldfinch is one of the most commonly seen birds in Renaissance paintings featuring the Christ Child. This is not just because its attractive appearance made it a favourite pet with children, but also because of the legend that it acquired the red spot on its head when it plucked out a thorn that was digging into Christ's brow as he carried his cross towards Calvary, and was splashed with a drop of his blood. Here the infant St John the Baptist is offering a goldfinch to Christ, who strokes it – a chilling reference to his future Passion – while Mary looks on impassively. Raphael painted this panel as a wedding present for a friend, but the painting was smashed into seventeen pieces when the owner's house fell down forty years later. It was nailed together again, and has been patched up over the centuries, but its original glory was revealed only in 2008, when ten years of painstaking restoration work were completed.

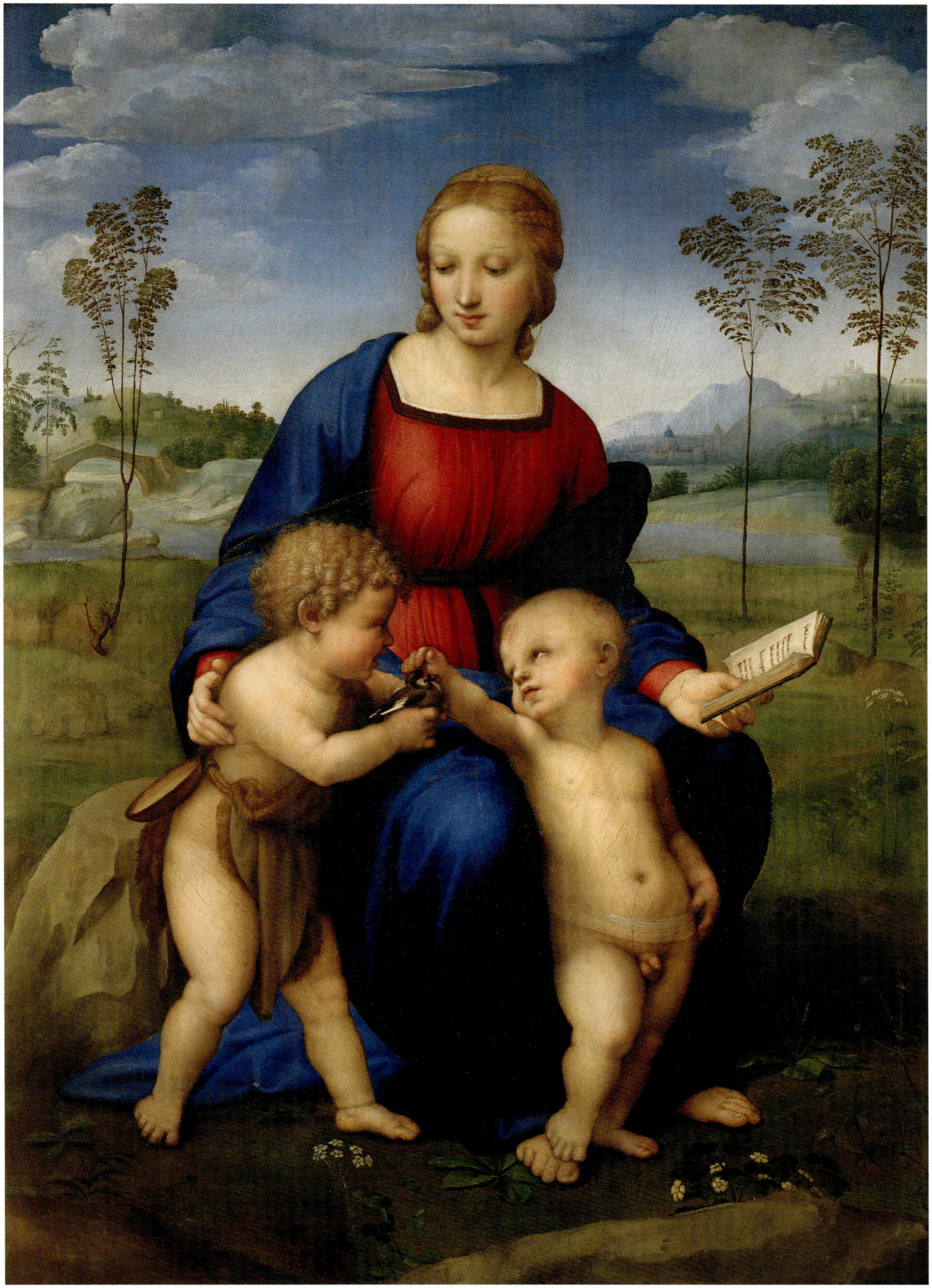

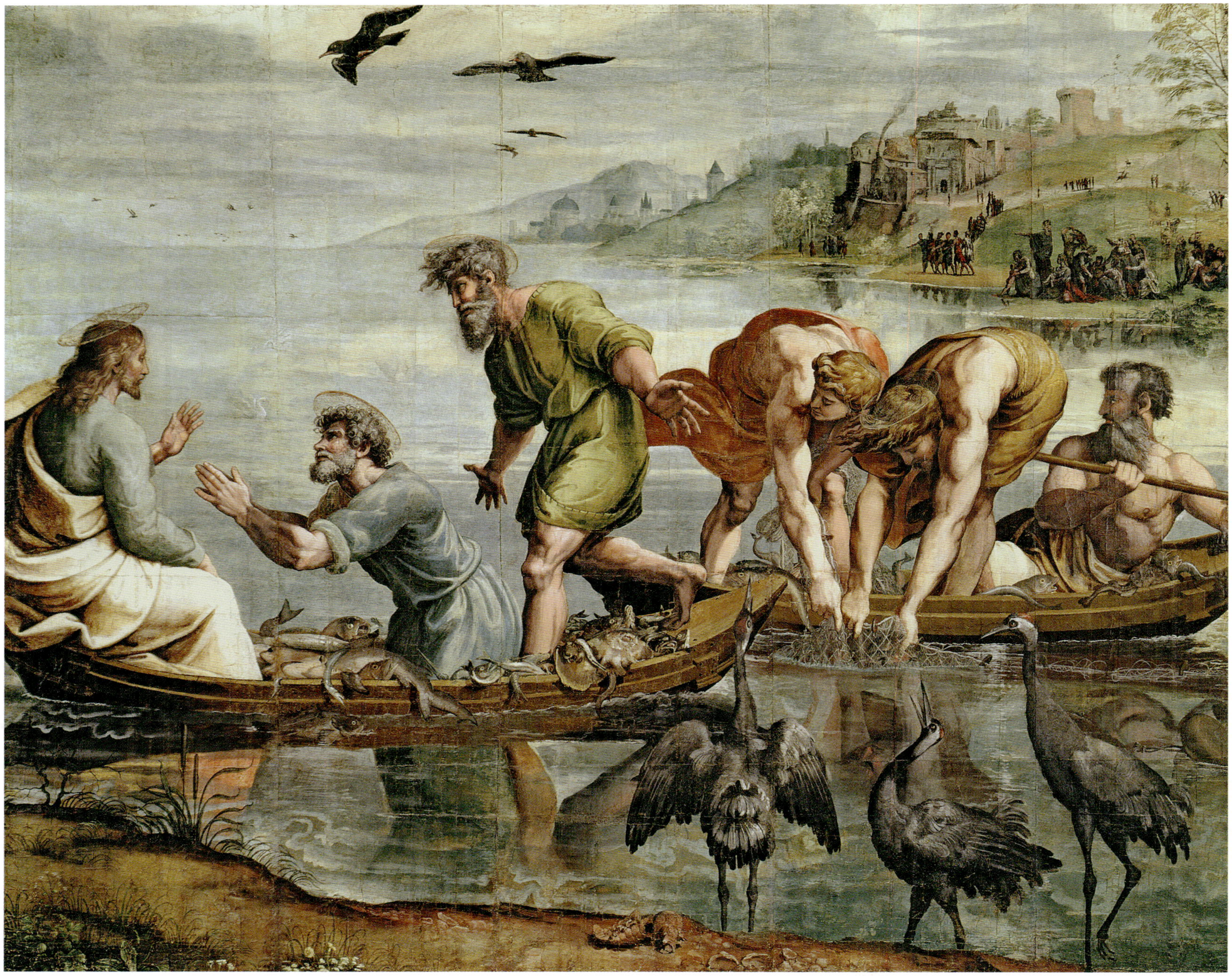

Raphael (Raffaello Sanzio)
(1483–1520)
The Miraculous Draught of Fishes
1515–16
Gouache and charcoal on paper mounted on canvas
319 × 399 cm (125⅝ × 157⅛ in.)
Victoria and Albert Museum, London

In 1515 Pope Leo X commissioned Raphael to produce a set of cartoons (designs) for ten tapestries depicting the lives of the saints Peter and Paul for the lower walls of the Sistine Chapel in Vatican City. The scene here is described in St Luke's Gospel: Christ comes across a poor fisherman, Simon Peter, who has had a fruitless night fishing in Lake Gennesaret (the Sea of Galilee). Jesus urges Simon Peter to let down his nets again, and the fisherman makes a miraculous catch, after which he joins Christ as an Apostle. The composition contains some remarkable bird symbolism. On the shore stand three cranes, said to be the most vigilant of birds. They had become a symbol of papal authority, since the Pope watched over his Church in the same way that the crane guarded its flock. The beautifully painted birds were probably not from the hand of Raphael, however, but by Giovanni da Udine, one of the artists in his workshop, who was renowned for his skill in painting animals. Flying above the fishermen are two ravens, which – unlike the cranes – had an ambiguous reputation as representatives of the corrupt clergy, although they could equally have been included to represent the banishment of such deceit. In the final tapestry the ravens were changed into seagulls. The swans, which can just be made out swimming on the waters, were said to bring good luck to sailors, although they were also common symbols of pride and deceit. It has been suggested that their proximity to the ravens may allude to a contemporary proverb about how difficult it was to convert sinners: 'One may as well try to make ravens white or swans black.'

Master of the Nuremberg Dominican Cycle

Pentecost

c. 1511–13
Oil on panel
103.5 × 103 cm (40¾ × 40½ in.)
Germanisches Nationalmuseum, Nuremberg

The Acts of the Apostles (2:1–4) tells how, ten days after witnessing the Ascension of Christ, the twelve Apostles returned to Jerusalem for the Jewish feast of Pentecost. As they were seated together in a room, the house was filled with a noise like a strong wind, flames appeared above them and they were filled with the Holy Spirit and began to talk in tongues, since the Spirit had 'given them the power of utterance'. Here, the Holy Spirit takes the form of a dove, which descends in a blaze of light to hover over the head of the enthroned Virgin Mary, who personifies the Church. A tongue of fire sits on the head of each Apostle. The unnamed artist who painted this panel would have been a contemporary of Nuremberg's most famous son, Albrecht Dürer (1471–1528; see pp. 14, 100 and 147), and something of an echo of Dürer's work can be sensed here.

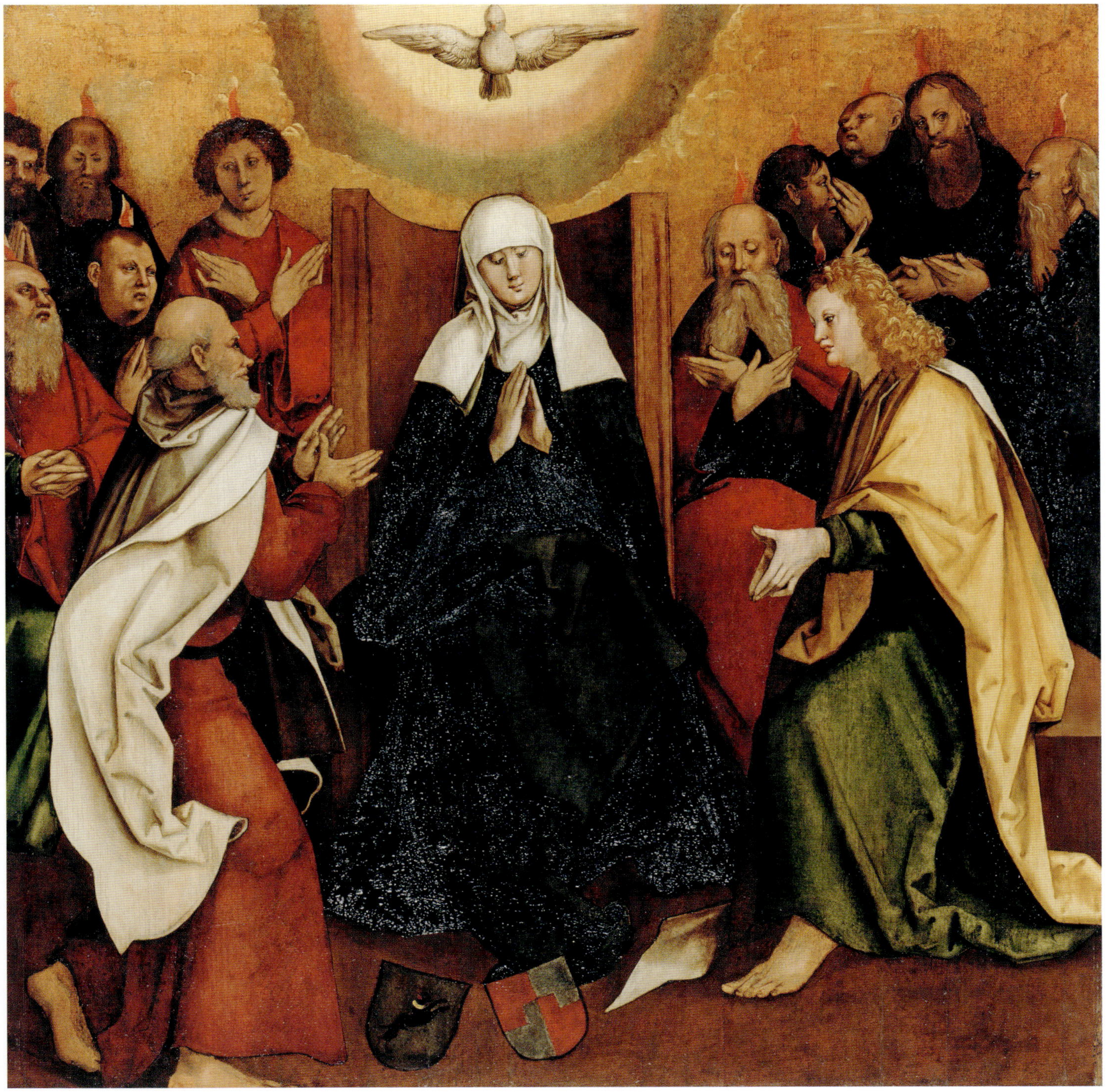

Hans Baldung Grien (1484/85–1545)

Madonna with Parrots

1533
Oil on panel
91.5 × 63.3 cm (36 × 25 in.)
Germanisches Nationalmuseum, Nuremberg

Parrots have been kept as domestic pets since ancient times, and are mentioned in literary works by Aristotle, Pliny, Aesop and Ovid. In Renaissance paintings they were sometimes linked with the Immaculate Conception and motherhood. The Christ Child in Jan van Eyck's *Madonna and Child with Canon George van der Paele* (1436; Groeningemuseum, Bruges) caresses a ring-necked parakeet, and parrots also appear in paintings by Carpaccio, Mantegna, Cranach and Rubens. In Baldung Grien's picture, the way in which the parrot perching on the Madonna's shoulder appears to be pecking at her neck is intriguing. Perhaps it is actually 'talking' into her ear; the artist also produced a curious drawing of a nude man listening to a parrot. The parrot here is included in homage to the artist's patron, the Bishop of Strasbourg, who was very fond of the birds. Baldung Grien probably trained with Albrecht Dürer (who was also keen on parrots) in Nuremberg, and his varied and extensive output included religious works, allegory, mythology and erotic engravings. There is certainly a veiled eroticism about this alluring Madonna breastfeeding her child.

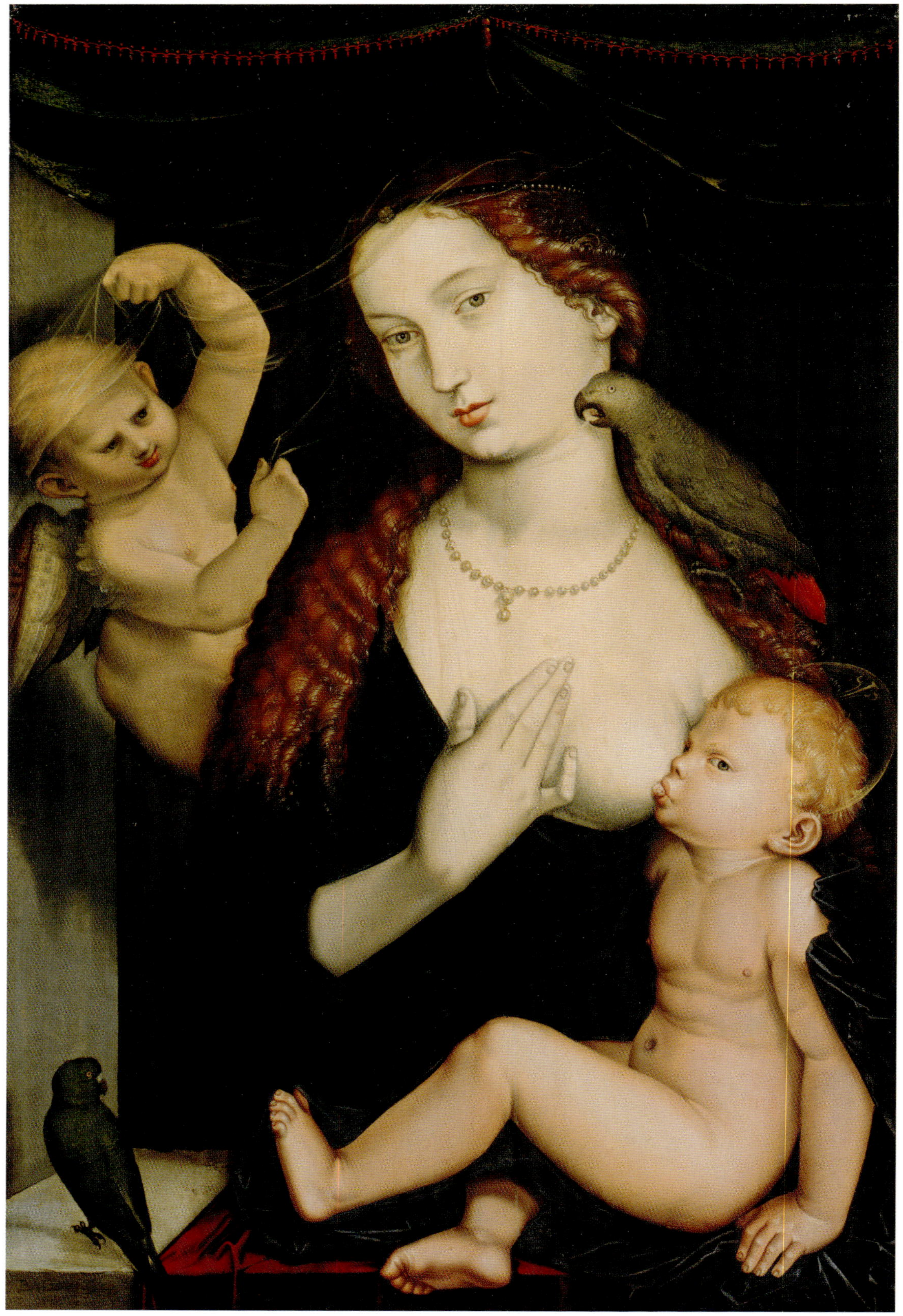

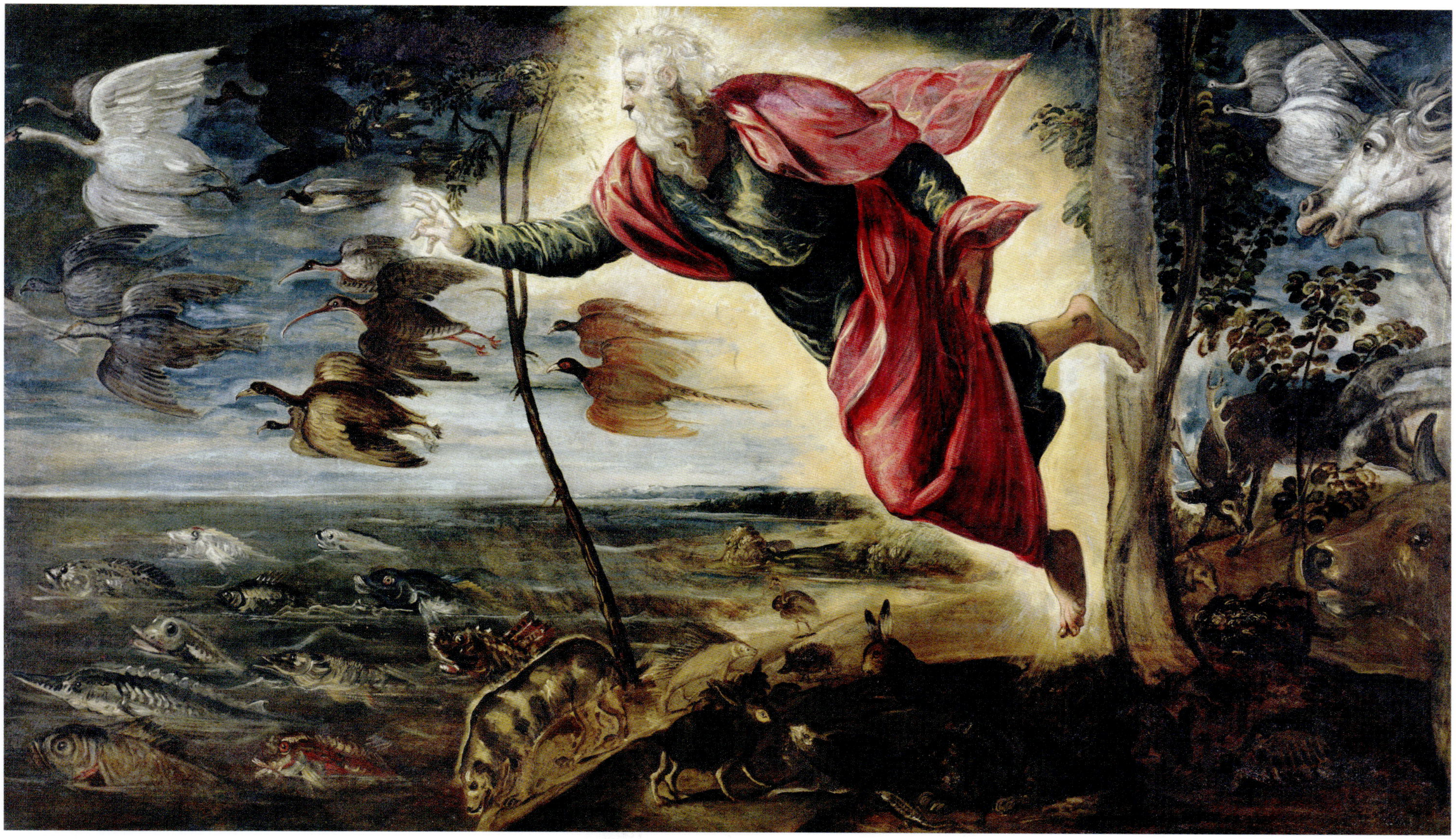

Tintoretto (Jacopo Robusti) (1519–1594)
The Creation of the Animals
c. 1550
Oil on canvas
150 × 258 cm (59 × 101½ in.)
Gallerie dell'Accademia, Venice

According to Genesis, God created the fish and the birds on the fifth day of Creation: 'God said, "Let the waters swarm with swarms of living creatures, and let birds fly above the earth in the open expanse of sky." God created the large sea creatures, and every living creature that moves, with which the waters swarmed, after their kind, and every winged bird after its kind' (1:20–22). Tintoretto's God dashes through the newly created firmament in a blaze of golden light, sending birds of all descriptions shooting through the skies. The birds dart out like missiles: the portrayal of their movement in flight is comically unrealistic, and they look like dead specimens. Behind God, animals (including a unicorn) await their turn; they will be created the following day. This is one of a series of paintings that Tintoretto produced early in his career for the Scuola della Santissima Trinità in Venice. It exhibits all the energy and dramatic effects of light and shade that came to characterize his mature work.

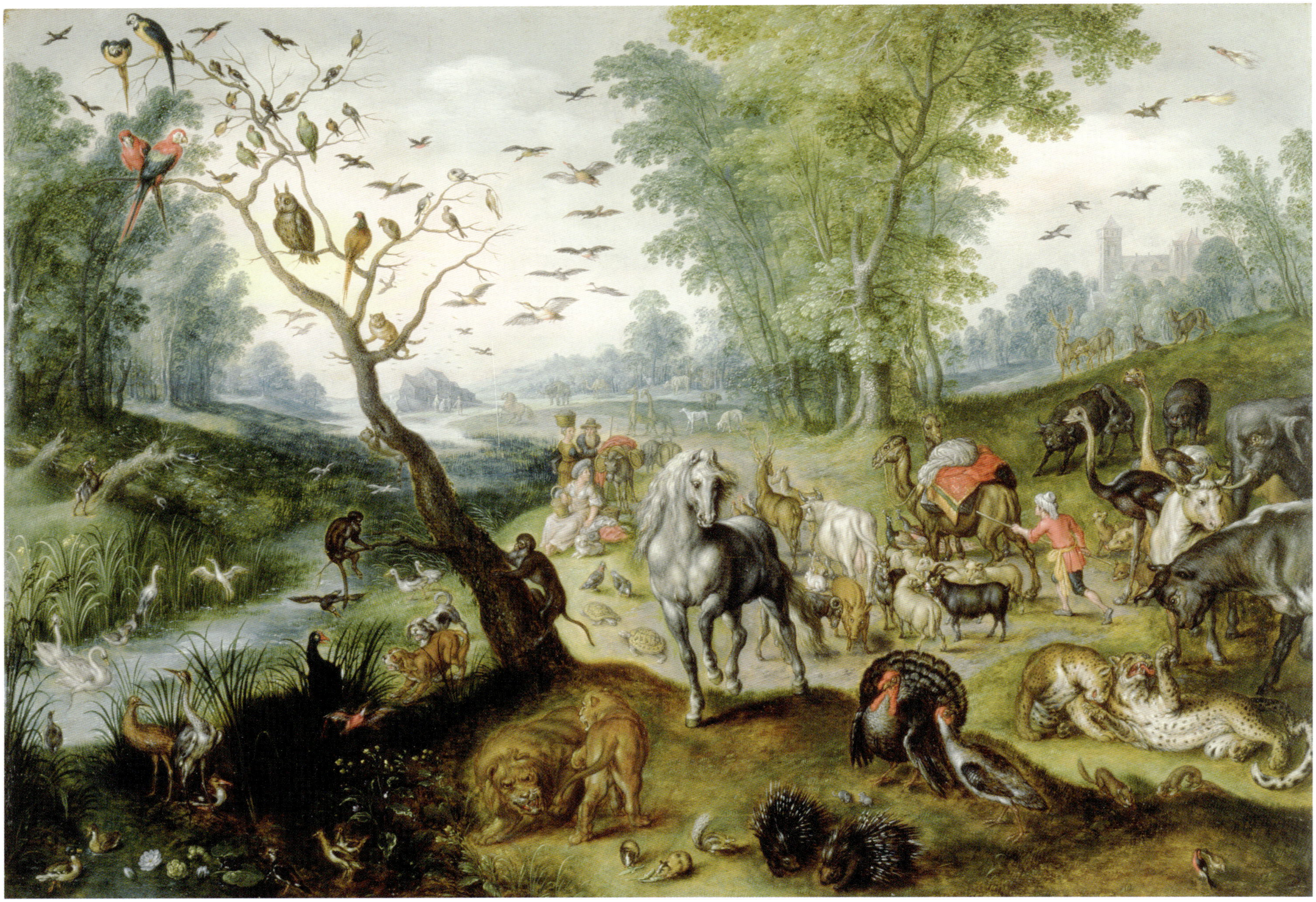

Jan Breughel the Elder (1568–1625) (after)
Noah's Family Assembling Animals Before the Ark

c. 1660
Oil on canvas
65.4 × 94.5 cm (25¾ × 37⅛ in.)
Walters Art Museum, Baltimore

The son of Pieter Bruegel the Elder, Jan Breughel specialized in paintings of paradisical scenes and still lifes of flowers, insects and birds. The subject of Noah's Ark was really just a pretext for him to indulge in a wildlife extravaganza. Pairs of creatures are about to board the tiny ark seen in the background, and among them are several recognizable species of bird. Some of them, such as the pigeons, ducks, herons and swans, were native to Europe, while others, including the macaws in the top left-hand corner, were more exotic imports. The turkeys in the foreground had been introduced to Europe from Central America in the 1530s, and by the time this work was painted they featured regularly on the banqueting table. The birds of paradise in the top right-hand corner were known from the bird skins imported from the 1520s onwards. Most of the birds and beasts in this picture may have been based on those the artist saw in the menagerie belonging to Archduke Albert and Isabella, the Counts of Louvain. Breughel painted in the park of their castle south of Brussels, where they kept their animals.

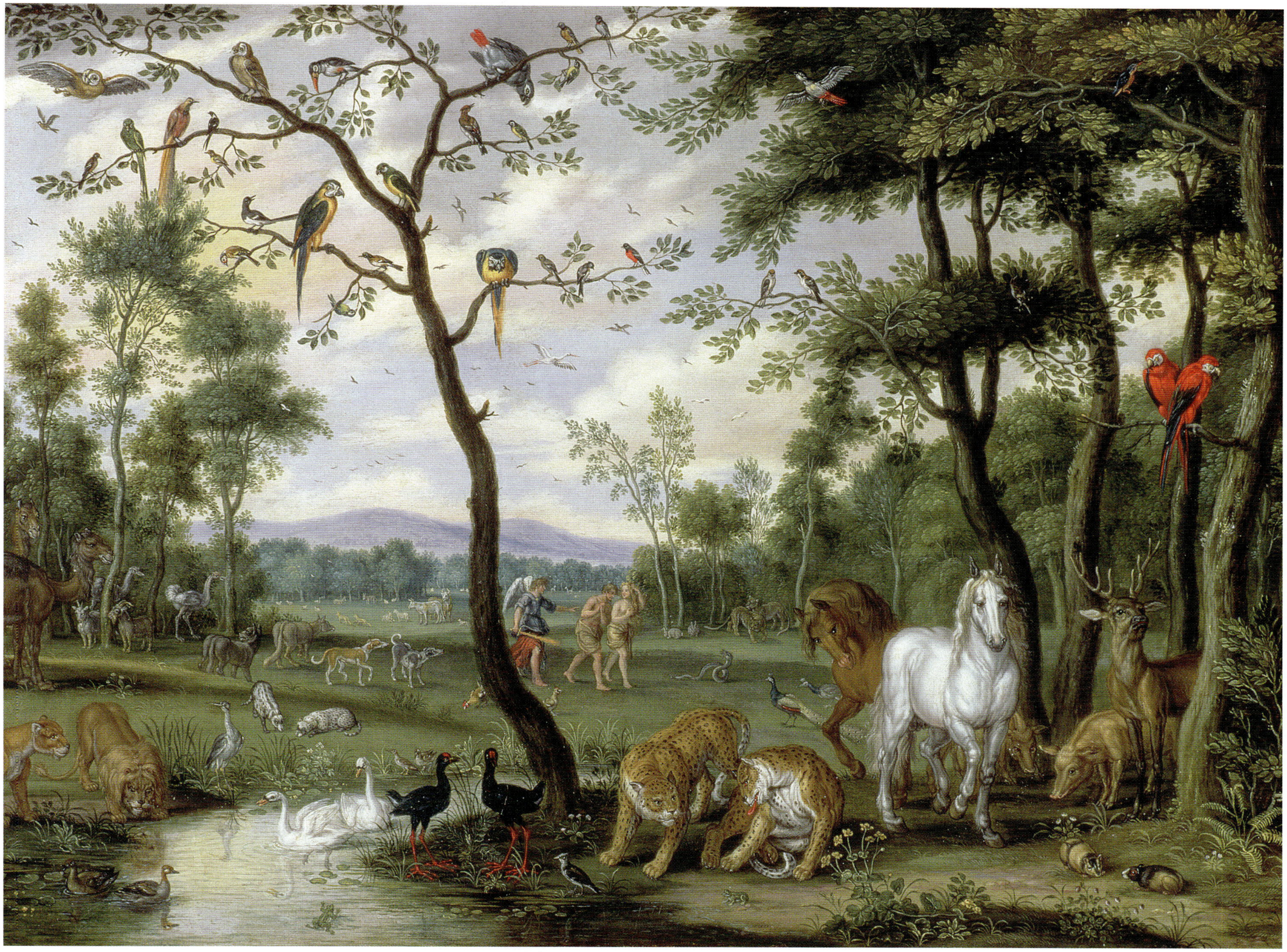

Jan Brueghel the Younger
(1601–1678)
Earthly Paradise

Mid-17th century
Oil on panel
42 × 57 cm (16½ × 22⅜ in.)
Private collection

Jan Brueghel the Younger spent much of his career carrying on the work of his more famous father, Jan Breughel the Elder (see opposite). He either made copies of his father's pictures, which were in great demand, or produced his own compositions, drawing on elements of his father's work. This picture is a classic example. In the background a shamefaced Adam and Eve are being expelled from the Garden of Eden, which resembles the kind of parkland seen in the artist's native northern Europe, although it is populated by several exotic creatures, many of which are also represented in pairs. Perched in the trees are some of the birds the unfortunate couple are leaving behind in this earthly paradise: barn owls, green parrots, birds of paradise, swallows, magpies, blue-and-yellow and scarlet macaws, African grey parrots, hornbills, waxwings and kingfishers. A further group of birds on the ground or in the water includes ducks, ostriches, grey herons, swans, black storks, chickens and peacocks.

Lubin Baugin
(1612–1663)
St Gregory the Great

17th century
Oil on panel
33 × 25 cm (13 × 9¾ in.)
Musée des Beaux Arts, Orléans, France

The dove (signifying the Holy Spirit) is the principal attribute of Pope Gregory the Great (*c*. 540–606). One of the four Latin Fathers of the Church, Gregory established the form of the Roman liturgy and the Gregorian chant, and wrote many theological commentaries, sermons and letters. The association with the dove arose from a story recorded by his disciple Peter the Deacon, who wrote that one day, when Gregory was dictating his homilies on Ezekiel to his secretary, he fell silent. The secretary looked behind the curtain that separated them and saw a dove seated on Gregory's head with its beak between his lips, placing the word of God in his mouth. Rather than transcribing this scene literally, artists have tended to show the bird perching on the Pope's shoulder or whispering in his ear. In this picture, it seems to have made a sudden and unexpected appearance – Gregory appears surprised and even alarmed as he looks up from his work. Baugin's composition, full of drama and movement, presents a distinct contrast with his calm and simple still lifes, which are much admired, and which feature in the film *Tous les Matins du Monde* (1991).

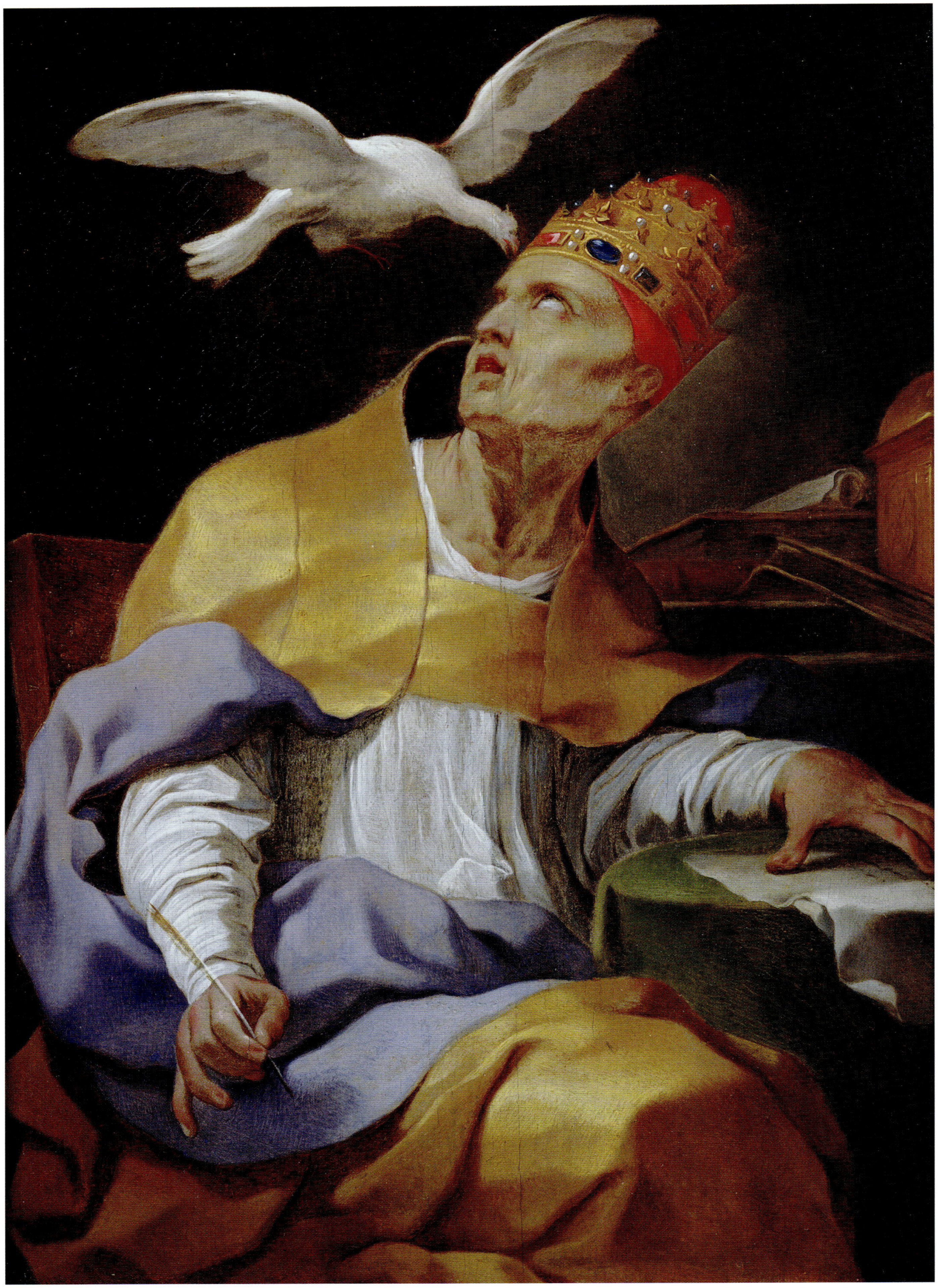

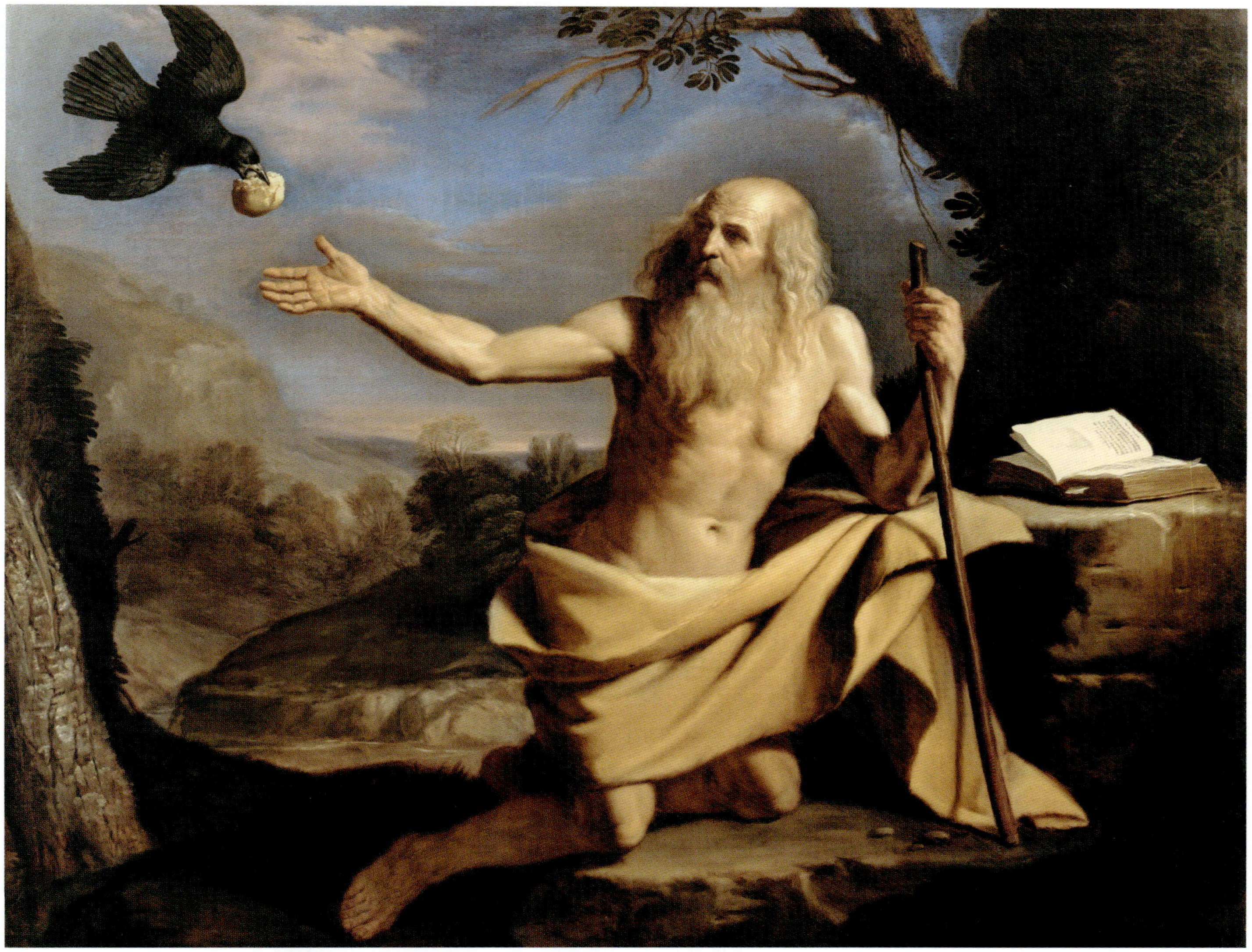

Guercino (Giovanni Francesco Barbieri) (1591–1666)
St Paul the Hermit Being Fed by a Raven
17th century
Oil on canvas
178 × 233 cm (70 × 91¾ in.)
Pinacoteca Nazionale di Bologna

Paul the Hermit, who was born in about AD 288 in Alexandria and is not to be confused with St Paul the Apostle, was the first of a number of early saints who chose to live a solitary life in the Egyptian desert, pursuing an existence of contemplation and avoiding persecution. According to legend he was fed by a raven, who brought him a loaf of bread every day in its beak. The fable was probably inspired by the biblical story that Elijah – who lived in the ninth century BC – was fed by ravens when he was living in the wilderness. (Guercino also depicted this episode in a painting of about 1620, in the National Gallery, London.) St Anthony the Great, St Benedict and St Onuphrius are similarly said to have benefited from such avian generosity. According to *The Golden Legend* (a collection of saints' lives written down in the thirteenth century), when St Anthony met Paul the Hermit in the desert a raven swooped down bearing two loaves of bread, one for each saint.

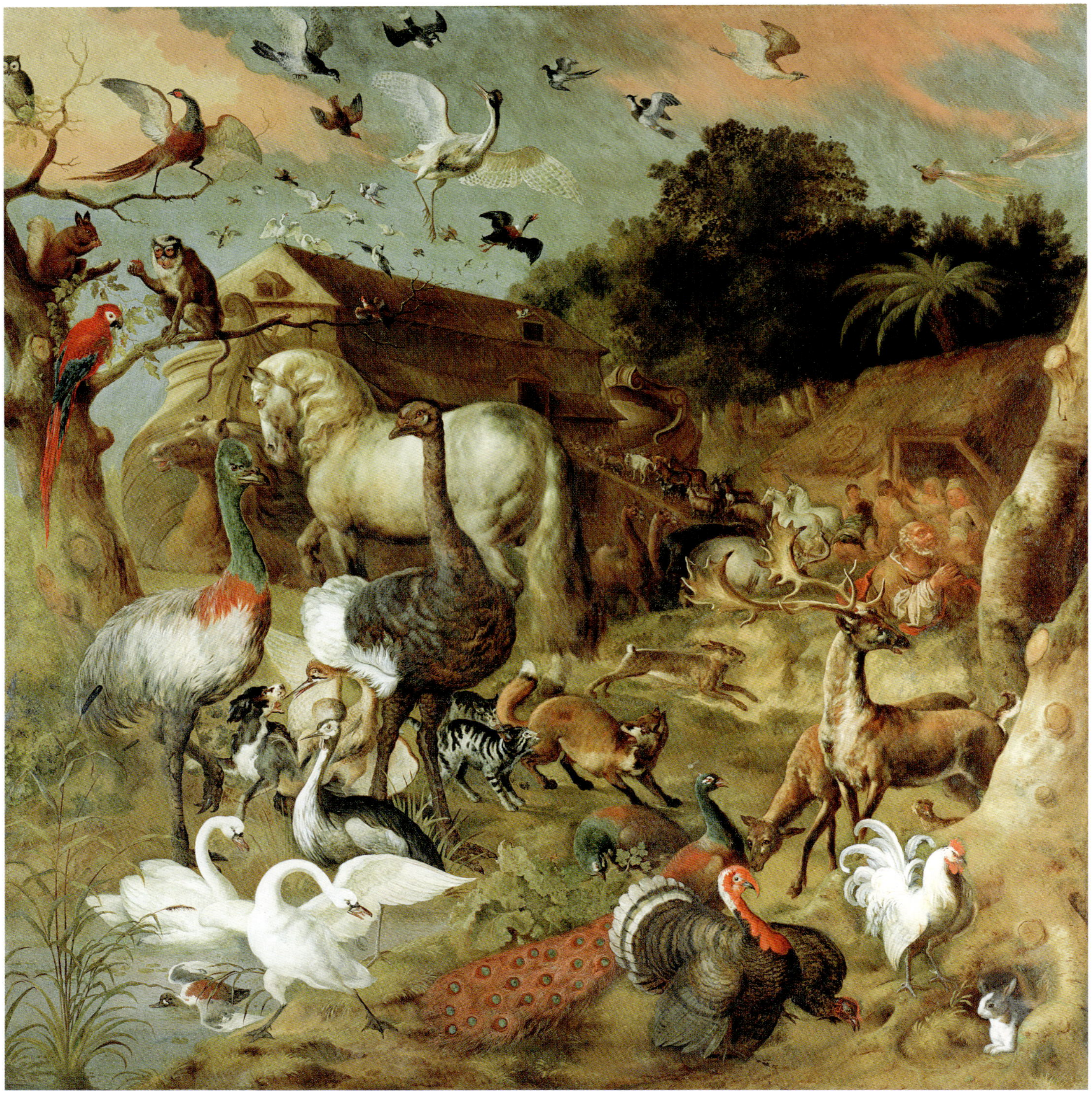

OPPOSITE

William Blake (1757–1827)

Eve Naming the Birds

1810
Tempera on canvas
74.9 × 61.1 cm (29½ × 24 in.)
Pollok House, Glasgow

The book of Genesis describes how God grants man dominion over all the beasts and fowl of the air (2:19). The task of naming them is given to Adam before Eve is created from his rib, but Blake, always a nonconformist, has decided to allow Eve her own role in the process. This picture of her giving names to the birds is a companion piece to one of Adam naming the beasts. Both compositions set the half-length figures in the Garden of Eden. Adam appears to bless the animals with a Christ-like gesture, but the gestures of the wide-eyed and innocent Eve are more ambiguous. One hand toys with her hair while the other is extended, palm outwards. Several birds flit around behind her. Blake was an individualist with his own idiosyncratic mystical philosophy, marrying his spiritual vision with a profound knowledge of the Bible.

Jan Griffier (*c.* 1645–1718)

Noah's Ark

c. 1710
Oil on canvas
487.6 × 487.6 cm (192 × 192 in.)
Bristol City Museum and Art Gallery

The subject of Noah's Ark has long provided artists with an excellent opportunity to depict a plethora of birds and animals. Here, swans, peacocks, turkeys, cockerels, ostriches, macaws, cranes and owls all wait their turn to board the ship in the background, along with assorted mammals. While some of the birds wait on the ground in pairs, others are flying in to join them. The Dutch artist Jan Griffier came to London after the Great Fire of 1666. He specialized in landscapes and river, marine and country-house views, and was also an expert etcher, producing an impressive series of plates of birds after compositions by the animal- and bird-painter Francis Barlow (see p. 169). Griffier may have sketched some of the animals seen here in private menageries or aviaries, as macaws and monkeys were popular pets at the time. The poses of the other animals and birds could have been based on examples seen in paintings by other artists.

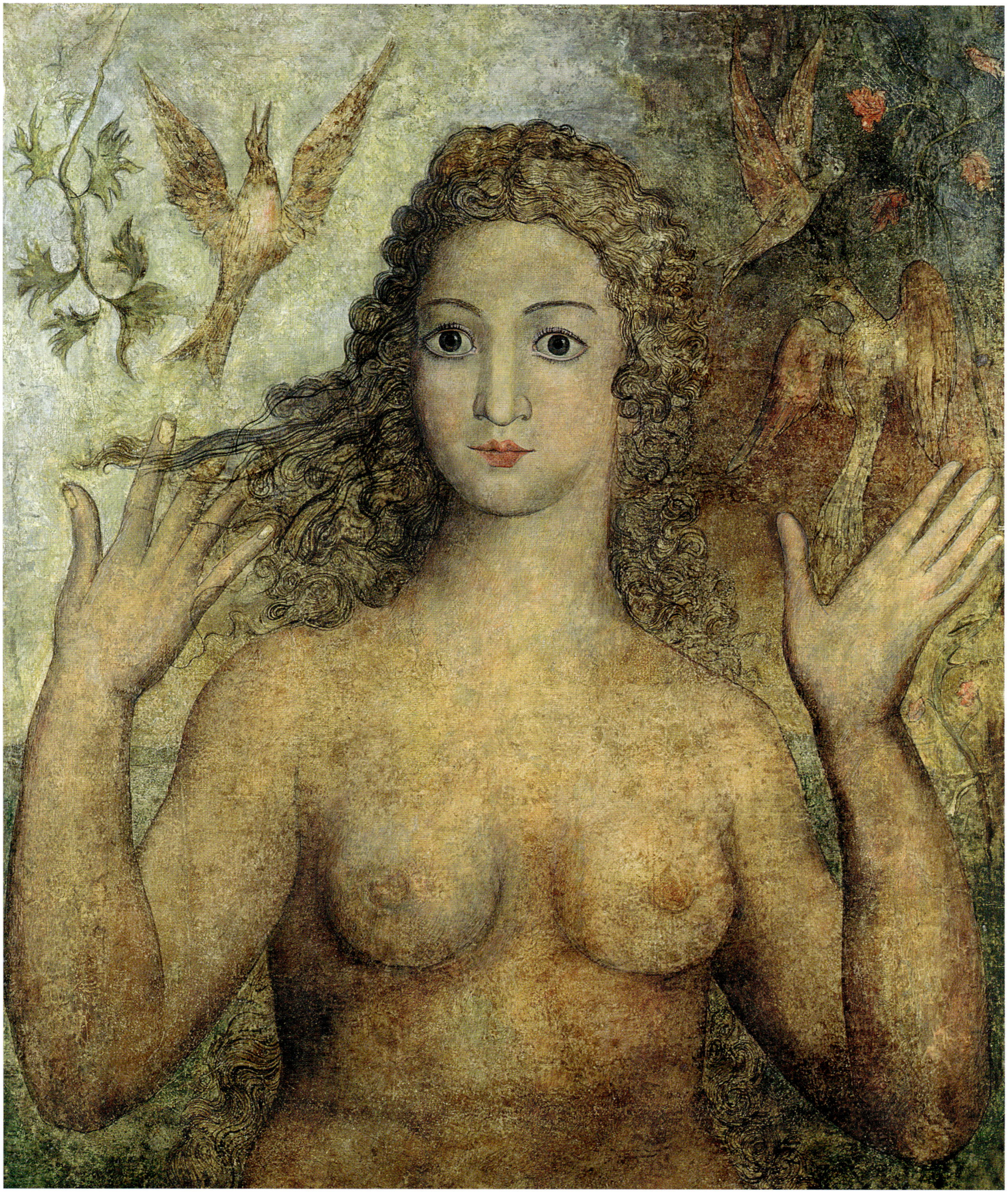

John Everett Millais (1829–1896)

The Return of the Dove to the Ark

1851
Oil on canvas
88.2 × 54.9 cm (34¾ × 21⅝ in.)
Ashmolean Museum, Oxford

The scene is an imagined one, based on a passage in Genesis that talks of the wives of Noah tending the dove that was released from the Ark and which returned bearing an olive branch, indicating that the flood waters were receding. The girls wear garments that are vaguely reminiscent of clerical garb, perhaps in keeping with the picture's message of hope and salvation. Millais originally planned to include the figure of Noah praying and several birds and animals in the background, and to create a frame with doves bearing olive branches in their beaks at each corner, but the plan was never realized. The picture was painted three years after the establishment of the Pre-Raphaelite Brotherhood, of which Millais was a founder member. The canvas, with its carefully transcribed naturalistic details (the dove's ruffled and slightly grimy feathers and the individually described strands of hay), enshrines the movement's emphasis on truth to nature.

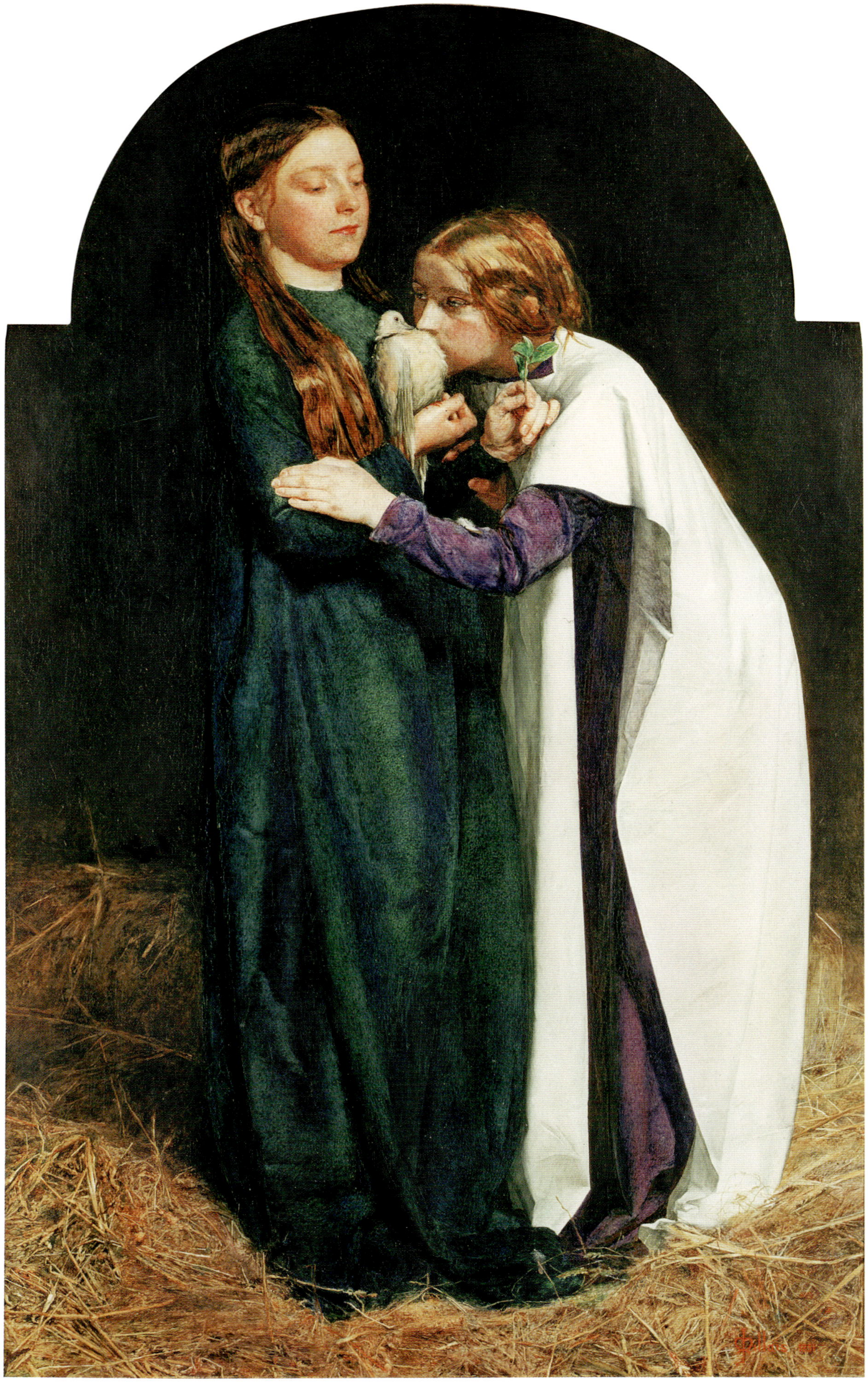

James Tissot
(1836–1902)
The Cock Crew

c. 1886–94
Watercolour and gouache on paperboard
17.5 × 9 cm (6⅞ × 3½ in.)
Brooklyn Museum, New York

In Christianity, the cock is associated with the Passion and the Resurrection, as well as with human frailty and repentance through its association with St Peter. The four Gospels all relate that during the Last Supper Jesus told Peter that he would deny him three times before the cock or rooster crowed, and – much to Peter's chagrin – the prediction came true. Perching atop a roof, Tissot's crowing bird, viewed from below against a night sky, does indeed convey a sense of doom, all the more believable because of the ordinariness of the bird. The artist enjoyed great success as a painter of beautiful women and fashionable society in Paris and London in the 1870s, but in 1882 a religious vision in the Church of St-Sulpice, Paris, convinced him to spend the rest of his life depicting subjects drawn from the Bible. This scene is from a series of 350 gouache illustrations of the life of Christ presented in an exhibition that toured to London, New York, Boston, Philadelphia and Chicago in 1896.

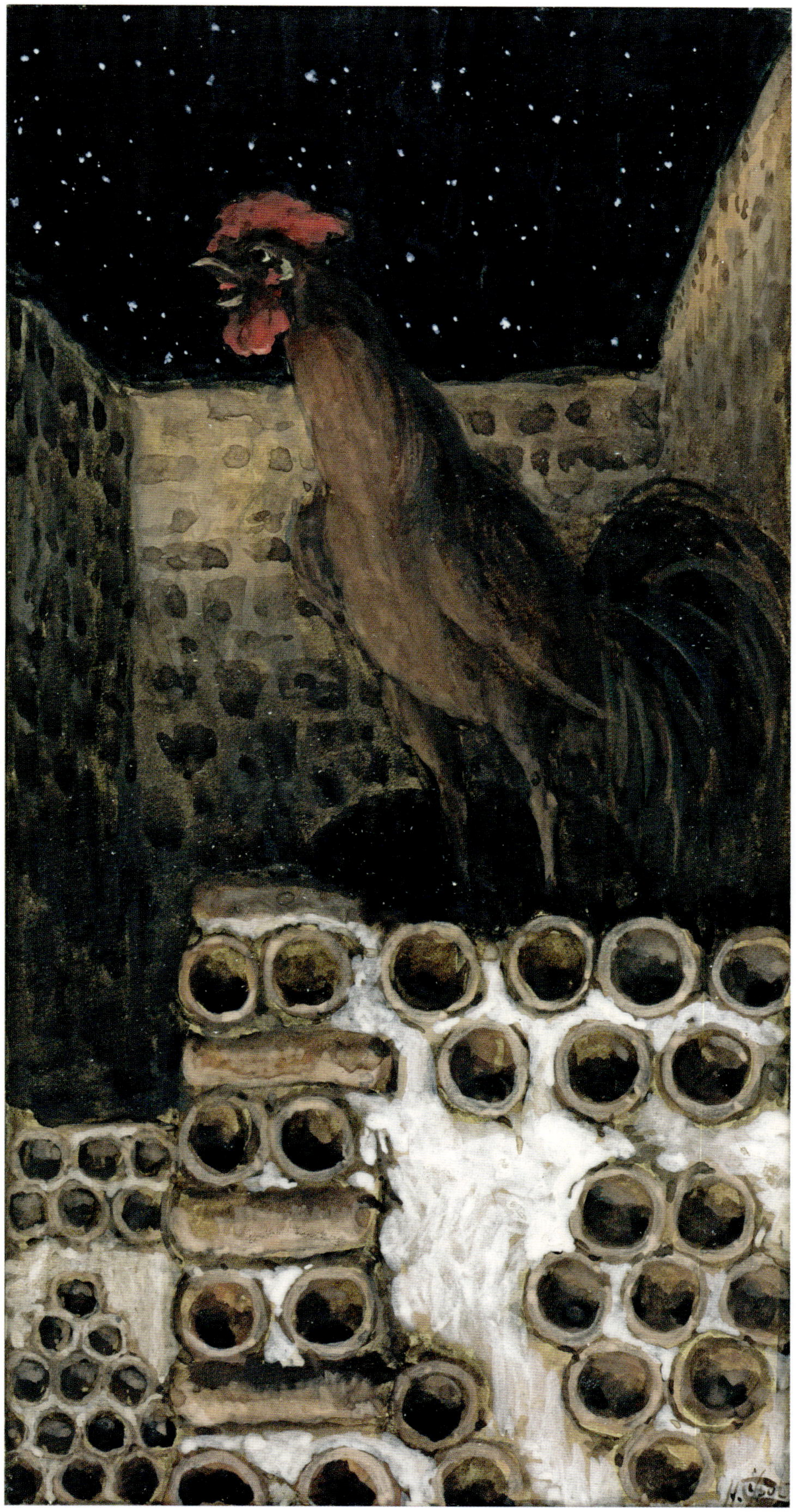

The Legendary Bird

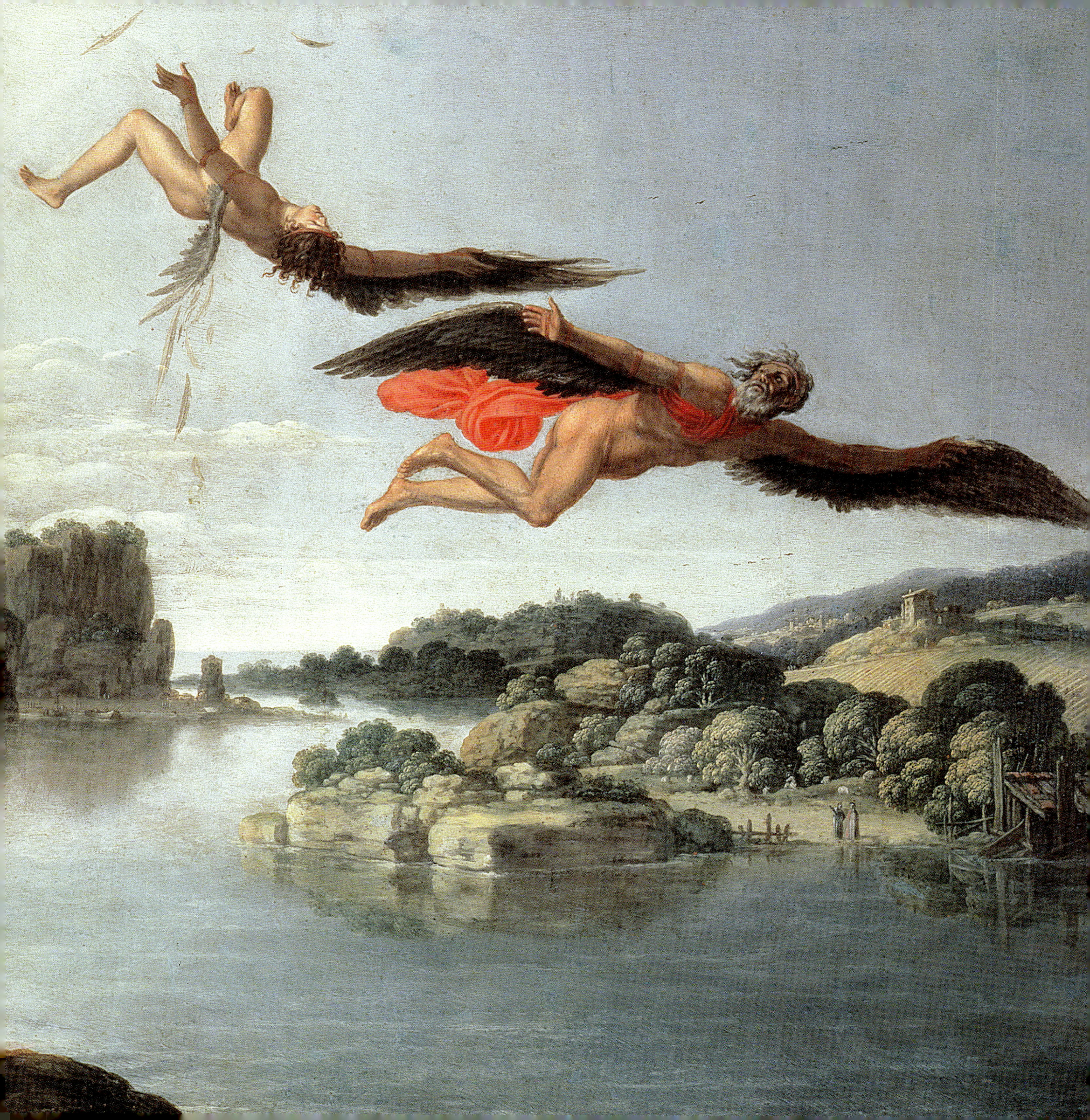

Centuries before the birth of Christ, and the advent of the idea that the Holy Spirit of God manifested itself as a dove, birds were central to the pagan legends of Europe. But whereas most birds associated with Christianity are benign and helpful in character, that is not so often the case in the stories of antiquity, where they can be tricksters, aiding and abetting mischievous or evil deeds. The Graeco-Roman myths in Ovid's *Metamorphoses* – which is full of tales of shape-shifting between gods and beasts – tell how Zeus (or Jupiter) transforms himself into a swan in order to seduce the wife of the king of Sparta (p. 94). The same god becomes an eagle in order to carry off the youth Ganymede (p. 103), and sends an eagle to pluck at the liver of his enemy Prometheus, subjecting him to continuous torture (p. 110). Another myth, relating to the labours of the god Heracles (Hercules), centres on his battle with a flock of fearsome birds that is threatening to destroy the town of Stymphalos in Arcadia (p. 100). The ultimate tribute to the power of these creatures occurs in Aristophanes' play *The Birds*, written in 414 BC, in which all the birds, under the leadership of a hoopoe, create a new city in the sky (Cloudcuckooland), gaining control over the communication between men and the gods.

In different world myths, birds bring life, death and thunderstorms (p. 121). They can sometimes speak, set events in motion, and steer or outwit people and gods. Many legends tell of people who gain the power to understand the language of birds. After tasting the magical blood of the dragon Fafnir, for example, the German hero Siegfried knows what the forest birds are saying (p. 118). Some birds are believed to have special abilities to tell the future or reveal the will of the gods. The power of prophecy has been ascribed to magpies, ravens and doves. Hybrid bird–humans, such as the sirin (or siren), occupy ambivalent roles, sometimes benevolent and at other times luring men to their death (p. 119).

Certain birds appear repeatedly in myth and legend, although not always in the same role in different cultures. The crow and the raven, for example, can be both oracles and symbols of malevolent forces. In Norse mythology, Wotan (or Odin) is always accompanied by two wise ravens, which tell him everything that happens on Earth (p. 117). Yet, according to Greek myth, the raven acquired its dark plumage as a punishment: Apollo turned its white feathers black after it failed in its duty as a guardian of his wife, and revealed the secret of her infidelity. The eagle usually has divine or royal associations in myth. By adopting the eagle as their symbol, innumerable kings, rulers and warriors have tried to suggest that they, too, possess divine or heroic qualities. In the ancient Near East and in Greece, the dove was a symbol of love and fertility, often associated with goddesses of love, such as Aphrodite or Venus (pp. 92 and 101). Owls are symbols of wisdom, patience and learning (p. 106), yet because they hunt at night they are also associated with secrecy and darkness. A multitude of particular and complex meanings is attached to other birds, too. Swans often serve as symbols of purity and feminine beauty, and both Celtic and Norse myths include tales of women who turn into swans (p. 115). Male beauty finds its avian counterpart in the splendidly exhibitionist peacock, which can suggest either foolish vanity or divine glory (p. 114).

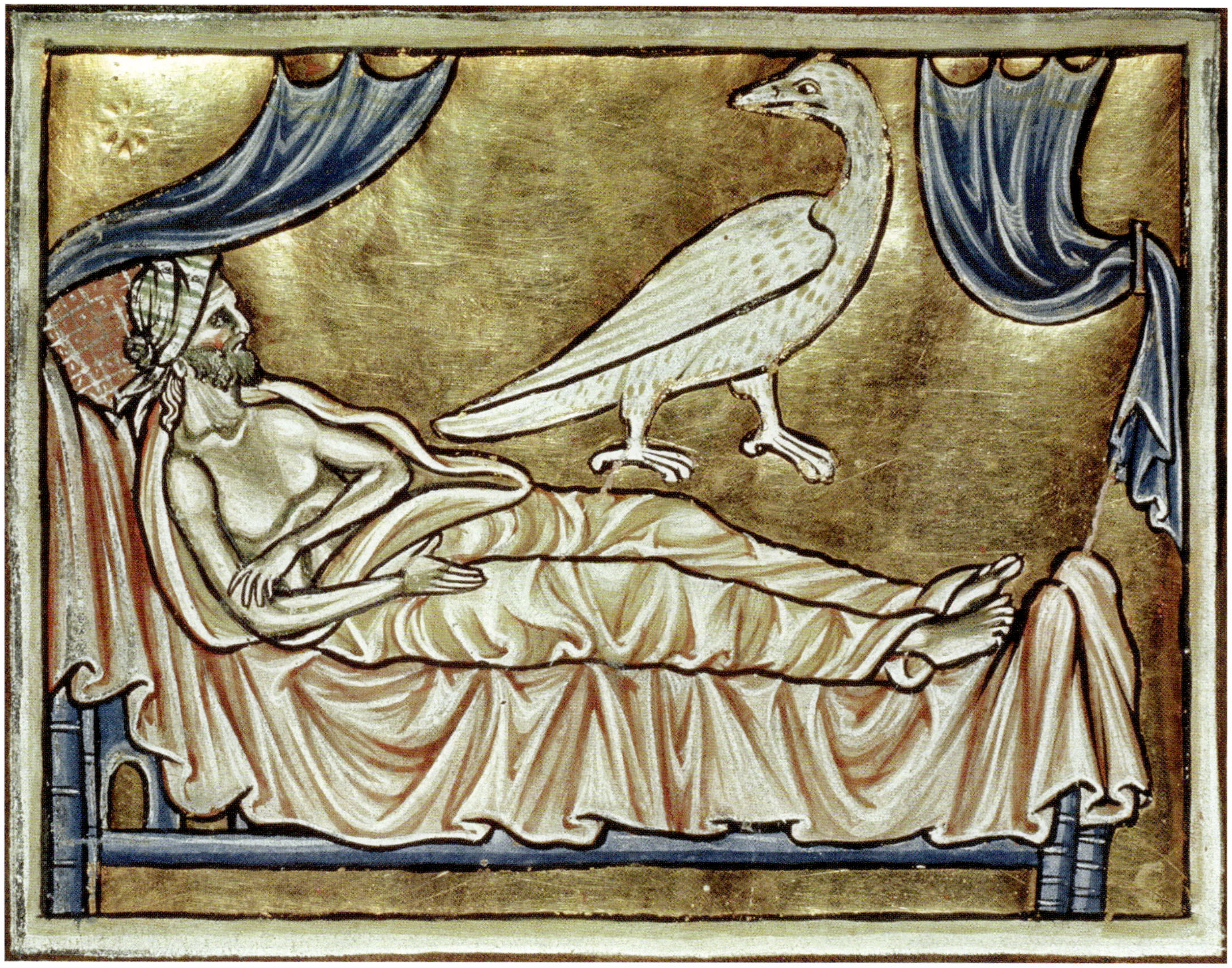

English
The Caladrius Bird, from a bestiary (MS Roy 12C XIX, f. 47v)
c. 1200–10
Vellum
15.8 × 22.2 cm (6¼ × 8¾ in.)
British Library, London

In Roman mythology, the caladrius bird would appear at sickbeds in royal residences. If it turned away from the invalid the person would die, but if it looked at his face he would live. (The prognosis is good for the person lying here, as the bird is clearly facing him.) It could also help to effect a cure by absorbing the sickness into itself and then flying towards the sun, which would burn off the illness. The medieval mind drew parallels between the caladrius and Christ, who took upon himself the spiritual disease of humanity through his Crucifixion and Resurrection. The bird is described as completely white. No convincing link to any particular species has been established, although it has been variously suggested that it is based on a dove, a swan and a plover. This illumination comes from an English bestiary produced in Durham. As is the case with many bestiaries, the text is based on the *Physiologus*, said to have been written by a Greek living in Alexandria in the fourth or fifth century AD.

Master of the Prayer Books (active *c.* 1500)
Venus Comes to the Rescue (from *Roman de la Rose*, Harley 4425 f. 138v)

c. 1500
Vellum
25.5 × 19 cm (10 × 7½ in.)
British Library, London

A team of white doves – a bird traditionally associated with Venus – flap their wings in unison as they draw her chariot into battle. The illumination comes from a Flemish manuscript of the *Roman de la Rose* (*Story of the Rose*), a thirteenth-century French poem. The verses tell of the Lover's quest for the rose, a symbol of his lady's love. In the early part of the poem, the Lover learns the arts of courtly love in a walled pleasure garden, but in the second part he has to win back his lover's heart after she is imprisoned in a castle. He calls on his army to assist him as he assails the castle, and Venus – representing carnal love – helps him to gain the ultimate victory. The manuscript was created in Bruges in about 1500, and is attributed to an anonymous Master of the Prayer Books on the grounds of its stylistic similarity with a group of religious manuscripts. But nothing further is known about this shadowy figure, who could have been an individual or a studio of artists working together.

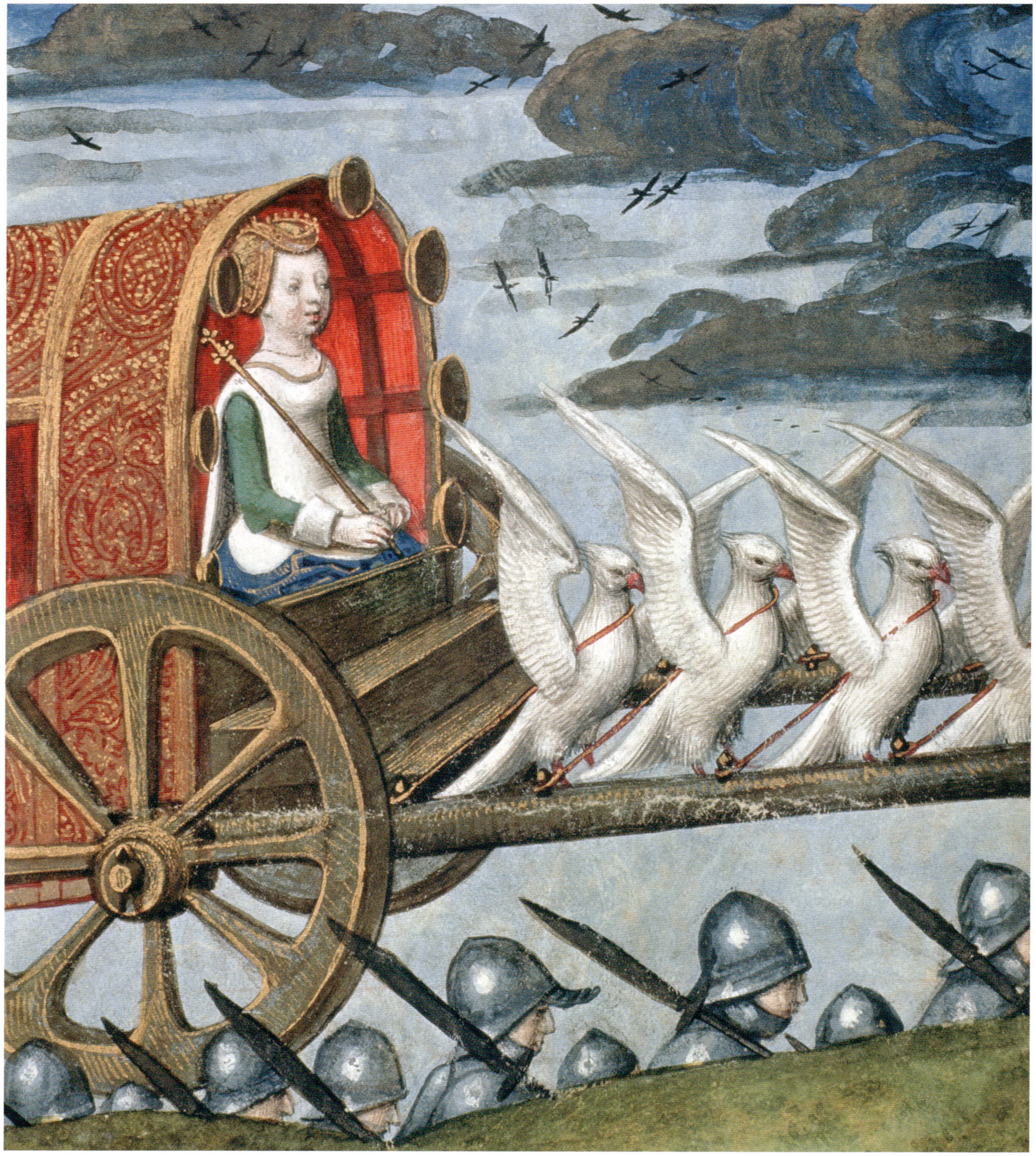

Fernando Gallego (1440–1507)
The Chariot of Mercury

c. 1480–90
Fresco
Museo de la Universidad, Salamanca, Spain

The Spanish painter Fernando Gallego was known primarily for his altarpieces and other religious works, painted in a meticulously detailed late Gothic style. One of his final commissions was for the ceiling vault of the library at the University of Salamanca, which he decorated with the constellations and signs of the zodiac. This detail shows the figure of Mercury, carrying his caduceus. Although the god usually relied on his winged sandals and helmet for speedy travel, here he has opted for a chariot, rather like the god Apollo. The planet Mercury rules the zodiac signs of Gemini and Virgo, and these are represented by the twins and the maiden on the chariot's wheels. The bird usually associated with Mercury is the cockerel, the herald of the new day, but the birds drawing his chariot here appear to be fantastic creations, with the features of different species, including the talons and wings of eagles.

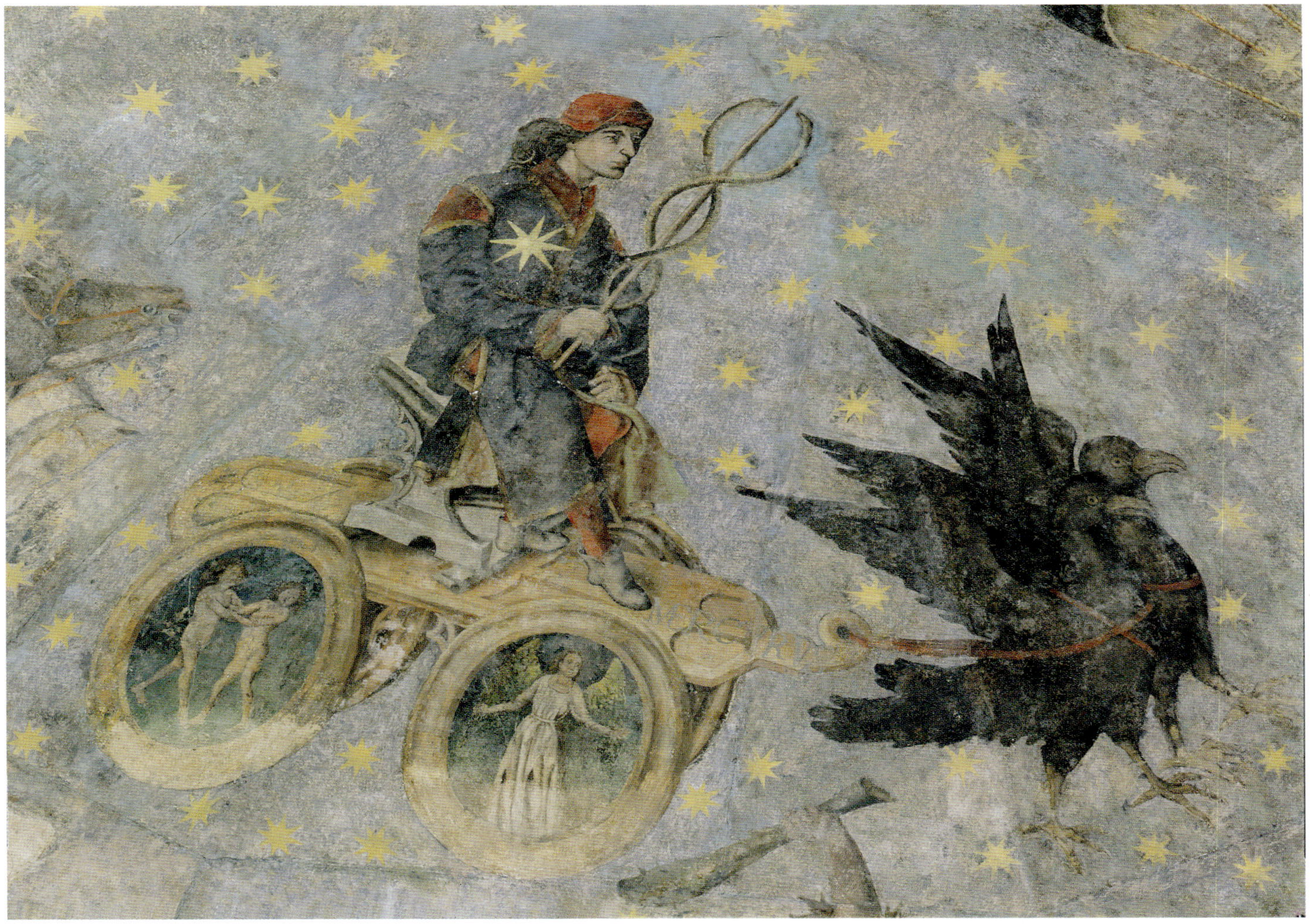

Correggio (Antonio Allegri) (*c.* 1490–1534)

Leda and the Swan

c. 1532
Oil on canvas
152 × 191 cm (59⅞ × 75⅛ in.)
Gemäldegalerie, Berlin

According to a Greek myth, later retold in Ovid's *Metamorphoses*, the god Zeus (Roman: Jupiter) assumed the form of a swan to visit Leda, the wife of the king of Sparta, while she was bathing. He seduced her, and she eventually produced two eggs, one of which contained Castor and Clytemnestra and the other Pollux and Helen. Scenes of the seduction were popular in Italian Renaissance art, and both Leonardo and Michelangelo created their own versions. Correggio's painting is one of a series of four subjects inspired by Ovid commissioned by Duke Federico II of Mantua. Leda seems to welcome her fate, embracing the swan in a highly erotic pose. Her companions receive the attentions of two more swans with some delight and amusement. Correggio, who came from Parma in central Italy, was celebrated for his dramatic, sensuous subjects, often rendered with a softness that owes something to Leonardo's melting outlines.

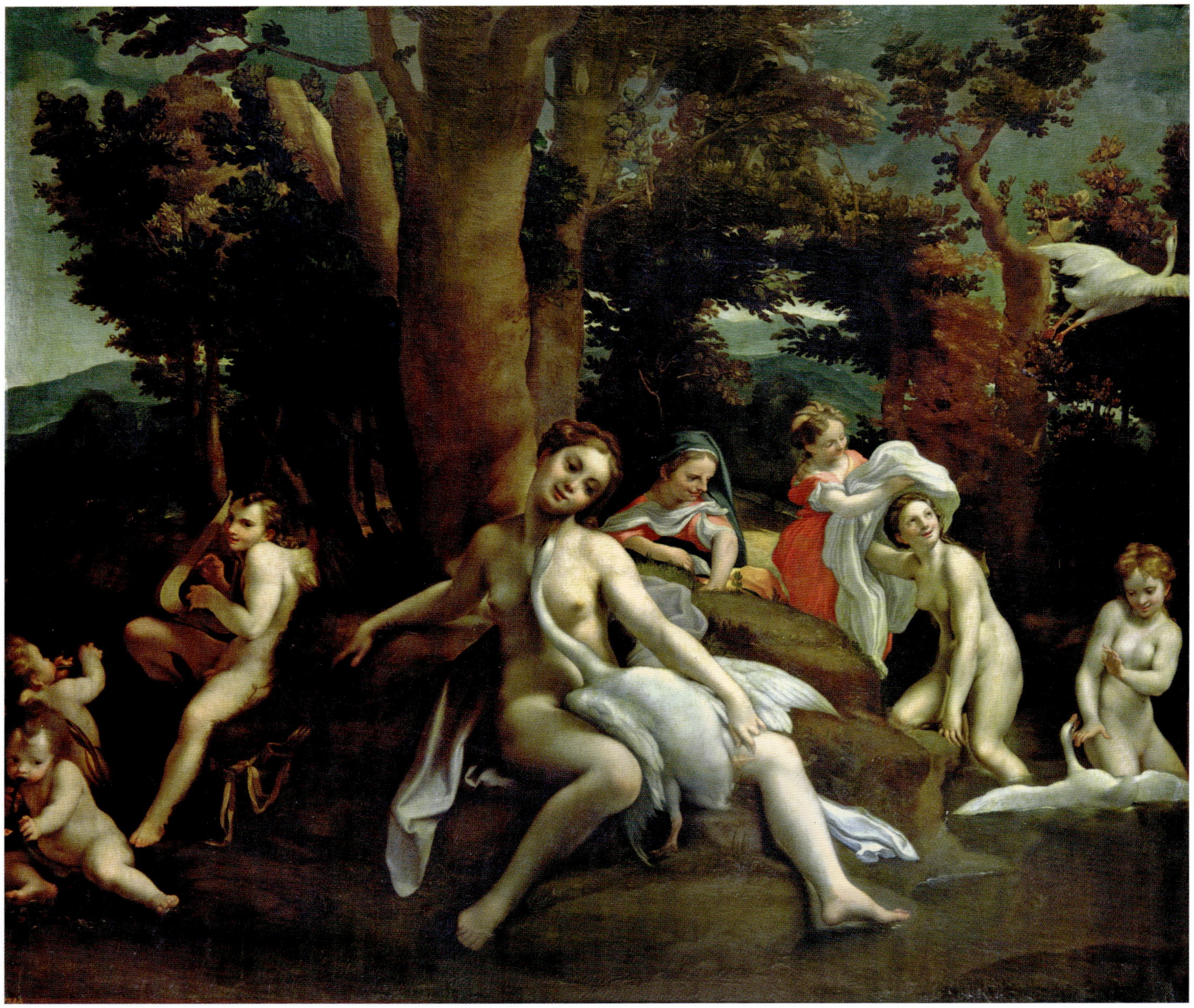

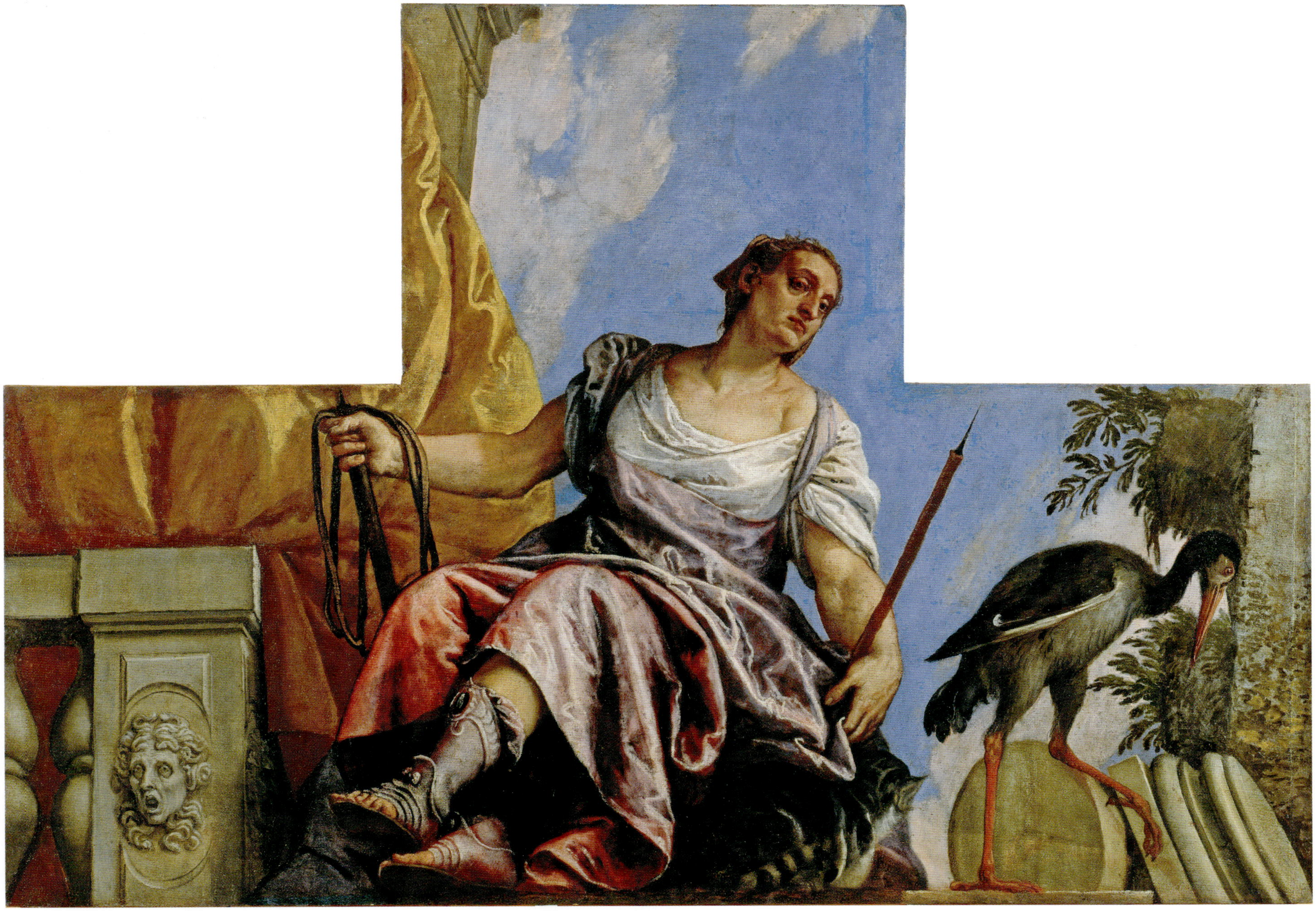

Paolo Veronese
(1528–1588)
Vigilance
1575–78
Oil on canvas
150 × 220 cm (59 × 86½ in.)
Sala del Collegio, Palazzo Ducale, Venice

Vigilance – one of the virtues traditionally required by rulers – was represented in Renaissance art as a female figure accompanied by a crane standing on one foot, holding a stone in its other claw. According to legend, when the watchful bird fell asleep it would drop the stone and immediately wake itself up and resume its watch, but Veronese's crane seems to be missing its stone. This is one of the eight virtues depicted by the Venetian artist in the borders of his ceiling in the Sala del Collegio (Council Chamber) in the Doge's Palace, where Venice's Cabinet of Government met under the chairmanship of the Doge. The other virtues are also identified by their accompanying attributes: a dog for Fidelity, a lamb for Gentleness, an ermine for Purity, a die and a crown for Reward, an eagle for Moderation, a cobweb for Dialectics and a cornucopia for Prosperity. The three central ceiling panels represent Mars and Neptune, Venice Ruling with Justice and Peace, and Faith and Religion.

Pieter Bruegel the Elder
(*c.* 1525/30–1569)
Netherlandish Proverbs

1559
Oil on panel
117.5 × 163.5 cm (46¼ × 64⅝ in.)
Gemäldegalerie, Berlin

Pieter Bruegel's painting contains about 100 vignettes illustrating popular sayings of his day, adding up to a humorous study in the follies of mankind. Birds play an important role in a number of them. In the centre left of the picture is a 'hen feeler', warning against counting one's chickens before they hatch. Above him, in the eaves, is a nest containing one egg, a metaphor for always having something in reserve. The fox and the crane dining together near the centre of the painting – an episode drawn from one of Aesop's fables – are two deceivers who try to outwit each other. In the background, a woman gazing out of a window at a stork illustrates a saying about wasting time. A man sitting on the shore with a flock of geese could be interpreted in two possible ways. The first, which illustrates the proverb 'Who knows why the geese go barefoot?', means that there is a reason for everything, even though it may not be obvious. The second – 'If I am not meant to be their keeper, I will let geese be geese' – advises against interfering in matters that are not your business. The crows beneath the gallows refer to the proverb 'Where the carcass is, there fly the crows'; in other words, if the evidence points to something it is probably true.

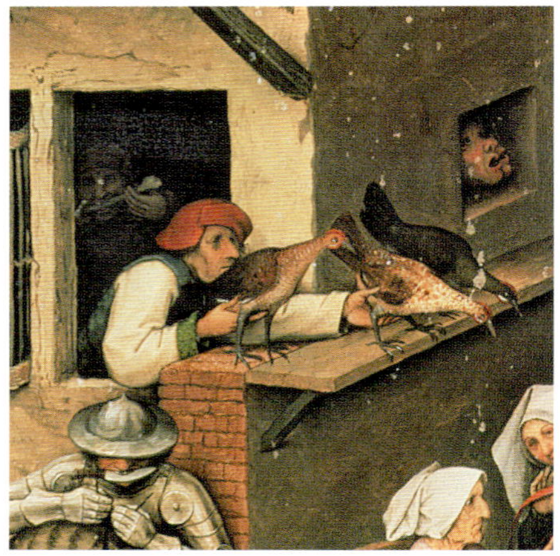

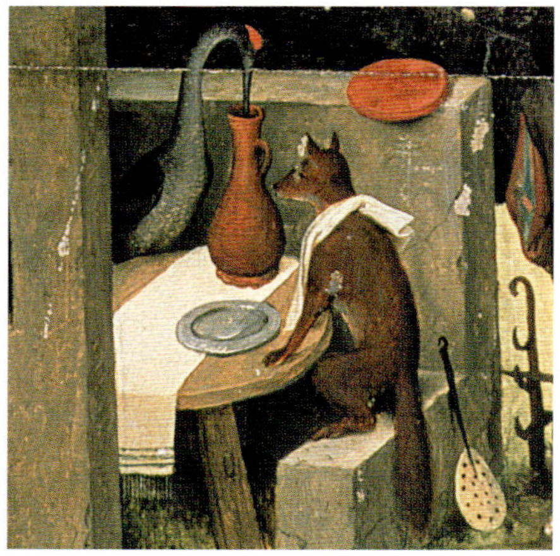

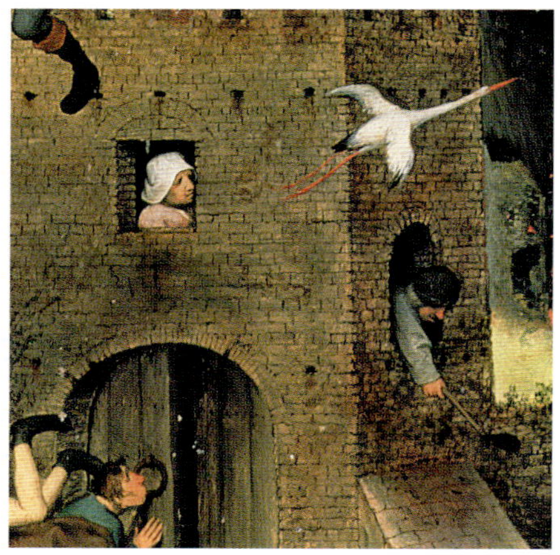

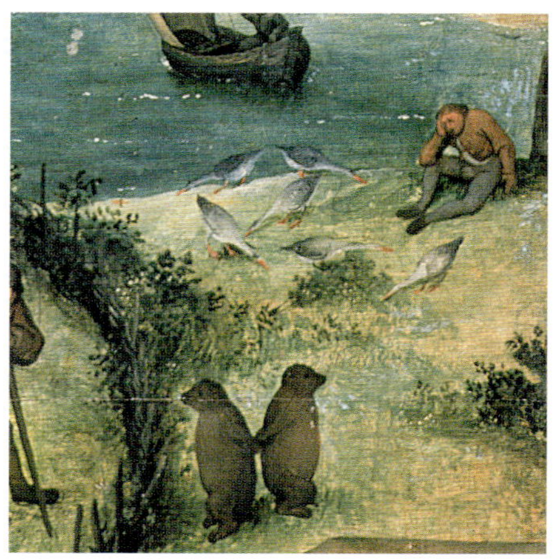

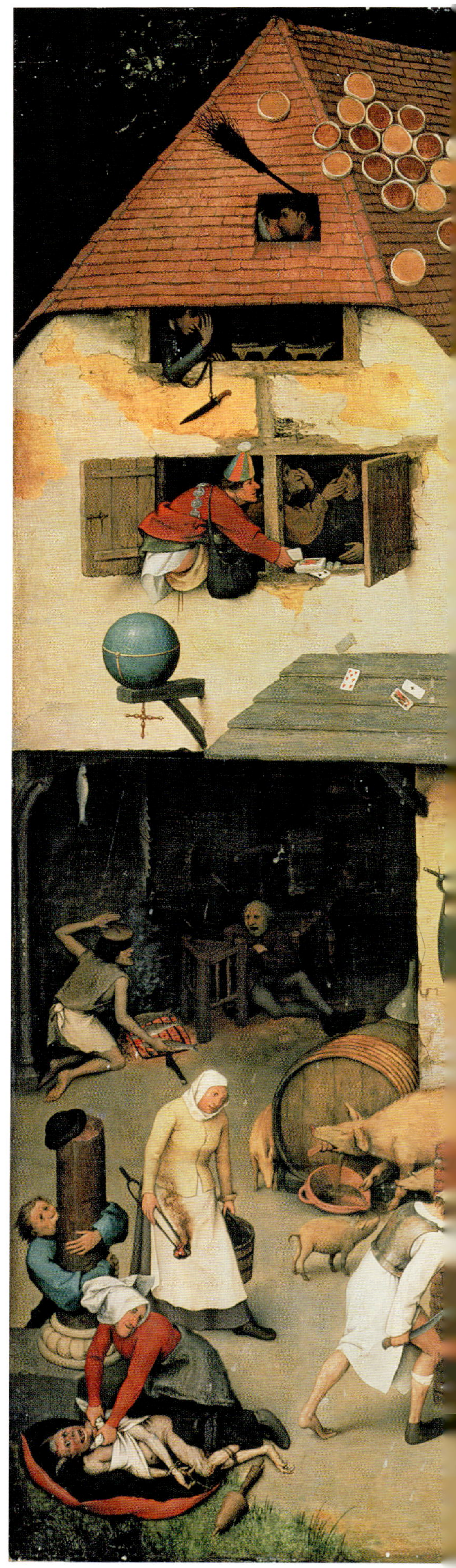

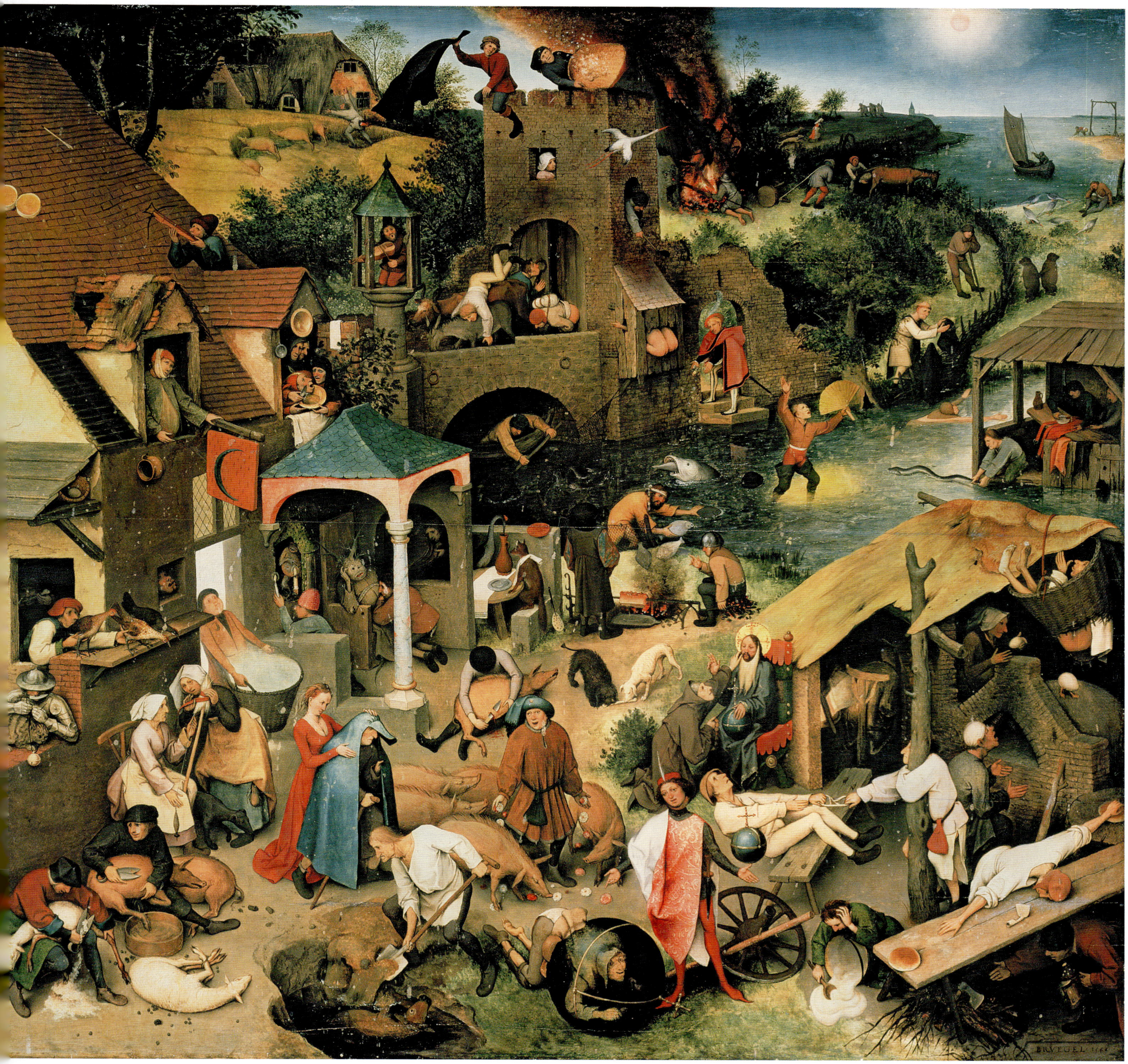

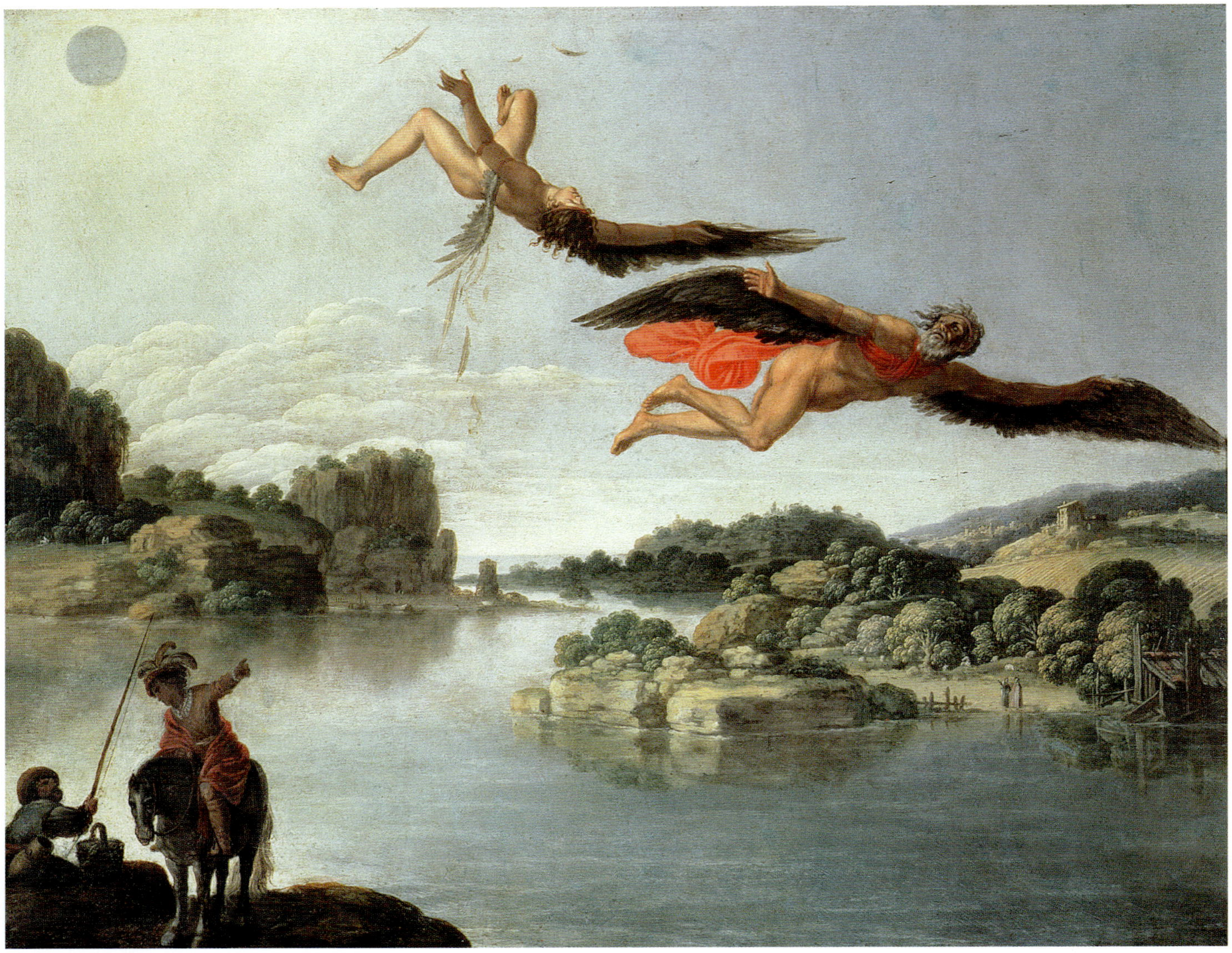

Carlo Saraceni
(*c.* 1579–1620)
Landscape with Fall of Icarus

c. 1600
Oil on canvas
40 × 52.5 cm (15¾ × 20⅝ in.)
Museo di Capodimonte, Naples

The human desire to fly like a bird informs the Greek myth of Daedalus and Icarus. Icarus is imprisoned with his craftsman father, Daedalus, on the island of Crete. As part of a plan to escape, Daedalus makes them both a pair of wings, which he attaches to their shoulders with wax. He sets off after instructing his son to follow him, flying neither too high nor too low. But Icarus soars up towards the sun, causing the wax to melt. His wings fall off and he plunges to his death. The story can be read in different ways: as a warning of the dangers of extremes and the value of moderation, or as a comment on the restless spirit of human intellectual enquiry. The theme was popular with artists from antiquity to the Baroque era. In paintings, Daedalus and Icarus are often shown flying over the sea, while country people in the adjoining landscape go about their daily business.

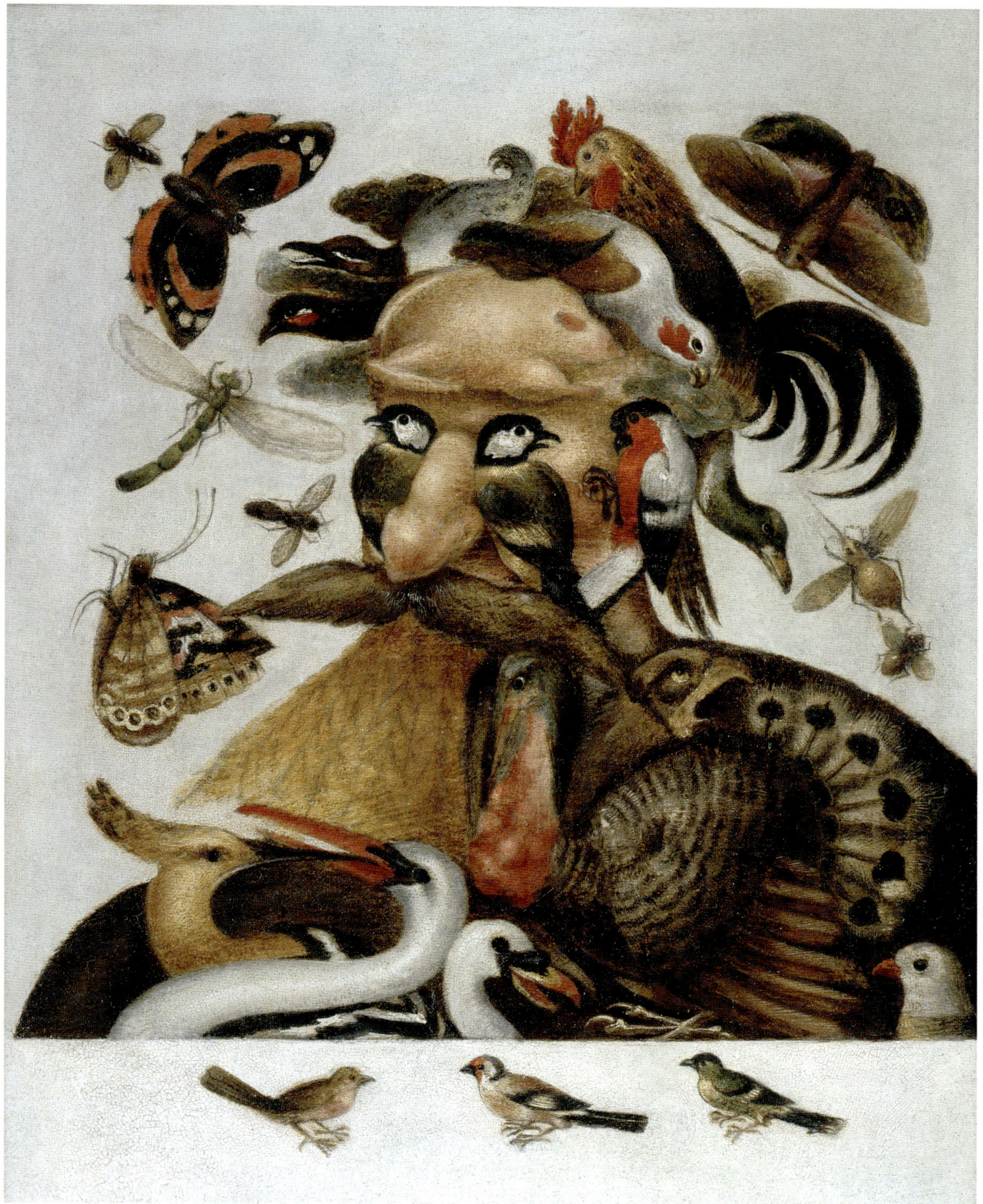

Giuseppe Arcimboldo (1527–1593) (follower of)
An Allegory of Air

16th century
Oil on copper
18.7 × 15.5 cm (7⅜ × 6⅛ in.)
Private collection

The Milanese painter Giuseppe Arcimboldo is famous for his fantasy compositions of human beings created from carefully observed flowers, fruit and animals, and his works were much copied and imitated. In common with many of his contemporaries, Arcimboldo produced series of paintings on the theme of the four seasons and the four elements. This picture, by one of his followers, is an amusing variation on the element of air. All the denizens of the sky – birds and insects – come together to make up one grotesque head. The ornithological accuracy of the picture is questionable, but among the identifiable birds are a hoopoe, swans or masked boobies, sparrows, a turkey cock, a cockerel, a dove, a bullfinch and a duck – although the artist has had to take a few liberties with scale to make them all fit into a convincing figure. A version of the subject produced by Arcimboldo for Emperor Maximilian of Austria (now known only from copies) placed greater prominence on the imperial eagle and peacock, which were symbols of Maximilian and the House of Habsburg.

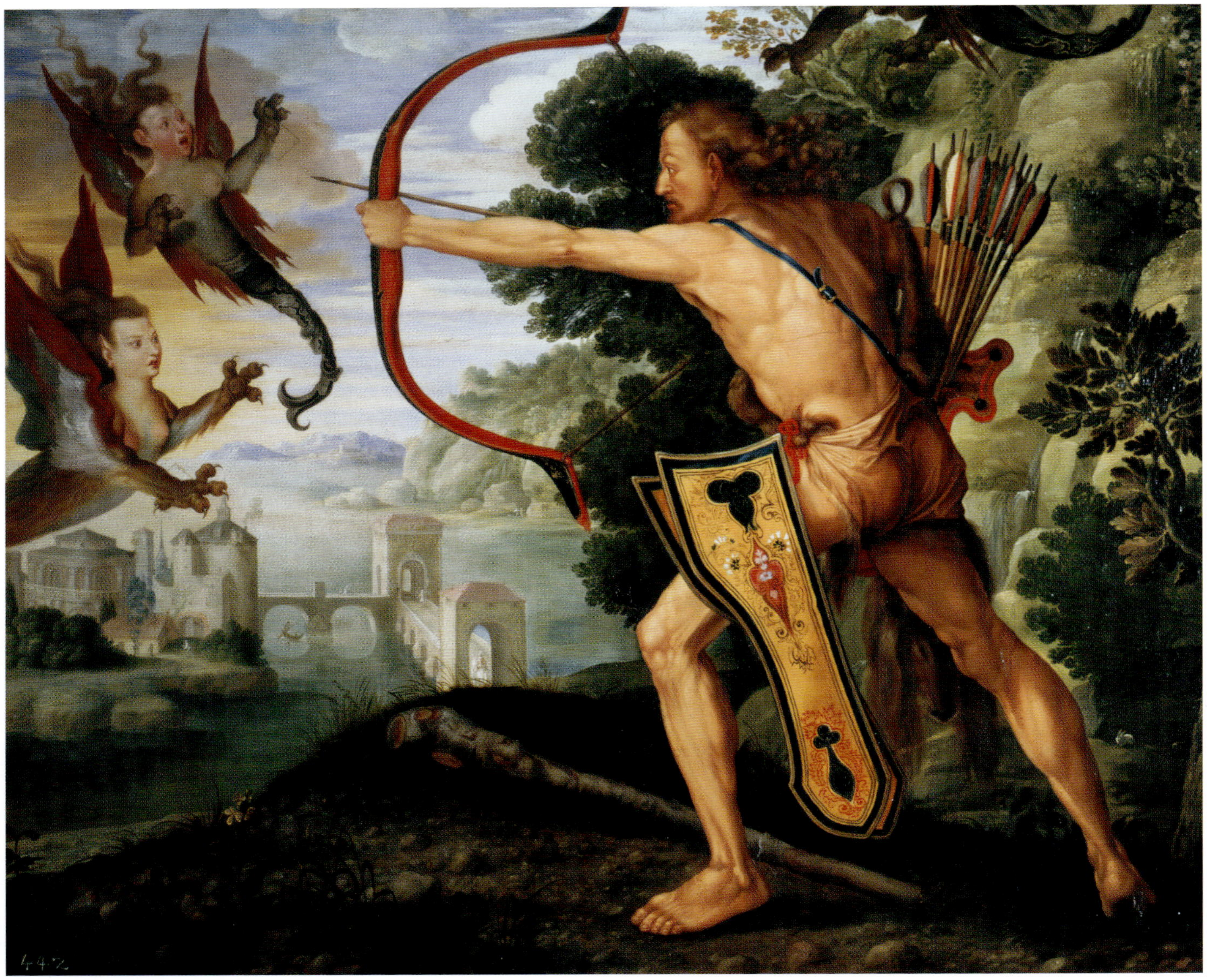

Albrecht Dürer
(1471–1528) (after)
Hercules and the Stymphalian Birds
1600
Oil on panel
90 × 113 cm (35⅜ × 44½ in.)
Kunsthistorisches Museum, Vienna

The Roman god Hercules (Greek: Heracles), the personification of physical courage, is set twelve tasks or 'labours' in which he must triumph over evil as a penance for killing his children in a fit of rage. His sixth task is to kill a flock of birds that has gathered at a lake near the town of Stymphalos in Arcadia, destroying the crops and killing the inhabitants. The birds are particularly vicious, with enormous claws, sharp beaks and feathers that are poisoned arrows, which can be aimed at potential victims. Hercules first scares the birds out of the trees by rattling a huge pair of clappers made by Vulcan (Greek: Hephaestus), god of the forge, and then shoots at them with a bow and arrow as they try to fly away. In Greek and Roman portrayals of the subject the birds are shown relatively naturalistically, but here they are composite half-female creatures more akin to the fearsome harpies of Classical myth.

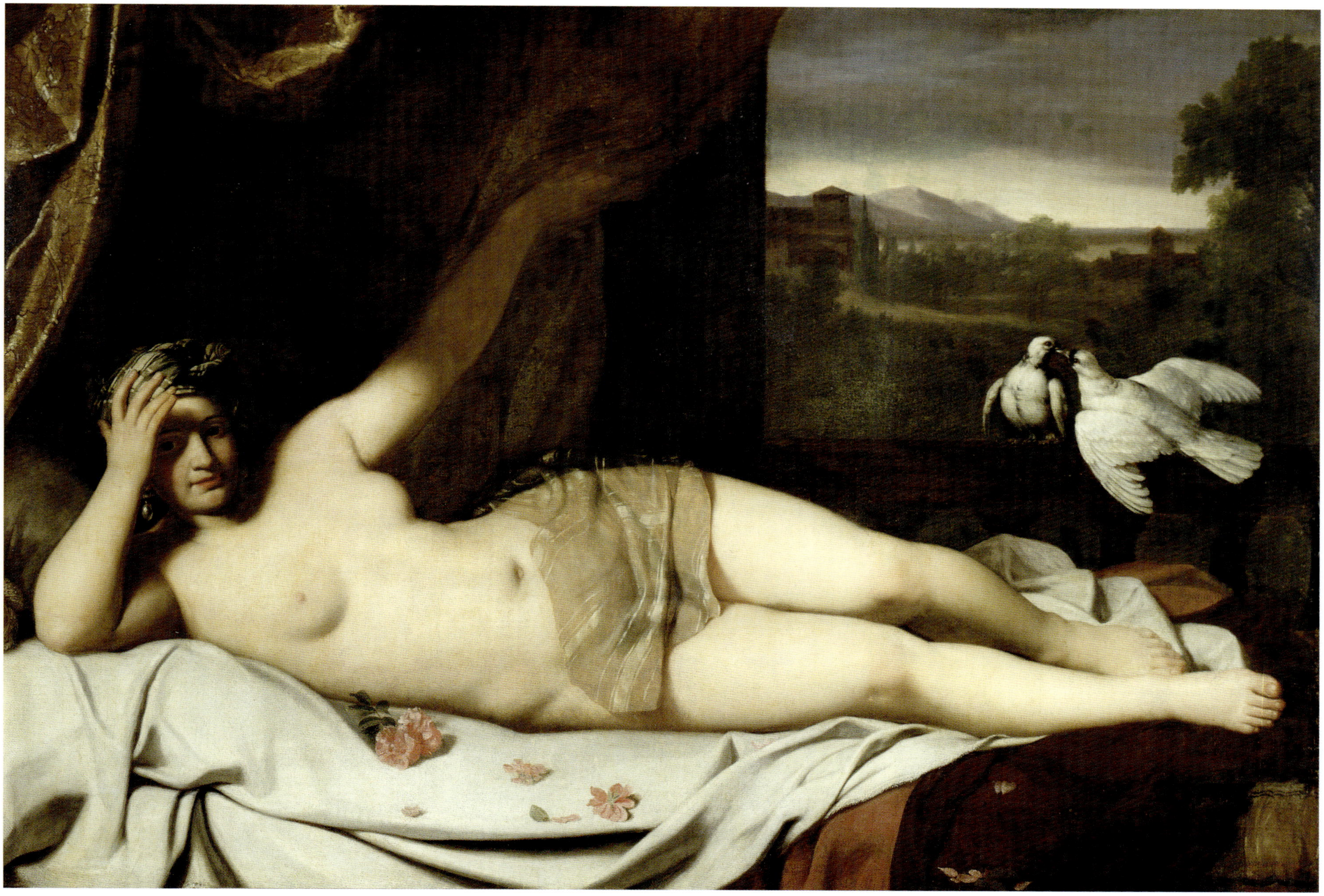

Domenichino (Domenico Zampieri) (1581–1641) (attrib.)
Venus
First half of the 17th century
Oil on canvas
121.9 × 168.9 cm (48 × 66½ in.)
York Art Gallery

Doves have a vast array of symbolic meanings, but have long been associated with love and constancy. They are an attribute of the Phoenician Astarte, the goddess of love and fertility, the Greek goddess Aphrodite and the Roman Venus. Many depictions of Venus show her with a pair of doves. Sometimes the birds draw her chariot; at other times they are simply companions playing about her person or present in the landscape. Doves also carry overtones of lust, and this Venus, reclining on her bed strewn with rose petals, is certainly making a flagrant display of her sexual charms while her birds bill and coo in the background. Originally from the Italian town of Bologna, Domenichino travelled to Rome and Naples, where he worked on prestigious church commissions. This Venus, however, definitely suggests profane rather than sacred love.

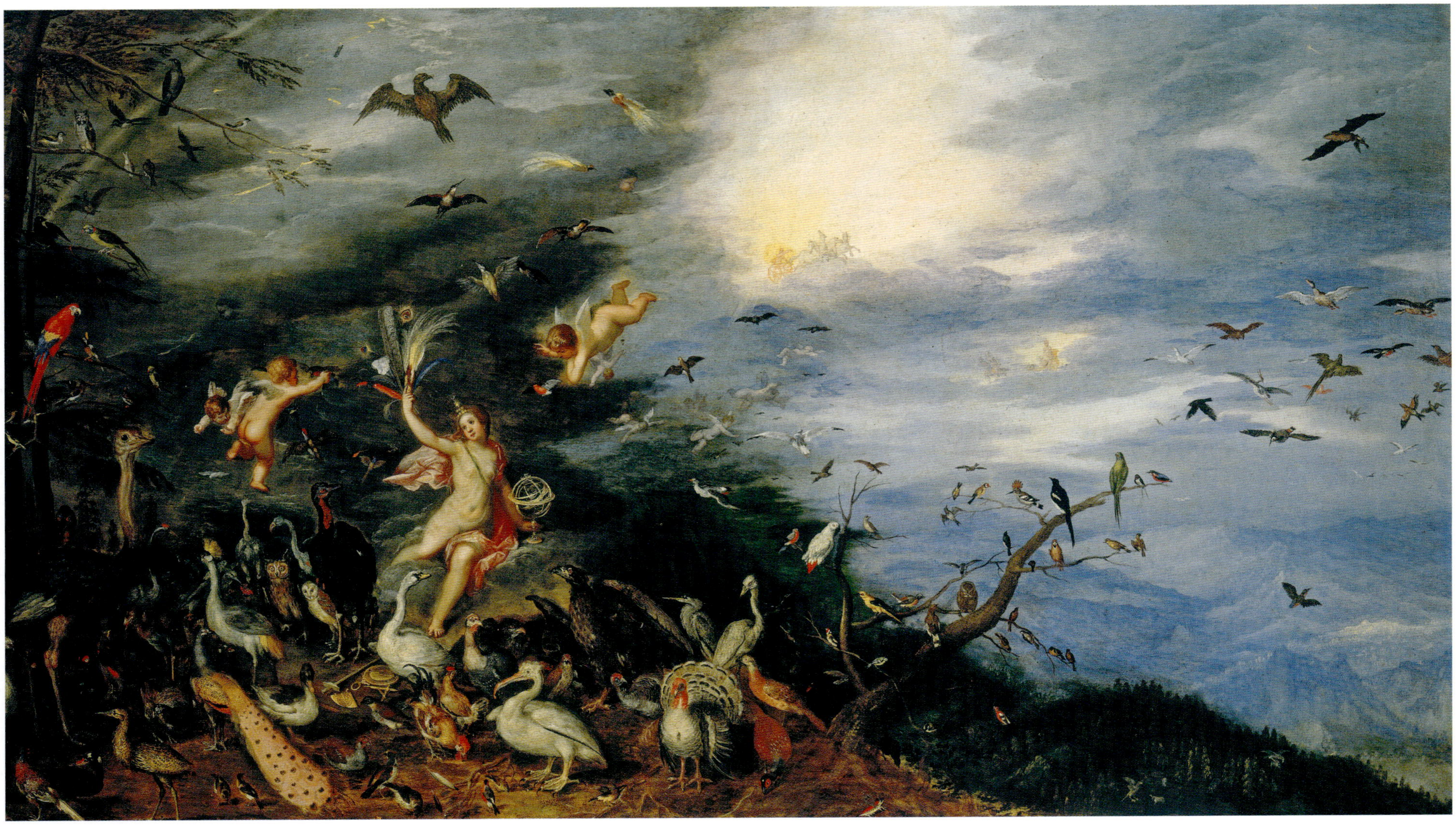

Jan Breughel the Elder (1568–1625)
An Allegory of Air
c. 1611
Oil on panel
55 × 93 cm (21⅝ × 36⅝ in.)
Galleria Doria Pamphilj, Rome

The four elements – earth, air, fire and water – were a popular theme in the sixteenth and seventeenth centuries, and artists often produced them as separate pictures in sets of four. They usually focus on a figure accompanied by appropriate attributes. In the case of air, that might be a youth, a god or a goddess surrounded by birds – the obvious inhabitants of the skies. An entire aviary seems to have been unleashed into the heavens in the Flemish painter Jan Breughel's version of the theme, which has the goddess Urania, the muse of astronomy, as the central character. In addition to an astrolabe, she is carrying the feathers of several birds. Birds even threaten to overrun the Earth: prominent in the foreground is a peacock, sacred to the goddess Juno (who is herself often included in allegorical depictions of air), a pelican, a turkey and owls. A colourful parrot perches on a branch, and an eagle and several other species fly overhead. Breughel, whose reputation was based on his meticulously detailed floral still lifes and depictions of Paradise, was the son of the more famous Pieter Bruegel the Elder, whose tastes were decidedly more terrestrial.

Peter Paul Rubens
(1577–1640)
The Kidnapping of Ganymede

1611–12
Oil on canvas
207 × 207 cm (81½ × 81½ in.)
Fürstlich Schwarzenberg'sche Verwaltung, Vienna

The Greek writer Homer tells how the god Zeus (or Jupiter, as he is in Roman mythology) fell in love with Ganymede, the son of the king of Troy. So enamoured was he of the boy's beauty that he transformed himself into an eagle and swooped down to abduct him, carrying him off to Mount Olympus, where he was granted immortality and served as a cup-bearer to the gods. The theme was a great favourite with artists from Classical times onwards, since it offered moments of high drama and action combined with homoerotic possibilities. Rembrandt's version of the scene shows Ganymede as a terrified, urinating infant gripped by the eagle's beak and talons, and Correggio depicts him as a seductive boy clinging on to the bird. Rubens (who painted the episode on more than one occasion) chose to portray him as a golden-haired youth. Here he is borne aloft on the eagle's wings, and, far from putting up a struggle, he appears to be enjoying his celestial transport.

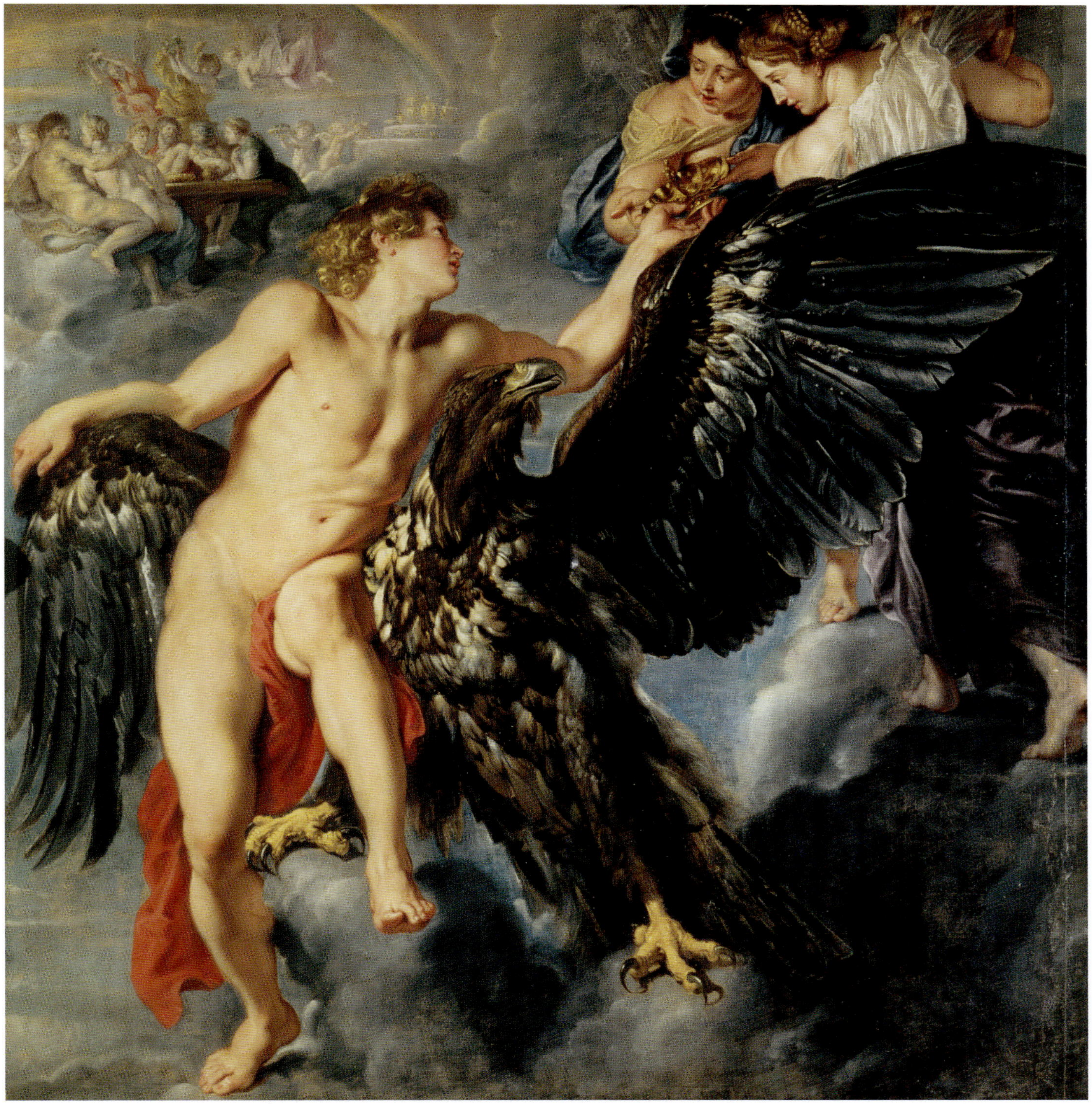

Peter Paul Rubens (1577–1640)

Juno and Argus

1611
Oil on canvas
249 × 296 cm (98 × 116½ in.)
Wallraf-Richartz-Museum, Cologne

Just as the eagle is the emblem of Jupiter (or Zeus), so the peacock is that of Juno (Hera). Ovid's *Metamorphoses*, a rich source of inspiration for artists, tells how Juno, the wife of Jupiter, has to endure his constant infidelity. When her husband seduces Io – and changes her into a heifer to conceal her – Juno asks for the heifer as a gift, and sets the hundred-eyed giant Argus to watch over her. Jupiter sends his messenger Mercury to recover Io, and he charms Argus to sleep before beheading him. As revenge, the wrathful Juno takes Argus's hundred eyes and sets them in the tail of the peacock. Rubens shows Argus's decapitated corpse lying in the foreground, while one of Juno's companions holds the head to pluck out the eyes. But the scene is celebratory rather than grisly, with pride of place given to the two splendid birds, the luscious female figures and the playful putti, who clutch at the feathers.

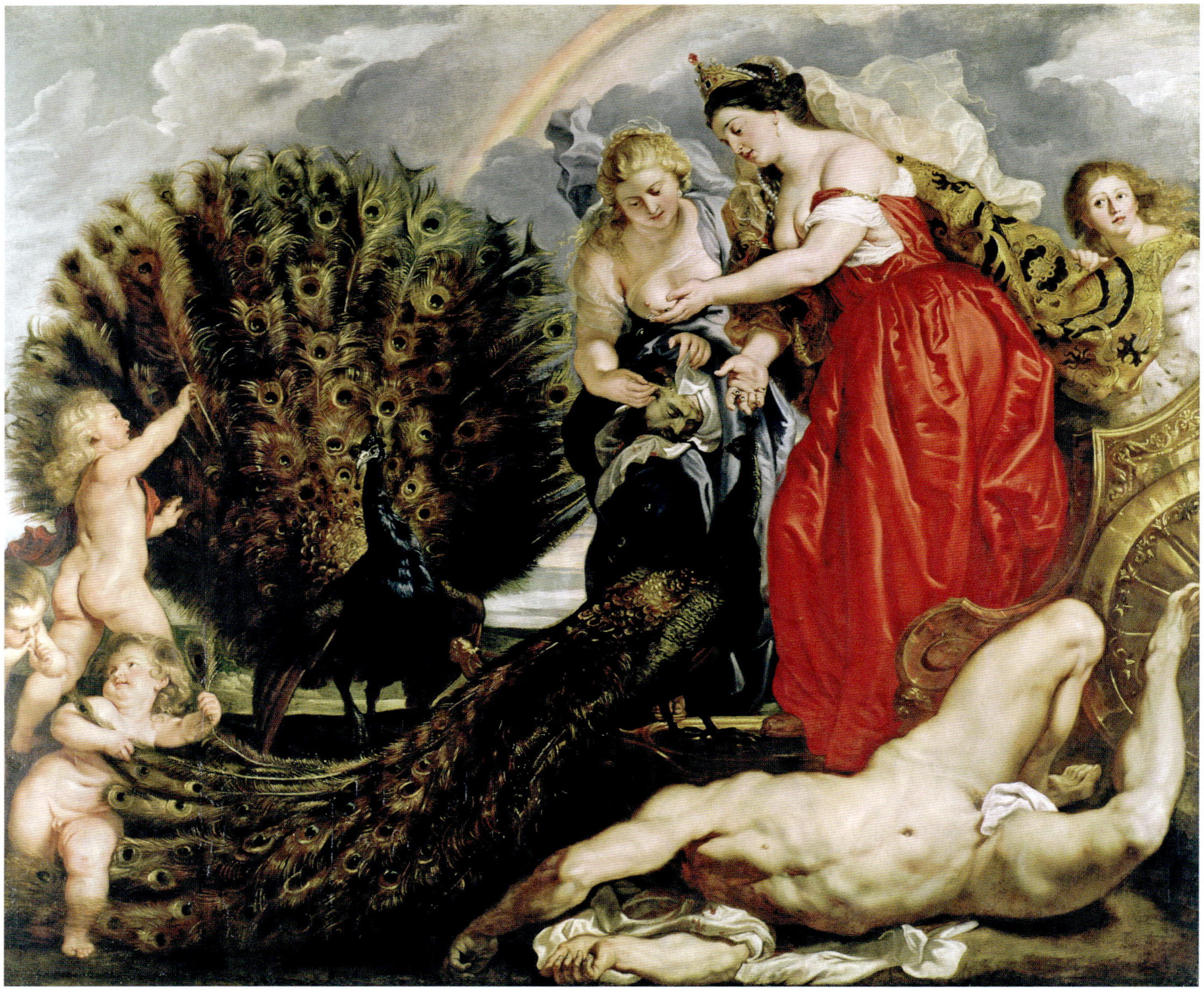

Frans Snyders
(1579–1657) (studio of)
The Fox and the Crane
c. 1630–40
Oil on canvas
119 × 201 cm (46⅞ × 79⅛ in.)
Private collection

This painting illustrates a classic tale of revenge, as told in Aesop's fables, which are said to have been written down in the fifth century BC. It also shows the folly of playing a joke on someone unless you are prepared to have it returned. A wily fox invited a crane to supper, but the meal, served in a flat dish, was a soup made of pulses, which the crane found impossible to eat as it slipped out of his beak. When the crane reciprocated the invitation he served the meal in a long-necked flagon, perfectly accessible with his long beak but well out of reach of the fox. The fox in this painting certainly looks hungry and peeved in comparison to the nonchalant bird enjoying its food. The picture was created in the studio of Frans Snyders, a Flemish artist who specialized in still life and animal paintings, and who was sometimes employed by other artists, such as Rubens, to paint the animals in their composite canvases.

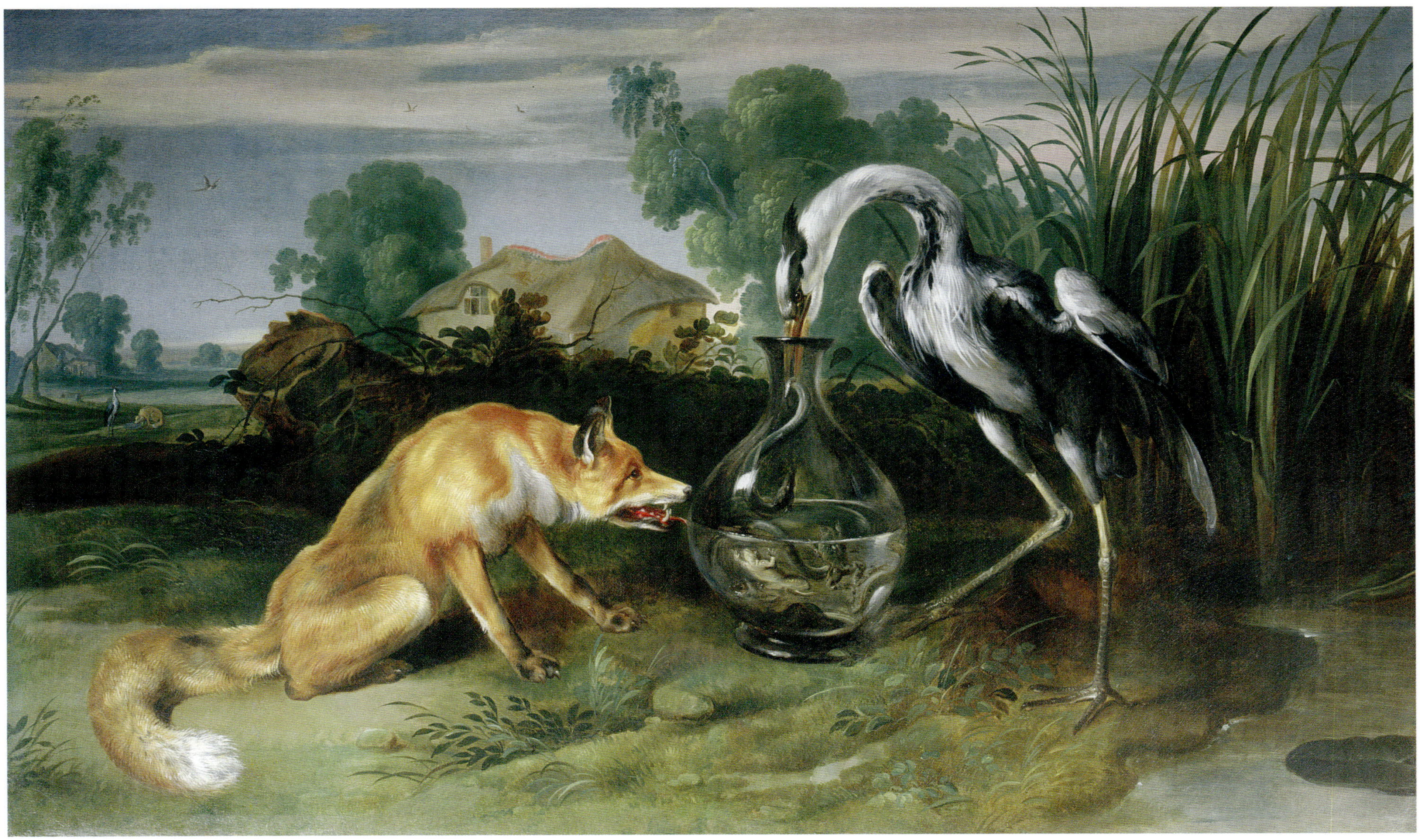

Simon Vouet
(1590–1649)
Allegorical Portrait of Anne of Austria as Minerva
1644
Oil on canvas
202 × 172 cm (79½ × 67¾ in.)
The State Hermitage Museum, St Petersburg

The Roman goddess Minerva (Greek: Athena) was said to have spread the virtues of civilization. Although in her earliest form she was a goddess of war (hence the armour in which she is often portrayed), she fought only for justice. But, above all, she was seen as the embodiment of wisdom and was invoked as a patroness of learned institutions. The owl with which she is frequently shown alludes to this aspect of her character. This portrait of Anne of Austria, the widow of Louis XIII, created by the French court artist Simon Vouet depicts the queen in the guise of Minerva. Prominent among the goddess's traditional attributes is the owl, seen peeping out from behind Anne's right foot. The implication is that the French queen possesses the goddess's finest qualities, particularly her good judgement.

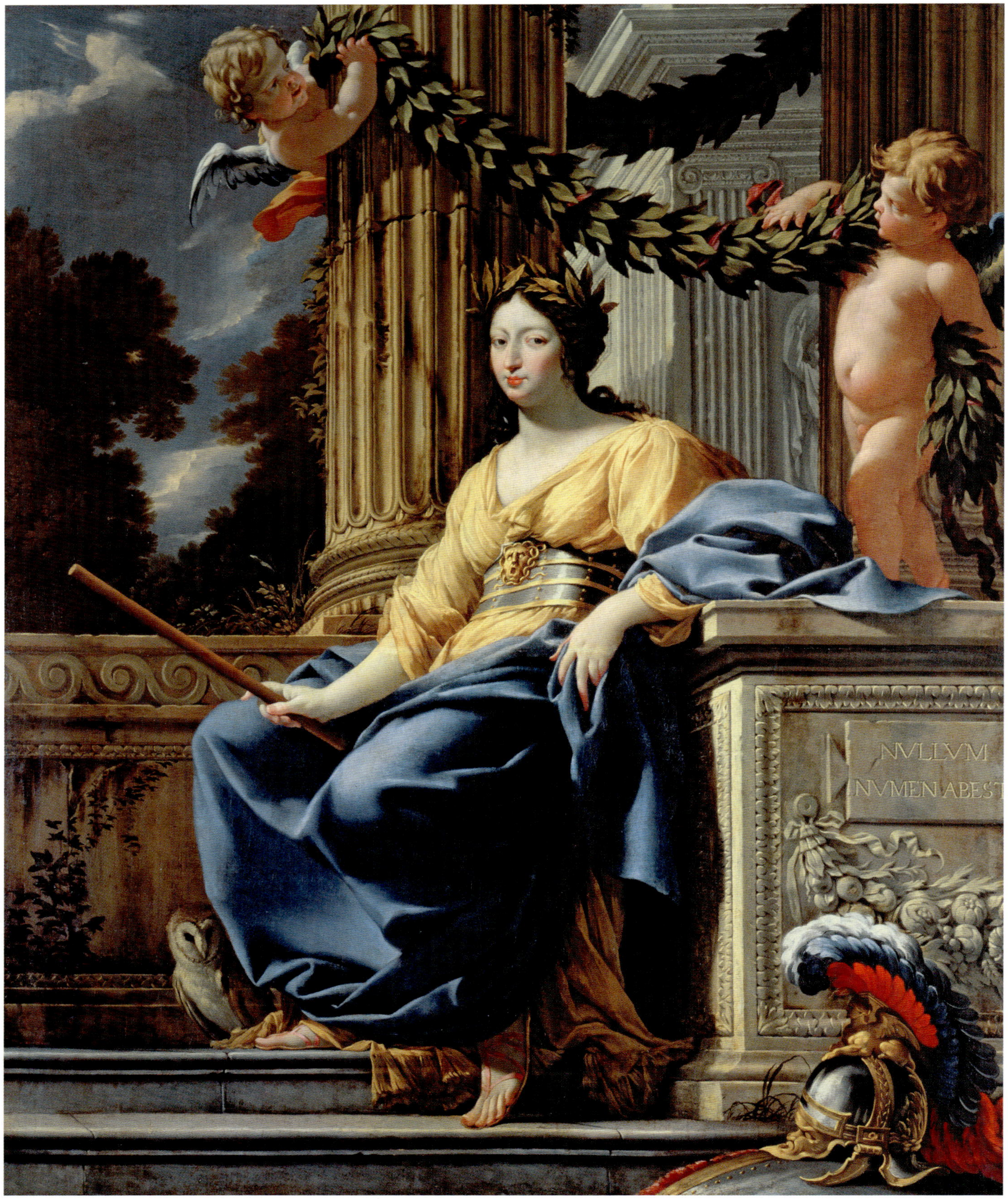

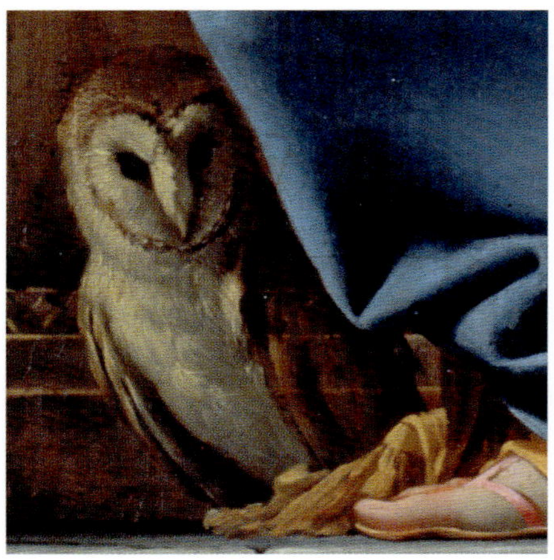

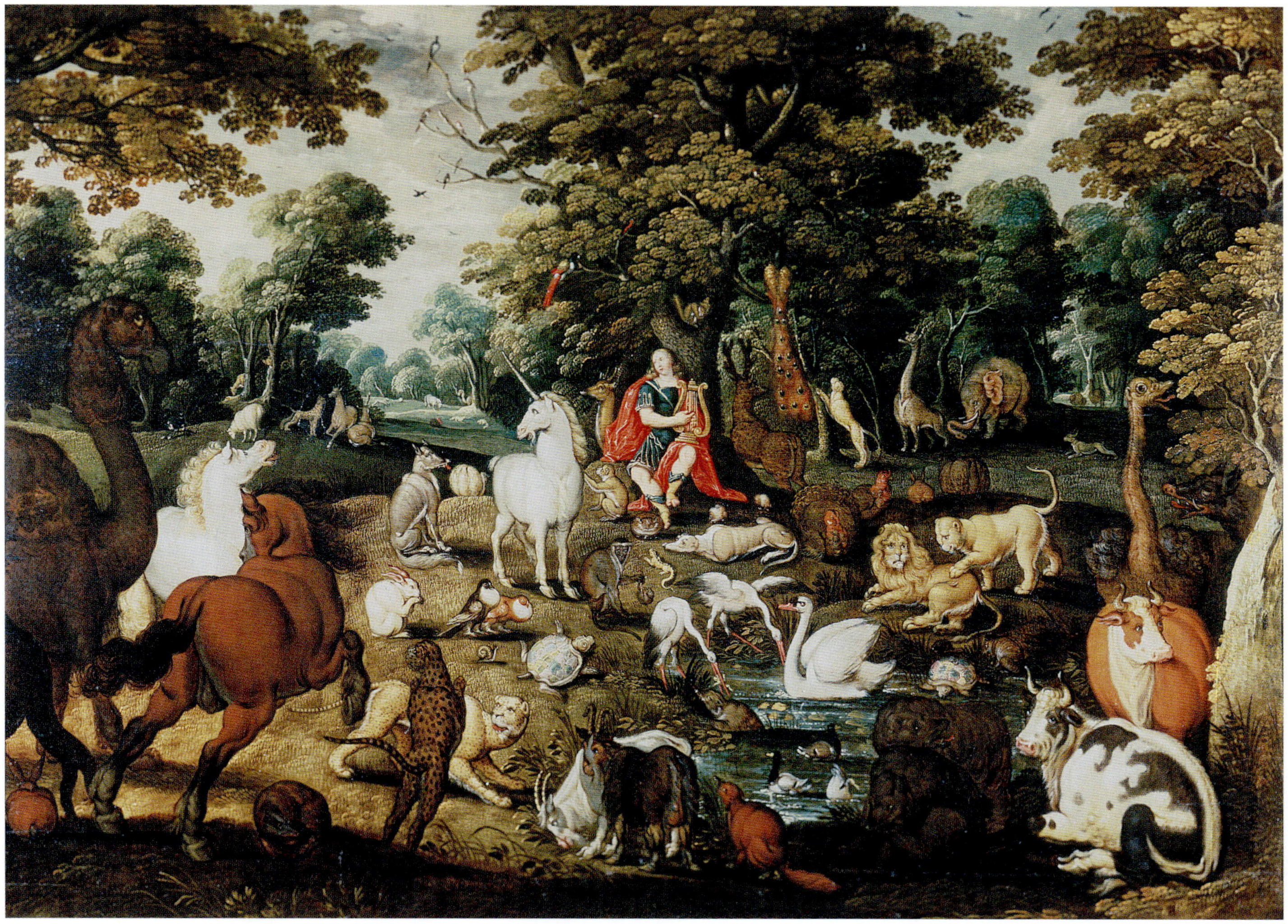

Jacob Bouttats
(1660–1718)
Orpheus Charming the Animals
n.d.
Oil on canvas
Dimensions unknown
Private collection

The Greek myth of Orpheus was a favourite theme for northern European artists in the Renaissance and Baroque periods. The Thracian poet is said to have played his lyre so sweetly that the animals and birds gathered around him, and were charmed into subduing their innate hostilities. He has certainly attracted a vast menagerie in this painting, including some mythical animals, such as the unicorn. Prominent among the creatures are the waterfowl (including a magnificent mute swan in the middle of the pond, and storks flapping wings that lack the customary black tips) and birds with puffed-out chests, which could be based on pigeons. A peacock and a macaw perch on branches near the singing poet, and smaller birds fly in from the distance, drawn by the melodies, while an ostrich squawks away on the right. The Flemish artist Jacob Bouttats specialized in paintings of the animal kingdom, focusing on such subjects as Noah's Ark and Paradise, in the tradition of Jan Breughel the Elder.

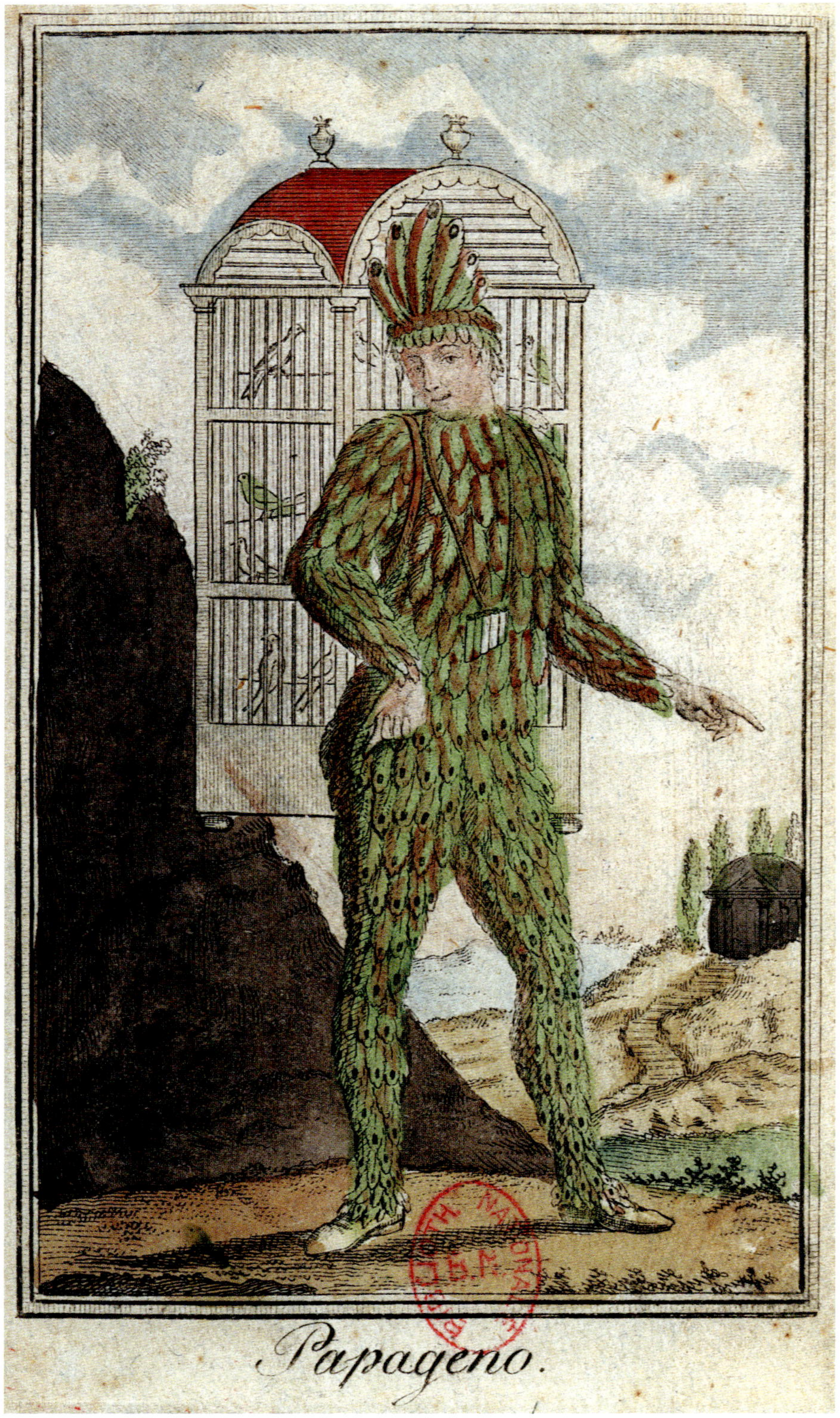

Italian

Papageno, the Bird Catcher

c. 1791

Coloured engraving

Bibliothèque-Musée de l'Opéra de Paris

In Mozart's opera *The Magic Flute*, Papageno is the bird-catcher, in a costume composed entirely of bird feathers. He is also equipped with a set of pan pipes to charm the birds (perhaps imitating their mating calls), and magic bells. He is the comical foil to the hero, Tamino, and accompanies him on his mission to rescue Pamina, to whom Tamino is promised in marriage. Papageno manages to fail the various trials of initiation that Tamino passes, but still wins his own woman in the end – Papagena, a beautiful female bird-catcher. This engraving appeared as the frontispiece to the original edition of the libretto of *The Magic Flute*, and it shows the baritone Emanuel Schikaneder (who also wrote the libretto) in his role as the first Papageno. The character's name is immediately suggestive of a parrot (*pappagallo* in Italian), and the green colour of his costume suggests the parrot's bright plumage.

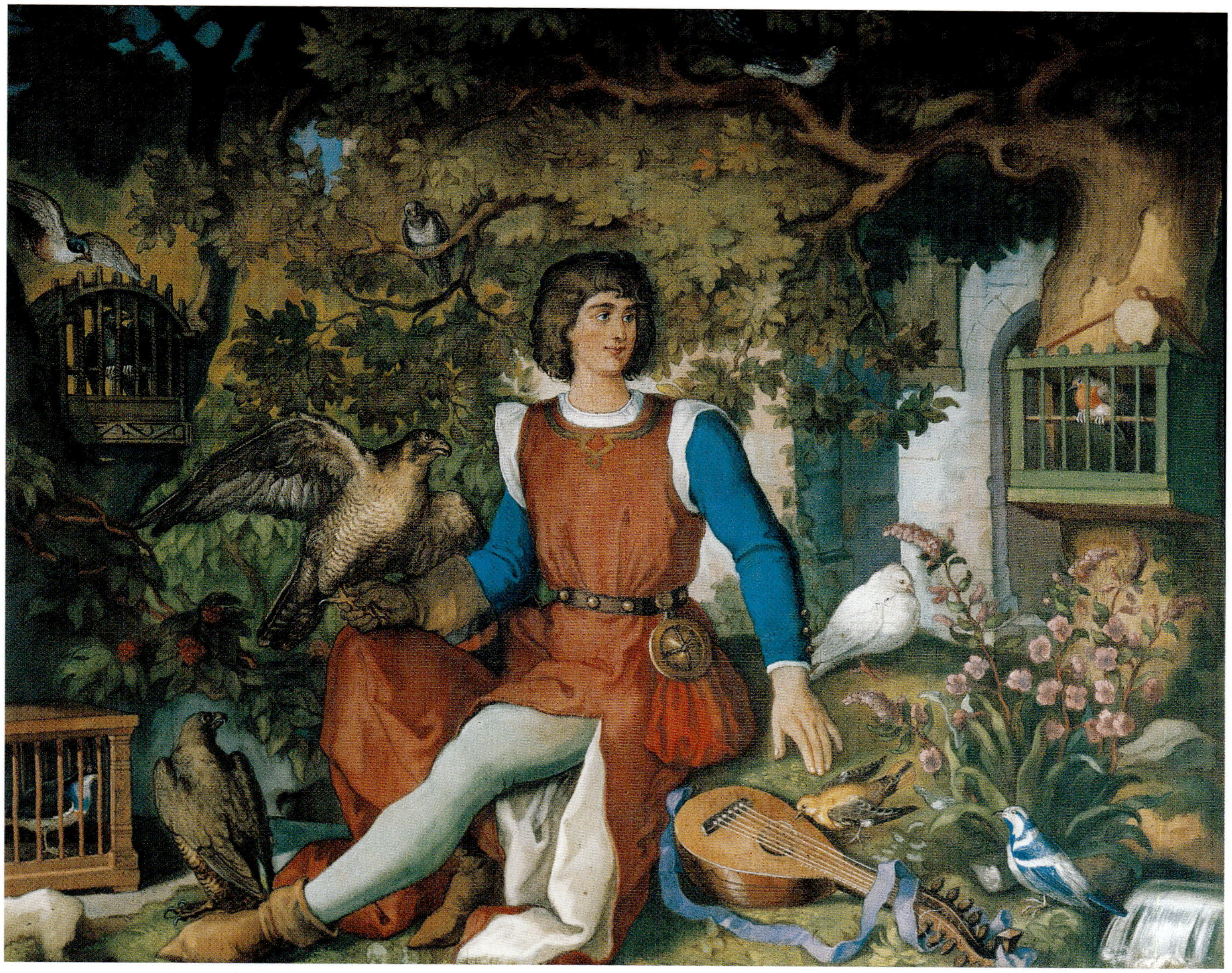

Eduard Ille
(1823–1900)
Portrait of Walther von der Vogelweide
c. 1881–92
Mural
Schloss Neuschwanstein, Bavaria

Walther von der Vogelweide (*c.* 1170–*c.* 1230) was a celebrated German medieval lyric poet or *Minnesinger*. Not much is known about him other than what can be gleaned from his surviving poems and lyrics. It is assumed that he belonged to the minor nobility, and his name means 'bird meadow': a gathering-place of birds common in many German towns, where hawks and songbirds were caught. He appears as a character in the Tannhäuser saga, and the composer Richard Wagner introduced him into two of his operas. This is one of the murals illustrating Walther's life in King Ludwig of Bavaria's castle, Neuschwanstein. It shows the poet surrounded by birds, which have inspired his songs. As befits a young nobleman, he has a hawk on his wrist, but he is also captivated by the tunes of the caged birds around him, and has laid down his lute to listen to them. Henry Longfellow's poem about Walther pays tribute to the poet's tender feeling for birds, stating that on his death he left a bequest so that the monks at Würzburg, where he was buried, could feed them every day.

Richard Westall (1765–1836)

Lady Charlotte Harley as Hebe

c. 1813
Oil on canvas
Dimensions unknown
Treasurer's House, Martock, Somerset

Richard Westall's portrait of a young aristocratic girl shows her in the guise of the Greek goddess Hebe (Roman: Juventus), the personification of youth and beauty. She is the daughter of Zeus and Hera (Jupiter and Juno), and a cup-bearer and handmaiden to the gods, feeding them nectar to grant them everlasting youth. Here the eagle of Zeus drinks from the cup of nectar she holds, while two doves – attributes of Aphrodite – flit around in the sky above her. Portraitists in the eighteenth century sometimes showed their female sitters as Hebe as a way of paying tribute to their youthful beauty. The lovely Lady Charlotte inspired the figure of Ianthe in Lord Byron's *Childe Harold's Pilgrimage* (the poet was one of her mother's lovers). Charlotte married Anthony Bacon, a hero of the Battle of Waterloo, and was the great-great-grandmother of the painter Francis Bacon.

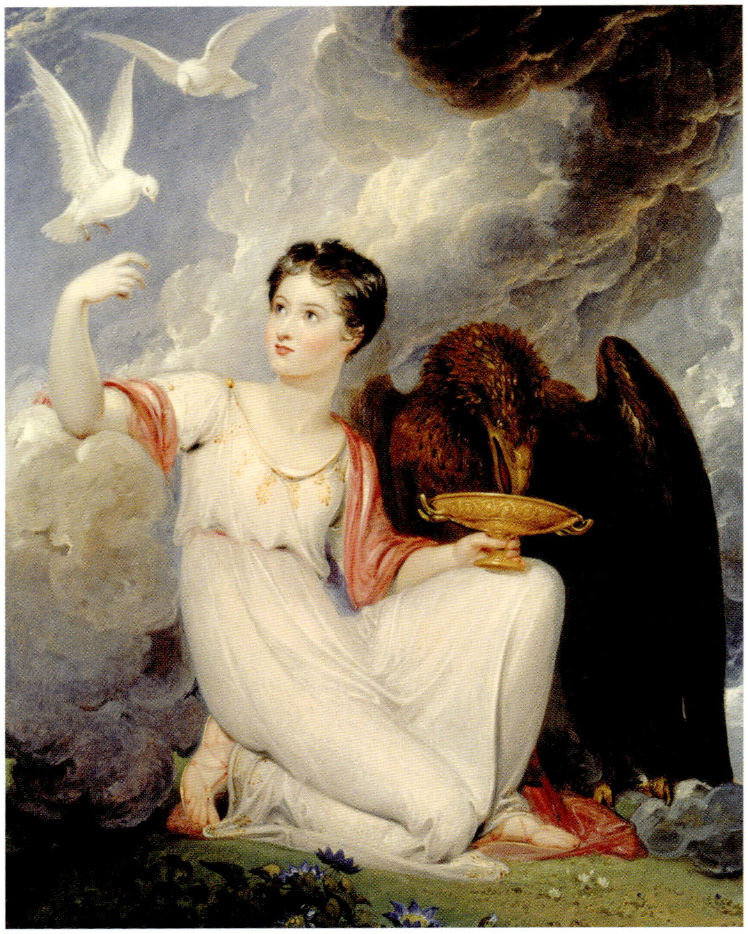

Jean-Louis-Cesar Lair (1781–1828)

The Torture of Prometheus

1819
Oil on canvas
290 × 228 cm (114⅛ × 89¾ in.)
Musée Crozatier, Le Puy-en-Velay, France

In Roman mythology, the Titan Prometheus created a human being from clay and stole fire from the gods. He was punished by Jupiter, who had him chained to a rock and sent an eagle to feed on his liver every day. The liver renewed itself overnight, allowing the whole cycle to begin afresh each morning. Eventually Hercules released him from this torture by killing the eagle. The scene of Prometheus bound has been depicted by artists since antiquity; the images usually show Prometheus naked and outstretched on a rock, shackled by his wrists and ankles, while the eagle pecks away at his side. The French artist Lair has replaced the rock with a column, portraying his Prometheus as a perfect youth, in keeping with the Neoclassical taste of his time. The Prometheus myth is similar to the Greek legend of Tityus, a giant who tried to rape Apollo's mother and was punished by being pegged to the ground while two vultures tore at his liver.

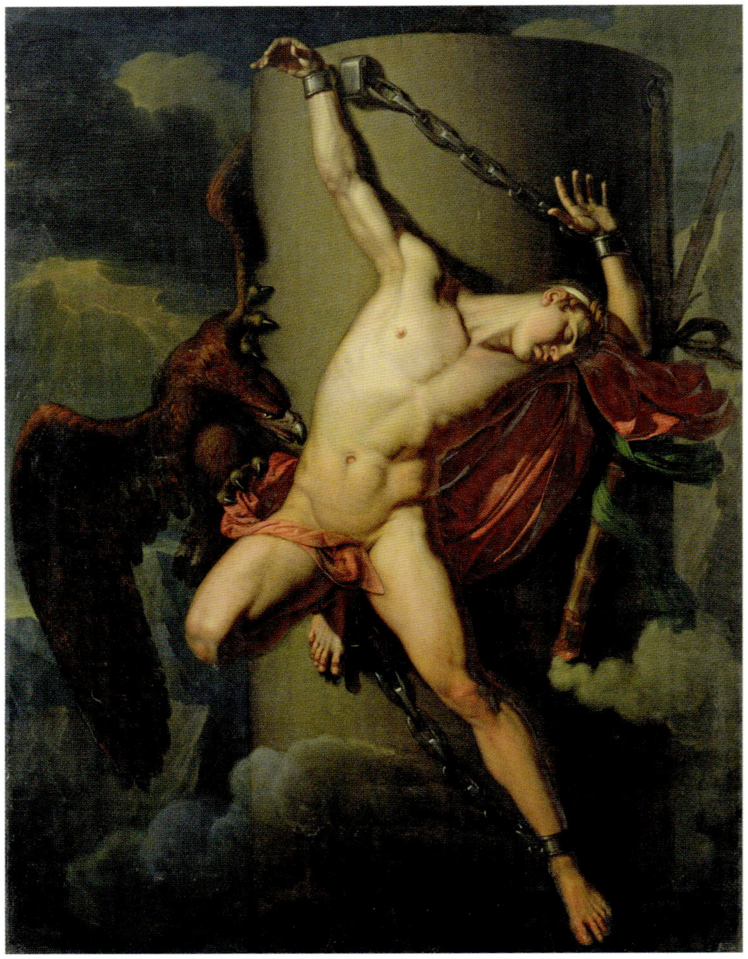

Sebastiano Mazzolino
(active 19th century)
An Allegory of Spring
19th century
Oil on canvas
61 × 48.3 cm (24 × 19 in.)
Private collection

There is a long tradition, dating back to antiquity, of representing the four seasons as figures. In Roman frescoes, spring is usually personified as a young woman with garlands in her hair, and in some Renaissance works the figure is identified as the goddess Flora. Painters in the nineteenth century sometimes added a tame bird to their allegories of spring; perhaps in a cage, being captured or held on a piece of string. This young woman is holding her pet bird on a short leash, allowing it a gentle flutter but keeping a vigilant eye on it to ensure that it does not stray. Despite the wealth of blooms and décolletage, the viewer's eye inevitably follows the young woman's to rest on the bird as it struggles to escape. Little is known about the artist, but the picture has a companion showing a maiden as summer with corn in her hair.

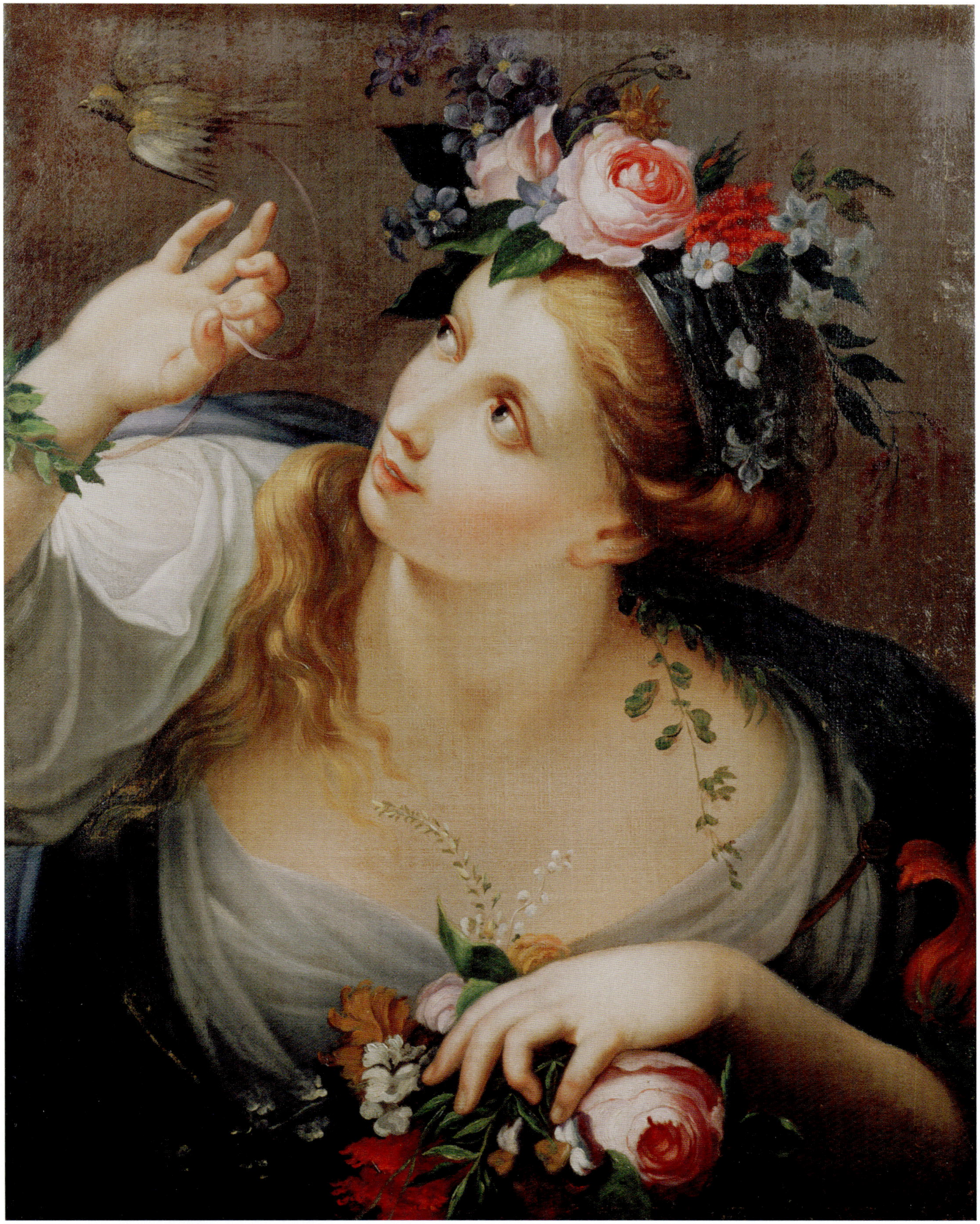

Gustave Doré
(1832–1883)
Harpies

1861
Engraving
Dimensions unknown
Bibliothèque des Arts Décoratifs, Paris

In Inferno XIII of his *Divine Comedy*, the Italian poet Dante describes travelling through a terrible wood haunted by harpies. These composite demons have broad wings, human faces and necks, clawed feet and fat bellies covered with feathers. They call out dreadful lamentations as they nest in trees that encase the bodies of those who have committed suicide. This engraving is one of a complete set produced by the French artist Gustave Doré to illustrate the *Divine Comedy*. His harpies are ugly bird–women, who perch menacingly in the branches looking towards the approaching figures of Dante and Virgil. The extreme tonal contrast serves only to heighten the horror of the image. The notion of the harpy has its origins in Greek mythology, where the word denotes a hideous winged female monster associated with the wind and storms, and which steals food or snatches people away.

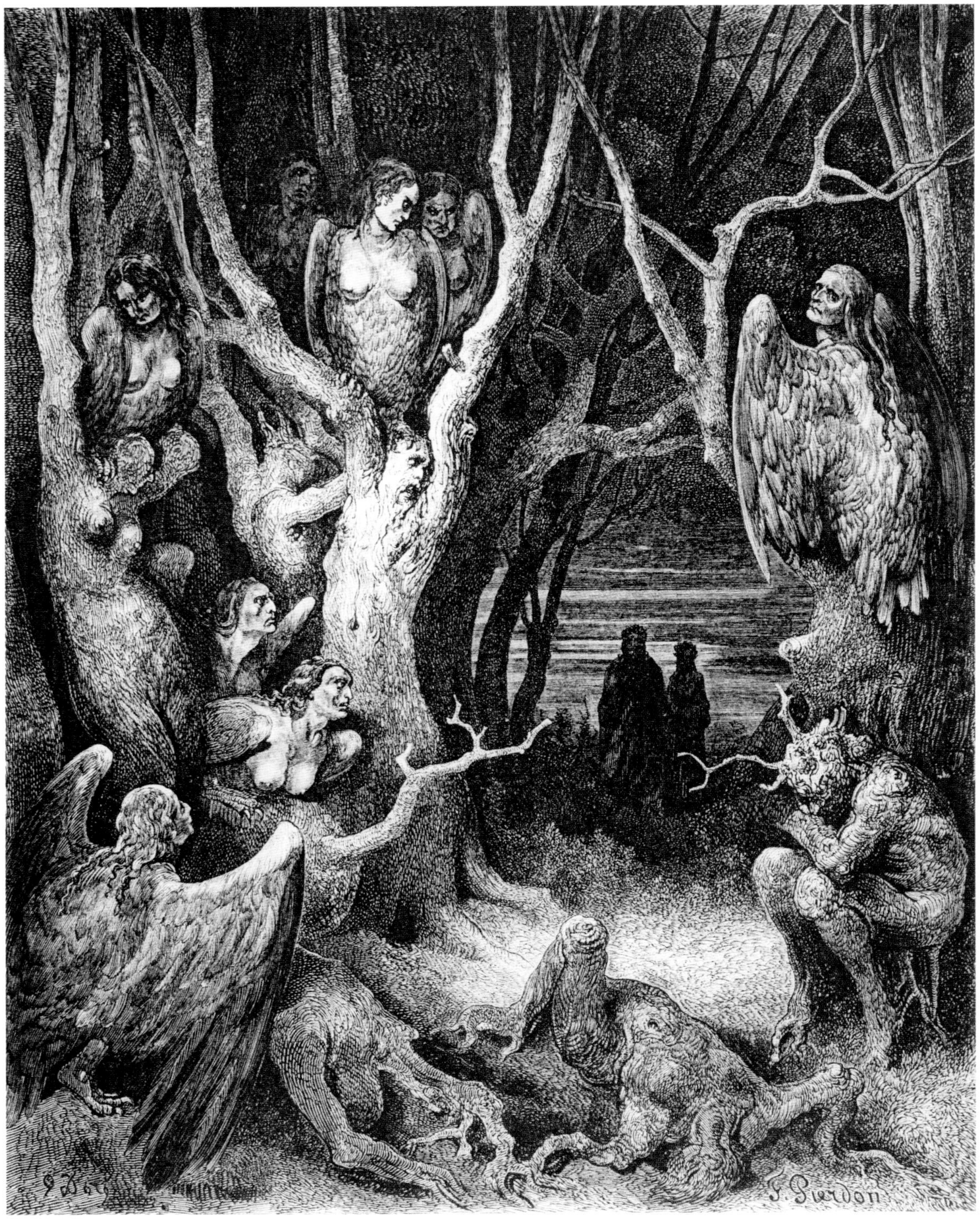

John Anster Fitzgerald
(1832–1906)
The Death of Cock Robin

c. 1865
Oil on canvas
Dimensions unknown
Private collection

John Anster Fitzgerald painted fairy subjects and dreamlands, often with a dark undertow. He produced a number of canvases illustrating the English ballad *Who Killed Cock Robin?*, which was first published in 1744 although its folk origins are probably older. The poem begins with the sparrow owning up to the murder, and moves on to the funeral arrangements. The owl volunteers to dig the grave, the rook to act as the parson, and the dove to take on the role of chief mourner. The kite offers to carry the coffin, the wren, cock and hen volunteer as pall-bearers and the thrush offers to sing a psalm. The poem ends: 'All the birds of the air fell a-sighing and a-sobbing,/ When they heard the bell toll for poor Cock Robin.' But in this picture it is the fairies who are the robin's chief mourners, and there is not another bird in sight.

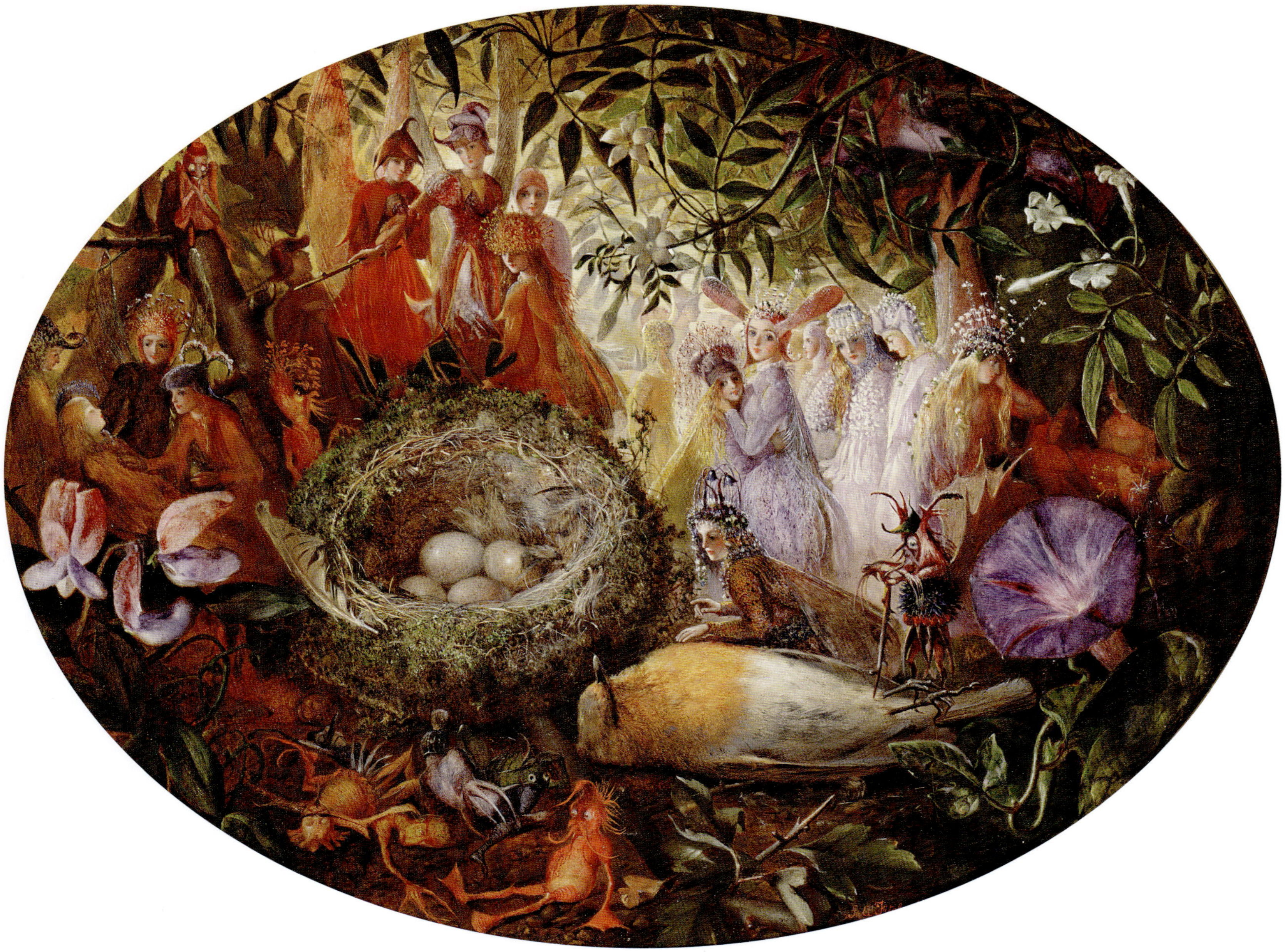

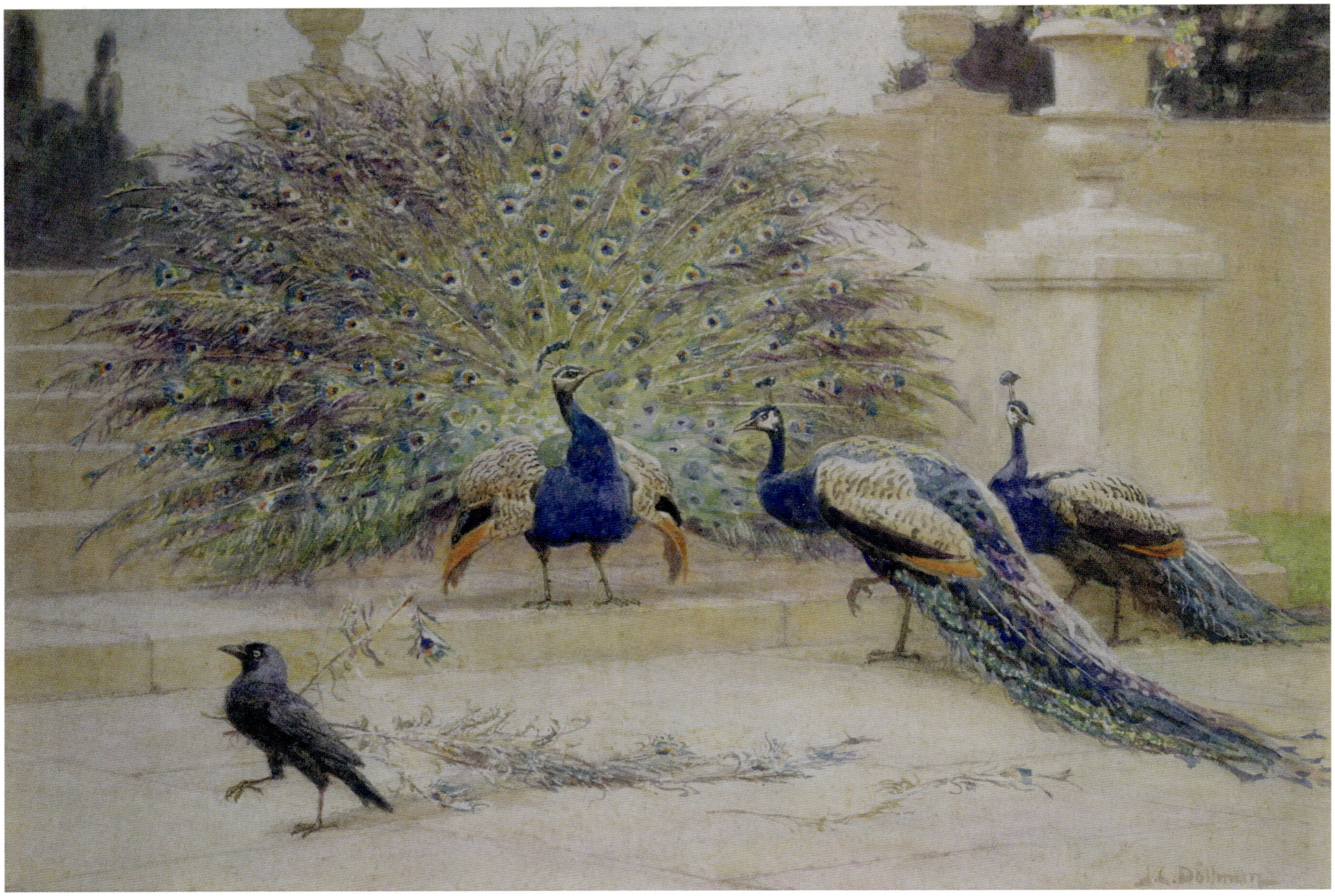

John Charles Dollman
(1851–1934)
The Borrowed Plume
n.d.
Watercolour on paper
25.4 × 37.4 cm (10 × 14¾ in.)
Private collection

One of Aesop's fables tells the story of a vain jackdaw, who decided that by decking himself out in colourful feathers he would be able to pass as a peacock. Strutting about in his borrowed finery, he abandoned his previous companions and attempted to mix with these elegant birds. But the peacocks soon spotted the imposter in their midst by his affected strutting, and stripped him of his new plumage, returning him to the other jackdaws, who now despised him. The moral of the tale is that those who try to ape the outward show of their superiors rarely get away with it, and are usually mocked by their equals. Dollman shows the bedraggled jackdaw marching off with his wounded pride, trailing a few remaining peacock feathers, while one of his tormentors fans out his tail in a magnificent display.

Walter Crane
(1845–1915)
The Swan Maidens

1894
Oil and mixed media on paper
27.2 × 20 cm (10⅝ × 7⅞ in.)
Private collection

Myths from around the world tell of human beings who transform themselves into swans – indeed, that is the premise behind Tchaikovsky's famous ballet *Swan Lake*, which is based on a Russian folk tale. Walter Crane's painting illustrates a European version of the legend, in which a young hunter falls in love with a swan maiden when he sees her bathing with her six sisters. He steals her swan robe so that she cannot fly away, and marries her. They live happily together and have children. But one day one of their children finds the hidden swan cloak and gives it to her mother, who uses it to fly back to her family. The husband has to undertake a long and difficult journey before he finds her and they are reunited. Crane has chosen to depict the beginning of the narrative, as the seven maidens have just finished bathing together and are putting on their swan garments. The girl in the pool is clearly the one who will be left behind in the land of the mortals.

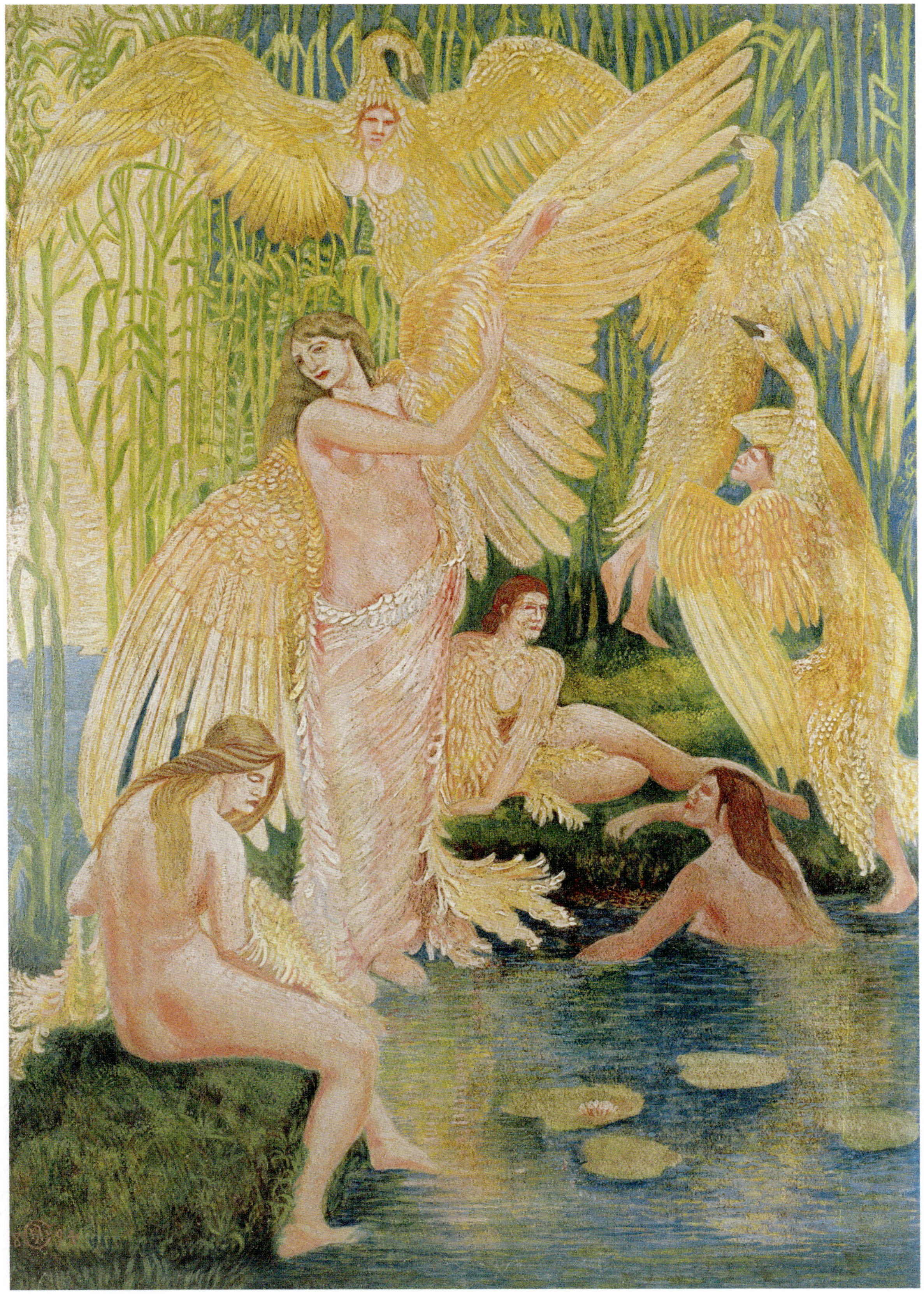

Sir Edward John Poynter (1836–1919)

Lesbia and Her Sparrow

1907
Oil on canvas
49 × 37 cm (19¼ × 14½ in.)
Private collection

The mythical Lesbia was based on Clodia Metelli, the lover of the Latin poet Catullus, who lived in the first century BC, and she is the subject of more than twenty poems by him. Two of the verses centre on her pet sparrow, saying that she loved it more than herself, that it treated her as a mother, nestling in her breast, nipping at her fingers, never straying far from her lap, and chirruping to her alone. Catullus recorded Lesbia's extreme grief and endless weeping when it died. The Victorian painter Edward Poynter portrays her gazing fondly at the tame bird perching on her wrist, unaware of its sad fate to come. The inclusion of the birdcage implies that it is a captive rather than a wild bird. In art, sparrows in the hands of young women can stand for wantonness or lust, and it has been suggested that the bird here carries erotic overtones as well as symbolizing the poet's enduring love.

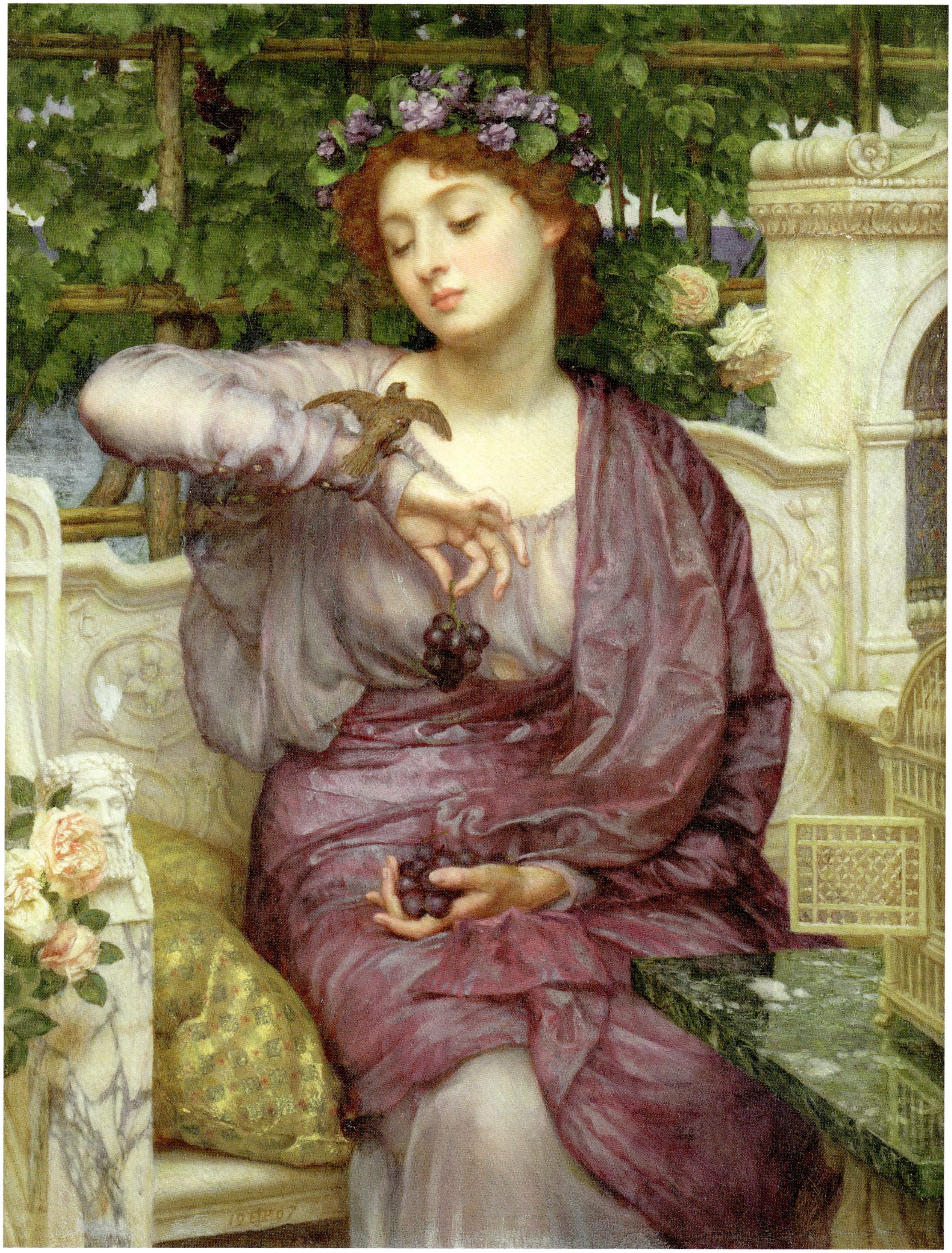

Arthur Rackham
(1867–1939)
The Ravens of Wotan

1924
Colour lithograph
Dimensions unknown
The Stapleton Collection

In Wagner's opera *Twilight of the Gods* (*Götterdämmerung*), which draws on various Norse myths, the two ravens, Hugin (Mind) and Munin (Memory), are constantly bringing messages to the god Wotan. Arthur Rackham's illustration – one of a suite of images based on Wagner's Ring cycle – shows the two ravens alone in a bleak landscape, the very epitome of menace. They play a small but important part in the drama. Just before his death in the third act of *Twilight of the Gods*, the hero, Siegfried, is distracted by the ravens, and when he turns to observe them his enemy Hagen thrusts a spear into his back and kills him. Then, in the climactic scene of both this opera and the whole of the Ring cycle, Brünnhilde sends the ravens forth to summon the fire god Loge, sending him to Valhalla to set fire to the great palace of the gods.

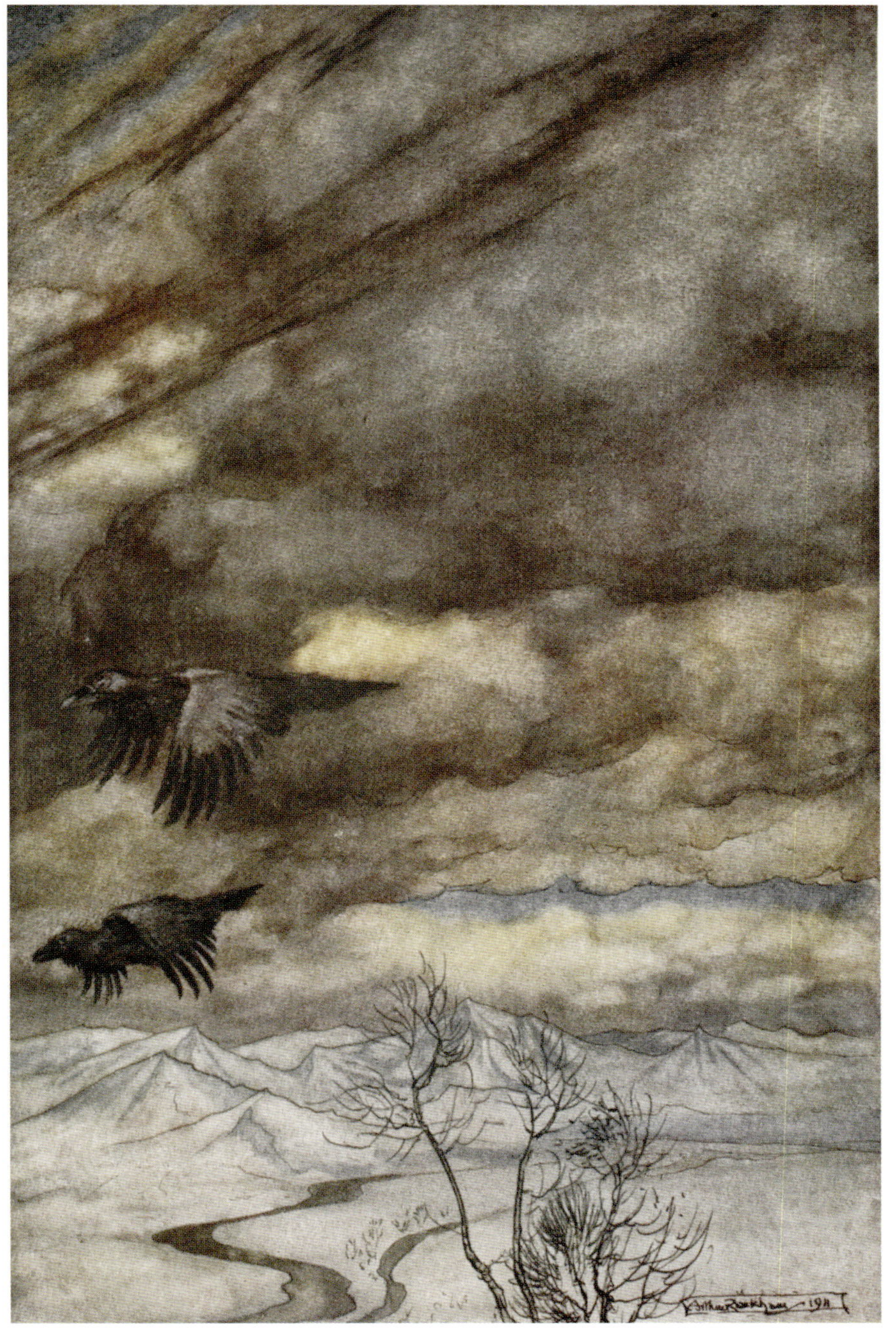

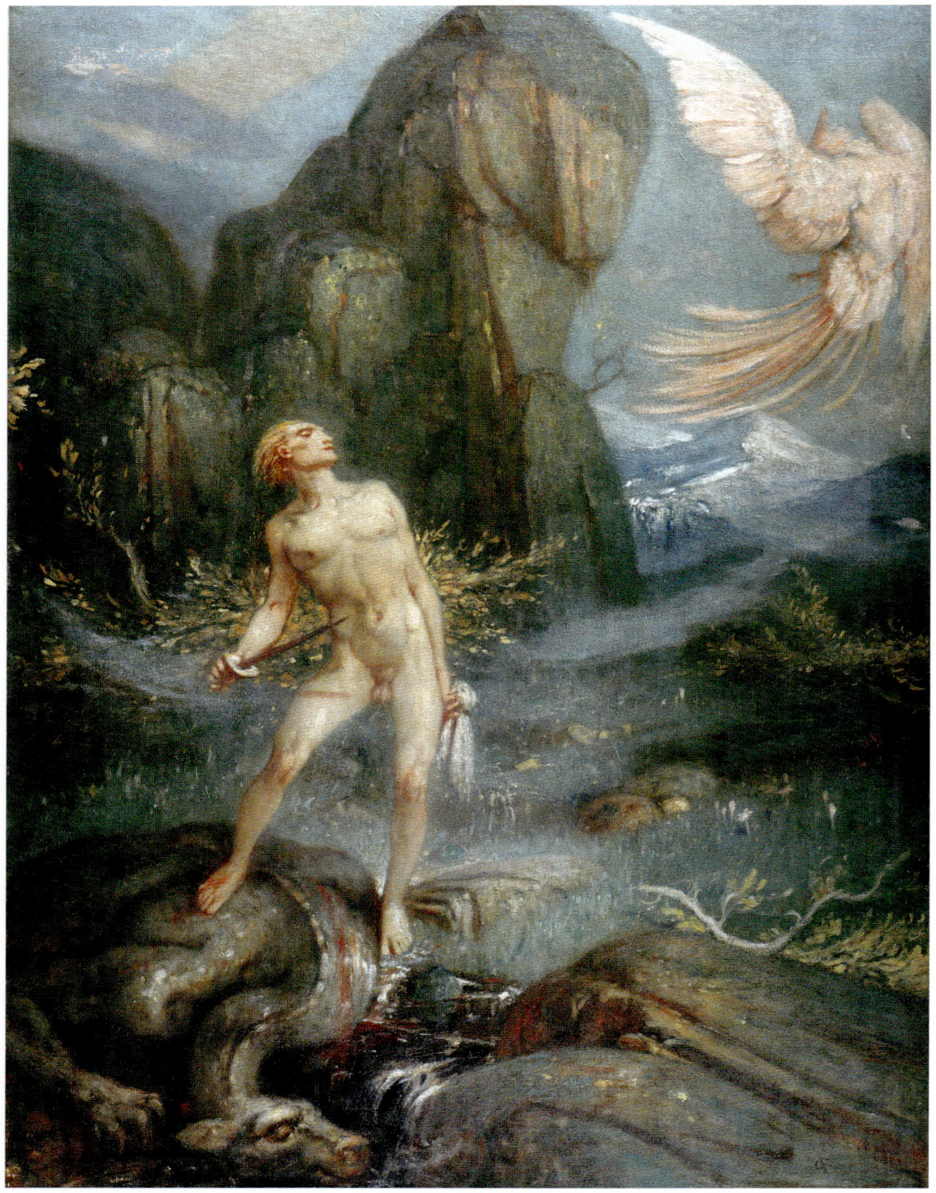

Charles Ricketts
(1866–1931)
Siegfried and the Magic Bird
c. 1930
Oil on canvas
117 × 90 cm (46 × 35⅜ in.)
Herbert Art Gallery & Museum, Coventry

An ancient Norse myth, retold in Wagner's Ring cycle, tells how Siegfried kills Fafnir the dragon, and when he tastes the creature's blood he acquires the ability to understand what a forest bird is saying to him. The instructions the bird gives him play a crucial role in subsequent events, leading him to the magical Ring and ultimately to the maiden Brünnhilde. It is a tale of daring and heroic deeds, but there is not much Teutonic muscularity about this scene, which contains more than a hint of theatrical decadence. That may be partly because of Ricketts's work as a theatre designer, his friendship with Oscar Wilde and those in his circle, and his admiration for the work of the *fin-de-siècle* artist Gustave Moreau. The bird is not a humble denizen of the forest but a fantastical creature whose message causes the naked Siegfried, standing on top of the dragon's corpse, to swoon with ecstasy.

Russian school
Icon depicting a sirin

18th century
Oil on panel
41 × 32 cm ($16\frac{1}{8}$ × $12\frac{5}{8}$ in.)
Ikonen-Museum, Recklinghausen, Germany

The Russian sirin, like the harpy, is half woman and half bird. In common with the siren of Greek myth, who lured sailors to their death, the sirin was originally said to be dangerous to humans, as anyone who heard it sing would forget everything to follow it, and ultimately die. Not surprisingly, people would attempt to scare it away with loud noises. However, in the seventeenth and eighteenth centuries the creature's malevolent aspects were toned down, and the sirin became associated with happiness and world harmony, since it was said to live near Eden. The sirin is usually depicted wearing a crown, and sometimes its head is surrounded by a nimbus like that of a saint; the halo and the faintly ecclesiastical garb on the sirin's upper body here certainly have a Christian resonance. Two other bird–women feature in Russian myth: the *alkonost*, with its song that also lulls human beings into forgetfulness, and the *gamayun*, or bird of wisdom.

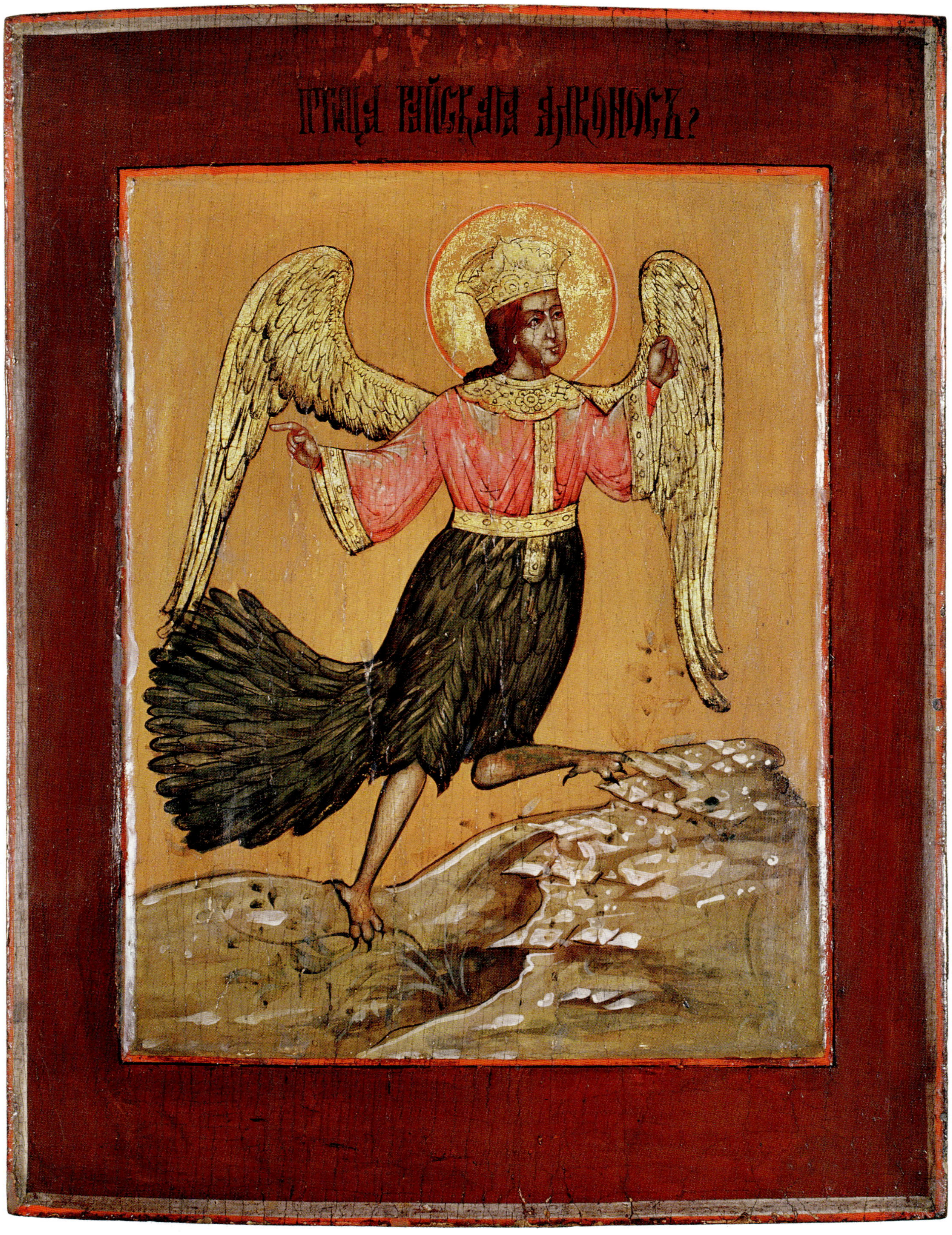

Aztec

An Eagle Knight (detail)

Date unknown

Stone

Museo del Templo Mayor, Mexico City

Birds feature prominently in the mythology of the Aztecs, the ancient inhabitants of Mexico. The country's capital city is even said to have been founded when the god Huitzilopochtli (whose name means 'the hummingbird of the south', or 'the left-handed hummingbird') guided the Aztecs to an island in the middle of a lake, where an eagle was spotted perching on a cactus plant. To this day the golden eagle is Mexico's national emblem and appears on its flag. Eagle knights were a special elite warrior class in the Aztec army, and were venerated for their bravery. The headgear of the eagle warrior was the bird's head, and this detail of a statue shows the soldier's face emerging from the beak. His body is covered with feathers, his feet are talons and he has wings. The extraordinarily modern-looking sculpture was found during the excavation of one of the city's main temples, the Templo Mayor, which was constructed some time after 1325 and rebuilt many times before it was destroyed by the Spanish in 1521.

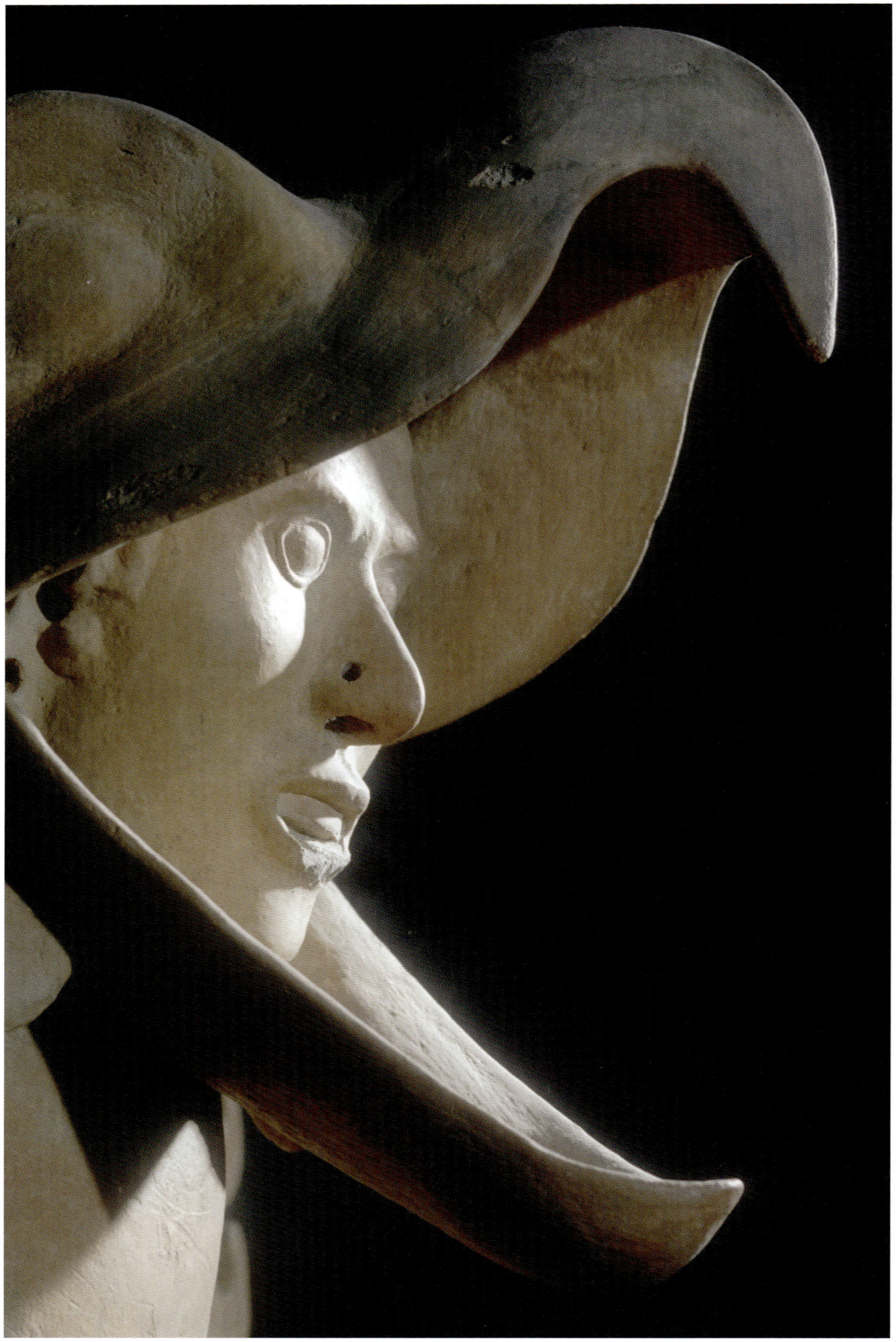

Haida artist
Thunderbird

Date unknown
Painted wood
Dimensions unknown
Peter Newark American Pictures Collection

In Native American legend, the thunderbird is one of the great forces of nature – a cause of the rainstorms that water the vegetation. When it flaps its wings it stirs the wind and brings thunder, and lightning flashes from its eyes and beak. It keeps lightning snakes under its wings to help kill whales, its favourite food. The thunderbird appears frequently in the songs and art of North America, where it is usually shown with a hooked beak and multicoloured wings. Debates have raged over whether it is based on any particular bird, but the creature it resembles most is an eagle. This statue was made by an artist of the Haida people, who live on the Pacific North-west coast of America, and are known for their stylized wooden carvings (particularly totem poles) as well as for their weaving and jewellery-making.

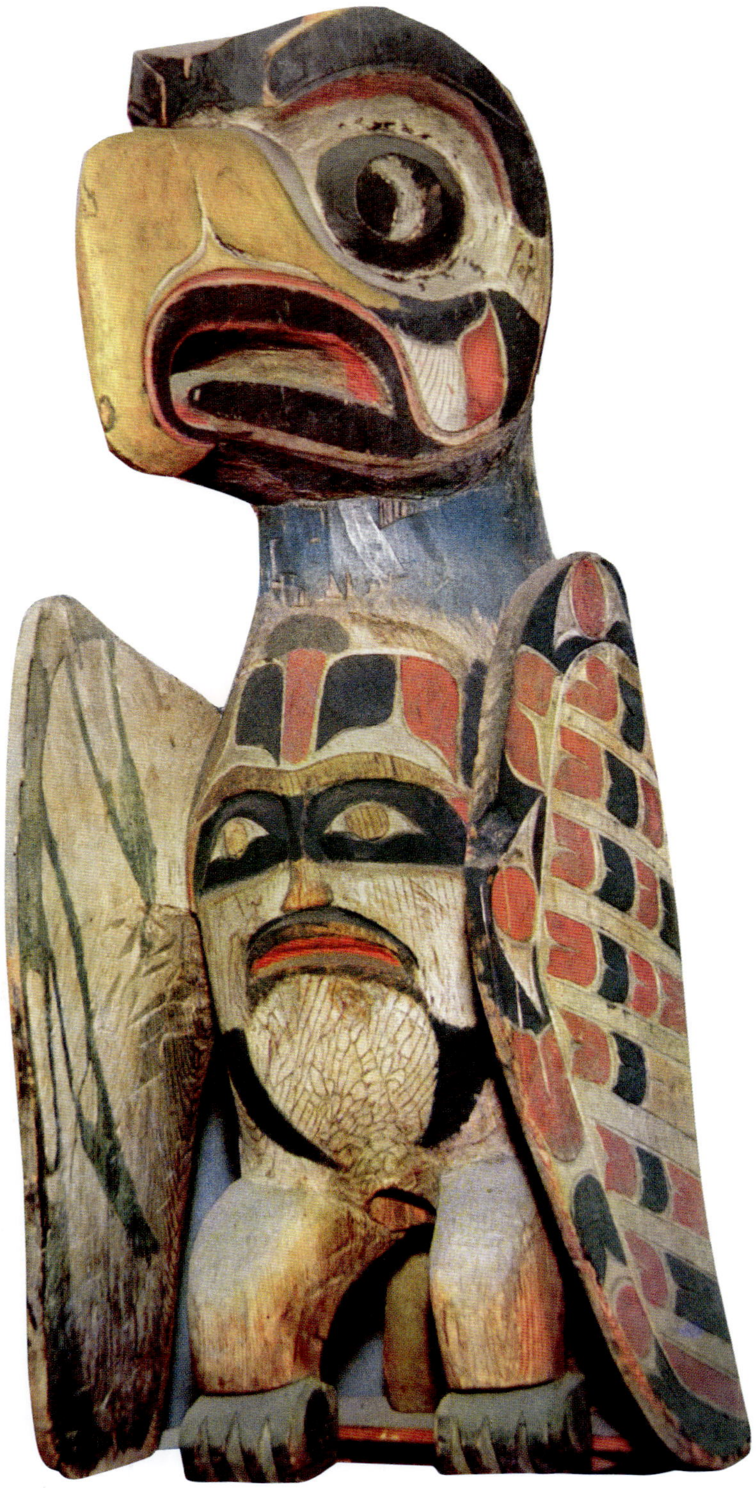

The Hunter and the Hunted

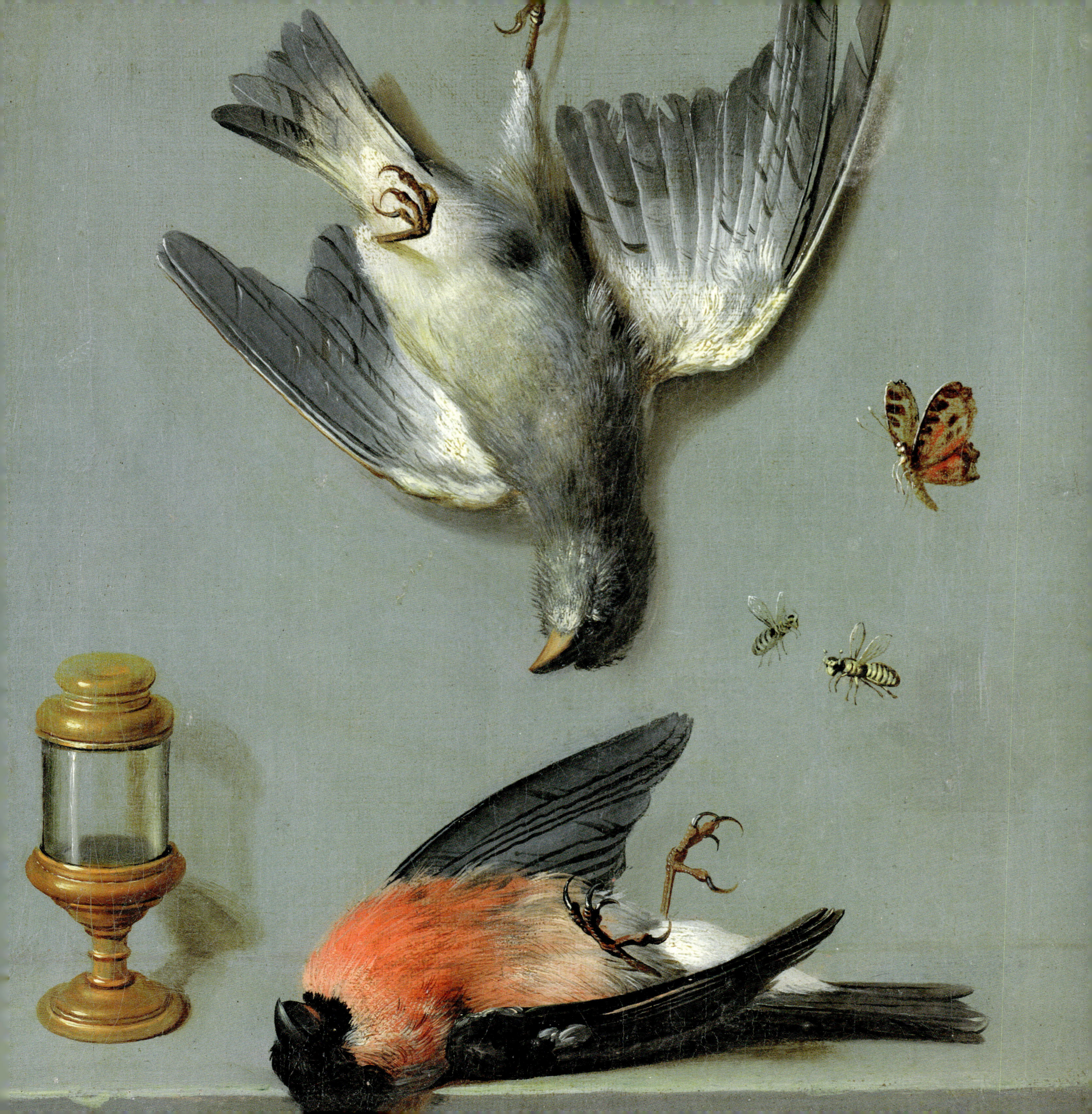

Men and women have hunted birds for food and for pleasure since time immemorial, as can be seen in early frescoes from ancient Egypt and Etruria, which depict men and youths in hot pursuit of them. But the use of trained birds of prey, such as falcons and hawks, to hunt other birds or small animals is a highly specialized sport bound up with class distinction, privilege and power. There is evidence to suggest that it originated in the Far East, and was introduced to Europe in the fourth century AD. During the Middle Ages and the Renaissance, when the sport was at its height in Europe, it was the noble pastime of kings and princes, and valued as useful training for war. Indeed, Frederick II of Hohenstaufen, the Holy Roman Emperor himself, even wrote a treatise on the subject in the thirteenth century.

A person's social standing dictated the type of bird he or she could use for hunting. *The Boke of St Albans* (1486), which details gentlemanly pursuits, including falconry, sets out fifteen birds of prey considered by the author, Dame Juliana Berners, to be appropriate for each rank. It is revealing more for the social status it accords each bird than as a practical guide to the sport. An emperor would use an eagle, vulture or merlin; a king a gyrfalcon; and a prince a falcon gentle. Lower down the social scale, a yeoman could use a goshawk, priests a sparrowhawk, and servants and children a kestrel. Interestingly, although it was intimately bound up with chivalry, hunting with birds was one sport open to women, as can be seen in some fifteenth-century miniatures. The illumination for the month of August in the fifteenth-century book of hours created for the Duc de Berry shows richly dressed women on horseback with falcons, as does the leaf from a fifteenth-century treatise on falconry reproduced opposite. Even the English queen Elizabeth I is said to have greatly enjoyed hunting with falcons. The popularity of the sport in royal and courtly circles had positive artistic consequences, as many of the artists employed by the nobility were required to produce hunting scenes to showcase the prowess of their masters, and this encouraged them to observe the birds and other creatures they kept at close quarters.

From the seventeenth century onwards, firearms gradually superseded hawks and falcons as hunting accessories; gunpowder was certainly a more efficient way of destroying large numbers of birds very rapidly. Painters were quick to pick up on the trophies of the hunt caught in this way, portraying mountains of game and birds piled high as evidence of the hunters' skill. More modest still lifes of dead game and hunting equipment, such as the one produced by Johannes Leemans (p. 131), pay a quieter tribute to the enjoyment of hunting. Hunting and trapping birds, or persuading them to fight one another, could also provide an excellent metaphor for amorous pursuit, and the French painters François Boucher and Jean-Léon Gérôme were among the many who exploited its erotic potential (pp. 133 and 139).

But hunting birds has not always been perceived as a noble pursuit. The Victorian artist G.F. Watts was horrified by the carnage, and his eloquent painting of a heron wounded in the name of sport accords the bird the heroic status of a sacrificial beast (p. 136). George Clausen's ragged boy scaring crows in a freezing winter field conveys the reality of keeping crops free of pests in the daily battle to make a living from the soil (p. 140). And Bruno Liljefors eliminated people from his hunting scene altogether, choosing to concentrate on the way birds hunt each other naturally, without human intervention. Although it was stage-managed by the artist, his composition conveys a real sense of nature red in tooth and claw (p. 137).

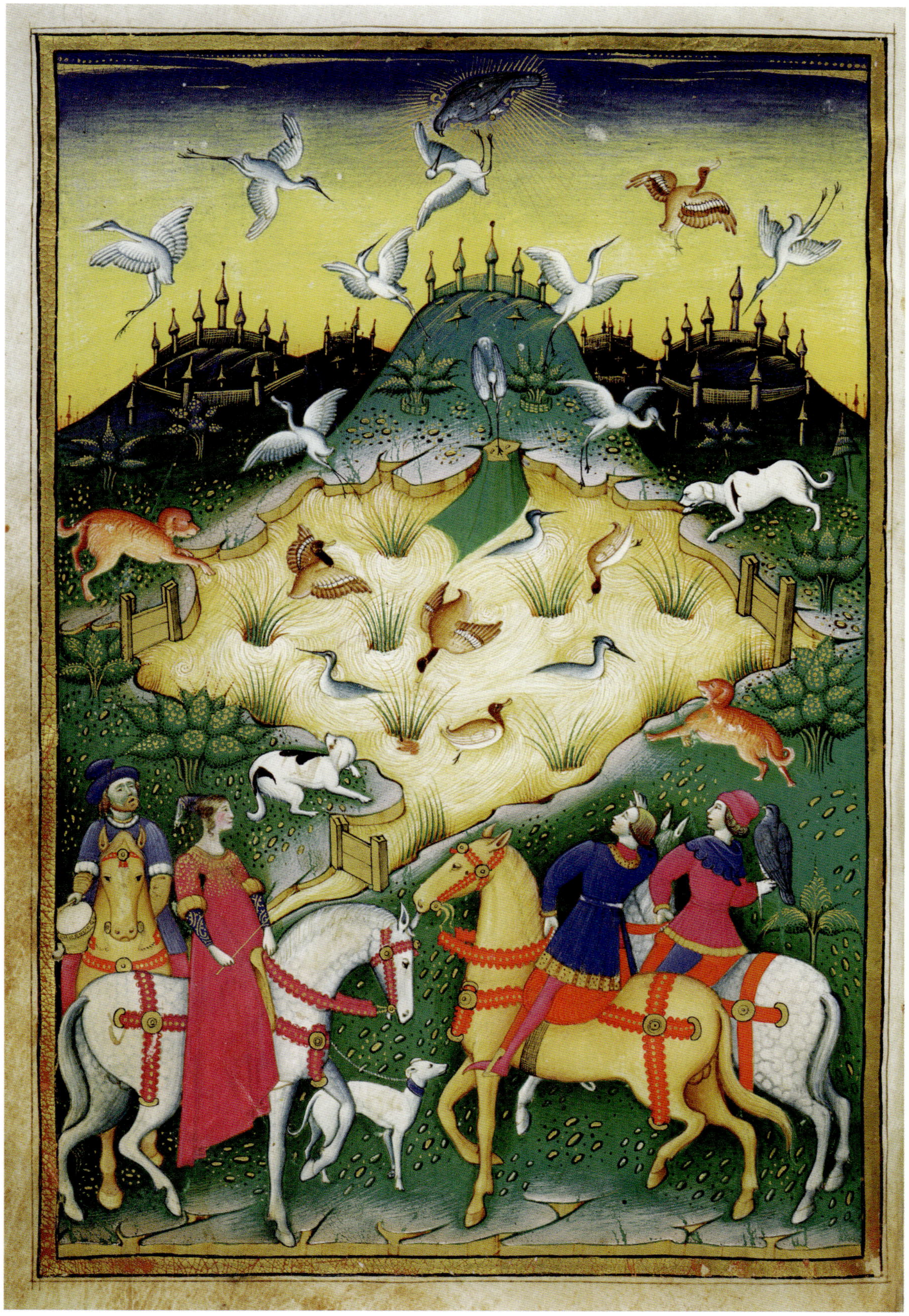

Italian

Hawking

1459

Illumination on vellum

21 × 15 cm (8¼ × 5⅞ in.)

Musée Condé, Chantilly, France

This illumination is from a richly illustrated fifteenth-century treatise on hunting, containing various texts in Latin and Arabic on falconry and hunting with dogs. The book once belonged to Francesco Sforza, Duke of Milan – a man who was evidently fond of falcons, as he is said to have wept at the death of his favourite. Falconry was expensive to maintain, requiring staff with specialist knowledge of the birds, so it was a sport of the nobility and princes, although it was not restricted to men. Indeed, hawking was an acceptable accomplishment for aristocratic ladies, and it is interesting that here a woman is enjoying the sport along with the male hunters. The hunt appears to be taking place near a pond or marsh, and the falcons have succeeded in bringing down an enormous number of waterfowl.

Follower of Giacomo Jaquerio (active 1403–1453)
The Fountain of Life (detail)

1418–30
Fresco
Castello della Manta, Saluzzo, Italy

The walls of the Baronial Hall in Castello della Manta in Piedmont, northern Italy, are decorated with an extraordinary set of frescoes in the International Gothic style. One wall depicts the nine heroes and nine heroines of antiquity, while another bears a scene of the Fountain of Youth, a legendary spring that was said to restore the youth of anyone who bathed in its waters. People are shown journeying towards the fountain from far and wide, arriving, disrobing, bathing and frolicking in the water, and continuing on their way, rejuvenated. Amid the throng of people old and young, and the various lovers indulging in amorous behaviour, are two falconers on horseback. One releases a falcon, while the other (seen here) has two hooded falcons on his wrist; their hoods will be removed when a suitable prey is found. In the fifteenth century the fortified castle of Manta was transformed into a splendid court, where French was spoken and Parisian fashions worn. Presumably the falconing scene reflects the courtly pursuits of its inhabitants.

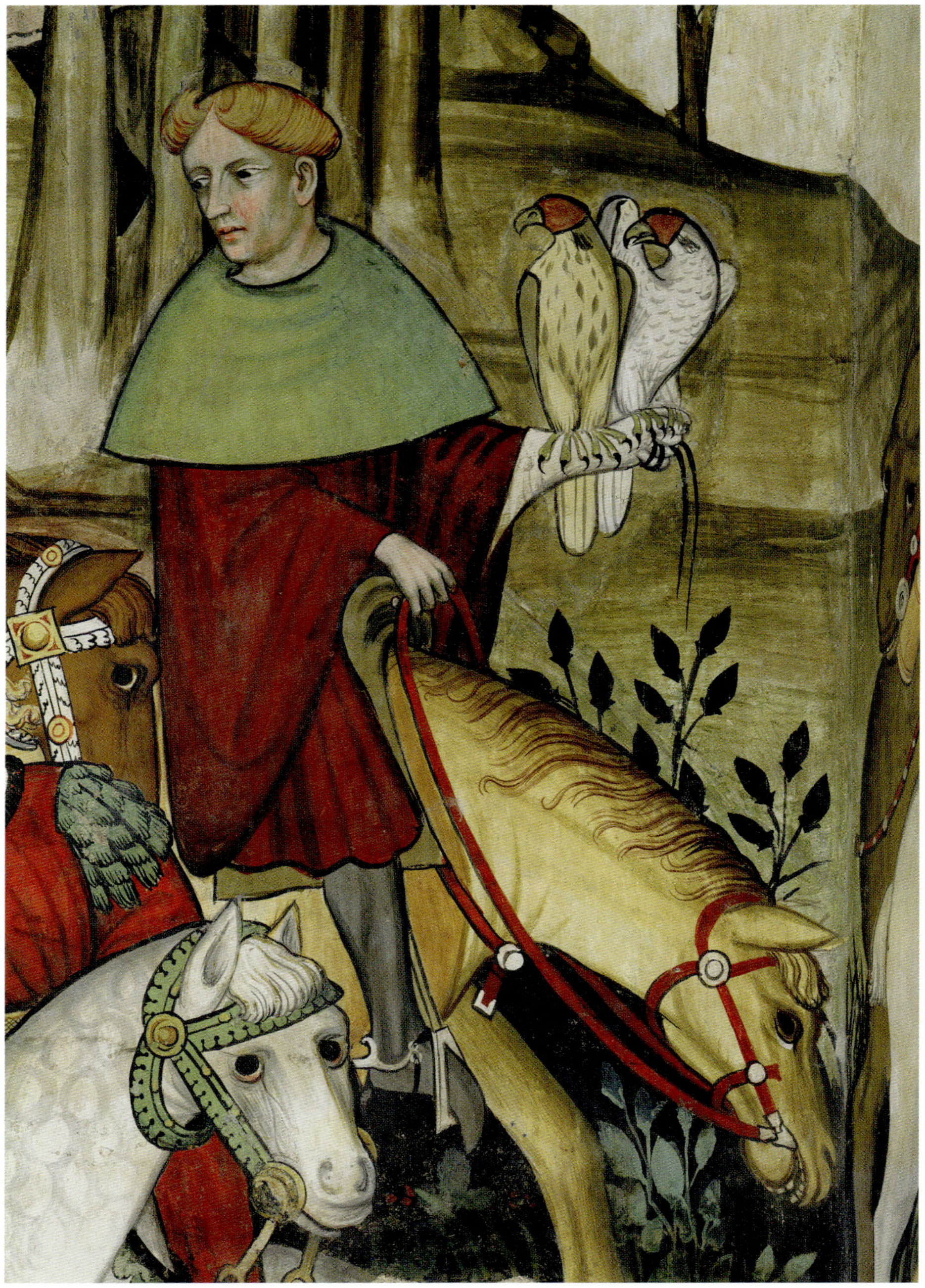

OPPOSITE

Franco-Flemish
The Flight of the Heron

First half of the 16th century
Tapestry
322 × 315 cm (126¾ × 124 in.)
Burrell Collection, Glasgow

An unfortunate grey heron tumbles out of the sky, having been set on by a falcon; other falcons swoop down to join in the kill. Hunting herons with falcons was a popular activity during the medieval and Renaissance periods. The thirteenth-century treatise by the Holy Roman Emperor, Frederick II of Hohenstaufen, *De Arte Venandi cum Avibus* (*The Art of Hunting with Birds*), devotes several pages to the sport, recommending two falcons as being better than one, and a hunting dog (seen here) as useful for retrieving dead birds. This particular hunt is taking place over a pond – the river or marshland being the heron's natural habitat and its traditional refuge from the hunt. While herons have long been hunted for food, they were also once pursued for their highly valued feathers. This Franco-Flemish tapestry, in which plants, animals and humans are all shown with careful attention to detail, encapsulates the aristocratic enjoyment of falconry.

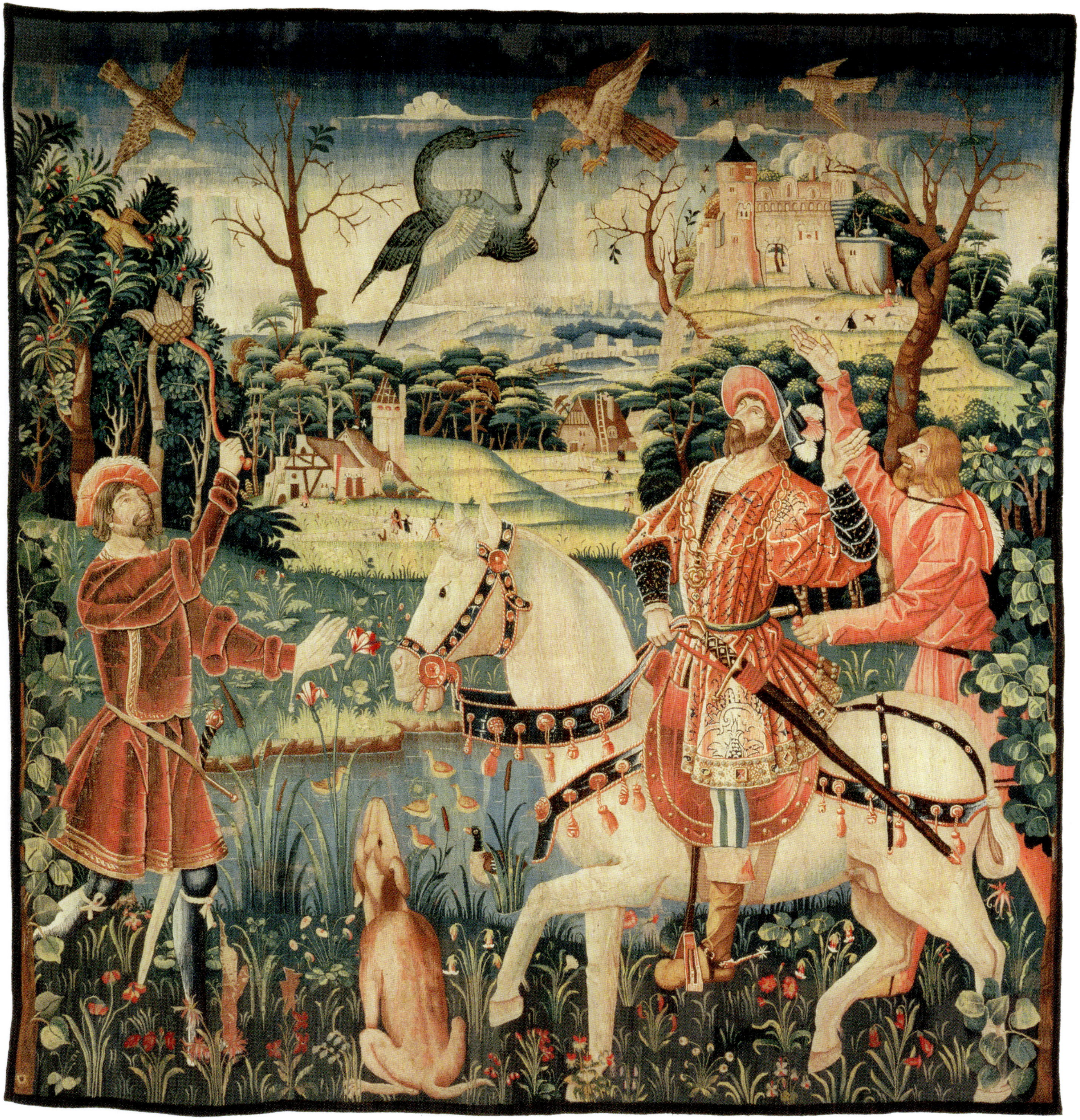

Pieter Bruegel the Elder
(*c.* 1525/30–1569)
Winter Landscape with Bird Trap

1565
Oil on canvas
39 × 57 cm (15⅜ × 22⅜ in.)
Kunsthistorisches Museum, Vienna

This is one of Bruegel's most popular and widely copied compositions. In a chilly, snow-clad winter landscape, skaters are making their way up and down a frozen river; some adults are playing hockey or curling; and children are spinning their tops. But in this apparently carefree scene lurks a sense of menace. Prominently placed among the trees on the right-hand side is a bird trap: a heavy slab of wood, probably an old door, tilted upwards and resting on a branch, which will fall the instant the rope attached to it is pulled, flattening the birds underneath. Crows – unwelcome predators – cluster around the trap, innocent of their impending fate. One does not have to look far for the allegorical meaning that inevitably underlies such motifs in Dutch paintings. Just as the trap can easily kill the birds, so the ice can give way and kill the skaters. Life is a precarious business.

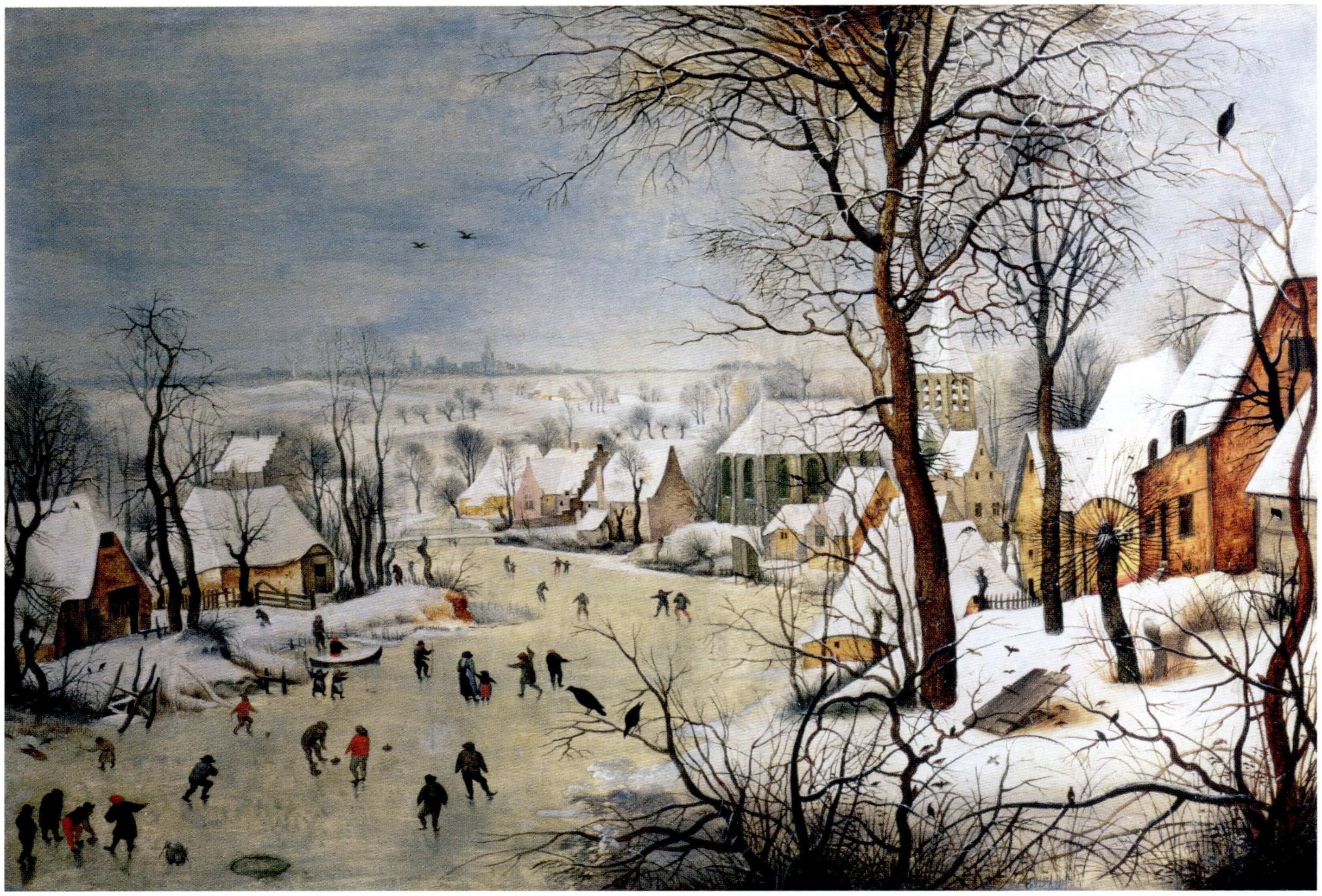

Lucas Cranach the Elder (1472–1553)
Still Life with Birds

c. 1530
Watercolour and gouache on vellum
34.6 × 20.3 cm (13⅝ × 8 in.)
Gemäldegalerie Alte Meister, Dresden

The corpses of two waxwings hang from a nail. The shadows they cast on the wall behind lend the painting a convincingly *trompe l'œil* quality. Waxwings breed in the forests of northern Europe, venturing further afield in severe winters in search of berries and other fruit – perhaps the reason why these two have been hunted. Although Cranach is best known for his religious works, which reflect the concerns of the Protestant Reformation (he was a friend of Martin Luther), and his mythological paintings, his portrayals of wildlife were equally accomplished. He produced lively scenes of his employers, the Electors of Saxony, dashing through the countryside with dogs in pursuit of stags or boar, based on studies of individual animals and sketches from nature. The waxwings reveal the artist's habit of direct observation.

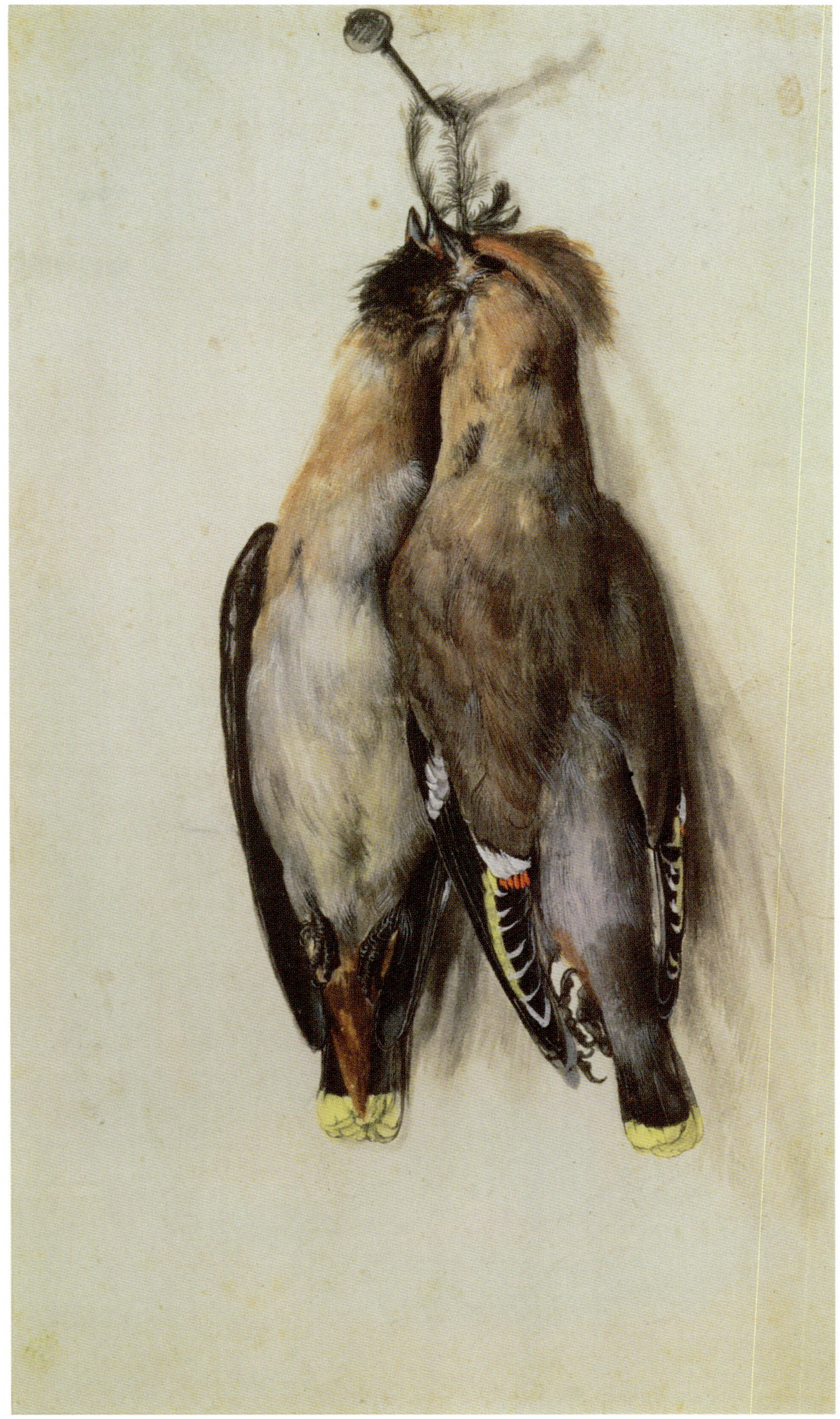

Rembrandt Harmensz. van Rijn (1606–1669) (workshop)
Man with a Hawk

1643
Oil on canvas
109 × 94 cm (42⅞ × 37 in.)
Private collection

The greatest Dutch artist of all, Rembrandt produced a large number of portraits, not all of which have identified sitters. This painting, which is signed by him, was long believed to be wholly by Rembrandt's hand, but recent scholars have suggested that it was produced by others in his workshop, and that the clothing in particular was painted by his pupil Ferdinand Bol. A later painting of a man with a hooded falcon, also from Rembrandt's studio and dated 1662–65, in the Göteborgs Konstmuseum, Sweden, has been identified as St Bavo, the medieval Dutch saint whose attribute is a falcon. The Netherlands was an important centre for European falconry at the time this picture was painted, and the sport was a popular one, although it was primarily associated with aristocrats. Attaching a falcon to the wrist of the young man would certainly have added prestige to the portrait.

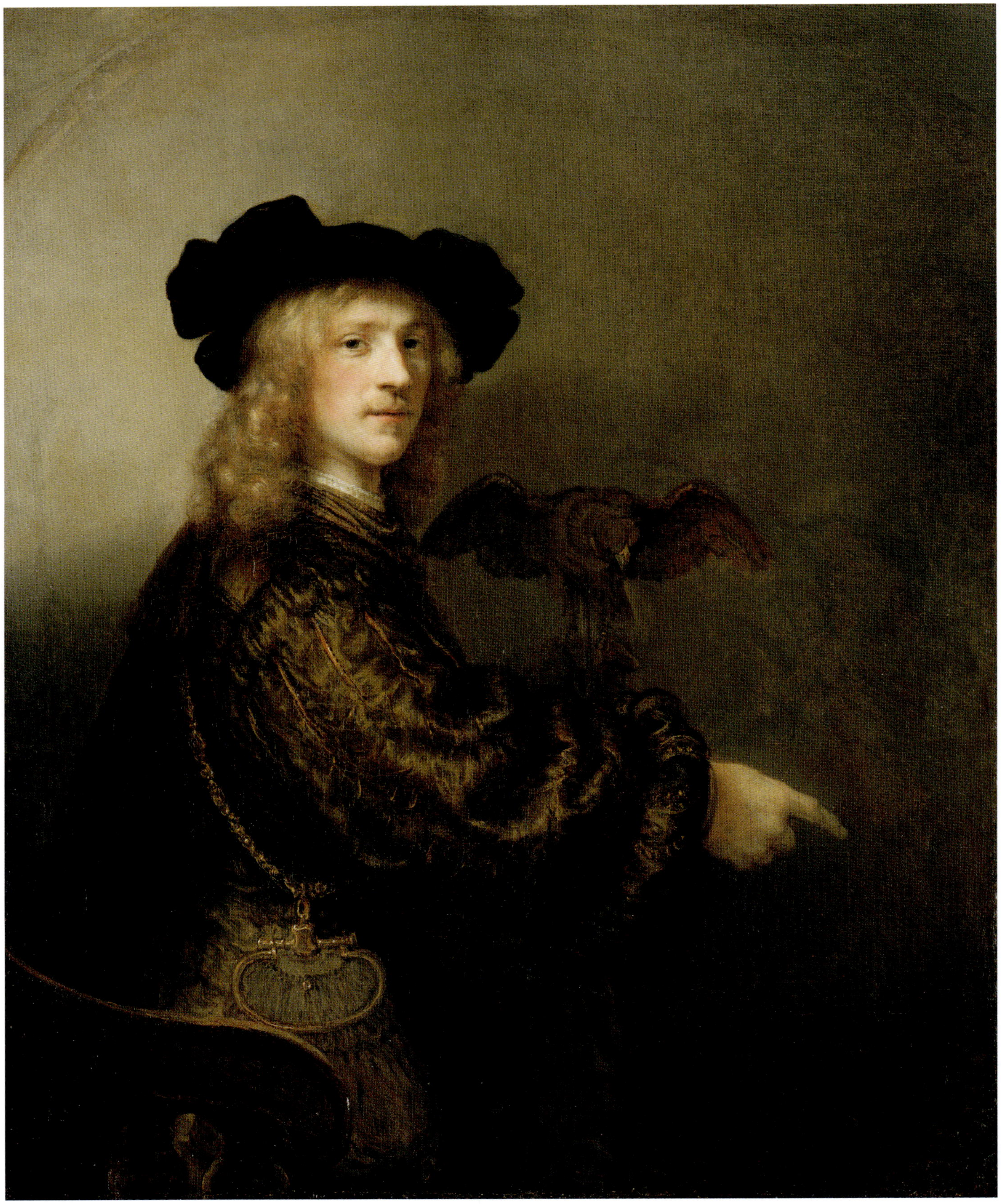

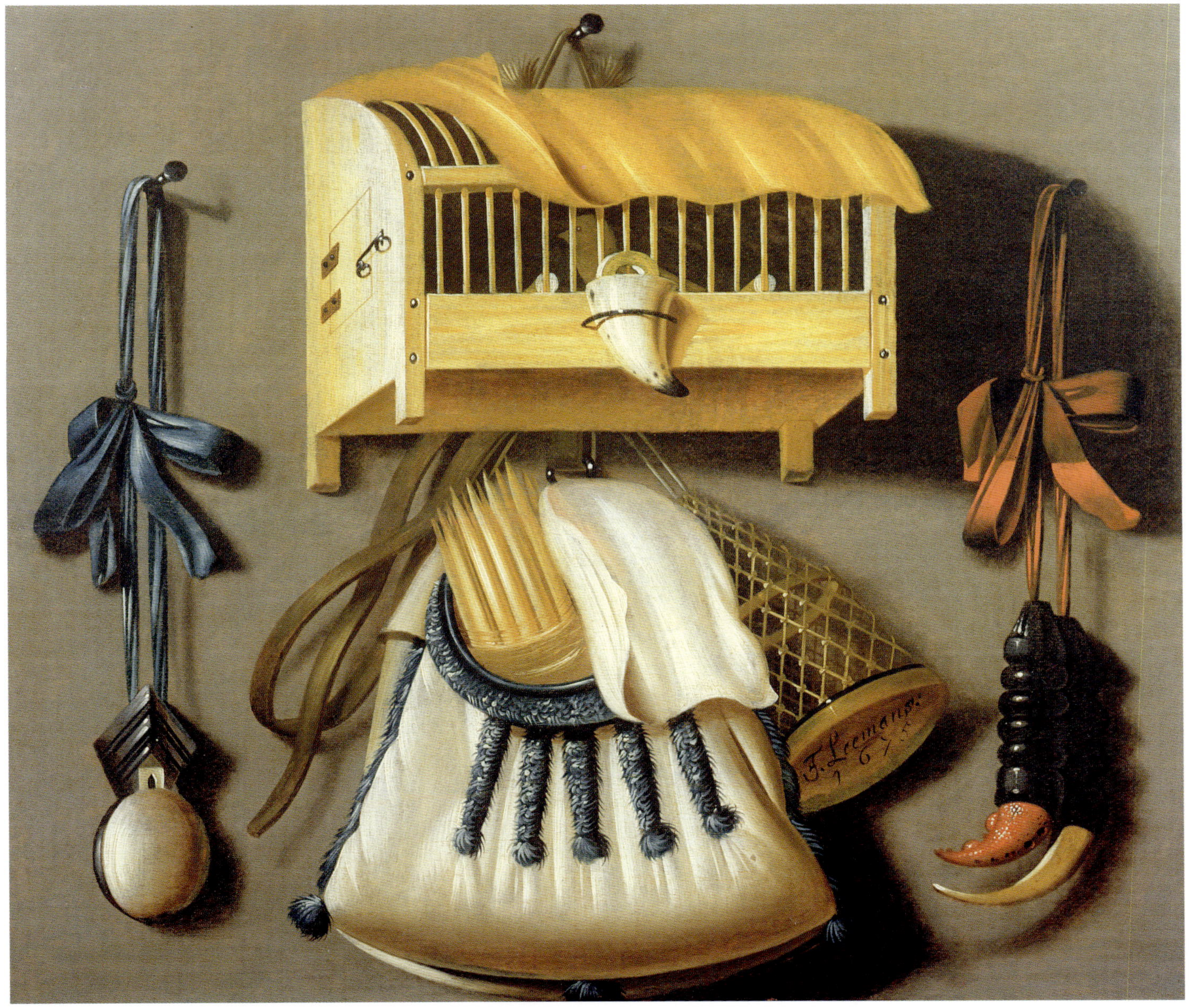

Johannes Leemans
(*c.* 1633–1688)
Trompe l'œil of hunting equipment and a birdcage
c. 1664–84
Oil on canvas
Dimensions unknown
Private collection

Paintings of game and hunting equipment were popular in the Dutch town of Haarlem in the second half of the seventeenth century, and Johannes Leemans was one of the most successful exponents. He specialized in painting *trompe l'œil* pictures of hunting equipment and birdcages, usually depicted against plain walls. Although he did not repeat his compositions exactly, they generally show a birdcage with a powder bag below it, and bird whistles to either side. Some also feature powder horns, trumpets and rifles. The birdcage would probably have held a small bird, such as a kestrel, which would have been used in hunting other birds. Perhaps it was no accident that hunting was the artist's central motif, for Leemans himself seems to have been a violent man, who is alleged to have murdered an army sergeant. He would have gained first-hand knowledge of weapons from his grandfather, who was an armourer.

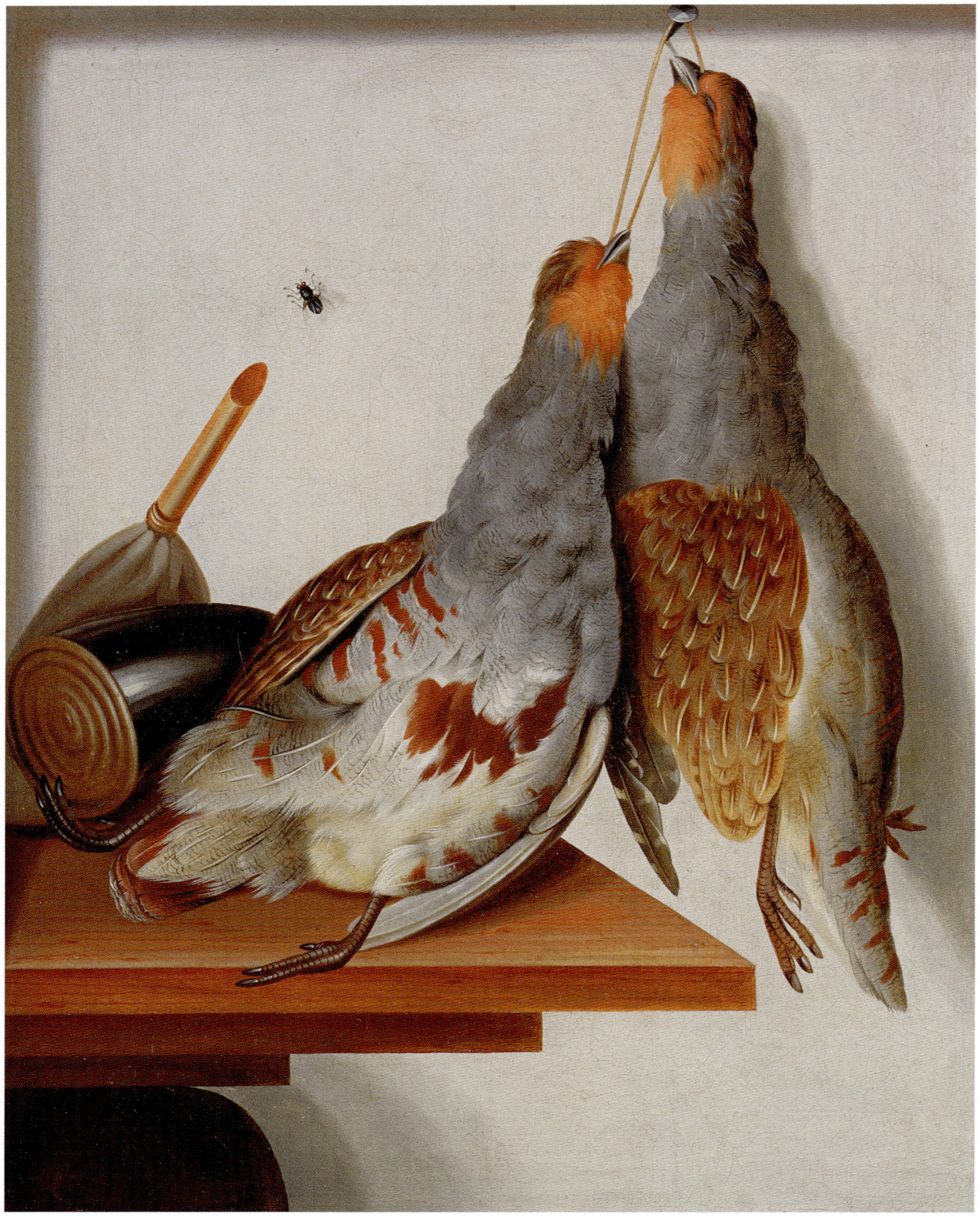

Cornelis Biltius
(1653–*c.* 1690)
Trompe l'œil of two partridges hanging from a nail
Second half of the 17th century
Oil on canvas
51.4 × 43.8 cm (20¼ × 17¼ in.)
Private collection

Little is known about Cornelis Biltius, an obscure Dutch artist who produced a number of paintings of dead birds and game. He belonged to a circle of artists working in The Hague, all of whom specialized in *trompe l'œil* still lifes, which were much in demand on the Dutch art market in the latter half of the seventeenth century. These two partridges – and the fly on the wall – are painted with such skill that one could almost believe they were real, although there are no unpleasant details to reveal that they have been hunted. Partridges and their close relatives pheasant and grouse have been pursued by European hunters for centuries. In medieval times they were chased with dogs, which were used to flush them out of hiding and into the air so that human hunters could shoot them down with bows and arrows. After the advent of firearms they were simply shot, and retrieved by the hunting dogs.

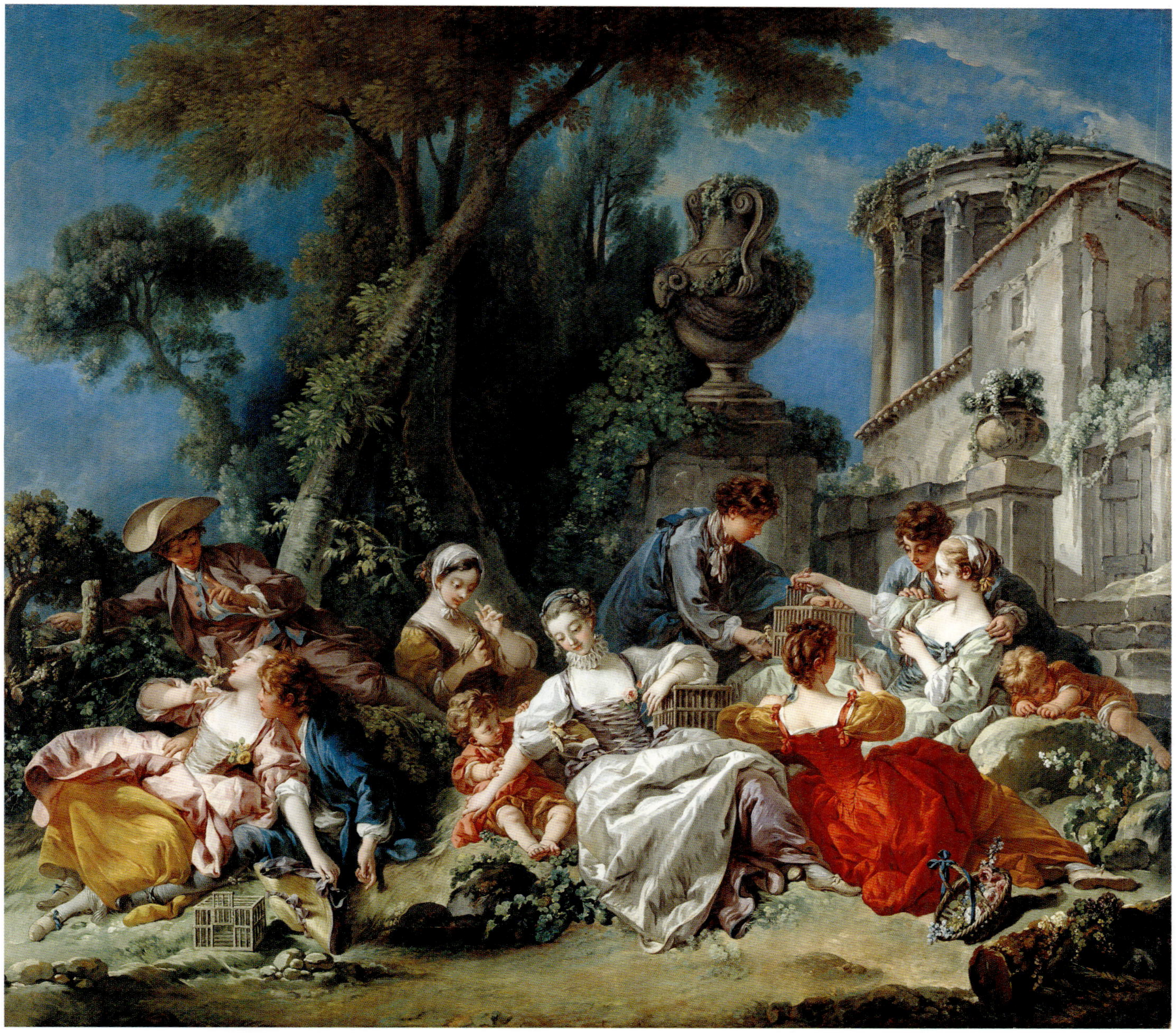

François Boucher
(1703–1770)
The Bird Catchers
1748
Oil on canvas
294.6 × 337.8 cm (116 × 133 in.)
Private collection

This composition and its pendant, *The Fountain of Love*, relate to a suite of tapestries showing countryside themes that were woven at Beauvais and are known as *The Noble Pastoral*. Despite the title of the painting, there is nothing unpleasantly predatory about the image. Indeed, the mood is light-hearted and flirtatious, as one would expect from a leading exponent of the French Rococo. Several fashionable couples are enjoying amorous dalliances in front of a ruined classical temple. Some are catching birds, others are playing with them, holding them on their fingers to their lips, or on lengths of string. In the eighteenth century, if a man gave a small caged bird to his loved one it told her that she held his heart captive. The link between captive birds and lovers can also be seen in other works by Boucher and his followers that show pretty young couples with a birdcage, or plump cupids capturing birds.

Jean-Baptiste Huet (1745–1811)

A Dog Attacking Geese

1769
Oil on canvas
128 × 162 cm (50⅜ × 63¾ in.)
Musée du Louvre, Paris

This picture helped to establish Huet's reputation as one of the leading animal painters in eighteenth-century France. Its enthusiastic reception at the Paris Salon in 1769 led to the artist's acceptance at the Académie Royale. In common with his English contemporary George Stubbs (see below), Huet showed a fine grasp of the anatomy of animals and birds, and even published studies of animal skeletons. But there is an element of melodramatic fantasy here, as well as anthropomorphism, that Stubbs would never have countenanced. One can easily read the assembled geese as a family, as the adults protect the young ones from the dog's attack. In a comic touch, the dog itself – a type of French mastiff – looks almost as frightened as the chicks. Geese are highly territorial animals and will respond aggressively to an intruder; these look as though they may even scare off the aggressor that has broken into their enclosure.

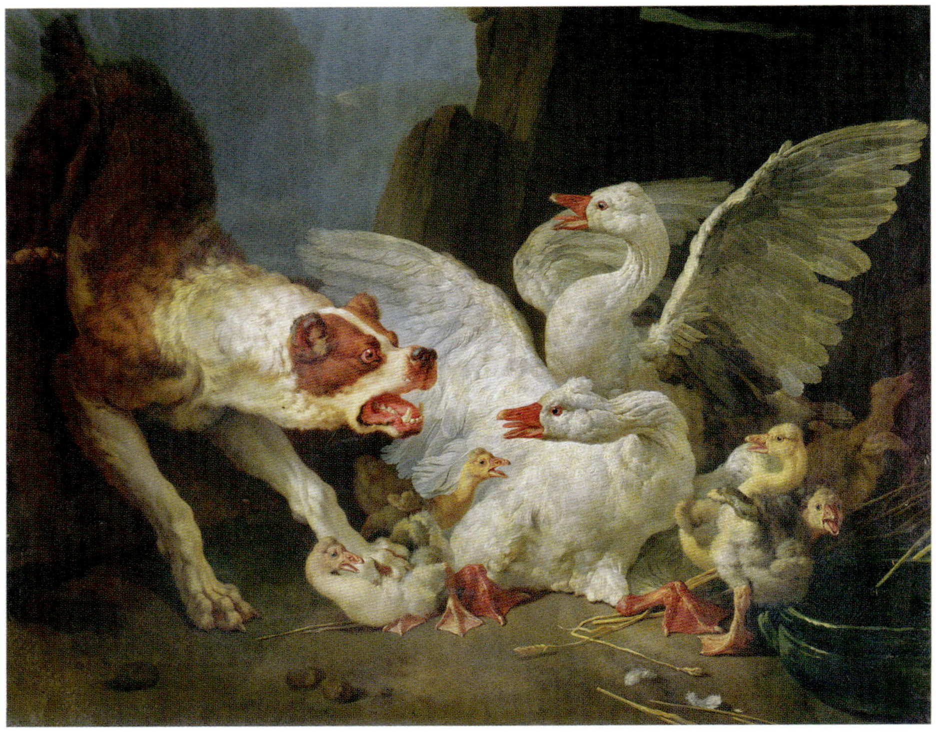

George Stubbs (1724–1806)

Greenland Falcon

1780
Oil on panel
81.3 × 99.1 cm (32 × 39 in.)
Yale Center for British Art, Paul Mellon Collection, New Haven, Connecticut

The British artist George Stubbs was a master of animal painting, and made extensive anatomical studies. At the end of his life he even began work on a study that compared the anatomy of humans, tigers and birds, although it was left incomplete at his death. It is therefore no surprise that his study of a Greenland falcon (or gyrfalcon) bears the hallmarks of careful observation and thorough understanding of the bird's physical structure. The falcon was a prized hunting bird, reserved in medieval times for royalty and nobility. This one certainly exhibits an almost regal hauteur, although it is a captive on its perch. Stubbs shows it resting on the wood on the pads of its feet, its neck feathers ruffled from wearing a hood. The countryside in the background is no doubt where it has just been hunting.

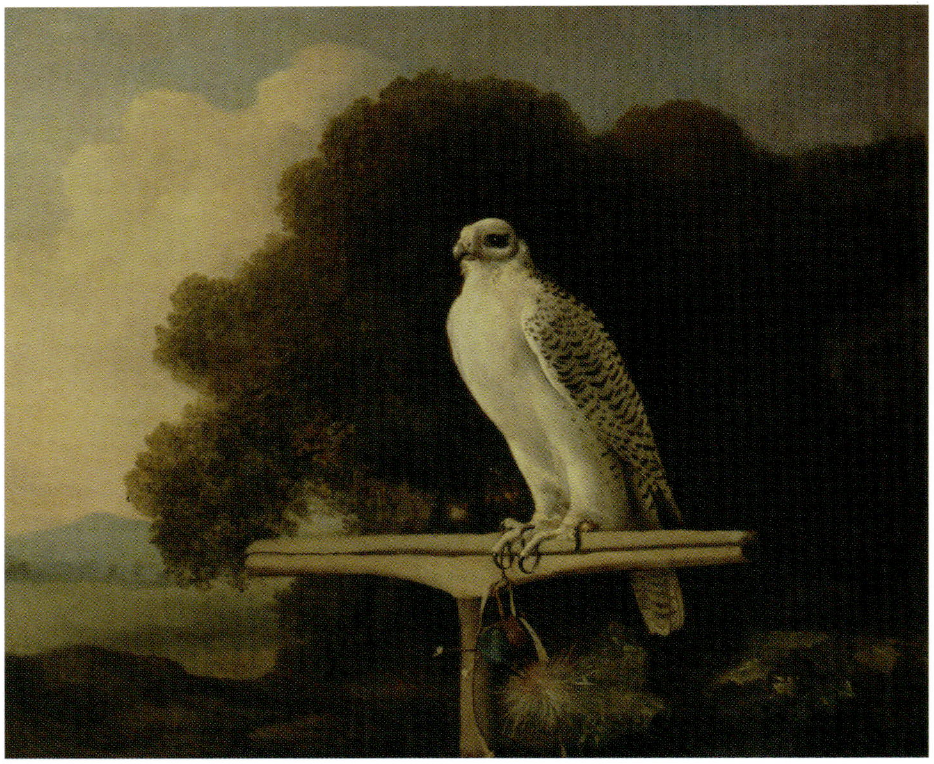

Jean-Baptiste Oudry (1686–1755)

Still Life with Birds and Insects

1713
Oil on canvas
Dimensions unknown
Musée des Beaux-Arts, Marseille

A dead male bullfinch lies beneath another bird, which may be a greenfinch, while wasps, a bee and a butterfly that are still very much alive flit around the corpses. This is a relatively early work by the French artist Oudry, who later came to specialize in grand and magnificent still lifes of dead game and elaborate hunting scenes, painted for the French king Louis XV. The artist was a keen observer of live creatures, and became particularly skilled at presenting birds and animals in motion. This picture, however, relies for its effect on stillness and simplicity. Its format is derived from Dutch still lifes of the preceding century. A great deal of Oudry's time was spent designing tapestries for the Beauvais and Gobelins factories, and he also produced a series of illustrations for Jean de La Fontaine's fables.

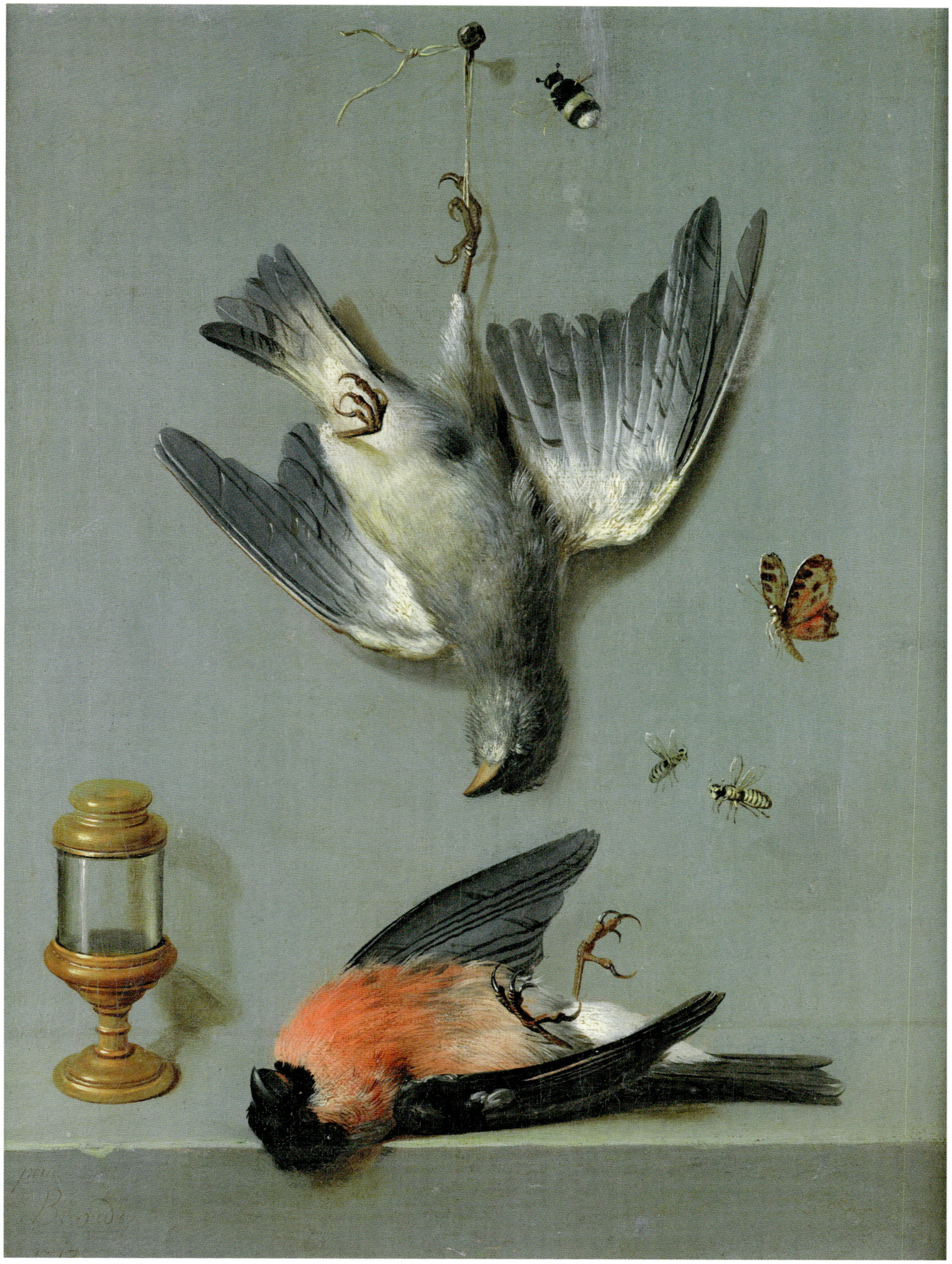

George Frederic Watts (1817–1904)

The Wounded Heron

1837
Oil on canvas
91.4 × 71.1 cm (36 × 28 in.)
Watts Gallery, Compton, Surrey

At the tender age of twenty, the Victorian painter G.F. Watts spotted a dead heron in a London poulterer's shop, and was so inspired by its beauty that he brought it back to his studio and used it as the basis for this imagined scene of medieval hawking. The falconer can be seen dashing through the landscape in the background, but since the bird effectively fills the picture space it is a still-life study as well as an image of considerable pathos. The subject may also be based on an episode Watts remembered from his childhood, when he accidentally crushed his pet bird. The artist's love of birds and his horror at their needless slaughter lasted his entire life. In 1898–99 he produced *A Dedication* ('To those who love the beautiful and mourn over the senseless and cruel destruction of bird life and beauty') in protest against the use of exotic feathers on clothes and hats (p. 30).

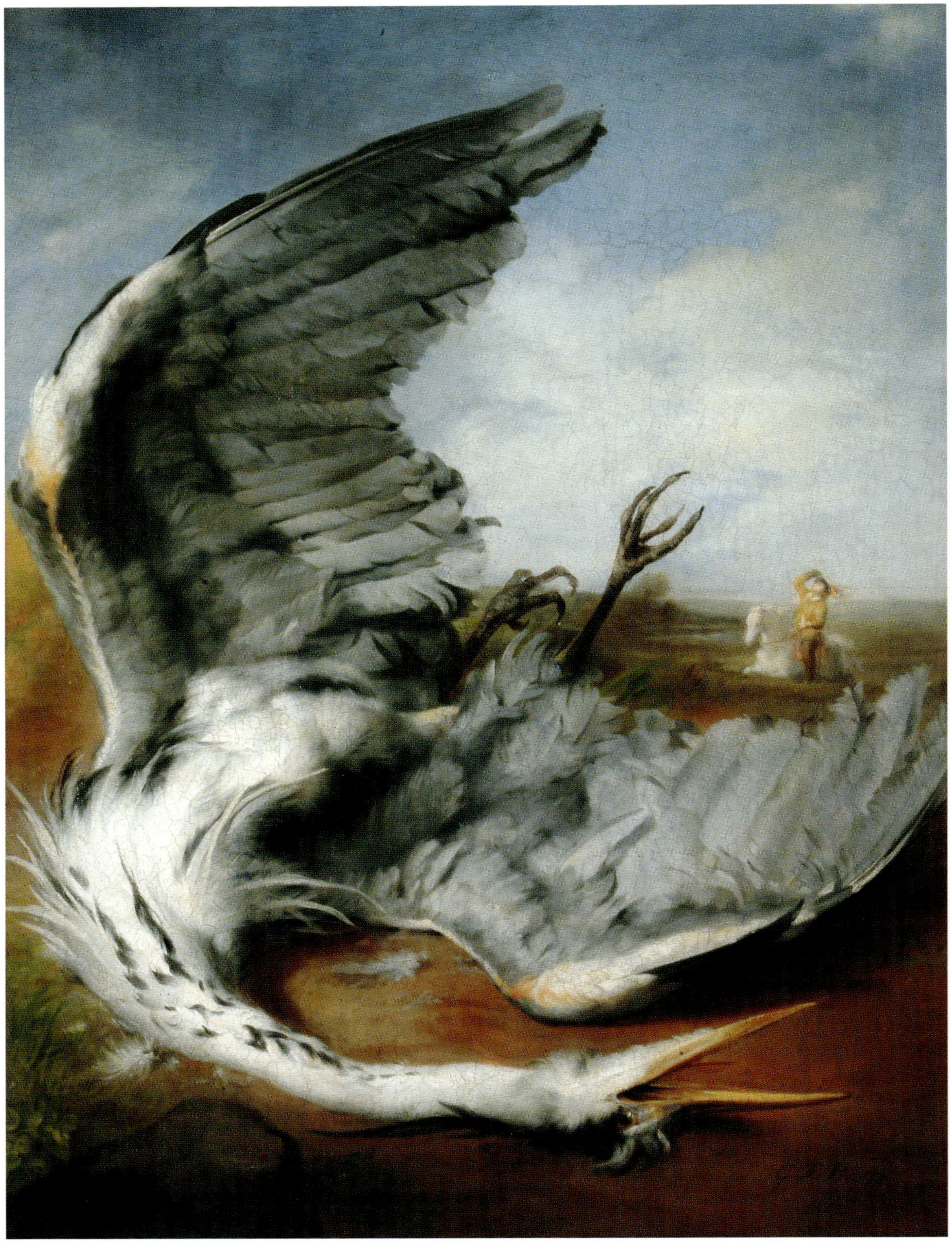

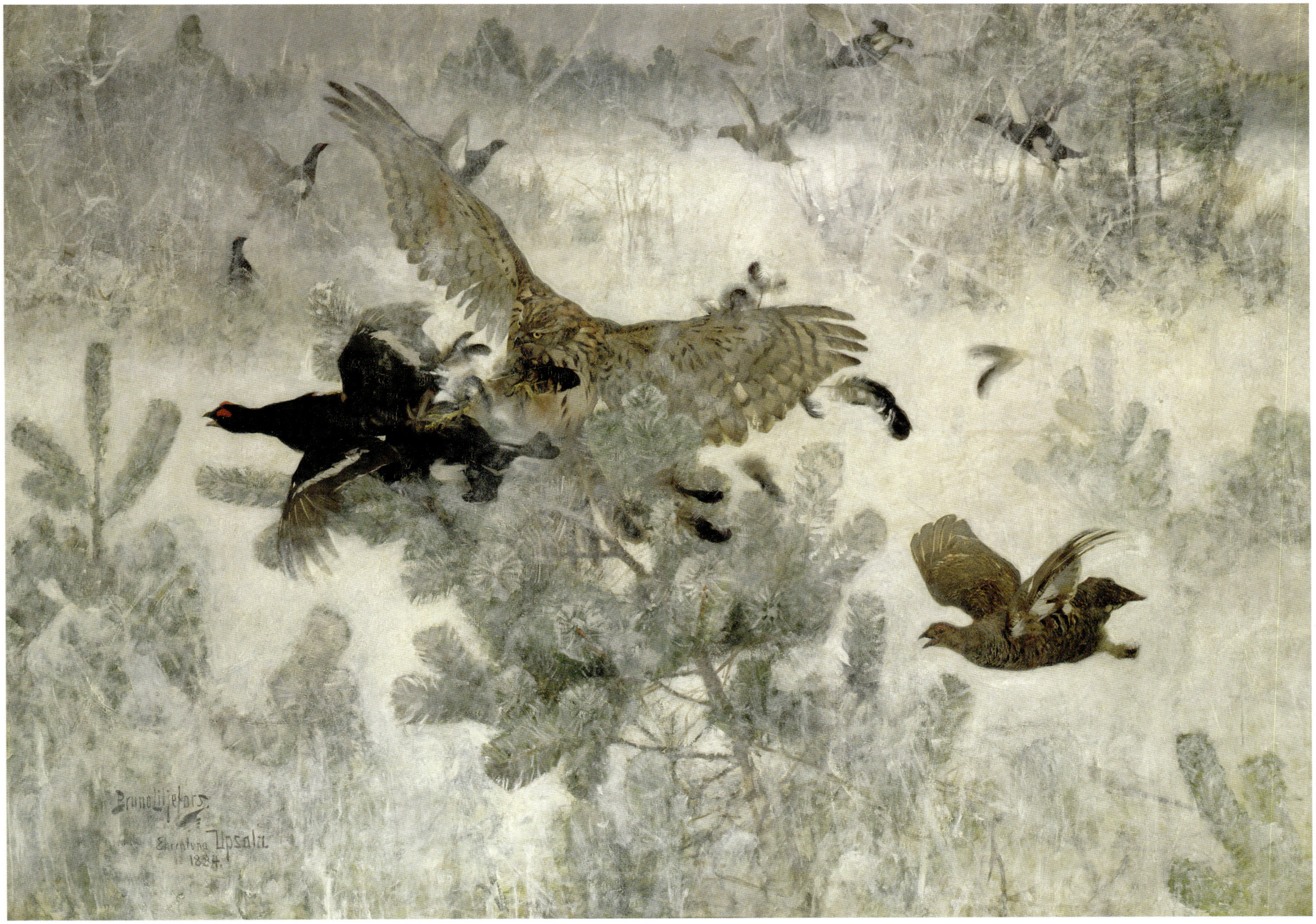

Bruno Liljefors
(1860–1939)
Hawk and Black Game

1884
Oil on canvas
143 × 203 cm (56¼ × 79⅞ in.)
Nationalmuseum, Stockholm

Bruno Liljefors was the most important Swedish wildlife artist of his day, drawing on his own experience as a hunter to depict the thrill of the chase. He also kept a small menagerie of animals and birds, enabling him to observe them at close quarters. He had studied in France and, like the Impressionists, made a habit of painting outdoors rather than in the studio. For this picture he placed a young hawk that he had killed himself among some dead grouse in the bushes near his home. But such is the animation of the scene that it is impossible to tell that the birds were dead rather than alive. Liljefors was fascinated by the way that wild creatures blend in with the countryside where they live, and the birds here, depicted with an almost monochrome palette, look entirely at one with the snowy landscape.

George L. Seymour (active 1876–1916)
The Arab Hunter

n.d.
Oil on panel
45.4 × 29.8 cm (17⅞ × 11¾ in.)
Private collection

During the nineteenth century a number of European artists turned to the Middle East and north Africa for their subject matter, and images of Arab hunters and falconers became a highly popular motif. The British painter George L. Seymour had trained in Paris under the French artist Jean-Léon Gérôme (see opposite), who was a prime exponent of such Orientalist subjects. Here, Seymour depicts a young hunter, who looks like a Nubian, bedecked with the tools and rewards of his trade – a gunbelt, a decorated powder flask and some dead birds, including what appears to be a sand partridge – and with an *ubuk*, or pipe, tucked into his belt. It is an image redolent of pride and dignity. Although the practice of hawking was popular in Arab lands, the man is not shown with the falcon but appears rather to have relied on firepower for his kill.

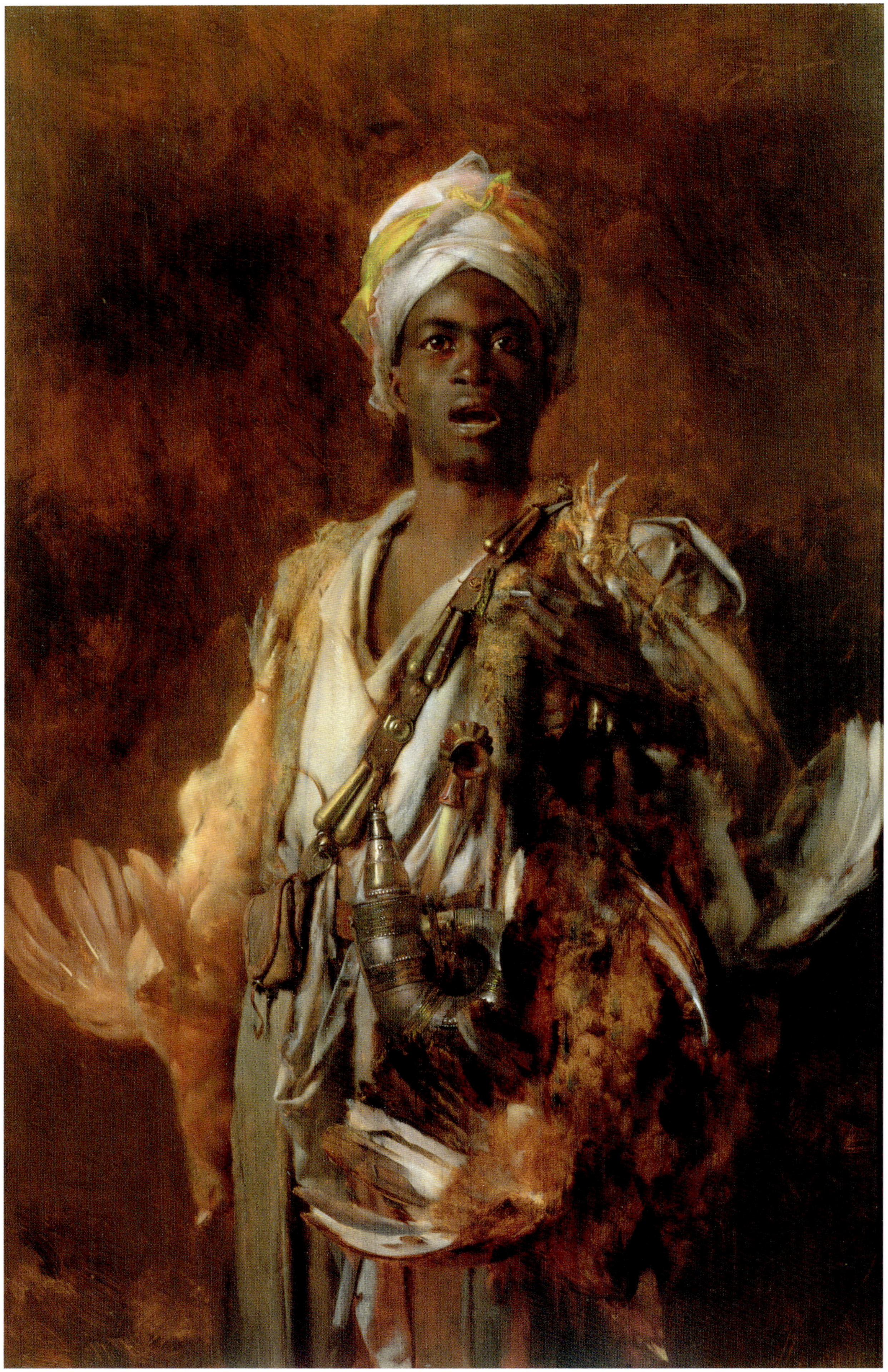

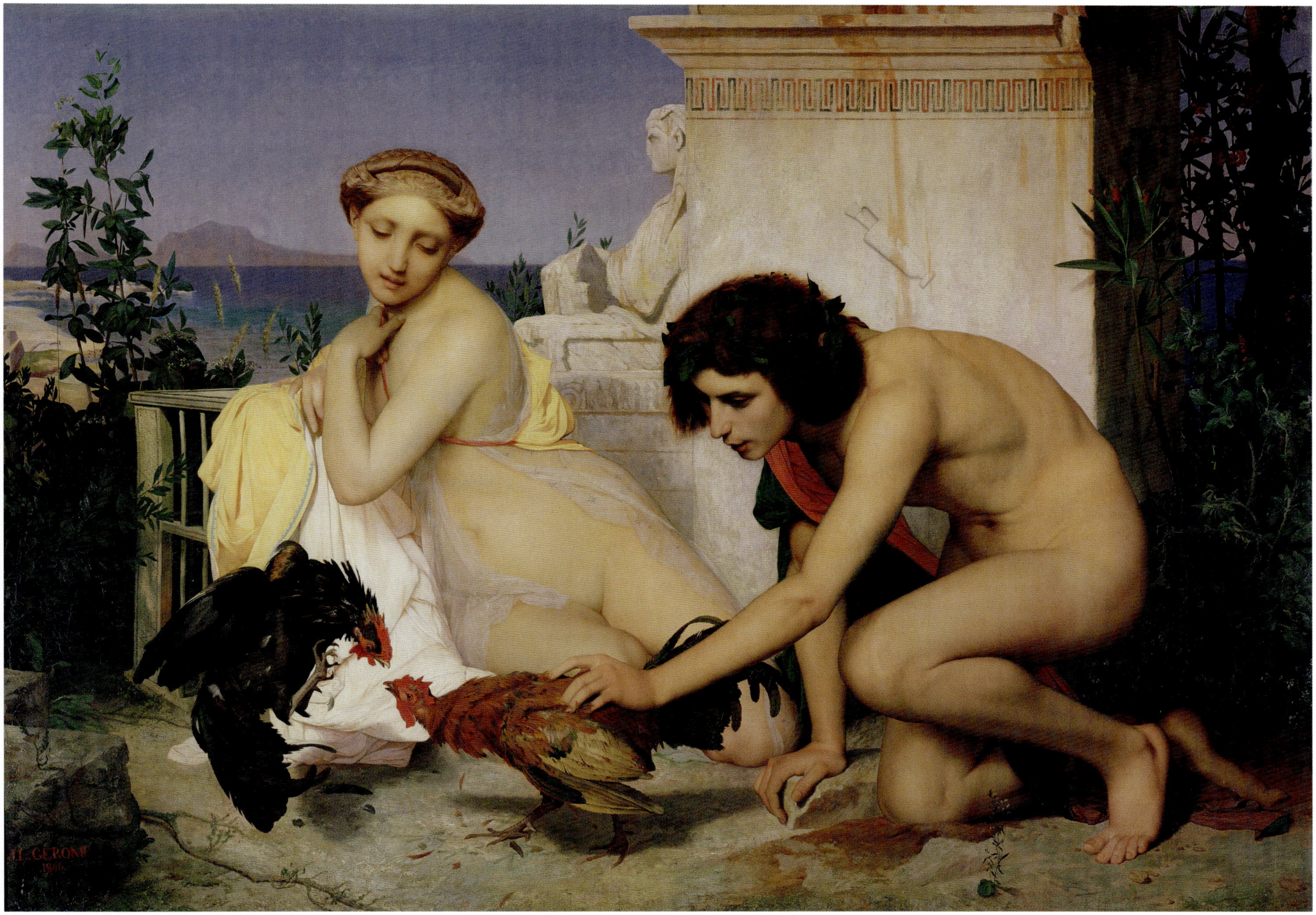

Jean-Léon Gérôme
(1824–1904)
Young Greeks Encouraging Cocks to Fight
1846
Oil on canvas
143 × 202 cm (56¼ × 79½ in.)
Musée d'Orsay, Paris

This work, with which the young French painter Gérôme made his name at the Paris Salon, is a curious one. A naked youth is encouraging a pair of cocks to fight, perhaps in the hope of impressing the young girl. Everything is delineated with the sharp focus typical of the Neoclassical style. Cockfighting may seem an unusually bloodthirsty entertainment for a pair of adolescent lovers, but it is hard to avoid reading a sexual subtext into the picture. The sport was documented in ancient Greece, and it has since enjoyed popularity throughout the world, although it is now illegal in many countries, including the United Kingdom and the United States. Typically, a pair of roosters specially bred for their stamina and aggression are pitted against each other in combat until one of them dies. The game usually takes place in a special ring, or cockpit, and bets are placed on the outcome.

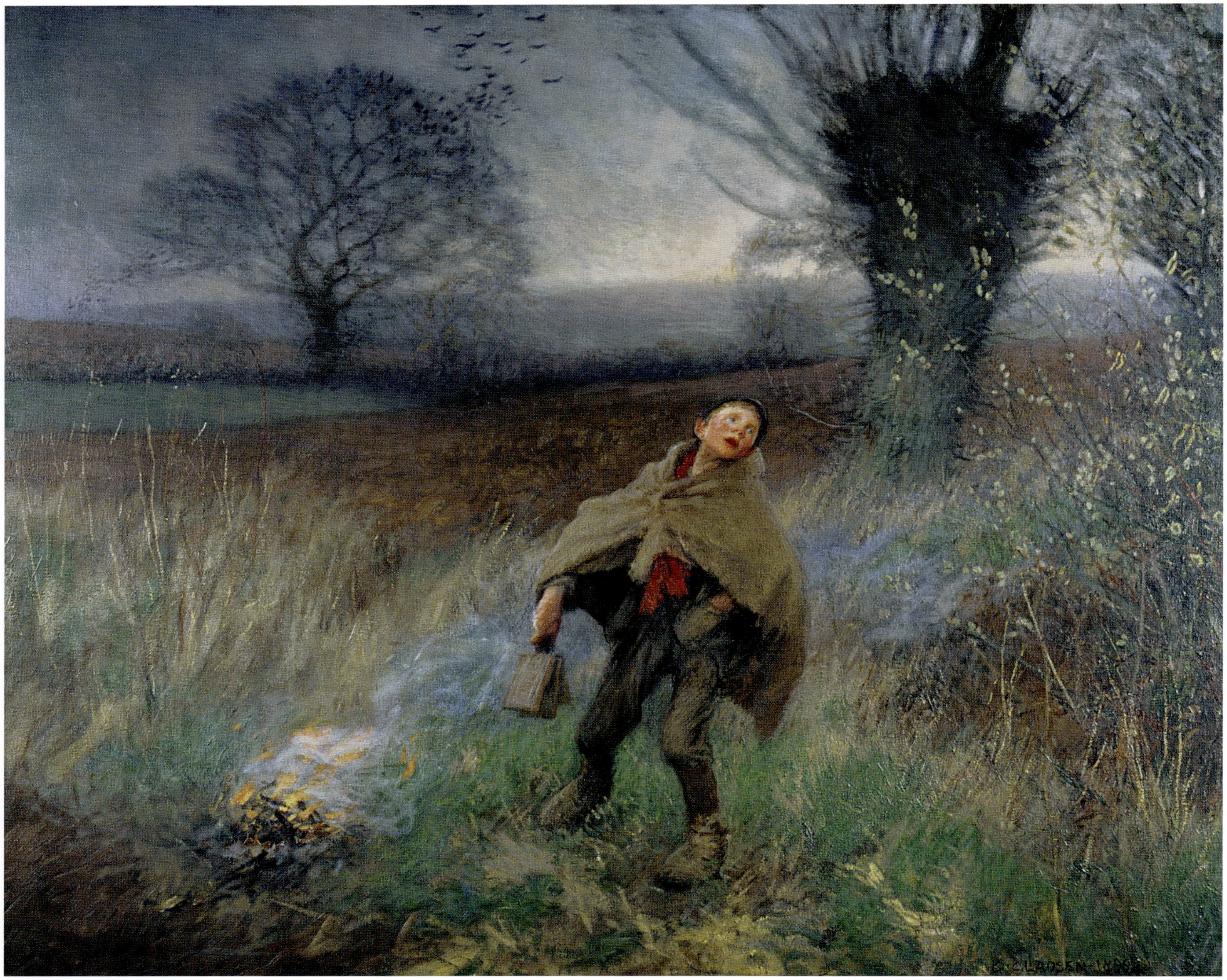

Sir George Clausen (1852–1944)

Bird Scaring, March, 1896

1896
Oil on canvas
102.2 × 128 cm (40 × 50⅜ in.)
Harris Museum & Art Gallery, Preston

Flocks of hungry birds are a nuisance for farmers because of their tendency to devour seeds and crops. The boy here is acting as a live scarecrow, frightening off the birds from a field with a wooden clapper, which would have made a loud noise when waved around. Unlike the elegant hawking scenes, in which richly clad lords and ladies enjoy their sport, this image shows the harsh reality of farming life. The lonely young lad standing in the freezing field seems to encapsulate rural poverty; indeed, he looks more hunted than the birds he is scaring away. In Victorian England, children as young as eight were employed in this way. George Clausen specialized in scenes of rural life, which he depicted without sentimentality. But his presentation of the unvarnished truth was not to everyone's taste, and when this picture was first exhibited at the Royal Academy in London, it drew harsh criticism for its perceived ugliness.

Claude Monet
(1840–1926)
Hunting Trophies
1862
Oil on canvas
104 × 75 cm (40⅞ × 29½ in.)
Musée d'Orsay, Paris

Monet produced a number of still lifes at the start of his career – perhaps because they meant he did not have to go to the expense of hiring a model – but they did not figure largely in his mature work. At this early stage in his artistic evolution Monet had not yet adopted the high-key colour that was to characterize his Impressionist canvases, and this composition is dominated by subtle tones of brown and beige. The edible birds – which include a pheasant, a blackcock, a common snipe, a red grouse and a woodcock – are beautifully observed, as is the hunting dog that eyes them. There was a long tradition in northern European art of painting the spoils of a day's hunt, ranging from the opulent canvases depicted by such great Flemish artists as Frans Snyders to Jean-Siméon Chardin's much humbler kitchen scenes. But it was a work by the French artist Constant Troyon showing a dog with a partridge in its mouth, exhibited at the Paris Salon in 1859, that seems to have been Monet's most direct source of inspiration for this picture.

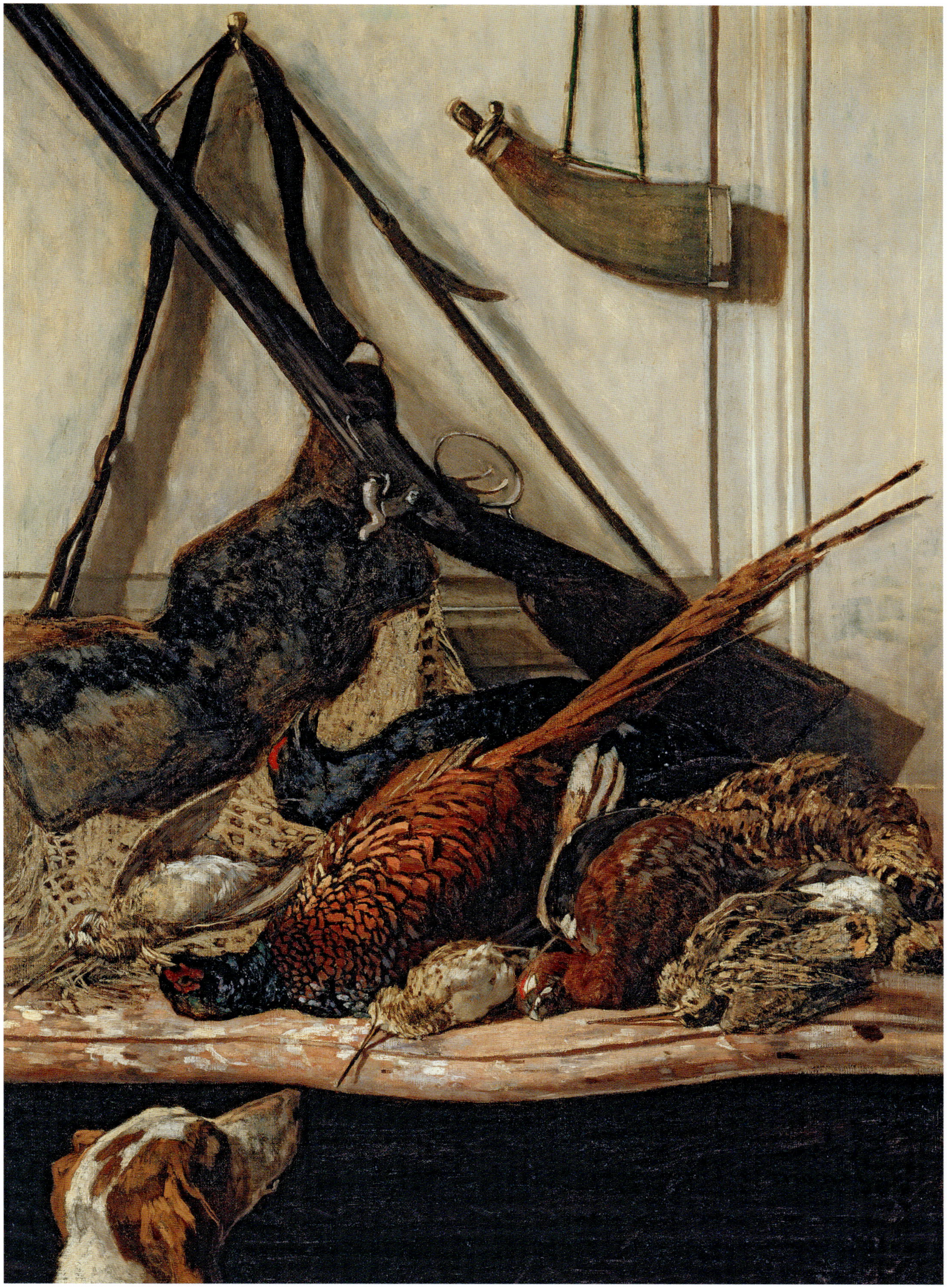

The Bird Observed

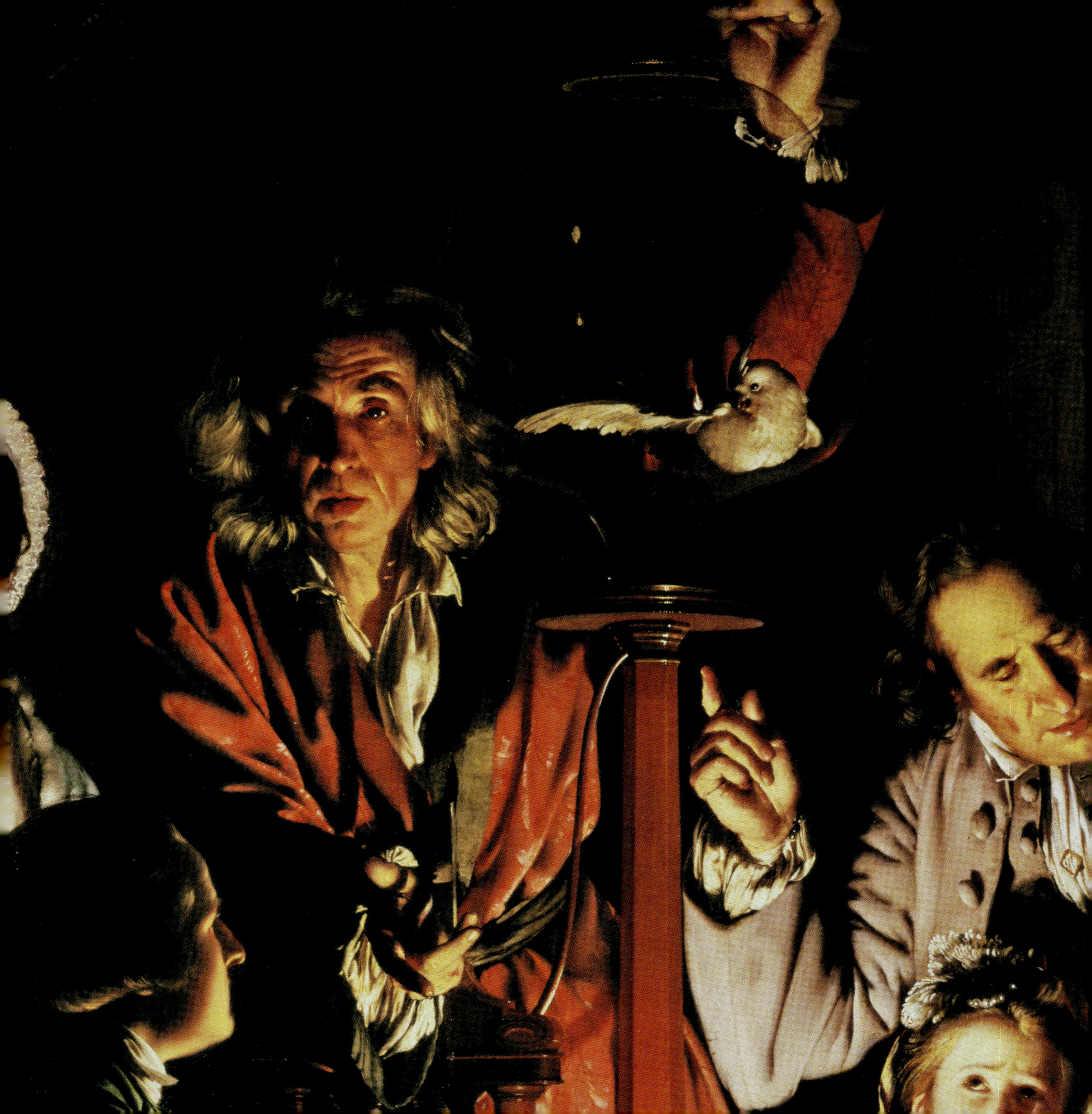

The earliest attempts to write a natural history of birds were made in the first century AD by the Roman writer Pliny the Elder, as part of a mammoth encyclopedia of the natural world. Pliny's work formed the basis for medieval bestiaries: fantastic compendia of folk tales and images of animals and birds. Some of the bird stories to be found in bestiaries are based on observation of birds' habits, but it was not until the Renaissance that Western artists made concerted attempts to arrive at a scientific understanding of avian life. They may not have had today's sophisticated binoculars or photographs and film for reference, but some of the watercolours they produced as preparation for frescoes and oil paintings demonstrate just how acute were their powers of observation. As early as the 1430s, Pisanello was studying birds belonging to the Gonzaga and Este households (opposite). At the end of the fifteenth century Leonardo da Vinci scrutinized birds in flight in an attempt to produce his own flying machine, and slightly later Albrecht Dürer produced a meticulously delineated wing of a blue roller that still astonishes today (p. 147). The freshness of these Renaissance drawings indicates that they could have been based only on a study of real birds, rather than the models seen in pattern books typically used by medieval illuminators.

The spirit of ornithological enquiry was given fresh impetus from the fifteenth century onwards by the species brought back to Europe by explorers and traders who travelled to new continents. The exotic birds they discovered did not have a cultural context in Europe, or an existing set of attributes, and so new ways of describing and classifying them were needed: ones that were not based on existing knowledge, traditions or symbolism, but were informed by first-hand observation. This, in turn, led to a tradition of ornithological illustration that found expression in prints and books. John White's remarkable watercolours of birds he had observed in North America and Mark Catesby's mammoth compendium of the flora and fauna of Carolina, Florida and the Bahamas are two outstanding examples of a genre that was to reach its apogee in the nineteenth century in the work of John James Audubon (pp. 146, 151 and 155). His *Birds of America* took bird illustration to new heights, and proved that it was entirely possible to marry accurate observation with artistic interpretation.

European artists in search of exotic bird life did not necessarily have to travel far afield to observe unfamiliar species. Before the establishment of modern zoos, there were privately owned menageries, many of which housed foreign creatures. Roelandt Savery did not have to journey to Mauritius to record the legendary dodo, but could do so comfortably in northern Europe at Prince Maurice of Nassau's establishment (see p. 149). The taxidermist's art also ensured that dead birds brought back from far-flung shores were available to those who wanted to study non-native birds, even if the specimens were not always padded out with due regard to anatomical truthfulness. Sir Ashton Lever's museum of natural history, which opened to the public in London in 1775, contained three rooms full of stuffed birds. At this date, taxidermists also played a crucial role in advancing scientific understanding of bird species. But plenty of artists have been happy to study the native birds they encountered in daily life (p. 153), subjecting them to the same detailed artistic enquiry as any imported exotic creature.

Pisanello (Antonio Pisano) (*c.* 1395–1455)

Five Jays

c. 1434–45
Watercolour on paper
Dimensions unknown
Musée du Louvre, Paris

Pisanello's ability to paint birds and animals was praised by his contemporaries. Although he sometimes used long-standing patterns for depicting these creatures, he refreshed these standard models with direct observation from life; his meticulous records of plants, flowers, animals and birds show his evident delight in the natural world. As a court artist in the Gonzaga and Este households, Pisanello also had plenty of opportunity to see at close quarters the menageries of beasts and birds that were kept for hunting. About 400 drawings by the artist and his workshop survive, most of them in the so-called Vallardi Album in the Louvre. The drawings were probably made to be used in unspecified future commissions, rather than with particular projects in mind. The studies of birds are particularly delicate and well observed. Some were made from dead specimens and others from live birds. Here, the same jay has been depicted from different angles, so presumably the watercolour was made from a living bird.

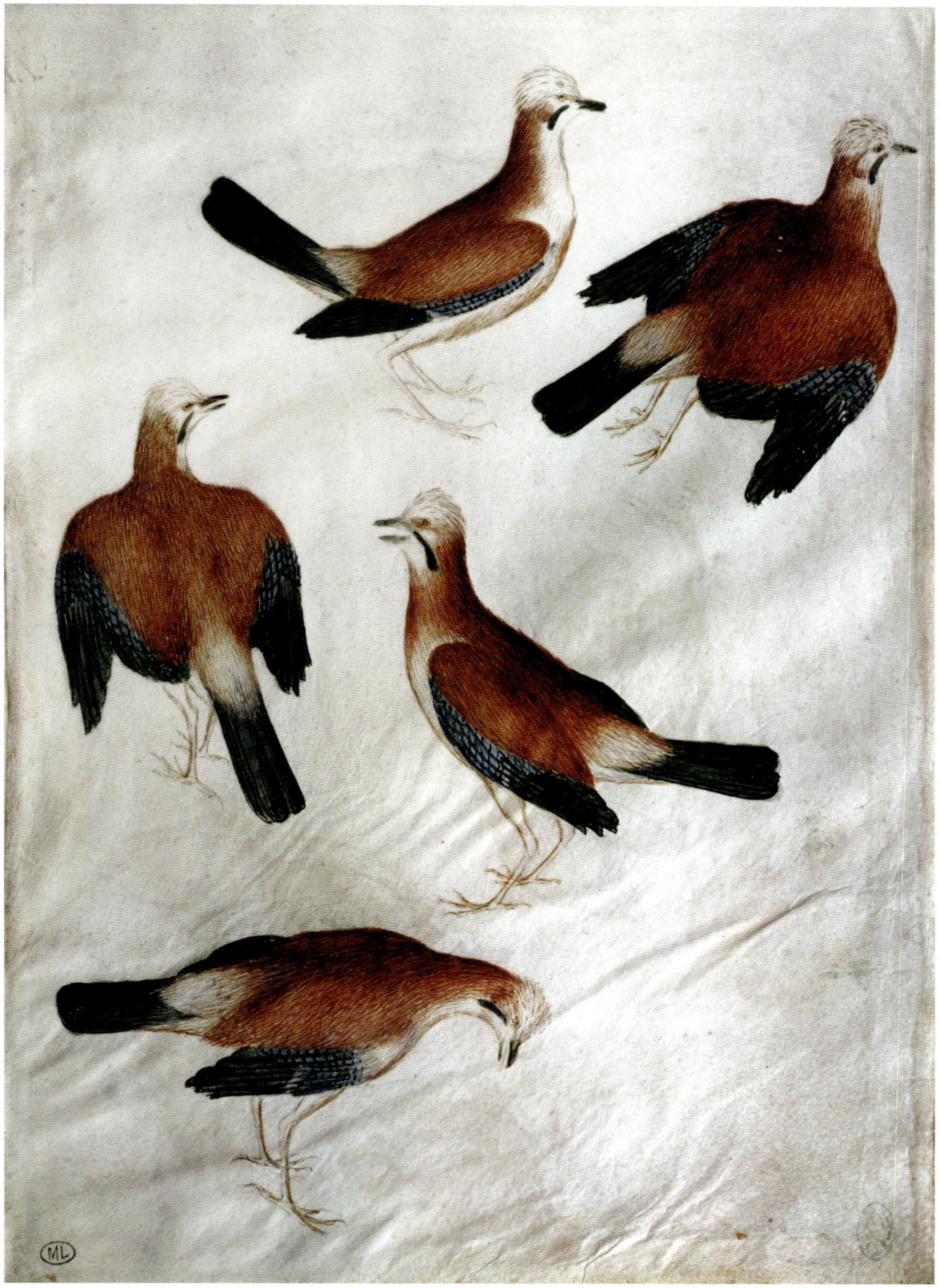

John White
(c. 1540–c. 1593)
Greater Flamingo

c. 1585
Watercolour
29.6 × 19.7 cm (11⅝ × 7¾ in.)
British Library, London

More than two centuries before John James Audubon set out on his massive quest to document all the birds of America, the artist John White produced this extraordinary image of an American flamingo. White, a British adventurer, sailed to North America five times during the reign of Elizabeth I, and was one of the first people to attempt to colonize the New World. In 1585, under the patronage of Sir Walter Raleigh, he led an expedition to found a settlement in Virginia at Roanoke. The colony was mysteriously abandoned, but White did leave watercolour drawings showing everything he found that was unknown in England at the time: plants, animals, birds and the daily life of the Algonquin people. This beautifully drawn flamingo, with spindly legs and plumage picked out in subtle gradations of pink, is one of those watercolours. They were engraved by Theodor de Bry and published as a book in 1590. White's folio was rediscovered a hundred years after his death by Sir Hans Sloane, whose collections were to form the basis of the British Museum. Sloane himself spent some time as a physician in Jamaica, and brought back a collection of 'curiosities' that included more than 1000 bird specimens.

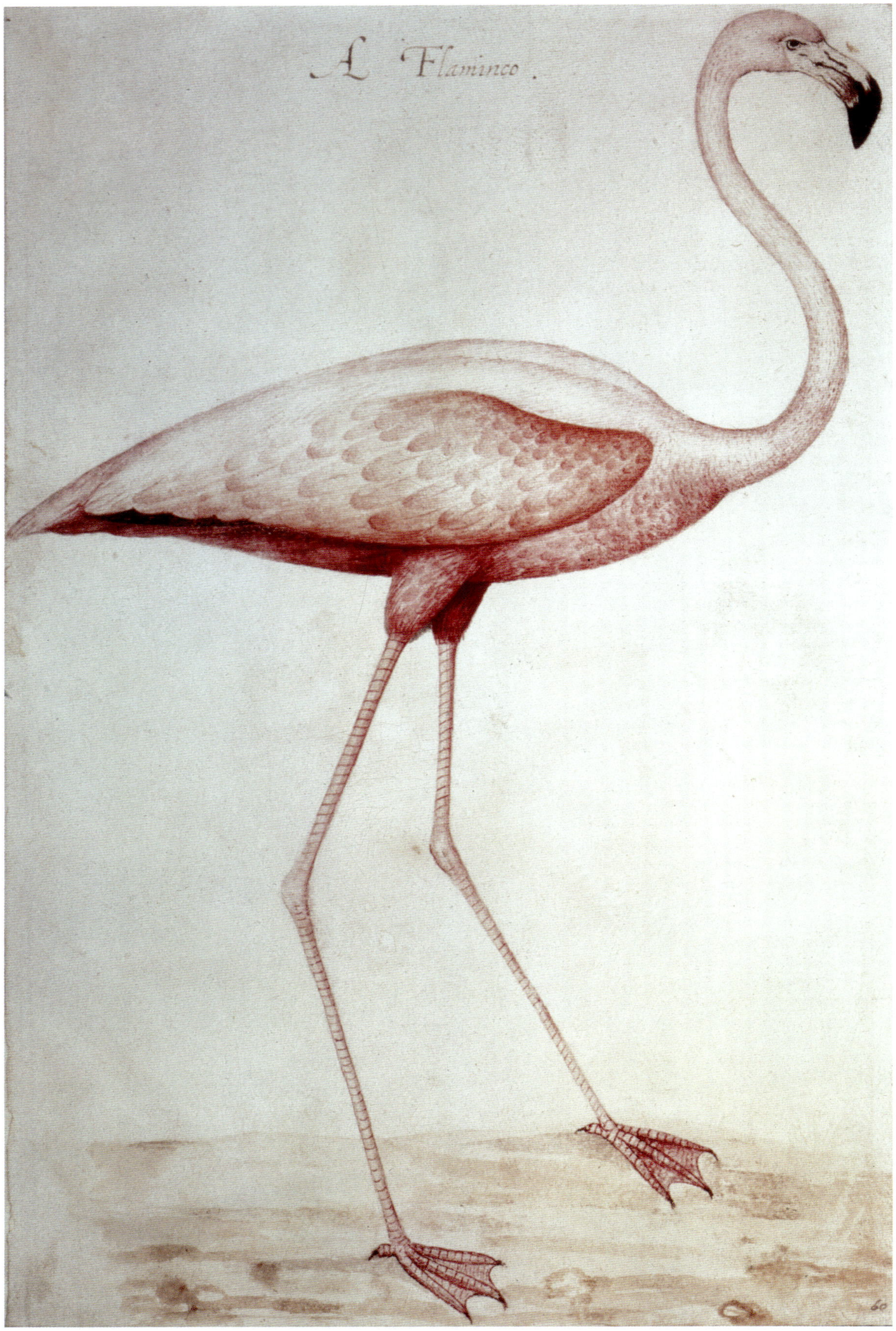

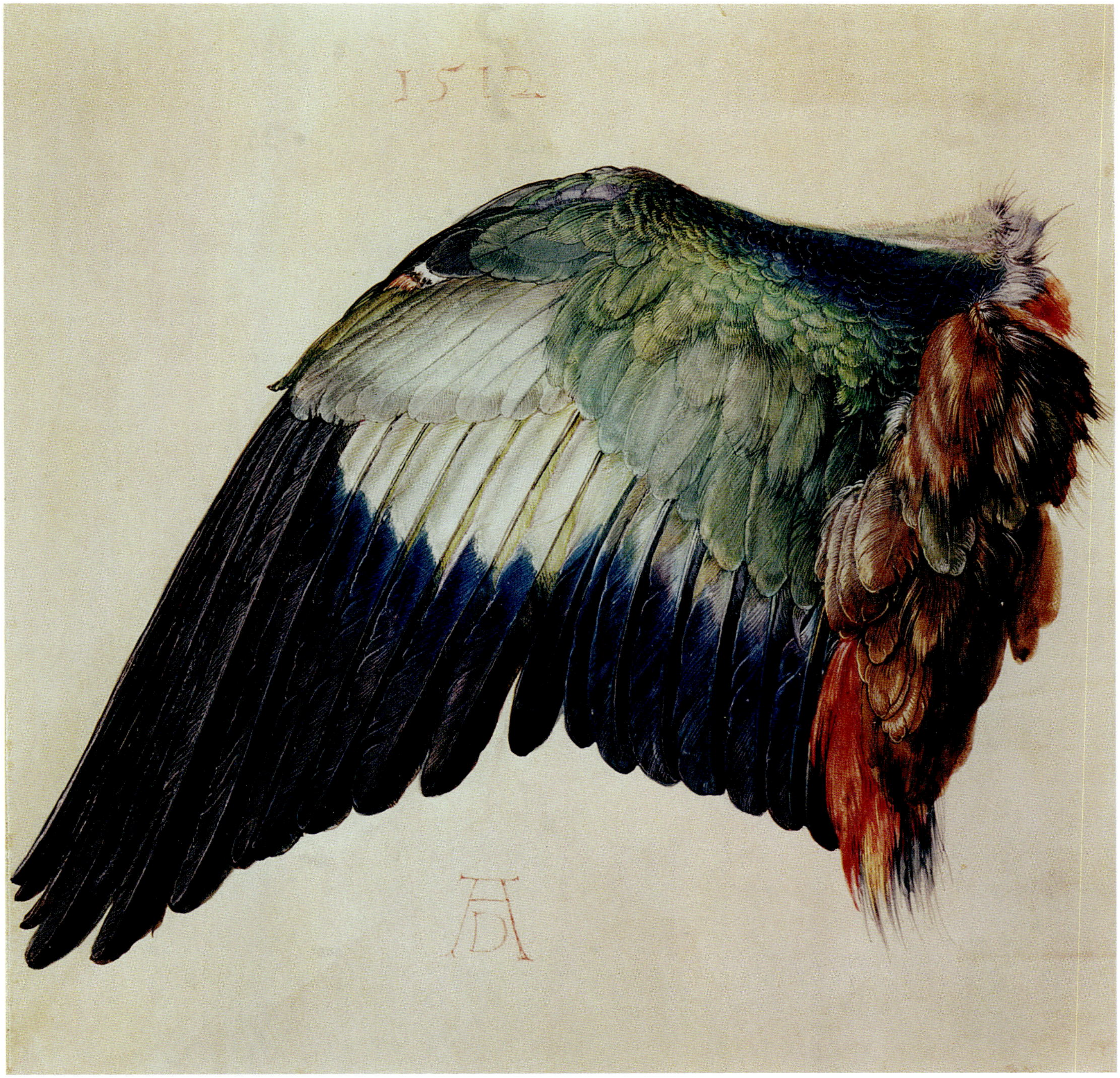

Albrecht Dürer
(1471–1528)
Wing of a Blue Roller

1512
Watercolour and gouache on vellum with gold
19.7 × 20 cm (7¾ × 7⅞ in.)
Graphische Sammlung Albertina, Vienna

Dürer was one of the first artists to make nature studies, and his astonishing powers of observation are evident here, in this study of the wing of a roller, a colourful bird found in southern and central Europe. The artist was fascinated by birds; in 1506 he brought back feathers from Venice for his friend Willibald Pirckheimer. He also produced a still-life study of a dead roller hanging from a nail; it, like this drawing, is in the collection of the Albertina in Vienna. Dürer's love of birds is evident in many of his paintings as well as his drawings. His *Virgin and Child with Animals*, also in the Albertina, contains several different types of bird: a woodpecker, a stork, swans, two owls and a parakeet. He also produced a painting of the Madonna and Child with a siskin (a type of finch) on Christ's arm (in the Gemäldegalerie, Berlin).

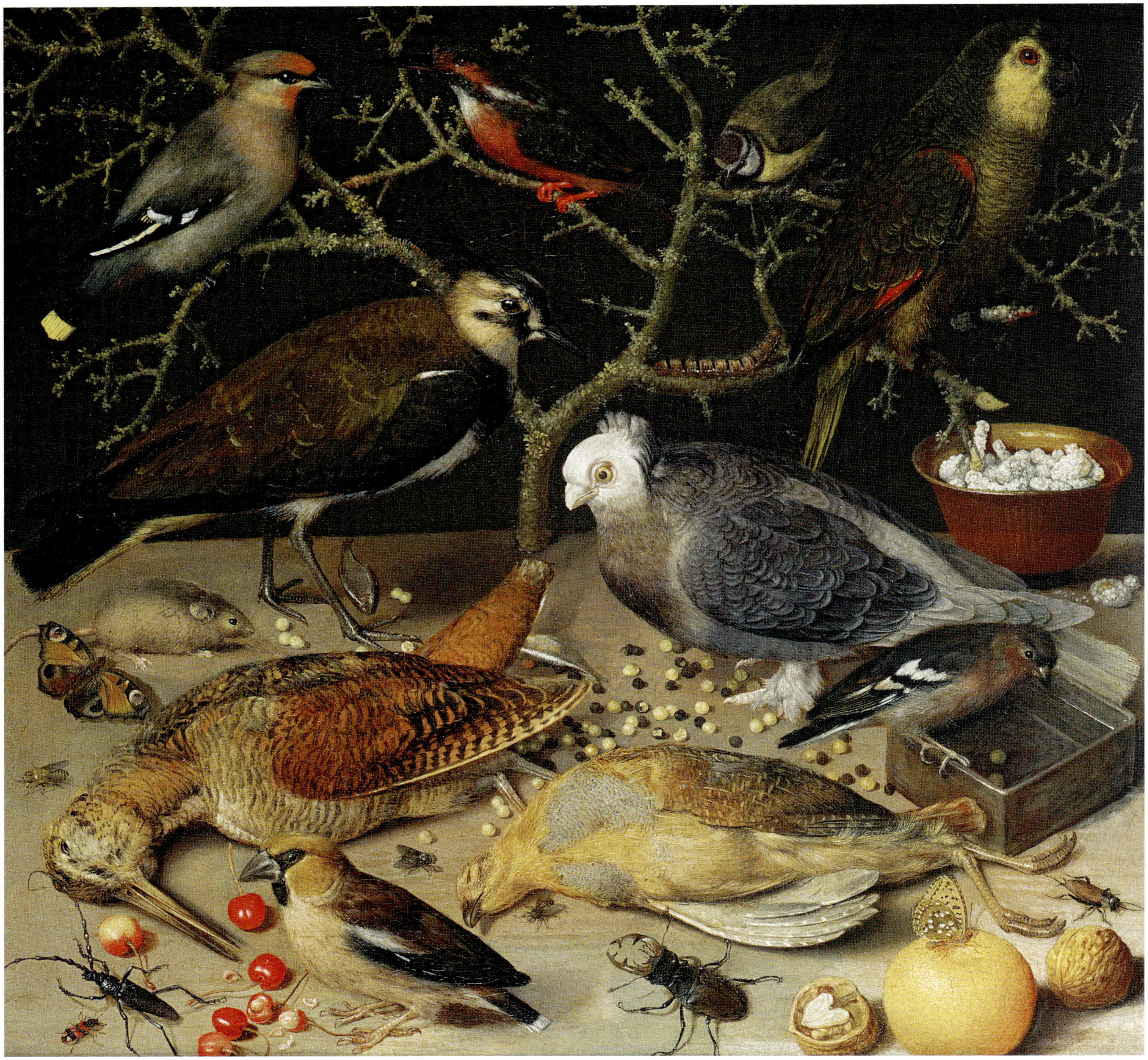

Georg Flegel
(1566–1638)
Still Life of Birds and Insects
1637
Oil on canvas
52.5 × 54.5 cm (20⅝ × 21⅜ in.)
Private collection

Flegel's still life is hardly still. It includes no fewer than ten birds (eight of which are shown alive), a mouse and various lively insects. A dead woodcock and partridge – tasty game birds – lie on the table. The artist seems to have been particularly fond of parrots, as they appear in other paintings, and he has included one perched in the branches here. Its neighbours on the mossy twigs are a waxwing, a kingfisher and a blue tit. Below them, a lapwing and a dove parade around the table, while a chaffinch perches on a box that contained the seeds or peppercorns that have spilled on to the surface, and a hawfinch appears to inspect the cherries. Flegel is an important Baroque still-life painter; he specialized in scenes of tables laid for meals, or covered with fruit and flowers.

Hans (Jan) Savery
(1589–1654)
The Dodo

1651
Oil on canvas
Dimensions unknown
Oxford University Museum of Natural History

The orthodox image of the now-extinct dodo – a giant flightless pigeon – is based on eight studies of the bird produced by the Dutch artist Roelandt Savery in the 1620s. This later version based on Savery's pictures, painted by his nephew Hans or Jan, is widely thought to have inspired the writer Lewis Carroll to include a dodo in his *Alice's Adventures in Wonderland*. The bird became extinct in the 1690s, but Roelandt Savery studied one when it was brought from its native Mauritius to Prince Maurice of Nassau's menagerie. The ornithologist George Edwards (1694–1773), who once owned one of Roelandt Savery's dodo paintings, claimed that it was painted 'in Holland from the living bird'. A contemporary report described the dodo as 'round and fat, few weigh less than fifty pound'. But modern research has challenged this observation and Savery's image, questioning whether the bird's bones would have supported the weight. Oxford University Museum of Natural History now displays a slimmed-down reconstruction of the dodo.

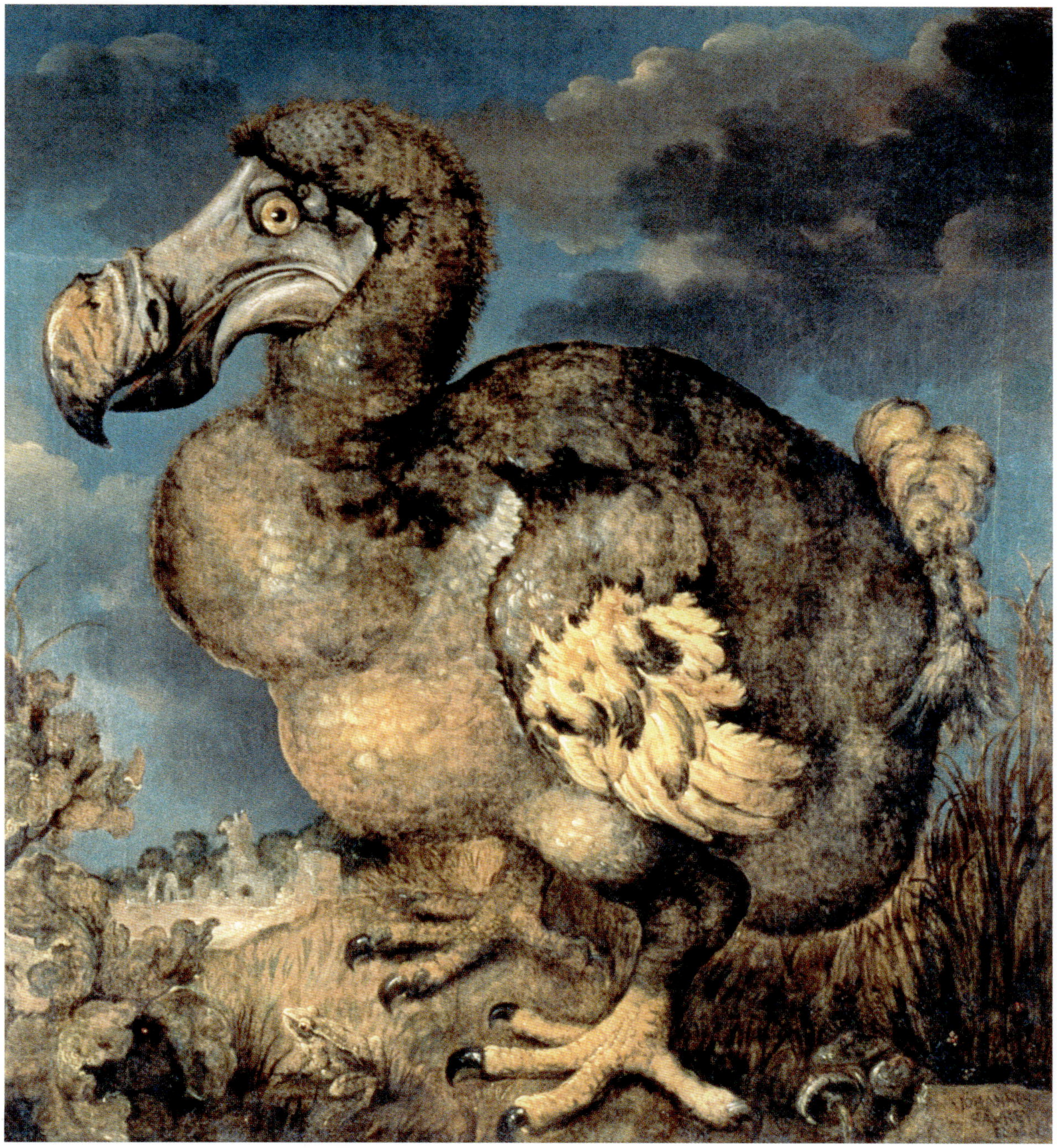

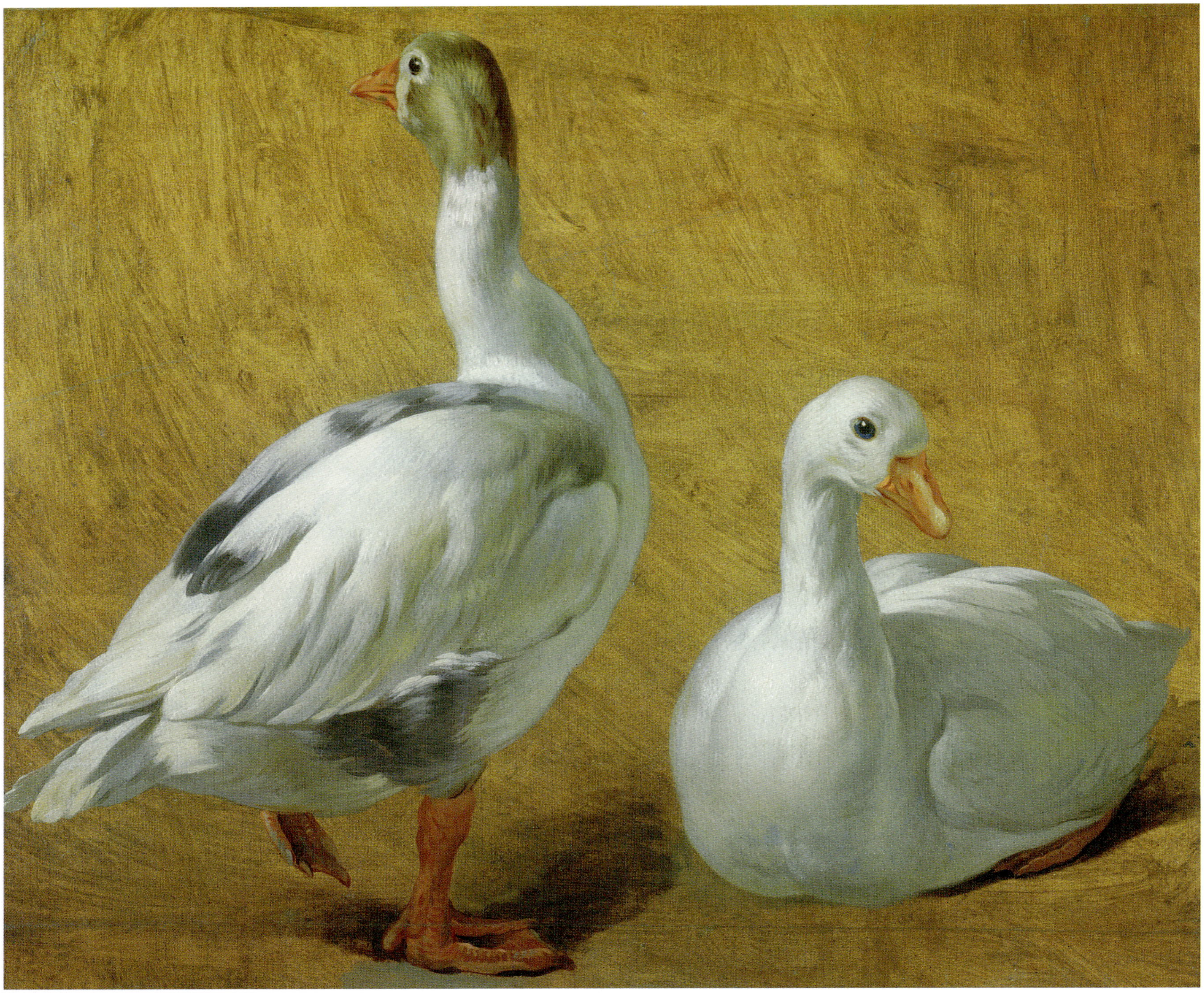

Alexandre-François Desportes
(1661–1743)
Study of Geese
First half of the 18th century
Oil on canvas laid on paper
52 × 64.3 cm (20½ × 25¼ in.)
Private collection

The French painter Desportes is best known for his scenes of hunting and piles of game – the trophies of the hunt – which he produced for the French kings Louis XIV and XV. He would follow the royal hunt around with a notebook in which he jotted sketches of the animals and birds in action. These domestic geese probably had a quieter life than the game birds pursued by the royal court, but they too would have ended up in the kitchen, since goose was enjoyed and foie gras (made from the livers of force-fed geese) served at royal banquets. In common with all the creatures in Desportes's studies, they have been faithfully observed, and their charming informality aligns them with modern artistic tastes. Desportes's role as court animal painter was eventually taken over by his younger contemporary Jean-Baptiste Oudry, who was equally adept at painting birds (p. 135).

Mark Catesby
(1682–1749)
A Blue Grosbeak and Sweet Bay

c. 1728–29
Watercolour and gouache over graphite with gum arabic
37.5 × 26.4 cm (14¾ × 10⅜ in.)
The Royal Collection

Often referred to as the father of American ornithology, the British naturalist Mark Catesby made two lengthy trips to America, where he collected plant specimens and studied the wildlife. His *Natural History of Carolina, Florida and the Bahama Islands*, published between 1731 and 1743, was the first comprehensive survey of the flora and fauna of south-eastern North America, which was then part of the British colonies. The 220 illustrations, engraved by Catesby himself, were compiled from sketches he had made and specimens he had collected during lengthy trips to Virginia, Carolina, Florida and the West Indies. Catesby's style was fairly flat, with minimal shading; he was aiming for an 'exact manner' that would provide an accurate record of what he had observed. Most of the plates combine flora and fauna, with the animals or birds placed near their source of food. Here, the blue grosbeak perches on a sweet bay tree, the seeds of which appear to drop into its mouth.

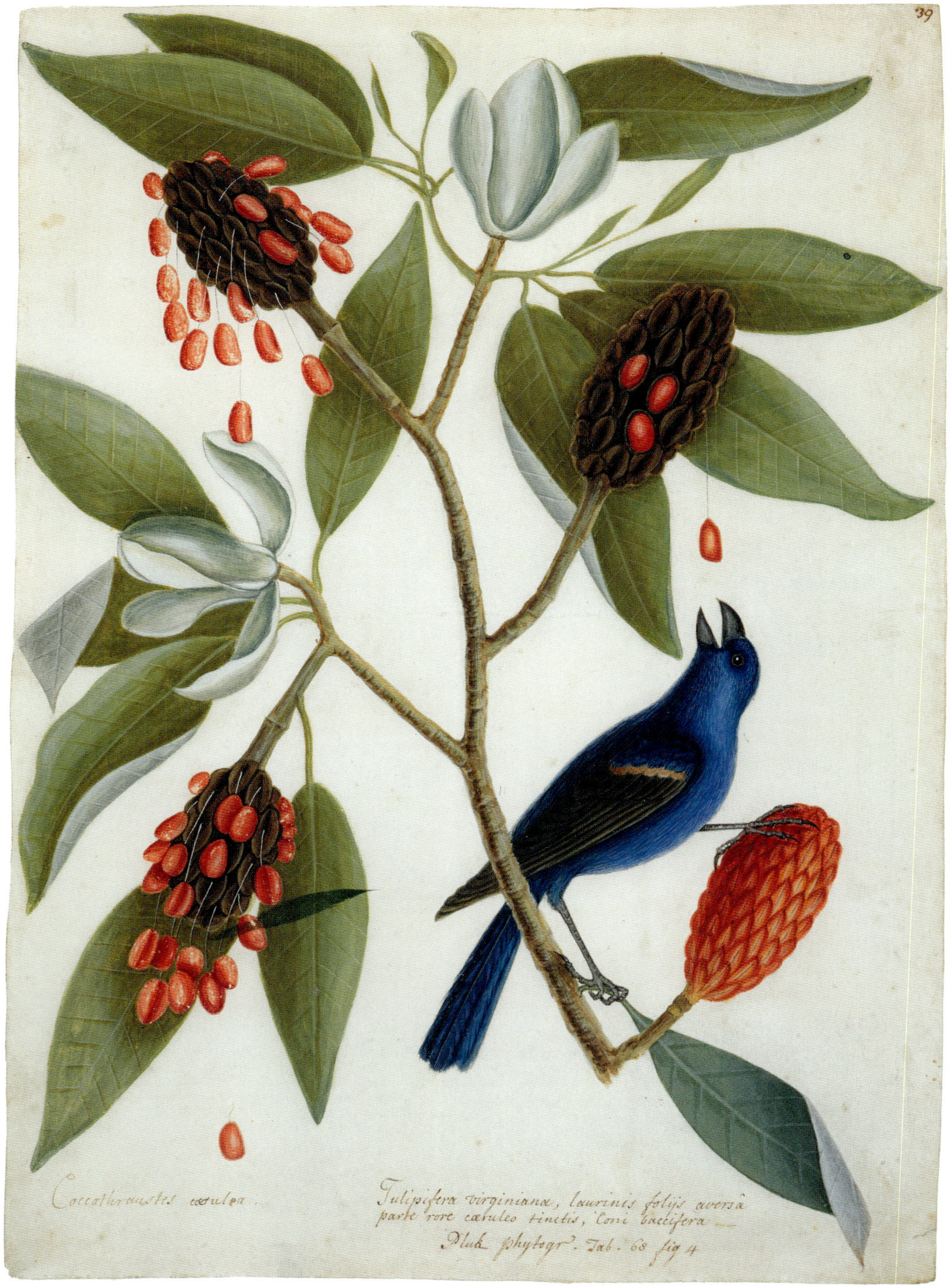

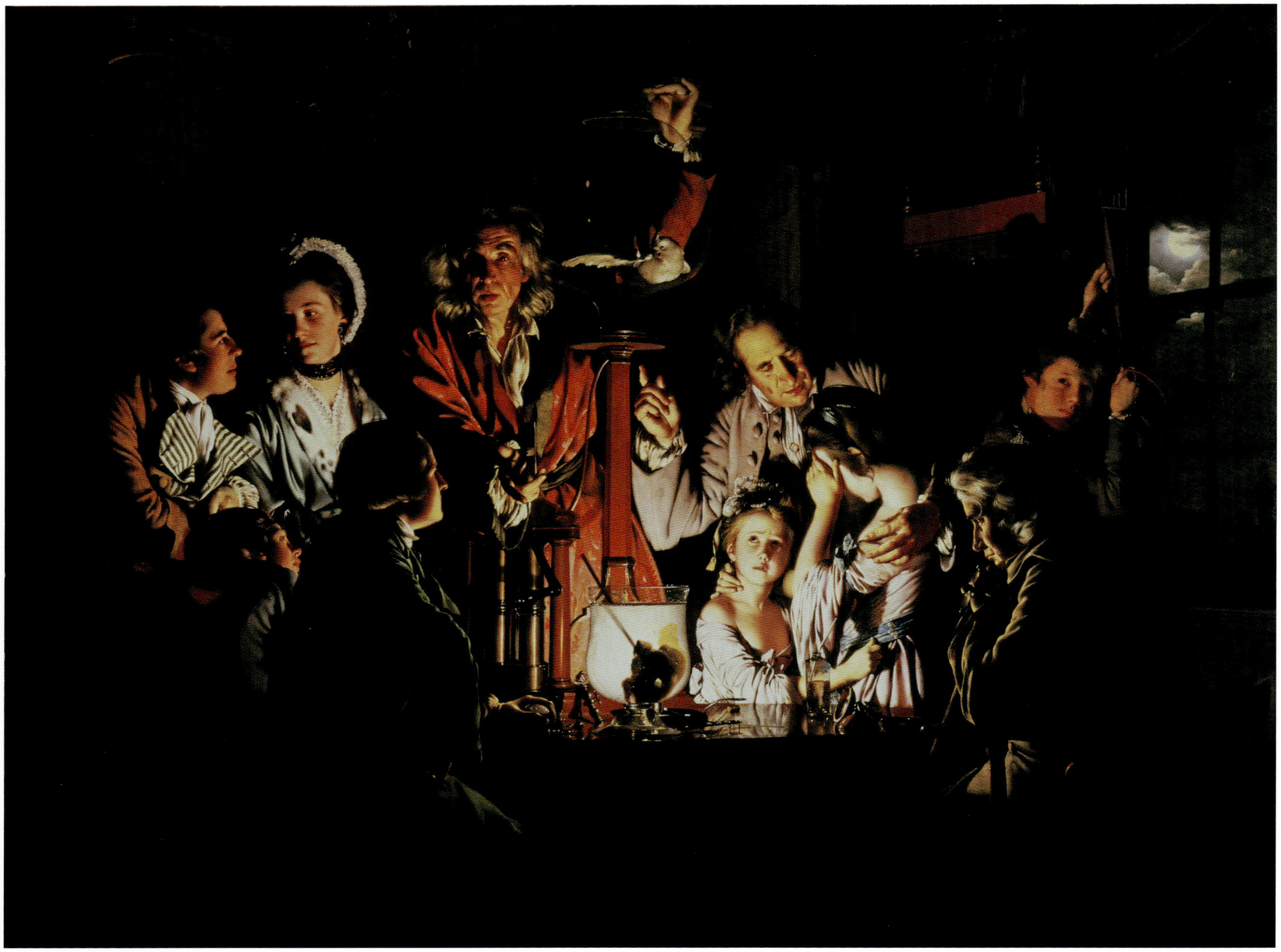

Joseph Wright of Derby (1734–1797)
An Experiment on a Bird in the Air Pump

1768
Oil on canvas
182.9 × 243.9 cm (72 × 96 in.)
The National Gallery, London

A scientific demonstration is taking place in a drawing room, where a travelling lecturer on natural philosophy is showing how an air pump can create a vacuum by withdrawing air from a glass chamber. The white cockatoo is flapping around inside, but appears to be sinking fast. Will it be allowed to die, or will the scientist let it live? Since a cockatoo was a more expensive bird than the sparrows or larks generally used in such experiments, it is likely that the experimenter does not intend to harm it. The spectators react in various ways: the two young girls are fearful for the bird, the men appear detached but curious, while the young lovers have eyes only for each other. When this work was painted, science was largely the province of interested amateurs. Joseph Wright was affiliated with the Lunar Society, whose members met every month near the full moon (so they could ride home by moonlight) to discuss science and nature; the full moon glimpsed through the window probably alludes to these gatherings. By 1768 the air pump had been around for a century, and scientific demonstrations involving birds or animals in vacuums were commonplace.

Ramsay Richard Reinagle (1775–1862)

An Ornithologist

1802

Oil on canvas

147.3 × 147.3 cm (58 × 58 in.)

Yale Center for British Art, New Haven, Connecticut

Sir Ashton Lever opened his natural history collection to the London public in 1775. Among the huge number of fossils, shells and animals on display were several stuffed birds brought back from the voyages of Captain Cook. The man responsible for their preservation was a Mr Thomson, who is probably the subject of this portrait. At this date taxidermy was not as sophisticated as it is now, but from the late seventeenth century onwards, curiosity about the natural world, and a desire to preserve newly discovered species, fuelled improvements in the preservation of the bird skins that were imported from the New World. However, the birds were not always padded out with much regard to musculature, since that was often unknown, as were the normal stance or flying habits of many species. Nonetheless, the three rooms full of stuffed birds in Lever's museum made it a useful source of reference for many artists, including Reinagle himself, before it was disbanded in 1806.

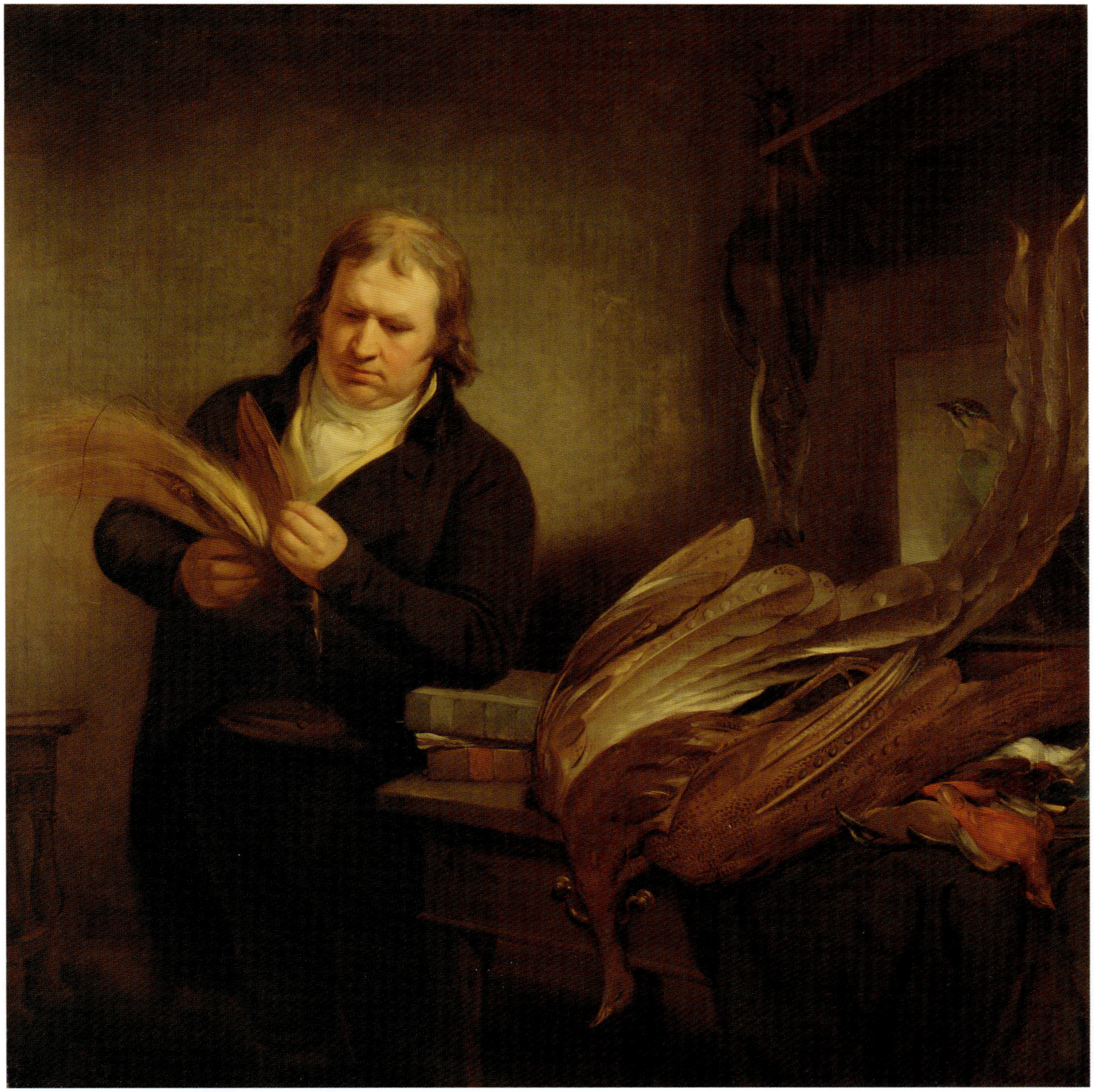

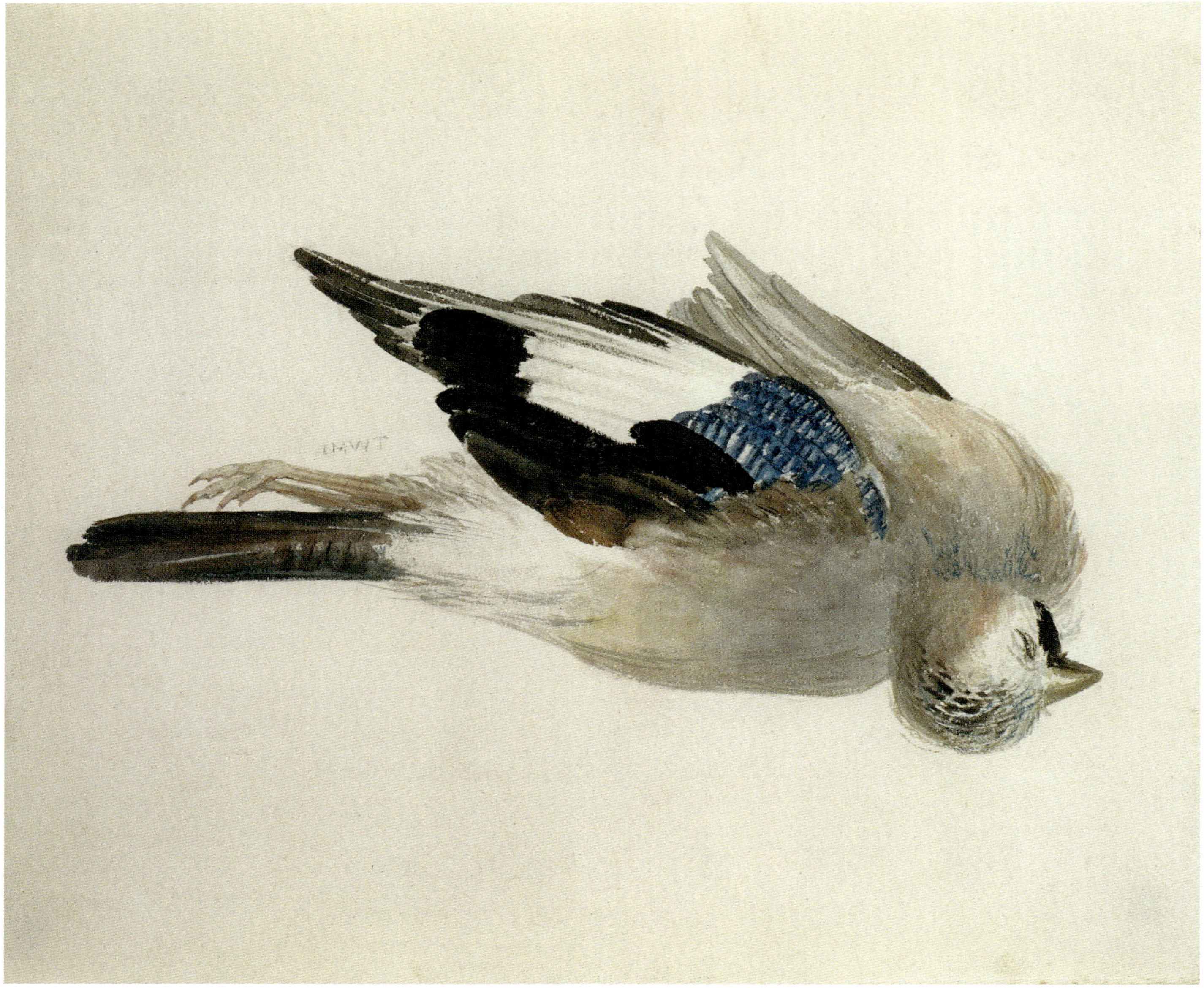

J.M.W. Turner
(1775–1851)
Jay
c. 1816
Pencil and watercolour on paper
9.1 × 23.2 cm (3½ × 9⅛ in.)
Leeds City Art Gallery

Turner, who is better known for his panoramic landscapes and observation of skies and sea, could also be an acute observer of smaller details in nature. In 1815–16 he produced twenty drawings of birds for a book on ornithology by his close friend and patron Walter Fawkes of Farnley Hall in Yorkshire, where he was a frequent visitor. While he was staying at the hall he took part in grouse shooting on the moors, seizing the opportunity to make several studies of native birds, two of them sketched from living examples and the rest from dead specimens. Fawkes's book, which ran to five volumes, included feathers and other conspicuous features of each bird. There is something poignant about this dead jay, the flash of blue on its wing introducing the only note of brilliant colour in this study of a lifeless corpse. The gamekeepers may have regarded the jay as a pest, since it eats the eggs and the young of several game birds.

John James Audubon (1785–1851)
Ivory-billed Woodpecker

1829
Coloured engraving
38.3 × 25.6 cm (15 × 10 in.)
Victoria and Albert Museum, London

Probably the best known of all the bird illustrators, Audubon realized early on that his heart lay in natural history rather than trade, and after a series of failed commercial ventures he devoted all his energy to an ambitious scheme to illustrate all the bird species of North America. Failing to interest American publishers, he eventually found an English publisher – Robert Havell – who was prepared to take on the mammoth project of producing *The Birds of America*, each copy of which contained 435 large colour illustrations representing 491 species. Audubon worked from specimens he had shot himself, pinning them to a board, often in highly dramatic poses. The board was covered with a grid, and he ruled the paper on which he drew with a similar grid to allow him faithfully to reproduce the bird's proportions. The artist produced his watercolours as quickly as possible before the plumage of his birds faded, but the prints owe their vividness of hue to the skill of the men who hand-coloured each plate, interpreting the originals as faithfully as possible. A number of Audubon's birds are now extinct; the ivory-billed woodpecker is a rare sight indeed.

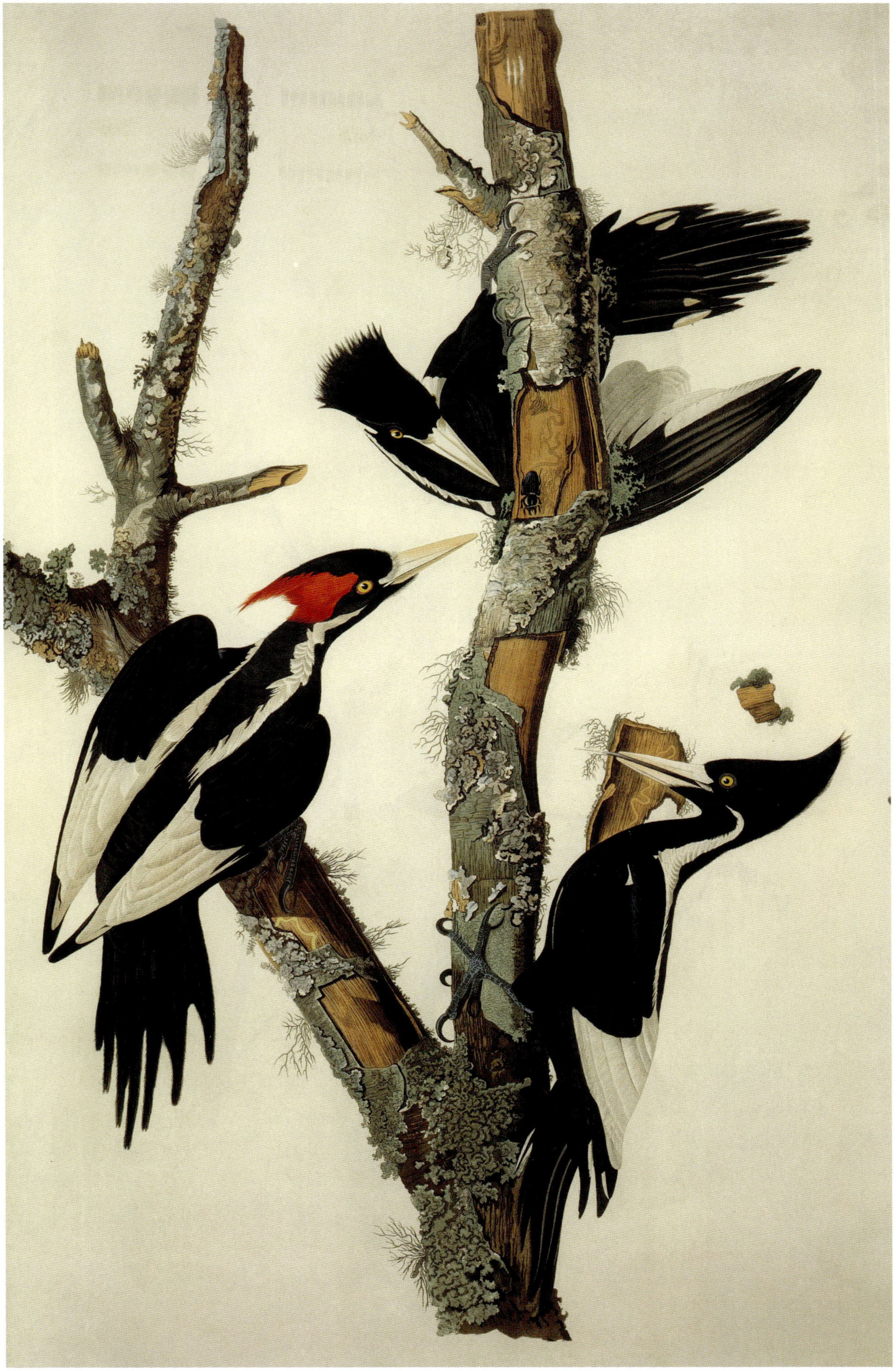

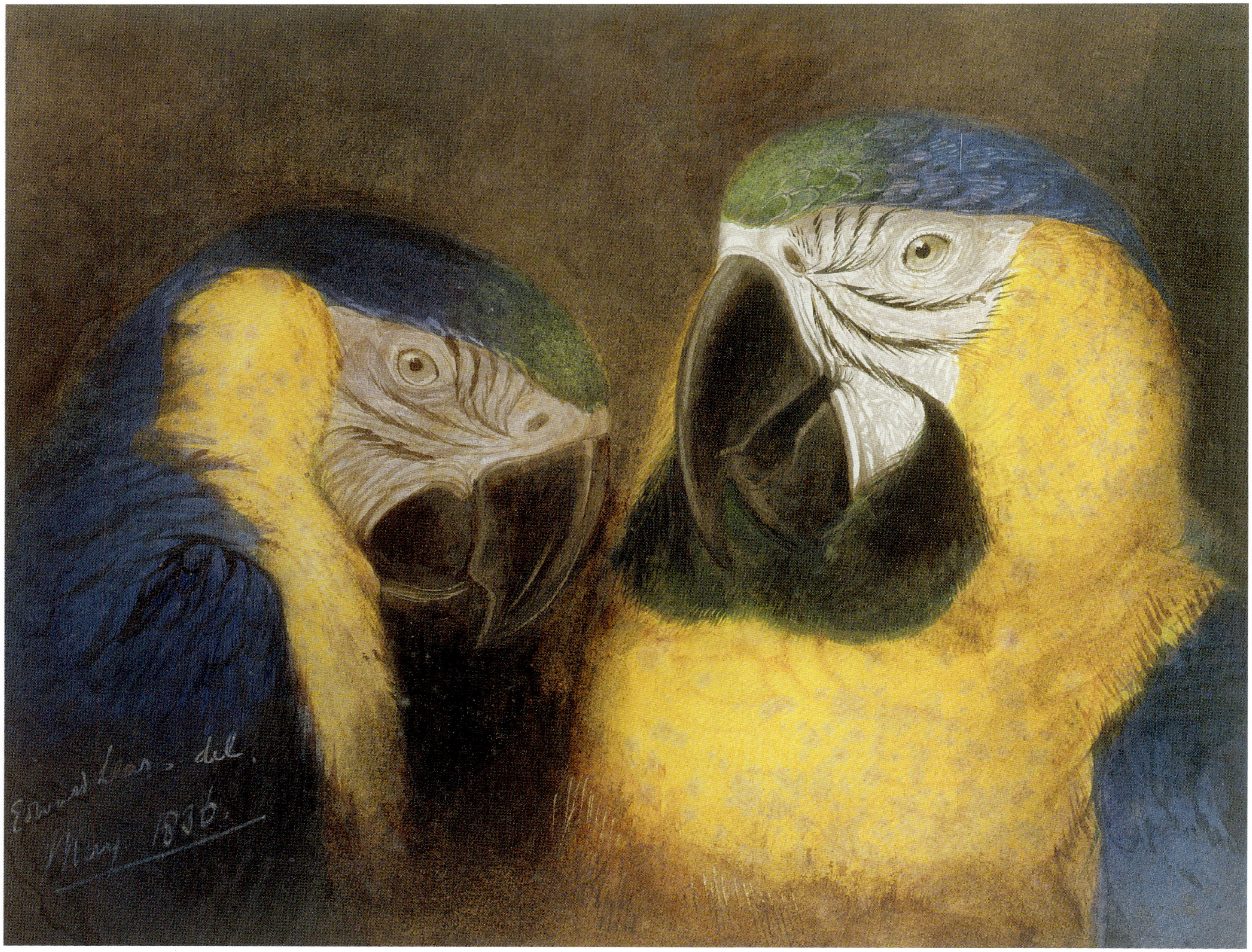

Edward Lear
(1812–1888)
Study of Heads of Ara ararauna *(Linn.), Brazil, May 1836*
1836
Watercolour on paper
Dimensions unknown
Knowsley Hall, Merseyside

Famous for his nonsense poems and comic verses, such as 'The Owl and the Pussycat', Edward Lear was also a keen and highly skilled painter of natural history. When the Zoological Society of London opened its collection of live animals to its members in 1828, he was one of its first visitors, having obtained permission to draw the parrots there with a view to compiling a book on all the known parrot species. His *Illustrations of the Family of Psittacidae, or Parrots* was published in 1830–32. It was not a financial success, but Lord Stanley (the future 13th Earl of Derby) was so impressed with it that he invited Lear to paint the rare birds and animals in his menagerie at Knowsley, near Liverpool. This was where Lear had the opportunity to capture the likeness of these colourful macaws. Because he preferred to observe his subjects from life rather than portray dead or stuffed specimens, his birds invariably have a liveliness about them. Indeed, these two look so animated that they could almost be having a conversation.

John Gould
(1804–1881)
engraved by Walter and Cohn
Marvellous Spatuletail

c. 1849–61
Colour lithograph
54.5 × 36.5 cm (21⅜ × 14⅜ in.)
Natural History Museum, London

A keen observer of birds from his teens, John Gould set up in business as a taxidermist, and in 1827 was appointed 'curator and preserver' of the museum collection at the Zoological Society of London. His greatest ambition, however, was to produce the best illustrated bird books, an endeavour in which he achieved great success. As he was not an expert draughtsman himself, he asked his wife, Elizabeth, to translate his rough sketches of birds into delicate watercolours and drawings on lithographic stone. He also collaborated with Edward Lear, whose depictions of birds were remarkable (opposite), although he lacked Gould's business acumen. Gould eventually published books on birds from all over the world – Europe, the Himalayas and Australia – and even helped Charles Darwin to identify the birds he brought back from the second *Beagle* voyage, in 1837. Gould particularly loved hummingbirds, and produced a five-volume work on them. This example, a native of Peru, is indeed as marvellous as its name implies. The male has two long feathers three times the length of its body, which it uses in courtship displays.

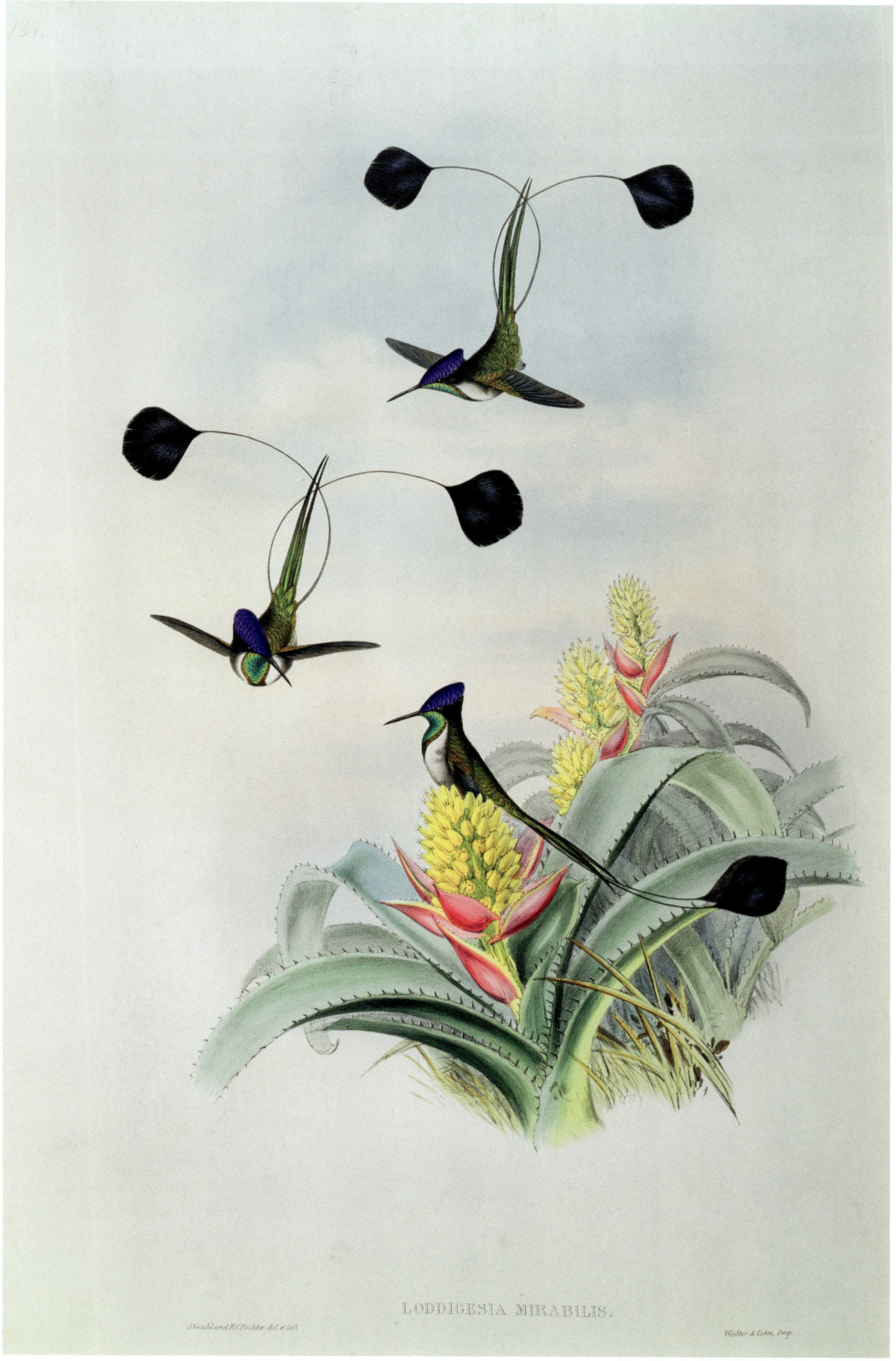

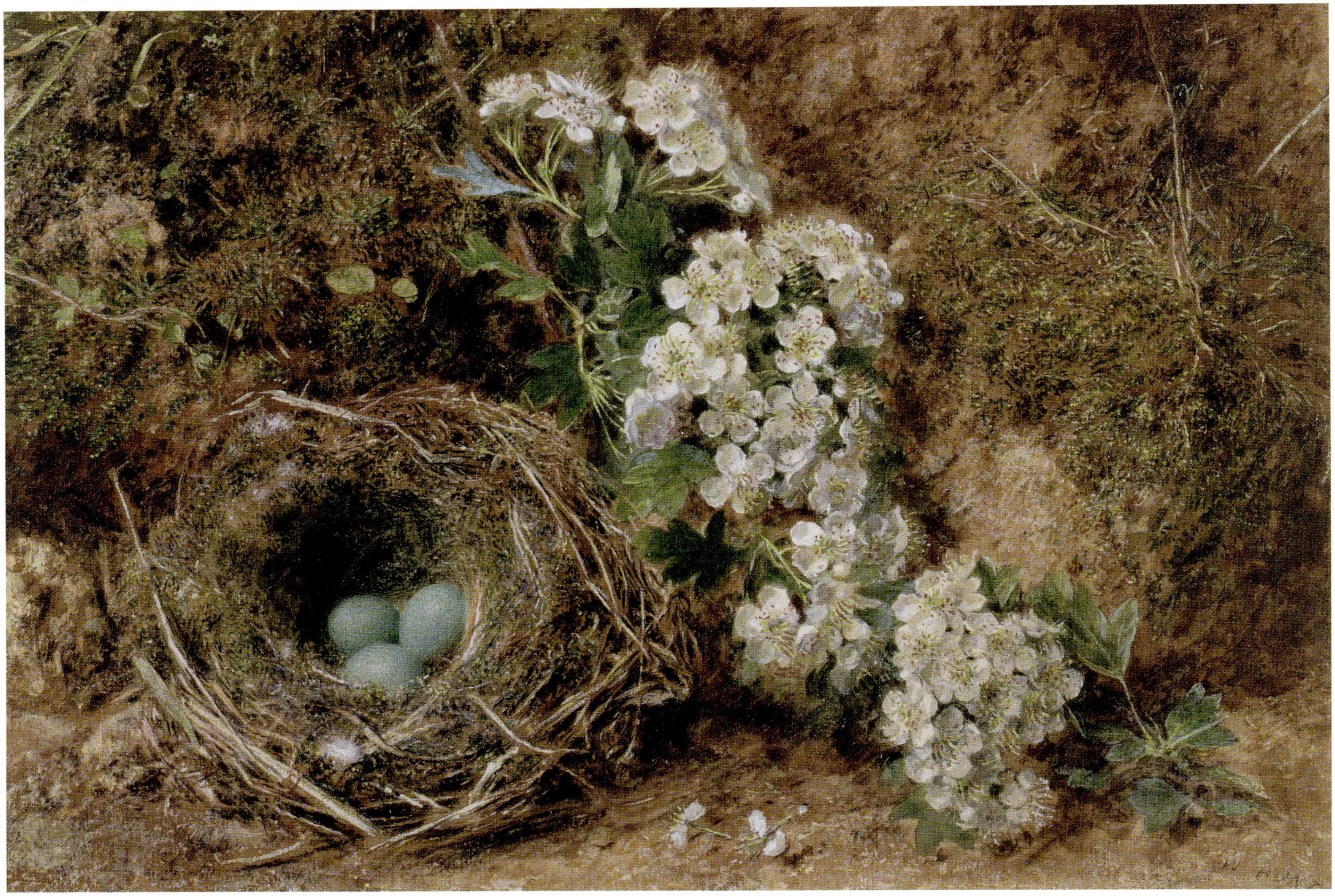

William Henry Hunt
(1790–1864)
May Blossom and a Hedge Sparrow's Nest
1845
Gouache on paper
19.7 × 28.6 cm (7¾ × 11¼ in.)
Bolton Museum and Art Gallery

William Henry Hunt was a painter and watercolourist of rustic genre scenes, fruit and flowers, landscapes, architectural studies and candlelit scenes. He was enormously prolific, and exhibited almost 800 pictures at the Old Watercolour Society during his lifetime. Although his subject matter was quite wide-ranging, in later life he naturally chose to concentrate on his most popular and lucrative theme – birds' nests in hedgerows – a speciality that earned him the nickname 'Bird's Nest' Hunt. The birds' nests, often paired with seasonal blooms, were delineated in microscopic, almost hallucinatory detail. The influential critic John Ruskin was a great admirer of his powers of observation and collected his work. John Clare, famous for his nature poetry, was moved to comment on a hedge sparrow's nest in his poem 'Bird's Nest':

And still hedge sparrow moping in the shade
Near the hedge bottom, weaves of homely stuff,
Dead grass and mosses green, an hermitage
For secrecy and shelter rightly made;
And beautiful it is to walk beside
The lanes and hedges where their homes abide.

John Atkinson Grimshaw (1836–1893)
A Dead Linnet

1862–63
Oil on board
16 × 24 cm (6¼ × 9⅜ in.)
Leeds City Art Gallery

John Atkinson Grimshaw is famous today for his moonlight scenes, but his earliest works were still-life studies of fruit, flowers, birds' nests and dead birds. These pieces of direct observation were one way in which the artist learned his trade, as he does not seem to have taken formal instruction from anyone. At the time, such still lifes as this were very fashionable, influenced by the example of 'Bird's Nest' Hunt (opposite). Sixty years before Grimshaw captured the beauty of this dead bird, the poet William Wordsworth had been captivated by a live one fluttering about the boughs of a fruit tree in bloom. He was moved to pay tribute to this lovely bird in his poem 'The Green Linnet', which ends:

Amid yon tuft of hazel trees,
That twinkle to the gusty breeze,
Behold him perched in ecstasies,
Yet seeming still to hover;
There! where the flutter of his wings
Upon his back and body flings
Shadows and sunny glimmerings,
That cover him all over.

My dazzled sight he oft deceives,
A brother of the dancing leaves;
Then flits, and from the cottage-eaves
Pours forth his song in gushes;
As if by that exulting strain
He mocked and treated with disdain
The voiceless Form he chose to feign,
While fluttering in the bushes.

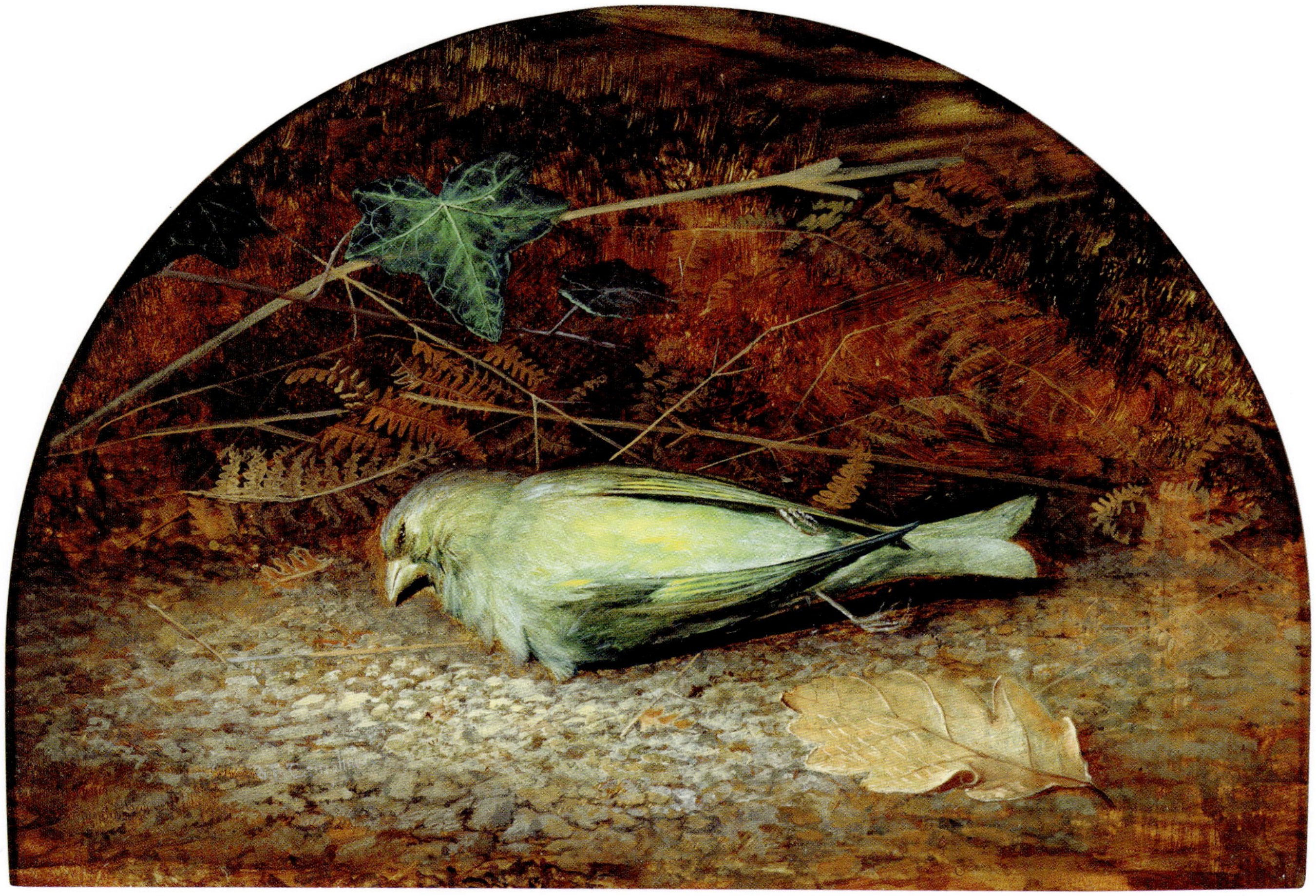

John Ruskin
(1819–1900)
Study of a Peacock Feather

1873
Watercolour on paper
21.1 × 13.2 cm (8¼ × 5⅛ in.)
Sheffield Galleries and Museums Trust

John Ruskin was a talented watercolourist as well as an art critic and social theorist, and he used his own drawings to illustrate his lectures when he was Slade Professor of Fine Art at the University of Oxford in the 1870s. Among these visual aids were studies he had made of birds' skulls and feathers. It is possible that these drawings were inspired by the studies Turner had made of birds at Farnley Hall in Yorkshire in 1815–16, as Ruskin saw them when he visited the hall in 1851 (p. 154). Ruskin also had his own collection of bird illustrations, including works by John Gould, John James Audubon, Thomas Bewick and Edward Lear. There are a number of Ruskin's meticulous drawings of peacock feathers in existence, and although they are all precisely delineated they have a poetry that transcends their scientific function. Ruskin must have been moved by the sheer perfection and beauty of the plumage, for he wrote: 'I have to draw a peacock's breast feather without having heaven to dip my brush in.'

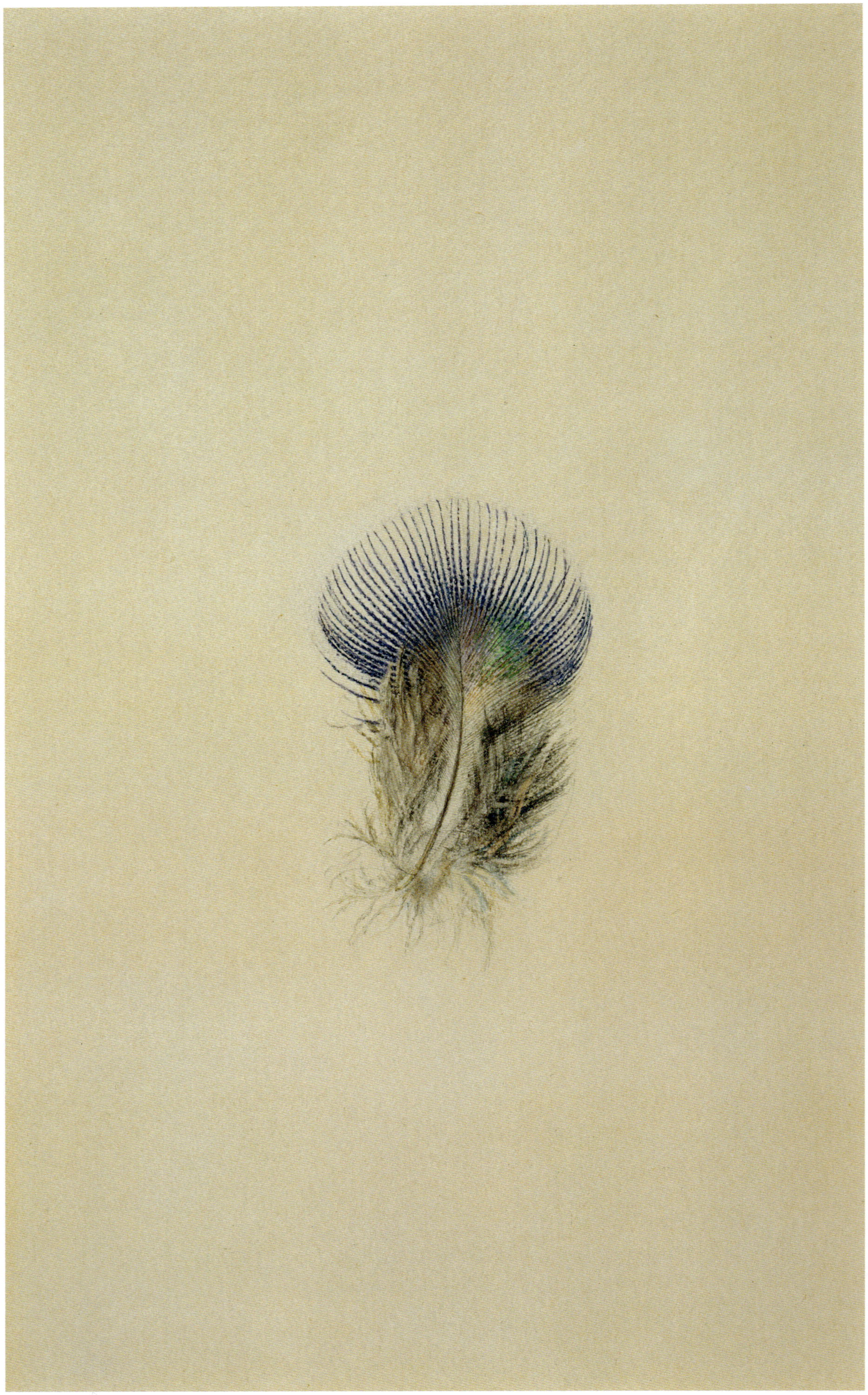

Martin Johnson Heade
(1819–1904)
Two Hummingbirds

c. 1865–75
Oil on canvas
29.4 × 21.8 cm (11½ × 8½ in.)
Brooklyn Museum, New York

The American artist Martin Johnson Heade started his career as a portraitist, then turned his attention to landscape, focusing particularly on the flat salt marshes of the American north-east coast. Three trips to South America, in 1863–64, 1866 and 1870, signalled another change of artistic direction, one that allowed him to give full expression to his obsession with hummingbirds. Heade had been fascinated by them since boyhood, and late in life claimed that he had raised and tamed hummingbirds for more than fifty years. When he went to Brazil in 1863 it was with the aim of preparing illustrations for a book on them. The book failed to materialize, either because of financial difficulties or because Heade was not satisfied with the quality of the reproductions, but he put his studies to good use in an extensive series of paintings featuring hummingbirds (frequently in conjunction with giant orchids) set against lush and mountainous landscapes. Heade's paintings naturally invite comparison with the work of Audubon and Gould, but he always placed his birds in fully realized tropical habitats, infused with exotic romanticism.

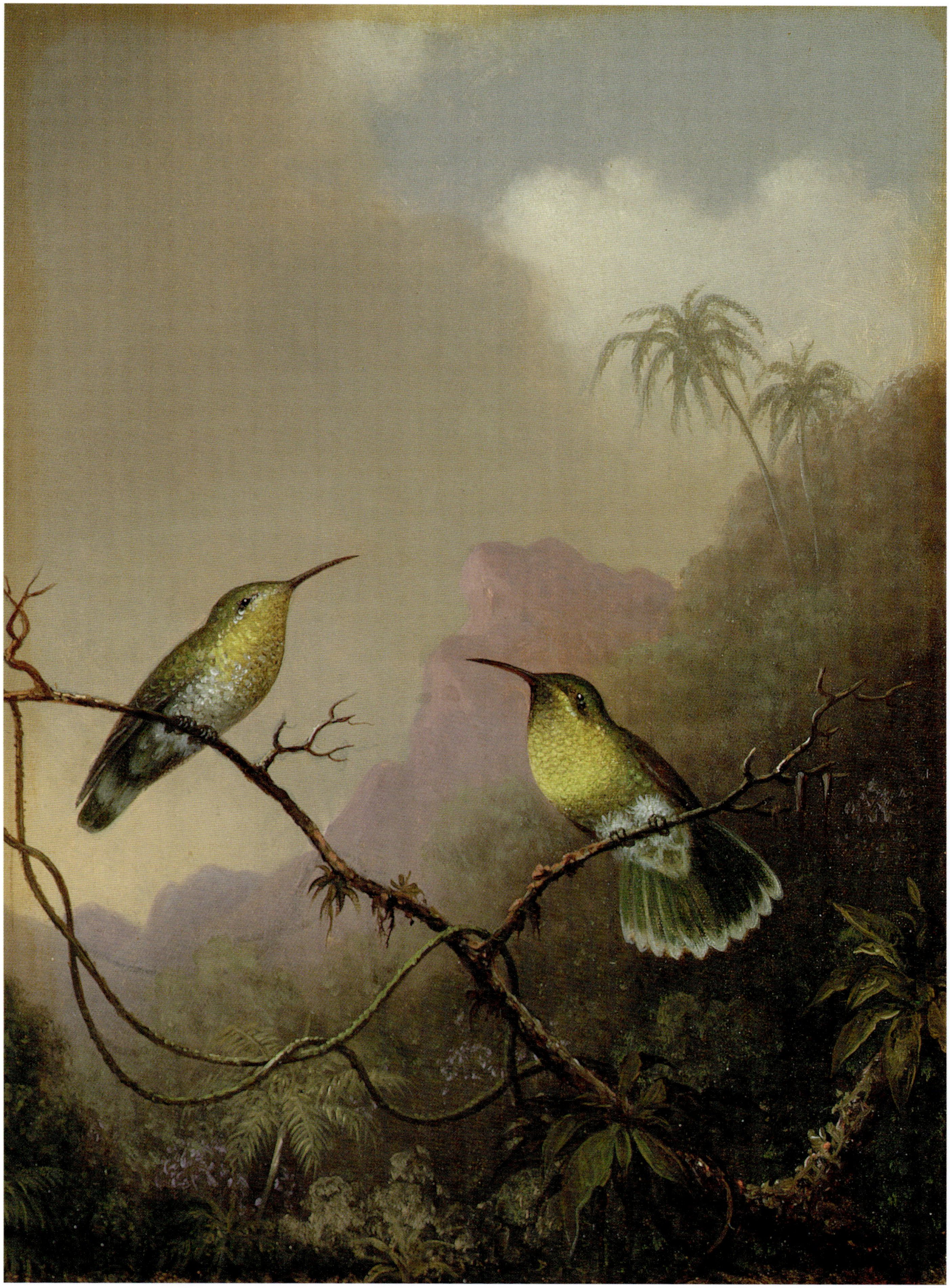

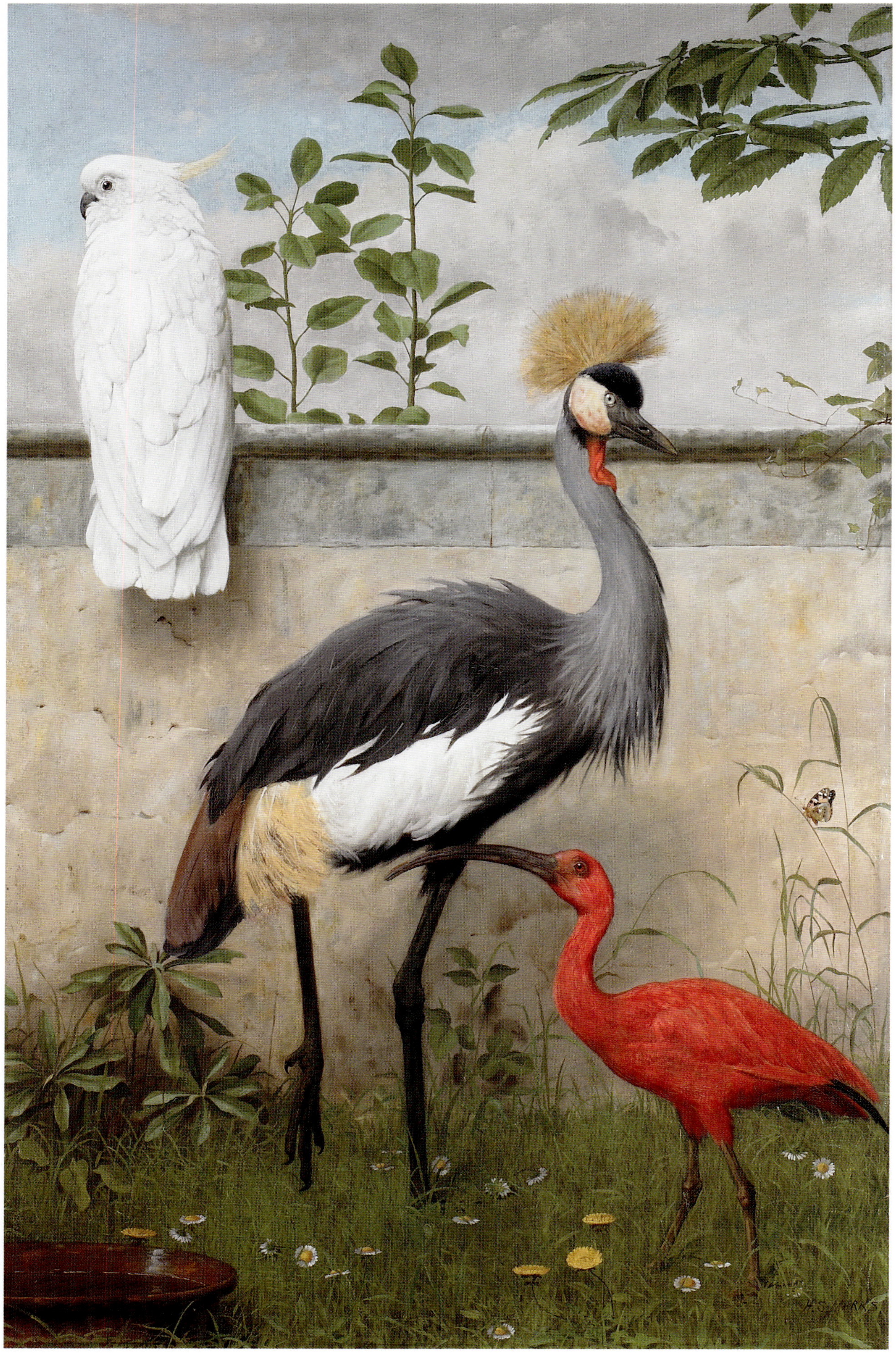

Henry Stacy Marks
(1829–1898)
Crested Crane, Cockatoo and Scarlet Ibis

c. 1874–80
Oil on canvas
Dimensions unknown
Private collection

In 1874 Henry Stacy Marks's patron, the Duke of Westminster, commissioned him to produce twelve decorative panels of birds for his country house, Eaton Hall in Cheshire. Previously known as a painter of historical and literary subjects, the artist honed his powers of bird observation with several visits to London Zoo. He is now best remembered for his bird subjects, which were very popular with the Victorian public, partly because of their light-hearted tone. A number of these pictures place the birds within a narrative in recognizably human situations – getting married or in a board meeting, for example – but this anthropomorphizing tendency is less in evidence here. Although the individual birds are painted with great attention to detail, this particular grouping would never occur in nature, since the crested crane is native to sub-Saharan Africa, the scarlet ibis to South America and the white cockatoo to Indonesia. Ruskin, who was a friend of Stacy Marks, greatly admired his bird studies.

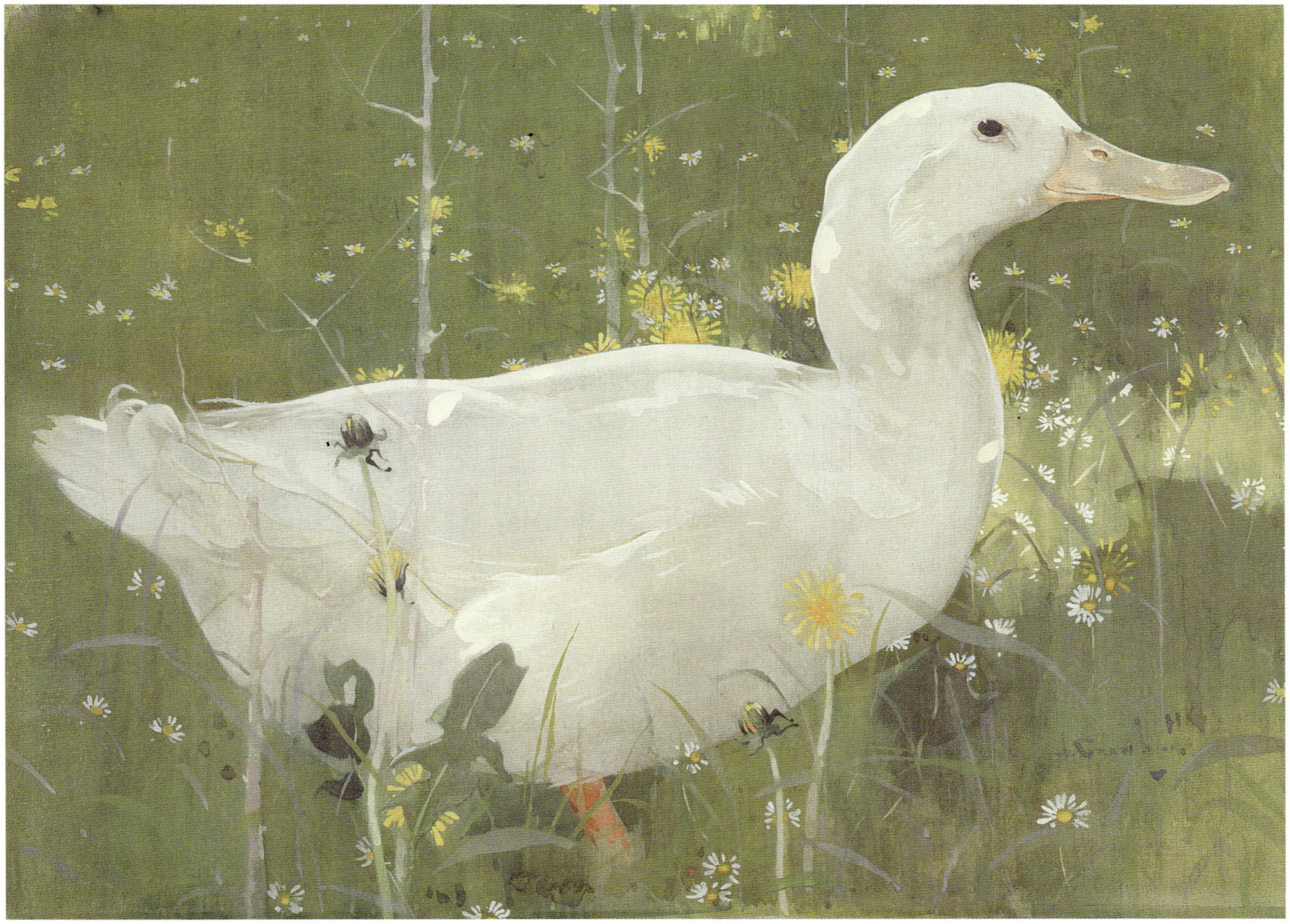

Joseph Crawhall (1861–1913)
The White Drake

c. 1895
Gouache on canvas
40.6 × 57.2 cm (16 × 22½ in.)
Private collection

Although he was born in Northumbria, Crawhall is generally thought of as a Scottish artist because of his close association with the group of painters known as the Glasgow Boys, who were influenced by contemporary French painting. Indeed, this work has all the freshness of a French Impressionist picture. Crawhall specialized in sensitive watercolours and gouaches of animals and birds. He worked mainly from memory, but would study his subjects intensely before attempting to distil their essential character. While many Victorian painters sentimentalized domestic animals, Crawhall did not attempt to infuse his subjects with human characteristics. This white drake, seen in dappled sunlight in a meadow filled with dandelions, daisies and reeds, is both believable and decorative. Crawhall's drake has a quiet dignity, but many people find ducks innately comic – a quality encapsulated in Disney's much-loved cartoon character Donald Duck, who was created in 1934.

Archibald Thorburn (1860–1935)

Ptarmigan

1903
Oil on canvas
30.4 × 50.8 cm (12 × 20 in.)
The Fleming Collection

In common with his Scandinavian contemporary Bruno Liljefors (p. 137), the Scottish artist Archibald Thorburn specialized in depicting birds in their natural environment. He was one of the first artists in the British Isles to go out into the field and sketch birds from life, at a time when others were basing their studies on dead or stuffed examples. Although he established his reputation as an illustrator of books on birds, and is most highly regarded as a watercolourist, Thorburn also produced a number of oil paintings. These generally show game birds, wildfowl and birds of prey in the Scottish mountains and grouse moors. This picture is a wonderful evocation of ptarmigan in their breeding ground in the Scottish Highlands, probably Inverness-shire, where the artist frequently worked. He was a great supporter of the Royal Society for the Protection of Birds, designing several Christmas cards for the organization and serving as its vice president.

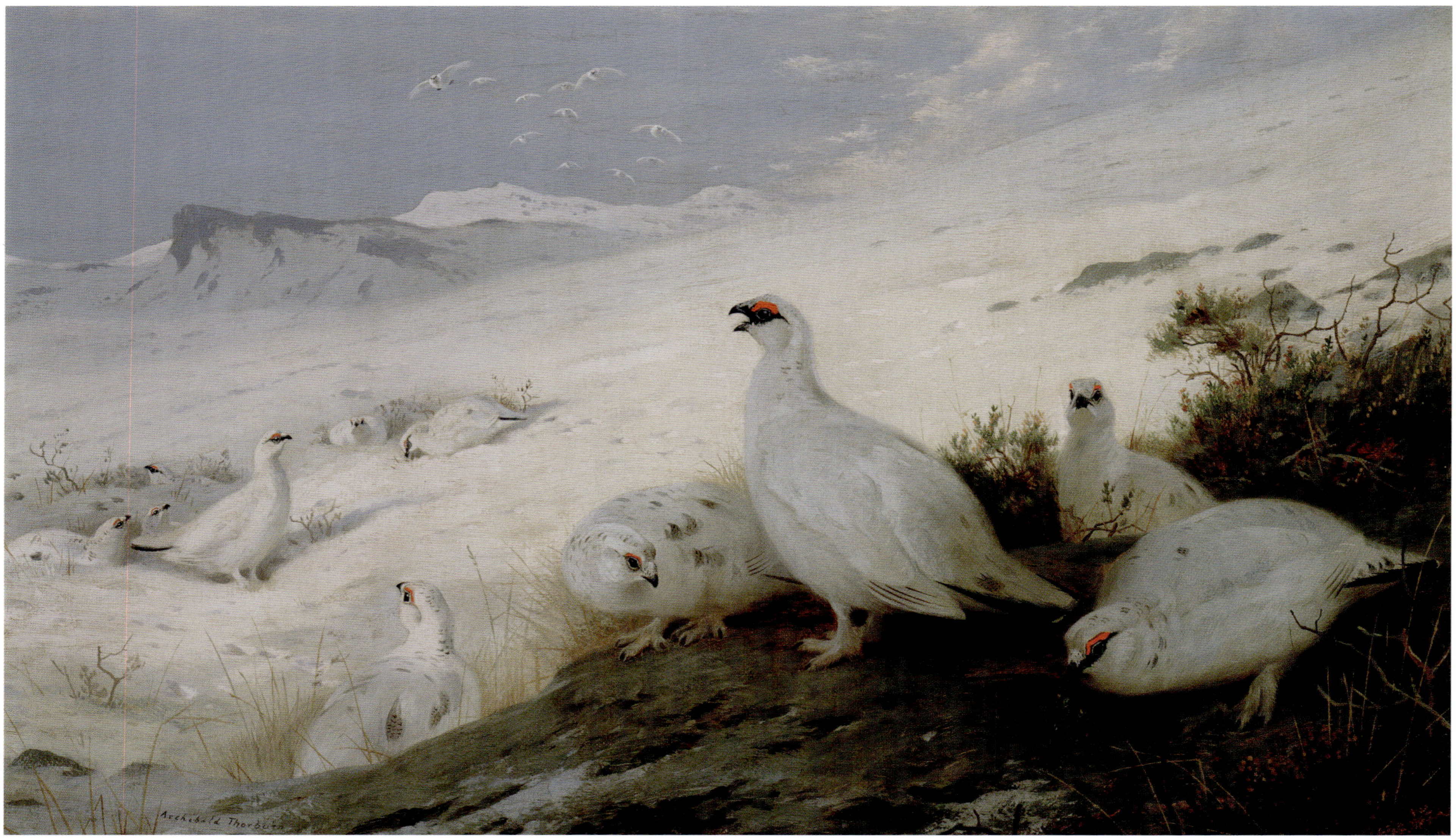

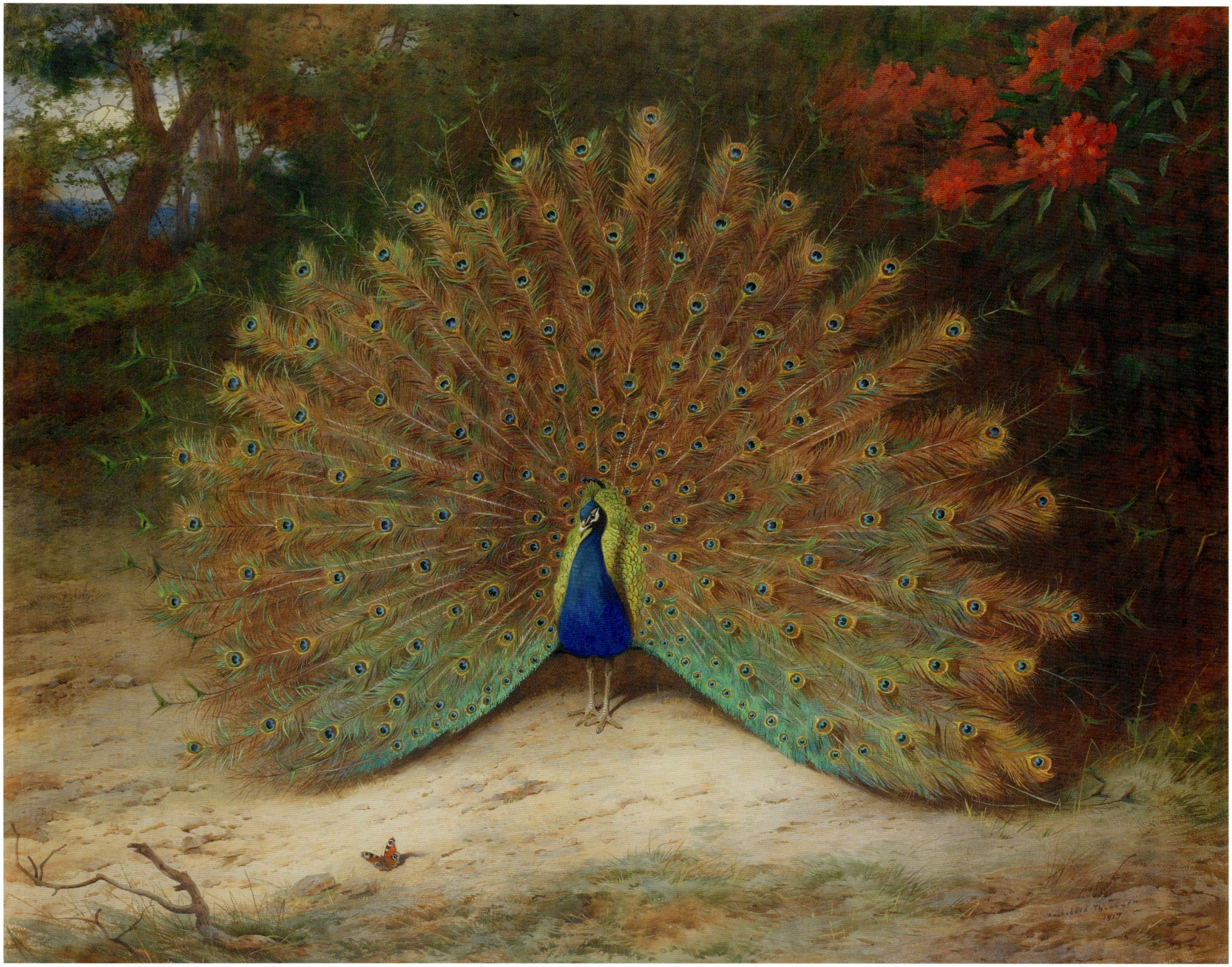

Archibald Thorburn (1860–1935)

Peacock and Peacock Butterfly

1917
Watercolour
87.5 × 111.5 cm (34⅜ × 43⅞ in.)
Private collection

A magnificent peacock fans out its tail feathers, completely outshining the peacock butterfly with delicate markings that spreads its wings in the foreground. Thorburn recalled that he had nightmares about painting the enormous number of eyes on the peacock's tail, but the effort was clearly worth it. His obituarist, writing in the *Scottish Naturalist* in 1936, said that 'of all his pictures … the most daring was a gigantic one … of a peacock in full display in front of a rich rhododendron in full bloom; a gorgeous sunset and woodland as the background'. He went on to praise the picture's rich colour and accuracy of detail. This watercolour is one of Thorburn's largest works, conceived on a grand scale that suits its splendid subject. Thorburn liked portraying birds in their natural habitat, but the extravagance of the bird's plumage seen against the English parkland serves to underline its status as an exotic import.

The Sociable Bird

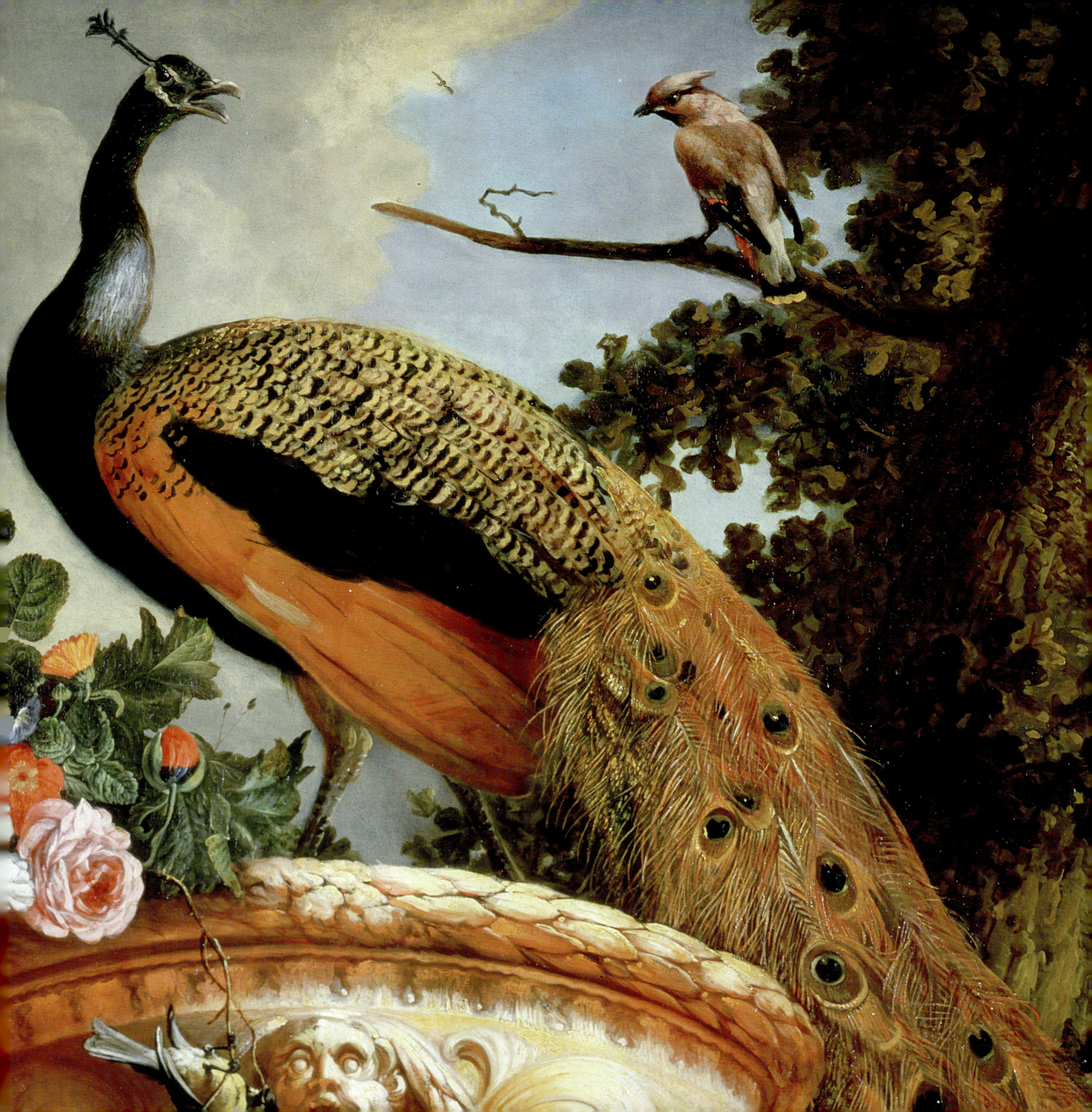

Large assemblies of birds appear in subject paintings from the Renaissance onwards. They are seen in depictions of biblical stories, such as Noah's Ark or the Garden of Eden, or mythical ones, such as Orpheus charming the animals. But it was not until the seventeenth century that a distinctive genre developed in which birds themselves provide the narrative.

The fact that birds appear to chirrup and chatter among themselves has given rise to the fantasy that they feel similar emotions to people, and that they are capable of arranging their own societies and relationships along human lines. The fanciful notion of different species of bird assembling socially is a seductive one with an ancient tradition. The Persian poet Farid ud-Din Attar's *Conference of Birds*, written in 1177 as an allegory on the Sufi search for God, describes birds gathering for a pilgrimage in order to choose a king. Each of the thirty birds on the pilgrimage has its own special character and story to tell. Geoffrey Chaucer's *Parliament of Fowls*, written two centuries later, describes a dream in which Lady Nature allows all the birds to assemble on St Valentine's Day to choose a mate. The conceit has very little to do with the way most birds behave, but it proved a fertile idea for such artists as Carl Wilhelm de Hamilton (p. 176), offering them the perfect chance to produce pictures that showed off their prowess in depicting a large variety of colourful birds crammed together in one large, vibrant composition.

While poets and artists may have enjoyed imagining this annual avian festival of love, some went further and invented the idea of a birds' concert. In his poem *A Concert of Birds*, the poet William Browne (*c.* 1590–1645) imagined such a scene, in which birds spontaneously gathered together in trees and bushes, each adding his own voice, from the thrush's countertenor to the crow's deep bass (p. 170). From the mid-seventeenth century the concert motif provided a focal point (and comic potential) for many paintings in which birds are shown gathered together. At this date musicians were beginning to take an interest in the sounds birds make; in 1650 the German scholar Athanasius Kircher even published a book containing musically notated birdsong. In paintings it is usually the owl that holds the musical score (pp. 172 and 183). The phenomenon of mobbing the owl, which occurs in nature, also provided an excellent pretext for painting bird compositions with a touch of anthropomorphic humour (p. 171, bottom).

Most of the pictures in this chapter were painted in the seventeenth and eighteenth centuries by Dutch, Flemish and English artists. This was an era when European traders and voyagers ventured far afield to Asia, Africa and South America, bringing back new, exotic birds (or bird skins) that had never been seen before outside their native lands. Some of these species found their way into menageries set up by royalty and aristocrats: patrons who were keen to commission artists to provide a visual record of their new trophies. Wealthy merchants, enriched by trade with the New World, also wanted showy, decorative pictures for the reception rooms of their recently constructed houses. Artists in The Netherlands, England, France and Italy were only too eager to meet the demand by providing paintings of birds, flowers and fruit in opulent settings.

Not all the artists based their compositions on an obvious narrative, such as a concert or a parliament, but all showed birds interacting with one another in an attempt to provide a link between them. Birds were often represented in highly unlikely combinations and exotic habitats (often vaguely Italianate) that bore no relation to reality, but which possess a whimsical charm.

Francis Barlow
(1626–1704)
Jay, Green Woodpecker, Pigeons and Redstart
c. 1650
Oil on canvas
76.2 × 63.8 cm (30 × 25⅛ in.)
Yale Center for British Art, New Haven, Connecticut

Francis Barlow is the earliest known British animal-painter; when he began his career, most of the artists specializing in this area were from the Low Countries. Although he was based in London, he made several expeditions to the countryside and produced a number of canvases showing native British birds against a landscape. Other paintings depict the more exotic species he was able to observe in the Earl of Lauderdale's aviary at Ham House, south-west of London, and Charles II's menagerie in St James's Park. The king's collection of birds included ostriches (presented by the Moroccan ambassador), cassowaries, peregrines and eagles, all of which found their way into Barlow's compositions. His pictures of hunting, fishing and falconry have earned him the title of 'the father of British sporting art'. Barlow's observations were disseminated through his etchings of birds and also his books: *Birds and Beasts in Sixty-Seven Excellent and Useful Prints* (1655) and *Birds and Fowles of Various Species* (1658).

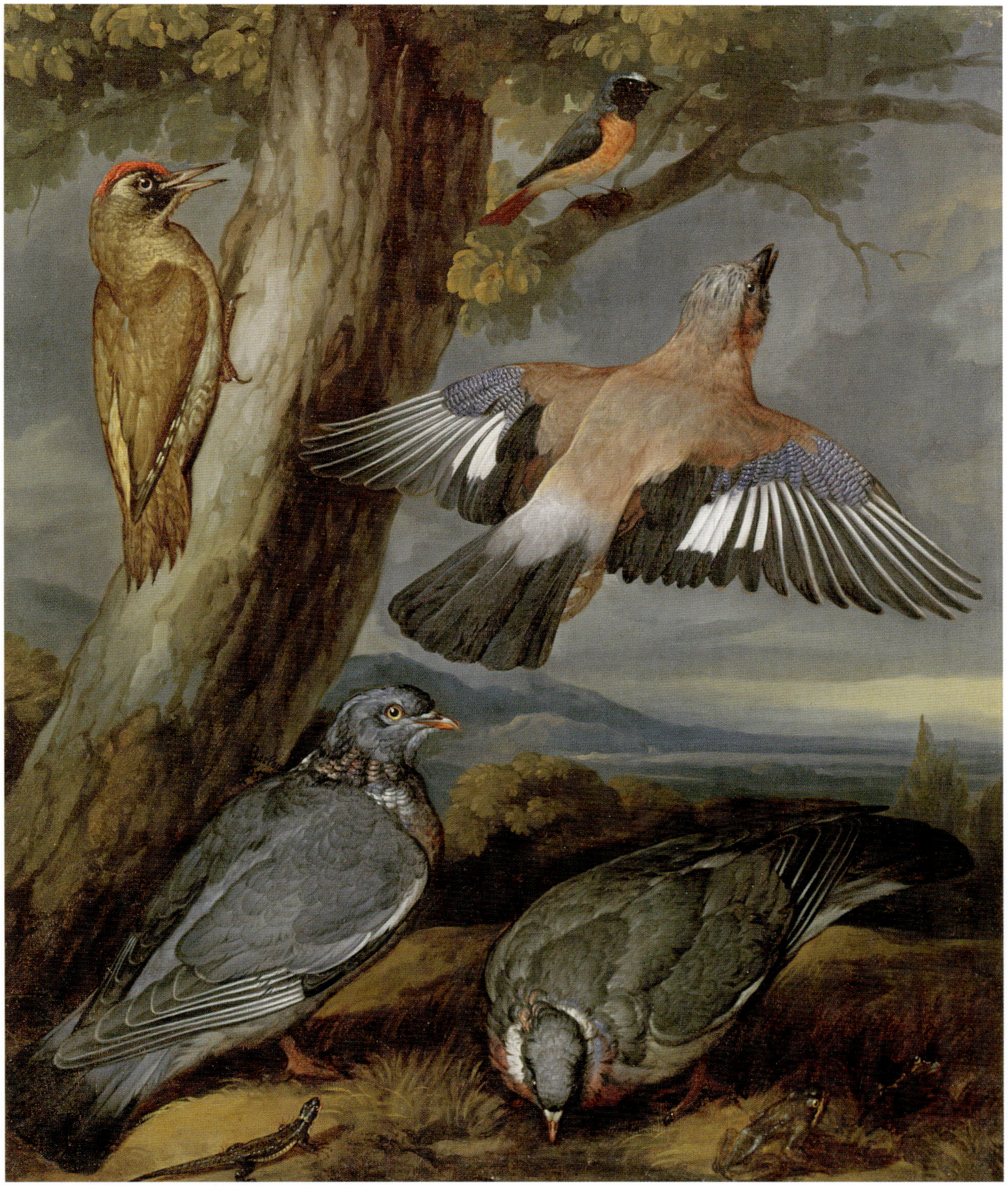

Flemish school
Birds of Britain

Late 17th or early 18th century
Oil on canvas
147.5 × 96.5 cm (58 × 38 in.)
Anglesey Abbey, Cambridgeshire

Fifty birds have gathered in what appears to be an English country park to take part in a bird concert. On the ground is a scroll of music, and the owl – which always occupies an important place in depictions of bird concerts – is holding a conductor's baton in its claw. The poet William Browne describes such a scene in the opening lines of his verse *A Concert of Birds*:

The mounting lark (day's herald) got on wing,
Bidding each bird choose out his bough and sing.
The lofty treble sung the little wren;
Robin the mean, that best of all loves men;
The nightingale the tenor, and the thrush
The countertenor sweetly in a bush.
And that the music might be full in parts,
Birds from the groves flew with right willing hearts.

All the birds can be identified, including the lark, wren, robin, nightingale and thrush mentioned in the poem, although if all the birds had sung in unison it would have made the most appalling cacophony, rather than the melodious symphony Browne imagined.

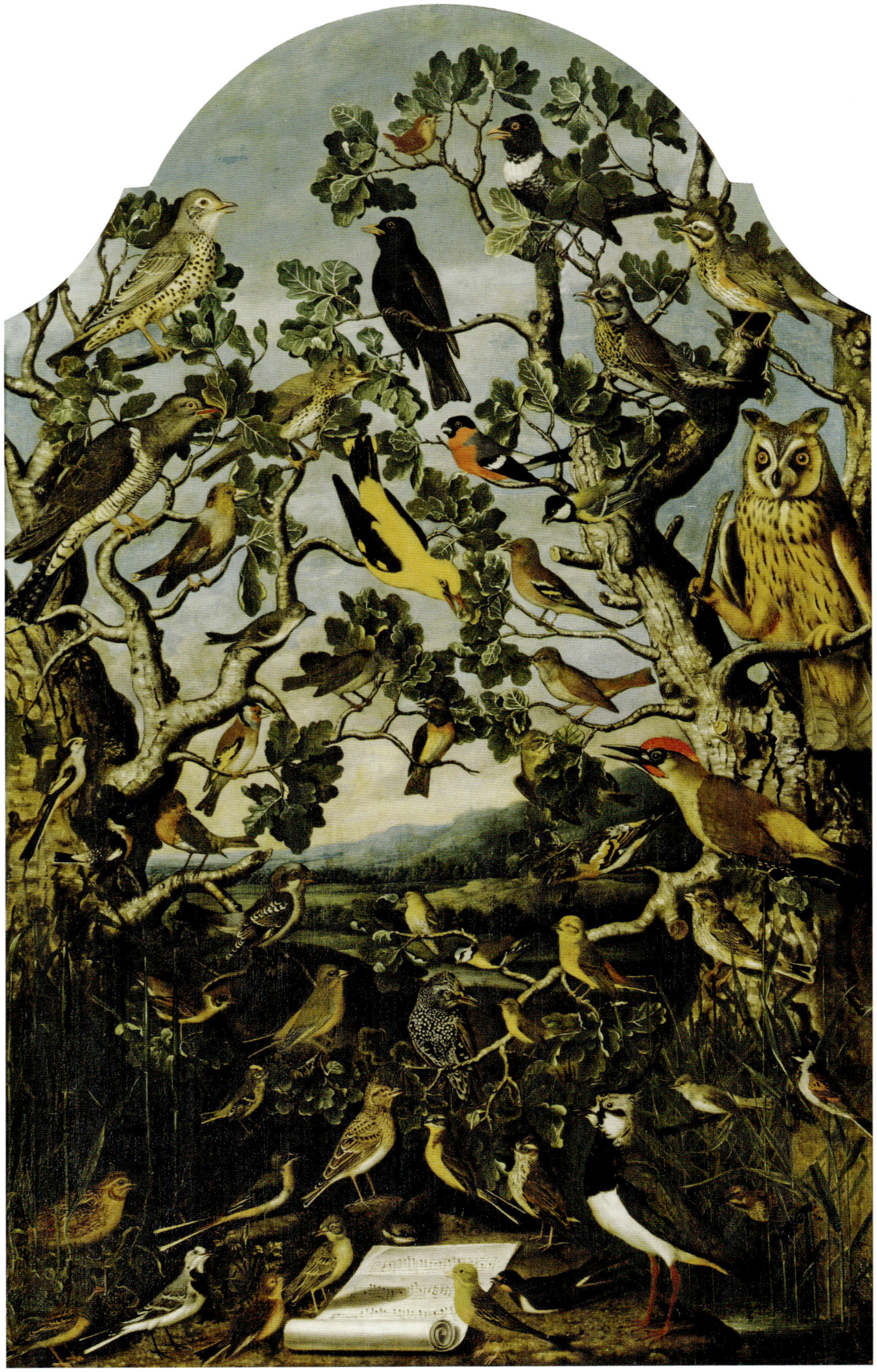

Charles Collins
(*c.* 1680–1744)
British Birds

1736
Oil on canvas
35 × 45.5 cm (13¾ × 18 in.)
Anglesey Abbey, Cambridgeshire

This painting comes from a set of twelve pictures of British birds, signed by Charles Collins. They depict 115 individual birds, many shown in pairs, representing 58 species. The birds are placed in vaguely Italianate rather than British landscapes, some of which feature buildings. Nine of the canvases are at Anglesey Abbey; the location of the other three is unknown. Collins followed the practice established by Francis Barlow (see p. 169) and Peter Casteels before him (see p. 182), and had these compositions made into a set of prints entitled *Icones Avium cum nominibus anglicis*, in which each bird was identified with its English name. Among those seen here are a goldfinch, a sparrow, a red crossbill and a grey shrike. The artist's accuracy of observation must have been one of the reasons he, together with Peter Paillou, was commissioned to paint watercolours of all the species of bird and mammal in Britain for the collector Taylor White. But this picture and its companions are so much more than simple ornithological illustration; the birds genuinely seem to interact with one another.

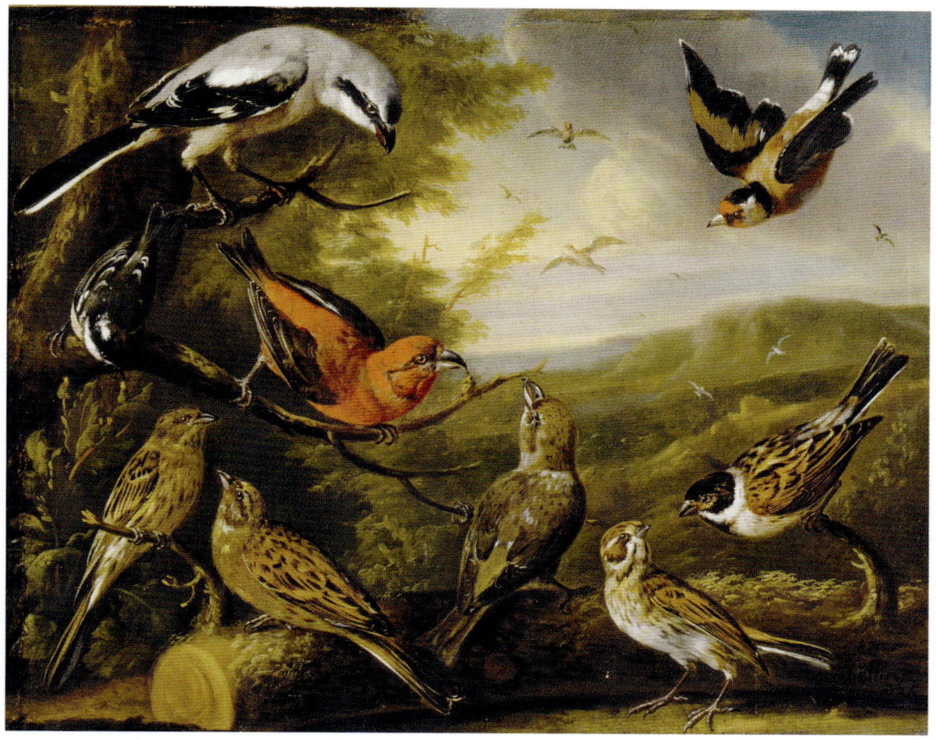

Tobias Stranover
(1684–1731)
Mobbing the Owl

Early 18th century
Oil on canvas
15 × 18.8 cm (5⅞ × 7⅜ in.)
Anglesey Abbey, Cambridgeshire

The Romanian artist Tobias Stranover settled in England, where he married the daughter of the bird painter Jakob Bogdány (see p. 177). The two artists may have collaborated on a number of occasions, as their compositions are quite similar. Owls hunt for food at night and sleep during the day. Because they are predators, they are feared by many smaller birds, and are often attacked or harassed by groups of them. Nor is this limited to one species: once one bird begins the attack, others soon join in. Stranover shows a host of birds that have discovered an eagle owl napping in a tree during daylight hours, and are indulging in a little gentle teasing. A number of exotic birds are striking up a discordant chorus to infuriate the owl. The attached verse reads:

Minerva's bird on wisdom ever bent
Is mock'd by those on lighter thoughts intent.
The ruffled sage, his anger clearly shows
At those who gaily flit beneath his nose.

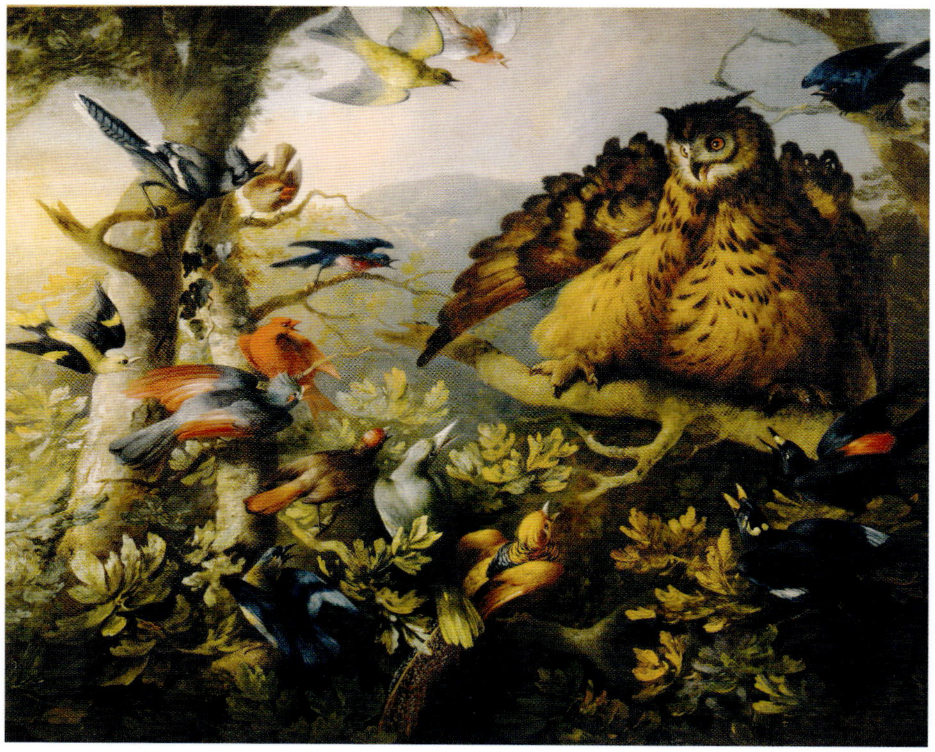

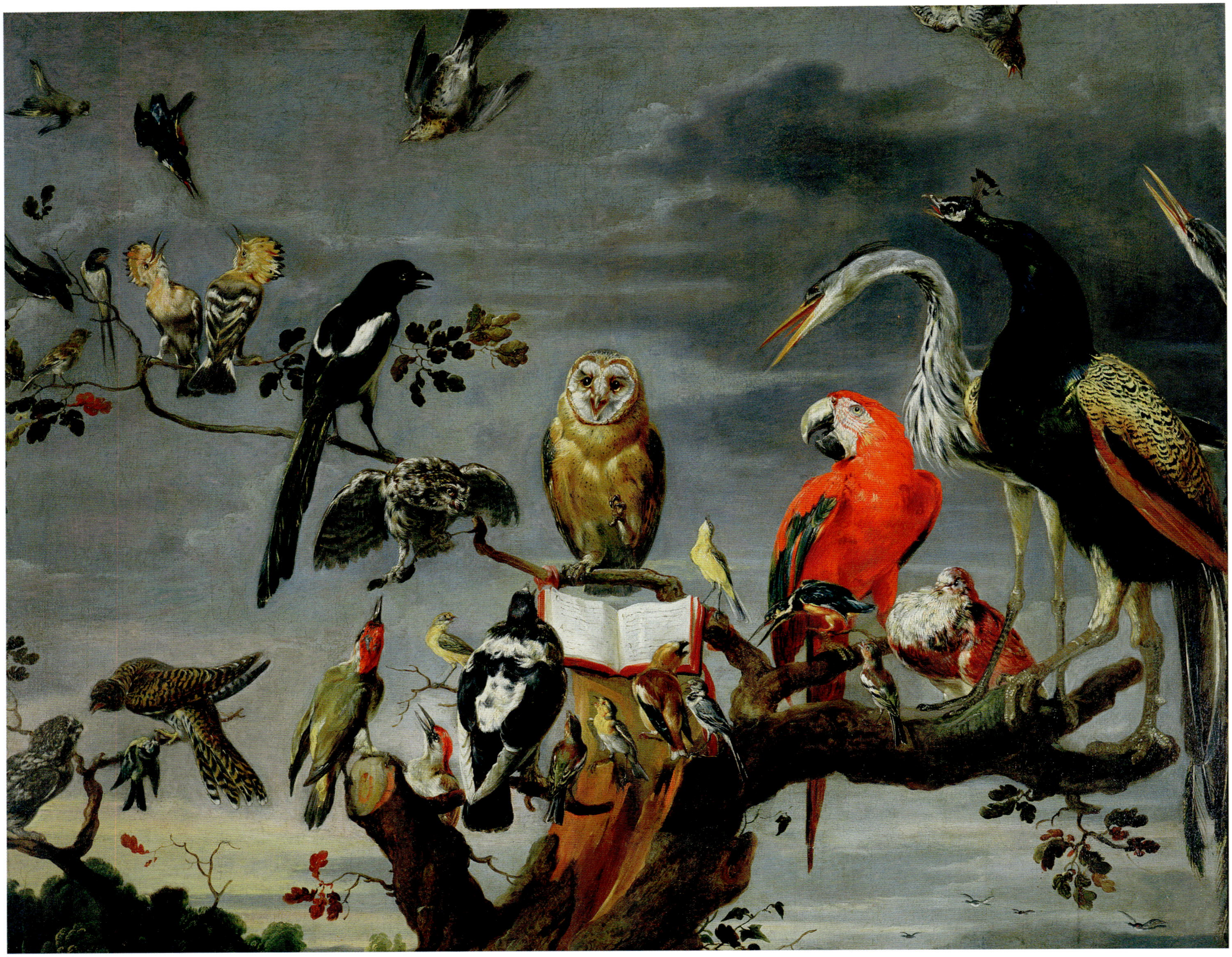

Frans Snyders
(1579–1657)
A Concert of Birds
1630s
Oil on canvas
134.6 × 175 cm (53 × 68⅞ in.)
Michaelis Collection, Cape Town

Several birds are gathering round an owl, which presides over the assembled company and the musical score. It sits impassively on a branch, while many of the other birds strain to read the music. The lively scene is given further animation by the fact that some birds appear to be soaring out of the picture space or entering the scene. Among the birds in the choir are a scarlet macaw, a magpie, a green woodpecker, a pigeon, a grey heron, two hoopoes, grey and yellow wagtails, a swallow and a kestrel. Highly prolific and influential as a painter, Snyders was the grand old man of Flemish still-life and animal painting; during his career he produced more than 300 pictures as well as collaborating with Rubens, who frequently asked him to paint the still-life elements and animals in his compositions.

Philip Reinagle
(1749–1833)
Birds on a Seashore

Late 18th century
Oil on canvas
212.2 × 305.5 cm (83½ × 120¼ in.)
Private collection

This painting is one of three bird pictures commissioned by George Walpole, 3rd Earl of Orford, for his home, Houghton Hall in Norfolk. It is based on studies made in the private museum in London that belonged to the collector Sir Ashton Lever, containing a large number of stuffed birds as well as shells, fossils, animals and reptiles. Reinagle has attempted to place the birds on a naturalistic stormy seashore, but the species he has chosen actually come from different habitats and would probably not have been found together in this setting. The sombre beach scene is relieved by the brilliant colour of the scarlet ibises in the centre, the flamingoes in the background and the vivid corals (which would, of course, have been growing in the water and not on the shore). The king penguin demolishing a fishy meal in the foreground adds a faintly comic touch.

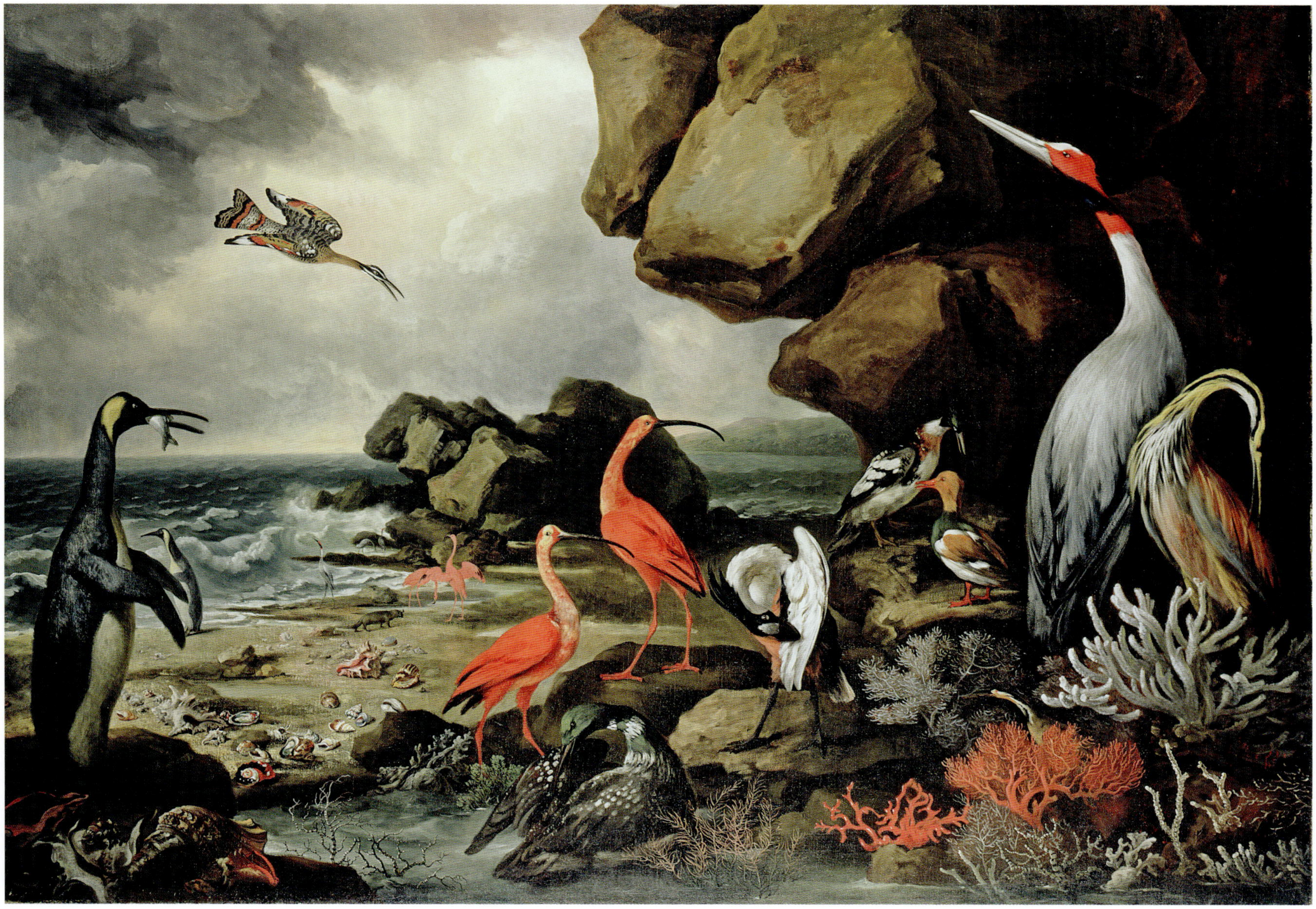

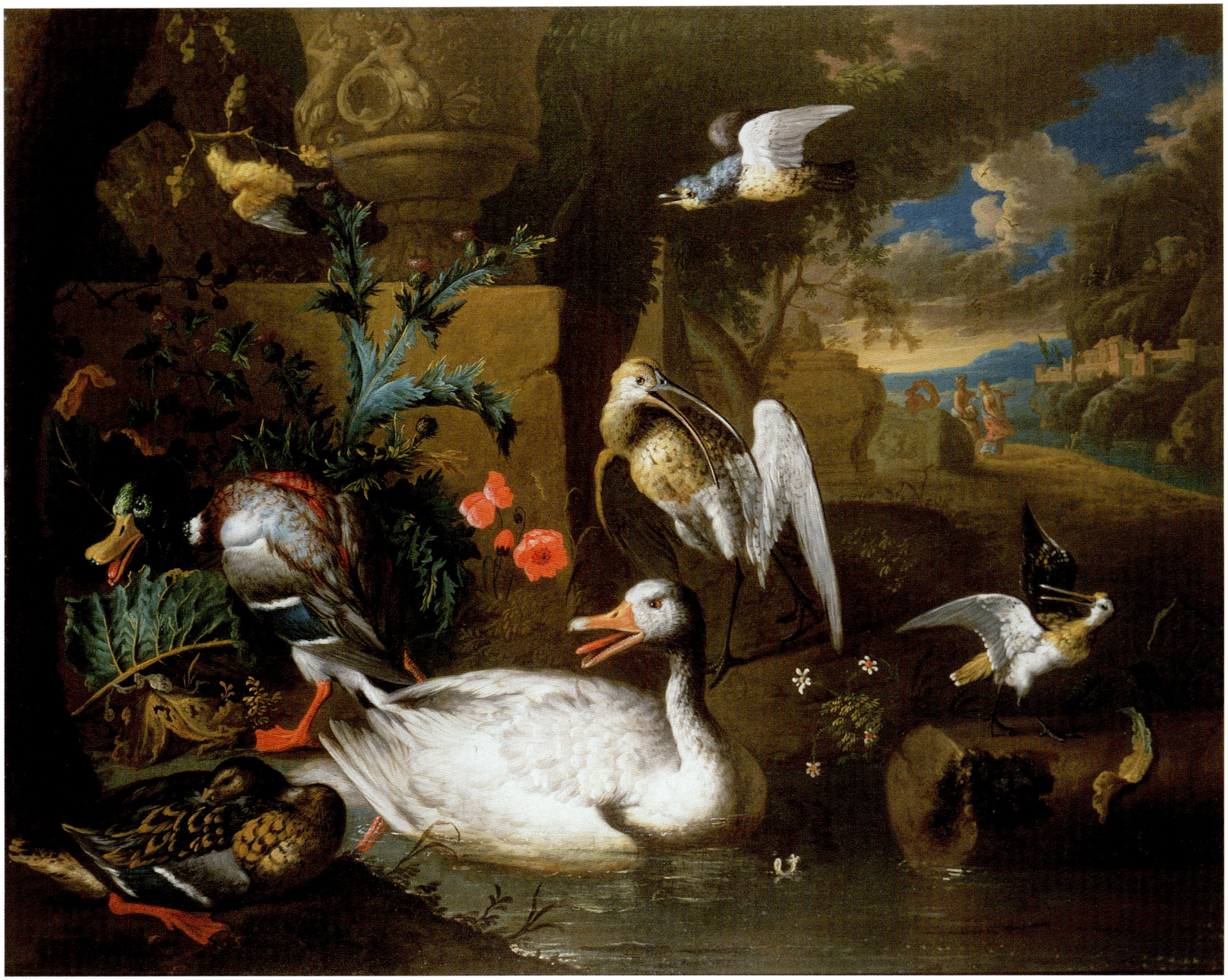

Jan van Oolen (1651–1694)

A Brace of Mallard, a Duck, a Curlew and a Snipe

Second half of the 17th century
Oil on canvas
110 × 134.7 cm (43¼ × 53 in.)
Private collection

The Dutch artist Jan van Oolen has painted an animated scene that includes some recognizable species, but he has used his imagination to add a few embellishments or alterations. The birds are placed in a vaguely Italianate park, complete with a classical urn and a castle in the background. Yet these are not the aristocratic or imported exotic birds that might have been found in such a seemingly elevated setting, but natives of northern Europe. A male and female mallard are shown in the company of a domestic goose (the 'duck'), a strange creature that resembles a curlew with its long, curved beak, and a snipe. It is hard to identify with any certainty the bird flying in from the top right-hand corner. Van Oolen's work is often confused with that of Melchior de Hondecoeter (see opposite and p. 179), whom he deliberately imitated. His brother Adriaen was also a painter of birds, and his work is very similar.

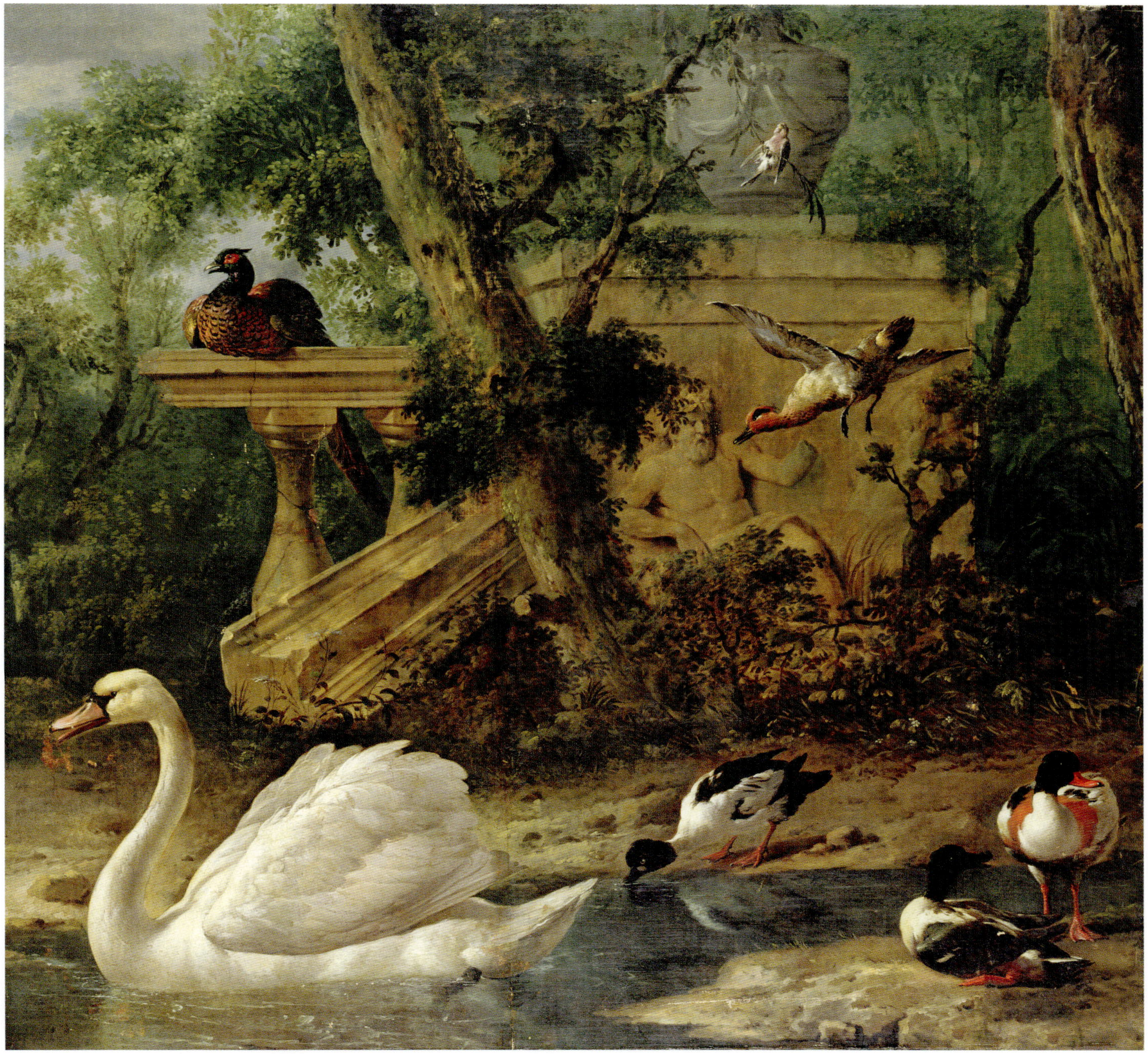

Melchior de Hondecoeter (1636–1695)

Birds in a Garden

Second half of the 17th century
Oil on canvas
215 × 233 cm (84⅝ × 91¾ in.)
National Museum Cardiff

De Hondecoeter's park, with its characteristic classical accessories – an urn and entablature – is home to some elegant waterfowl. A swan glides by on the lake, while a shelduck, a goldeneye and a teal gather at the edge of the water, preparing to take a dip. Only the pheasant sits aloof on the balustrade. The details of each bird are faithfully observed: De Hondecoeter bred his own birds in his garden so that he could see them at close quarters and record details of their plumage as accurately as possible. The inventory compiled on his death even included a special device that he used to keep dead birds in the right position while he painted them. Unlike some of his contemporaries, he was careful to record birds in their correct relative sizes. His compositions are always animated, and he often introduces a narrative, sometimes including a dramatic element by showing the birds fighting or fleeing from a common foe. Many of his paintings were created for country houses and palaces; this one once adorned a drawing room in Cavendish Square, London.

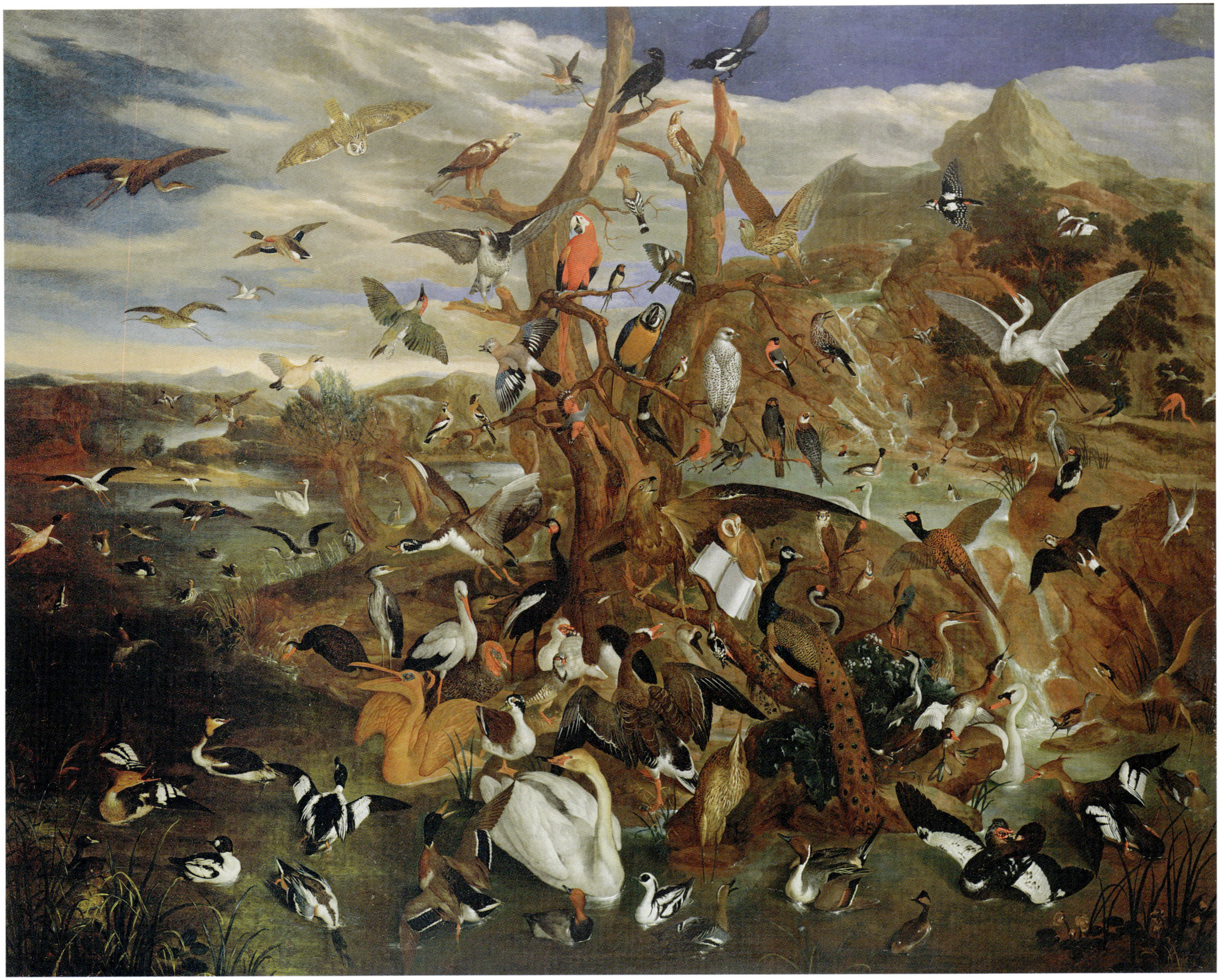

OPPOSITE

Carl Wilhelm de Hamilton (1668–1754)

The Parliament of Birds

Date unknown
Oil on canvas
Dimensions unknown
Alan Jacobs Gallery, London

Geoffrey Chaucer's lengthy poem *A Parliament of Fowls*, written in about 1380, describes how birds come together on St Valentine's Day to choose their mates. Altogether Chaucer mentions thirty-six species of bird, including the eagle, the crane, the jay, the kite, the sparrow, the lapwing, the peacock and the pheasant – all of which can be seen here. Hamilton has added some extras, too, since well over sixty birds are shown in his picture. Chaucer sets out in some detail the positions occupied by the birds:

The foules of ravine
Were hyest set, and than the foules smale
That eten, as hem Nature wolde enclyne,
As worm or thyn of which I tell no tale;
And water-foul sat lowest in the dale;
But foul that lyveth by sed say on the grene.

The artist has followed this scheme, placing a crow and a magpie (like ravens) at the top of the picture, followed by smaller birds in the branches of the tree, while birds that eat seeds are placed on the green and waterfowl are lowest of all in the composition.

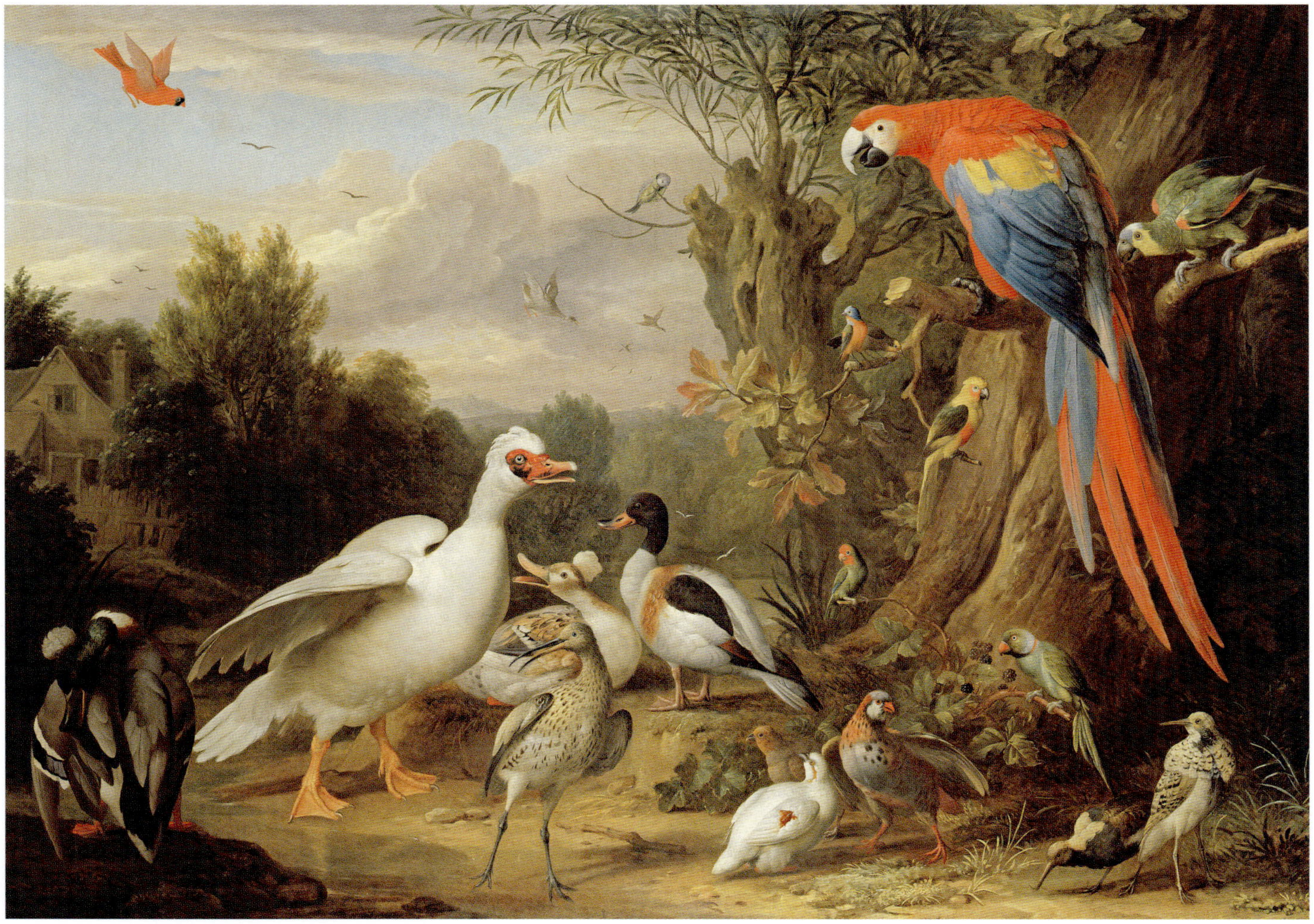

Jakob Bogdány (1660–1724)

A Macaw, Ducks, Parrots and Other Birds in a Landscape

c. 1708–10
Oil on canvas
142.2 × 207.5 cm (56 × 81⅝ in.)
Yale Center for British Art, New Haven, Connecticut

Jakob Bogdány left his native Hungary in 1684 and travelled to Amsterdam, where he learned about painting in the Dutch manner, and produced flower pieces. By 1688 he was working in London, where he later found patronage as a bird painter at the court of Queen Anne. His paintings often combine native British birds with more exotic specimens that could have been observed in menageries, so here a scarlet macaw from South America dominates a scene that includes a mallard drake, a Muscovy duck, a shelduck, partridges and an Amazon parrot, while a red cardinal from North America – kept as a caged bird in England – flies into the composition from the upper left. The sheer number of Bogdány's paintings, and the fact that the same birds reappear in them, suggests that he was operating a studio to keep up with demand. His son-in-law Tobias Stranover (see p. 171, bottom) certainly borrowed motifs from him, and may have been a collaborator.

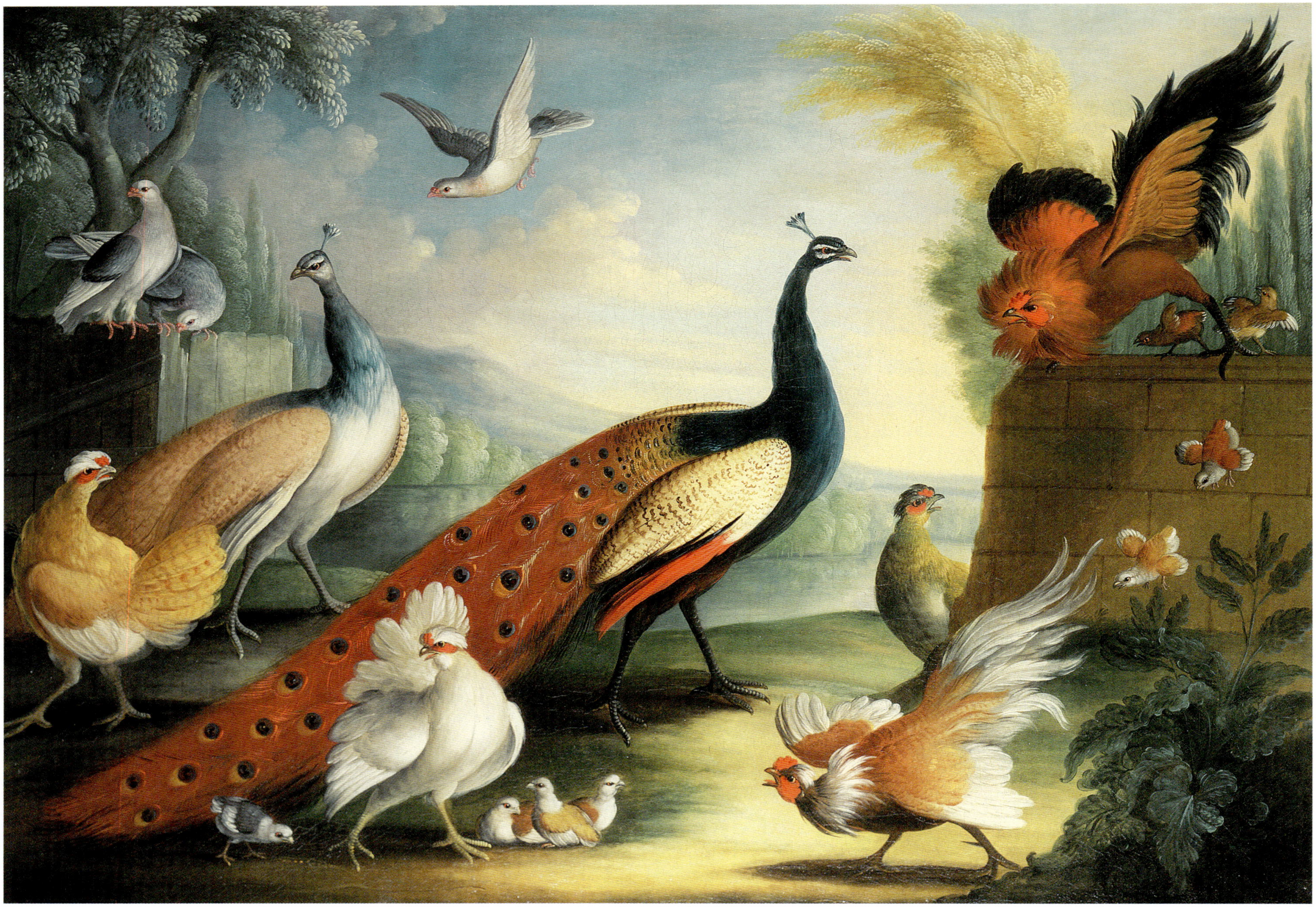

Marmaduke Cradock
(1660–1717)
Two Peacocks, Doves, Chickens and a Rooster in a Parkland
n.d.
Oil on canvas
89.5 × 127.7 cm (35¼ × 50¼ in.)
Private collection

Originally from Somerset, Marmaduke Cradock forged a career in London, where he specialized in painting pictures of birds. Together with Francis Barlow (see p. 169), he established the English school of animal painting in the closing years of the seventeenth century. Since he did not tend to work for aristocrats, he did not have access to the rare imported species that were kept in the private menageries owned by the nobility. His birds tend to be native British species or fancy fowl – although he often included a peacock, adding an exotic note to his compositions of birds shown in idyllic parkland settings. What is interesting here is the manner in which the birds appear to communicate with one another, and the way in which the angry rooster seems to be defending his chicks from the strutting peacock as they take their first perilous flight to the ground.

Melchior de Hondecoeter (1636–1695)

A Peacock on a Decorative Urn

Second half of the 17th century
Oil on canvas
Dimensions unknown
Private collection

In common with many Dutch painters of the Golden Age, Melchior de Hondecoeter came from an artistic family. His grandfather and father were both painters, and he studied with his uncle Jan Baptist Weenix in Italy, where he absorbed the practice of using Italianate landscape backgrounds. His pictures generally feature both indigenous and exotic birds in parkland settings. Here, an impressive peacock perches on an imposing classical bowl; its peahen partner, appropriately enough, occupies a less prominent position behind it. A red-rumped swallow flies off to the left, while a waxwing sits on a branch above and a great tit hangs on a stem that has escaped from the foliage in the container. An Amazon parrot in the foreground gazes at the peacock's magnificent train. De Hondecoeter's lively depictions of birds made him much in demand among the wealthy owners of menageries in The Netherlands, and the Dutch king William III even commissioned him to paint his collection of animals at his palace, Het Loo.

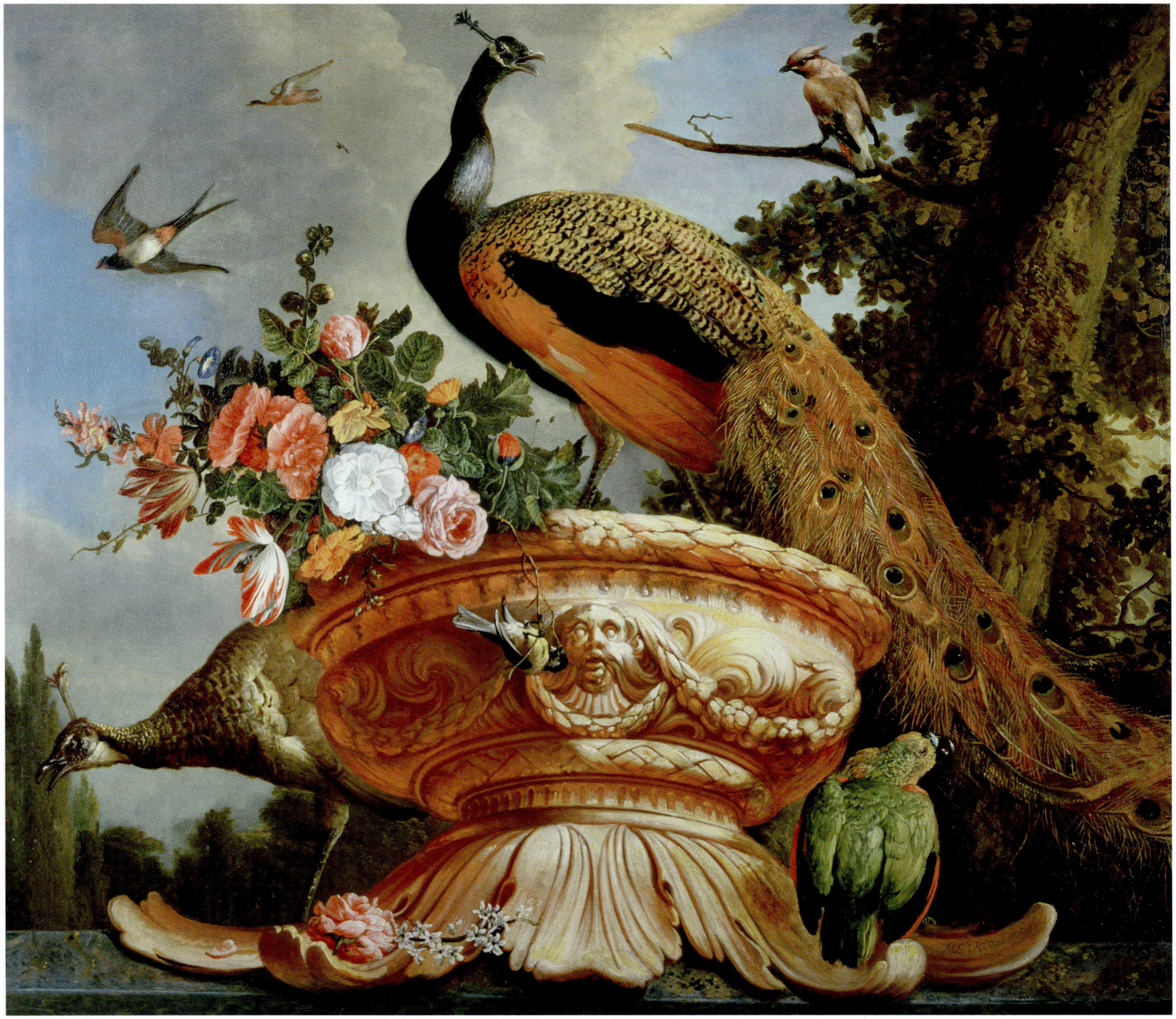

Johannes van Bronckhorst (1648–1726)

An Assembly of Exotic Birds

c. 1710
Oil on canvas
55 × 73 cm (21⅝ × 28¾ in.)
Private collection

A pastry cook turned artist, Bronckhorst lived in the Dutch port of Hoorn, and specialized in paintings of insects, flowers and birds. He favoured the imported exotic birds seen here, portrayed with plenty of space around them so that their form and plumage could be fully appreciated. Although they are grouped in a landscape setting, in reality these birds would have been seen together only in aviaries, as they come from different parts of the world. The foreground is dominated by a pair of greater flamingoes from southern France or Spain; one is displaying by flapping its wings. To their left are two types of pheasant – silver, shown in flight, and a golden pheasant just below it – both of them native to the Far East. A great curassow from South America struts into the picture from the left, while the ubiquitous scarlet macaw perches on a branch above. A western-crowned pigeon, a native of Papua New Guinea, stares out across the lake.

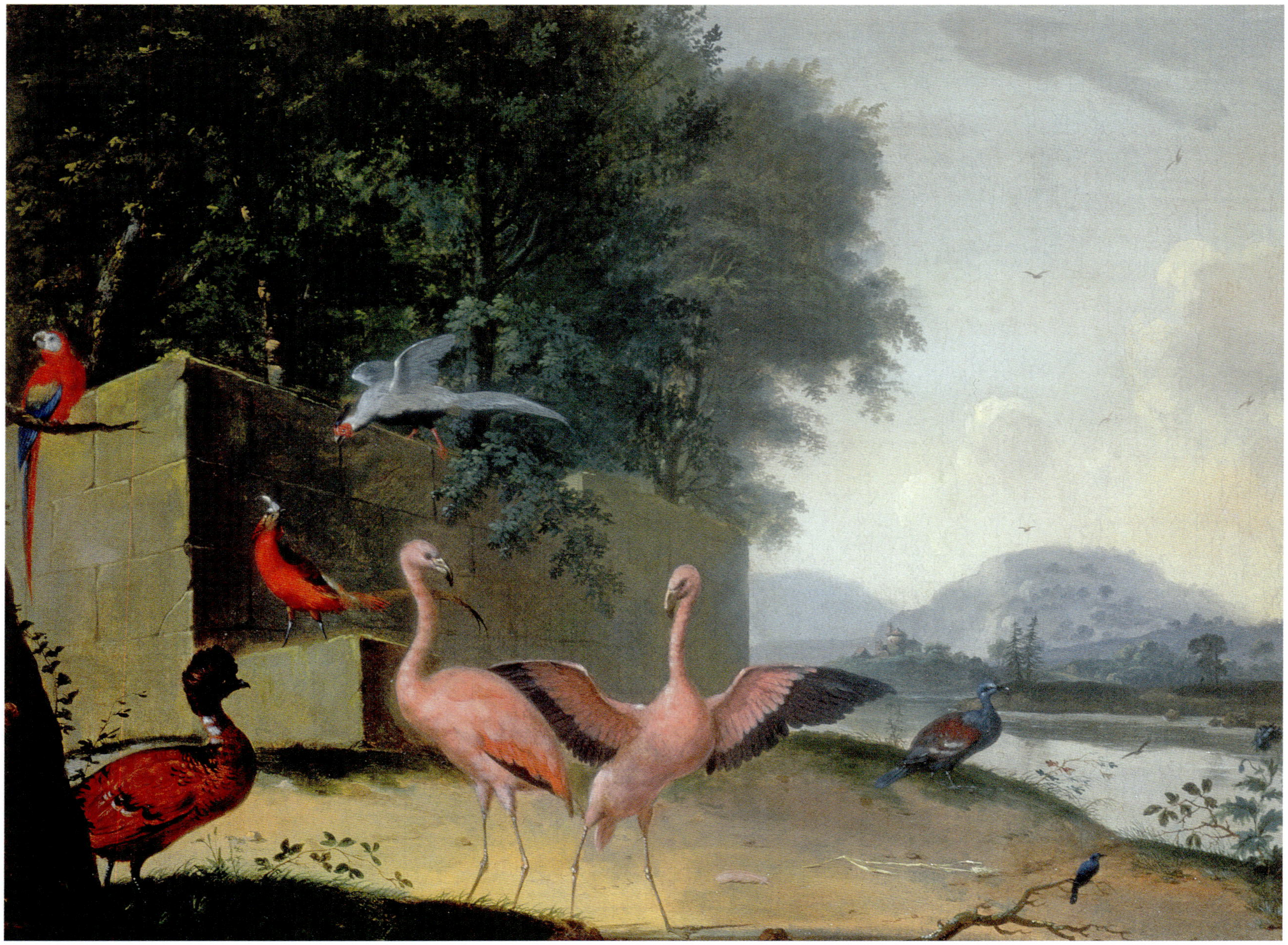

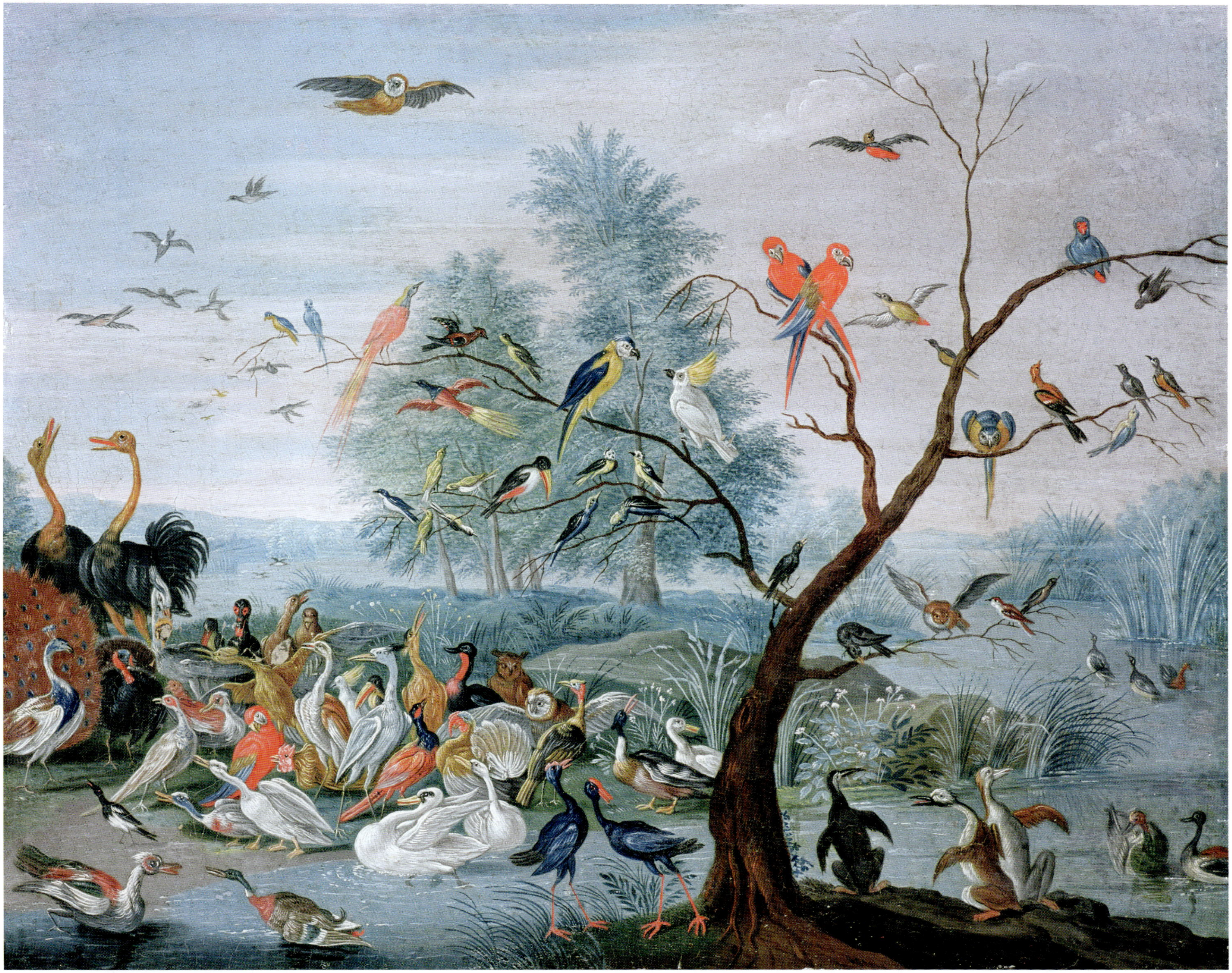

Jan van Kessel the Elder (1626–1679)

Tropical Birds in a Landscape

17th century
Oil on panel
27.5 × 35.6 cm (10¾ × 14 in.)
Private collection

Birds from all over the world gather in this improbable scene by the prolific Flemish artist Jan van Kessel, who was the grandson of Jan Breughel the Elder. It is possible to identify a number of them, including different kinds of owl, scarlet and blue-and-yellow macaws, birds of paradise, a sulphur-crested cockatoo, a hornbill, herons, mallards, ostriches, a red-breasted merganser, mute swans, a crowned crane, a cuckoo, a starling and a turkey. In the foreground are three creatures that are supposed to represent penguins, but the artist has given them animal-like haunches. The scene is pure fantasy, since these birds would never have been seen together in the wild. Nor would Kessel have actually painted or sketched them from life, since he worked chiefly from stuffed samples or skins in museum cabinets. But this element of inaccuracy detracts little from the animation and charm of the scene.

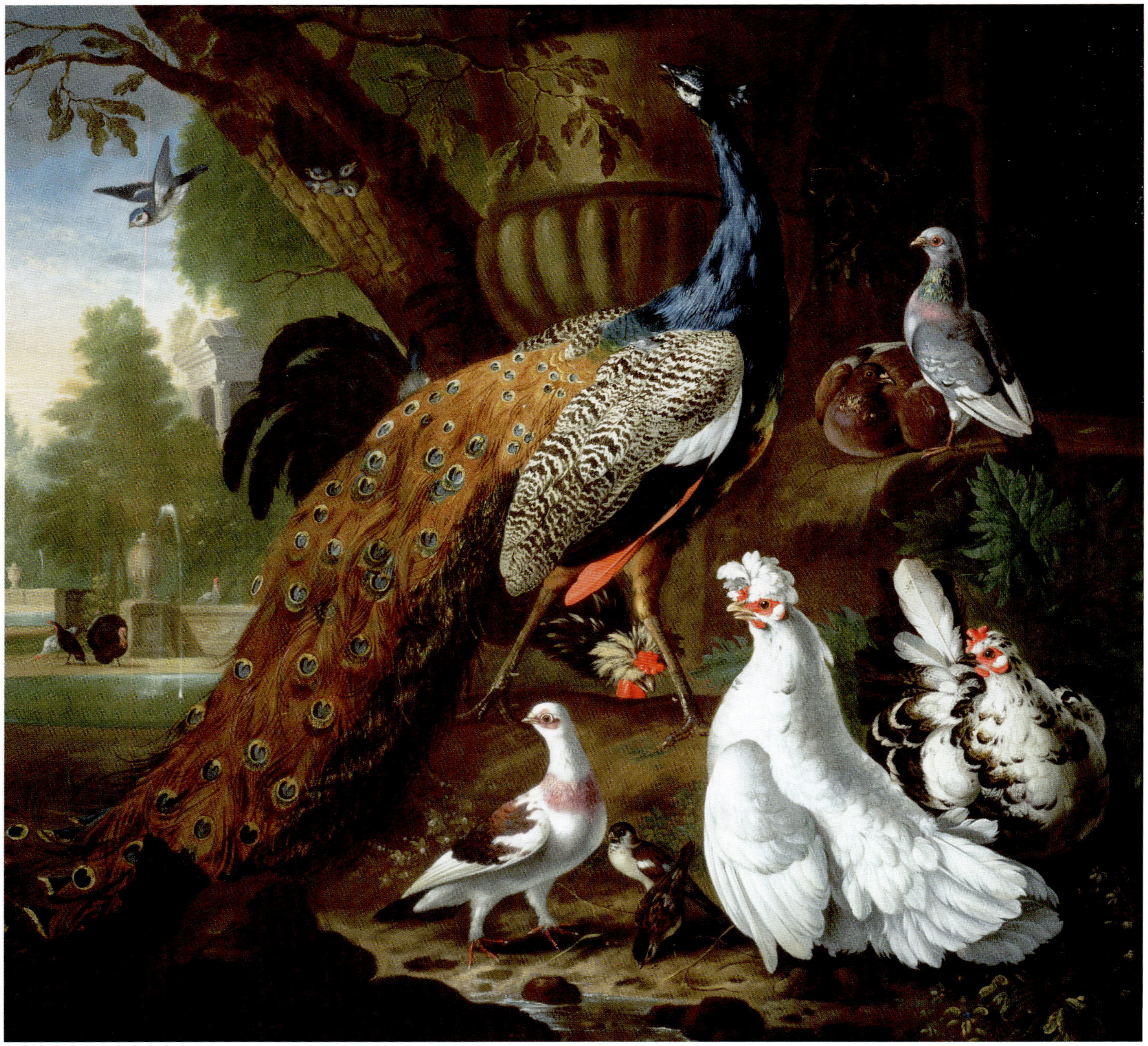

Peter Casteels III
(1684–1749)
A Peacock in a Classical Landscape
1719
Oil on canvas
122 × 134.5 cm (48 × 53 in.)
Private collection

Born and trained in Antwerp, Peter Casteels III followed in the footsteps of many of his countrymen, who emigrated to England in search of a market for their pictures. He made a living as a painter of flowers and exotic birds, as an importer of fine pictures and as a textile designer. In this painting he sets an assembly of birds – some exotic and some more domestic – in a classical landscape complete with urns, a temple and tinkling fountains. A magnificent peacock presides over the scene, although it is leaving the display to the turkey in the background. A black cockerel pecks around behind the peacock, while different breeds of pigeon and fancy poultry strut about in the foreground. A charming touch is added by the tiny blue tits waiting in the oak tree while their parent flies off in search of the next meal. In 1726, in common with other artists of the late seventeenth and early eighteenth centuries who published their work as prints, Casteels issued a set of twelve plates of birds based on his own compositions, entitled *Icones Avium*.

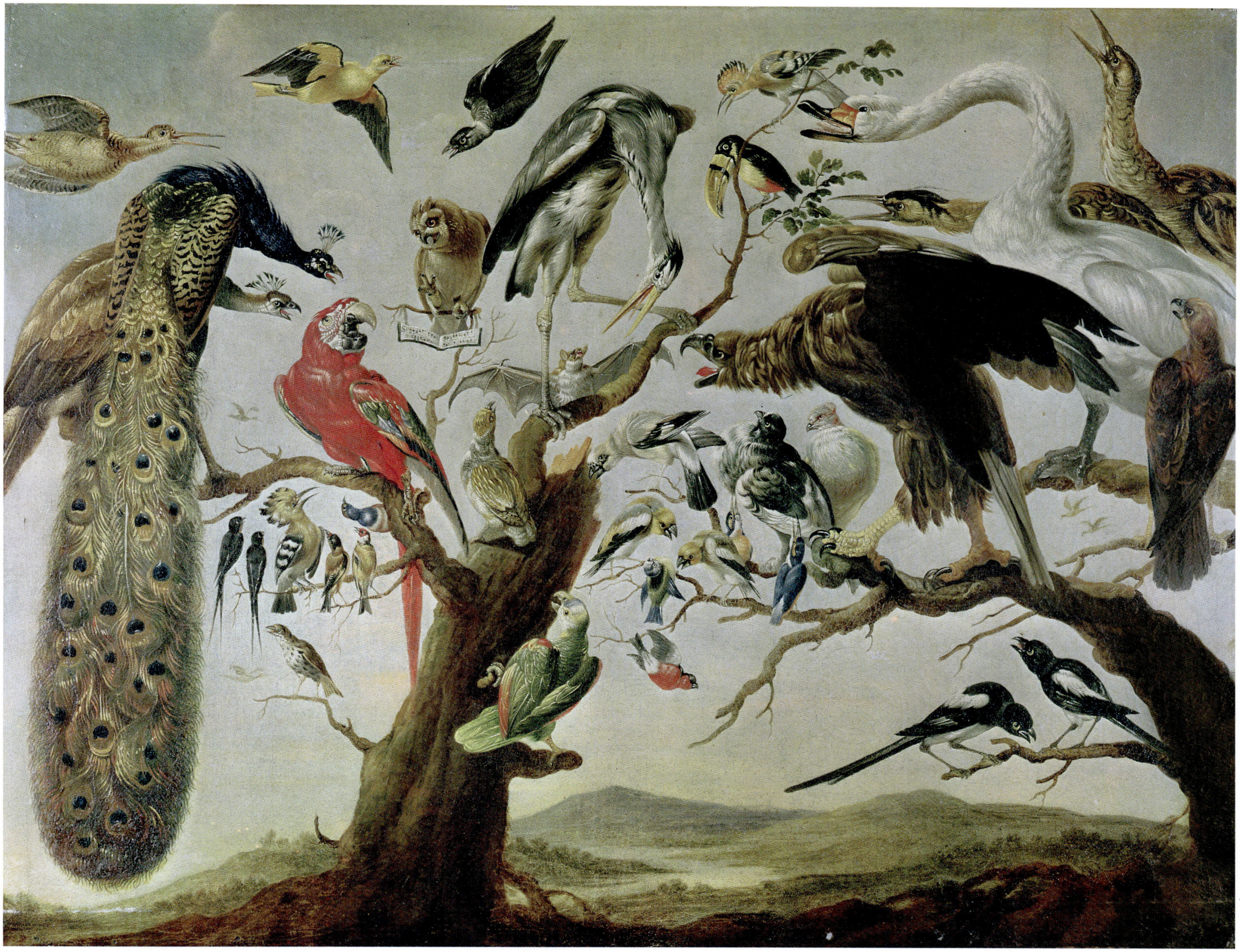

Frans Snyders
(1579–1657) (after)
The Birds' Concert
First half of the 17th century
Oil on canvas
135 × 175 cm (53⅛ × 68⅞ in.)
Musée des Beaux-Arts, Dunkirk

In this amazing assembly of birds, some are very accurately observed while others appear to be a mix of more than one species. But all have open beaks, and are participating in what must be a deafening chorus. Among the identifiable birds, the right-hand side is dominated by two bitterns, a mute swan (presumably not that mute in this instance), two types of eagle and two magpies. In the centre are hoopoes, a toucan, a kingfisher, a grey heron, hawfinches, blue tits, a bullfinch, swallows, a thrush, goldfinches, a scarlet macaw and the inevitable owl in its usual role as choirmaster. Below it, a bat adds its squeaky accompaniment to the concert. A peacock, a peahen and a woodcock dominate the left-hand side. This canvas is a copy of Frans Snyders's *Bird Concert* (1630s), which once belonged to Horace Walpole and hung at Houghton Hall, Norfolk, but which is now in the State Hermitage Museum in St Petersburg.

The Eastern Bird

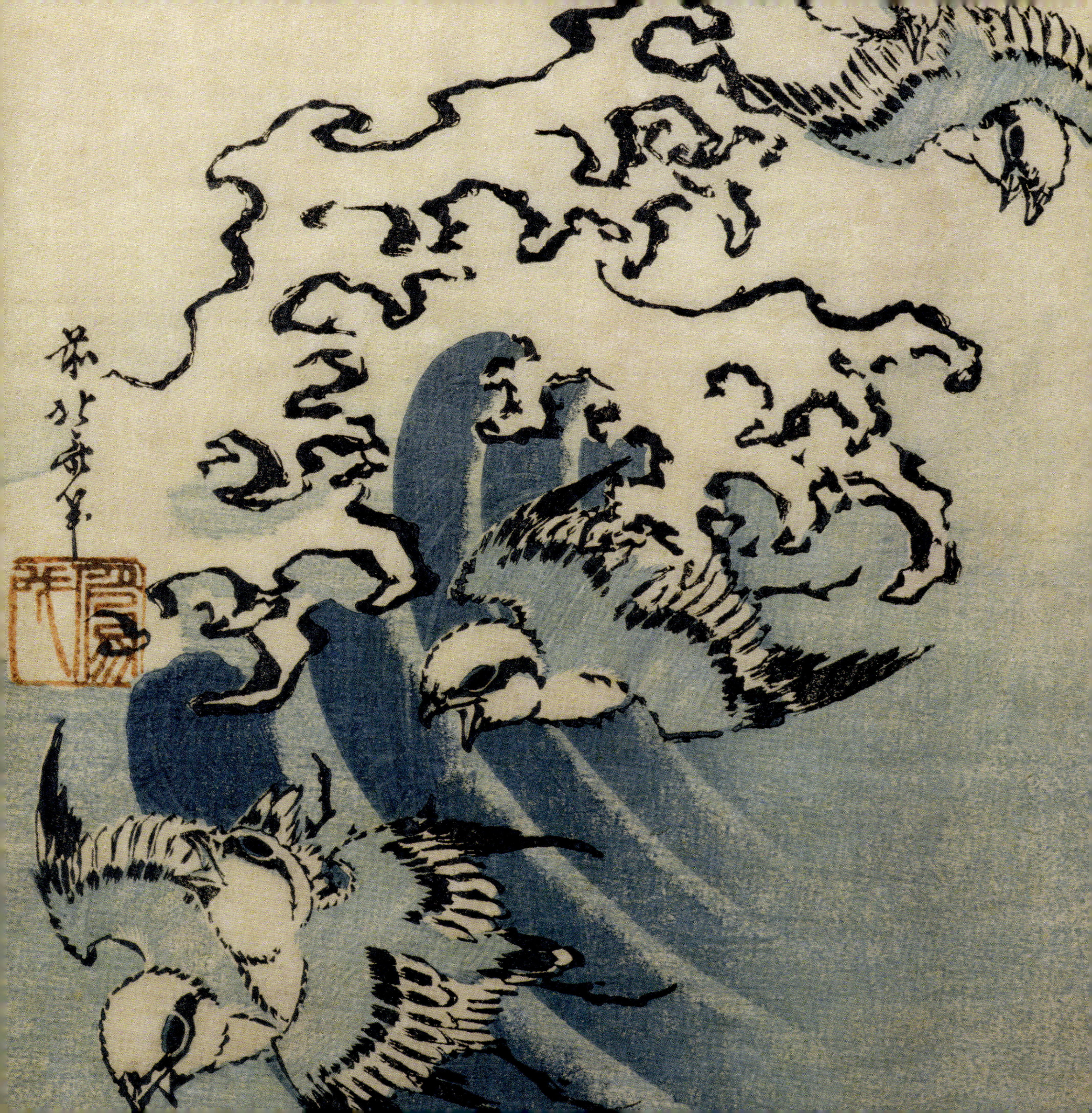

Images of birds have always been used as decoration for furniture, snuff bottles, ceramics, clothes and other household goods in the Far East, but they assumed a central place in Chinese fine art as long ago as the tenth century, when scenes of birds and flowers developed into a branch of painting in its own right. During a long apprenticeship, Chinese artists would observe living birds rather than dead ones, and some of them came to specialize in just one species. Although the genre waxed and waned in popularity over the centuries and under various dynasties, it never disappeared. In Japan, the long tradition of bird and flower images reached its apotheosis in prints from the late eighteenth century onwards, fostered by an intense interest in nature on the part of poets and the general public. Japanese artists also showed birds swooping into view in their landscapes and townscapes, adding movement and dynamism to the composition.

The bird painting of China and Japan is characterized by elegance and simplicity. While Chinese artists superbly convey the delicacy and liveliness of birds in sensitive brush paintings and watercolours, Japanese artists have tended to exploit the graphic qualities of birds in flight in their boldly designed screens, hanging scrolls and woodblock prints. Perhaps the sensitivity of Far Eastern artists to the beauty of birds has something to do with the reverence for the natural world in Buddhist thought, and the notion of birds and animals as sentient beings.

The myths and legends of the Far East are rich in birds. A bird in Far Eastern art is very rarely just a bird: it usually carries a symbolic significance that transcends its superficial appearance. Bird symbolism was built into the very fabric of Chinese society: for centuries civil officials sported badges bearing different types of bird (such as cranes, quail, geese and peacocks) to denote their rank and status. Birds are frequently linked with auspicious signs: the anonymous Chinese artist who painted quail and grasshoppers among flowers would have been well aware of the fact that these birds were associated with bravery, and that a pair could represent peace and prosperity (p. 188). Similarly, Bian Shoumin's geese and Ando Hiroshige's mandarin ducks were depicted specifically because of their associations with marital fidelity (pp. 189 and 193). The crane is particularly celebrated in Chinese and Japanese legend, since it is thought to live for centuries (pp. 194–95). In art it symbolizes longevity, particularly when coupled with a pine tree, another symbol of long life.

Far Eastern thought also abounds with imaginary birds, and these fantastical creatures find their way into decorated manuscript pages, paintings and murals. The phoenix is a prime example (pp. 192–93). As a bird associated with immortality, it was closely linked with royalty, and was adopted as a symbol by both Chinese and Japanese empresses. In Hindu art and literature, where birds and animals are revered and often represented as gods and goddesses, there are plenty of examples of helpful birds coming to the rescue of humans. In the epic poem the *Ramayana*, the demigod Jatayu or Jatayus takes the form of a giant bird in order to save the kidnapped goddess Sita (p. 200). Helpful birds also play their part in Islamic legend: the mythical simurgh comes to the rescue of the infant prince Zal in the *Shahnama* or *Book of Kings* (p. 202), and a giant bird helps a poor young man to marry the woman of his dreams by transporting him across the heavens and out of danger (p. 199).

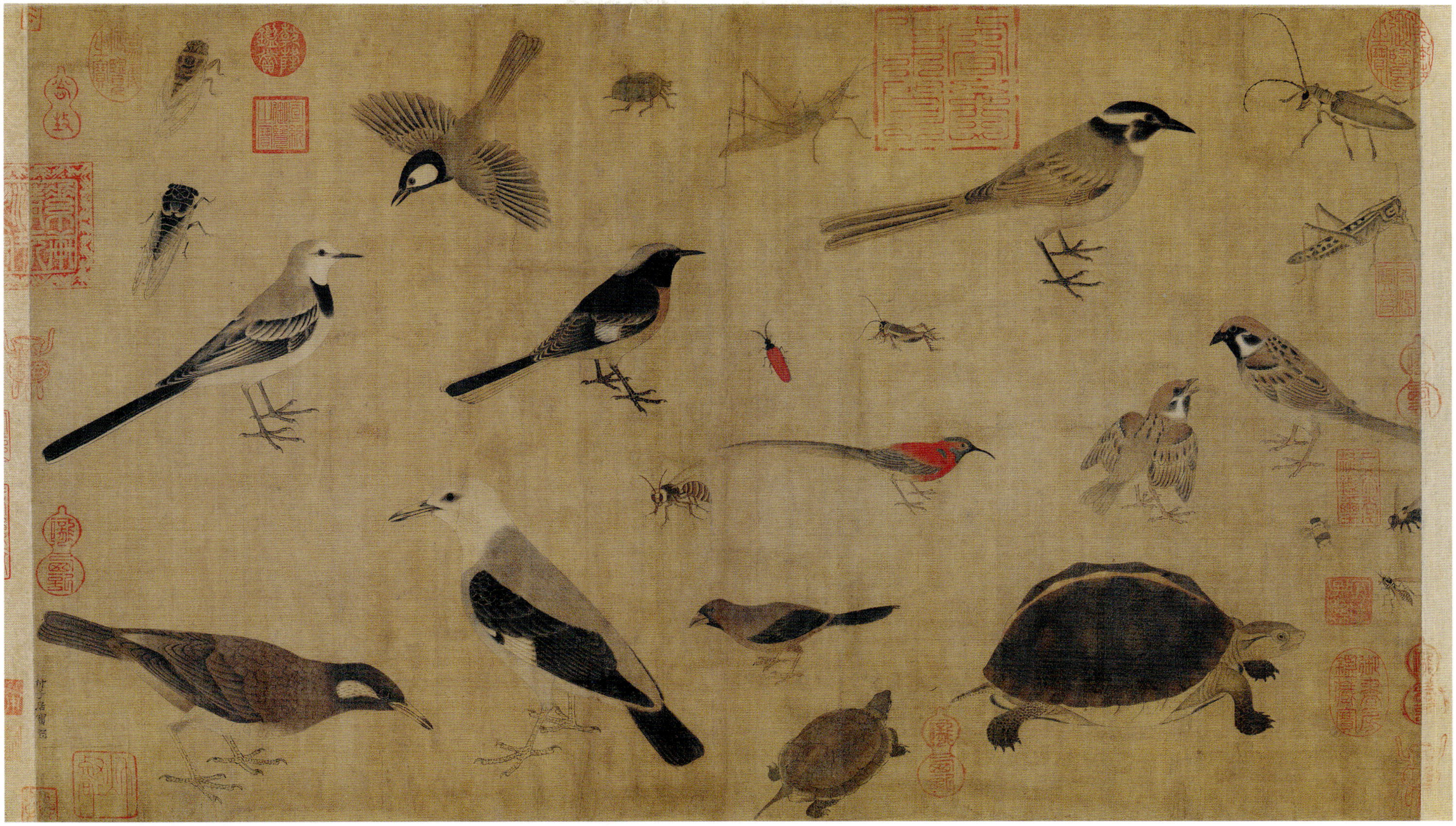

Huang Quan
(*c.* 903–965)
Animals Sketched from Nature
c. 934
Handscroll, colours on silk
41.5 × 70 cm (16¼ × 27½ in.)
The Palace Museum, Beijing

These remarkable studies of birds, made in tenth-century China, far surpass paintings by contemporary European artists in their accuracy and delicacy. Huang Quan was the leading painter of birds and flowers during the Five Dynasties period (907–60). He worked at the Imperial Painting Academy in western Szechuan, and probably sketched these creatures from life in order to teach his eldest son how to draw. Huang is said to have been able to render birds so realistically that, when he painted six cranes on the wall of the imperial palace, a living crane stood beside them, confusing them with real birds. And when he painted a mural featuring flowers and such birds as sparrows and pheasants, a white eagle swooped down to carry off his 'prey'. Whether or not the stories are pure fantasy, Huang certainly had the ability to depict birds with characteristic liveliness. Among the various creatures shown here we can identify ten birds (including a wagtail, a sparrow and a tit), two turtles and twelve insects.

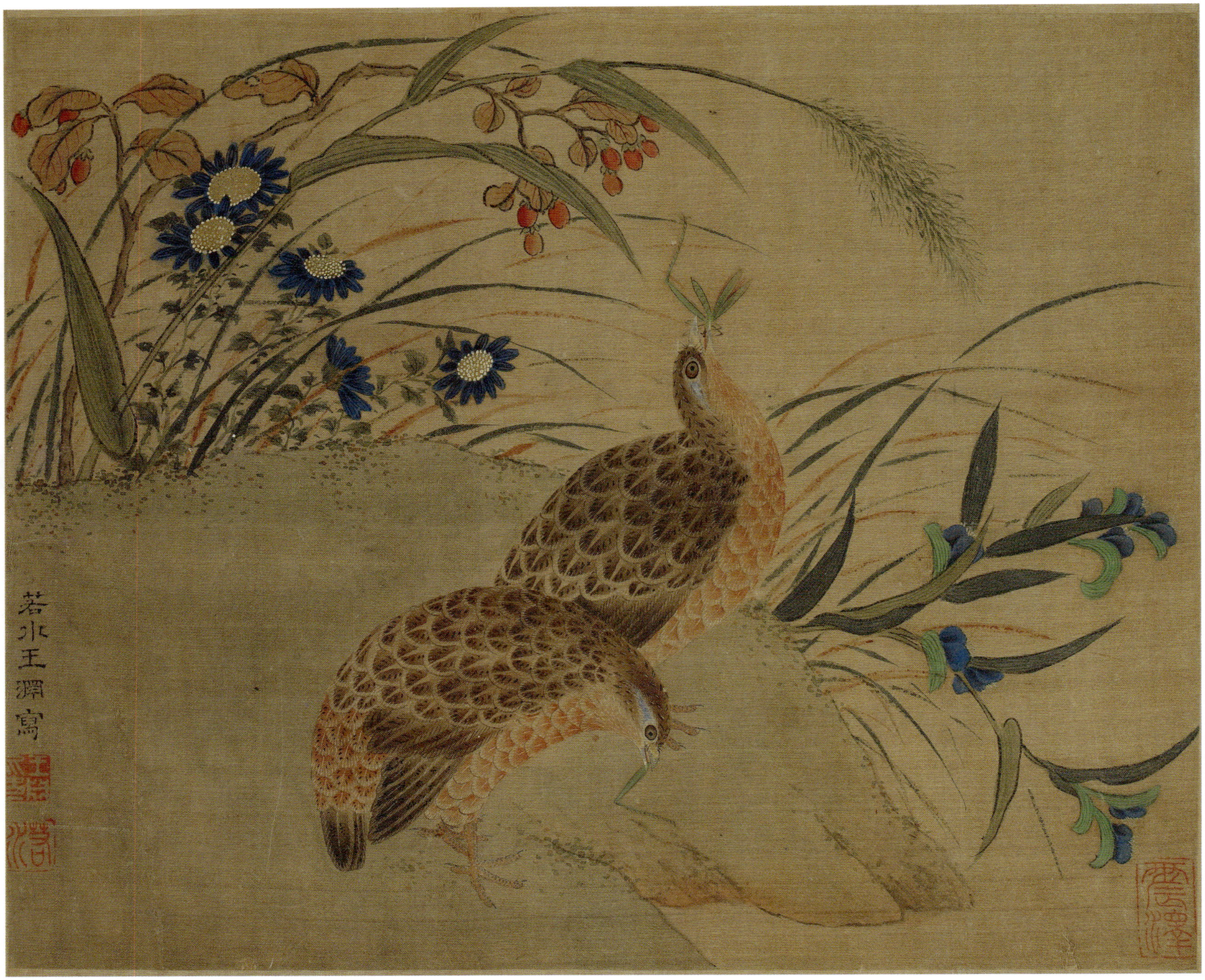

Chinese

Two Quail Eating Grasshoppers under Flowers

Qing Dynasty (1644–1912)
Ink and colours on silk
27.5 × 34 cm (10¾ × 13⅜ in.)
Freer Gallery of Art, Smithsonian Institution, Washington, D.C.

In China, the quail carries a host of associations. It is admired for its courage and fighting spirit, which is why it was used as a badge of the eighth- and ninth-rank civil servants during the period when this work was painted. Its dull, ragged appearance also links it with poverty, and it was, in addition, associated with the spring season. In Chinese art it can symbolize something quite specific. The word for 'quail' sounds like that for 'peace', and a pair of quail often represents peace and prosperity or a loving couple. The grasshoppers on which these quail are feeding have their own associations: the word for 'grasshopper' sounds similar to that for 'official', and when a grasshopper is shown outside its cage it can stand for peasants who have left their villages and risen to higher positions. The insect is also associated with fertility and good luck.

Bian Shoumin
(1683–1752)
One Hundred Geese

Early 18th century
Pen and ink on paper
197.1 × 96.3 cm ($77\frac{5}{8}$ × 38 in.)
Brooklyn Museum, New York

The Chinese artist Bian Shoumin, who was also noted for his poetry and calligraphy, made a particular study of geese, and even lived for a time near a lake so that he could observe them on their migration route. The fruits of first-hand observation and the deft hand of the calligrapher are evident in this hanging scroll, which depicts each bird with a few fluent strokes of the brush. The wild goose is an ancient motif in Chinese art and society, although Chinese artists generally preferred to portray it with claws rather than webbed feet. It was associated with the fourth rank of officials and was also a favourite of the military, since its behaviour and flight formation resembled those of an army. The Chinese also believed that wild geese mate for life, so a picture of a pair could represent marital fidelity and prosperity. A flock of geese could also suggest winter and snow.

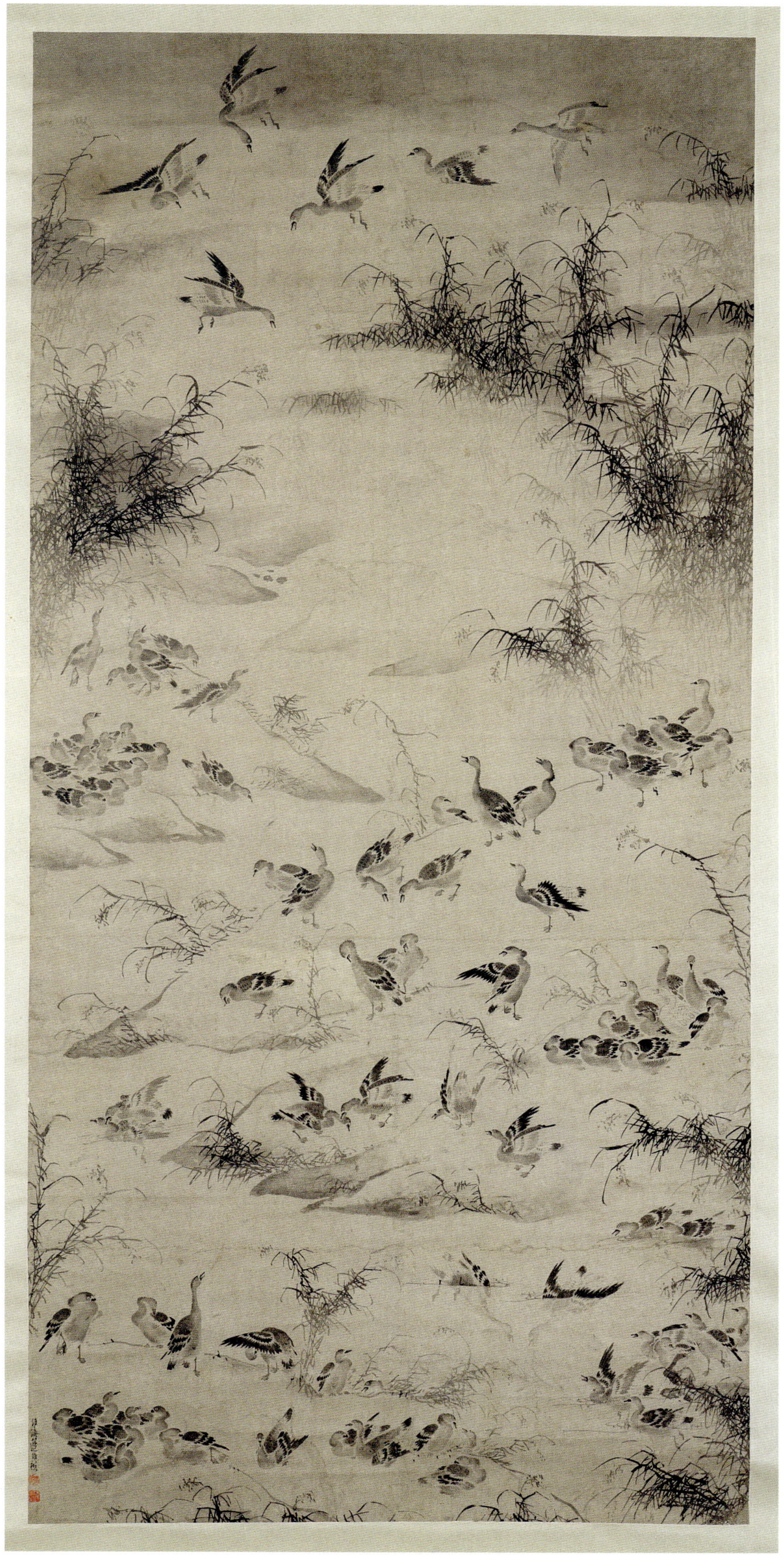

Kano Motonobu (1476–1559)

Pheasants and Peonies

1513 or 1535
Ink and wash on paper
174.5 × 99 cm (68⅜ × 39 in.)
Kyoto National Museum

The Japanese artist Kano Motonobu was an official court painter to the Ashikaga shoguns (military rulers). His work married elements of the Chinese monochromatic style with the Japanese preference for decorativeness and colour. Here, the colourful birds and flowers are set in a more subdued landscape. The artist was commissioned to paint a series of eight sliding door panels depicting birds and flowers of the four seasons for the temple of Daisen-in in the Daitokuji monastery in Kyoto. The panels would together have formed one grand central scene, and this is a detail from one of them. Originally installed in the Hojo Hall in the temple, the paintings are now mounted as hanging scrolls in the Kyoto National Museum. The season represented here is summer, and the peonies are in bloom. The pheasant is linked with the Shinto sun goddess Amaterasu, and conveys the promise of abundance.

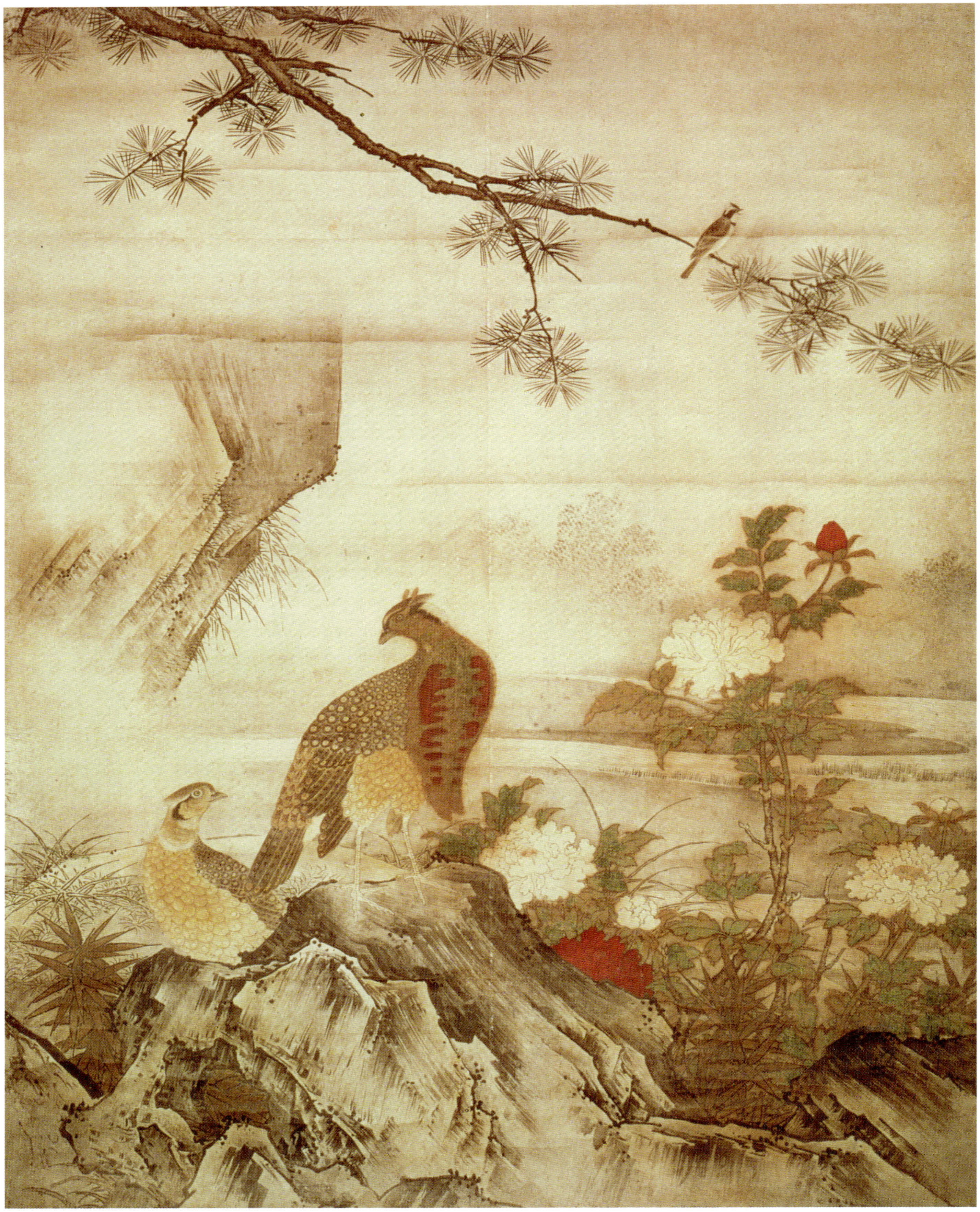

Katsushika Hokusai
(1760–1849)
Waves and Birds

c. 1825
Colour woodblock print
71 × 52 cm (28 × 20 in.)
Victoria and Albert Museum, London

Hokusai's most famous print is *The Great Wave off Kanagawa* (1831), which shows three tiny fishing boats being tossed about by gigantic waves, the foam of which breaks into claws that seem to grasp for the hapless fishermen. Man appears powerless in the face of vengeful nature. The artist produced a similar composition, *Fuji Seen from the Sea*, in 1834, in which the waves moved from right to left, the foam breaking into a multitude of birds, which may be plovers or gulls. The birds seem to neutralize the potentially destructive energy of the sea. The wave in *Waves and Birds*, which was created a few years earlier, is seen in close-up. A flock of friendly finches flies over stylized swirls of spume. The birds are beautifully observed; during this period the artist was creating several detailed images of flowers and birds.

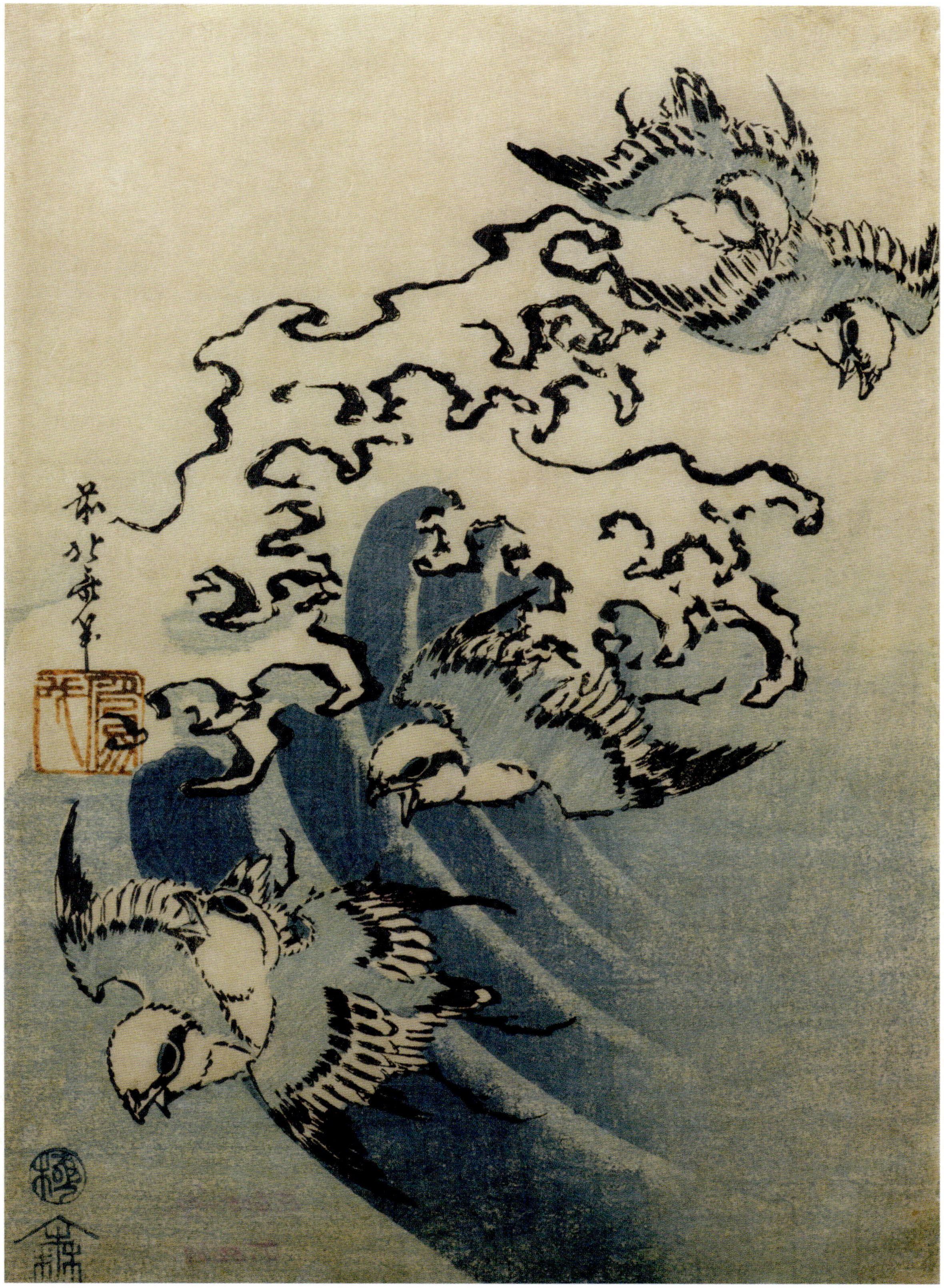

Katsushika Hokusai
(1760–1849)
Phoenix (detail)

1835
Eight-panel folding screen: ink, colour, cut gold leaf and sprinkled gold on paper
Museum of Fine Arts, Boston

The legendary phoenix features in ancient myths from East and West as a generalized symbol of rebirth and renewal, although its precise significance and appearance vary in different cultures. In Japan it is called the *Ho-o* or 'immortal bird', in reference to its lengthy life cycle. It was adopted as a symbol of the imperial household, specifically linked to the empress, and was said to appear at the beginning of a new era, or at the outbreak of peace after conflict. It was a popular motif on Japanese furniture from the medieval period onwards, and was also commonly used to decorate gold and silver lacquered boxes. Hokusai's phoenix is mounted on a folding screen; the artist has clearly assembled his mythical creature from parts of different birds, endowing it with an elaborate tail train that slightly resembles that of a peacock. At the age of eighty-nine, the artist painted an even larger, brilliantly coloured phoenix measuring 30 square metres (323 sq. ft) on the ceiling of the Ganshoin Temple in Obuse, central Japan.

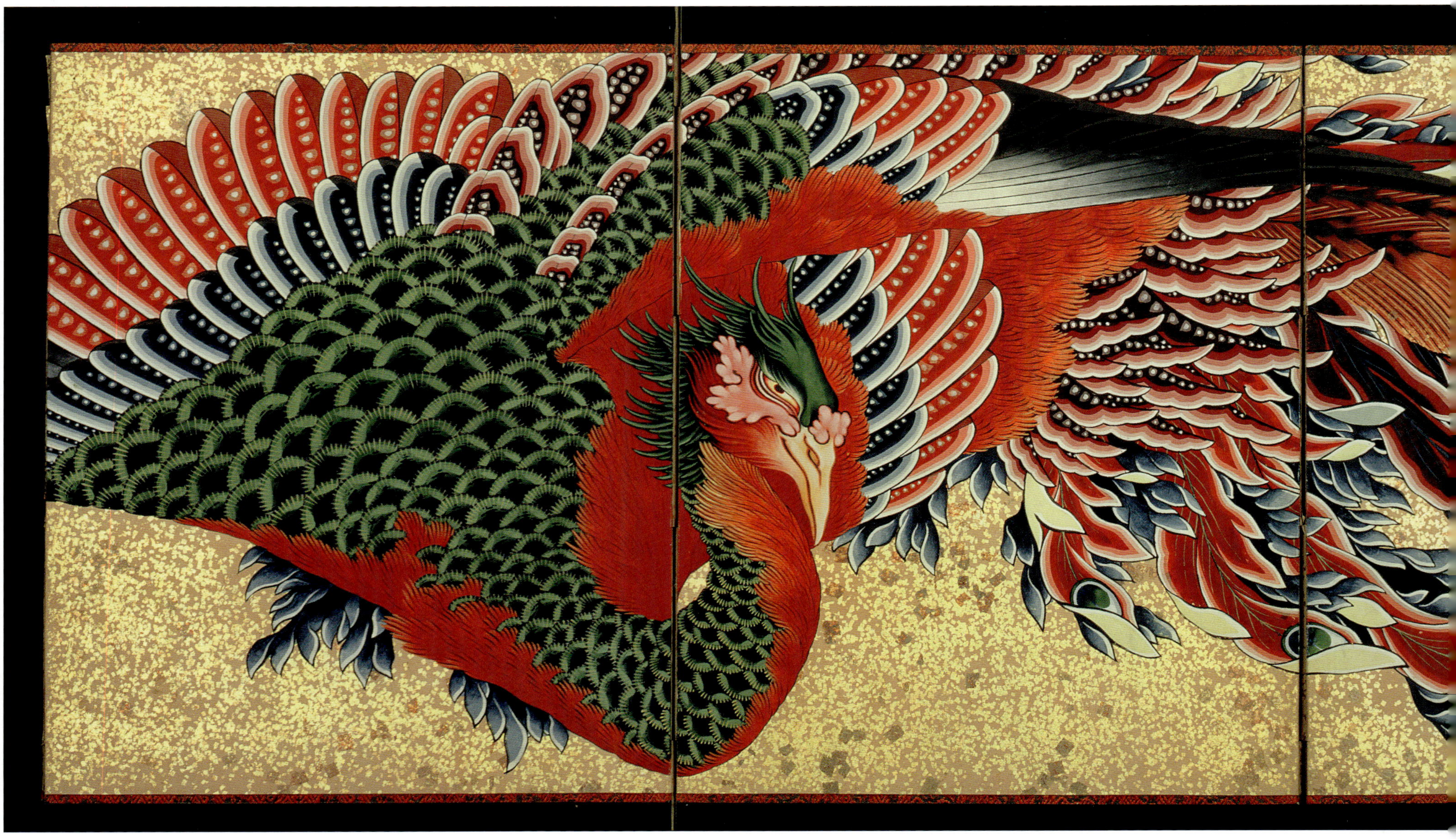

Ando Hiroshige (1797–1858)
Mandarin Ducks

c. 1832
Colour woodblock print
38 × 17.5 cm (15 × 6⅞ in.)
The Whitworth Art Gallery, University of Manchester

Together with Hokusai, Hiroshige was one of the leading landscape artists in nineteenth-century Japanese printmaking. However, he began his career focusing on images of beautiful women, and during the 1830s he specialized in prints of birds and flowers – a theme that had a long tradition in Chinese and Japanese art. The subject also chimed with a prevailing interest in nature in contemporary poetry. The haiku inscribed on this print reads:

The morning tempest
Sees even mandarin ducks
Go separate ways.

Mandarin ducks, which are thought to be monogamous, became a symbol of marital fidelity in Far Eastern art and literature, and pairs were often presented to couples as a wedding present. But this verse suggests that the tumultuous weather has driven even this loving pair apart. The swiftly flowing current of the river is indicated by bold swirls of blue.

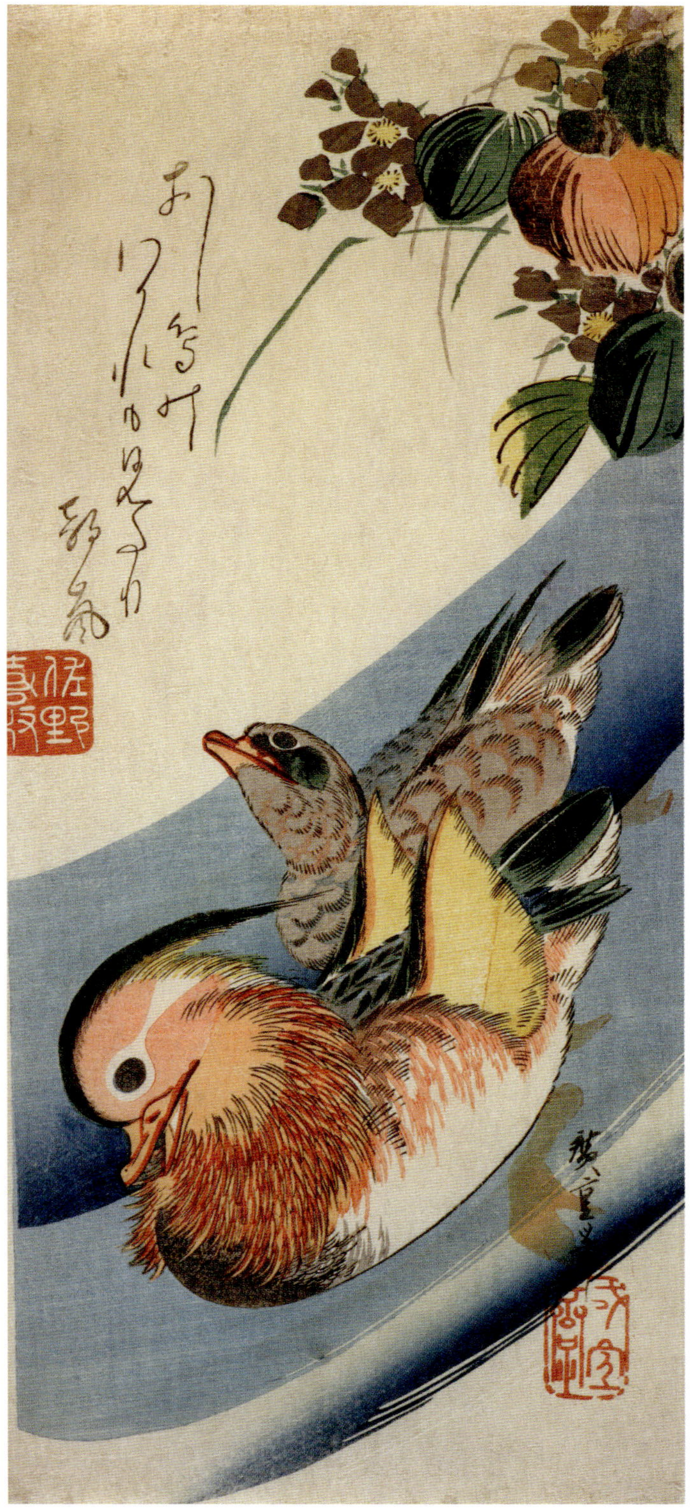

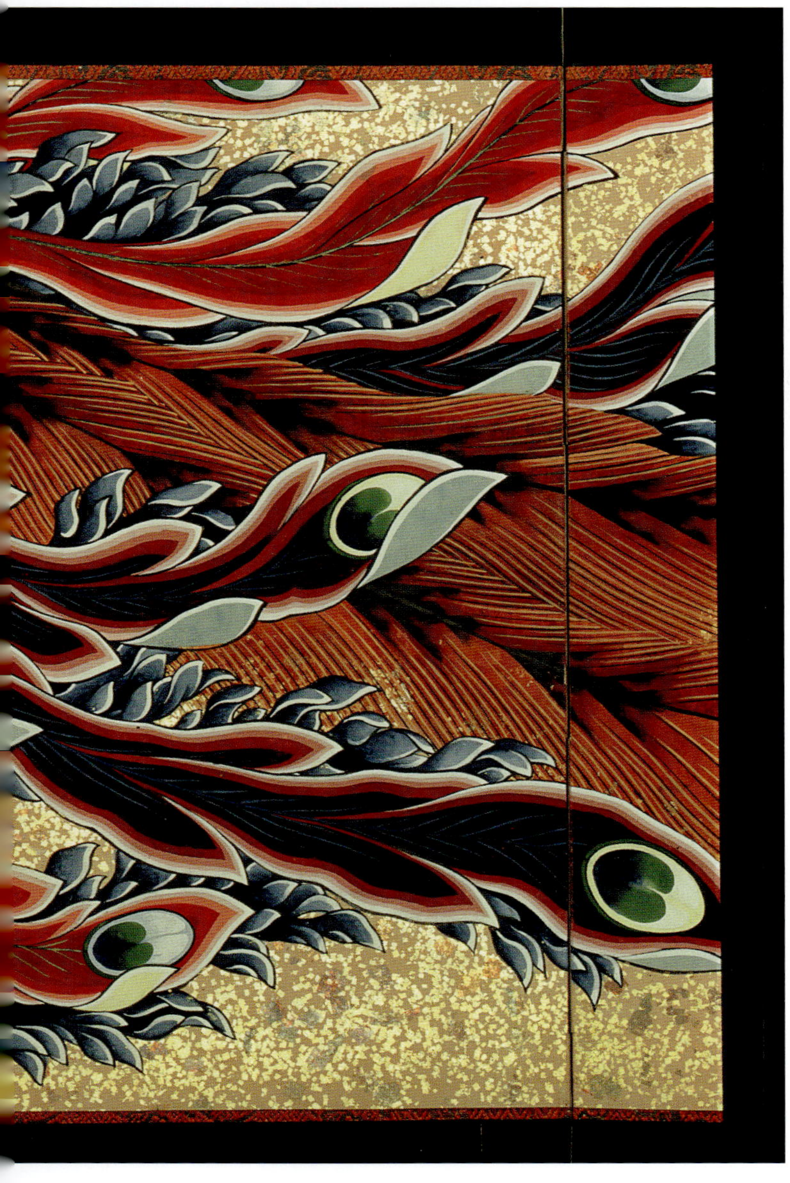

Suzuki Kiitsu
(1796–1858)
Reeds and Cranes

19th century
Six-panel folding screen: colour on gilded silk
177.5 × 369 cm (69⅞ × 145¼ in.)
Detroit Institute of Arts

The crane is a popular motif in Japanese art and literature, and not just because of its natural grace and beauty. The traditional saying that it lives for a thousand years has led to it being regarded as a symbol of good fortune and longevity. Its habit of mating for life has also caused it to represent fidelity. The painter and poet Kiitsu was a master of the Rinpa school of painting, which favoured the depiction of such simple subjects as birds and flowers against a background of gold leaf. Some of these cranes are strutting about the reed beds, while others have just taken off in flight. A companion screen, also in the Detroit Institute of Arts, shows the entire flock of cranes soaring above the Earth and into the golden distance. Six-fold screens like these were used as portable space dividers in Japanese homes, and the panels generally bear a single image rather than six separate ones.

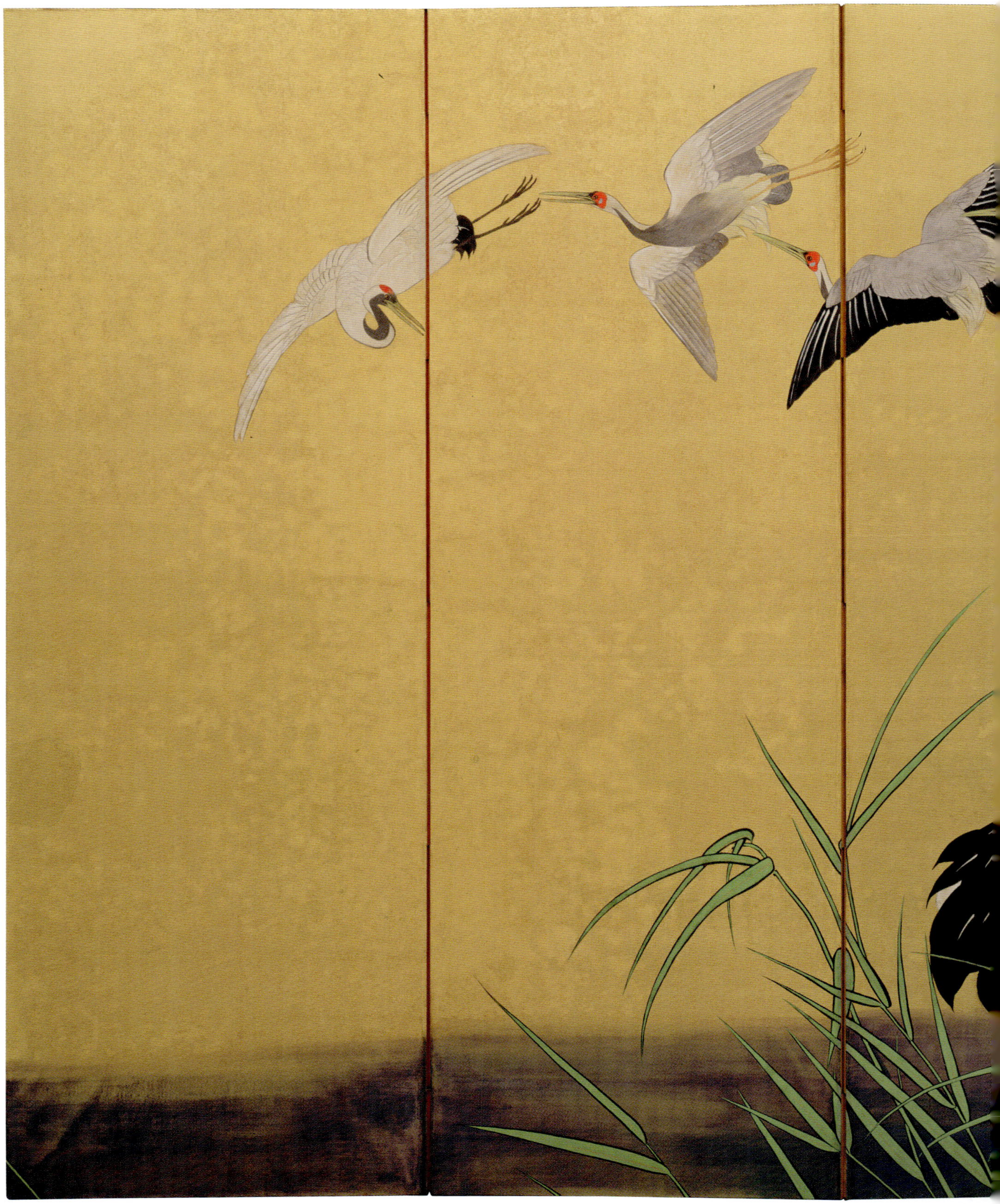

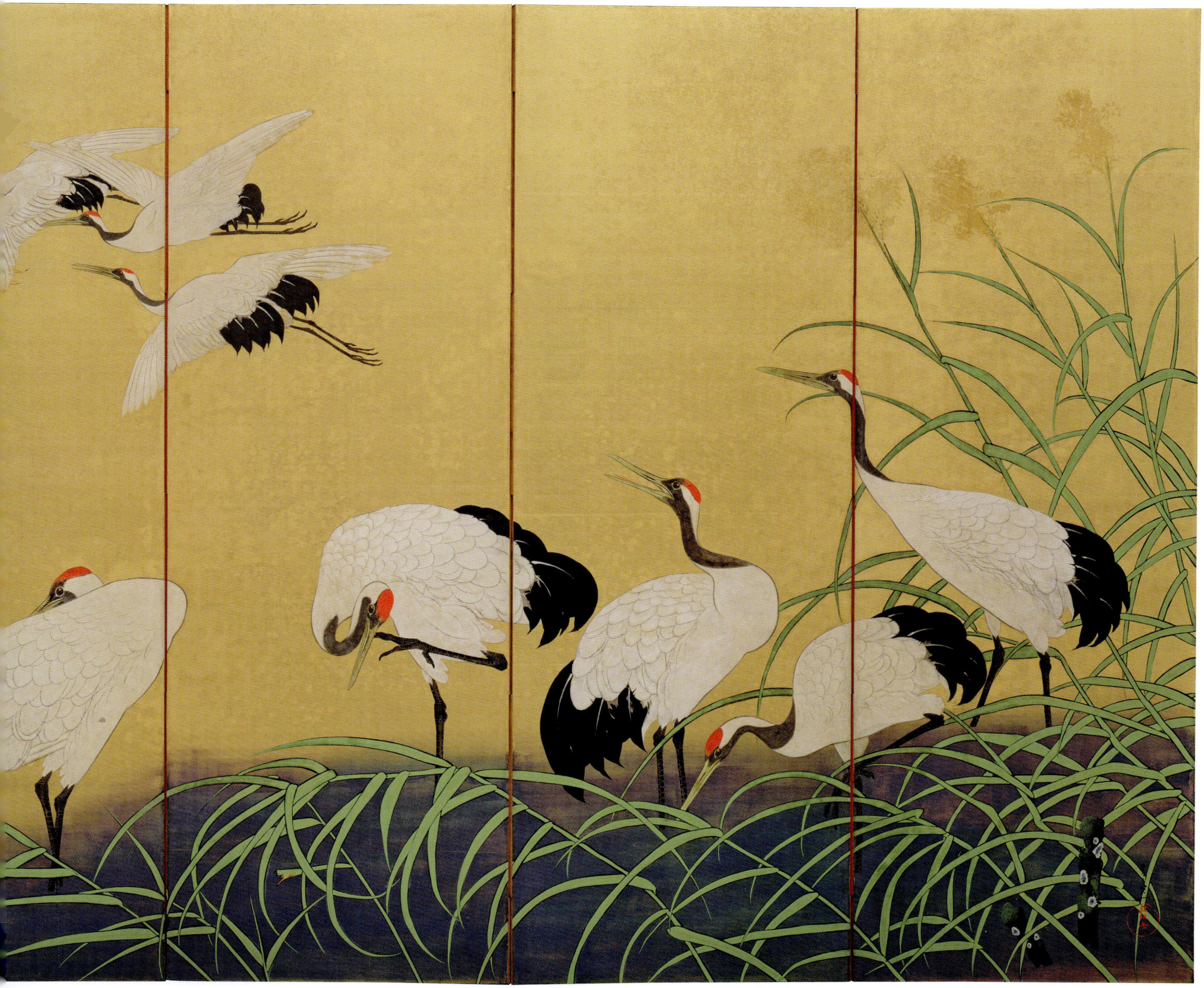

Ando Hiroshige
(1797–1858)
Sakasai Ferry

1857
Woodblock print
34.2 × 22.9 cm (13⅜ × 9 in.)
Brooklyn Museum, New York

One Hundred Famous Views of Edo was Hiroshige's last great series. It depicts scenes in and around the ancient Japanese capital (subsequently renamed Tokyo) from interesting and unusual viewpoints, presented in a vertical format. This print shows the Nakagawa River with a small settlement on its banks. White herons or egrets are feeding among the reeds and flying overhead, as little boats punt along to the landing. Some years earlier the artist had specialized in studies of birds (p. 193), and his knowledge of them is evident in the way he has captured the essence of the egrets in a few simple but fluid strokes. The white heron or egret appears in Japanese art as a symbol of purity. Its habit of standing still with its eyes closed for long periods of time has led to its association with the Buddhist practice of meditation.

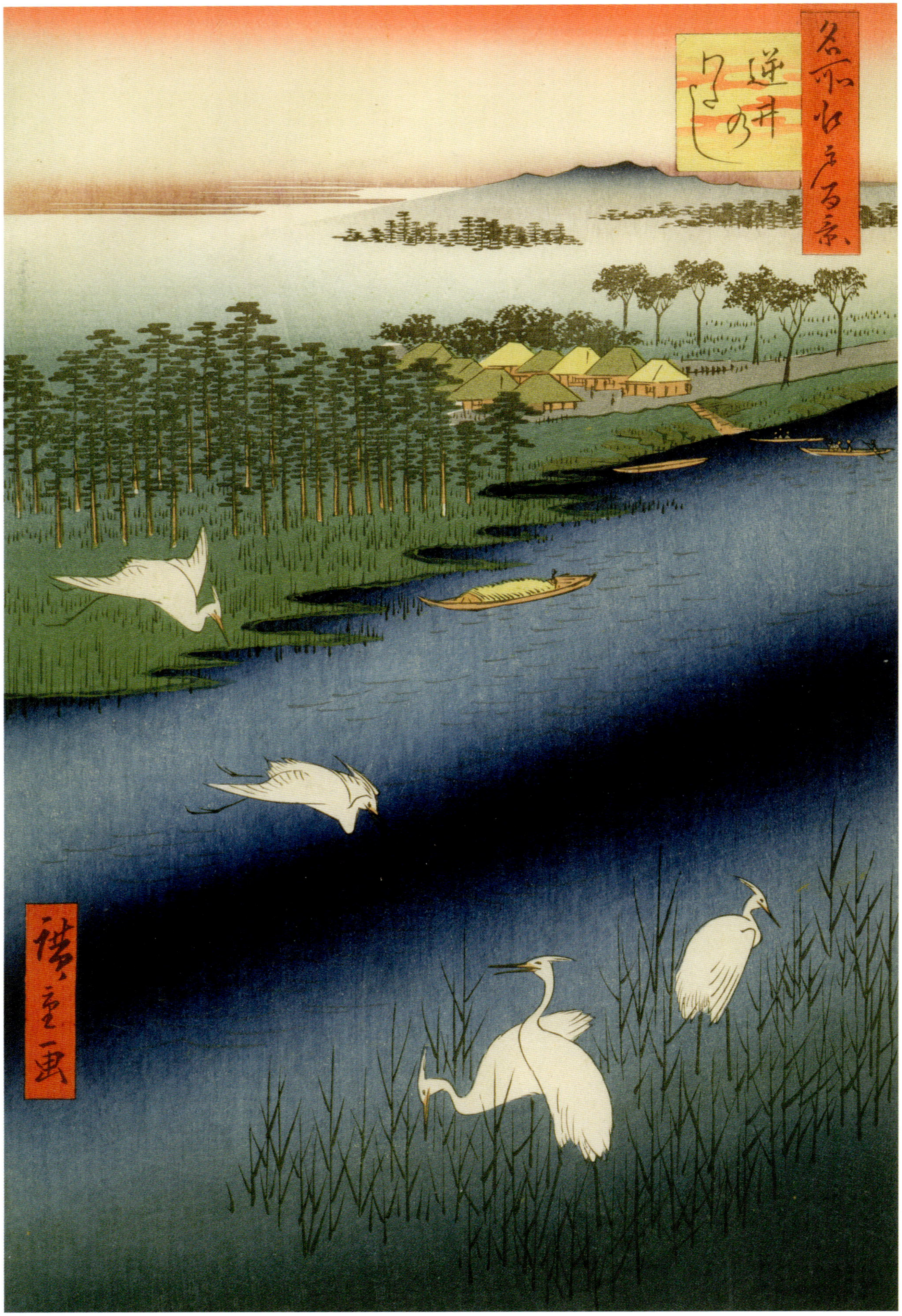

Shibata Zeshin
(1807–1891)
Crows in Flight at Sunrise

1888
Colour woodblock print
Dimensions unknown
University College London Art Museum

Shibata Zeshin worked as a painter and printmaker, and was a master of design. The pleasing graphic simplicity of this print is typical of his work, which is characterized by its balance and boldness. The association of the flying crows with the glowing sunrise may not be accidental, for the crow has long been linked in Japanese myth with the sun and the sun goddess Amaterasu. An ancient legend tells how a monster threatened to devour the sun, but the rulers of Heaven created a crow, which flew down the monster's throat and choked it. The crow is also associated with the mythical first emperor, Jimmu-Tenno, who was wandering around looking for a place to found his new kingdom when he caught sight of a crow sent by the sun goddess. He followed the crow to Yamoto (now part of Higashimatsushima, Miyagi Prefecture), where he settled in 660 BC, becoming the ancestor of all Japanese emperors.

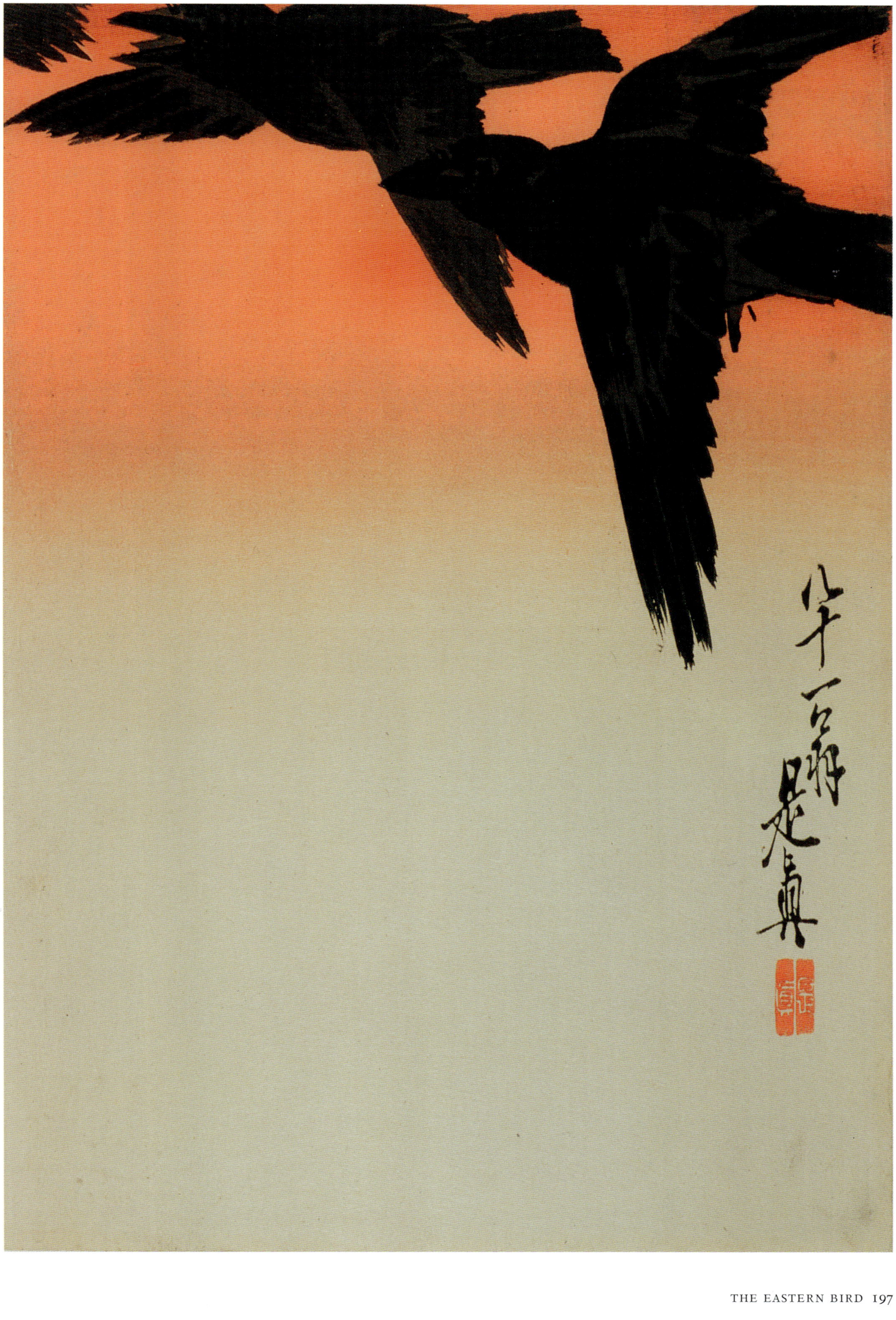

Indian (Deccan school)

Two Cranes by the Edge of a Pond

17th century

Gouache and watercolour

12.5 × 18.5 cm (5 × 7¼ in.)

Musée Guimet, Paris

Two cranes are looking for their meal at the water's edge, and one has managed to catch a fish in its beak. This delightfully decorative watercolour was produced in the Indian sultanate of Bijapur, some time in the seventeenth century. The art created in the area of the Deccan, where the sultanate was located, shows a strong Persian influence, as many artists from Persia came to live there, although in time their traditions mingled with native Hindu ones. Bijapur art is distinguished by the use of rich, dark colours – such as the olive that forms the backdrop for this picture – and dense vegetation. The crane carries many different but related associations in Asian cultures. It can symbolize lifelong fidelity and love, because of its habit of monogamous bonding for life, as well as virtue and knowledge. In Indian art, white cranes are also associated with the rainy season, and they are sometimes shown flying in a row below the monsoon clouds.

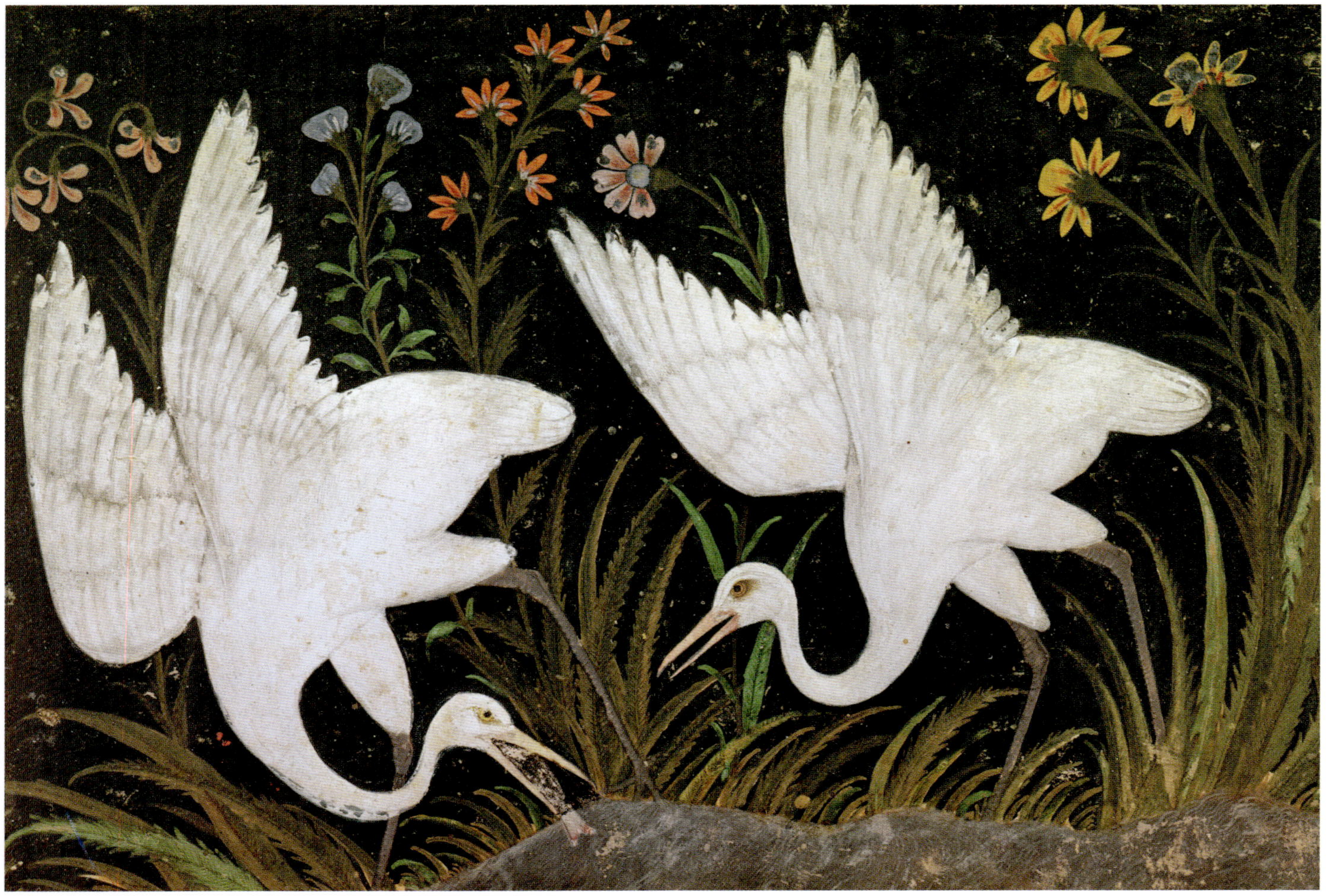

Islamic school

The Merchant from Isfahan Flying

14th century
Gouache on paper
Dimensions unknown

Institute of Oriental Manuscripts, Russian Academy of Sciences, St Petersburg

This is an illumination from *The Wonders of Creation and the Oddities of Existence*, a compilation originally put together in 1270 by Zakariya Qazwini, an Iraqi judge, covering geography, astronomy, natural history and travellers' tales. One of the fables it contained was that of the Merchant from Isfahan. A young man who has set his heart on marrying the girl of his dreams is given a task to perform before permission for the marriage is granted: he must go to Isfahan and find out why a merchant there has imprisoned his wife. On the way he is befriended by a giant bird or simurgh when he defends her offspring from attack. In return the bird helps him to solve the riddle and spirits him through the air, away from the man who threatens to kill him, and back to his home town where he can claim his bride. This is a wonderfully graphic and humorous image of the young man clinging on to the legs of the gigantic bird as he speeds through the air.

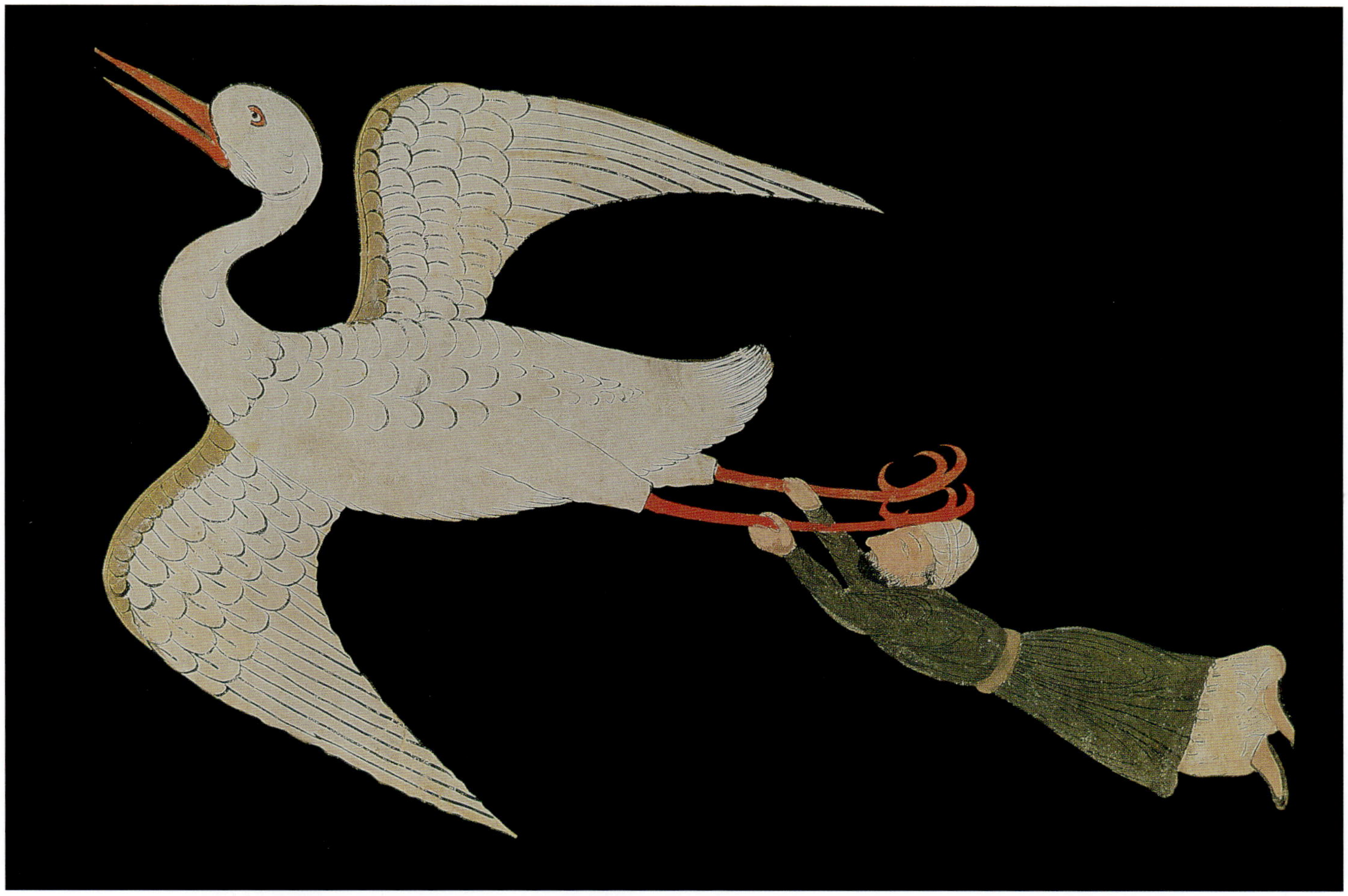

Shyam Sundar (Mughal dynasty)
The Vulture Jatayus Hears Sita's Plea and Gives Battle to Ravana, from *The Ramayana of Valmiki*, vol. 1, f. 132r

16th century
Opaque watercolour, ink and gold on paper
27.5 × 15.2 cm (10¾ × 6 in.)
Freer Gallery of Art, Smithsonian Institution, Washington, D.C.

This watercolour illustrates an episode in the Hindu epic poem the *Ramayana*. The valiant demigod Jatayus, who takes the form of a bird, tries to rescue Sita, the wife of Rama, when she is kidnapped by Ravana, the king of Lanka, who abducts her in his winged chariot. Despite the fact that he is elderly, Jatayus's bravery enables him to kill Ravana's charioteer and mules. But in the end Ravana gets the better of him, and cuts one of his wings, sending him tumbling to the ground. Jatayus lives just long enough to tell Rama what has happened, so that Rama can set in train the events that will lead to Sita's rescue. The scene here conveys the chaos of battle, with Jatayus's feathers scattering in combat and the distraught Sita in the background. Jatayus is described variously as a vulture and as an eagle; in this illustration he more closely resembles the latter.

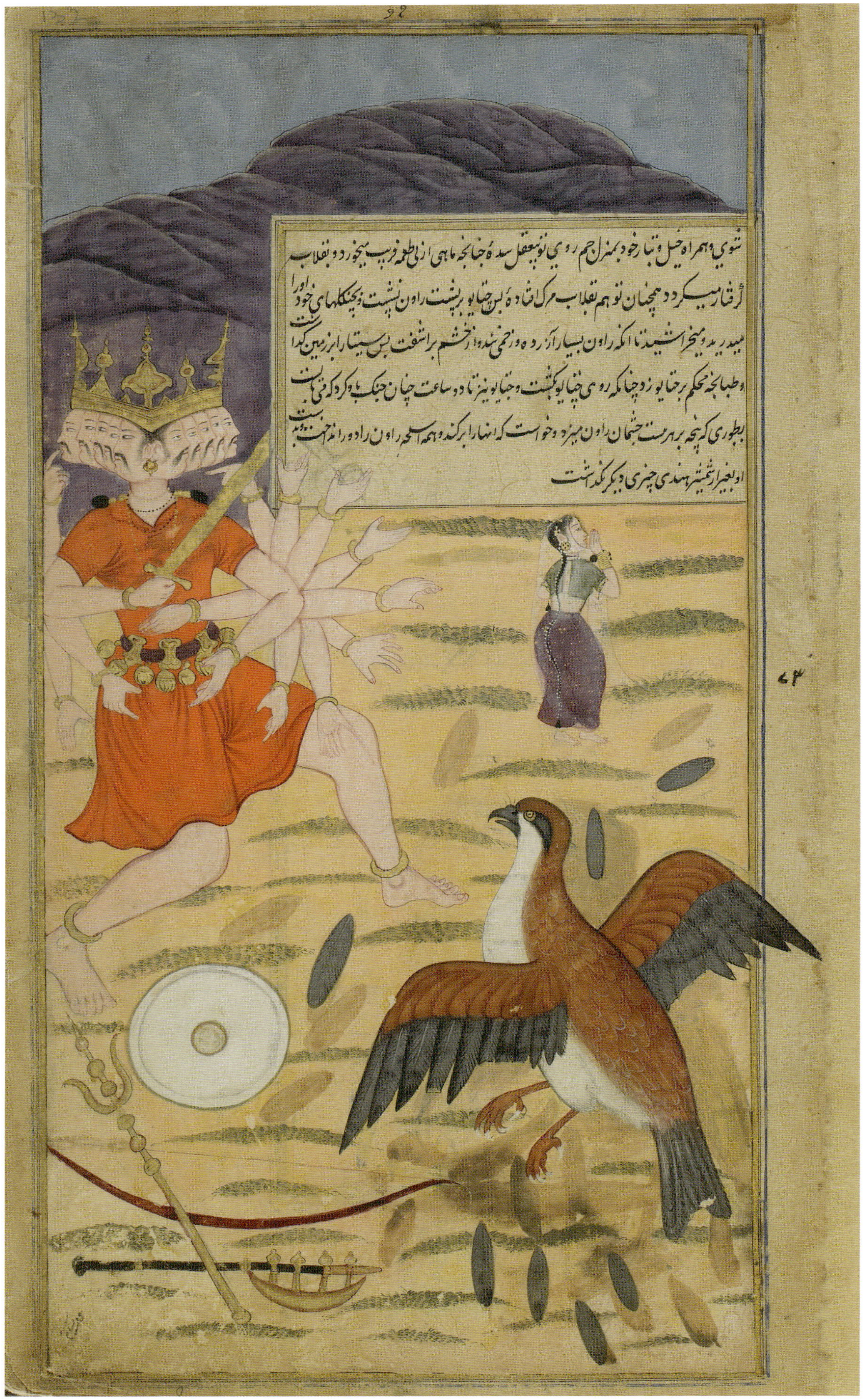

Indian

A Fowler Kills a Bird

16th century
Gouache, watercolour, ink and gold on paper
27.5 × 15.2 cm (10¾ × 6 in.)
Freer Gallery of Art, Smithsonian Institution, Washington, D.C.

The poetic form of the *Ramayana*, one of the great classics of Indian literature, is said to have been inspired by the death of a heron – an episode illustrated in this miniature. The Hindu sage Valmiki, who is alleged to have composed the epic poem, was washing in the River Ganges when he heard birdsong. As he moved closer he discovered two krauncha birds (herons) in amorous dalliance in the branches of a tree. A moment later the male was shot by a hunter's arrow and the female left disconsolate. Overcome by sorrow for the bird, Valmiki spontaneously uttered a verse: 'O hunter! May you suffer ignominy for hundreds of years! For you have mercilessly killed one of the krauncha birds engaged in harmless love play.' These few lines gave birth to a new style of metred poetry, which would form the basis of both the *Ramayana* and the *Mahabharata*.

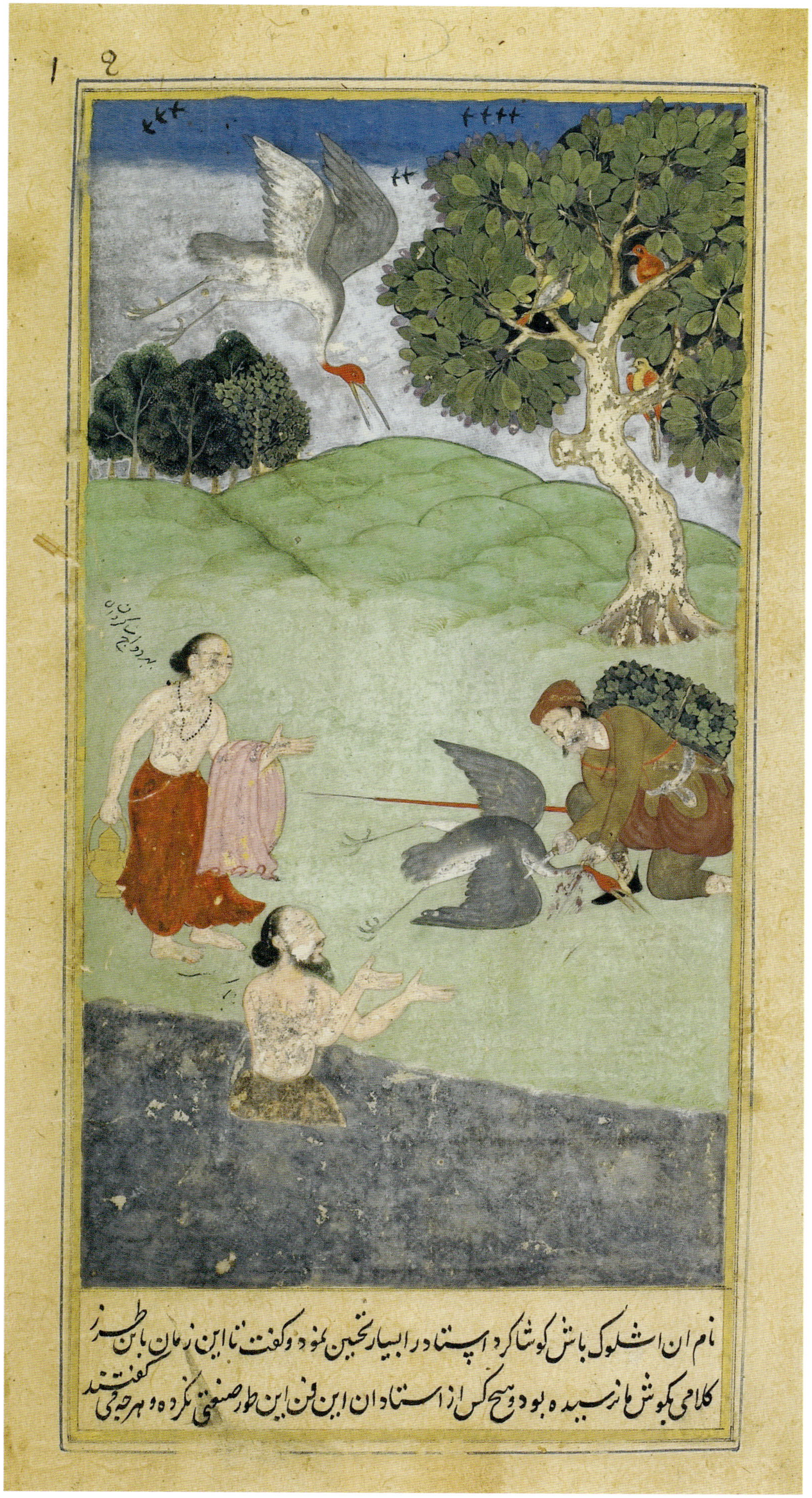

Persian

Zal Being Rescued by a Simurgh

16th century
Gouache and watercolour on paper
Dimensions unknown
Chester Beatty Library, Dublin

Unlike the harpy, which is also a composite bird–woman, the simurgh is a benevolent creature. It appears in Persian art in various guises, sometimes with a dog's head and sometimes with a human one, and usually with copper-coloured wings. It features in the Iranian epic poem the *Shahnama*, or *Book of Kings*, which was completed about 1010. This illustration from a sixteenth-century manuscript of the poem shows an episode in which the simurgh comes to the rescue of the baby prince Zal, who has been cast out by his father because he is an albino. On hearing the cries of the infant the simurgh flies to the mountain peak where he has been abandoned, and rescues him, eventually raising the child as its own. The anonymous artist who produced this illumination has successfully conveyed the grace and beauty of the bird with trailing plumage as it flies across the page, clutching the baby in its claws.

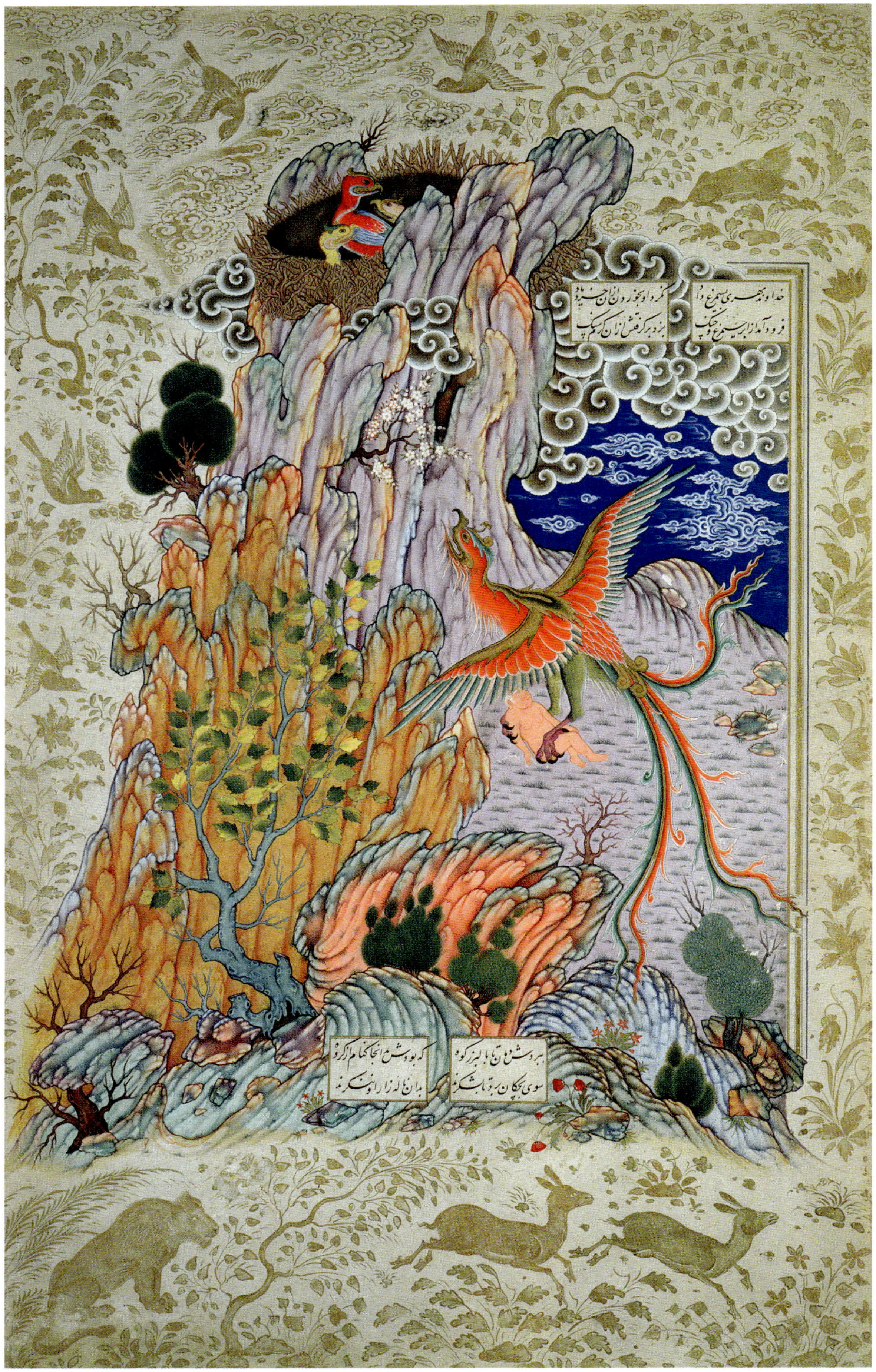

Ustad Mansur
(active 1590–1630)
A Turkey Cock (detail)

c. 1612
Opaque watercolour and gold on paper
Victoria and Albert Museum, London

Mughal art – a unique synthesis of Indian and Persian styles – reached its artistic height in the illuminated books produced in the sixteenth and seventeenth centuries under the patronage of the emperors Akbar, Jahangir and Shah Jahan. Fascinated by the natural world, Jahangir (ruled 1605–27) was a keen observer of birds, animals and flowers, and even kept his own menageries and aviary. A consignment of exotic birds and animals arrived at his court in 1612, sent by one of his trusty servants, who had been asked to buy all kinds of rarities from the Portuguese colony of Goa. Captivated by their unusual appearance, Jahangir asked his artists to paint the creatures for his illustrated memoirs, the *Jahangirnama*. One of the birds the emperor found most amazing was this turkey cock; he was particularly intrigued by the way it spread its feathers and strutted like a peacock. The artist charged with capturing it in a work of art was Ustad Mansur. His simple device of placing the turkey in isolation against a plain background seems to emphasize its strangeness.

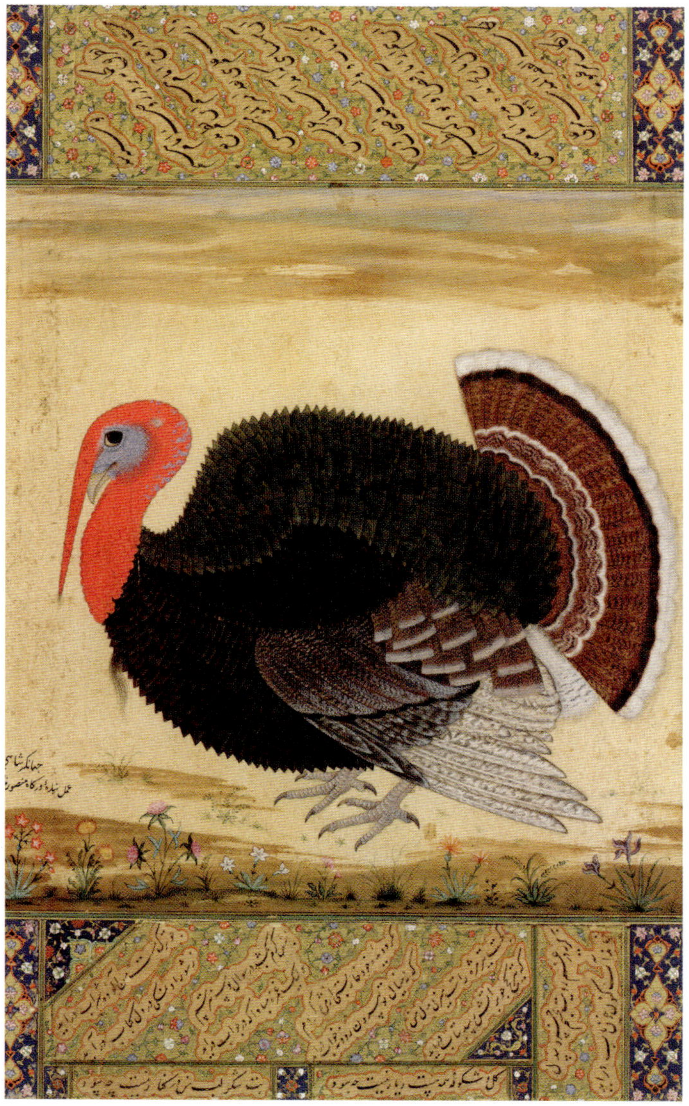

Mughal
Jewelled Falcon

c. 1640
Gold with enamel and inlaid rubies, emeralds, diamonds, sapphires and onyx
23.4 cm (9⅛ in.) high; 8.3 cm (3¼ in.) in diameter
Museum of Islamic Art, Doha

This luxurious piece, inlaid with precious jewels and enamel, was made in the Imperial Mughal workshop and belonged to the emperor Shah Jahan (ruled 1628–56). It was probably part of the decoration of a throne, or it may have been carried on a staff in court processions. The Muslim rulers associated falcons with kingship, victory and power, whereas the Sufi poet Rumi took a more spiritual view of the bird, seeing it as a symbol of the human soul. The arts reached dizzy heights of magnificence under Shah Jahan, who commissioned several landmark buildings, including the Taj Mahal. In his palace in Delhi he had a peacock throne, which took the form of a jewelled pavilion; on its roof stood a pair of peacocks, their tails encrusted with rubies, emeralds and sapphires.

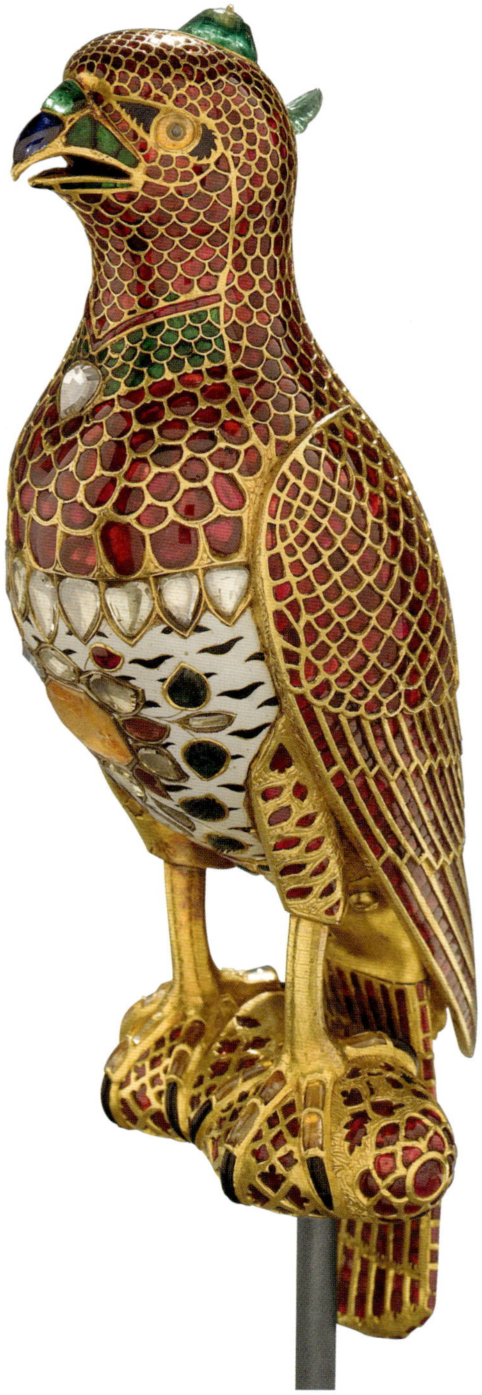

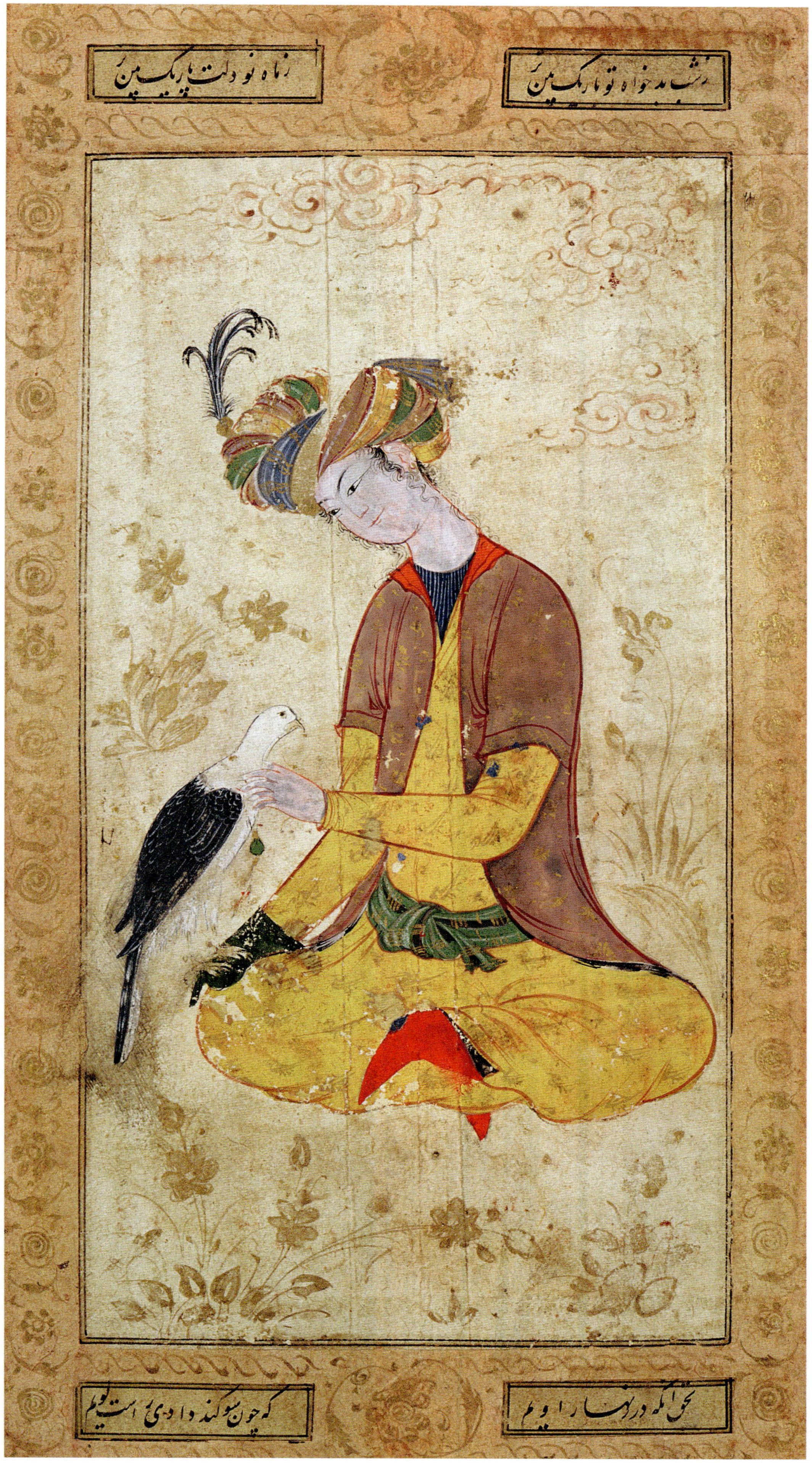

Mughal

A Hunter Stroking His Falcon

Early 17th century
Ink, gouache and gold on board
Dimensions unknown
Musée du Louvre, Paris

Using falcons to capture quarry began as a way of hunting food, but developed into an elite competitive sport. It has been practised for centuries, although its precise origins are difficult to pin down. According to one legend, falconry was invented in Persia under King Tahmooreth around 8000 BC, at least 2000 years before Zoroaster. Whatever the truth of how it began, falconry became known as the sport of kings in the Middle and Far East, and for centuries was limited to royalty and nobility. This youthful Persian hunter gazes affectionately at the sporting bird perched on his wrist, while stroking its neck. There are several images in Mughal painting of courtiers and officials holding falcons, reflecting the prestigious standing of falconry in Persia and Mughal India.

Indian (Deccan school) Finch, poppies, dragonfly and bee

c. 1650–70
Gouache and gold on paper
29.2 × 19.7 cm (11½ × 7¾ in.)
Brooklyn Museum, New York

Mughal emperors, including Jahangir, who commissioned their court artists to paint botanical and ornithological studies, helped to spread a taste for such subjects through Indian art. The anonymous painter who produced this picture has clearly observed the plants and wildlife he depicts in some detail, but he has rendered them in highly decorative colours. The bird – a variety of Indian finch – is painted in fanciful, slightly surreal hues that suggest that the image originated in the state of Golconda, in the south central region of India known as the Deccan. There were strong cultural links between this area and Persia, and Deccan art shows an affinity with the gem-like productions of Persia.

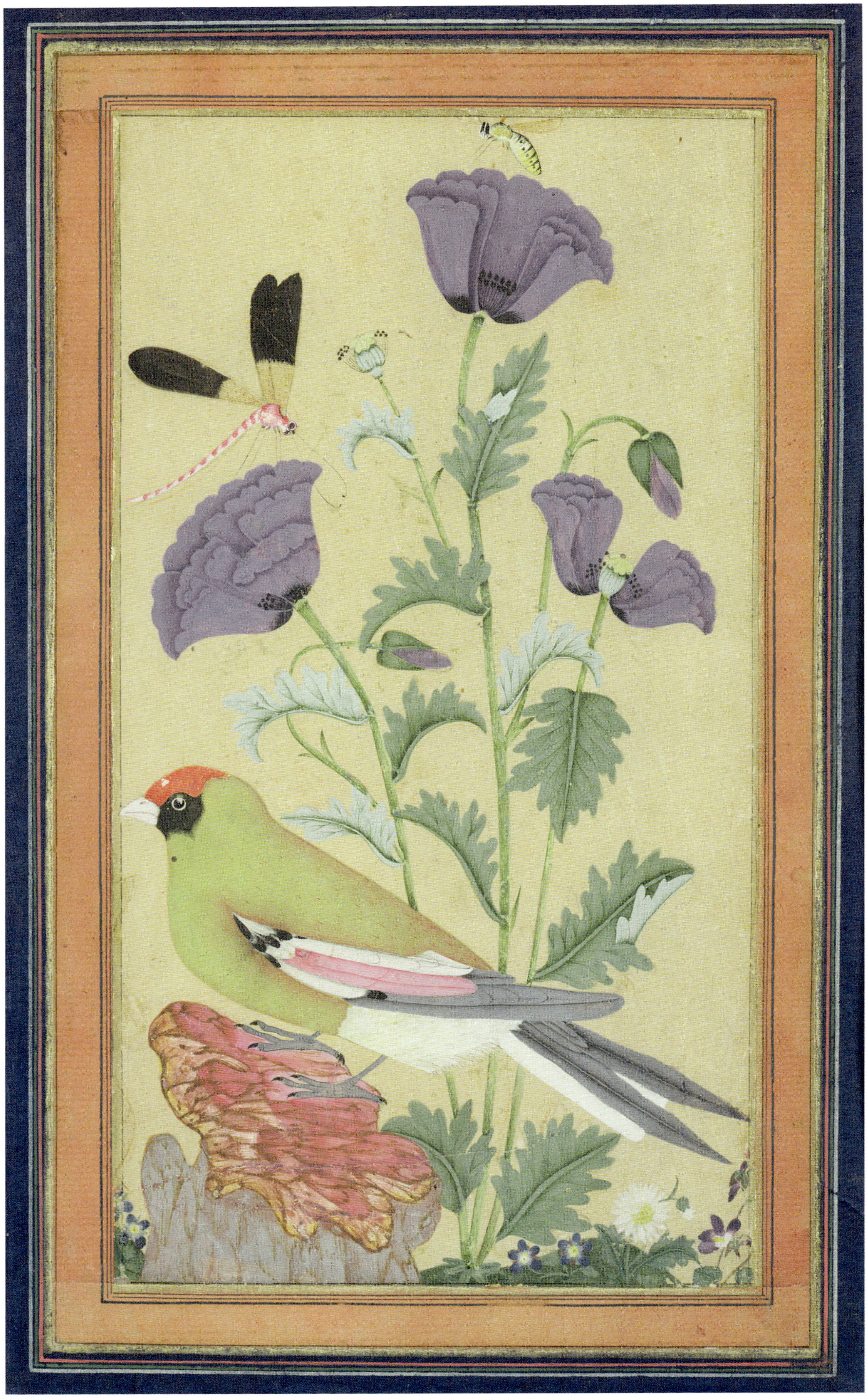

Mughal

Eight Pigeons and a Pigeon-cote on a Hill

Early 18th century
Gouache and gold on paper
21.2 × 13.2 cm (8⅜ × 5⅛ in.)
The Fitzwilliam Museum, Cambridge

Pigeon breeding in India dates back to the early years of Mughal rule, and the Mughal emperors seem to have had a particular affection for the birds. After he came to the throne, Akbar (ruled 1556–1605) is said to have kept more than 20,000 pigeons, and his successors Jahangir (ruled 1605–27) and Shah Jahan (ruled 1628–56) shared his affection for pigeons and pigeon flying. The birds can be seen in Mughal paintings carrying secret messages to lovers or confidential military instructions to soldiers. The eight birds in this picture, however, are simply pecking about on the ground. It has been suggested that these are Lahore or Sherajee pigeons – large, gentle, ornamental birds – which were originally bred in Persia, and imported to Lahore by the Mughal emperors. Their pigeon-cote resembles a tent. The birds are clearly enormous in comparison with the trees in the background, but the picture's naive sense of scale and perspective is part of its charm.

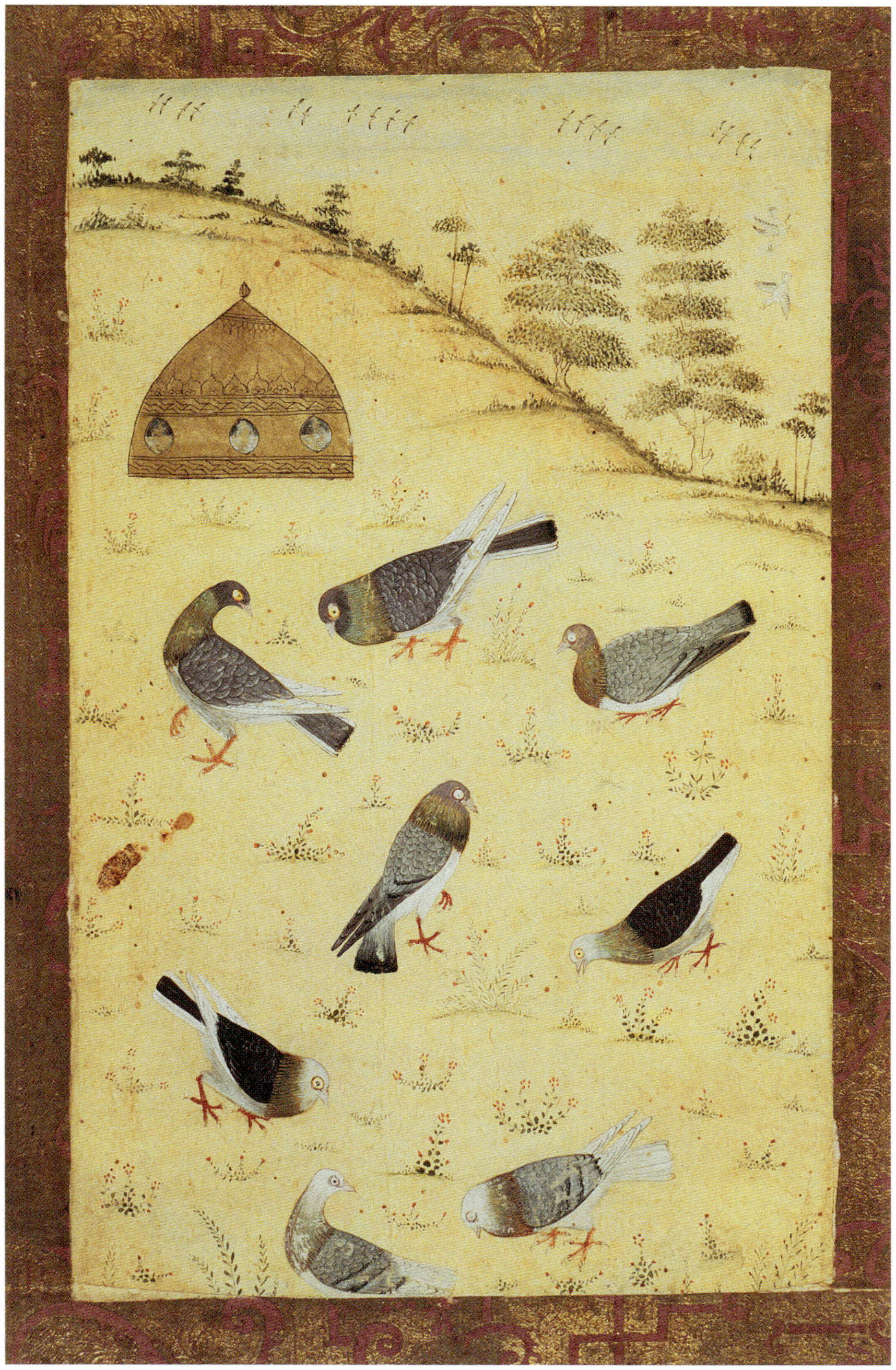

Turkish
Tile with two parrots

17th century
Fritware painted in polychrome under a colourless glaze
25.4 × 24.8 cm (10 × 9¾ in.)
The Fitzwilliam Museum, Cambridge

The small town of Iznik (the modern name for ancient Nicea) in north-western Turkey was the centre of production for ceramic vessels and tiles during the Ottoman Empire. Although the production of ceramics began there in the fifteenth century, it was at its height during the sixteenth and seventeenth centuries, when the repertoire of motifs expanded to include not only plants, and such flowers as carnations, tulips and hyacinths, but also fantastic birds and animals. In this tile, which is decorated in the typical Iznik colours of red, emerald green, blue and black, two green parrots perch either side of a blue vase containing a red carnation and sprays of blue hyacinth. The birds' markings bear some resemblance to those of the Alexandrine parakeet, so named because Alexander the Great is credited with introducing the species from the Punjab to various Asian and European countries in the fourth century BC, but – as is the case with many depictions of creatures on ceramics – accuracy was not necessarily the craftsman's prime concern.

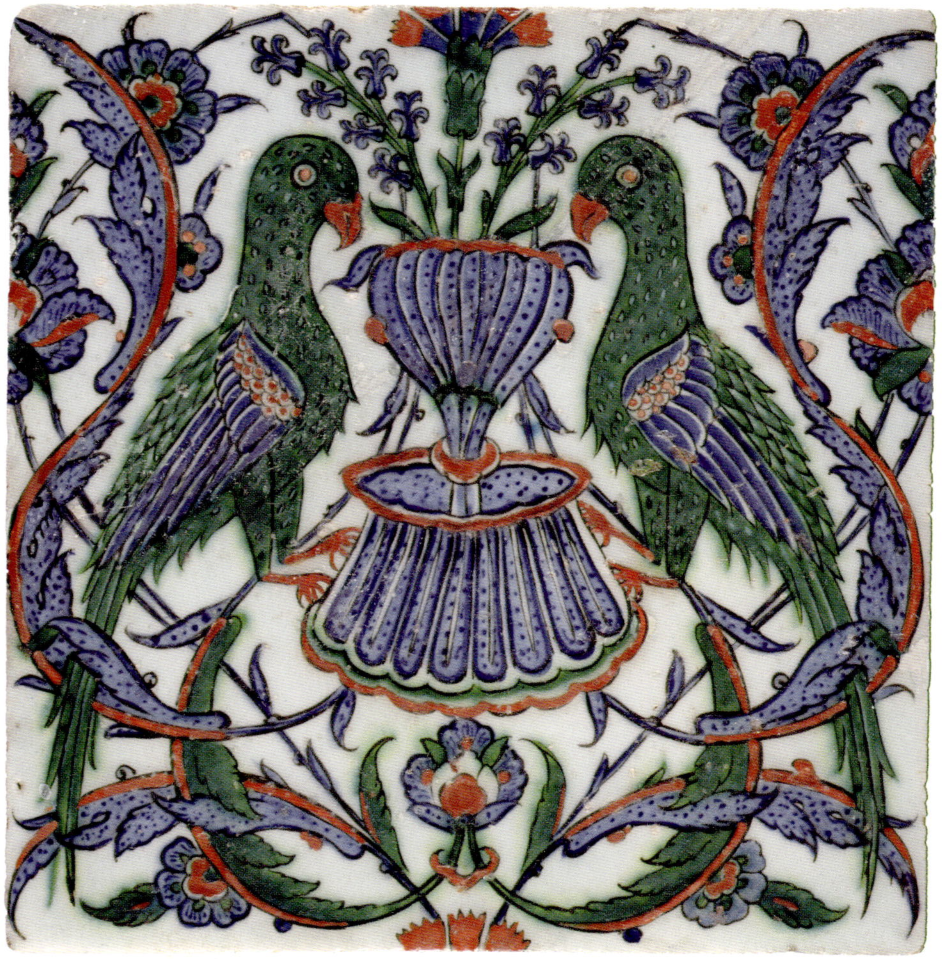

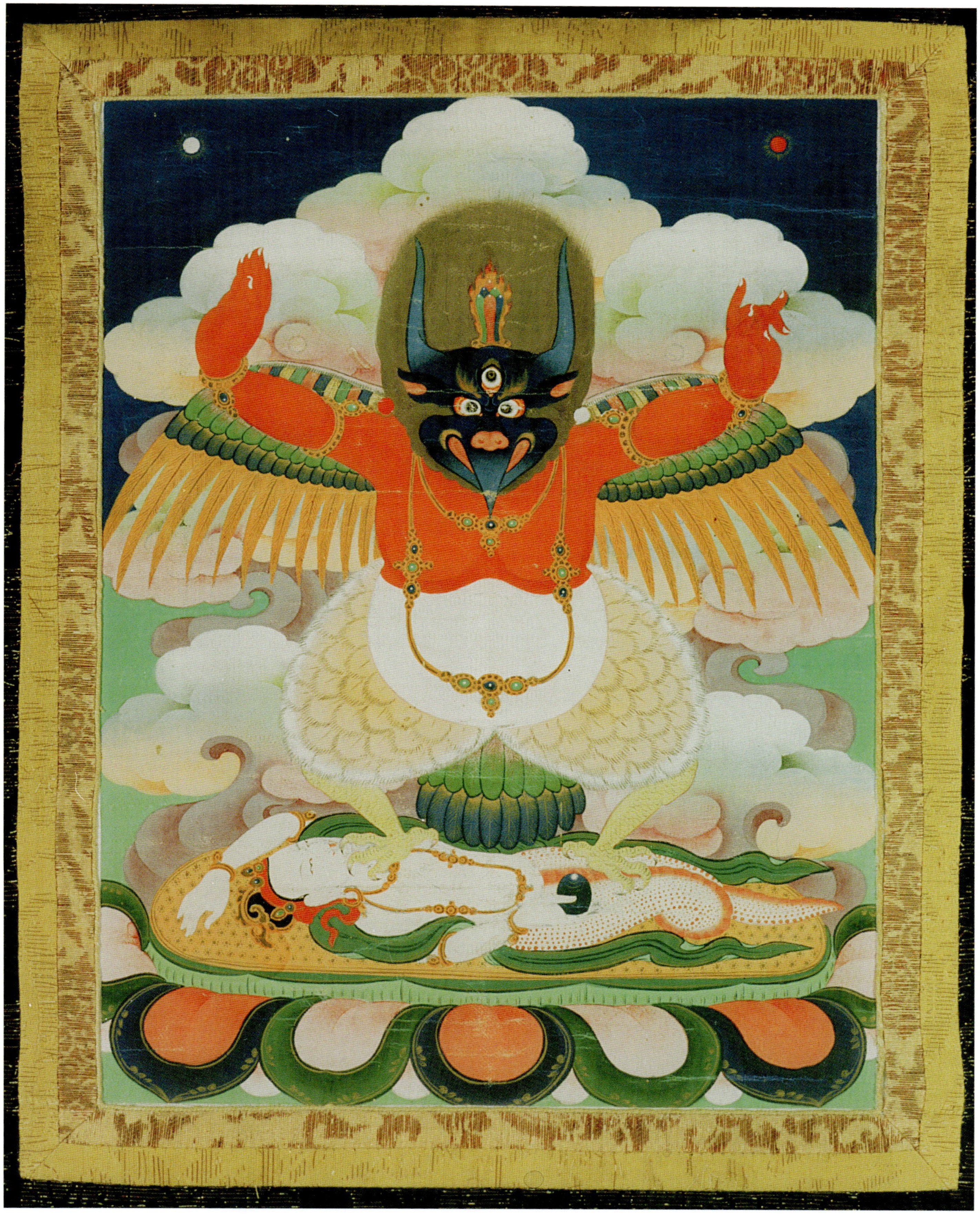

Tibetan
Thangka showing garuda trampling a dying naga
19th century
Cloth
32 × 24 cm (12⅝ × 9⅜ in.)
National Museum of Scotland, Edinburgh

The garuda, which appears in both Hindu and Buddhist mythology, is a mythical winged creature that combines human features with those of large birds, such as the eagle. It is the sworn enemy of the nagas, the serpent-like beings it hunts, and this Tibetan *thangka* (a painted textile depicting a religious subject) shows a garuda trampling one to death. While the garuda is important and indeed ubiquitous in countries as far apart as India, Nepal, Indonesia and Thailand, and makes frequent appearances in the art of the Far East, it varies widely. It can have the face of a bird or a human, and human or bird-like limbs. But it is always vast in scale and enormously powerful and fast in flight. It has been adopted by some countries as a national or military symbol, and has lent its name to Indonesia's national airline.

The Domestic Bird

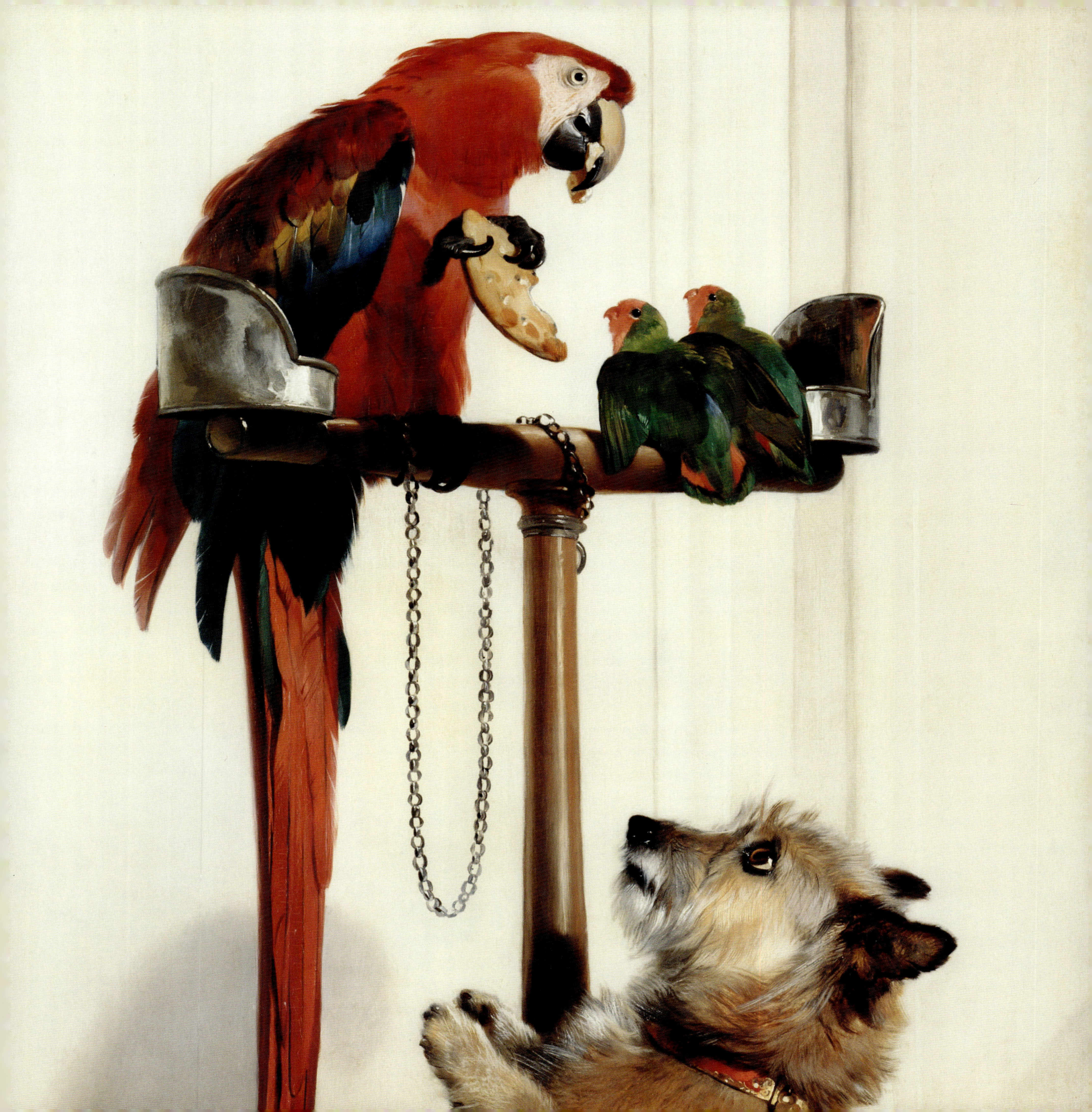

Birds entered the domestic sphere along with farmyard animals millennia ago, as providers of food or as hunting accessories, but it was not long before they also entered our hearts as pets and daily companions. William Blake may have thundered 'A Robin Redbreast in a Cage/ Puts all Heaven in a Rage', but there is evidence that birds were kept in cages or aviaries as far back as ancient Egypt and Greece. No doubt their owners were as enchanted by their beauty and song as we are today.

The home has traditionally been the domain of women, so it is hardly surprising that when birds are depicted in scenes of domestic life it is generally in the company of women and children. Men, when they are portrayed on their own rather than in mixed company, are more commonly shown with birds that have some practical purpose, such as the hawks or falcons used in hunting. But single women are portrayed tenderly embracing doves and pigeons, weeping over dead canaries, suggestively canoodling with parrots, or relaxing in parks or gardens with such showy birds as peacocks and swans that complement their beauty.

Pet birds appear as incidental details in many Renaissance paintings and portraits – Crivelli's *Annunciation*, for example, shows a goldfinch in a cage (p. 14, right) and Carpaccio's two Venetian ladies sitting on their balcony are accompanied by tame birds (p. 17, right) – but, with the burgeoning of genre scenes in the seventeenth century, images of domesticated birds began to multiply. A number of Dutch paintings of everyday life depict pet birds simply for their anecdotal value or decorative colour; these pictures provide a lively counterpart to the kitchen or market scenes featuring heaps of dead birds and plucked poultry. But painted birds can also come freighted with meaning in pictures that illustrate proverbs. An owl, for example, could represent wisdom or its reverse – stupidity – as is the case with Jan Steen's evocation of an unruly classroom (p. 217) and Frans Hals's image of a madwoman (p. 214).

Caged birds could convey a subtext of love or lust, especially when shown with a female owner. In Dutch prints and texts, birds are associated with lasciviousness, and the Dutch verb *vogelen* ('to bird') is slang for sexual intercourse. If the bird has escaped its cage, there might be suggestion of flirtation or lost virginity. That is the implied narrative in two eighteenth-century French paintings: Greuze's picture of a young girl mourning the death of her pet canary (p. 223, bottom), and Boilly's canvas of an amorous couple with an escaped bird (p. 227). Birds are also the subject of numerous superstitions, in which they appear to ordinary people as harbingers of doom. That is the case with the single magpie that appears in the kitchen of a Cornish fisherman's wife (p. 235), and the raven whose cry causes a horse to stumble, bringing down a farmer's wife and her cargo of eggs (p. 226).

The sheer beauty of parrots, and their endearing ability to mimic human speech, have given them an affectionate place in the home, and their colourful plumage has also been a gift to artists. Initially associated in art with the Virgin Mary, they eventually became beloved pets, first of kings and nobles, and then in bourgeois households. By the nineteenth century artists were showing parrots as companions to women, sometimes scantily clad or nude women, as a kind of stand-in lover (p. 221).

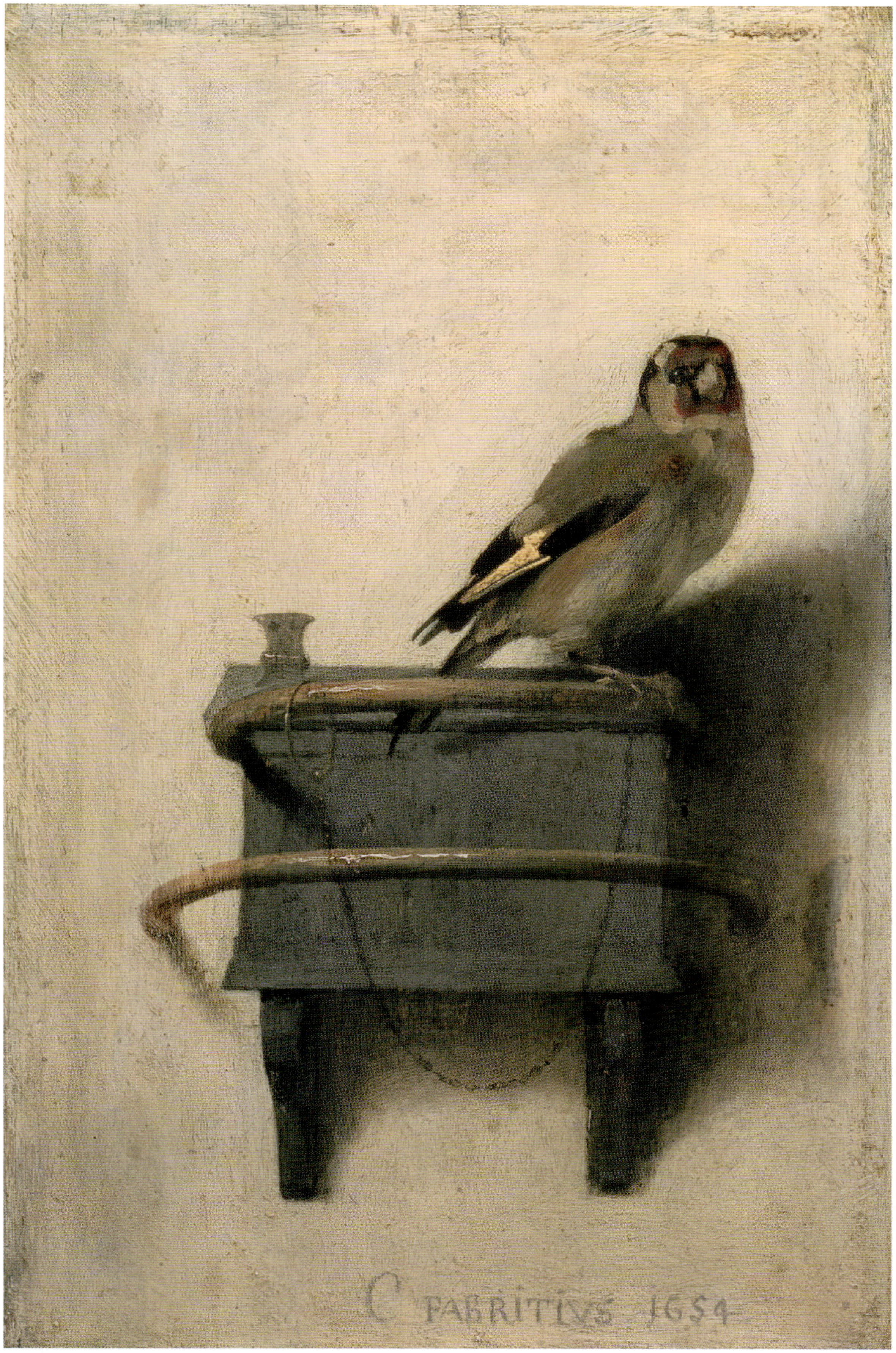

Carel Fabritius (1622–1654)
The Goldfinch

1654
Oil on panel
33.5 × 22.8 cm (13⅛ × 9 in.)
Mauritshuis, The Hague

Rembrandt's most gifted pupil, Carel Fabritius died at a relatively tender age when an arsenal in his native Delft exploded, killing him and destroying his studio and much of his work. Only about a dozen paintings by him are known to have survived, including this masterly study of a goldfinch, attached to a wall-mounted feeding box by a delicate chain. Painted on an intimate scale, it is a superb piece of painterly illusionism. The bird is pretty much life-size, and at a quick glance the viewer might almost be fooled into thinking that he was looking at a real one, although it is quite freely painted. The perspective indicates that the picture was designed to be seen from below, and it has been suggested that it was kept nailed to a wall at the same height as a real feeding box. Goldfinches were popular pets in The Netherlands at this time, and their owners enjoyed getting them to perform tricks, such as drawing their own drinking water from a bowl in a tiny bucket on a chain (see p. 22). The goldfinch's Dutch nickname, *putterje*, means 'drawer of water'.

Gustave Courbet (1819–1877) after Frans Hals (1581/85–1666)
Malle Babbe

1869
Oil on canvas
85 × 71 cm (33½ × 28 in.)
Hamburger Kunsthalle, Hamburg

The French artist Gustave Courbet was so intrigued by Frans Hals's portrait of 1633 showing a woman with an owl on her shoulder that he made this faithful copy. *Malle* means 'mad' in Dutch, and the woman's leering grin certainly suggests a manic quality. Although this was probably intended as a character study rather than a portrait, there was actually a real 'Malle Babbe' in Haarlem in Hals's time; she lived in a workhouse for the mentally ill. The meaning of the owl has been long debated. Traditionally owls were an attribute of Athena, the goddess of wisdom, and associated with calm and moderation. But in Dutch paintings of the Golden Age an owl could also stand for the reverse: witchcraft, stupidity, licentiousness and drunkenness. Since Malle Babbe is clutching an outsize pewter tankard, the last association must surely apply here.

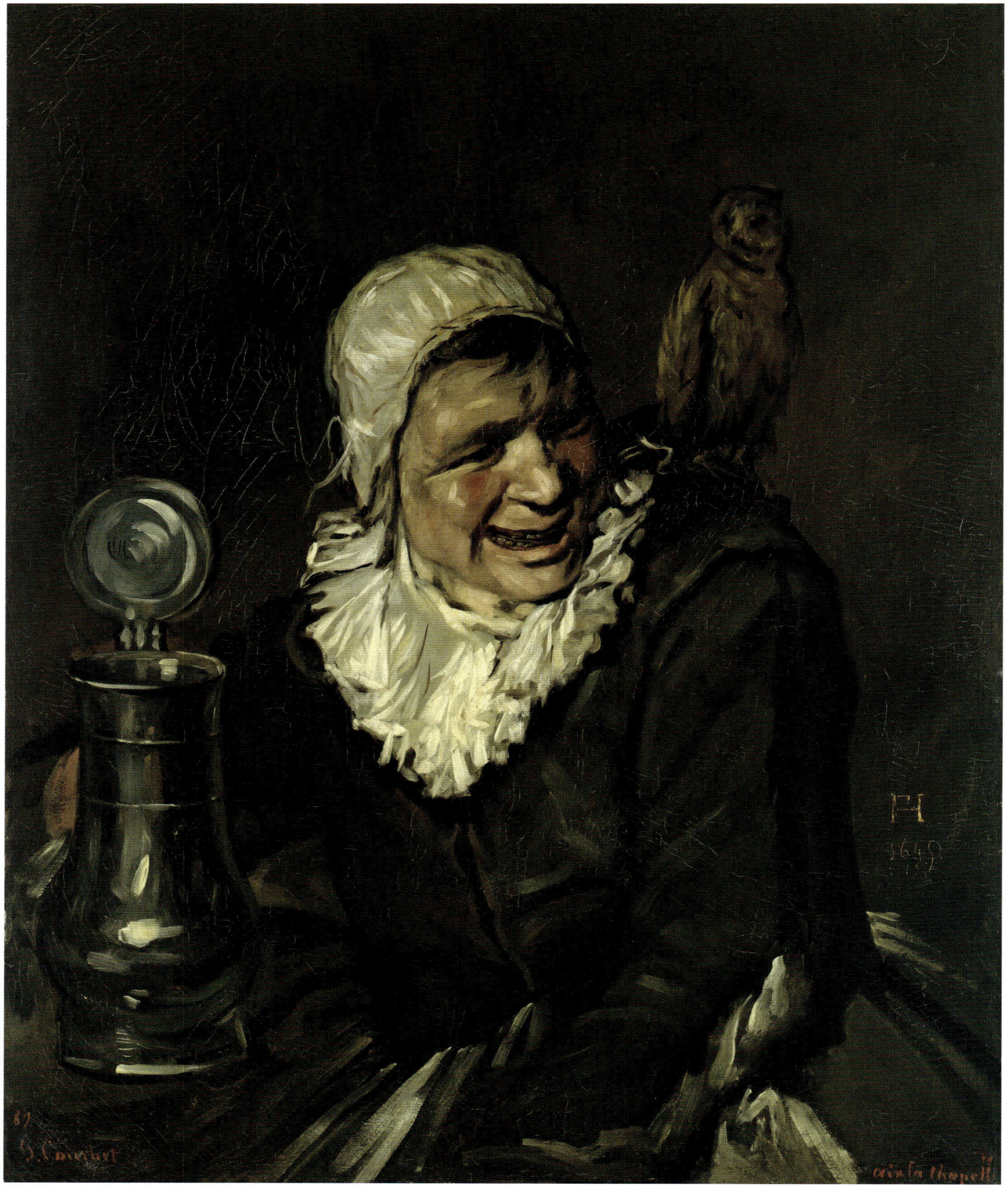

Gabriel Metsu
(1629–1667)
A Woman Sewing, with a Parrot

c. 1650
Oil on canvas
35 × 27 cm (13 ¾ × 10⅝ in.)
The Pushkin Museum of Fine Arts, Moscow

Metsu's lady in her well-ordered home, intent on her lacemaking, seems to exemplify the virtues of industriousness, docility and modesty that would have been desirable in a middle-class young woman in seventeenth-century Amsterdam. Her pet parrot is perching on top of its cage. To judge from the frequency of its inclusion in paintings, the parrot was a fairly common household pet in The Netherlands at the time, although it was obviously not a native bird. Caged birds were traditionally associated with love and erotic yearning. The parrot's various symbolic meanings include garrulousness, desire and lust, and the fact that it has been let out of its cage here could allude to flirtation or loss of virginity – an interesting undercurrent to the domesticated virtue the woman appears to embody.

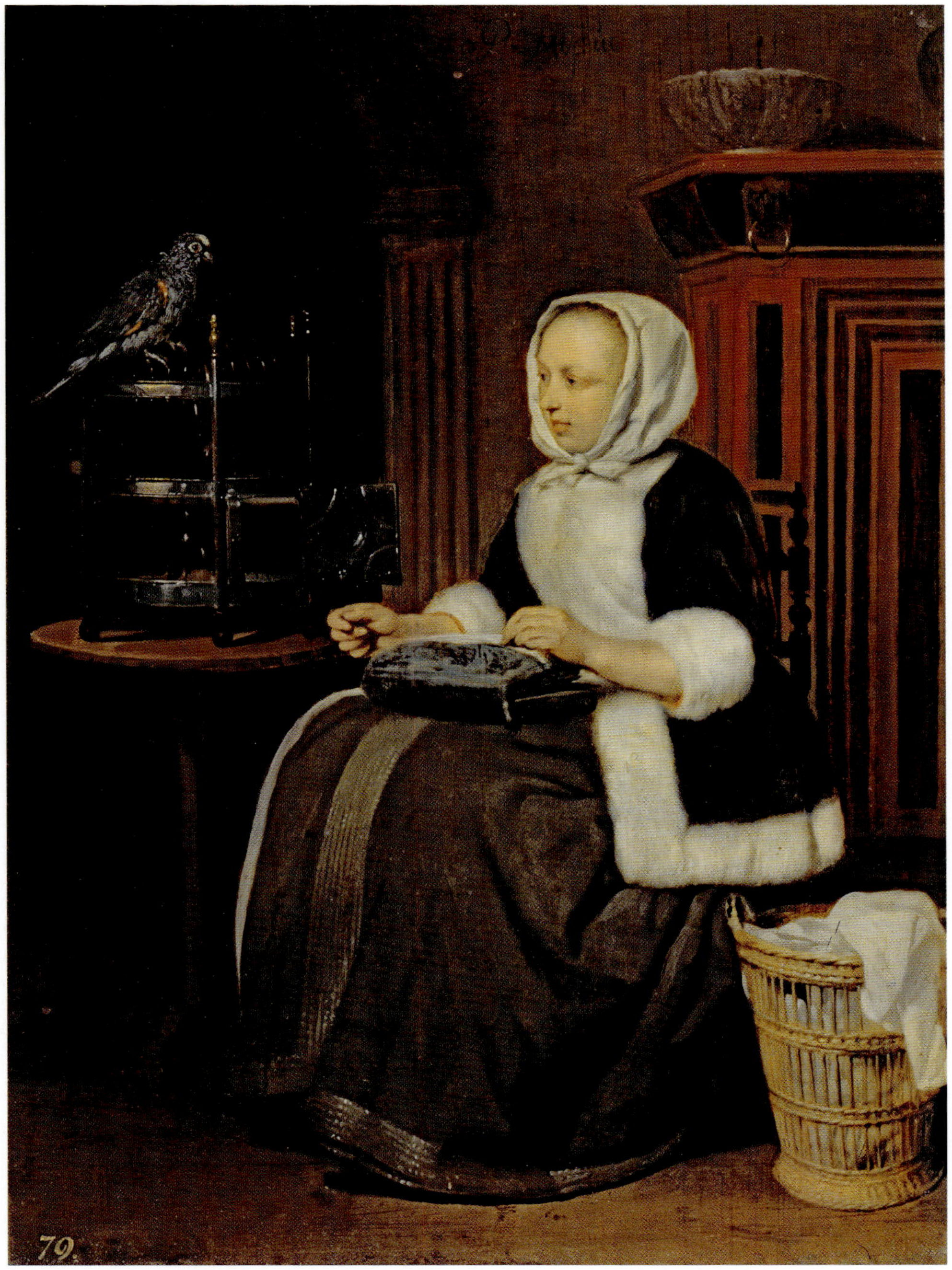

Frans Snyders
(1579–1657)
The Poulterer's Shop

c. 1612–15
Oil on canvas
188.1 × 152 cm (74 × 59⅞ in.)
National Museum Cardiff

A kitchen maid is selecting the ingredients for a meal. Laid out before her is a tempting array of birds, including a cockerel, pigeons, a mallard and a bittern, as well as a hare and a cauliflower, celery and artichokes; but she is opting for chickens. Snyders – who specialized in paintings of animals and still lifes – painted these creatures with remarkable fidelity to nature. The accuracy of his observation has enabled scholars to identify fifty species of bird in his paintings of pantries, food stalls and banquets, and his pictures have been used as evidence of historic eating habits. The artist originally intended this as a pure still life, to include the carcass of a roe deer in the foreground, but this plan was abandoned, and the figures were added by a painter from Rubens's workshop. This kind of artistic collaboration was common at the time, and Snyders was often called on to paint the animals in Rubens's canvases. There was frequently an erotic element in scenes involving kitchen maids, and there is certainly something rather suggestive in the man's expression here.

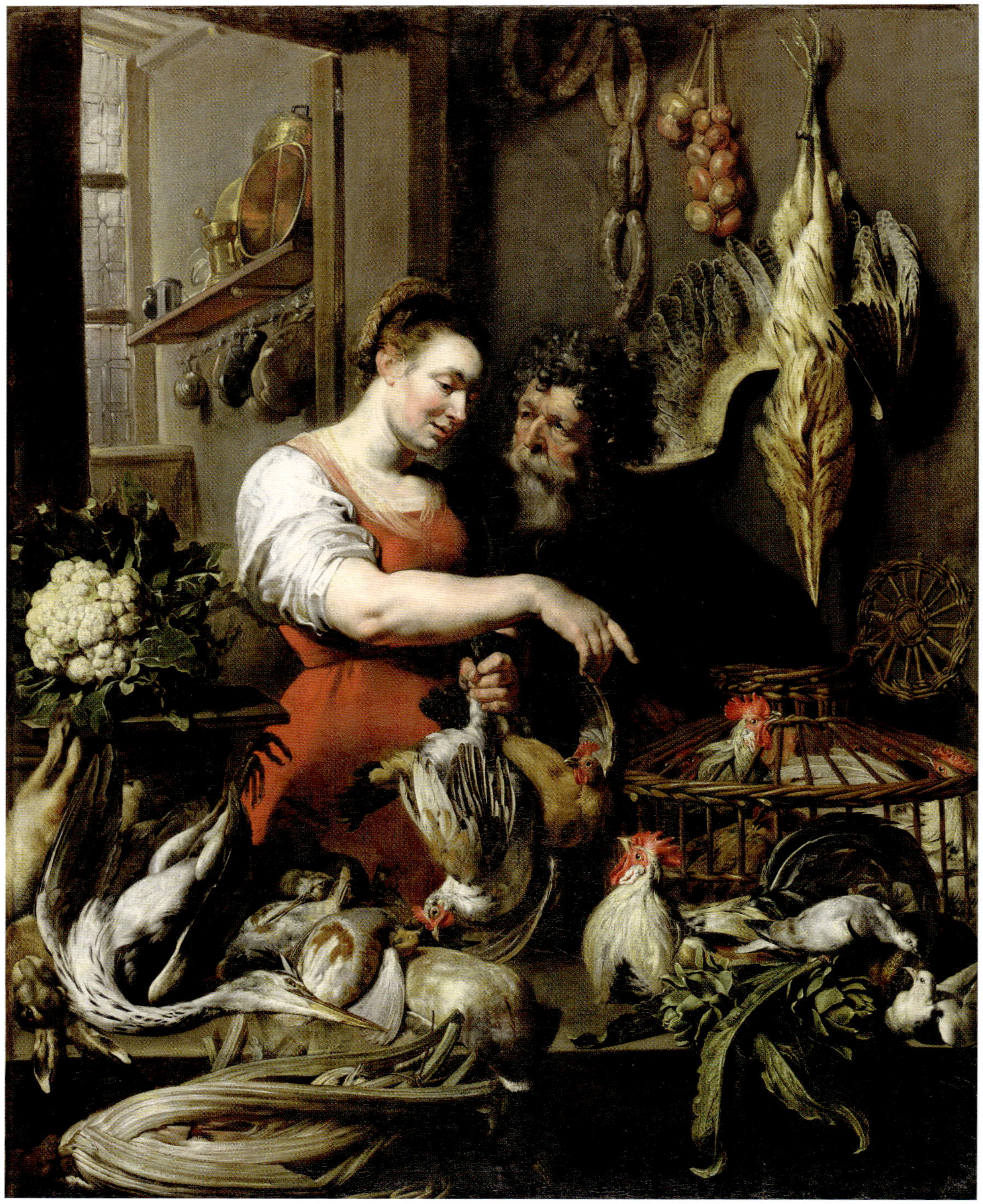

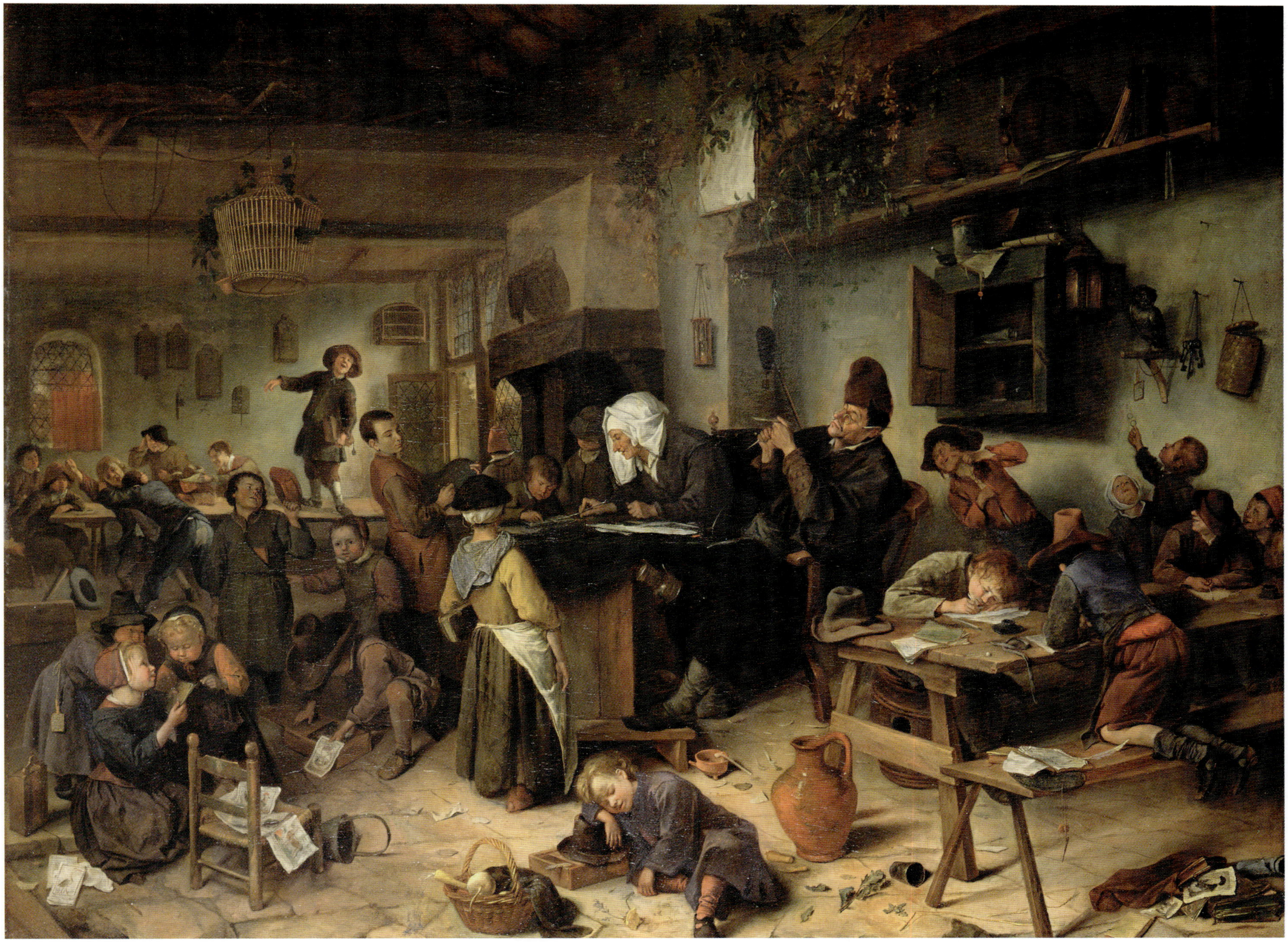

Jan Steen
(1626–1679)
A School for Boys and Girls

c. 1670
Oil on canvas
81.7 × 108.6 cm (32⅛ × 42¾ in.)
Scottish National Gallery, Edinburgh

Mayhem rules in Jan Steen's Dutch classroom, where the teacher and his wife seem oblivious to the antics of their pupils. The artist has played a subtle joke on his subjects and audience by basing his composition loosely on Raphael's *School of Athens*, which depicts a gathering of the finest scholars of antiquity. And since Steen was also fond of illustrating popular sayings of the day, there is one at the heart of this picture. At the far right a boy offers a pair of glasses to an owl – the traditional symbol of wisdom, associated with the goddess Athena – perched on a wall above him. This illustrates the Dutch proverb 'What use are spectacles or a candle if the owl does not want to see?', encapsulating the painting's underlying theme of the foolishness of mankind.

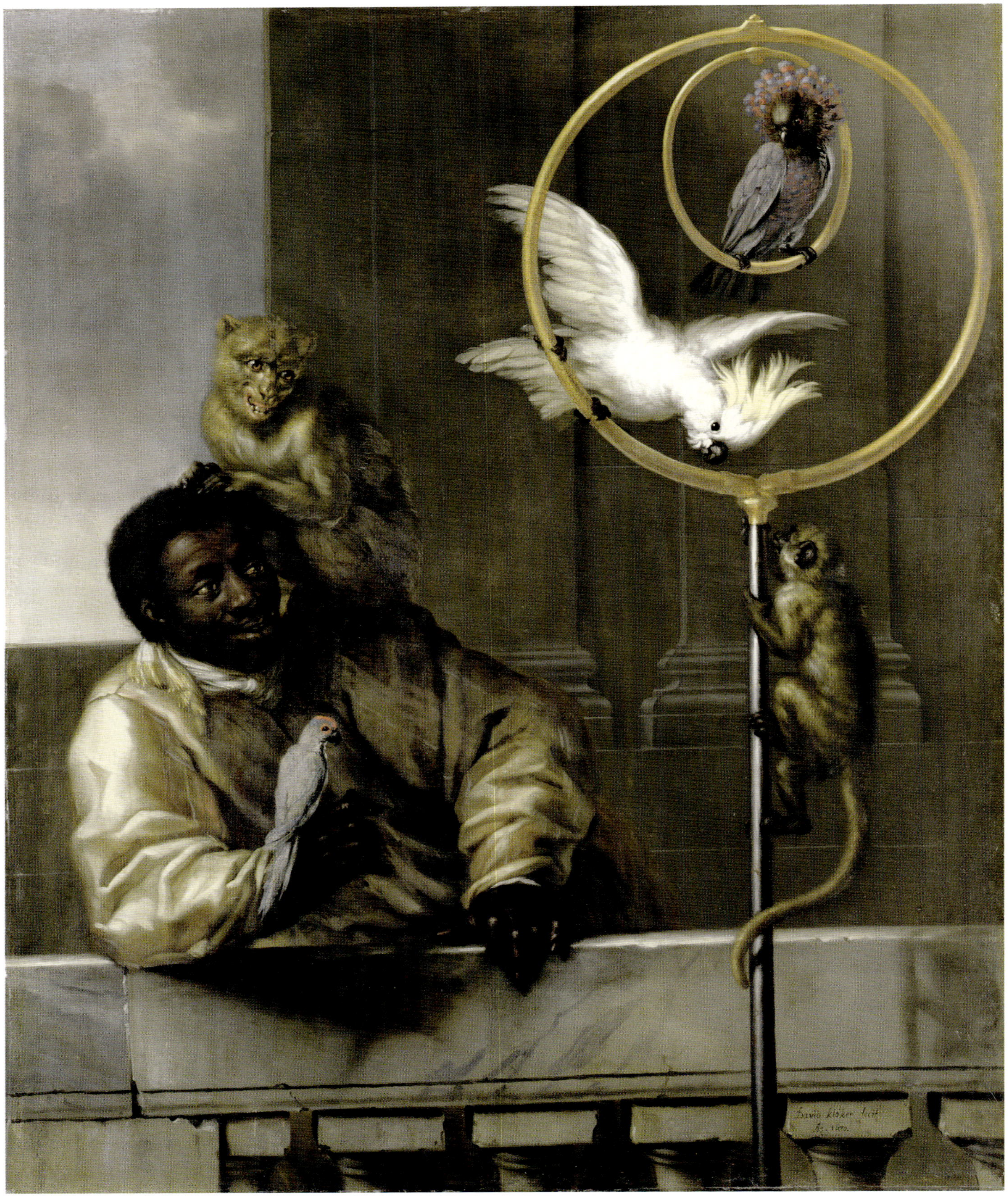

David Klöcker Ehrenstrahl
(1628–1698)
Boy with Parrots and Monkeys
1670
Oil on canvas
144 × 120 cm (56⅝ × 47¼ in.)
Nationalmuseum, Stockholm

The German artist David Klöcker Ehrenstrahl was appointed court painter to the Swedish king Charles XI in 1661, and in addition to portraying members of the court he captured the likenesses of animals in the royal menagerie – including dogs, squirrels, polar bears, camels and elks – on a number of occasions. The king is said to have kept many exotic birds, including parrots, in his palaces, and the young man in this painting may have been one of his animal-keepers. He certainly seems entirely at home with the monkeys and birds around him, and one cannot help feeling that the artist has sensed an affinity between his exotic appearance and the tropical animals in his care – one of them a sulphur-crested cockatoo. The other two parrots are probably imaginary. Ehrenstrahl was equally adept at painting birds in their natural habitat in the Swedish landscape; another of his paintings in the Nationalmuseum in Stockholm shows blackcocks (black grouse) in the woodland in springtime.

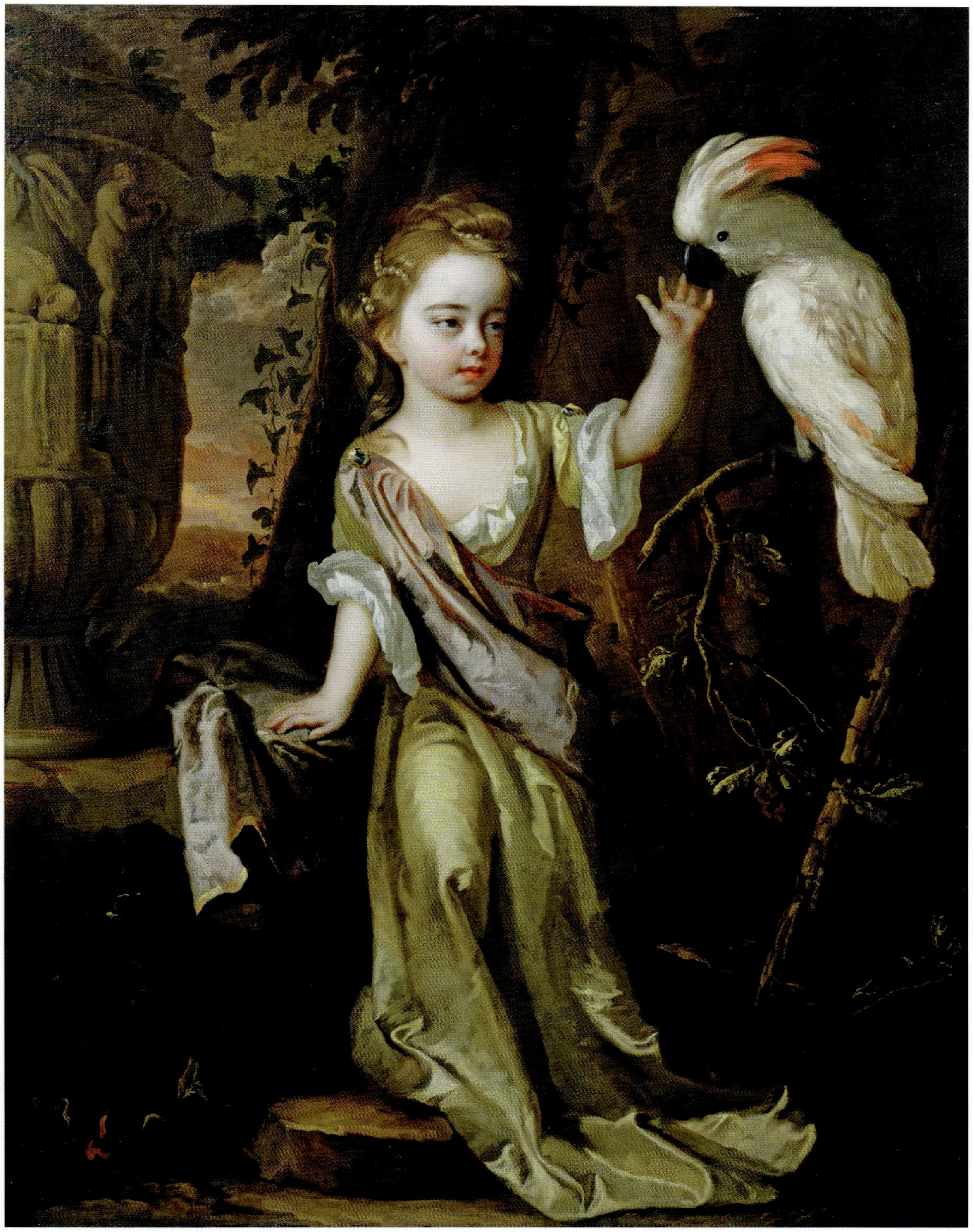

Michael Dahl (1659–1743)

Portrait of a Young Girl with a Cockatoo

c. 1690
Oil on canvas
127 × 101.2 cm (50 × 39¾ in.)
Private collection

The parrot's increasing popularity as a domestic pet and smart accessory is recorded in European art from the seventeenth century onwards. The Swedish portrait painter Michael Dahl trained with David Klöcker Ehrenstrahl (see opposite) before settling in London, where he became a serious rival to the portraitist Sir Godfrey Kneller and enjoyed the patronage of Queen Anne. This unidentified little girl stands beside a classical urn in a vaguely defined parkland setting, her luxurious dress a miniature version of adult attire. But she exhibits an endearingly childish curiosity as she reaches out to touch her pet, showing little fear of its sharp beak. The salmon-crested cockatoo was not painted by Dahl, but was most probably the work of the bird specialist Jakob Bogdány (p. 177), a Hungarian painter who, like Dahl, came to work in London.

Jean-Baptiste van Loo (1684–1745)

Portrait of Peg Woffington

c. 1738
Oil on canvas
91.5 × 71 cm (36 × 28 in.)
Private collection

The motif of an anonymous young woman with a caged bird at a window was popular in the late seventeenth and early eighteenth centuries, but this picture is a portrait of a recognized sitter. The beautiful Irish actress Margaret (Peg) Woffington was one of the leading figures on the early Georgian stage, and a lover of the renowned actor David Garrick. This portrait, which exists in a number of versions and was clearly painted when she was in her prime, shows her with two birds, inviting speculation as to their allegorical significance. The dark one is in a cage, while the paler one, probably a canary, is at liberty and rests on her shoulder. Could this be an allusion to the contradictions inherent in the actress's life, which combined comparative freedom and confinement? Van Loo was a French artist who won attention during the few years he spent in England with his portraits of theatrical personalities.

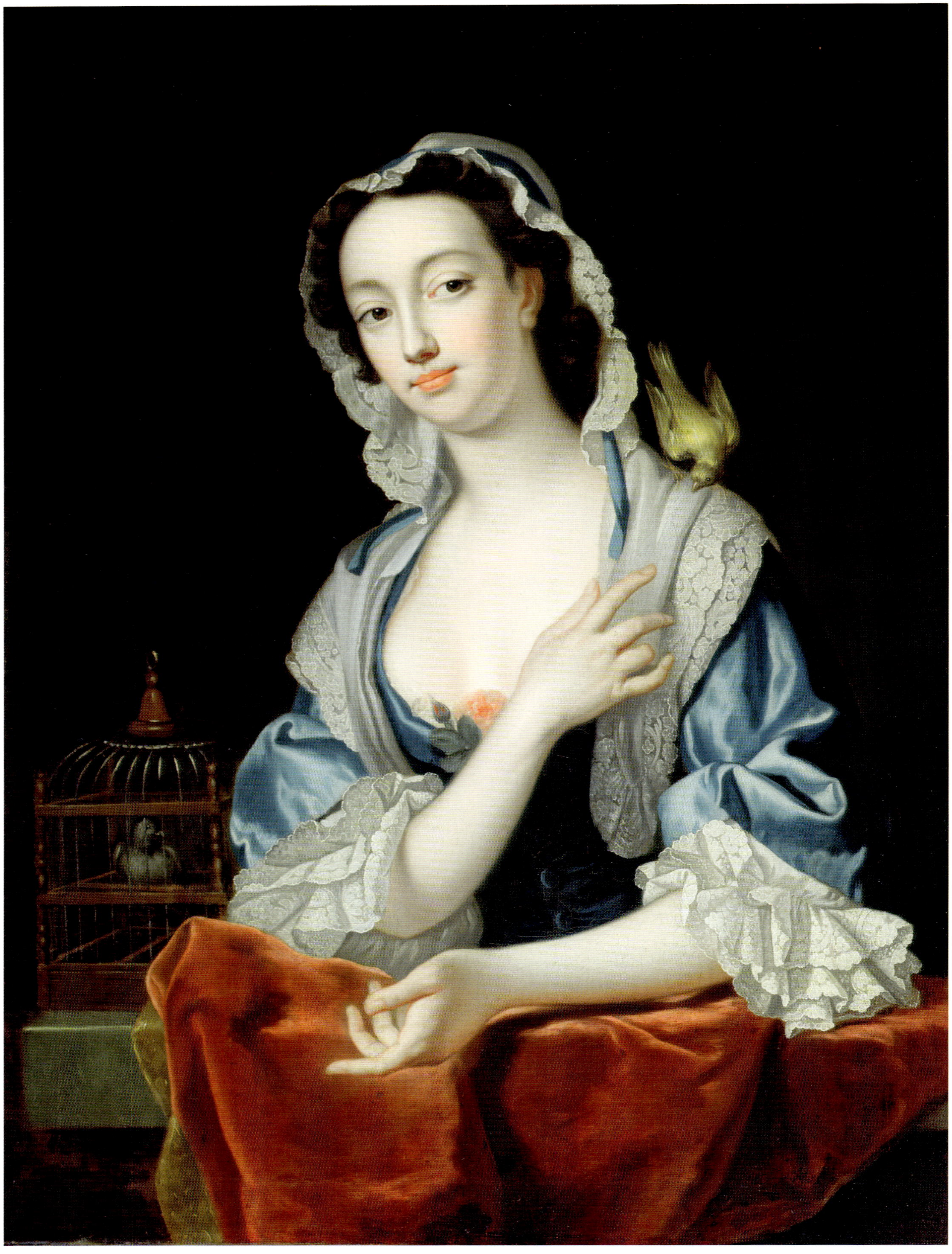

Giambattista Tiepolo (1696–1770)

A Young Woman with a Macaw

c. 1760
Oil on canvas
70 × 52 cm (27½ × 20½ in.)
Ashmolean Museum, Oxford

The Venetian artist Giambattista Tiepolo is celebrated for his ambitious fresco cycles that decorate churches in Venice and palaces in Germany and northern Italy. But this intimate canvas, which is not related to those grand schemes, depicts a voluptuous young woman with one breast bared, fondling a scarlet macaw, its brilliant red feathers dazzling against her pale flesh. The subject and treatment are reminiscent of the courtesan pictures painted by Tiepolo's Venetian predecessors Giorgione and Paolo Veronese. The portrait, which may show one of the artist's daughters, was probably painted for Empress Elizabeth Petrovna of Russia, for whom Tiepolo was producing a series of half-length fantasy female figures late in 1760. The pictures may have been intended to form part of a decorative scheme representing an allegory of the seasons or the senses. The subject of a woman with a parrot became popular among nineteenth-century French artists: Eugène Delacroix, Gustave Courbet, Édouard Manet and Pierre-Auguste Renoir all produced variations on the theme.

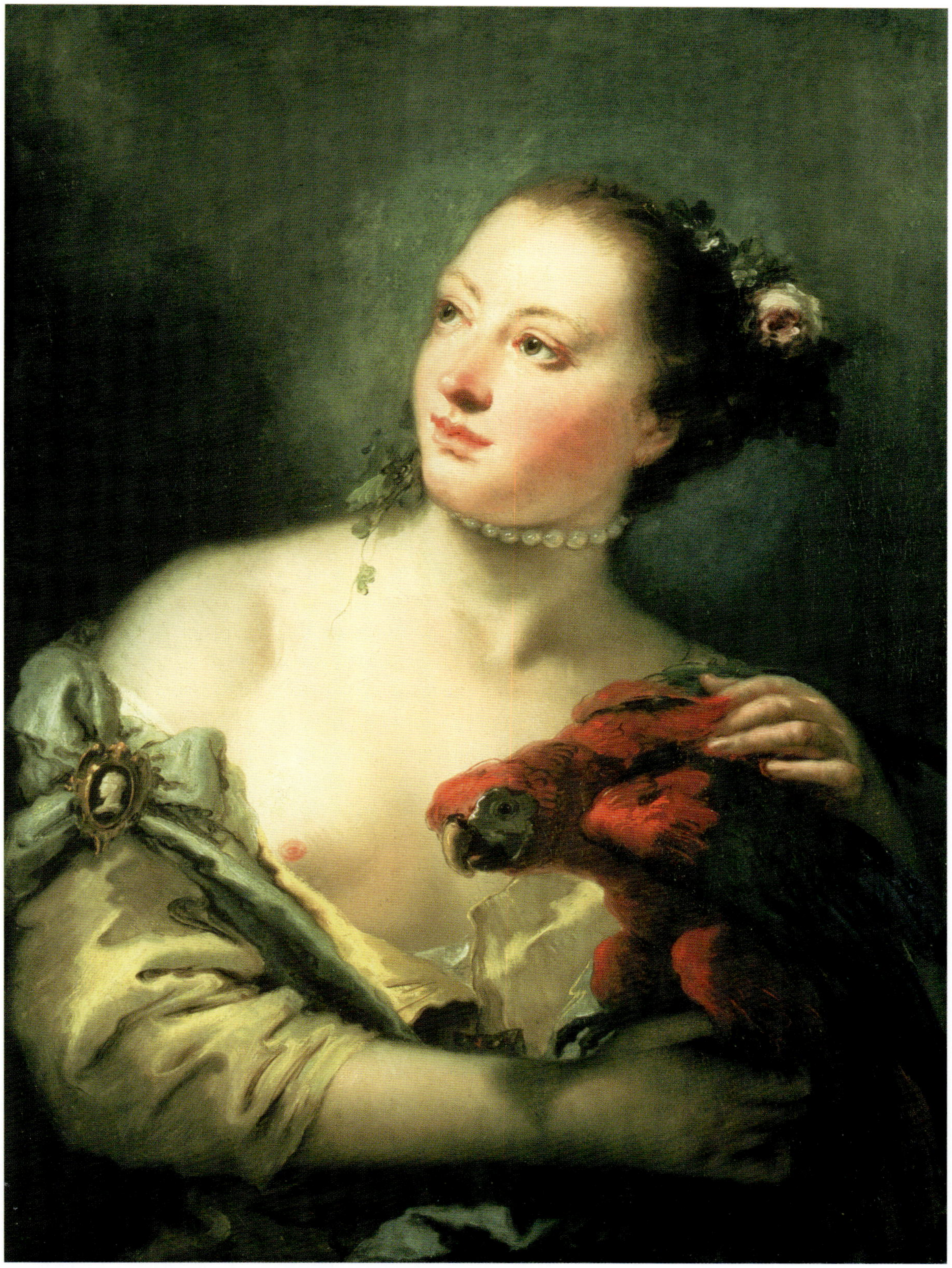

Jean-Siméon Chardin (1699–1779)

The Bird Organ

1751
Oil on canvas
50 × 43 cm (19⅝ × 17 in.)
Musée du Louvre, Paris

A well-dressed lady has temporarily abandoned her embroidery to amuse herself by teaching her pet canary (*serin* in French) to sing. Perched on her knees is a *serinette*, or cylinder organ. The woman would have turned the handle to play her favourite melody, repeating it until the bird was able to sing the notes. The birdcage on a pedestal table has an attachment for a screen to shield the bird from the light. Canaries were usually deprived of light during this exercise so that they had nothing to distract them, but Chardin obviously could not hide his birdcage from the viewer or the point of the picture would have been obscured. The painting is reminiscent of Dutch genre scenes of the previous century in its depiction of the quiet pleasures of a well-to-do bourgeois household, although it was actually commissioned by King Louis XV, and may at one stage have belonged to the brother of the king's mistress, Madame de Pompadour.

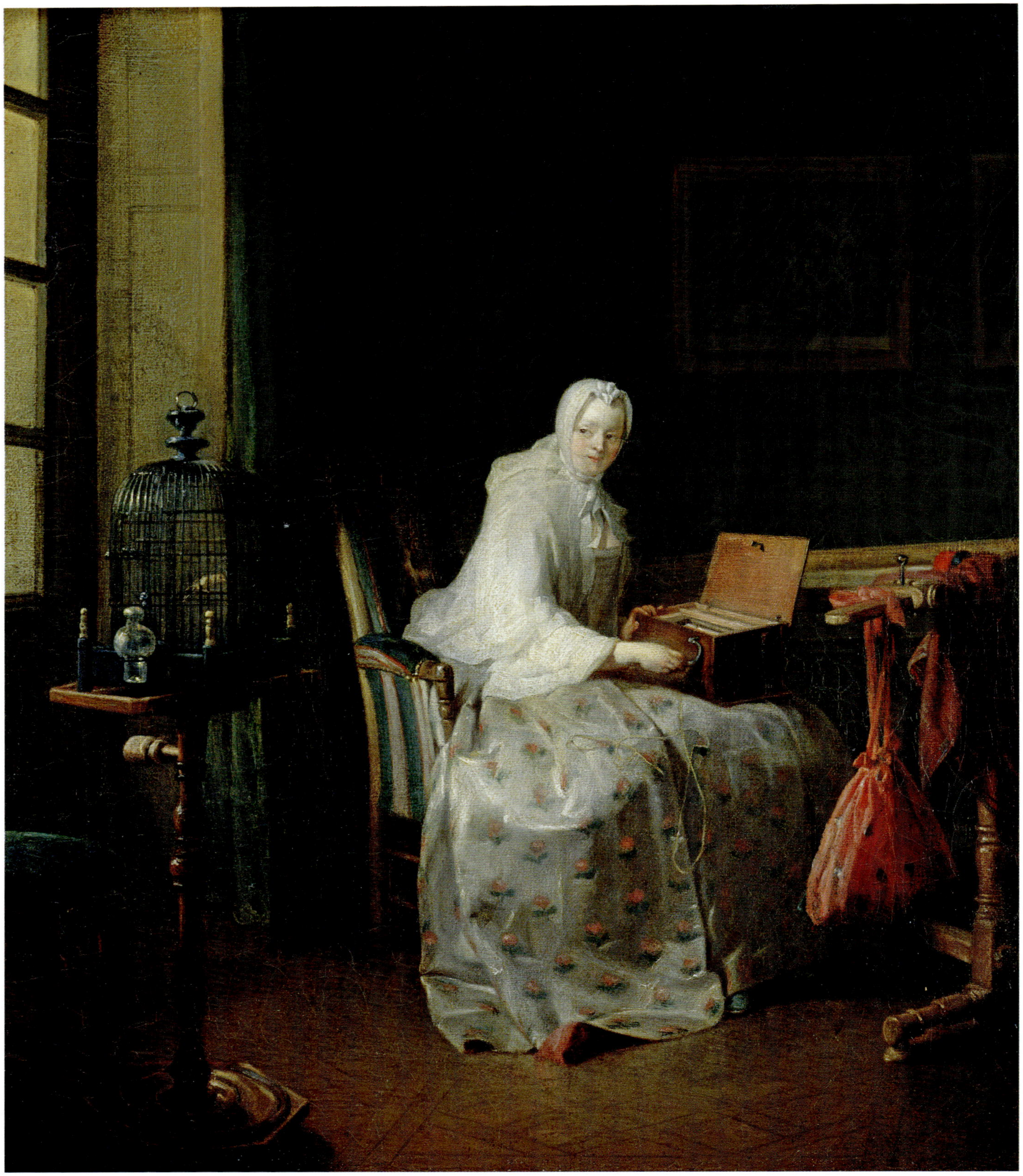

Johann Christian von Mannlich (1741–1822) (attrib.)

Young Woman Fastening a Letter to the Neck of a Pigeon

c. 1760
Oil on canvas
58.4 × 48.9 cm (23 × 19¼ in.)
Philadelphia Museum of Art

The use of homing pigeons to carry messages between rulers, merchants and military men dates back to antiquity, and pigeons were still being employed in the nineteenth century to send information when Paris was under siege in the Franco-Prussian War, and normal methods of communication were blocked. But this painting attributed to the German artist Johann von Mannlich presents a more light-hearted, romantic view of the pigeon post, as a young woman ties a love letter to the neck of a very phallic-looking dove with a blue ribbon. Doves or pigeons are the birds of Venus, so they would have been fitting bearers of erotic missives. The motif must have been a familiar one: a decade earlier, the French king's mistress Madame de Pompadour had commissioned François Boucher to paint a similar scene (now in the National Gallery of Art, Washington, D.C.), in which two young ladies attach a letter to the neck of a dove with a blue ribbon.

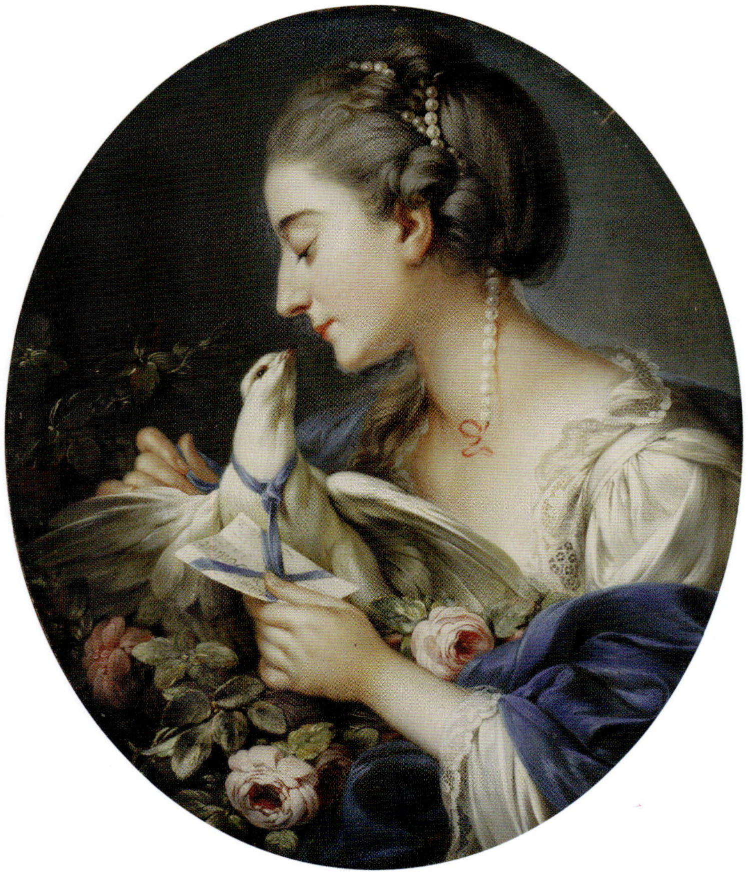

Jean-Baptiste Greuze (1725–1805)

A Girl with a Dead Canary

1765
Oil on canvas
53.3 × 46 cm (21 × 18⅛ in.)
Scottish National Gallery, Edinburgh

While Chardin's young woman (opposite) is teaching her pet canary to sing, Greuze's girl is grieving over hers, whose feathers, originally painted with a yellow glaze, have faded to white. Its corpse lies on top of a cage garlanded with leaves that put the viewer in mind of a funeral wreath. But is there another reason for the girl's tears? When this painting was shown at the Paris Salon, it provoked a lengthy commentary from the critic Denis Diderot, who longed to console the girl, but then paused to reflect that such extravagant mourning could not have been caused simply by the death of her bird. In order to explain it, he invented an entire narrative in which the girl had been seduced while her mother was out, and possibly neglected to feed her bird because of her distraction. So the girl is actually mourning her lost virginity – a reading that gains some support from the association of caged birds and the amorous arts in Renaissance emblem books and in Dutch seventeenth-century paintings.

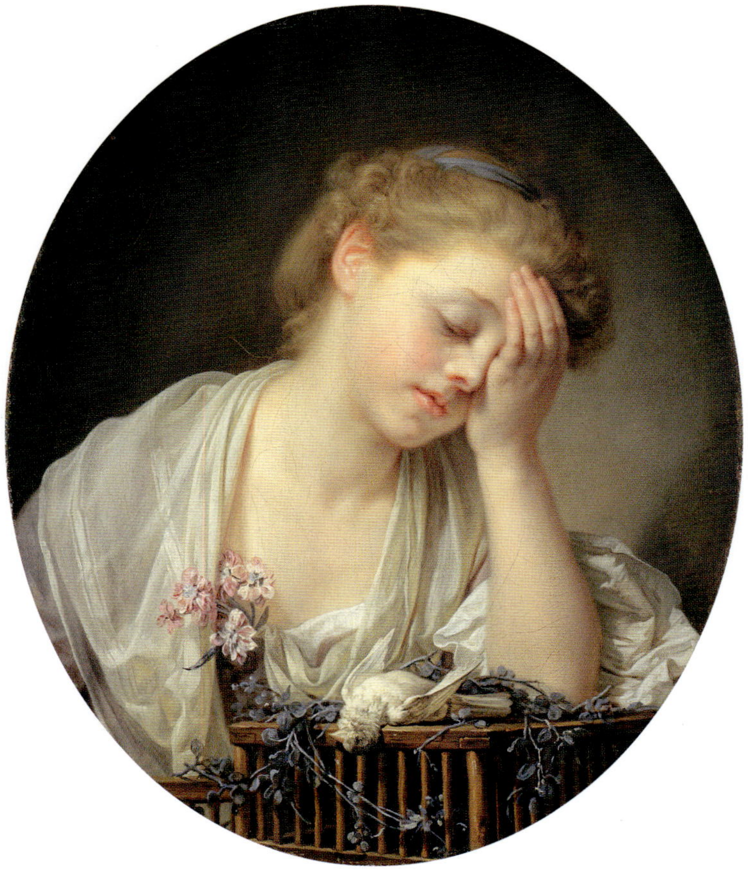

Joseph Wright of Derby (1734–1797)
The Synnot Children

1781
Oil on canvas
152.4 × 125.8 cm (60 × 49½ in.)
National Gallery of Victoria, Melbourne

One of Joseph Wright's best-known paintings is *An Experiment on a Bird in the Air Pump* (p. 152). He returned to the theme of a captive bird in this work, a portrait of the three children (Marcus, Walter and Maria) of Sir Walter Synnot, a wealthy Irish landowner. The central anecdote is an ingenious way of animating a group portrait, while at the same time posing a puzzle for the onlooker. Walter has taken a pet dove from its cage, his bold stare confronting the spectator in much the same way as that of the scientist in the *Experiment* picture, while Marcus reaches for the bird and Maria crosses her breast in a gesture that suggests dismay. Is it simply a melodramatic dispute between two brothers, the younger one who wants to set the bird free and the elder one who wants to put it back in its cage? The attitude of Walter, who raises his hand in a gesture more usually associated with Christ, suggests a visual joke: the dove is, after all, associated with the Holy Spirit.

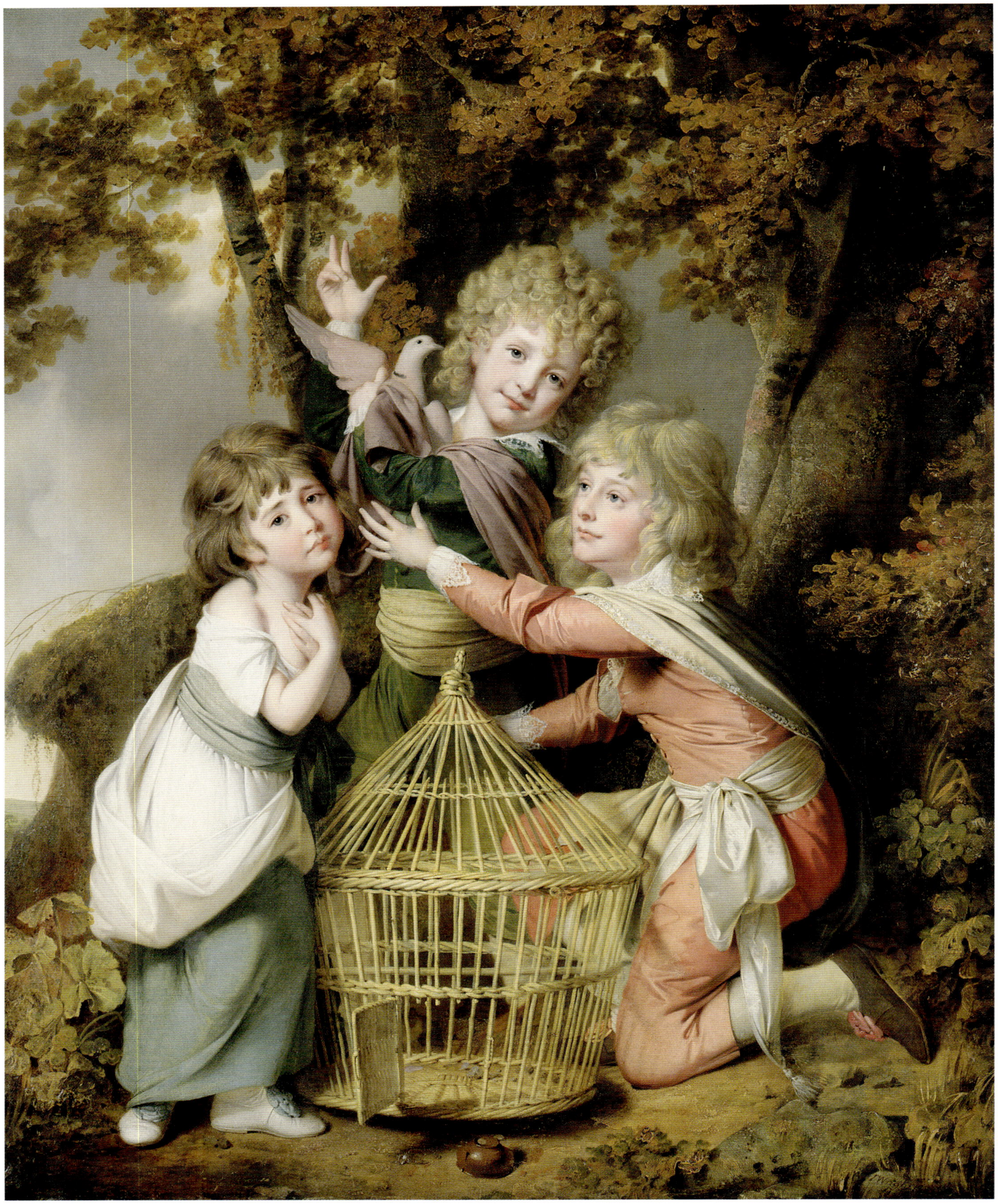

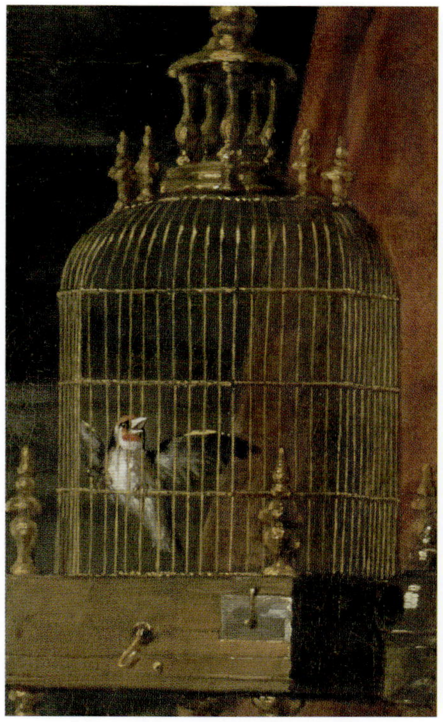

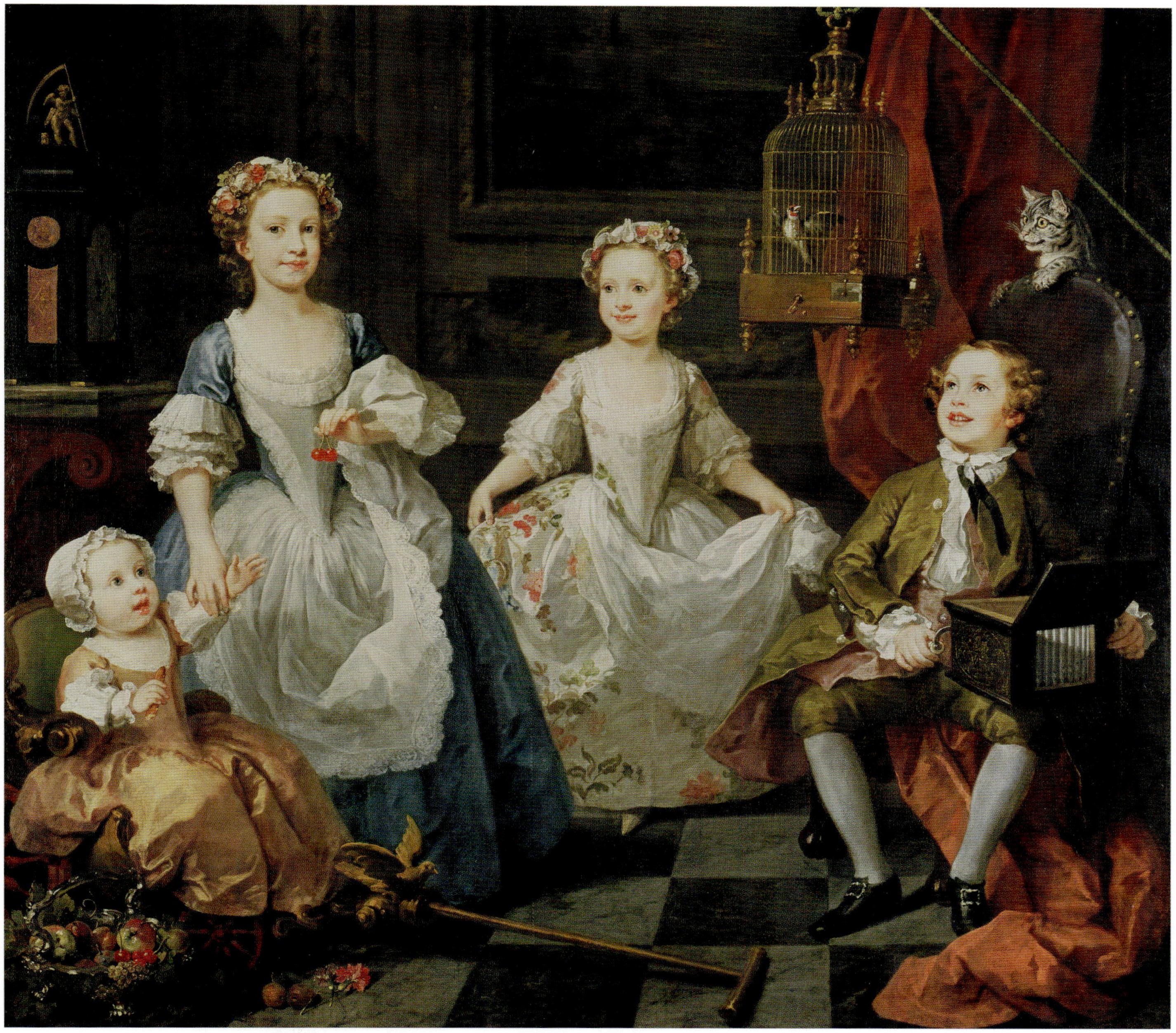

William Hogarth
(1697–1764)
The Graham Children

1742
Oil on canvas
160.5 × 181 cm (63 ⅛ × 71 ¼ in.)
The National Gallery, London

The ancient antagonism between cat and bird provides an amusing anecdote in this portrait of Henrietta Catherine, Anna Maria, Richard Robert and baby Thomas – the children of Dr Daniel Graham, Apothecary to King George II. Richard Robert plays a bird organ, which imitates birdsong (rather like the one in the painting by Chardin on p. 222), inspiring the pet bullfinch in its cage to start its own song. This has alerted the cat, which has climbed the back of the chair and sits poised to pounce on the bird, which flaps frantically as it attempts to escape, although it remains safely behind bars. Thomas sits in a little cart with wheels, its long handle decorated with a gilded carving of a dove. It may have had a mechanism that made the dove's wings flap as it was towed along. This is actually a posthumous portrait of Thomas, who died before the painting was completed.

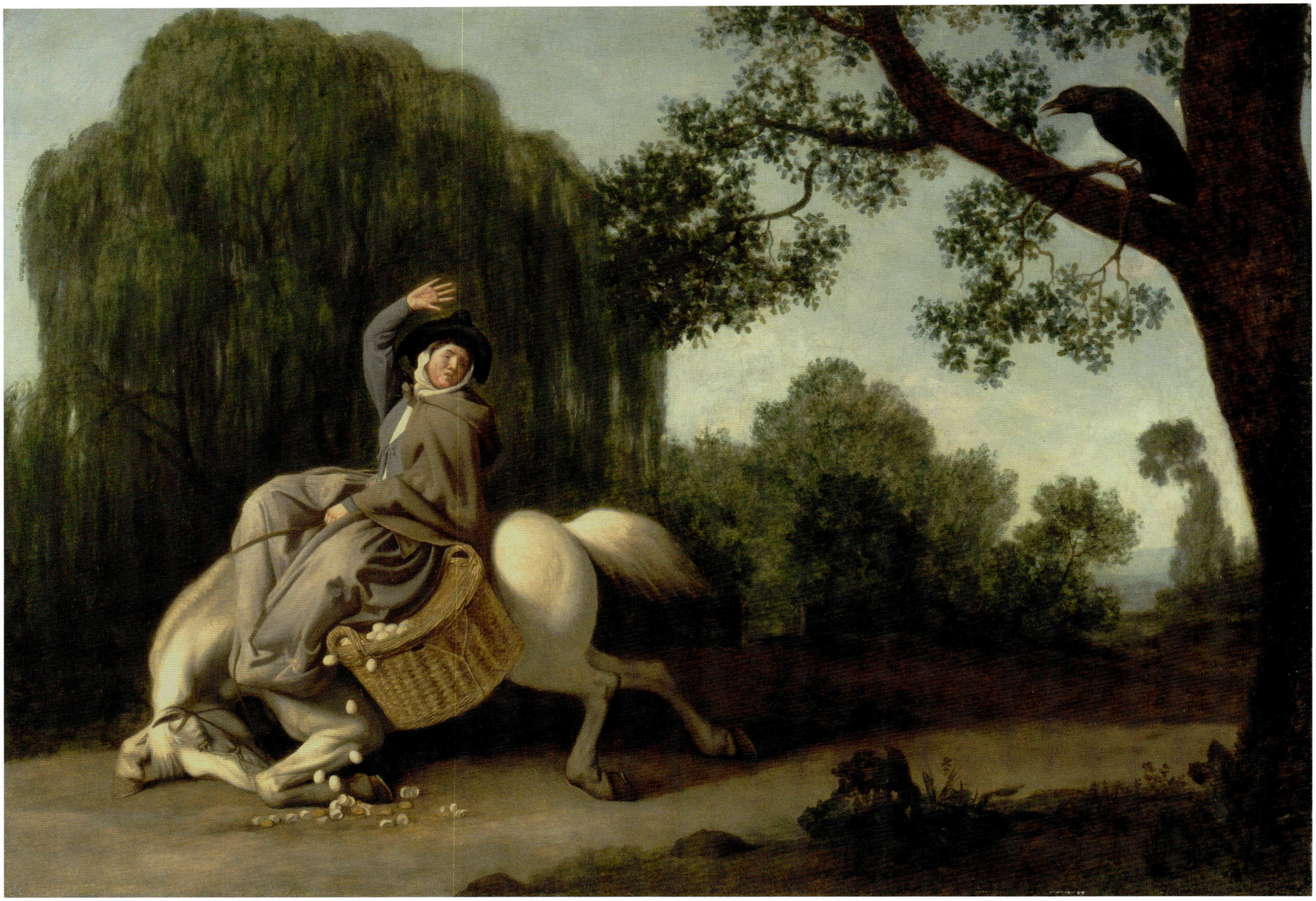

George Stubbs (1724–1806)

The Farmer's Wife and the Raven

1786

Oil on millboard

67.2 × 98 cm (26⅜ × 38½ in.)

Yale Center for British Art, New Haven, Connecticut

An ancient superstition warning that it is bad luck to hear a raven call from the left supplies the subject for this painting, and the poem on which it is based. John Gay's verse tells the tale of a farmer's wife on her way to market, and of her encounter with a raven, a catalyst for a disaster caused by her own bad planning. As she rides to market with her panniers full of eggs, her elderly horse is startled by a raven croaking in a tree and stumbles to the ground, smashing the eggs. The farmer's wife shakes her fist at the bird, cursing it: 'Thou croaking toad,/ A murrain take thy whoreson throat!/ I knew misfortune in the note.' But the raven points out that the misfortune is the woman's fault: had she chosen a better horse, it would not have fallen, however many ravens squawked at it. Although the eye is drawn immediately to the intertwined figures of falling horse and farmer's wife, her raised arm points to the tree, where the instigator of the unfortunate incident sits happily on a branch.

Louis-Léopold Boilly (1761–1845)

Couple with an Escaped Bird

c. 1790
Oil on canvas
40 × 32 cm (15¾ × 12⅝ in.)
Musée du Louvre, Paris

By the time the French artist Louis-Léopold Boilly painted this sexually charged scene, in the late eighteenth century, there was a long-established symbolic connection between caged and escaped birds and amorous behaviour. Here, the erotic connection between the escaped bird – which looks like a canary – and the young woman on the verge of losing her virginity could not be clearer. The young man's state of undress and his lascivious gaze, together with the woman's gesture towards the fragile bird, all ram home the point. It was certainly not lost on the Committee of Public Safety, which, during the height of the French Terror, condemned this picture for its erotic content, and the artist for painting works that were 'of an obscenity repugnant to Republican morals'. Only the discovery of a patriotic painting depicting the revolutionary hero Marat saved Boilly from serious consequences. After this episode, Boilly turned away from sensual subjects to concentrate on history and genre scenes and portraiture.

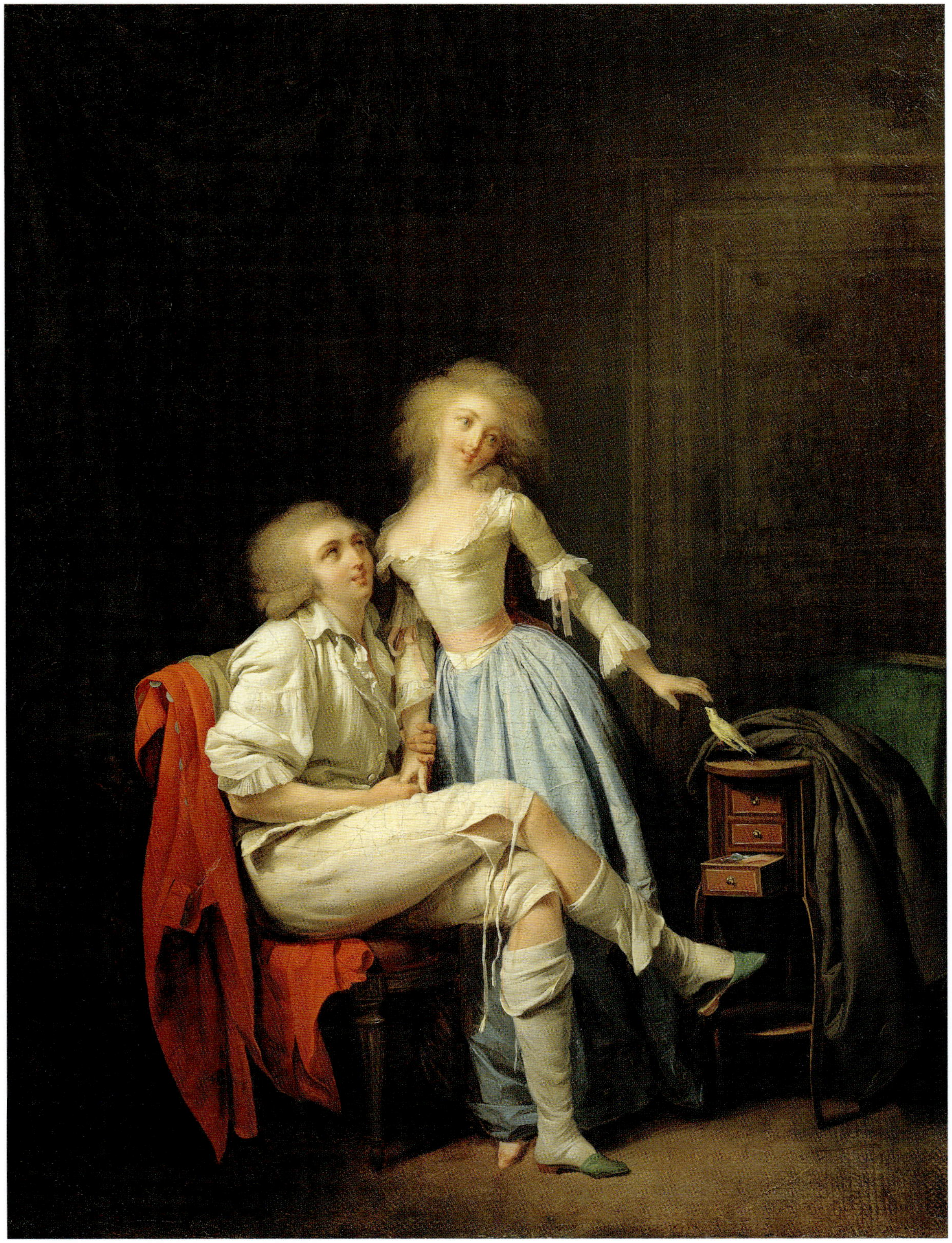

Walter Howell Deverell (1827–1854)
The Grey Parrot

1852–53
Oil on canvas
53.5 × 35.2 cm (21 × 13⅞ in.)
National Gallery of Victoria, Melbourne

Parrots appear in nineteenth-century French paintings by Eugène Delacroix and Gustave Courbet as erotic accompaniments to nude women, but this British picture is the very image of respectability. The young woman is enjoying the affectionate company of her pet bird as she reads her book by a window. If parrots imitate human behaviour, this one is conducting itself with modesty and decorum. At about the time he painted this canvas, Deverell produced *A Pet* (Tate), which shows the same young woman peering into a birdcage. Deverell was intimately connected with the Pre-Raphaelite circle; he shared a room with Dante Gabriel Rossetti and is credited with having discovered Lizzie Siddal, the Pre-Raphaelite model par excellence who became Rossetti's wife. Deverell's life was cut short by kidney disease, and this tranquil picture was painted in his last year, when he was living in the London suburb of Kew.

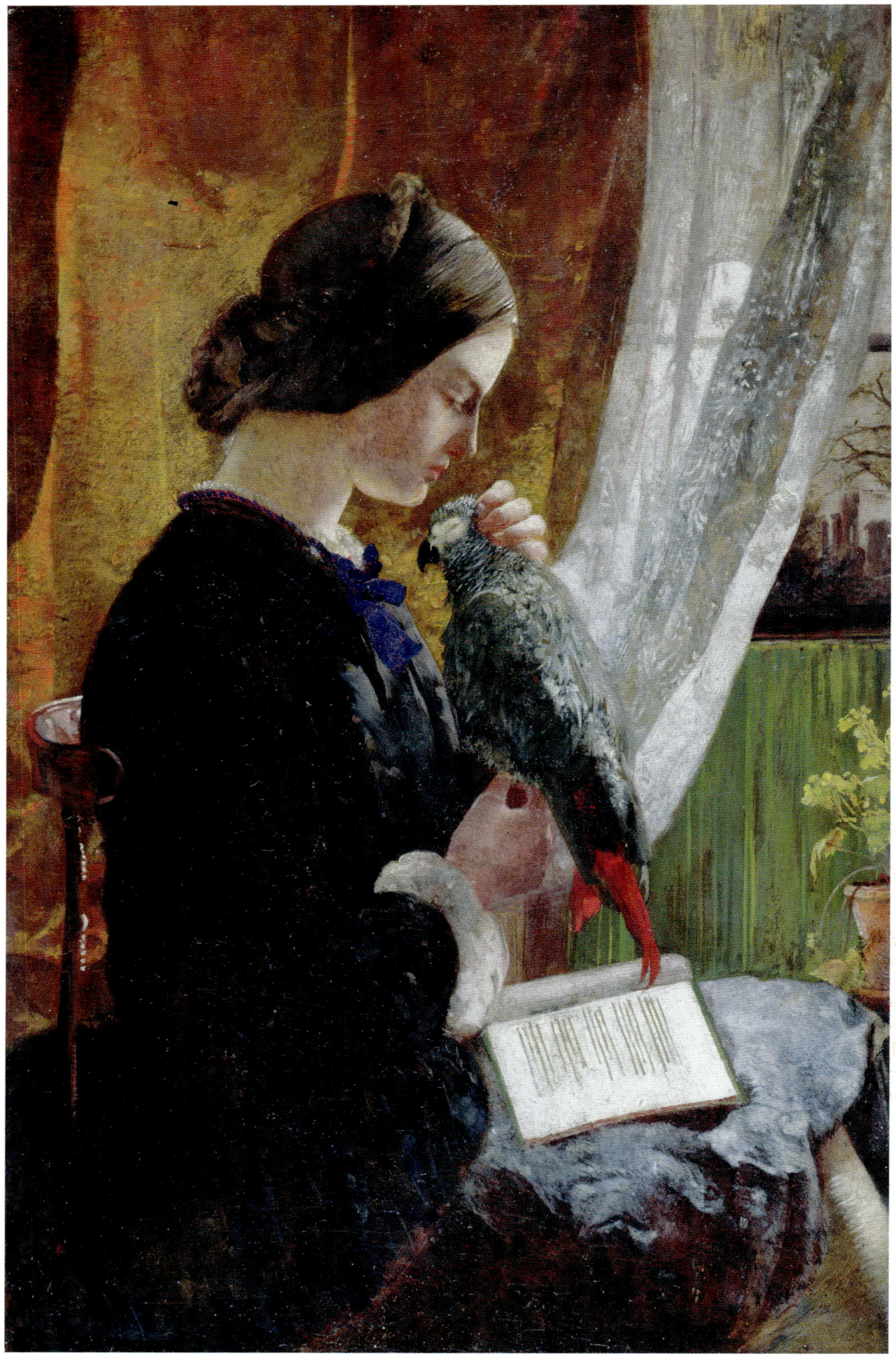

Sir Edwin Landseer
(1802–1873)
Islay, Tilco, a Macaw and Two Love Birds
1839
Oil on canvas
130.2 × 71.8 cm (51¼ × 28¼ in.)
The Royal Collection

In common with many British monarchs, Queen Victoria was a passionate animal-lover, and commissioned several portraits of her pets. Edwin Landseer has captured some of her favourites here: the terrier Islay, the toy spaniel Tilco, a magnificent scarlet macaw and two lovebirds. Although it is chained to a stand, the macaw has the upper hand, as it munches on a biscuit while Islay asks for a bite and the lovebirds look on, hoping to be offered a crumb or two. Victoria had evidently taught Islay to sit up and beg, so Landseer cleverly worked the dog's characteristic pose into the composition. Tilco appears to have given up on the biscuit quest, and has set about destroying some royal correspondence instead. In its mouth is a dark-blue feather, but it is not clear whether it is one plucked from the macaw or a quill pen. Landseer was a master painter of animals, frequently investing them with human characteristics.

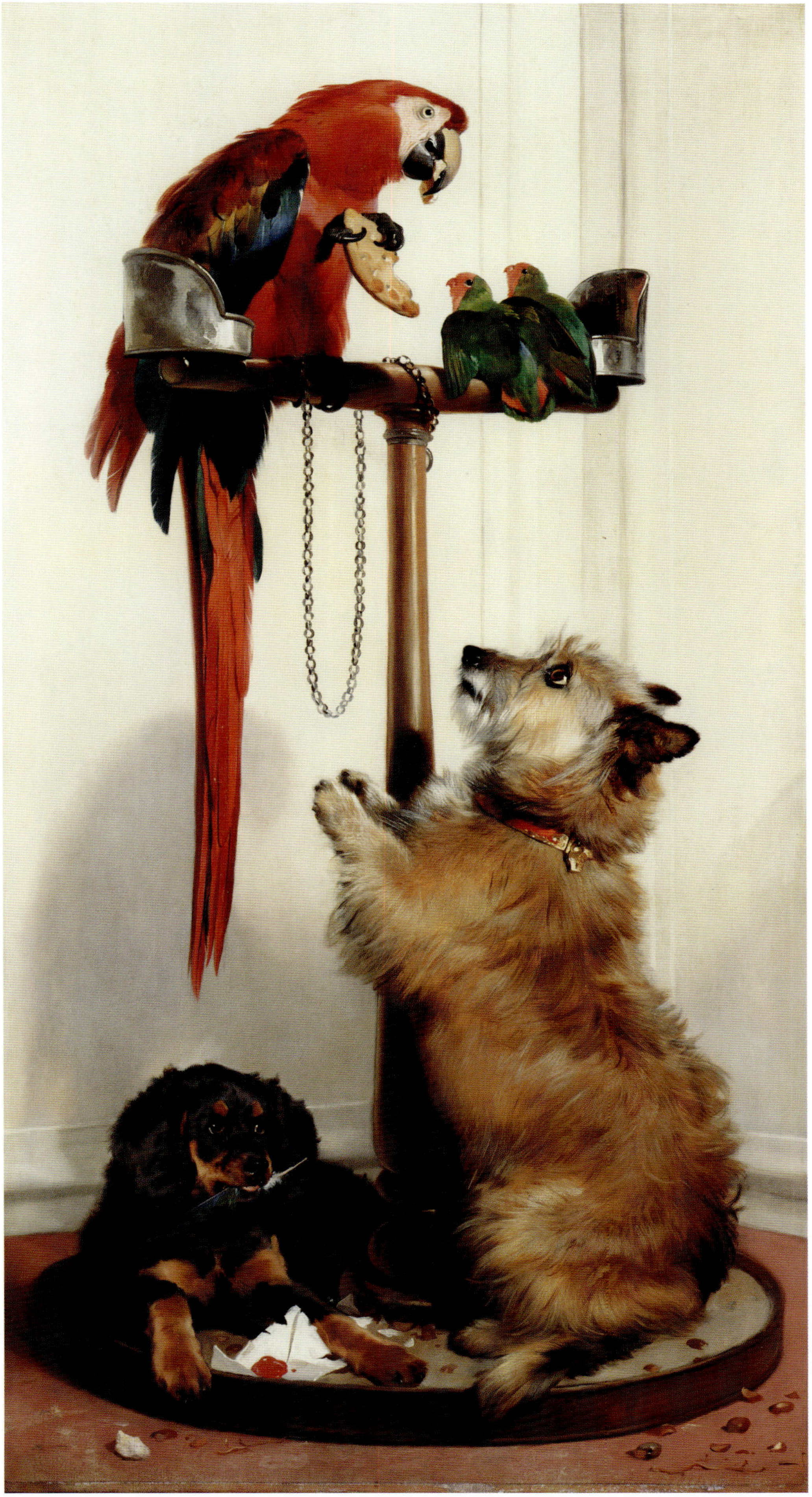

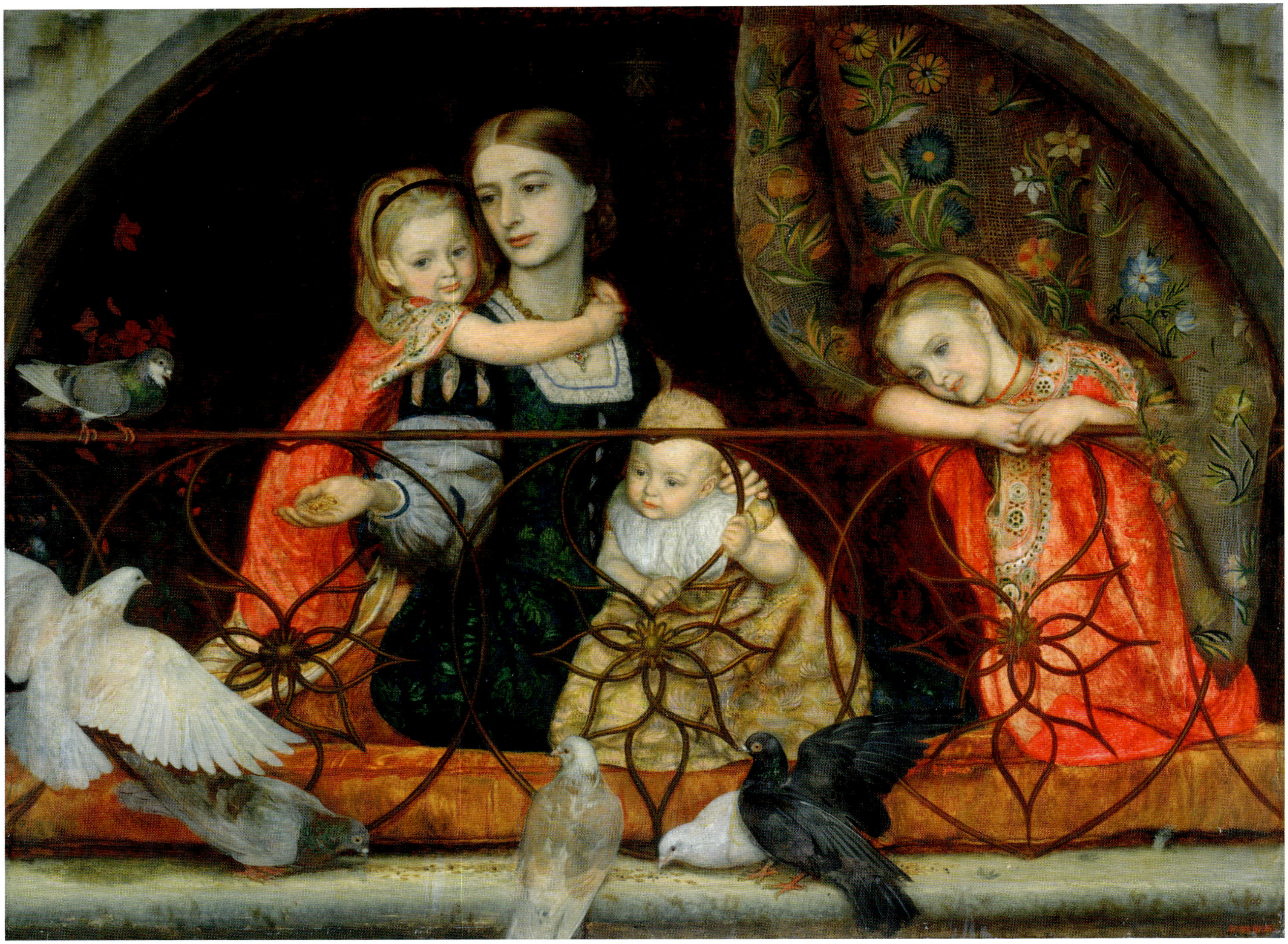

Arthur Hughes
(1832–1915)
Mrs Leathart and Her Three Children
c. 1863–65
Oil on canvas
77.4 × 104.1 cm (30½ × 40⅞ in.)
Laing Art Gallery, Newcastle upon Tyne

The pigeons that flutter around St Mark's Square in Venice provided the inspiration for this charmingly informal portrait of a young mother and her three children. The artist, Arthur Hughes, was a gifted member of a second generation of Pre-Raphaelite artists, and the picture was commissioned by James Leathart, a Newcastle industrialist and collector of Pre-Raphaelite work. The unusual format was suggested by a similar scene witnessed by the artist on a visit to Venice in 1863. Certain details indicate that he had also been looking at Italian Renaissance painting: the sumptuous fabric of the costumes, the slashed sleeves of the mother's dress, and the alcove or balcony format, with a half-drawn curtain. When the picture was first exhibited, it was described by *Athenaeum* magazine as 'one of the sweetest and most tender family pictures we know'.

John Frederick Lewis
(1805–1876)
Caged Doves

c. 1864
Oil on panel
76.2 × 53.3 cm (30 × 21 in.)
Private collection

The British artist John Frederick Lewis set up home in a large Mamluk house in Cairo in 1841, and spent the next decade painting Orientalist scenes, which found a ready market at home. Among his most popular themes was the harem, that fascinating enclosed world of women that the Victorian public imagined to be a place of unbridled sensual pleasure. Here one of its inhabitants – typical of the fair-skinned women favoured by the Ottoman sultans – is playing with the birds that are normally caged but are free to fly around in the safety of home. The parallel with her situation is an obvious one. Doves have had a long association with beautiful women because of their traditional link to the goddess Venus. Lewis appears to have kept a number of animals and birds in his grand home in Cairo. When the writer William Makepeace Thackeray visited him there in 1845, he observed: 'Pigeons were flapping and hopping and fluttering, and cooing about. Happy pigeons ... no doubt, fed with the crumbs from the henna-tipped fingers of Zuleikah.'

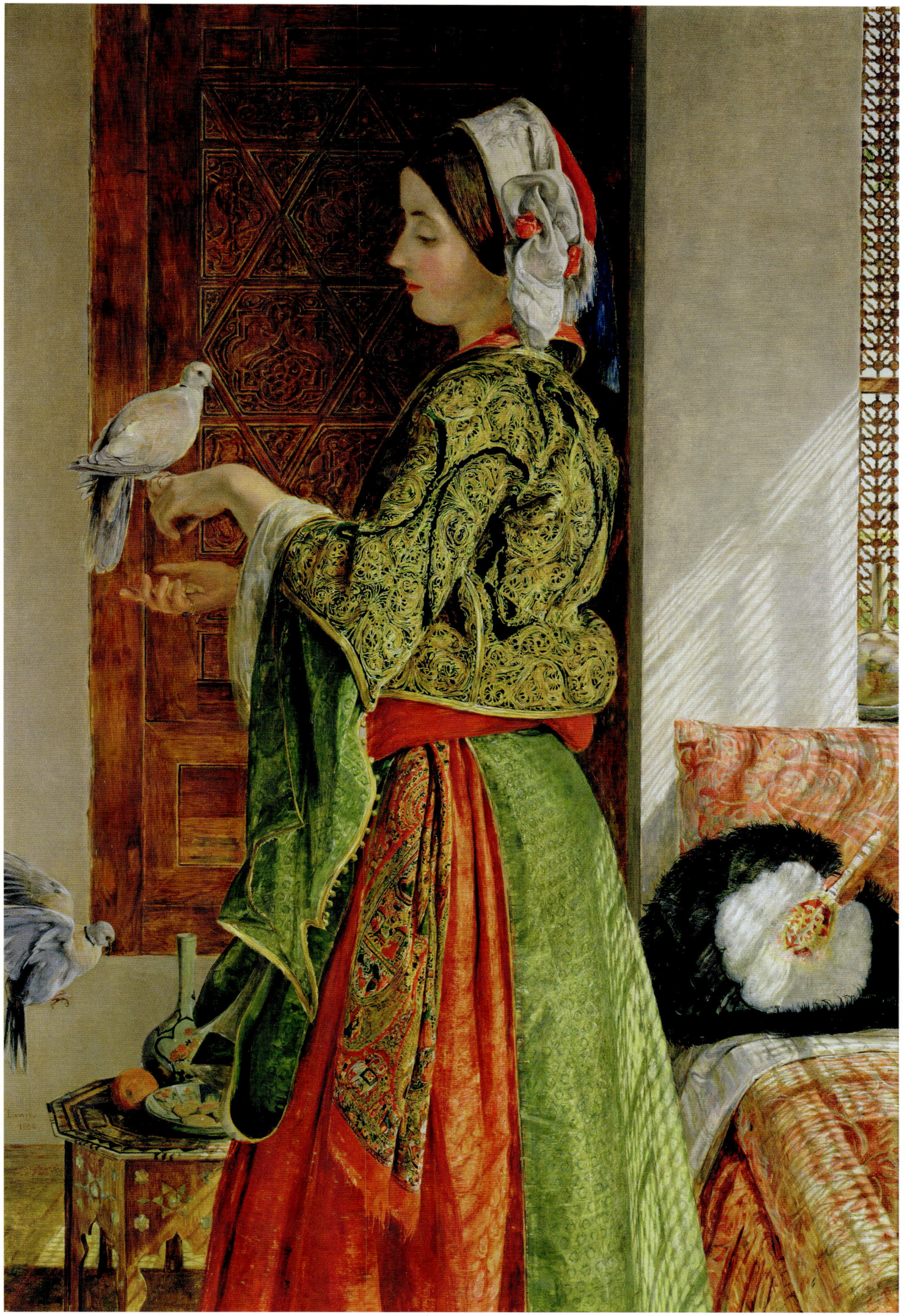

James Archer
(1824–1904)
Girl with a Linnet

1865
Oil on canvas
Dimensions unknown
Private collection

The linnet was a popular bird in Victorian and Edwardian England, and was mentioned in poems by William Wordsworth, William Butler Yeats and Alfred Lord Tennyson. It was generally kept as a caged pet, but in this painting it is impossible to tell whether the bird is captive or has just flown in through the window. The girl stands stock-still as it perches on her finger, her pose unconsciously echoing that seen in the countless portraits of men with hawks. Her expression of total concentration seems to indicate that she is trying not to move so that she does not frighten the bird away. A Scot by birth, Archer settled in London in 1862. He specialized in portraiture, particularly pictures of children in historical dress, and scenes drawn from Arthurian legend. His paintings of children show some similarity to those of the Pre-Raphaelite artist Sir John Everett Millais.

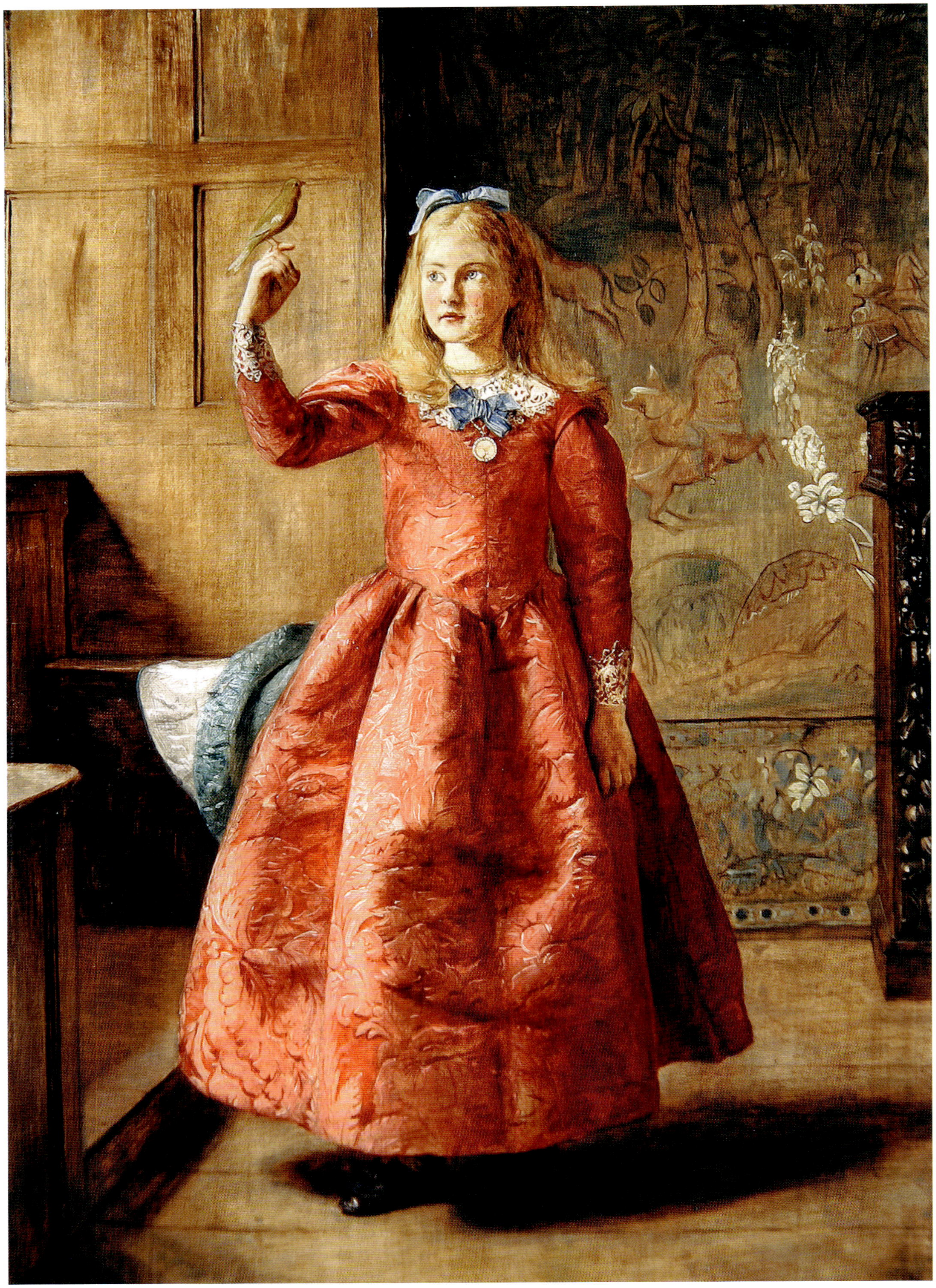

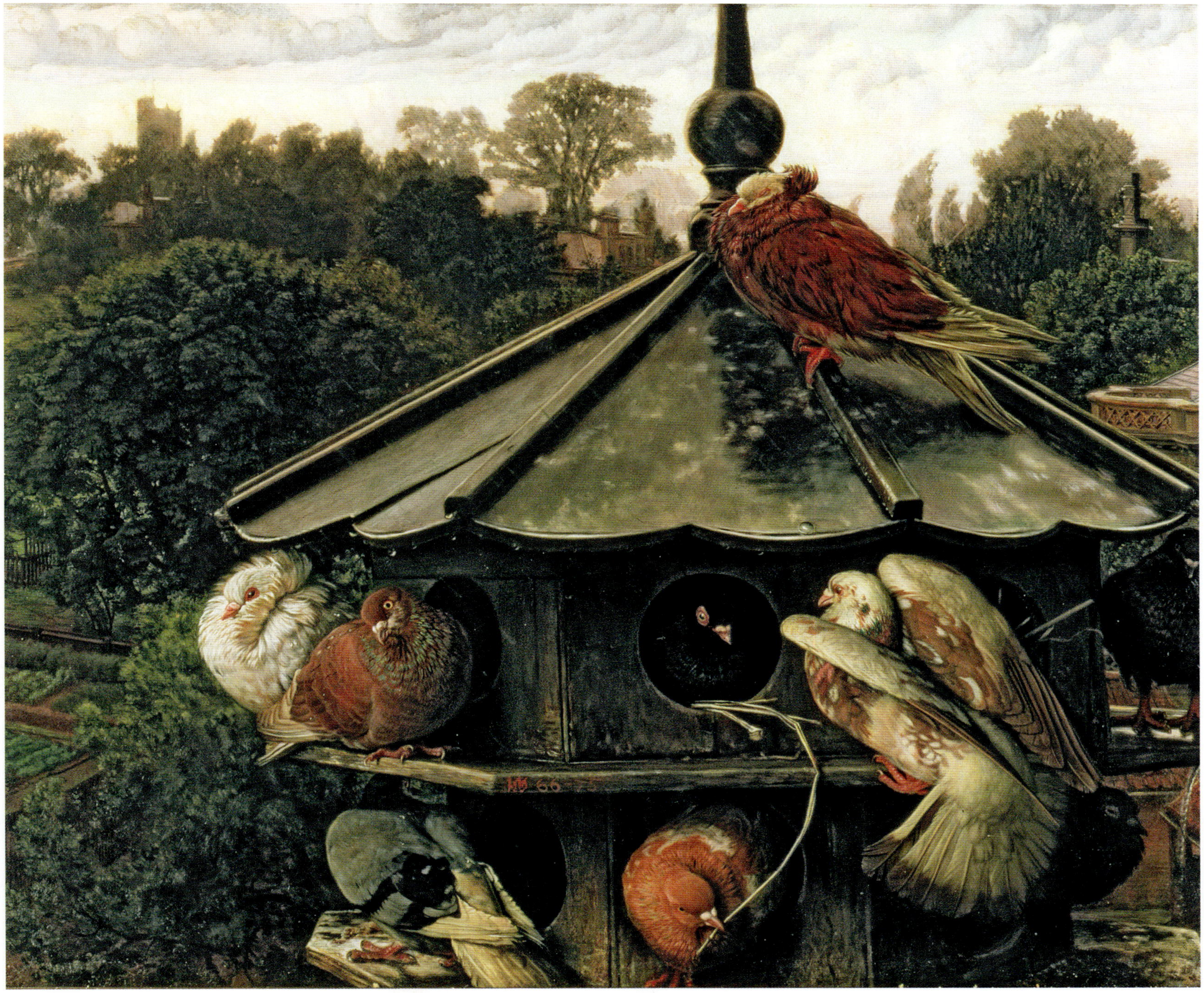

William Holman Hunt (1827–1910)

The Festival of St Swithin, or The Dovecote

1866–75
Oil on canvas
73 × 91 cm (28¾ × 35¾ in.)
Ashmolean Museum, Oxford

According to folklore, if it rains on St Swithin's Day (15 July) it will continue to rain for the following forty days. The pigeons here are having to cope with some foul weather. One braves it out on the roof of the dovecote, while others take shelter inside. The forty days of rain naturally evoke thoughts of the biblical Flood, and so the domestic dovecote appears as a kind of Noah's Ark, offering a lifeline to the threatened birds. (Actually, pigeons and doves were traditionally encouraged to nest in dovecotes because they were an important source of food.) Holman Hunt was one of the founding members of the Pre-Raphaelite Brotherhood, and this picture displays the obsessive attention to detail that characterizes the work of that group. In his quest for authenticity, Hunt even bought the birds (which all have different plumage) and the dovecote. Although he designed the composition for his sister Emily to work on, she gave up on the project and Hunt completed it, producing what he said was his most highly finished work.

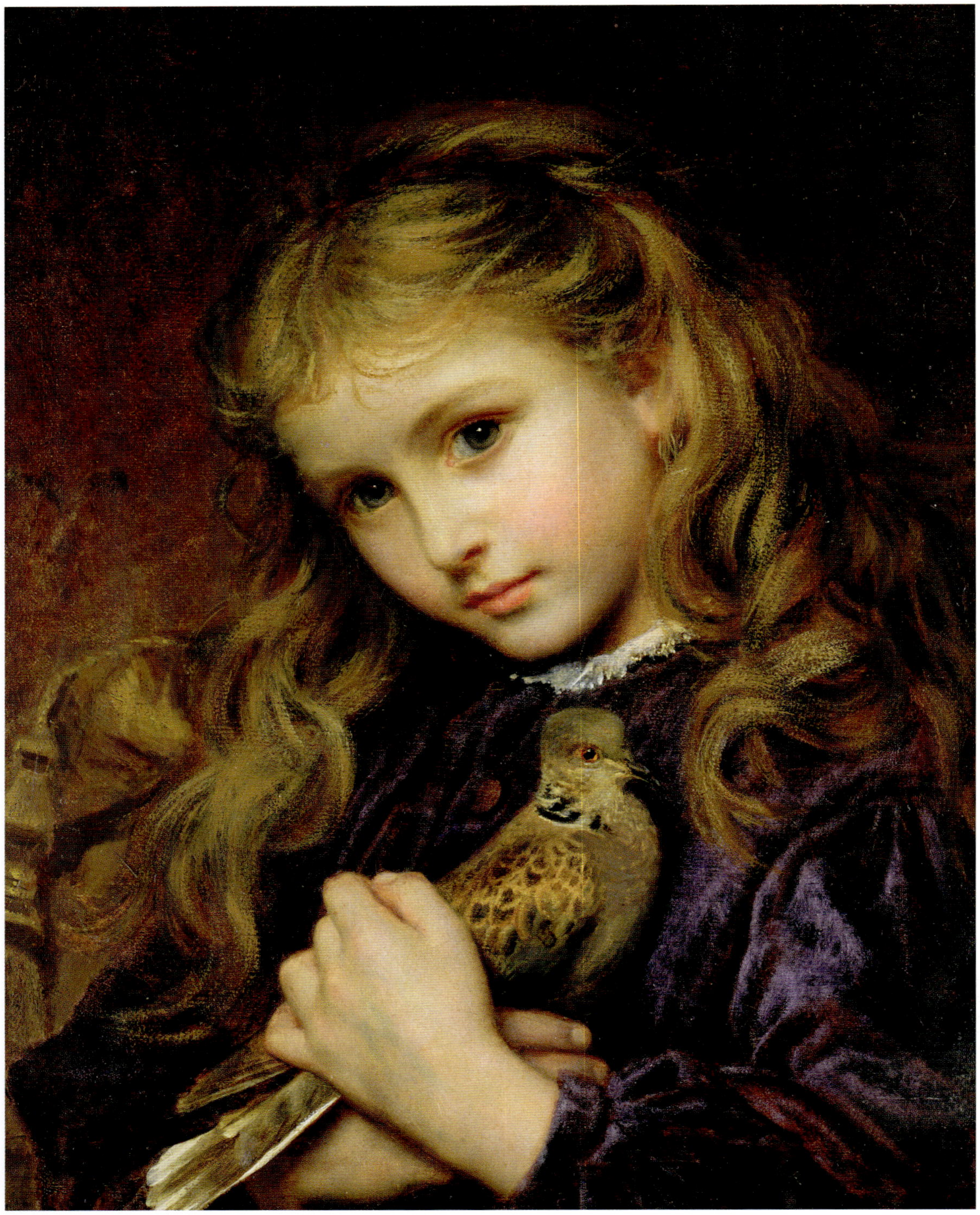

Sophie Anderson (1823–1903) *The Turtle Dove*

n.d.
Oil on canvas laid on board
35.6 × 29.8 cm (14 × 11¾ in.)
Private collection

Victorian painters had a tendency to sentimentalize animals and children, especially when the two were brought together in one picture. But Sophie Anderson's depiction of a young girl cradling a dove is affecting in its tenderness, and just escapes the mawkish. The artist began her career as a portraitist, and later specialized in paintings of women and children. She was loosely associated with the Pre-Raphaelite movement, and this painting shows all the attention to detail that characterized Pre-Raphaelite art: the distinctive black-and-white markings on the bird's neck, for example, are well observed. Doves are, of course, sacred to the goddess of love, but the mood here is innocent and gentle rather than lewd. One wonders whether the girl is enjoying the soft purring sound the turtle dove makes, which might remind her of a pet cat.

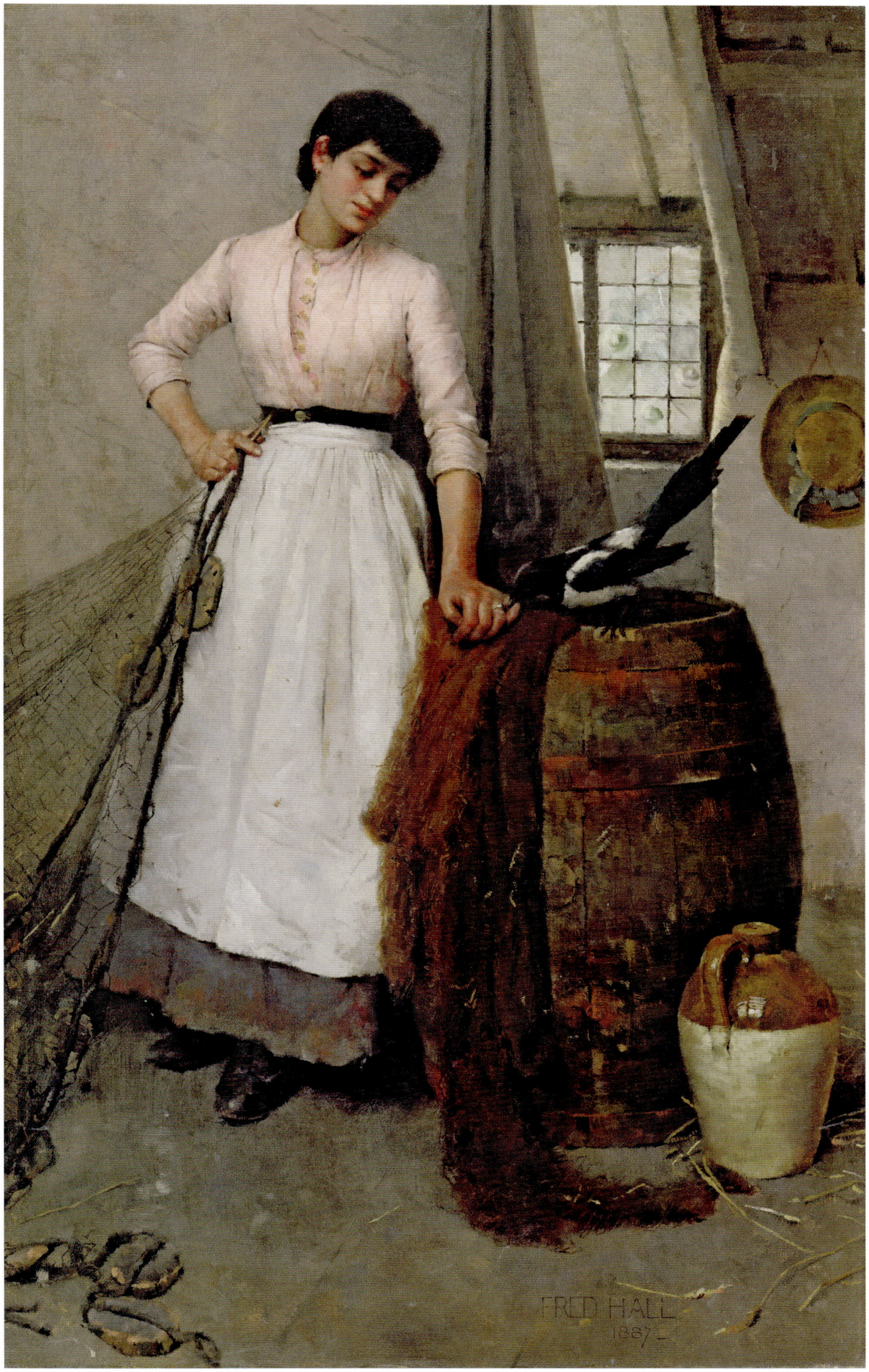

Fred Hall
(1860–1948)
One for Sorrow

1887
Oil on canvas
81.3 × 50.8 cm (32 × 20 in.)
Yale Center for British Art, New Haven, Connecticut

An ancient West Country rhyme about the magpie, dating from about 1750, goes: 'One for sorrow, two for joy, three for a wedding, four for a death.' There are many later variants, some of which substitute 'a girl' for three, and 'a boy' for four, but all agree that seeing a magpie on its own is never good news. Here, one has flown into a humble cottage and alighted on a barrel. Magpies are attracted by shiny objects, and the bird's attention is focused on the young woman's wedding ring. She may well be concerned at this harbinger of doom, which has arrived on its own and without the partner that would have allayed the bad luck. The fact that she is holding a fishing net indicates that she is a fisherman's wife, so perhaps the woe foretold is that of loss at sea. The theme was a common one among painters based in the Cornish village of Newlyn, where Fred Hall set up home in 1884.

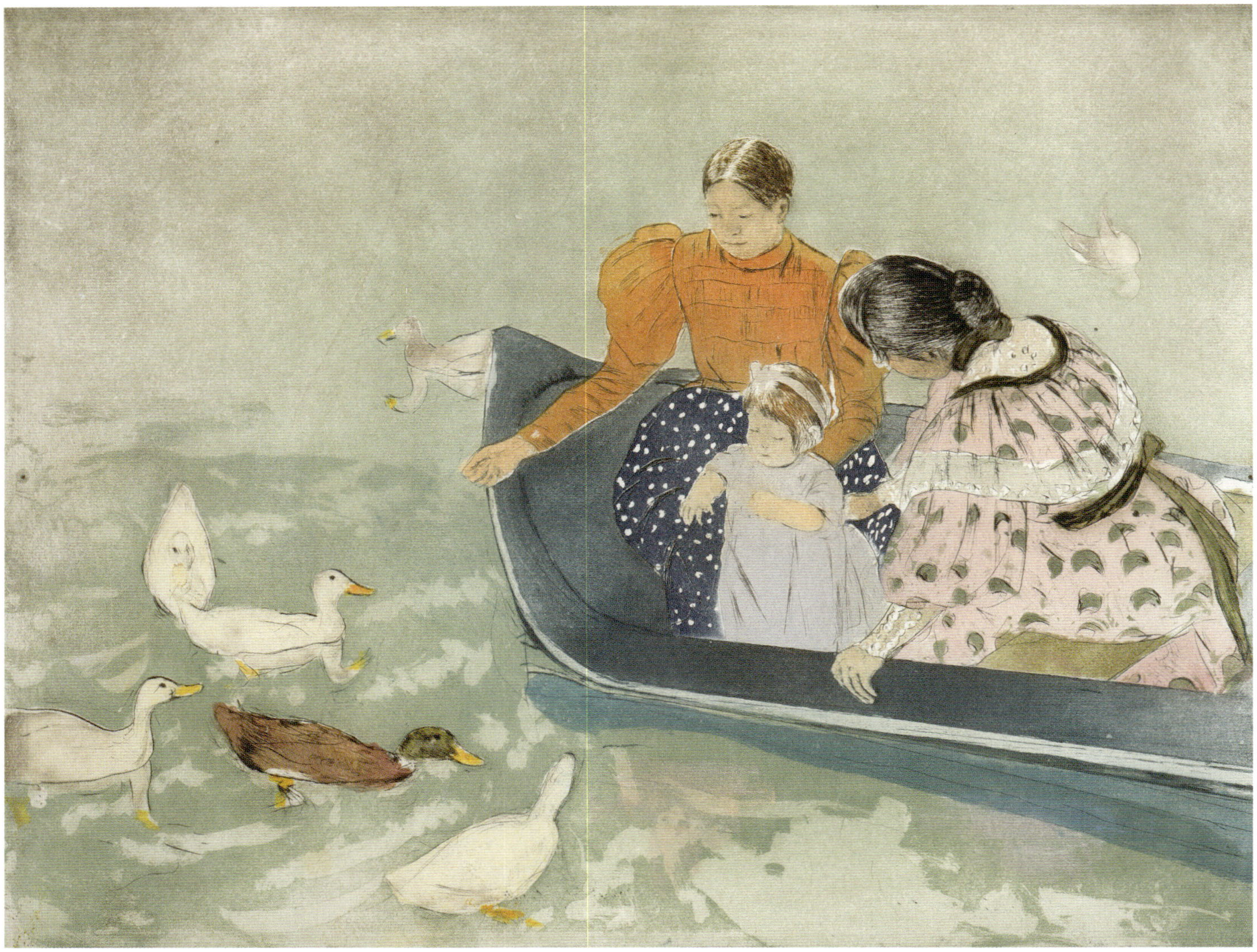

Mary Cassatt
(1844–1926)
Feeding the Ducks
1895
Dry point and aquatint on paper
29.8 × 40 cm (11¾ × 15¾ in.)
Allen Memorial Art Museum, Oberlin College, Ohio

The common childhood pleasure of feeding ducks in the park is portrayed here with tenderness. The American artist Mary Cassatt had studied in Paris in the 1870s and exhibited with the Impressionists, sharing their predilection for subjects drawn from everyday life. Shortly before she produced this print, she was working on a painting called *Summertime* (now in the Metropolitan Museum of Art, New York), showing a woman and a girl in a boat on a lake feeding waterfowl. She wrote to a friend: 'I am now painting with my models in the boat and I sit on the edge of the water and in these warm still September days it is lovely.' This print explores the same subject, but instead of a young girl, the child is a toddler, taking faltering steps towards the birds that clearly mesmerize her. The boldness of line owes something to Japanese woodblock prints by Katsushika Hokusai (see pp. 191–93) and Kitagawa Utamaro, whose work Cassatt had discovered a few years earlier.

Edmond Aman-Jean (1858–1935/36)

Young Girl with a Peacock

1895

Oil on canvas

105 × 68 cm (41¼ × 26¾ in.)

Musée des Arts Décoratifs, Paris

Towards the end of the nineteenth century peacocks came to enjoy a special place in the affections of avant-garde artists and designers. Their glorious plumage became the motif par excellence of the Aesthetic movement in the 1870s and Art Nouveau during the 1880s and 1890s. No English 'artistic' interior of the period was complete without a vase of peacock feathers, and in Paris the gallery set up in 1895 by Siegfried Bing, La Maison de l'Art Nouveau, helped to spread the peacock craze through the objects for sale, which included many Japanese artefacts and prints with peacock decoration. The Parisian painter Edmond Aman-Jean, a friend of the more famous Georges Seurat, was celebrated for his elegant female portraits. Here, a young woman in an extravagantly printed dress takes a stroll around a garden in the company of a peacock. She avoids the viewer's gaze, apparently lost in her own thoughts, and to complement her pensive mood the bird avoids displaying itself.

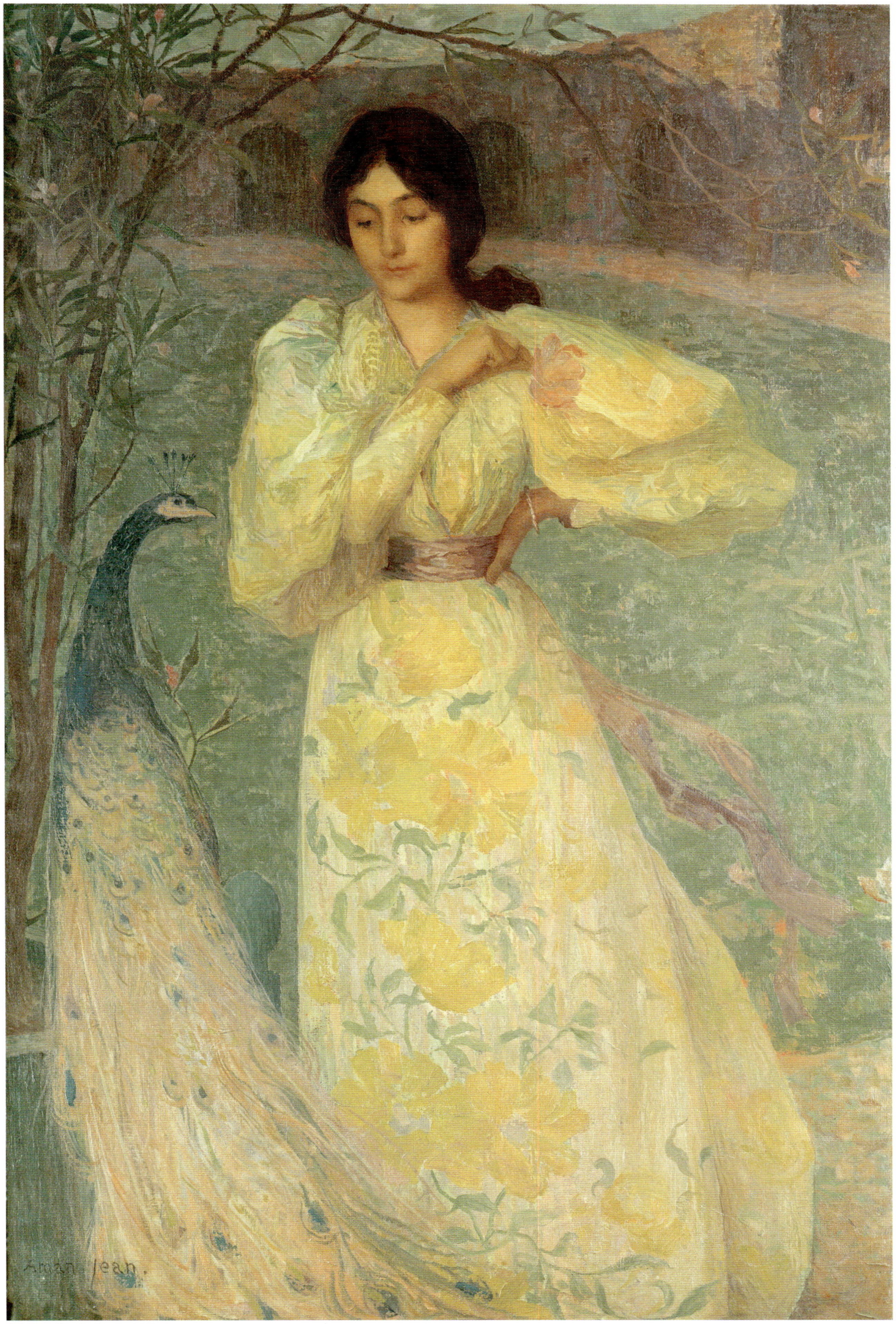

Rupert Bunny (1864–1947)
A Summer Morning

1897
Oil on canvas
97.9 × 129.5 cm (38½ × 51 in.)
Art Gallery of South Australia, Adelaide

Rupert Bunny was Australian by birth, but the many years he spent in Paris (where he lived for most of his career) left their mark on his art. This painting of willowy beauties in flowing gowns bears all the hallmarks of *fin-de-siècle* French sensibility. In the 1890s, the decade when it was painted, Bunny was focusing on depictions of women at leisure – in parks, by the seaside or at home – in a sun-drenched atmosphere redolent of ease and perpetual summer. It is hard to imagine that a swan would be delighted at the prospect of being fed the rose the beautiful woman offers it, but the picture aims at a dreamy evocation rather than literal truthfulness, and the elegant demeanour of the swans perfectly complements the graceful young women on the stepping stones. Tchaikovsky's ballet *Swan Lake*, composed some twenty years before this picture was painted, also plays on the natural affinity between female grace and the seductive beauty of the swan.

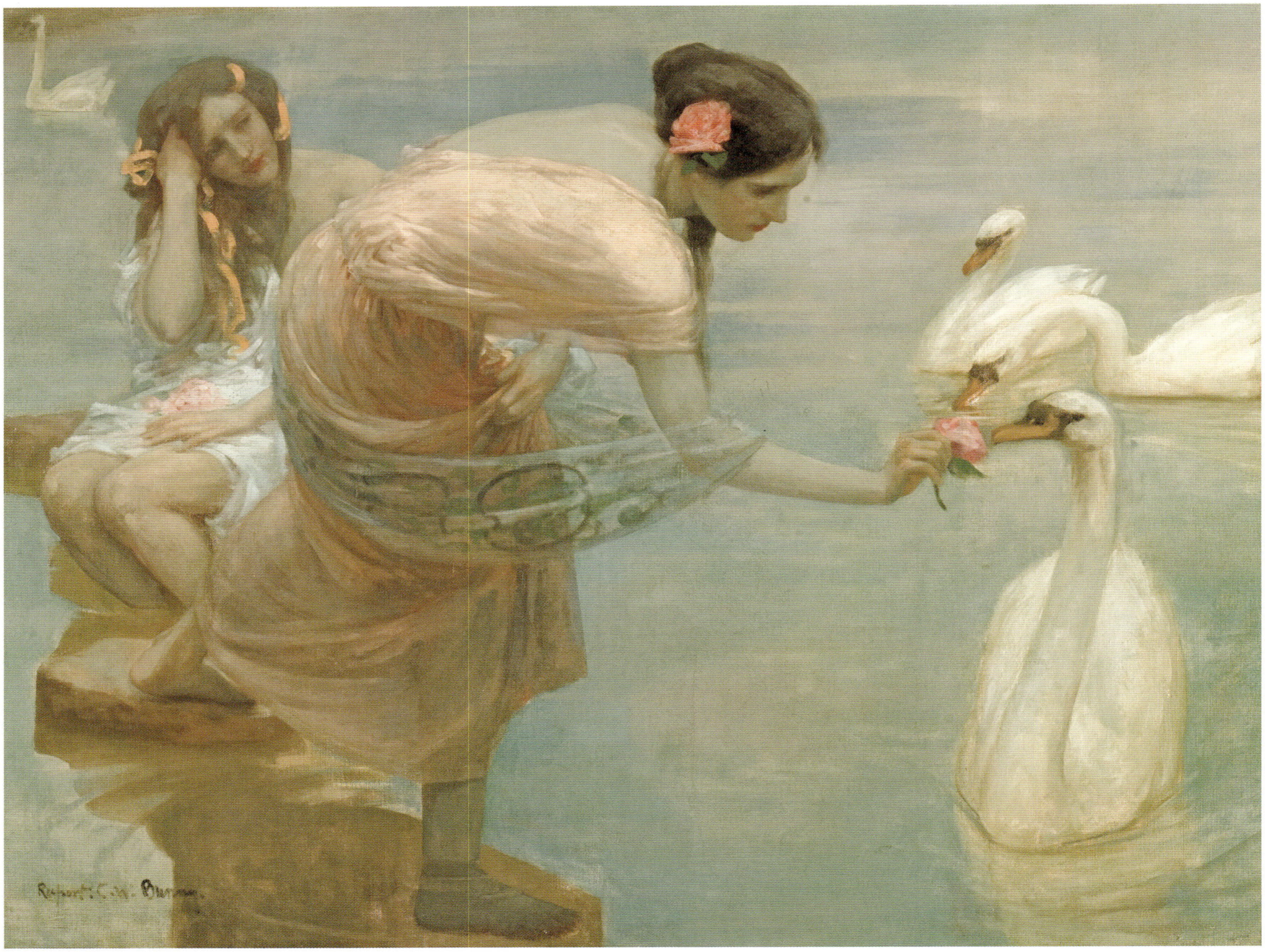

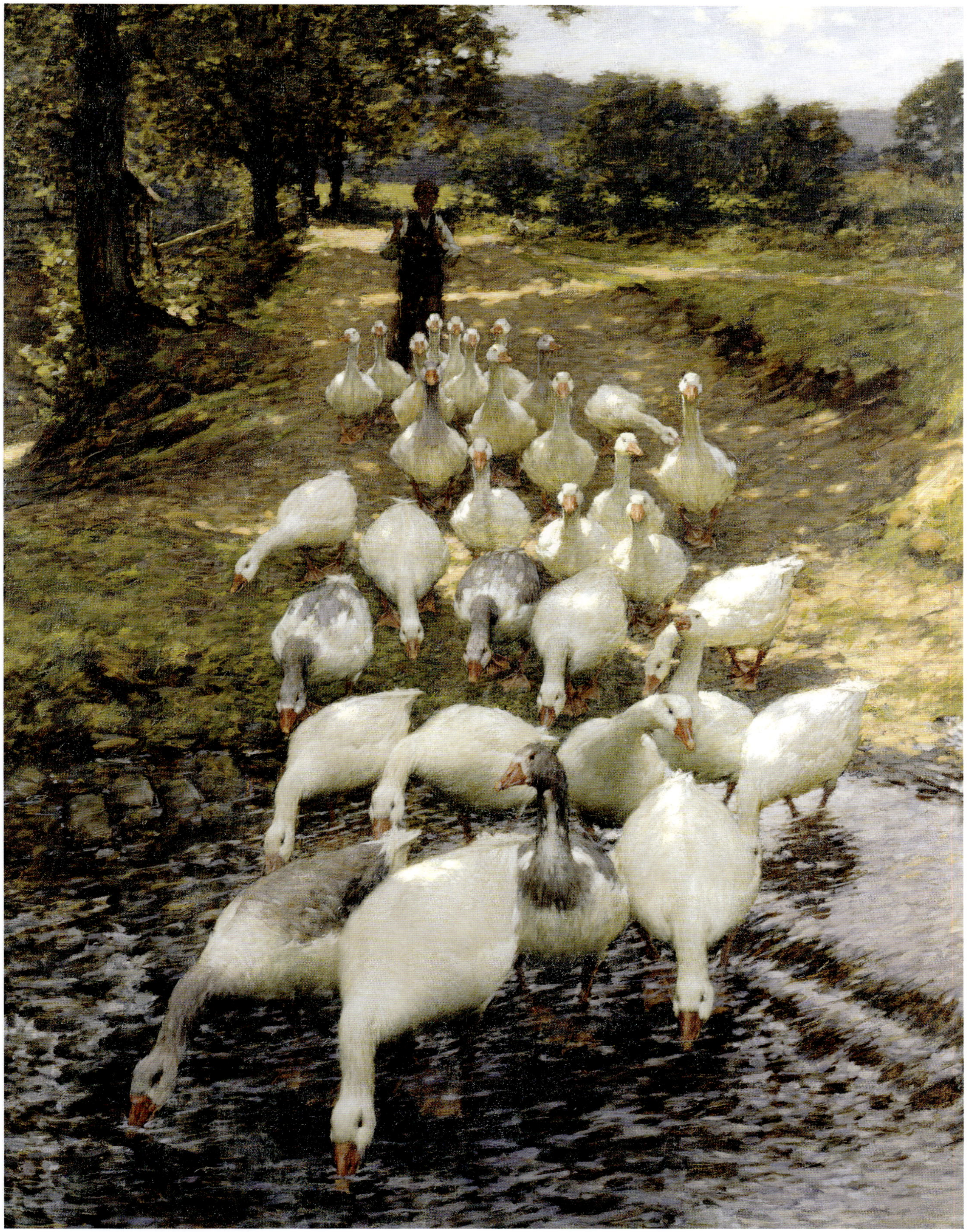

Henry Herbert La Thangue (1859–1929)
The Watersplash

1900
Oil on canvas
116.8 × 94 cm (46 × 37 in.)
Victoria Art Gallery, Bath

La Thangue's geese make their way through a Sussex country lane in dappled sunlight, pausing to drink at a watersplash before the farmer moves them on. The vertiginous perspective makes it appear as though they are about to cascade out of the picture and on to the viewer. Despite its inherent Englishness, this realistic evocation of rustic life owes a great deal to the example of the French painter Jules Bastien-Lepage, who had pioneered the painting of similar rural scenes in the open air in his native country. At the end of the nineteenth century, paintings of rural life became increasingly popular, partly because industrial expansion was depopulating the countryside and there was a growing fear that traditional manners and customs would disappear. La Thangue was keen to document ways of life that were under threat. At the time this picture was painted he was able to draw his subjects from the farms and villages near his home in Graffham, West Sussex, but after 1901 he extended his search for an uncontaminated rural idyll to Provence and Liguria.

The Modern Bird

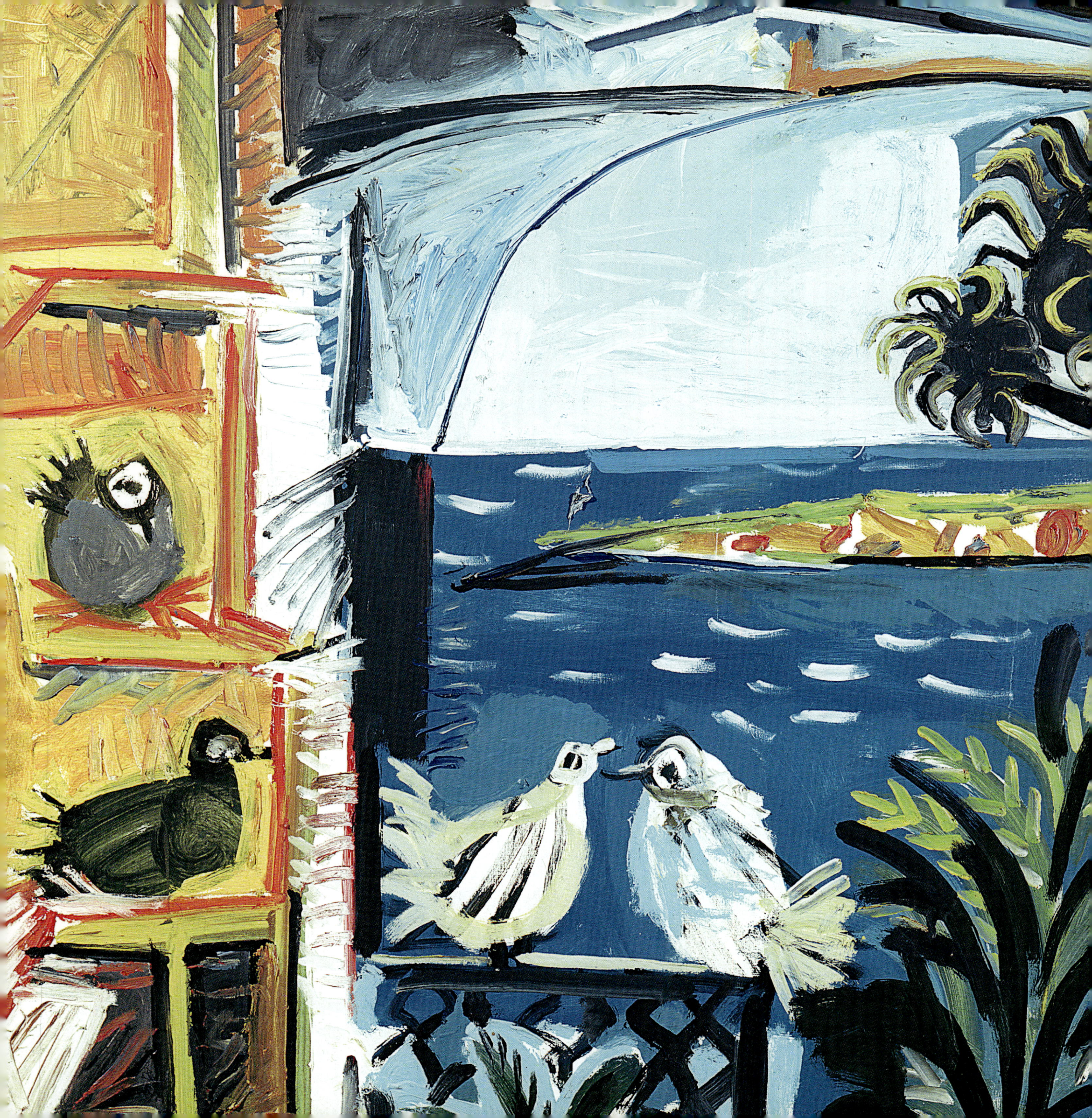

While the twentieth century saw a complete re-examination of the whole notion of representation in art, bird motifs never disappeared altogether. Indeed, birds are central to the work of some of the period's most radical innovators. Pablo Picasso and Georges Braque, who turned the world of art upside down when they developed Cubism, both produced a large number of canvases featuring birds later in their careers, after their experiments with pure abstraction (pp. 252 and 258). Picasso was particularly drawn to doves and pigeons, and produced one of the most startling reworkings of the dove's original iconography when he created his simple poster design for the dove of peace (p. 35).

But artists at the forefront of modernism have not kept within the confines of traditional bird symbolism or ornithological observation. They have been far more interested in extending artistic boundaries, often using birds as part of a wider pictorial or sculptural exploration. So the Futurist artist Giacomo Balla, who was interested in speed, urban life and contemporaneity, chose to concentrate on the dynamic trajectories of the flight of swifts seen against the facade of a building, rather than on the individual forms of the birds themselves (opposite). Henri Gaudier-Brzeska's sculpture of a bird swallowing a fish (p. 245), produced on the eve of the First World War, suggests nothing so much as a hand grenade, a perfect encapsulation of violence that is the complete opposite of the softer qualities more usually associated with birds. Constantin Brancusi's bird in flight, created at the beginning of the Second World War, is also utterly modern but in a different way: it is a streamlined, pared-down sculpture that distils the essence of a bird's pose with a bare minimum of information (p. 251).

Twentieth-century artists also felt freer than their predecessors to draw on their personal experience and imaginings, interpreting birds in a subjective way rather than necessarily plundering the repositories of world myth. Fuelled by new psychoanalytical theories, Surrealist artists conjured up subjects from the depths of their own psyches. So Max Ernst invented his own avian alter ego, Loplop, and constantly returned to bird motifs in his art, in which the boundary between birds and humans is blurred (p. 253). Salvador Dalí, too, fascinated by his colleague André Breton's dream, created his own vision of a bird in a state of metamorphosis (p. 256). And in Edward Burra's hands, innocent pots morphed into hybrid human–birds to become the stuff of nightmares (p. 255). Paul Klee's outwardly innocent evocations of birds in gardens or as part of twittering machines or abstract patterns seem light-hearted and joyful by comparison – more the stuff of dreams – although their apparent naivety is belied by the sophistication of his compositions (p. 246). Even artists who worked in a more conventional idiom, such as Stanley Spencer and Marsden Hartley, attached a subjective significance to birds because they depicted them in situations and places that were redolent with personal meaning (pp. 247 and 250).

There are hundreds of excellent wildlife artists working today who continue the tradition of painting birds with the utmost accuracy, aided by excellent binoculars, photography and film. But for others, birds continue to provide a starting point for wilder flights of imagination. Birds may be all around us, creatures that we see every day, but the possibilities they offer to artists – even those who work in the most contemporary idioms, such as video and installation – are inexhaustible.

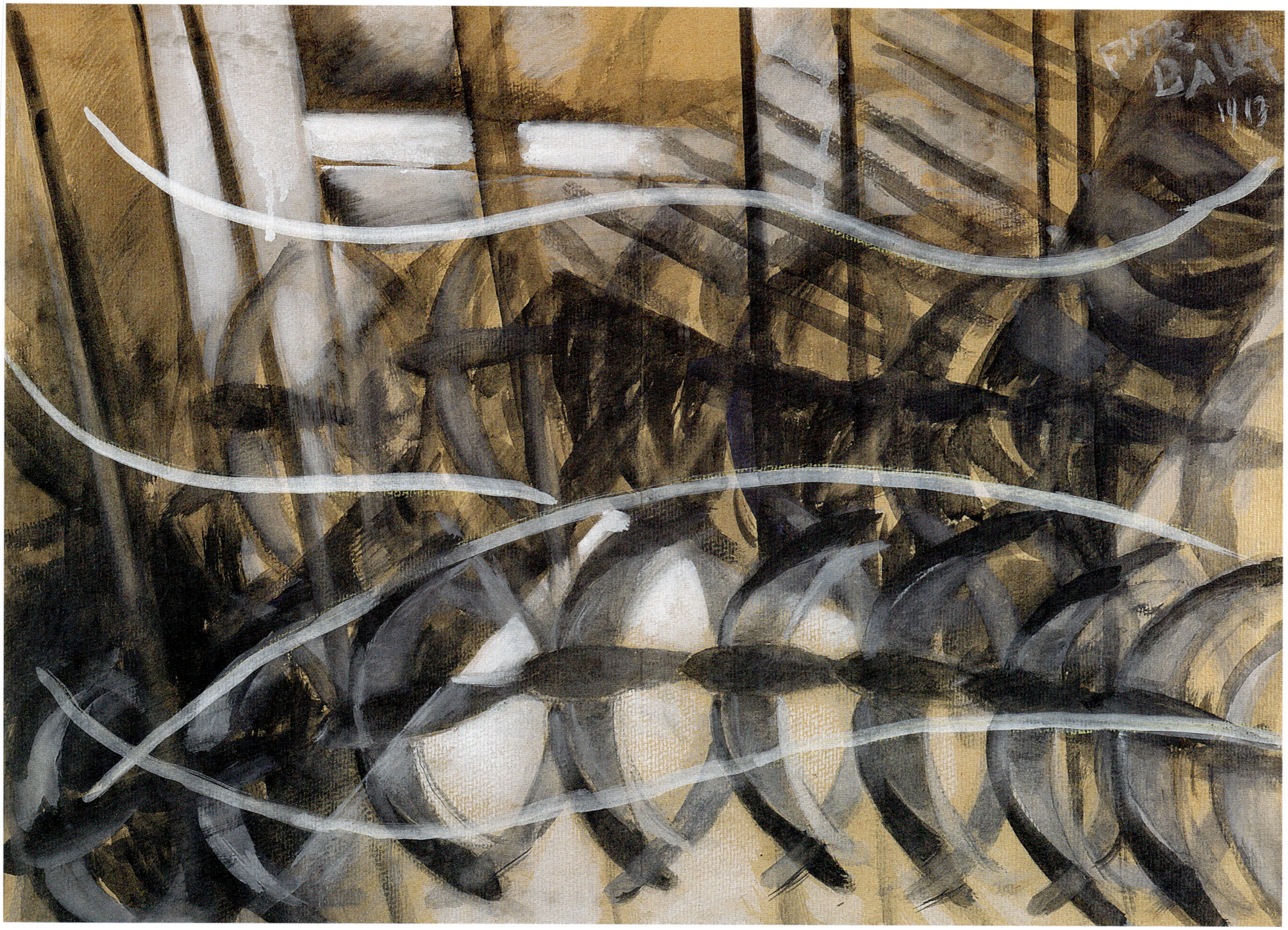

Giacomo Balla
(1871–1958)
Study for *Swifts: Paths of Movement + Dynamic Sequences*
1913
Tempera on paper
49 × 68 cm ($19\frac{1}{4}$ × $26\frac{3}{4}$ in.)
Private collection

Giacomo Balla was at the forefront of Italian Futurism, an artistic movement that sought to glorify everything that was dynamic and modern. But unlike some of his contemporaries, who investigated the speed of mechanical objects, Balla demonstrated an early concern with the movements of the natural world: people and animals running, and birds on the wing. In this study for one of his most famous canvases, he tracks the trajectories of birds flying outside a building. At this stage of his investigation, the birds are recognizable, but in later versions of the theme they became more abstracted, their bodies being subsumed into a linear pattern. Representing birds in the air has always presented a challenge for artists, but here Balla cleverly conveys the essence of the swift's swooping and darting flight, as well as its speed.

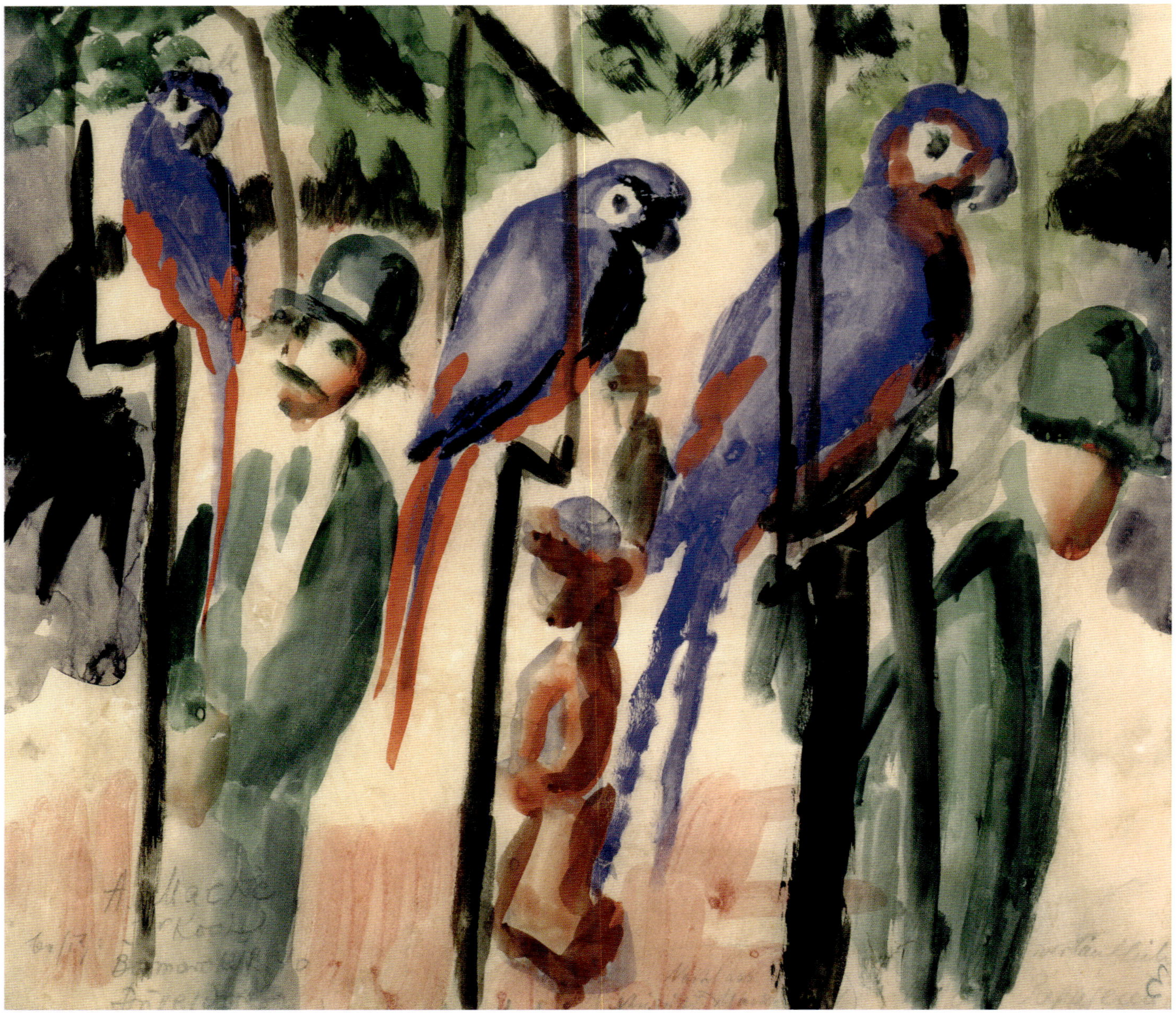

August Macke (1887–1914)
Blue Parrots

1914
Watercolour on paper
27 × 32 cm (10⅝ × 12⅝ in.)
Kunstmuseum Mülheim an der Ruhr, Germany

The German artist August Macke was drawn to scenes of people strolling at leisure through cities, reading newspapers, sitting in restaurants and window shopping. A visit to Amsterdam in the spring of 1912 inspired him to sketch people enjoying the zoological gardens there – a habit he continued in Cologne's zoo on his return to Germany. In this spontaneous watercolour we see a bowler-hatted man pausing to gaze at the blue parrots on their perches. Once the treasured pets of the aristocracy, parrots were now available for everyone to admire. The whole atmosphere is one of ease and grace, and there are no really wild or savage beasts to introduce a note of menace. Macke was one of the leading members of the Blue Rider group of artists, with Wassily Kandinsky and Franz Marc, but his own work tended less towards abstraction than that of his associates, showing a greater debt to French Fauvist painting.

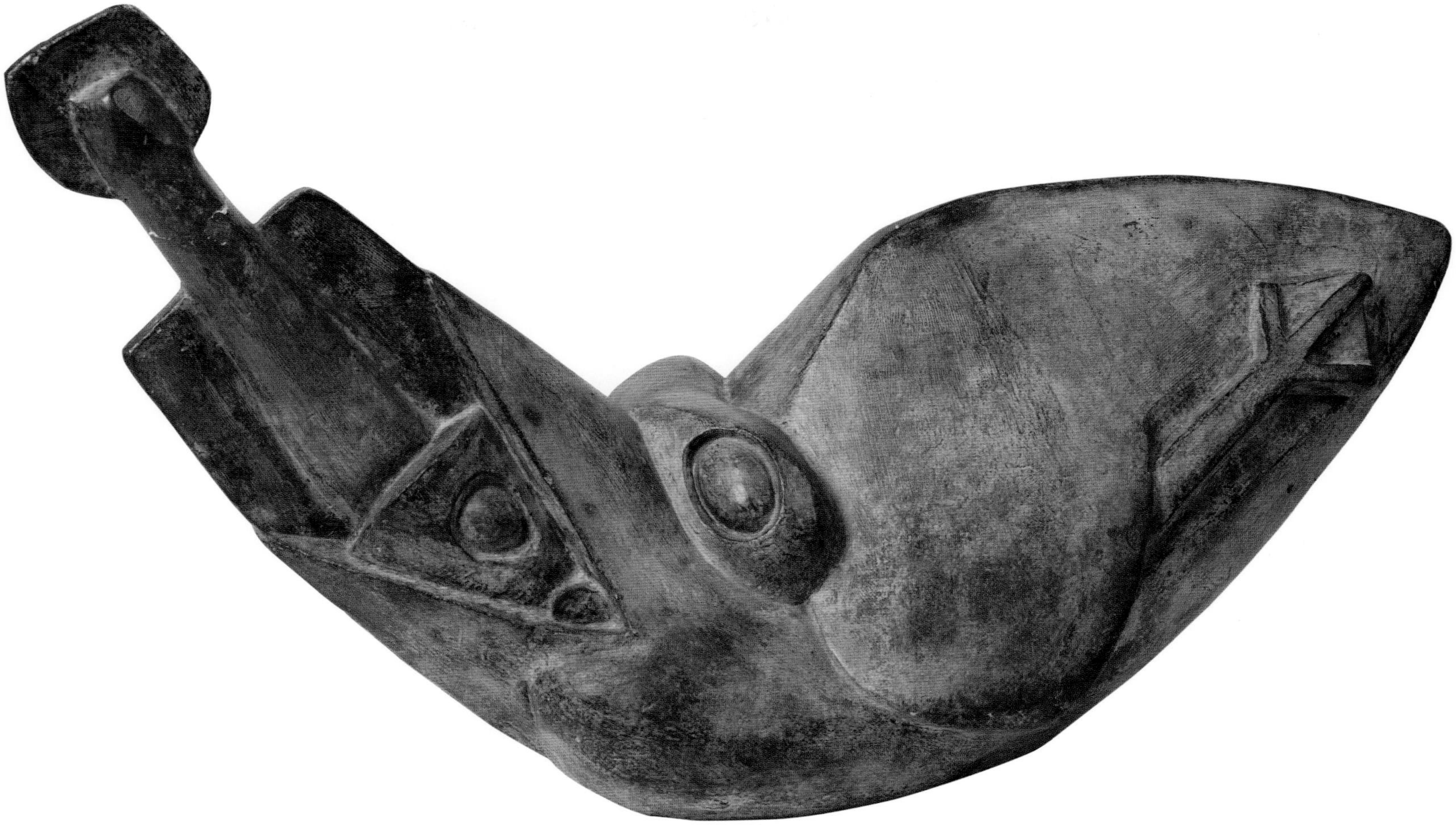

Henri Gaudier-Brzeska
(1891–1915)
Bird Swallowing a Fish
1914
Plaster
33 × 58 × 28 cm (13 × 22¾ × 11 in.)
Kettle's Yard, Cambridge

The French sculptor Henri Gaudier-Brzeska was an acute observer of animals and birds. This sculpture came about after he had observed a bird struggling to swallow a large fish in the Serpentine River in Hyde Park, London. He made a number of sketches of the incident, which later found three-dimensional expression in this piece. Lacking the money to cast it in metal, the artist carved it directly into plaster; in 1964 Henry Moore was commissioned to cast the sculpture in bronze. The work marries Gaudier-Brzeska's fascination with the natural world and the forms of the machine age. The shape of the fish, which appears to be about to choke the bird, has been likened to a torpedo or hand grenade. It is not surprising that many have seen the work as reflecting the mounting tension of war, which was just about to break out in Europe.

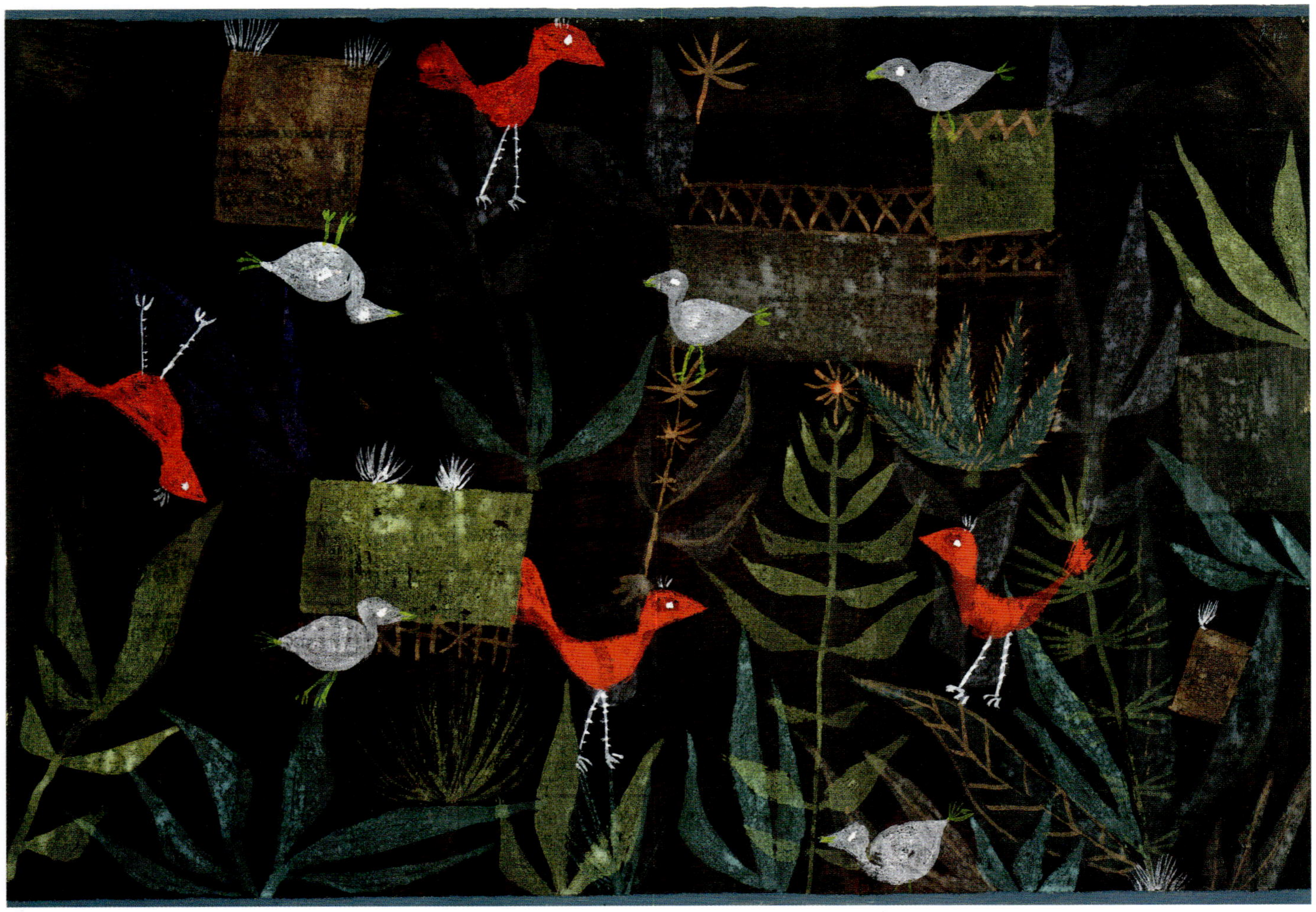

Paul Klee (1879–1940)

Bird Garden

1924
Watercolour on primed paper on cardboard
27 × 39 cm (10⅝ × 15⅜ in.)
Pinakothek der Moderne, Munich

Much of Paul Klee's work is infused with a sense of humour and playfulness. It is hard not to smile at this flock of red and white birds disporting themselves among stylized foliage evocative of an enchanted garden. The mood is light-hearted, the calculated naivety reminiscent of the children's drawings that fascinated the artist. Although it has been suggested that the imagery of birds and plants was inspired by wall mosaics Klee saw in the palace of King Roger in Palermo when he visited Sicily in 1924, the artist's fascination with birds predates his Italian trip. In 1923 he had produced a very similar watercolour, *Landscape with Yellow Birds* (in a private collection), which shows the creatures perching among vaguely vegetal forms. And in 1922 he had created a famous watercolour drawing (now in the Museum of Modern Art, New York) entitled *Twittering Machine*, in which a group of sketchily outlined birds forms part of a demonic musical box that is cranked into action by the turning of a handle. In 1979 *Bird Garden* was reproduced on a German stamp marking the centenary of the artist's birth.

Stanley Spencer
(1891–1959)
Separating Fighting Swans

c. 1932/33
Oil on canvas
91.4 × 72.5 cm (36 × 28½ in.)
Leeds Museums & Galleries

The English artist Stanley Spencer drew extensive inspiration from the daily life he observed around him in the Berkshire village of Cookham, where he had grown up and which he described as a 'holy suburb of heaven'. His paintings of the place frequently marry the literal with the visionary, conveying an almost childlike innocence. Swans are a feature of life on the River Thames at Cookham, and Spencer had earlier recorded the annual ritual of marking the birds in *Swan Upping at Cookham* (1915–19; Tate). Here, however, the artist features in his own painting, intervening to stop two swans fighting. Three figures of angels, sporting wings but clad in everyday dress, watch him from the bank. Spencer's marriage was in crisis when he painted this canvas, as he had fallen for another woman and separated from his wife. It is tempting to read something of this personal conflict into the picture.

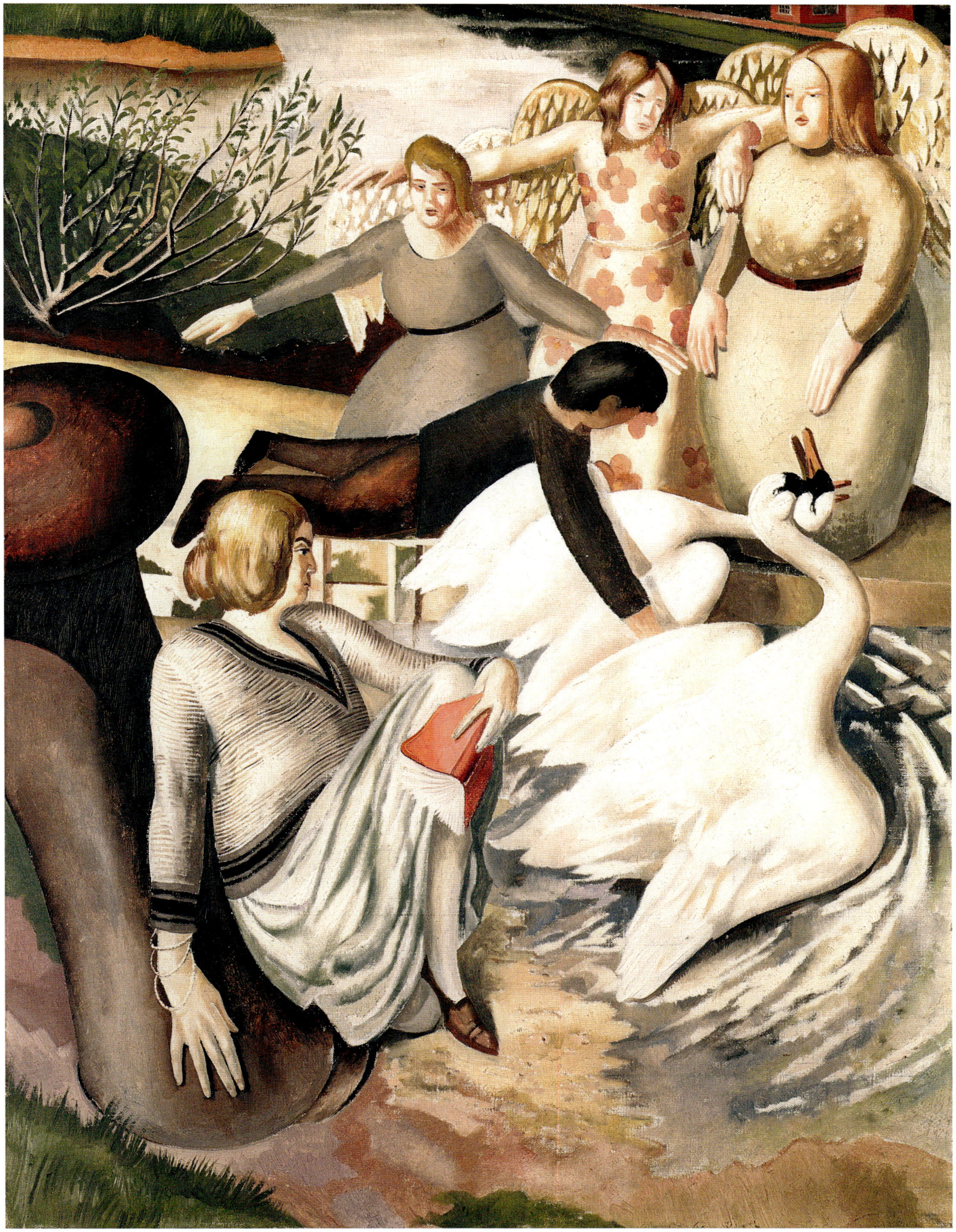

Marc Chagall
(1887–1985)
The Peacock Complaining to Juno
c. 1927
Gouache on paper
51 × 41.3 cm (20 × 16¼ in.)
Private collection

Birds appear in hundreds of Chagall's paintings. Red, green, blue and yellow ones dance over depictions of his native village in Russia and fly over embracing lovers, while clowns morph into bird-like creatures. However, this bird relates to one of Jean de La Fontaine's fables rather than to Chagall's personal history and mythology. The goddess Juno had given the peacock its splendid tail of many eyes (see p. 104), but the peacock complained that his pitiful voice made him the laughing stock of the bird kingdom, saying that he wished he had a song as tuneful as the nightingale's. The goddess rebuked the peacock, saying that each bird had its special attribute, and that if it did not like its rainbow colours and brilliant tail she would take the plumage from its back. Chagall has emphasized the bird's splendour by depicting its tail as though it is studded with gems that shine out against the dark background.

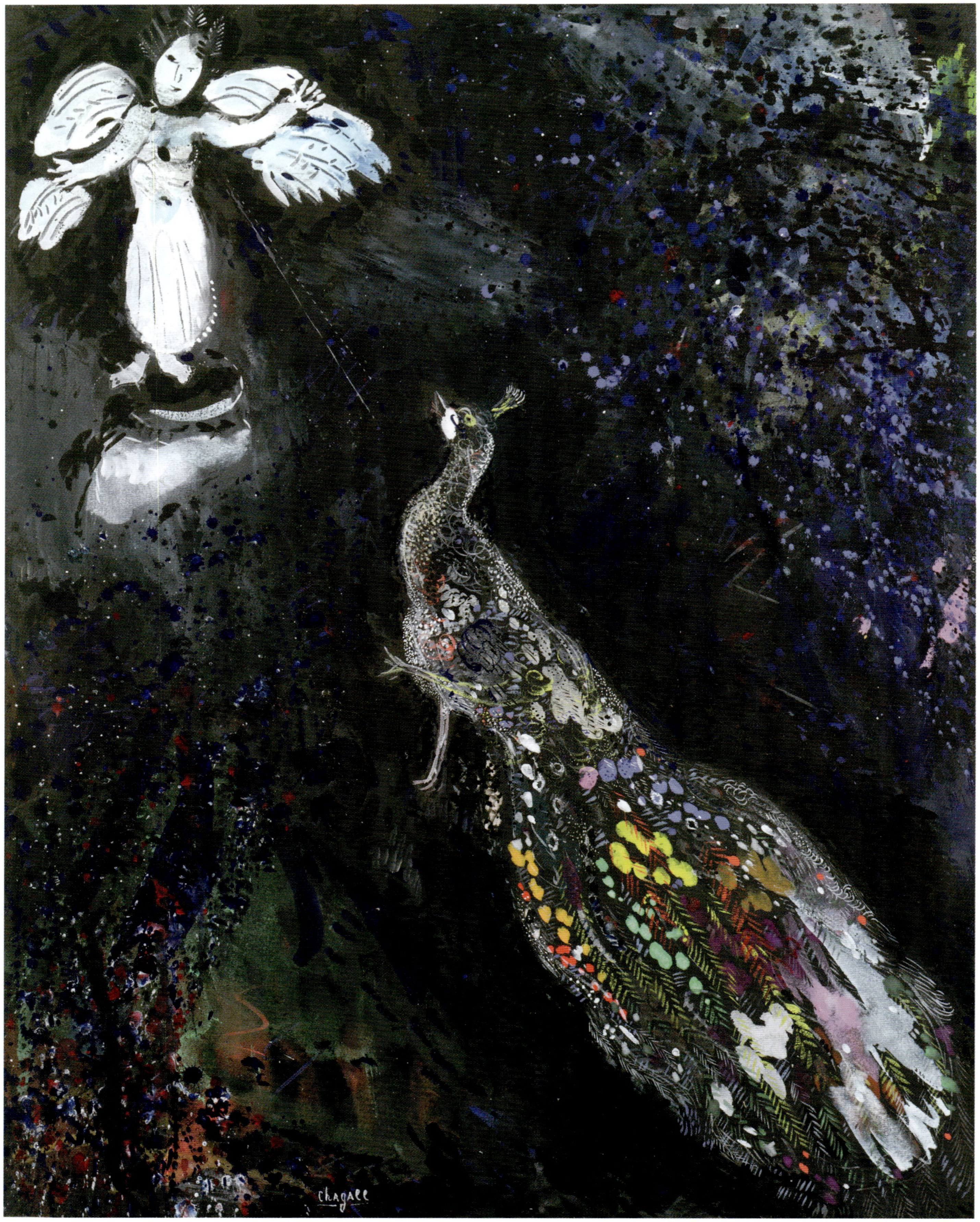

Gino Severini
(1883–1966)
Window with Pigeons

c. 1930–31
Tempera on paper
31 × 24 cm ($12\frac{1}{8}$ × $9\frac{3}{8}$ in.)
Galleria Alberto della Ragione, Florence

In the years before the First World War, Gino Severini was at the forefront of the Italian Futurist movement, becoming its ambassador among artists of the Parisian avant-garde, including Picasso and Braque. Futurism exalted everything that was fast, modern and dynamic, but Severini was more attracted to the human figure in motion than to machine imagery, and specialized in paintings of cabaret dancers in frenzied movement. In the inter-war years he and many of his fellow artists returned to a more conservative, figurative style of painting. He produced a number of decorative still lifes featuring musical instruments, pigeons, ducks and fish, inspired by the recently uncovered wall paintings at Pompeii. This picture is a fine example. The mood is tranquil and static, and, although the whole is very deliberately composed, one can almost believe that the Picasso-like birds have fluttered in through the open window.

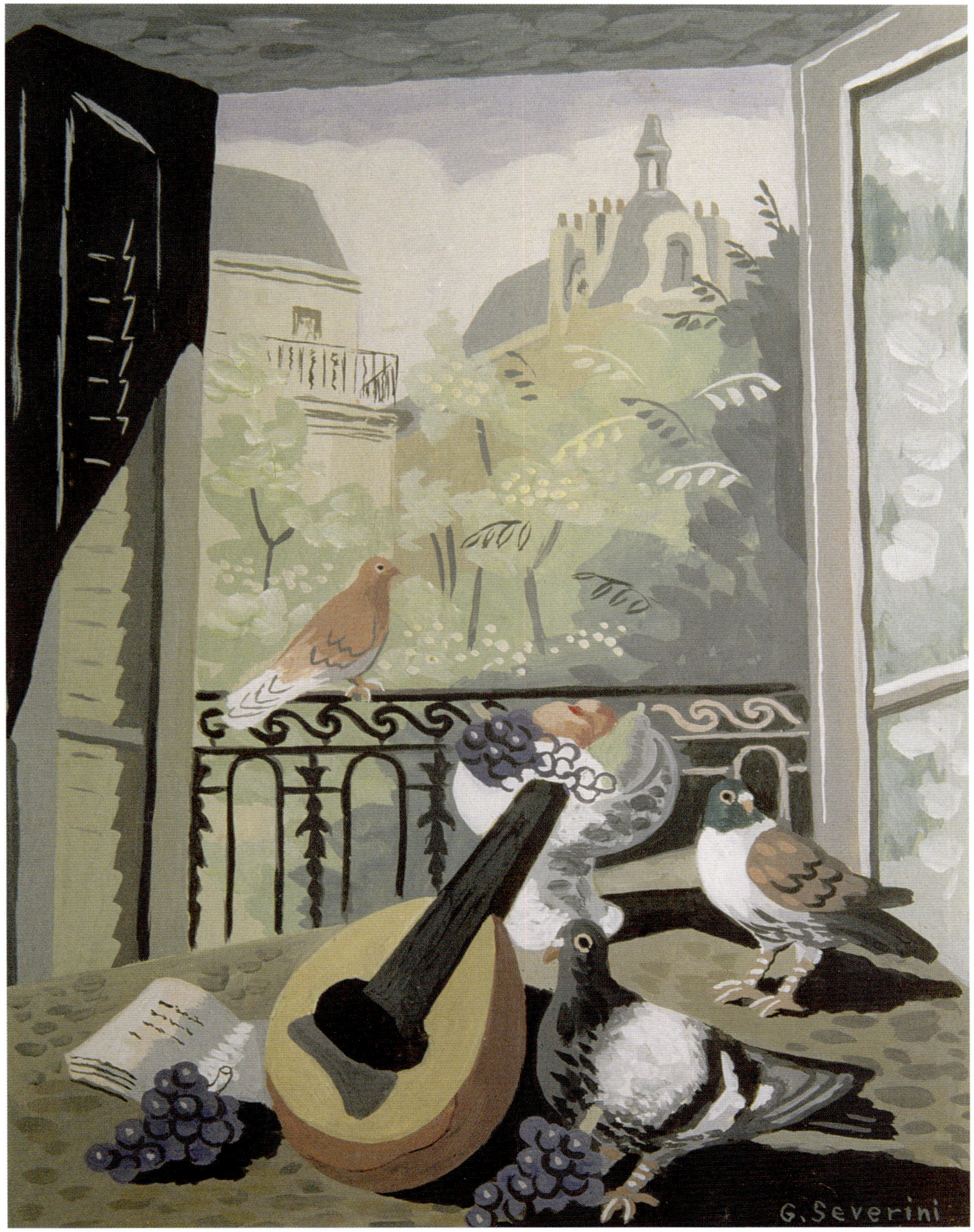

Marsden Hartley (1877–1943)

Birds of the Bagaduce

1939
Oil on board
71.1 × 55.8 cm (28 × 22 in.)
The Butler Institute of American Art, Youngstown, Ohio

After spending some years in New York and Europe, the American painter and poet Marsden Hartley returned to his native Maine in 1937, declaring that he wanted to become 'the painter of Maine' and show American life and subjects – as many other American artists were striving to do at the time. He painted this canvas while staying with his friends in West Brookville, on the edge of the Bagaduce River, near the coast. At first glance it appears to be a light-filled, joyous seascape, but it is underlined by personal tragedy, since Hartley had lost two close friends at sea, the poet Harold Hart Crane and the fisherman Alty Mason, only a few years previously. The sky – filled with clouds and birds – appears to dominate the small boats bobbing about on the choppy water. While the boats seem fragile beneath the vast expanse of the heavens, the seabirds are free to roam over the waves.

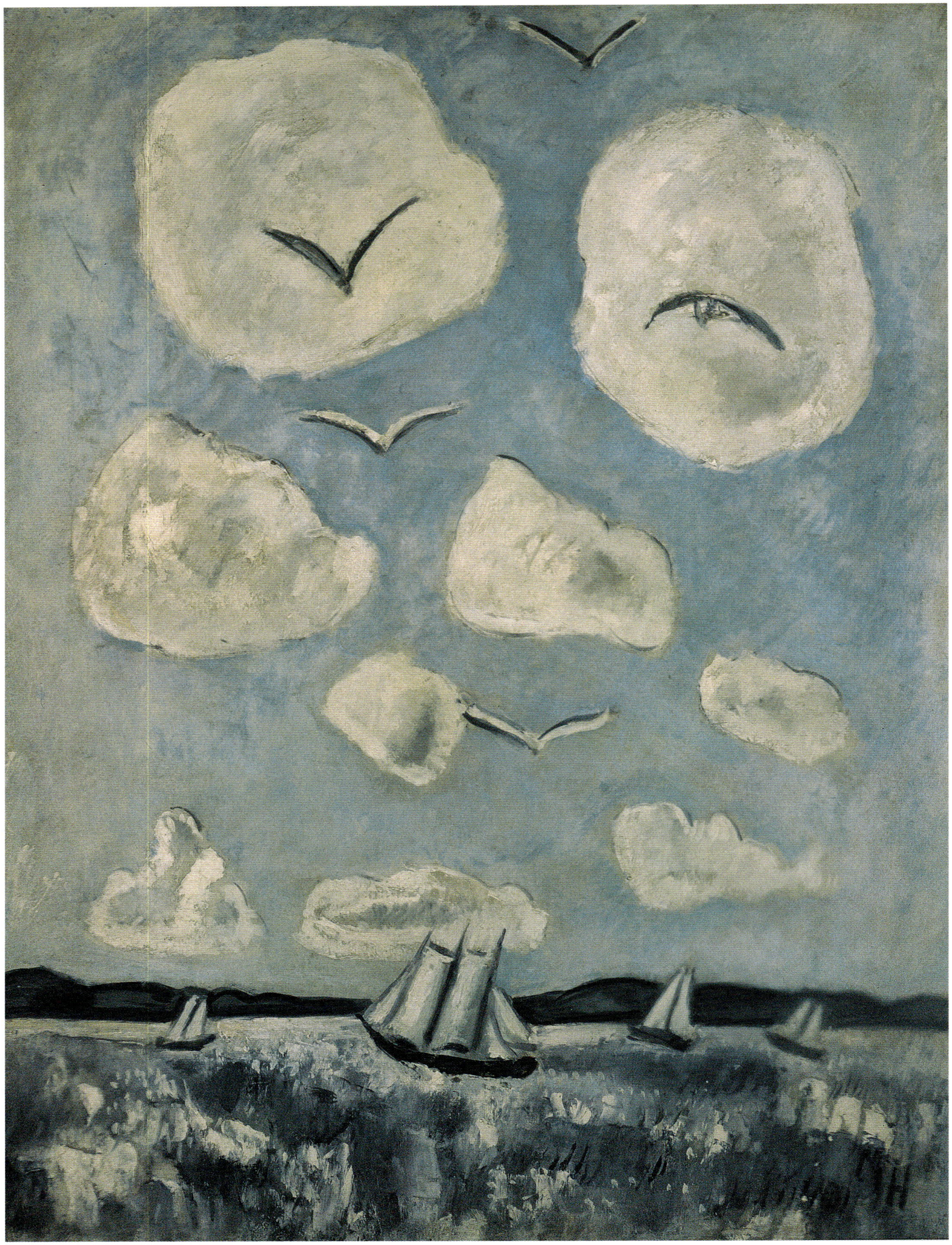

Constantin Brancusi
(1876–1957)
The Bird in Space

1940
Bronze
193 cm (76 in.) high
Centre Pompidou, Paris

The Romanian artist Constantin Brancusi settled in Paris, where he associated with the leading artists of his day, including Henri Matisse, Fernand Léger, Amedeo Modigliani, Marcel Duchamp and Auguste Rodin. For two decades – from the 1920s to the 1940s – he investigated the theme of the bird in flight, producing seven versions of this sculpture in marble and nine in bronze, all of which have the highly finished surface associated with streamlined objects. Dispensing with such characteristic avian features as wings and feathers, Brancusi pared the form down to an absolute minimum. Body, head and beak are one elongated oval, balanced on a slender cone suggestive of the bird's feet. The creature appears to thrust upwards, as though it is about to take flight. In 1926, when one of the bronze versions was sent to New York, customs officials refused to believe that it was a work of art exempt from import duty. Two years later a judge relented and classified it as a sculpture, saying that 'while some difficulty might be encountered in associating it with a bird, it is nevertheless pleasing to look at and highly ornamental'.

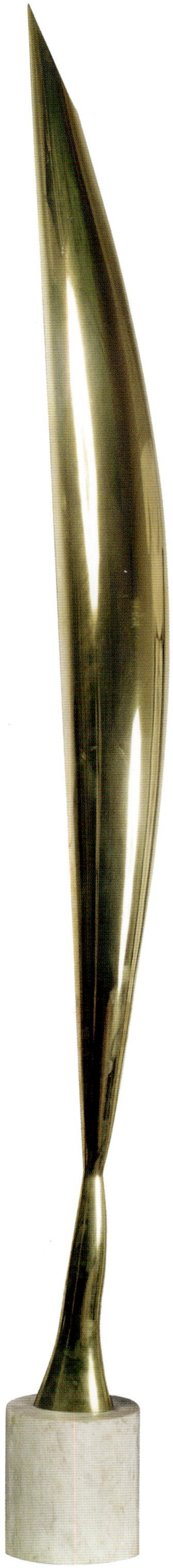

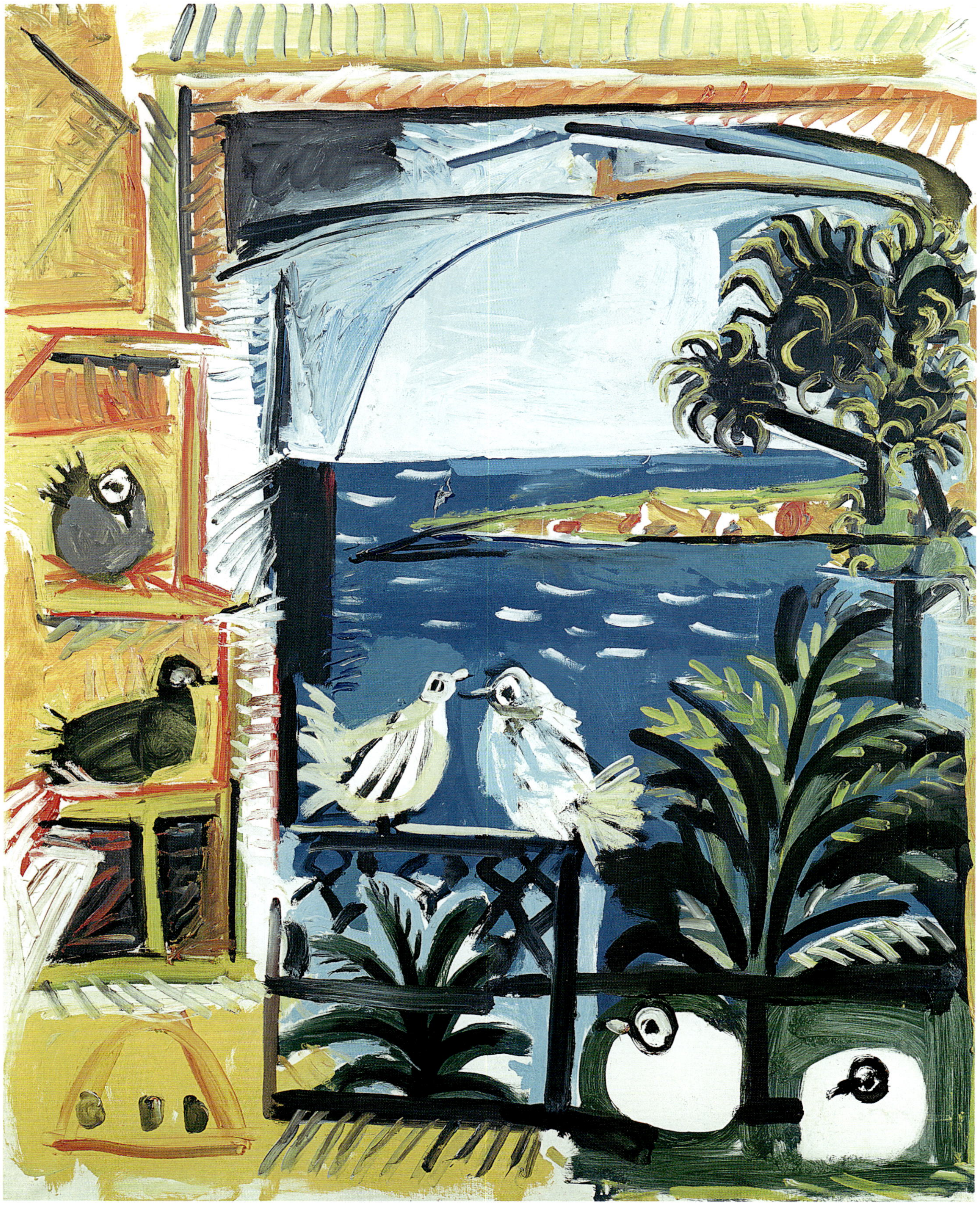

Pablo Picasso
(1881–1973)
The Pigeons, Cannes
1957
Oil on canvas
100 × 80 cm (39⅜ × 31½ in.)
Museu Picasso, Barcelona

In September 1957 Picasso was hard at work at La Californie, his home in Cannes, on a series of variations on the theme of Diego Velázquez's *Las Meninas*. He had abandoned the lower part of the house and moved his studio to the top floor, where he shared the space with pigeons of all types and colours, which nested in alcoves and perched on the railings of the balcony. For a few days he interrupted his intensive study of the Spanish Old Master to paint nine views out of the open window of his studio towards the Mediterranean, showing the birds on the railings, pecking about on the ground, clustered inside or flying into the distance. During this period Picasso also made a number of ceramics featuring birds, and pigeons and doves were particular favourites. He may have been especially fond of them because he began sketching them as a child, alongside his father.

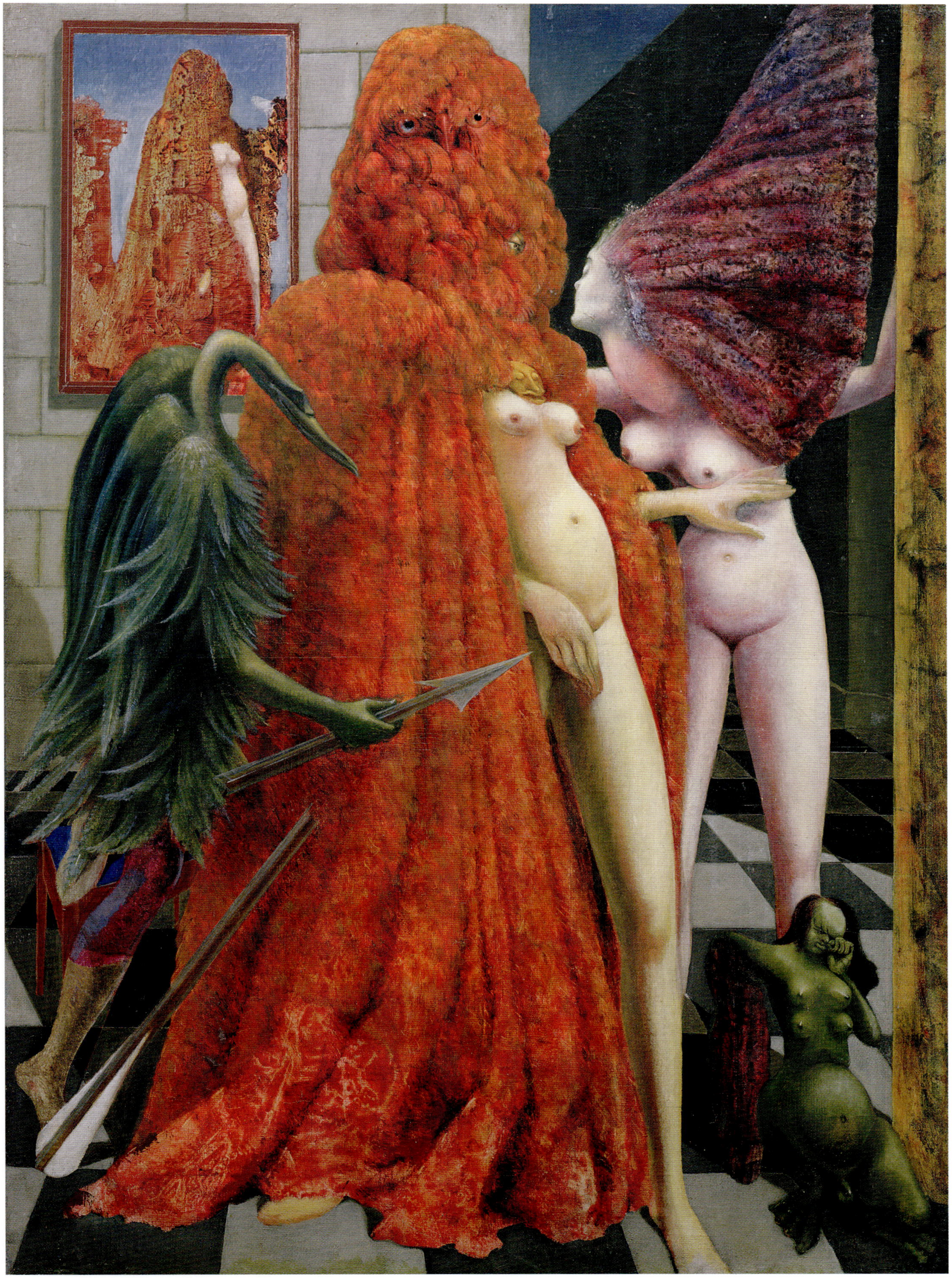

Max Ernst
(1891–1976)
The Robing of the Bride

1940
Oil on canvas
129.6 × 96.3 cm (51 × 38 in.)
Peggy Guggenheim Collection, Venice

The Surrealist artist Max Ernst was fascinated by birds, and even developed an artistic alter ego, Loplop, a kind of superior bird that appeared in several of his works. Ernst claimed that his avian obsession began when, as an adolescent, he awoke one night to find that his pet bird – a pink cockatoo – had died, and a few moments later his father came into his room to announce that his sister had been born. This led to a conflation of birds and humans in his imagination, and nowhere is this more evident than in this sinister and mesmerizing canvas. A bride – probably based on Ernst's lover, Leonora Carrington – wears a robe of tawny feathers, which almost totally obscures her face (we can make out only one eye), and which is surmounted by a mask-like owl head, staring straight out of the canvas. By her side is a diminutive green bird–man carrying a broken spear – an all-too-obvious reference to the way her strident sexuality has disarmed him. The birds are at the centre of a truly Surrealist nightmare.

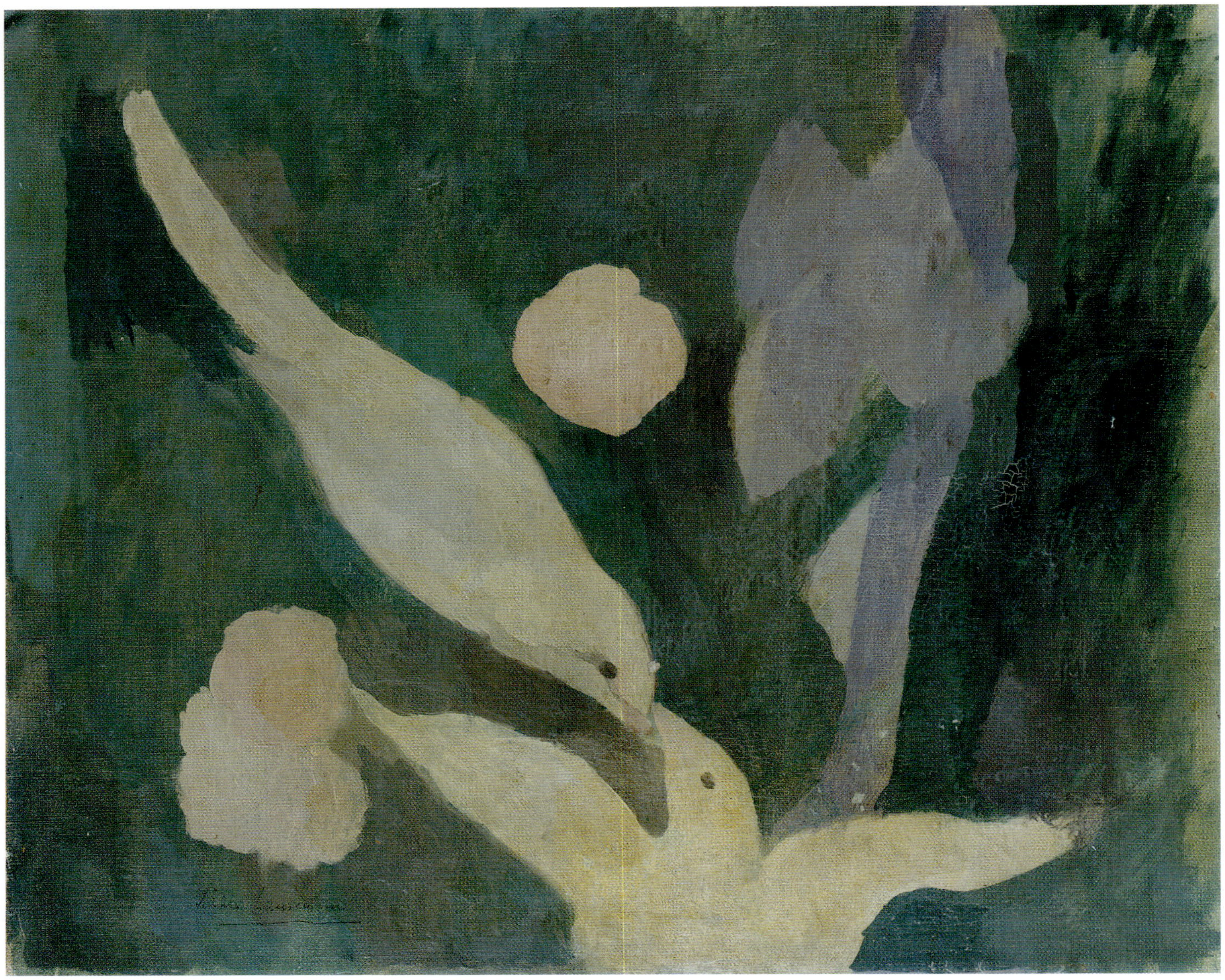

Marie Laurencin
(1883–1956)
Two Doves
n.d.
Oil on linen
36.5 × 45.5 cm (14⅜ × 18 in.)
Private collection

The work of the French artist Marie Laurencin has a soft and delicate quality that may derive from her early training as a porcelain painter at Sèvres. She was associated with artists and theoreticians at the heart of the Cubist circle in Paris – Braque, Guillaume Apollinaire and Picasso – but her own art was never one of hard edges or jarring forms. Instead, she developed an individual language for portraying such subjects as dreamy young women, dancers, animals and flowers, using the kind of pastel palette favoured in Rococo art. Here, two doves – a bird traditionally associated with Venus, the goddess of love – dally together, appearing almost to kiss or feed each other. It is an image of undeniable grace and charm infused with the gentle poetry characteristic of all Laurencin's work.

Edward Burra
(1905–1976)
Birdmen and Pots

1947
Watercolour on paper
82 × 57 cm (32¼ × 22⅜ in.)
Hove Museum & Art Gallery

Edward Burra once confessed that he felt that 'everything looks menacing. I'm always expecting something calamitous to happen'. A sense of threat certainly pervades this nightmarish scene. In Burra's hands inanimate objects – pots – become sinister through their association with the beady-eyed bird-men. But the robed figures with human hands in the foreground are ambiguous: are they people sporting bird masks, or are they actually hybrid creatures? Perhaps they are engaged in some sinister ritual of turning pots into birds, since two of those on the table appear to be in a state of metamorphosis. In the background, more bird-like creatures and an oval window resembling an eye add to the atmosphere of mystery. Burra stands alone in twentieth-century British art as an extraordinary individual who was fascinated by human eccentricity, and who explored the seedier side of modern urban life as well as the wilder shores of the imagination.

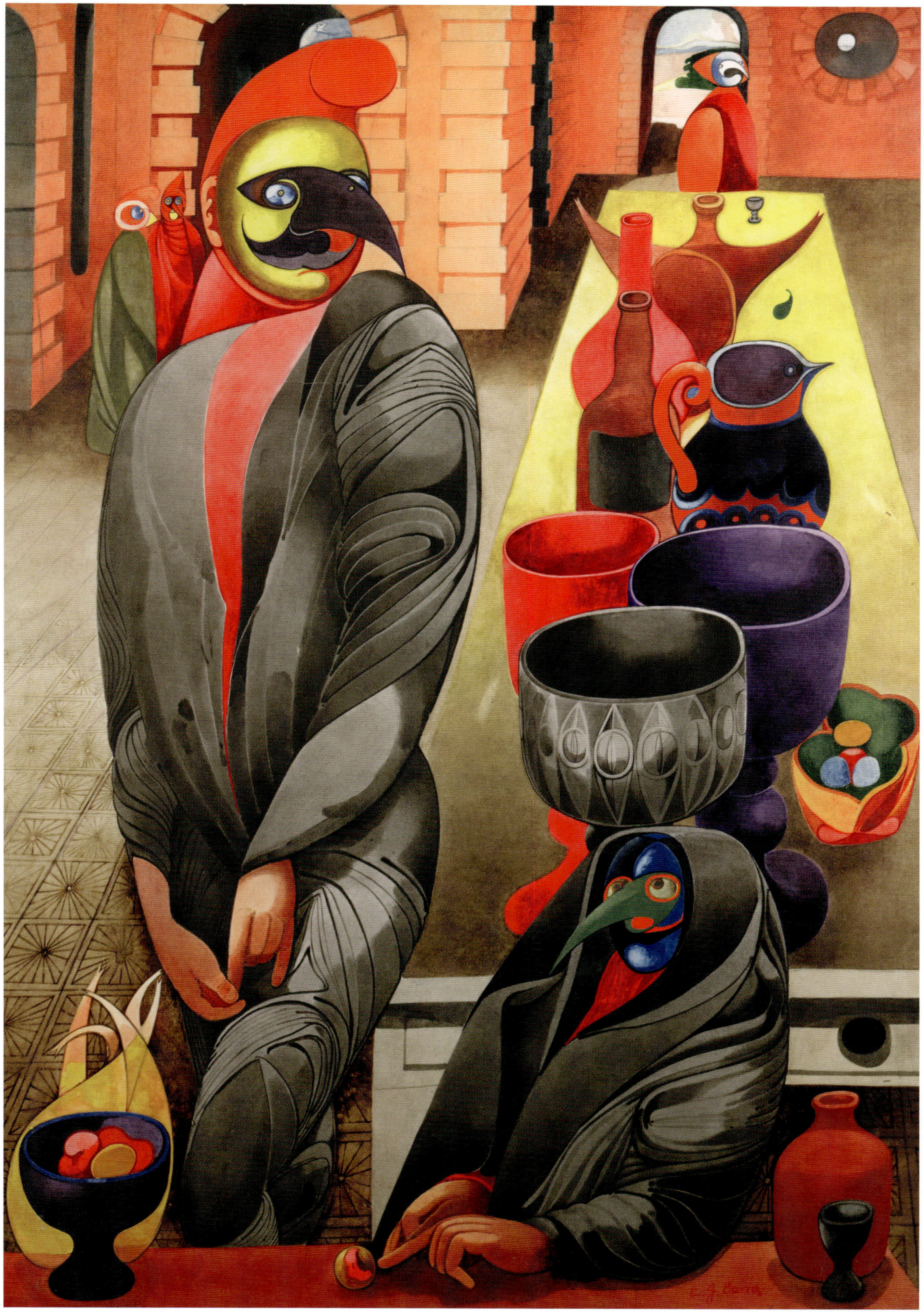

Salvador Dalí (1904–1989)
Bird

1928
Oil, sand and gravel on board
49 × 60 cm (19¼ × 23⅝ in.)
Scottish National Gallery of Modern Art, Edinburgh

Dalí created this picture shortly after he had become interested in Surrealist art and ideas, and it shows a clear debt to the work of Max Ernst, who had his own bird obsession (p. 253). It was inspired by a dream related by the Surrealist leader André Breton, in which he was swimming in the sea with friends when one of them shot at a group of birds flying overhead. When they were washed ashore, the dead birds had so changed that they resembled other creatures entirely, such as cows or horses. Dalí's family had a house in the Spanish fishing village of Cadaqués, which is where this picture was painted, and it incorporates bits of the beach, both sand and coarser gravel. Dalí gave his own insight: 'The interesting thing in this *Bird* is that with its side already monstrous, it carries in its entrails a thing that is a foetus and instead of the foetus being that of a bird, it's a cat! The moon is there as in many other canvases of this period.'

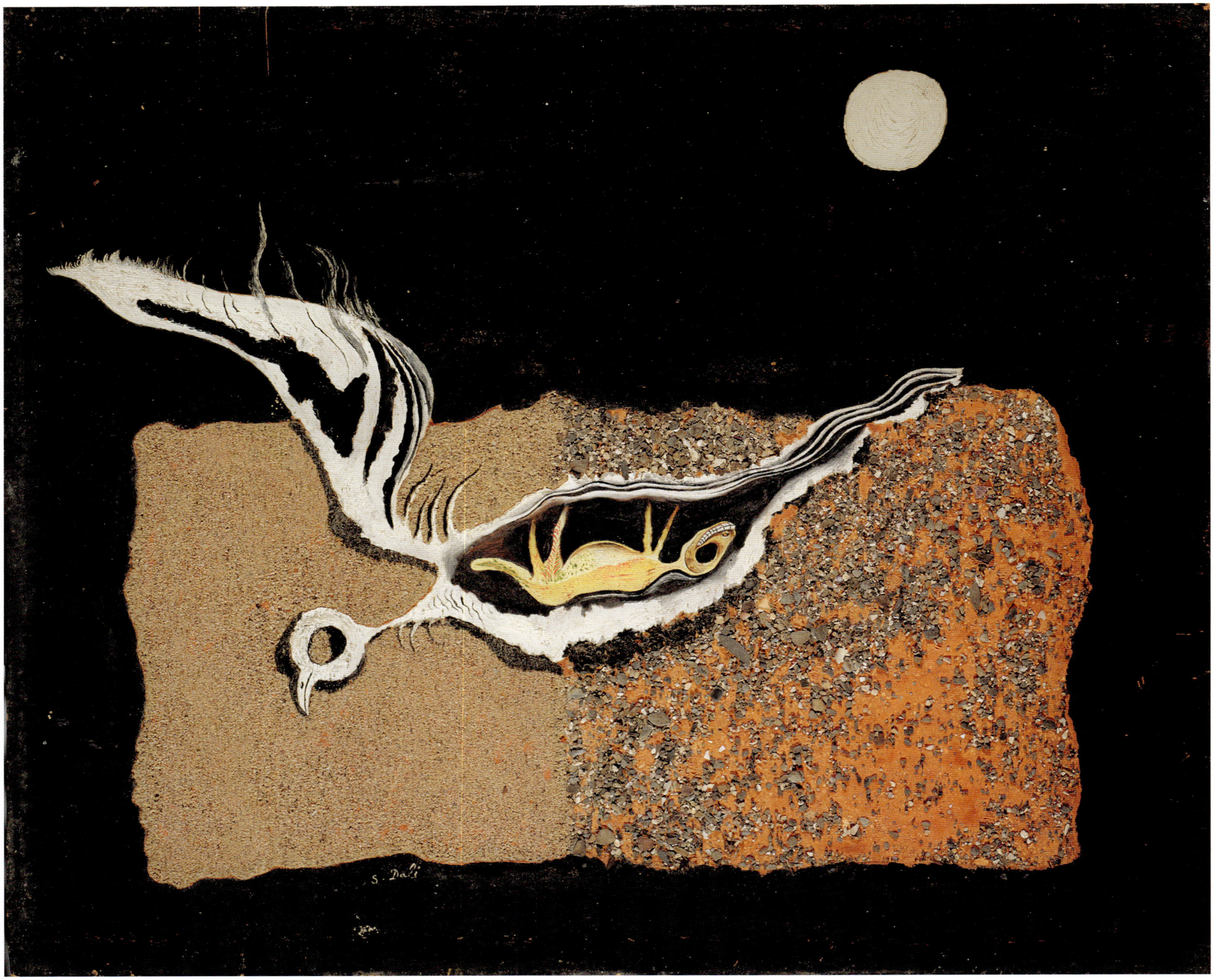

Lucian Freud
(1922–2011)
Sparrowhawk

1948
Pastel on paper
21.6 × 21.6 cm (8½ × 8½ in.)
Private collection

Lucian Freud claimed always to have been excited by birds, saying: 'If you touch wild birds it's a marvellous feeling.' He was particularly fond of birds of prey, and in the late 1940s kept in his studio a pair of sparrowhawks that he had bought in a London pet shop. He would take his rifle down to the canal in Regent's Park to shoot rats to feed his birds. One writer who visited the studio in 1947 commented on 'a live falcon which swoops around the room and alights on the master's wrist'. Freud was famous for his searching portraits of friends and family, and this bird has been subjected to the same full-frontal scrutiny as Freud's human subjects. This is clearly a portrait of a very specific creature with a predatory nature, its alert eyes reflecting its surroundings.

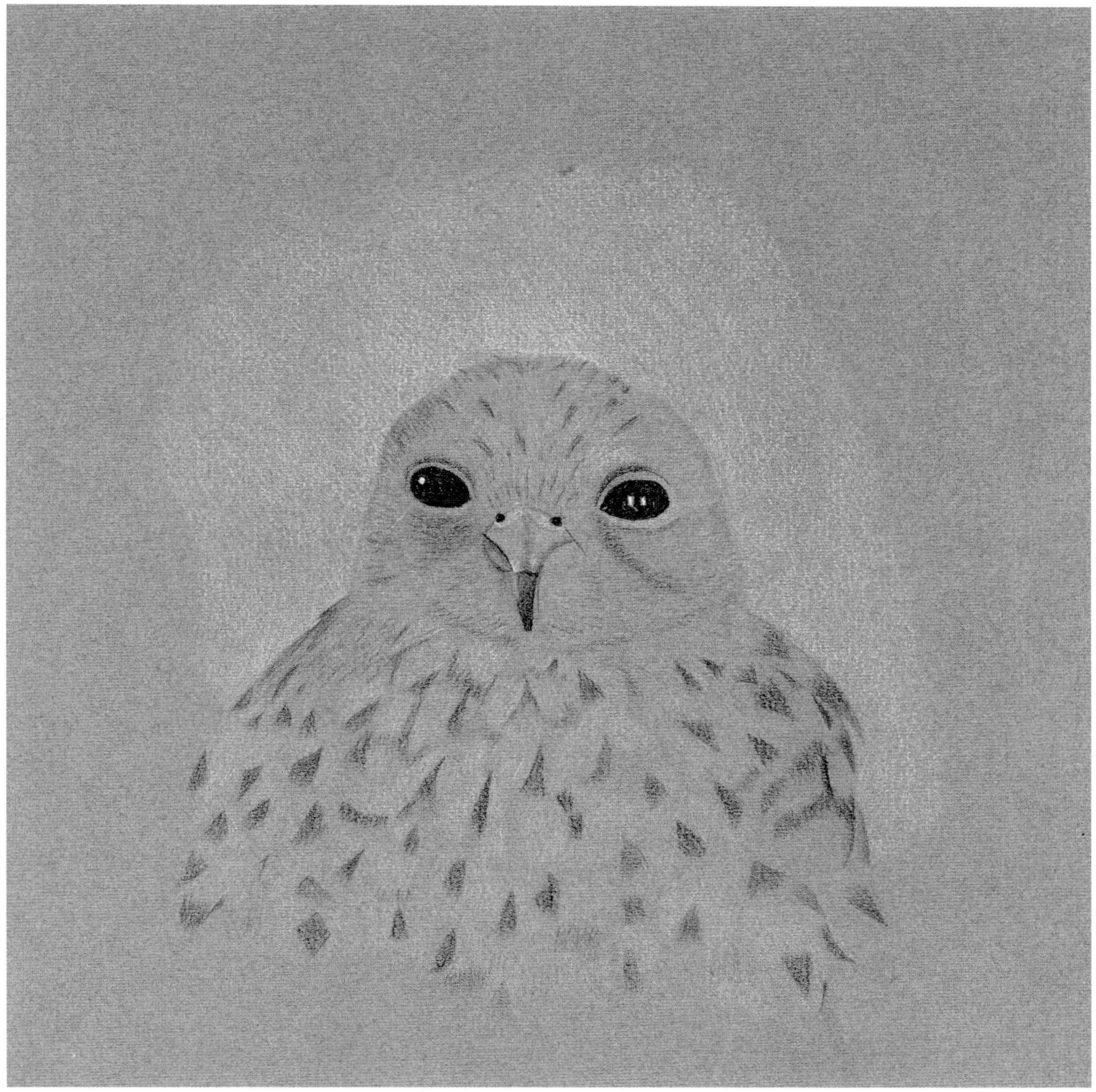

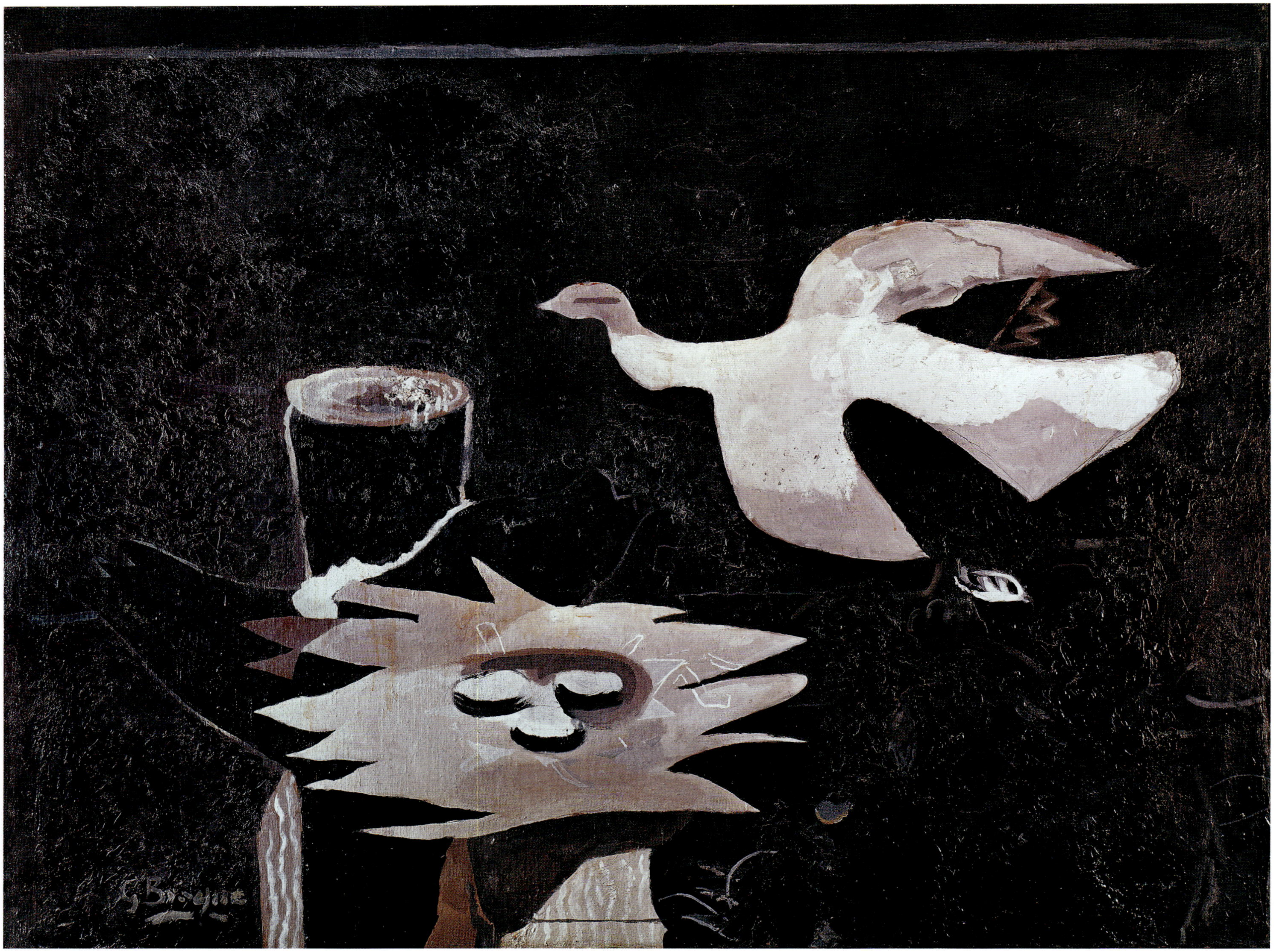

Georges Braque
(1882–1963)
The Bird and Its Nest
1955
Oil and sand on canvas
130.5 × 173.5 cm (51⅜ × 68⅜ in.)
Centre Pompidou, Paris

Birds make a frequent appearance in the work of Georges Braque. Beginning in the 1930s, he began to produce a series of pictures of his studio, all featuring a bird among the jumble of objects, paintbrushes, palettes and easels. At first the bird represented a picture within a picture, but eventually it took on a life of its own, and its distinctive silhouette in flight recurs in several works of the 1950s. In 1952 Braque was commissioned to decorate the ceiling of the Salle Henri II in the Louvre. He chose to fill the three ceiling panels with dark birds shown as simplified flat shapes outlined in white against a blue background. There is a little more detail in this picture, which he created three years later, as we can see that the bird is returning to its star-shaped nest containing three eggs. That year, Braque visited a bird sanctuary in the Camargue in the south of France, a trip that confirmed his avian fascination, but he always resisted any attempt by critics to read a symbolic significance into his favourite motif.

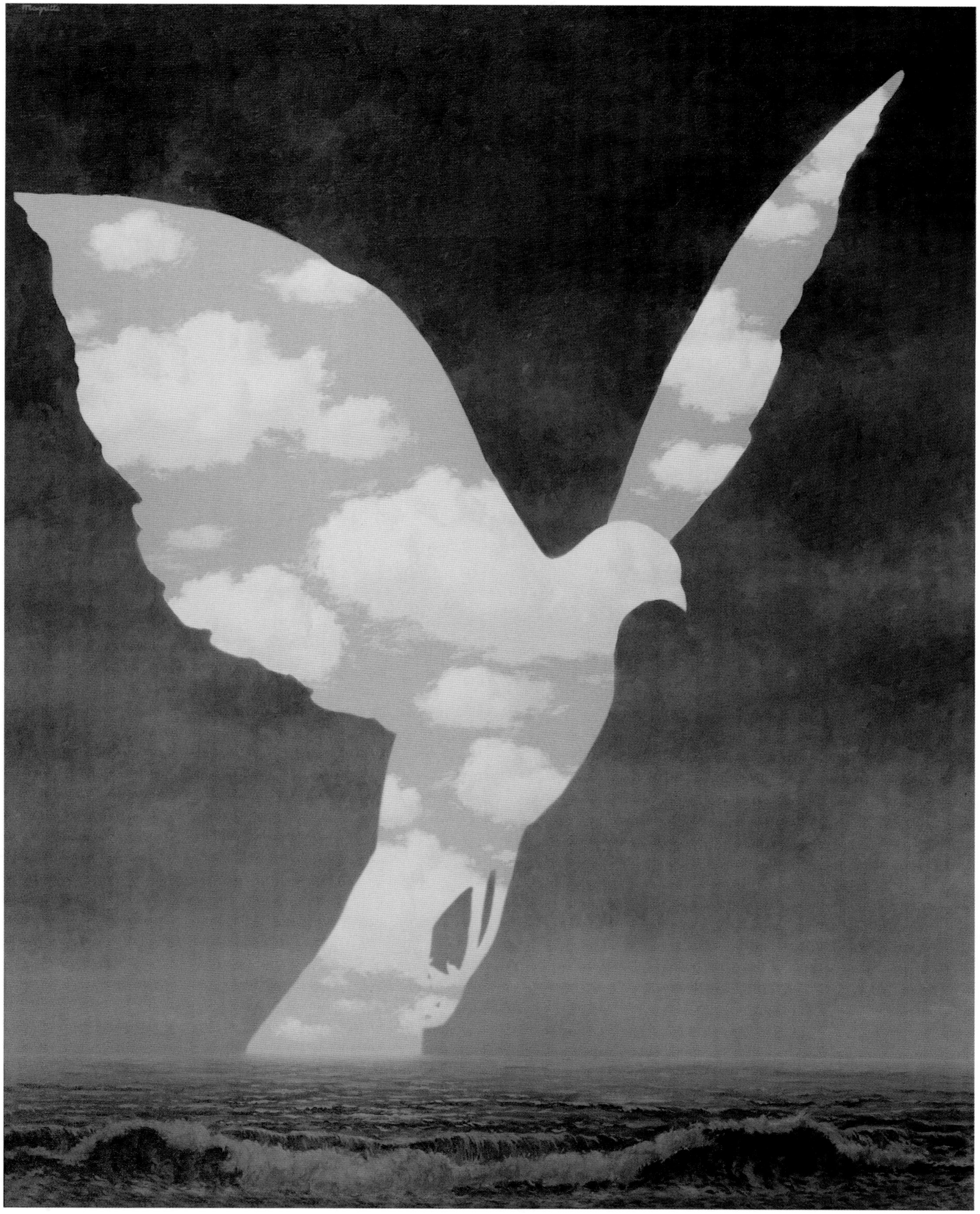

René Magritte
(1898–1967)
The Big Family
1963
Oil on canvas
100 × 81 cm (39⅜ × 31⅞ in.)
Private collection

The Belgian Surrealist painter René Magritte is well known for his memorable images, which bring together the banal and the exotic to disturbing effect. A number of his paintings seek to reconcile opposite states in order to reveal a less literal but more poetic reality. Several represent day and night simultaneously, and here a giant silhouette of a bird in flight reveals a cloudy daytime sky against a dusky background. The bird dominates the calm seascape, but there is a certain ambiguity about whether it suggests peace or menace. As is the case with so many of Magritte's canvases, the title is suggestive but baffling, and appears to have little relationship with the image. The bird is a constantly recurring motif in Magritte's work. In one painting, *Perspicacity* (1936; private collection), he shows himself at work on a painting of a bird in exactly the same pose as the one here, but using an egg as a model.

Craigie Aitchison (1926–2009)

Yellow Painting

1984
Oil and collage on canvas
30.5 × 40.6 cm (12 × 16 in.)
Private collection

The Scottish artist Craigie Aitchison does not fit neatly into any of the major art movements of the twentieth century. He was a loner who pursued his own idiosyncratic vision; his paintings had no obvious predecessors or imitators. But his simple, vibrant compositions, which feature a limited repertoire of birds, landscapes, dogs (usually Bedlington terriers) and scenes of the Crucifixion, found a ready public and a loyal following. Aitchison's bright palette was inspired by the early Italian masters Giotto and Piero della Francesca, whom he admired. The insistent two-dimensionality of the objects and beings he painted invests them with a disarmingly child-like quality, although the artist hated being described as naive. Because his figures are always shown in isolation against a flat background colour, they can sometimes appear rather vulnerable, almost fragile, but this painting of bird, berries, tree and butterfly communicates a sense of spontaneous joy.

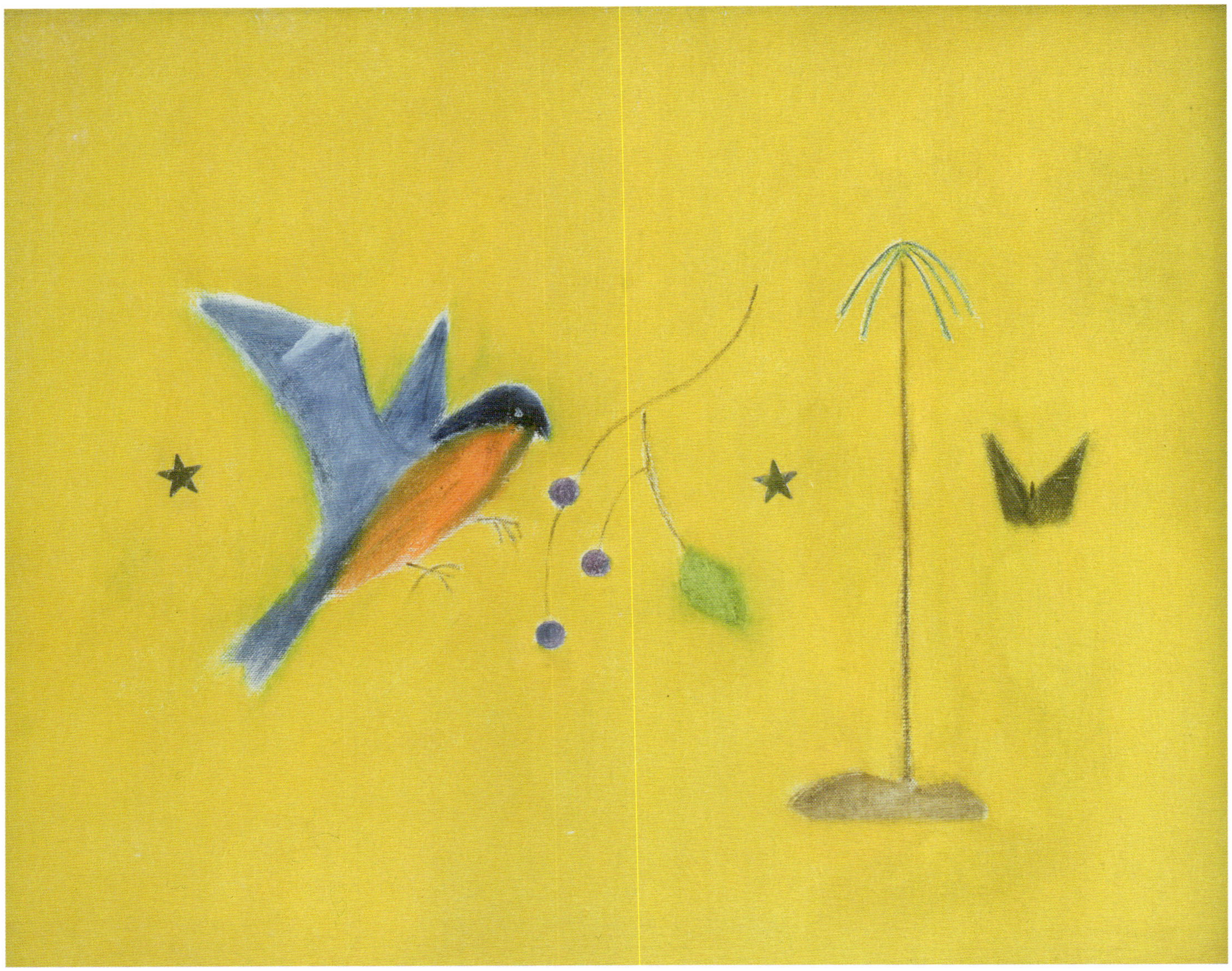

Cai Guo-Qiang
(born 1957)
Flying Together

2011
Styrofoam, resin, feathers and hide
Dimensions variable
Collection of the artist; on display at Mathaf, the Arab Museum of Modern Art, Doha

Twenty-seven falcons and a camel crowd together in mid-air in this installation by the leading Chinese artist Cai Guo-Qiang. The two creatures are icons of the Arab world, and the piece was commissioned by the Qatar Museums Authority for the artist's first solo exhibition in the region, which explored the historic trading links between the artist's home town of Quanzhou and the Middle East. Cai observed live falcons in the area, and his birds are so wonderfully lifelike that the viewer might assume that they are the result of the taxidermist's art; they are actually carefully constructed from styrofoam and feathers. The work is ambiguous: are the birds harming the camel or are they helping it to fly? The artist wants spectators to provide their own interpretation. He evidently enjoyed assembling the piece, saying: 'I'm just a big kid. I love things that move and fly.'

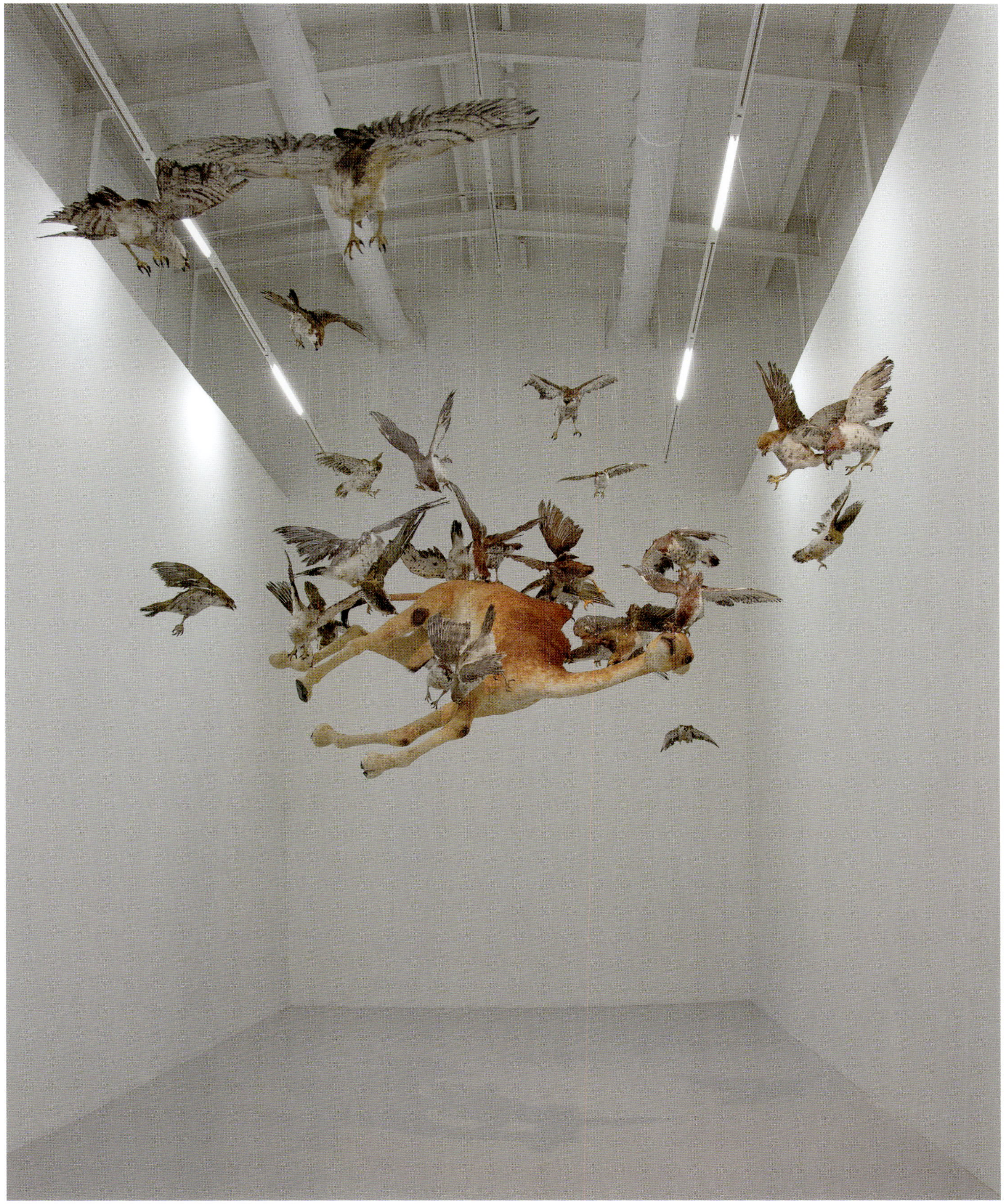

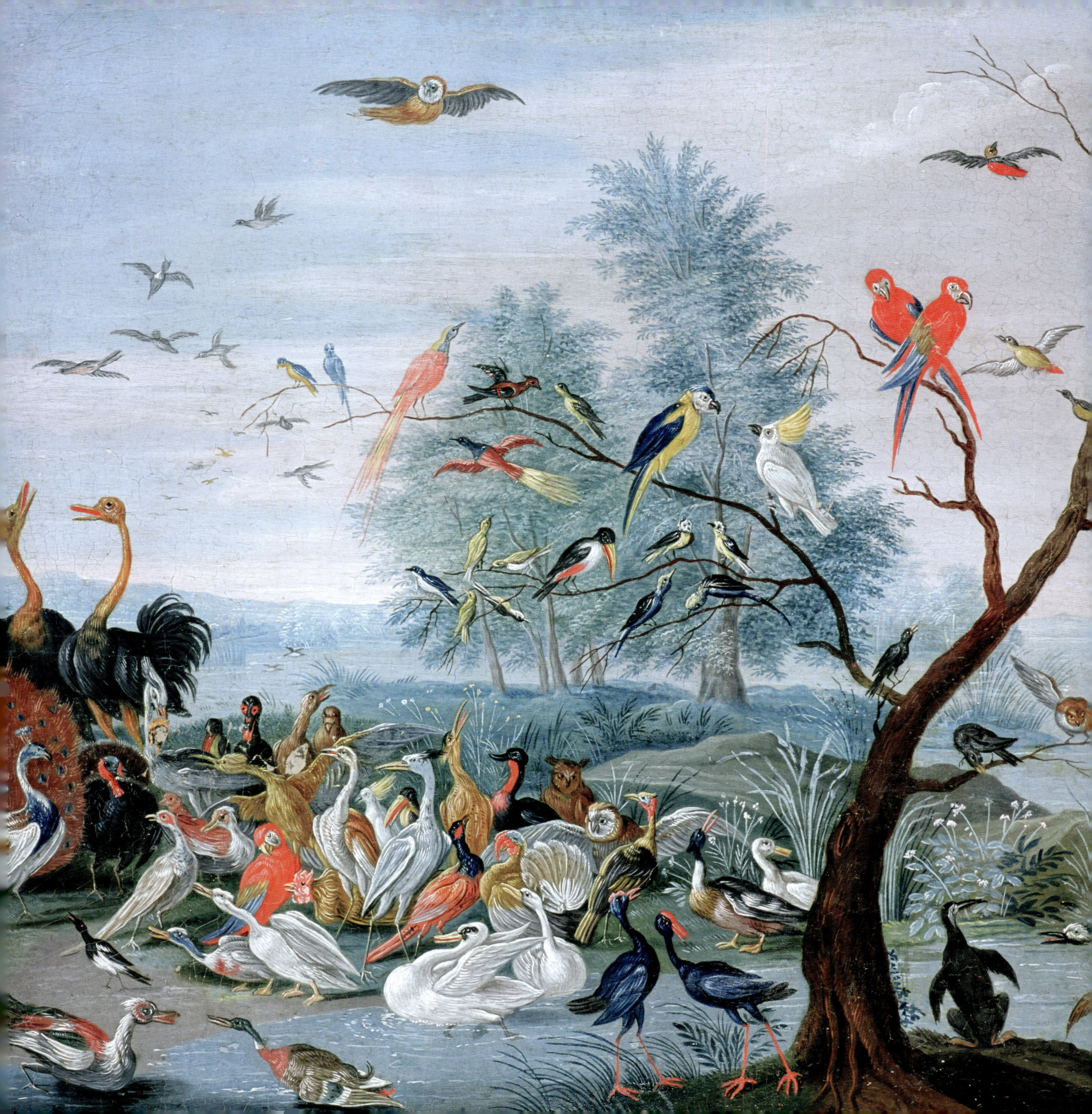

Timeline

c. 30,000 BC
An owl is etched on to the wall of the Chauvet Cave in southern France.

c. 30,000–17,000 BC
Snowy owls are depicted in the cave of Les Trois Frères in south-western France.

c. 17,000–16,000 BC
An auk is traced on the ceiling of the Cosquer Cave in southern France.

c. 15,000 BC
A bird on a stick and a bird–man are drawn in the Lascaux Caves in south-western France.

c. 2620 BC–1320 BC
Birds appear in the numerous wall decorations in the tombs of the valleys of the Kings, Queens and Nobles in Thebes, Egypt, as well as in Egyptian Books of the Dead. The scenes show evidence that birds are farmed as well as hunted.

c. 1323 BC
The pharaoh Tutankhamun is buried. His tomb contains a number of artefacts that relate to birds, including the famous vulture pendant.

c. 575–550 BC
The Laconian cup showing Zeus and the eagle is painted in southern Greece.

c. 520–510 BC
The Tomb of Hunting and Fishing in Tarquinia, Italy, is decorated with scenes featuring flocks of birds in flight.

c. 500 BC
The Greek author Aesop writes his fables, many of which use animals to illustrate a moral point. Birds appear as characters in several of the tales, and the stories later prove highly popular with artists.

414 BC
Aristophanes' play *The Birds* describes how all the birds gather together to create a new city in the sky to control communication between men and the gods.

c. 350 BC
The Greek philosopher Aristotle writes his *Historia Animalium*, which includes descriptions of some 140 bird species he recognized.

326 BC
Alexander the Great leads his army into the Punjab. When he returns home to Europe, he brings a green parrot, which becomes known as the Alexandrine parakeet.

2nd century BC
The Hellenic mosaic artist Sosos of Pergamon creates a composition showing doves perching on a bowl, which Pliny the Elder later describes as a supreme example of illusionism in mosaic art. It is much copied by successive generations of artists.

1st century BC–1st century AD
Mosaics and frescoes in the villas of Pompeii are decorated with scenes of birds in gardens, larders and river landscapes.

c. AD 8
The Roman poet Ovid completes his *Metamorphoses*, which describes the transformation of mythical figures into animal form. Artists from the Renaissance onwards draw upon the book for subject matter.

c. 77–79
Pliny the Elder writes his 37-volume *Historia Naturalis*, one volume of which is dedicated to birds. Medieval bestiaries later use it as a source of information.

2nd–3rd century AD
Birds appear in painted scenes in Roman catacombs.

c. 678–721
The Lindisfarne Gospels, produced by Eadfrith, Bishop of Lindisfarne, contains several stylized birds woven into its semi-abstract designs.

c. 800
The Book of Kells, a masterpiece of early Irish art, features a number of birds, including the eagle of St John.

c. 934
The Chinese artist Huang Quan produces a handscroll, *Animals Sketched from Nature*. His paintings of birds are so lifelike that they are said to fool real birds.

1177
The Persian poet Farid ud-Din Attar writes his *Conference of Birds*, an allegory on the soul's search for God.

c. 1240–50
Frederick II of Hohenstaufen, the Holy Roman Emperor, publishes a treatise on falconry, *De Arte Venandi cum Avibus* (*The Art of Hunting with Birds*), which includes several marginal illustrations of birds as well as ornithological observations.

1297–99
Giotto paints his famous *St Francis Preaching to the Birds* in the Upper Church of San Francesco in Assisi.

c. 1340
The margins of the Luttrell Psalter are decorated with everyday scenes featuring birds, including geese, hawks, hens and rooks.

c. 1380
Geoffrey Chaucer writes his long poem *A Parliament of Fowls*, which describes how birds gather on St Valentine's Day to choose their mates.

c. 1400–1407
The Sherborne Missal, produced in Dorset, contains about forty identifiable species of bird, including gannets, moorhens, storks, cormorants, wagtails, woodpeckers and robins.

c. 1434–45
Pisanello produces several detailed studies of birds from both dead and living examples.

1436
Jan van Eyck's *Madonna and Child with Canon George van der Paele* shows the Christ Child caressing a ring-necked parakeet.

1486
Dame Juliana Berners writes *The Boke of St Albans*; it describes which birds of prey are appropriate to each rank of society.

1486
Carlo Crivelli paints his *Annunciation, with St Emidius*, which includes several symbolic birds: a caged goldfinch, a dovecote with doves, a peacock and the Holy Spirit represented as a dove.

c. 1490–1500
Leonardo da Vinci makes detailed studies of the flight of birds in preparation for building his own flying machine.

c. 1500
Hieronymus Bosch's triptych *The Garden of Earthly Delights* contains several recognizable birds alongside fantasy hybrid creatures, such as a bird–man.

c. 1500–10
Beautifully painted birds feature in the work of Venetian artists including Vittore Carpaccio and Giovanni Bellini.

c. 1506
Raphael paints his famous *Madonna of the Goldfinch*, one of many paintings by Renaissance artists pairing the Virgin and infant Christ with a goldfinch.

1512
Albrecht Dürer draws his celebrated study of the wing of a blue roller – one of several studies of birds that he made around this time.

1515–16
Raphael produces a cartoon for the Sistine Chapel tapestries, *The Miraculous Draught of Fishes*, which features cranes and ravens.

c. 1526–28
Hans Holbein paints his portrait *Lady with a Squirrel and a Starling*.

c. 1532
Correggio produces a highly erotic *Leda and the Swan* for the Duke of Mantua.

1533
Hans Baldung Grien paints his *Madonna with Parrots*. The bird is in homage to his patron the Bishop of Strasbourg, a parrot-lover.

c. 1550
Tintoretto's large canvas *The Creation of the Animals* features birds darting across the sky.

1559
Pieter Bruegel the Elder's *Netherlandish Proverbs* includes a number of vignettes based on folk tales featuring birds.

1570s
Jacopo Zucchi's ceiling for the garden pavilion of the Villa Medici in Rome features a *trompe l'œil* pergola decorated with vines and birds.

c. 1585–90
John White makes five journeys to North America and sets up a colony in Virginia. The colony mysteriously vanishes, but White leaves a legacy of twenty-five watercolours of New World birds, as well as pictures of animals and the daily life of the Algonquin people.

1599–1603
Ulisse Aldovrandi publishes his three-volume *Ornithologia*, containing 685 woodcuts of birds.

1609
Peter Paul Rubens establishes his studio in Antwerp. He often includes birds in his work, many of them added by Frans Snyders.

c. 1610–15
Frans Snyders's scenes of kitchens and markets show several recognizable species of bird, helping modern scholars to reconstruct seventeenth-century eating habits.

1612
A consignment of exotic birds arrives at the court of the Mughal emperor Jahangir, who commissions his artists to paint them for his illustrated memoirs.

1626–28
Roelandt Savery bases his famous image of the now-extinct dodo on an example in Prince Maurice of Nassau's menagerie.

1629
Shah Jahan, the Mughal emperor, commissions a throne in the form of a small pavilion surmounted by peacocks. It takes pride of place at his palace in Delhi.

1633
Frans Hals's *Malle Babbe*, a character study of an elderly woman, shows an owl perched on her shoulder, possibly suggesting witchcraft, stupidity or drunkenness.

1639
Rembrandt paints a self-portrait with a dead bittern.

1650
Athanasius Kircher's musical encyclopedia *Musurgia Universalis* includes birdsong transcribed into musical notation, and a parrot saying 'hello' in Greek.

1650–76
Francis Barlow produces several paintings and etchings of birds. His compositions, which feature both native and exotic species, appear in his books *Birds and Beasts in Sixty-Seven Excellent and Useful Prints* (1655) and *Birds and Fowles of Various Species* (1658). He also illustrates Aesop's fables.

1654
Carel Fabritius produces his superlative study of a pet goldfinch next to a wall-mounted feeding box.

1676
Francis Willughby and John Ray publish their three-volume illustrated *Ornithologia*, which lays the foundations for modern ornithology.

c. 1685
Willem Wissing includes a cockatoo in his portrait of the English queen Mary of Modena. Parrots also feature in other seventeenth-century portraits, by Peter Lely, Godfrey Kneller and Michael Dahl.

1702
The French king Louis XIV appoints Alexandre-François Desportes as official painter of the royal hunt, and commissions the artist to record his menagerie.

c. 1705
Maria Sibylla Merian, a German artist specializing in insects and plants, travels to Surinam. The book she publishes on her return includes birds, focusing on aspects of their biology.

1731–38
Eleazar Albin, a German painter and writer, publishes his three-volume *Natural History of Birds*, the first bird book to be illustrated with hand-coloured etchings. It includes ten North American species. A later book on songbirds includes images of their eggs. Albin's designs are used by pottery firms as the basis of decoration for their wares.

1731–43
Mark Catesby publishes his *Natural History of Carolina, Florida and the Bahama Islands*, with 220 illustrations of flora and fauna, including birds.

1736
Charles Collins paints a set of twelve pictures showing British birds; these are later published as prints with the birds' names identified in English.

1742
William Hogarth's portrait *The Graham Children* shows a caged bullfinch being frightened by a cat.

1743–51
George Edwards publishes his four-volume *Natural History of Uncommon Birds*, with illustrations based on the specimens in Sir Hans Sloane's collection.

1749–1804
The French naturalist George-Louis Leclerc, Comte de Buffon, publishes his mammoth forty-four-volume encyclopedia *Histoire naturelle générale et particulière*, ten volumes of which are devoted to birds. About eighty artists are employed to produce the coloured plates, which are also sold separately. Almost 2000 of the plates feature birds.

1751
Jean-Siméon Chardin's *Bird Organ* shows a young woman teaching a canary to sing.

1753
Jean-Baptiste Oudry paints his *White Duck*, an exercise in tonal harmony. It is just one of his many carefully observed paintings of birds.

1758
Carl Linnaeus publishes the tenth edition of his *Systema Naturae*, a system of classification for the natural world. It lists 564 birds.

1759
Sir Hans Sloane's library and natural history collection, which includes an extensive avian section, opens in London to the public as the British Museum. The flora and fauna specimens later become part of the Natural History Museum.

1765
Jean-Baptiste Greuze's *Girl with a Dead Canary* depicts a young woman mourning her pet. Denis Diderot interprets it as an allegory on lost virginity.

1768
Joseph Wright paints *An Experiment on a Bird in the Air Pump*, which shows a white cockatoo at the centre of a scientific demonstration.

1768–79
Captain Cook's three voyages of discovery bring back over 200 new bird specimens from newly discovered parts of the world, as well as bird illustrations by Sydney Parkinson and William Ellis.

1775
Sir Ashton Lever opens his private natural history museum to the London public. On display are many stuffed birds brought back from Captain Cook's voyages.

1780s–1790s
Sarah Stone, a rare example of a female natural history painter, exhibits her paintings of birds at London's Royal Academy.

c. 1790
Louis-Léopold Boilly's *Couple with an Escaped Bird* provokes a scandal with its sexual innuendo.

1791
Mozart composes his opera *The Magic Flute*, which features the character of Papageno, the bird-catcher, who is traditionally represented covered in bird feathers.

1795
The British artist George Stubbs begins work on his comparative anatomical study of humans, tigers and birds. It is unfinished at his death.

1796–1808
The French naturalist François Levaillant commissions the artist Jacques Barraband to produce the illustrations for his books on the birds of Africa and such exotic species as parrots and birds of paradise.

1797
Thomas Bewick, a British artist, publishes his two-volume *History of British Birds*, containing 448 wood engravings.

1808–14
Alexander Wilson publishes his *American Ornithology*, the first guide to birds to be produced in America with coloured plates.

1815–16
J.M.W. Turner produces twenty watercolour studies of birds for his friend Walter Fawkes's book on ornithology.

1826
The Zoological Society of London is founded by Stamford Raffles. It opens the world's first scientific zoo two years later.

1827
John Gould, who started out as a taxidermist, becomes 'curator and preserver' to the newly established Zoological Society's museum collection in London. Over the next half-century Gould publishes many books on birds from around the world: the Himalayas, Australia, Europe and Great Britain. His wife, Elizabeth, and Edward Lear provide several of the illustrations, which feature a number of previously unknown species.

1827–38
John James Audubon publishes his multi-volume *Birds of America*, a groundbreaking work featuring 435 hand-coloured plates of birds shown life-sized.

1830s
The Japanese artist Ando Hiroshige begins to specialize in paintings of flowers and birds. Katsushika Hokusai, another Japanese artist, also paints birds, and his work is especially appreciated in the West.

1830–32
The youthful Edward Lear publishes his *Illustrations of the Family of Psittacidae, or Parrots*.

1836
Charles Darwin's voyage on the *Beagle* brings back several birds from the New World. In his identification of the birds Darwin is assisted by the ornithologist John Gould. It emerges that the mockingbirds, or mocking thrushes, on two islands in the Galapagos archipelago differ from each other. The observation is Darwin's first hint that species could evolve over time – a revolutionary theory that he published in 1859 in *On the Origin of Species*.

1839
Sir Edwin Landseer paints a portrait of Queen Victoria's pets, which include a macaw and lovebirds.

1841
The invention of oil paint in tubes makes it easier for artists to move out of the studio to paint outdoors.

1847
London Zoo begins admitting paying visitors to aid funding.

1851
At the Great Exhibition in London, John Gould displays 1500 hummingbirds mounted in glass cases. Stuffed birds are by now popular in Victorian homes.

1851
The German artist Josef Wolf is appointed official artist to the Zoological Society of London. His drawings and paintings have a liveliness that owes a great deal to the time he spends sketching out of doors.

1858
The British Ornithologists' Union is founded with the aim of promoting the study of birds in order to understand their biology.

1863–70
The American artist Martin Johnson Heade makes three trips to South America and studies hummingbirds.

1869
The Dutch artist John Gerrard Keulemans comes to London. He becomes one of the most prolific illustrators of books on birds in late Victorian Britain, recording many new species that were being brought back from expeditions all over the world.

1870s
The English critic John Ruskin produces exquisite watercolour studies of plumage and peacocks' feathers. Around this time the peacock motif is taken up enthusiastically by artists and designers of the Arts and Crafts, Aesthetic and Art Nouveau movements. The craze lasts until the turn of the century.

1874
The Duke of Westminster invites the artist Henry Stacy Marks to produce twelve decorative panels for his Cheshire home, Eaton Hall, which has a parrot house.

1875–76
Pyotr Ilyich Tchaikovsky composes his ballet *Swan Lake*, based on the Russian folk tale of a princess who is turned into a swan.

1876–77
J.A.M. Whistler designs the Peacock Room (now in the Freer Gallery of Art, Washington, D.C.) for the London residence of his patron Frederick Leyland.

1880s
The Swedish artist Bruno Liljefors begins to paint carefully observed pictures of birds and animals set in the landscape. His naturalism, married to an artistic sensibility moulded by Impressionism, earns him great praise.

1883–86
The photographer Eadweard Muybridge produces a sequence of images that capture the movement of a bird in flight.

1886
In New York, George Bird Grinnell founds the Audubon Society, dedicated to the preservation of birds and their eggs. It becomes a nationwide organization in 1905.

1889
Emily Williamson founds the Plumage League in Manchester to protest against the use of rare birds' feathers in clothing. It is the forerunner of the Royal Society for the Protection of Birds.

1895
The Danish illustrator Henrik Grönvold becomes the Natural History Museum's unofficial artist. He prepares many anatomical studies of birds for the museum and illustrates several bird books. These expensively produced hand-coloured lithographed volumes fall out of fashion after the First World War.

1898–99
The British artist G.F. Watts paints *A Dedication* as a protest against 'the senseless and cruel destruction of bird life and beauty'.

1899
The Scottish artist Archibald Thorburn, Vice President of the Royal Society for the Protection of Birds, designs the society's first Christmas card. He designs nineteen such cards before his death in 1935, donating all but one of the paintings free of charge to the society.

1907
A technique of aerial photography using time-delay cameras strapped to homing pigeons is developed by the German apothecary Julius Neubronner.

1908
Beatrix Potter's popular children's book *The Tale of Jemima Puddle-Duck* is published. The central character is a duck dressed in a bonnet and shawl.

1913
The Futurist artist Giacomo Balla paints *The Flight of Swifts*, which tracks the flight paths of birds outside a building.

1913–14
The portable 35-millimetre camera is invented by the German Oskar Barnack; it does not use plate-glass negatives and can be taken into the field, but it is not mass-produced until 1925.

1914
Henri Gaudier-Brzeska produces his sculpture *Bird Swallowing a Fish*, which marries the simplified shape of a diving bird with the forms of the machine age.

1915–19
Stanley Spencer records the annual ritual of marking swans on the River Thames in his *Swan Upping at Cookham*.

1920s
Max Ernst invents Loplop, a bird that represents his alter ego. It appears in several of his works.

c. 1920–40
Constantin Brancusi produces a number of pared-down sculptures of birds in flight.

1921
The Importation of Plumage (Prohibition) Act is passed in Britain, and the wearing of feathers begins to fall out of fashion.

1922
Paul Klee produces his watercolour *Twittering Machine*, showing sketchily outlined birds as part of a music box.

1934
Walt Disney Productions creates the much-loved cartoon character Donald Duck.

1941
The Mexican artist Frida Kahlo paints a self-portrait, *Me and My Parrots*, one of a number of paintings by her which feature pet birds.

1949
The World Peace Congress adopts Pablo Picasso's dove of peace as its emblem.

1952
Georges Braque decorates a ceiling in the Louvre, Paris, with simplified forms of birds on a blue background.

1953–79
The British wildlife painter Charles Tunnicliffe provides cover illustrations for the Royal Society for the Protection of Birds (RSPB) magazine. His bird illustrations also appear in several books for adults and children.

1963
Alfred Hitchcock makes *The Birds*, a terrifying film in which birds in a California town attack people with increasing viciousness.

2011
The Chinese artist Cai Guo-Qiang creates *Flying Together*, an installation featuring falcons and a camel, in Qatar.

2011
The *Ghosts of Gone Birds* exhibition in London features pictures of birds by a variety of artists, musicians and authors, who have all donated their work to raise funds for BirdLife International's Preventing Extinction programme.

Further Reading

BIRDS AND BIRD ART

John James Audubon, *The Audubon Reader*, ed. Richard Rhodes, New York (Albert A. Knopf) 2006

Simon Armitage and Tim Dee (eds), *The Poetry of Birds*, London (Viking) 2009

Janet Backhouse, *Medieval Birds in the Sherborne Missal*, London (British Library) 2001

Tim Birkhead, *The Wisdom of Birds: An Illustrated History of Ornithology*, London (Bloomsbury) 2008

Simona Cohen, *Animals as Disguised Symbols in Renaissance Art*, Leiden (Brill) 2008

Jonathan Elphick, *Birds: The Art of Ornithology*, London (Scriptum Editions) 2004

Graeme Gibson, *The Bedside Book of Birds*, London (Bloomsbury) 2005

David Hill, *Turner's Birds: Bird Studies from Farnley Hall*, Oxford (Phaidon) 1988

Christine E. Jackson, *Bird Illustrators: Some Artists in Early Lithography*, London (H.F. & G. Witherby) 1975

——, *Great Bird Paintings of the World, Volume 1: The Old Masters*, Woodbridge, Suffolk (Antique Collectors' Club) 1993

——, *Bird Painting: The Eighteenth Century*, Woodbridge, Suffolk (Antique Collectors' Club) 1994

——, *A Dictionary of Bird Artists of the World*, Woodbridge, Suffolk (Antique Collectors' Club) 1999

——, *Peacock*, London (Reaktion Books) 2006

Wilhelmina Mary Feemster Jashemski and Frederick Gustav Meyer (eds), *The Natural History of Pompeii*, Cambridge (Cambridge University Press) 2002

Maureen Lambourne, *The Art of Bird Illustration*, London (Quantum Publishing) 2002

Jeremy Mynott, *Birdscapes: Birds in Our Imagination and Experience*, Princeton, New Jersey (Princeton University Press) 2009

Peter Tate, *Flights of Fancy: Birds in Myth, Legend and Superstition*, London (Random House) 2007

David Turner, *Was Beethoven a Birdwatcher? A Quirky Look at Birds in History and Culture*, Chichester (Summersdale Publishers) 2011

Hope B. Werness, *The Continuum Encyclopedia of Animal Symbolism in Art*, London and New York (Continuum) 2003

Darryl Wheye and Donald Kennedy, *Humans, Nature, and Birds: Science Art from Cave Walls to Computer Screens*, New Haven, Conn., and London (Yale University Press) 2008

William Brunsdon Yapp, *Birds in Medieval Manuscripts*, London (British Library) 1981

ART HISTORY AND INDIVIDUAL ARTISTS

David Bindman, *Hogarth*, London (Thames & Hudson) 1981

Robin Blake, *George Stubbs and the Wide Creation: Animals, People and Places in the Life of George Stubbs, 1724–1806*, London (Chatto & Windus) 2005

Gian Carlo Calza, *Ukiyo-e*, London (Phaidon) 2005

Jean Clottes, *Cave Art*, London (Phaidon) 2008

Robert Descharnes and Gilles Néret, *Salvador Dalí, 1904–1989: The Paintings*, Cologne (Taschen) 2007

Matthi Forrer, *Hokusai*, Munich (Prestel) 2010

Wayne E. Franits, *Dutch Seventeenth-century Genre Painting: Its Stylistic and Thematic Evolution*, New Haven, Conn., and London (Yale University Press) 2004

Boris Friedewald, *Paul Klee: Life and Work*, Munich (Prestel) 2011

Andrew Graham-Dixon (editorial consultant), *Art: The Definitive Visual Guide*, London (Dorling Kindersley) 2008

John Guy and Deborah Swallow (eds), *Arts of India: 1550–1900*, London (V&A Publications) 1990

Peter Humfrey, *Painting in Renaissance Venice*, New Haven, Conn., and London (Yale University Press) 1996

Henri Loyrette (ed.), *Nineteenth-century French Art: From Romanticism to Impressionism, Post-Impressionism and Art Nouveau*, Paris (Flammarion) 2007

Sylvia Martin, *Futurism*, Cologne (Taschen) 2005

Susie Nash, *Northern Renaissance Art*, Oxford (Oxford University Press) 2008

Patrick O'Brian, *Picasso*, London (Collins) 1976

Eric Shanes, *Constantin Brancusi*, New York (Abbeville Press) 1989

Seymour Slive, *Dutch Painting: 1600–1800*, New Haven, Conn., and London (Yale University Press) 1998

Walter Spies, *Max Ernst: A Retrospective*, Munich (Prestel) 1991

Jane Stevenson, *Edward Burra: Twentieth-century Eye*, London (Jonathan Cape) 2007

Ingo Walther, *Art of the 20th Century*, Cologne (Taschen) 2005

Patricia Bjaaland Welch, *Chinese Art: A Guide to Motifs and Visual Imagery*, Tokyo (Tuttle Publishing) 2008

Norbert Wolf, *Dürer*, Munich (Prestel) 2010

Frank Zöllner and Johannes Nathan, *Leonardo da Vinci 1452–1519: The Complete Paintings and Drawings*, Cologne (Taschen) 2007

EXHIBITION CATALOGUES

Braque: The Late Works, exhib. cat. by John Golding, Sophie Bowness, Isabelle Monod-Fontaine, Menil Foundation, Houston, 1997

Chardin, exhib. cat. by Pierre Rosenberg, Galeries nationales du Grand Palais, Paris, 7 September–22 November 1999; Kunstmuseum and Kunsthalle, Düsseldorf, 5 December 1999–20 February 2000; Royal Academy, London, 9 March–28 May 2000; The Metropolitan Museum of Art, New York, 19 June–17 September 2000

Hiroshige, exhib. cat. by Matthi Forrer, Royal Academy of Arts, London, July–September 1997

The Parrot in Art: From Dürer to Elizabeth Butterworth, exhib. cat. by Richard Verdi, Barber Institute of Fine Arts, University of Birmingham, 2007

Pisanello, Painter to the Renaissance Court, exhib. cat. by Luke Syson and Dillian Gordon, The National Gallery, London, 2001

Index

Page numbers in *italic* refer to the illustrations

Picture credits

l = left; r = right; t = top; b = bottom

AKG Images: jacket front, 155; Alan Jacobs Gallery, London/The Bridgeman Art Library: 176; Allen Memorial Art Museum, Oberlin College, Ohio/R.T. Miller , Jr., Fund/ The Bridgeman Art Library: 236; Anglesey Abbey, Cambridgeshire/National Trust Photographic Library/John Hammond/ The Bridgeman Art Library: 170, 171t, b; Art Gallery of South Australia, Adelaide/ M.J.M. Carter AO Collection/The Bridgeman Art Library: 238; © The Artist/Image courtesy Mathaf:Arab Museum of Modern Art, Doha: 261; Ashmolean Museum, University of Oxford/The Bridgeman Art Library: 86, 221, 233; Basilica di San Marco, Venice/Giraudon/The Bridgeman Art Library: 62b; Bibliothèque des Arts Décoratifs, Paris/ Archives Charmet/The Bridgeman Art Library: 112; Bibliothèque de l'Opéra Garnier, Paris/Archives Charmet/The Bridgeman Art Library: 108; Bolton Museum and Art Gallery/The Bridgeman Art Library: 158; Bonhams/Private collection: 165; The Bridgeman Art Library: 42, 44; © Bristol City Museum and Art Gallery/The Bridgeman Art Library: 84; British Library, London/ The Bridgeman Art Library: 91, 92; British Library, London/© British Library Board. All rights reserved/The Bridgeman Art Library: 61, 146; © British Library Board. All rights reserved/The Bridgeman Art Library: 11, 13; British Museum, London/The Bridgeman Art Library: 8r, 45; Brooklyn Museum of Art, New York/The Bridgeman Art Library: 87; Brooklyn Museum of Art, New York/ Purchased with funds given by Susan Beningson, Dr and Mrs Richard Dickes, Asian Art Council & Carll H. de Silver Fund/ The Bridgeman Art Library: 189; Brooklyn Museum of Art, New York/Dick S. Ramsay Fund/The Bridgeman Art Library: 4, 161; Brooklyn Museum of Art, New York/Gift of Anna Ferris/The Bridgeman Art Library: 196; Brooklyn Museum of Art, New York/Ella C. Woodward Memorial Fund/The Bridgeman Art Library: 206; Burrell Collection, Glasgow/The Bridgeman Art Library: 127; © Butler Institute of American Art, Youngstown, Ohio/Museum Purchase 1957/ The Bridgeman Art Library: 250; Ca' d'Oro, Venice/The Bridgeman Art Library: 70; Castello della Manta, Saluzzo, Italy/Alinari/ The Bridgeman Art Library: 126; Catacombs of San Sebastiano, Rome/De Agostini Picture Library/V. Pirozzi/The Bridgeman Art Library: 54t; Christie's Images/photograph © Christie's Images/The Bridgeman Art Library: 116; Convent of St Tomas, Ávila, Spain/The Bridgeman Art Library: 68; © CORBIS: 7b; The Rt Hon. Earl of Derby/ The Bridgeman Art Library: 156; Detroit Institute of Arts/Founders Society Purchase/ The Bridgeman Art Library: 194–95; Egyptian National Museum, Cairo/ The Bridgeman Art Library: jacket back bl, 39, 46; © Estate of C.F. Tunnicliffe, photograph © Bonhams, London/The Bridgeman Art Library: 33; Fitzwilliam Museum, University of Cambridge/ The Bridgeman Art Library: 10, 20b, 207, 208; The Fleming-Wyfold Art Foundation/ The Bridgeman Art Library: 164; Freer Gallery of Art, Smithsonian Institution, USA/Gift of Charles Lang Freer/ The Bridgeman Art Library: 188, 200, 201; Freud Museum, London/The Bridgeman Art Library: 48; Fürstlich Schwarzenberg'sche Verwaltung, Vienna/The Bridgeman Art Library: 103; Galerie de Jonckheere, Paris/ The Bridgeman Art Library: 23, 81; Galleria dell'Accademia, Florence/The Bridgeman Art Library: 64; Galleria dell'Accademia, Venice/ Cameraphoto Arte Venezia/The Bridgeman Art Library: 79; Galleria Alberto della Ragione, Florence/The Bridgeman Art Library/© ADAGP, Paris and DACS, London 2012: 249; Galleria Doria Pamphilj, Rome/Alinari/The Bridgeman Art Library: 102; Gemäldegalerie, Berlin/The Bridgeman Art Library: 94; Gemäldegalerie Alte Meister, Dresden/© Staatliche Kunstsammlungen Dresden/The Bridgeman Art Library: 18l, 129; Gemäldegalerie Alte Meister, Kassel/ © Museumslandschaft Hessen Kassel/Ute Brunzel/The Bridgeman Art Library: 22; Germanisches Nationalmuseum, Nuremberg (Nürnberg)/The Bridgeman Art Library: 77, 78; Giraudon/The Bridgeman Art Library: 8l, 40, 41; Graphische Sammlung Albertina, Vienna/The Bridgeman Art Library: 147; R.G. Gunn/courtesy the Jawoyn Association: 7t; Hamburger Kunsthalle, Hamburg/ The Bridgeman Art Library: 26, 214; © Estate of the artist/Harris Museum and Art Gallery, Preston/The Bridgeman Art Library: 140; © Herbert Art Gallery & Museum, Coventry/ The Bridgeman Art Library: 118; Hermitage, St Petersburg/The Bridgeman Art Library: 28, 69, 106l, r; Ikonen-Museum, Recklinghausen, Germany/Giraudon/The Bridgeman Art Library: 119; Institute of Oriental Studies, St Petersburg/Giraudon/The Bridgeman Art Library: 199; The J. Paul Getty Museum, Los Angeles: 133; Johnny van Haeften Gallery, London/The Bridgeman Art Library: 148; © Kettle's Yard, University of Cambridge/ The Bridgeman Art Library: 245; Kunsthistorisches Museum, Vienna/ The Bridgeman Art Library: 100, 128; Kyoto National Museum/The Bridgeman Art Library: 190; Laing Art Gallery, Newcastle upon Tyne/© Tyne & Wear Archives & Museums/The Bridgeman Art Library: 230; © Lambeth Palace Library, London/ The Bridgeman Art Library: 62t; Leeds Museums and Galleries (City Art Gallery)/ The Bridgeman Art Library: 154, 159; Leeds Museums and Galleries (City Art Gallery)/ The Bridgeman Art Library/© The Estate of Stanley Spencer 2012. All rights reserved DACS: 247; Collection of the Earl of Leicester, Holkham Hall, Norfolk/ The Bridgeman Art Library: 20t; Louvre, Paris/The Bridgeman Art Library: 50, 227; Louvre, Paris/Giraudon/The Bridgeman Art Library: 134t, 145, 205, 222; Louvre, Paris/ Peter Willi/The Bridgeman Art Library: 74; Mauritzhuis, The Hague/The Bridgeman Art Library: 213; Metropolitan Museum of Art, New York/Giraudon/The Bridgeman Art Library: 32; Michaelis Collection, Cape Town/The Bridgeman Art Library: 172; Musée des Arts Décoratifs, Paris/Peter Willi/ The Bridgeman Art Library: 237; Musée des Beaux-Arts, Dunkirk/Giraudon/ The Bridgeman Art Library: 183; Musée des Beaux-Arts, Marseille/Giraudon/ The Bridgeman Art Library: 123, 135; Musée des Beaux Arts, Orléans/Giraudon/ The Bridgeman Art Library: 82; Musée de la Chasse et de la Nature, Paris/Archives Charmet/The Bridgeman Art Library: 27l; Musée Condé, Chantilly, France/Giraudon/ The Bridgeman Art Library: 55, 125; Musée Crozatier, Le Puy-en-Velay, France/Giraudon/ The Bridgeman Art Library: 110b; Musée Guimet, Paris/The Bridgeman Art Library: 198; Musée Lapidaire, Vienne, France/ Giraudon/The Bridgeman Art Library: 9t; Musée National d'Art Moderne, Centre Pompidou, Paris/Giraudon/The Bridgeman Art Library/© ADAGP, Paris and DACS, London 2012: 258; Musée National d'Art Moderne, Centre Pompidou, Paris/Giraudon/ The Bridgeman Art Library/© ADAGP, Paris and DACS, London 2012: 258; Musée Nationale du Bardo, Le Bardo, Tunisia/ The Bridgeman Art Library: 51; Musée d'Orsay, Paris/The Bridgeman Art Library: 139; Musée d'Orsay, Paris/Giraudon/ The Bridgeman Art Library: 141; Museo Archeologico Nazionale, Naples/Alinari/ The Bridgeman Art Library: 37, 52–53; Museo Correr, Venice/The Bridgeman Art

Library: 17r; Museo e Gallerie Nazionale di Capodimonte, Naples/Alinari/The Bridgeman Art Library: 89, 98; Museo Nazionale Archeologico, Tarquinia, Italy/Giraudon/The Bridgeman Art Library: 55; Museo Picasso, Barcelona/Giraudon/The Bridgeman Art Library/© Succession Picasso/DACS, London 2012: 241, 252; Museo del Templo Mayor, Mexico City/Bildarchiv Steffens/Henri Stierlin/The Bridgeman Art Library: 120; Museo de la Universidad, Salamanca, Spain/The Bridgeman Art Library: 93; Museum of Fine Arts, Boston, Massachusetts/William Sturgis Bigelow Collection/The Bridgeman Art Library: 192; The Museum of Islamic Art, Qatar JE.69.2001: 204; National Gallery, London/The Bridgeman Art Library: 14r, 19, 65, 67, 71, 143, 152, 225l, r; © National Gallery of Scotland, Edinburgh/The Bridgeman Art Library: 217, 223b; National Gallery of Victoria, Melbourne/Purchased through the Art Foundation of Victoria/The Bridgeman Art Library: 224; National Gallery of Victoria, Melbourne/Felton Bequest/The Bridgeman Art Library: 228; National Museum Wales/The Bridgeman Art Library: 175, 216; © National Museums of Scotland/The Bridgeman Art Library: 209; © Nationalmuseum, Stockholm/The Bridgeman Art Library: 137, 218; Natural History Museum, London/The Bridgeman Art Library: 157; His Grace the Duke of Norfolk, Arundel Castle/The Bridgeman Art Library: 12; © Oxford University Museum of Natural History/The Bridgeman Art Library: 149; Padua Baptistery, Padua/Alinari/The Bridgeman Art Library: 16b; The Palace Museum, Beijing: 187; Palazzo Ducale, Venice/Cameraphoto Arte Venezia/The Bridgeman Art Library: 95; Palazzo Medici-Riccardi, Florence/The Bridgeman Art Library: 66; Peggy Guggenheim Foundation, Venice/The Bridgeman Art Library/© ADAGP, Paris and DACS, London 2012: 253; Philadelphia Museum of Art, Pennsylvania/Gift of John T. Dorrance, 1965/The Bridgeman Art Library: 223t; Photo Scala, Florence – courtesy of the Ministero Beni e Att. Culturali: 75; Pinacoteca Nazionale, Bologna/Alinari/The Bridgeman Art Library: 83; Pinakothek der Modern, Munich/Bayerische Staatsgemäldesammlungen/The Bridgeman Art Library: 246; Prado, Madrid/The Bridgeman Art Library: 59, 72–73; Private collection/Accademia Italiana, London/The Bridgeman Art Library: 9b, 56; Private collection/photograph © Agnew's, London/The Bridgeman Art Library: 231; Private collection/Archives Charmet/The Bridgeman Art Library/© Succession Picasso/DACS, London 2012: 35; Private collection/photograph © Bonhams, London/The Bridgeman Art Library: 114; Private collection/The Bridgeman Art Library: jacket back br, 21b, 27r, 29r, 130, 162, 254, 257, 260; Private collection/The Bridgeman Art Library/© ADAGP, Paris and DACS, London 2012: 30r, 259; Private collection/The Bridgeman Art Library/Chagall ®/© ADAGP, Paris and DACS, London 2012: 248; Private collection/Charles Plante Fine Arts/The Bridgeman Art Library: 24l, 29l; Private collection/photograph © Christie's Images/The Bridgeman Art Library: 57, 173; Private collection/photograph © The Fine Art Society, London/The Bridgeman Art Library: 138, 163; Private collection/Giraudon/The Bridgeman Art Library/© Salvador Dalí, Fundació Gala-Salvador Dalí, DACS, 2012: 34; Private collection/Giraudon/The Bridgeman Art Library/© DACS 2012: 243; Private collection/© John Mitchell Fine Paintings/The Bridgeman Art Library: 150; Private collection/Johnny van Haeften Ltd, London/The Bridgeman Art Library: 15, 99, 132; Private collection/© Lawrence Steigrad Fine Arts, New York/The Bridgeman Art Library: 25, 220; Private collection/photograph © The Maas Gallery, London/The Bridgeman Art Library: 113, 234; Private collection/photograph © Peter Nahum at The Leicester Galleries, London/The Bridgeman Art Library: 115, 232; Private collection/Peter Newark Western Americana/The Bridgeman Art Library: 121; Private collection/photograph © Philip Mould Ltd, London/The Bridgeman Art Library: 111, 219; Private collection/photograph © Rafael Valls Gallery, London/The Bridgeman Art Library: 21t, 105, 107, 131, 167, 174, 178, 179, 180, 182; Private collection/photograph © Heini Schneebeli/The Bridgeman Art Library: 43; Private collection/The Stapleton Collection/The Bridgeman Art Library: 117; Pushkin Museum, Moscow/The Bridgeman Art Library: 215; Real Monasterio de El Escorial, El Escorial, Spain/Giraudon/The Bridgeman Art Library: 14l; Roy Miles Fine Paintings/The Bridgeman Art Library: jacket back tl, 24r, 181; The Royal Collection © 2011 Her Majesty Queen Elizabeth II/The Bridgeman Art Library: 151, 211, 229; © Estate of the artist, courtesy of Lefevre Fine Art, London/Royal Pavilion, Libraries & Museums, Brighton & Hove/The Bridgeman Art Library: 255; San Francesco, Upper Church, Assisi/Alinari/The Bridgeman Art Library: 63; Schloss Neuschwanstein, Bavaria/De Agostini Picture Library/A. Dagli Orti/The Bridgeman Art Library: 109; Scottish National Gallery of Modern Art, Edinburgh/The Bridgeman Art Library/© Salvador Dalí, Fundació Gala-Salvador Dalí, DACS, 2012: 256; Sheffield Galleries and Museums Trust/The Bridgeman Art Library: 160; Staatliche Gemäldegalerie, Berlin/The Bridgeman Art Library: 96–97 (all); Stadtisches Museum, Mulheim, Germany/The Bridgeman Art Library: jacket back tr, 244; Stirling Maxwell Collection, Pollok House, Glasgow/© Culture and Sport Glasgow (Museums)/The Bridgeman Art Library: 85; Thyssen-Bornemisza Collection, Madrid/J.P. Zenobel/The Bridgeman Art Library: 17l; Treasurer's House, York/National Trust Photographic Library/John Hammond/The Bridgeman Art Library: 110t; © Trustees of the Chester Beatty Library, Dublin/The Bridgeman Art Library: 202; © Trustees of the Watts Gallery, Compton, Surrey/The Bridgeman Art Library: 30l, 136; © UCL Art Museum, University College London/The Bridgeman Art Library: 197; Victoria and Albert Museum, London/The Bridgeman Art Library: 76, 185, 191, 203; © Victoria Art Gallery, Bath and North East Somerset Council/The Bridgeman Art Library: 239; Villa Medici, Rome/The Bridgeman Art Library: 16t; Wallraf Richartz Museum, Cologne/Giraudon/The Bridgeman Art Library: 104; © Walters Art Museum, Baltimore/The Bridgeman Art Library: 80; Whitworth Art Gallery, University of Manchester/The Bridgeman Art Library: 193; Yale Center for British Art, Paul Mellon Collection: 18r, 134b, 153, 169, 177, 226, 235; © York Museums Trust (York Art Gallery)/The Bridgeman Art Library: 101

The publisher has made every effort to trace and contact copyright holders of the illustrations reproduced in this book; it will be happy to correct in subsequent editions any errors or omissions that are brought to its attention.

ACKNOWLEDGEMENTS

I should like to thank Simon and Amanda Davey for generously sharing their knowledge about birds, and William Humble, Ian Chilvers, Jane Puttick and Debra N. Mancoff, who have also helped in different ways. I am very grateful to the team at Merrell Publishers, particularly Claire Chandler, Rosanna Lewis, Nicola Bailey, Tom Lobo Brennan, Nick Wheldon and Amanda Mackie.

First published in 2012 by Merrell Publishers, London and New York

Merrell Publishers Limited
81 Southwark Street
London SE1 0HX

merrellpublishers.com

British Library Cataloguing-in-Publication data:
Bugler, Caroline.
The bird in art.
1. Birds in art. 2. Birds in art – History.
704.9'4328-dc23

ISBN 978-1-8589-4568-2

Produced by Merrell Publishers Limited
Designed by Tom Lobo Brennan
Project-managed by Rosanna Lewis
Proof-read by Barbara Roby
Indexed by Hilary Bird
Printed and bound in China

Jacket, front: John James Audubon, *Ivory-billed Woodpecker* (detail; 1829), see p. 155
Jacket, back, clockwise from top left: Jan van Kessel the Elder, *Tropical Birds in a Landscape* (detail; 17th century), see p. 181; August Macke, *Blue Parrots* (detail; 1914), see p. 244; Henry Stacy Marks, *Crested Crane, Cockatoo and Scarlet Ibis* (detail; *c.* 1874–80), see p. 162; Egyptian, *Meidum Geese* (detail; *c.* 2620 BC), see p. 39
Frontispiece: Martin Johnson Heade, *Two Hummingbirds* (detail; *c.* 1865–75); see p. 161
Page 263: Van Kessel the Elder, *Tropical Birds in a Landscape* (as above)

For Bill

9 781858 945682